LAURENS COUNTY, S.C.: RABUN CREEK SETTLEMENT 1762-1848

by

Margaret Peckham Motes

CLEARFIELD

Other books by the author

Laurens & Newberry Counties, S.C.: Saluda and Little River Settlement 1749-1775, co-authored with Jesse H. Motes, III. Winner of the National Genealogical Society 1995 Award for Excellence (Methods and Sources.)

South Carolina Memorial: Abstracts of Land Titles – Vol. 1, 1774-1776, co-authored with Jesse H. Motes, III.

Butcher, Baker, Candlestick Maker and Other Occupations in Newburyport, Massachusetts – 1850 Census.

Books published by Clearfield Company, Baltimore, MD

Free Blacks and Mulattos in South Carolina – 1850 Census.

Blacks Found in the Deeds of Laurens and Newberry Counties, S.C.: 1785-1827: Listed in Deeds of Gift, Deeds of Sale, Mortgages, Born Free and Freed.

Irish in South Carolina – 1850 Census.

Migration to South Carolina: Movement from the New England and Mid-Atlantic States – 1850 Census.

Migration to South Carolina – 1850 Census from England, Scotland, Germany, Italy, France, Spain, Russia, Denmark, Sweden, and Switzerland.

North End Papers 1618-1880 Newburyport, Massachusetts – Development of the North End of the City. By Oliver B. Merrill, transcribed by Margaret Peckham Motes.

Printed for Clearfield Company by
Genealogical Publishing Company
Baltimore, Maryland
2011

ISBN 978-0-8063-5541-2

Made in the United States of America

CONTENTS

Preface... v
Acknowledgements.. vi
Sources... vii
Abbreviations... ix
Maps... x
- 1820 Map of Laurens County showing Rabun Creek................ xi
- 1883 Map of Laurens County, upper part of Rabun Creek........ xii
- 1883 Map of Laurens County, SC, area where
  Rabun Creek joins the Reedy River...................................... xiii
Introduction.. xiv
Petitions for Land from South Carolina Council Journals:
Vol. IV 1754- 756... 1
Petitions for Land from South Carolina Council Journals:
Vol. V 1757-1765.. 1
Petitions for Land from South Carolina Council Journals:
Vol. VI 1766-1770... 2
Petitions for Land from South Carolina Council Journals:
Vol. VII 1771-1774.. 4
Letter from John Pearson to his Excellency, Wm. Henry Lyttleton, Esq. 5
Meeting Houses, Ministers, Places of Public Worship and
Graveyards and Burying Grounds.. 6
Mills and House Tracts.. 9
Ancient Boundary and Old Indian Lines 11
Loyalists near Rabun Creek.. 13
Quakers in the Rabun Creek area.. 15
Settlers on Rabun Creek.. 19
Name Index.. 278
Place Index.. 327

PREFACE

The starting point for this book was to locate the earliest families who lived on Rabun Creek in Laurens County, SC. This was accomplished in part by use of the indices of the South Carolina Colonial Survey and Memorial records and the books on Laurens County which had indexed place names. The microfilm for these Colonial Records was purchased from the South Carolina Archives and on loan from the Church of the Latter Day Saints.

Brent H. Holcomb's books on the *Petitions for Land from the South Carolina Council Journals* provided the list of early settlers who petitioned for land and received grants on Rabun Creek. The Quaker Records by the late Rev. Silas Emmett Lucas provided information on the Quaker movement into this area. The late Sarah M. Nash's *Abstracts of Early Records of Laurens County, SC 1785-1820* provided a good reference to the deed books and will books on microfilm.

The deeds and wills filled in family connections and provided information on the sites of old mills, paths, wagon roads, Indian trails, Ancient Indian Boundary lines, forts, churches, ministers, neighbors and the names of Negros gifted to family members. Some deeds have a survey attached; these are noted as [Plat]. Some of the microfilm copies were difficult to read and are stated [Poor microfilm copy].

Some early deeds were not found and possibly not recorded. Many of the early settlers did not make the long trip to Charleston to record deeds. These deeds may have been land transfers within the family or with their neighbors—sometimes called "pocket deeds."

To establish the land record and chain of title the microfilm for the South Carolina Colonial Surveys, Memorials, Deeds of Laurens County, Last Will and Testaments, and Power of Attorney records were used. The latter records helped to establish early land transfers when those deeds were missing.

The original landowner's name has been used as the ownership of the land changed. The original land owners' names are in italics within the deed. This helps identify the original tract of land as it was sold from one person to another through the years.

Every attempt has been made to keep the spelling of surnames, creeks and rivers as they were found in the documents. The spellings of the surnames are often different in the same document. The name "Rabun Creek" is the current spelling. The name of the creek appears in numerous variations throughout these pages, e.g. Reaburns, Raborn, Raboun, Raburn, Raiborn, Raibourn, Raybans, Raybons, Rayborn, Raybornes, Raybournes, Rayburn, Rayburnes, Rayburns, Reighbourn, etc.

Margaret Peckham Motes
Newburyport, Massachusetts
July, 2011

v

ACKNOWLEDGEMENTS

This work has been put together with the use of many difference sources by historians and researchers who have abstracted the early records of Laurens County, South Carolina. A list has been provided of those authors whose works have been used in doing research or to acquire more information of the early settlers in the area along Rabun Creek.

I special thank you to Brent H. Holcomb, of Columbia, SC, for giving me permission, when I first thought about this project a few years ago to let me abstract the names of those who petitioned for land on Rabun Creek from his series of books on *Petitions for Land from South Carolina Council Journals South Carolina*. These petitions are an excellent source of information for those doing research in the early records of South Carolina.

Without the books by Brent H. Holcomb, Sara M. Nash's Laurens County Deeds and the many other researchers who have transcribed Laurens County records it would have been difficult to search the microfilm for the deeds and wills of those who lived in the Rabun Creek settlement.

Thank you to my good friend and graphic designer, Sarah Raleigh of Raleigh Design in Newburyport, prepared the cover for this book, and to Joe Garonzik, of Clearfield Company, for his correspondence and interest in the new work.

A special thank you goes to my husband, Jesse H. Motes "Skip" for his continued support and help with the maps and reviewing the text during this long process.

SOURCES

South Carolina Colonial Surveys and Plats

South Carolina Colonial Memorials

Microfilm of Laurens County Deed Books A-Q.

Microfilm of Laurens County Will Books A-F.

Barnwell, Robert W. Jr., *Loyalism in S.C. 1765-1785*, published as a thesis at Duke University, Durham, NC, 1941.

Brevard, Joseph, *An Alphabetical Digest of the Public Statue Law of South Carolina, Volume 3,* Charleston, SC, 1814.

Bundrick Glenda and Suber, Andy, *Newberry County South Carolina Probate Estate Abstracts Volume 2,* privately published, 1989.

Elliott, Colleen, *Laurens County, South Carolina Wills 1784-1840,* Southern Historical Press, Easley, SC, 1988.

Holcomb, Brent H., *Petitions for Land from the South Carolina Council Journals, Vol. IV: 1754-1756.* South Carolina Magazine of Ancestral Research, Columbia, SC, 1998.

Holcomb, Brent H., *Petitions for Land from the South Carolina Council Journals, Vol. V: 1757-1765.* SCMAR, Columbia, SC, 1998.

Holcomb, Brent H., *Petitions for Land from the South Carolina Council Journals, Vol. VI: 1766-1770.* SCMAR, Columbia, SC, 1999.

Holcomb, Brent H., *Petitions for Land from the South Carolina Council Journals, Vol. VII: 1771-1774.* SCMAR, Columbia, SC, 1999.

Holcomb, Brent H. *South Carolina Deed Abstracts 1783-1788,* Charleston Deed Bk. Z_5, 300, 301, SCMAR, Columbia, SC, 1996,

Holcomb, Brent H., *South Carolina Deed Abstracts 1783 -1788,* SCMAR Columbia, SC, 1996.

Ingmire, Frances Terry, *Laurens County South Carolina Will Book A-C 1777-1809,* privately published, n.d.

Langley, Clara A., South *Carolina Deed Abstracts 1719-1772, Vol. IV,* Southern Historical Press, Easley, SC, 1984.

The Laurens County Advertiser, Laurens Co., SC., December 4, 1979

Laurens District Chapter, South Carolina Genealogical Society, *Burying Grounds, Graveyards and Cemeteries, Laurens Co., South Carolina Vol I, 1990.*

Lucas, Rev. Silas Emmett , Jr., *Mill's Atlas, Atlas of the State of South Carolina,* Southern Historical Press, Easley, South Carolina, 1980.

McDowell, William, Jr., Colonial , *Colonial Records of South Carolina, Documents relating to Indian Affairs 1754 -1776,* Columbia, SC 1992.

Meriwether, Robert L.; *The Expansion of South Carolina 1727-1763,* Southern Publishers, Inc., Kingsport, TN, 1940.

Nash, Sara M., *Abstracts of Early Records of Laurens County, South Carolina 1785-1820.* Fountain Inn, South Carolina, Privately published, 1982.

Nash, Sarah M., *Ancestors and Descendants Nash, Gray, Fowler, King, Bailey, Mahaffey, Hopkins, Cureton and Others*" published privately, 1972.

Norfleet, Phil, *Biographical Sketch of Moses Kirkland*, South Carolina Loyalists and Rebels – website sc_tories.tripod.com, September 24, 2003.

Revill, Janie, *Some South Carolina Genealogical Records*, Southern Historical Press, Easley, SC. 1986.

Laurens County Historical Society & Laurens County Art Council, *The Scrapbook, A Compilation of Historical Facts About Places and Events of Laurens County, South Carolina*, published by Laurens County Historical Society & Laurens County Arts Council, Jacobs Press, Clinton, SC., 1982.

Young, Pauline, *Abstract of Old Ninety-Six and Abbeville District, Wills and Bonds*, Southern Historical Press, Easley, SC, 1977.

Wright, Robert K. Wright, Jr. and Mac Gregor, Morris J. , Jr., *Soldier-Statesmen of the Constitution*, Center of Military History, United States Army, Washington, D.C, 2004.

ABREVIATIONS

LCDBK A: 30   Laurens County Deed Book A pg. 30.
LCWBK B: 40   Laurens County Will Book B pg. 40.

[P13_150:3]   SC Colonial Plats Vol. 13, pg. 150, item 3 on page.
[M18_300:2]   SC Colonial Memorial Vol. 18, pg. 300, item 2 on page.

MAPS

Sections of two important Laurens County maps which show Rabun Creek were scanned and appear in this book. They are the Laurens County map, surveyed by Henry Gray, D.S. in 1820 found in Mill's *Atlas, Atlas of the State of South Carolina* and A *Complete Sketch Laurens County, SC Kyzer & Hellams, 1883.*

Rabun Creek is feed by many branches and streams as it runs into the Reedy River and flows downstream into the Saluda River. The maps show the South Fork, North Fork, and one unnamed branch coming off Rabun Creek.

The 1820 Mills' Atlas has the following families or mills on "Reaburns's Creek" or on one of its forks.

- Abercrombie's Mill
- Anderson's Mill
- Allen
- McNeis
- Boyd
- Killingworth
- Knight

The *Kyzer & Hellams 1883* map shows the dramatic changes in the population in the area when compared to the 1820 map. Several "burnt forts" located on Rabun Creek are also noted. The *Kyzer & Hellans, 1883* map gives the names of the residents; many of these surnames go back to the earliest settler, indicating that some descendants were still living in the area of Rabuns Creek.

The small branches and creeks which run into or near Rabun Creek often took the names of the property owner, e.g. Dirty Creek "formerly Hallams Branch of Reaburns Creek," Todd's Branch, Brown's Creek, Sherrill's Branch, Calhouns Branch, Peachlans/Peachland/Peachling Branch head of Durban Branch and Rabun Creek, Rockey Branch of Burrisses Creek, Burrisses Branch/Creek, O'Daniels Branch, Brown's Fork, on fork of Rabun Creek, Ritchey's Branch, Starmes Branch, McHergs or McHurgs Creek, Polks Branch, Williams Branch/Williams Creek, Hilly Branch, Bradshaws Branch, Hellams Branch, Indian Hut branch, Indian Creek, Widow Reed's Branch or Widow Reed's Spring Branch, O'Daniel's Branch, Jones Brach, Rock House Branch, School house Branch, Gutterys, Branch, Still House Branch, Moll Kelly's Branch, Kellett Branch, Dutchman's Creek, Allison's Creek, Raifords Creek, Indian creek, Warrior Creek, Mountain Creek and Bullet Branch, so named due the fact that it was swift and treacherous "dangerous as a bullet" during heavy rains.

The full names and other branches and creeks are listed in the place index.

**1820 Map of Laurens County, SC showing Rabun Creek.
Town of Laurensville, later Laurens, SC located in upper right.**

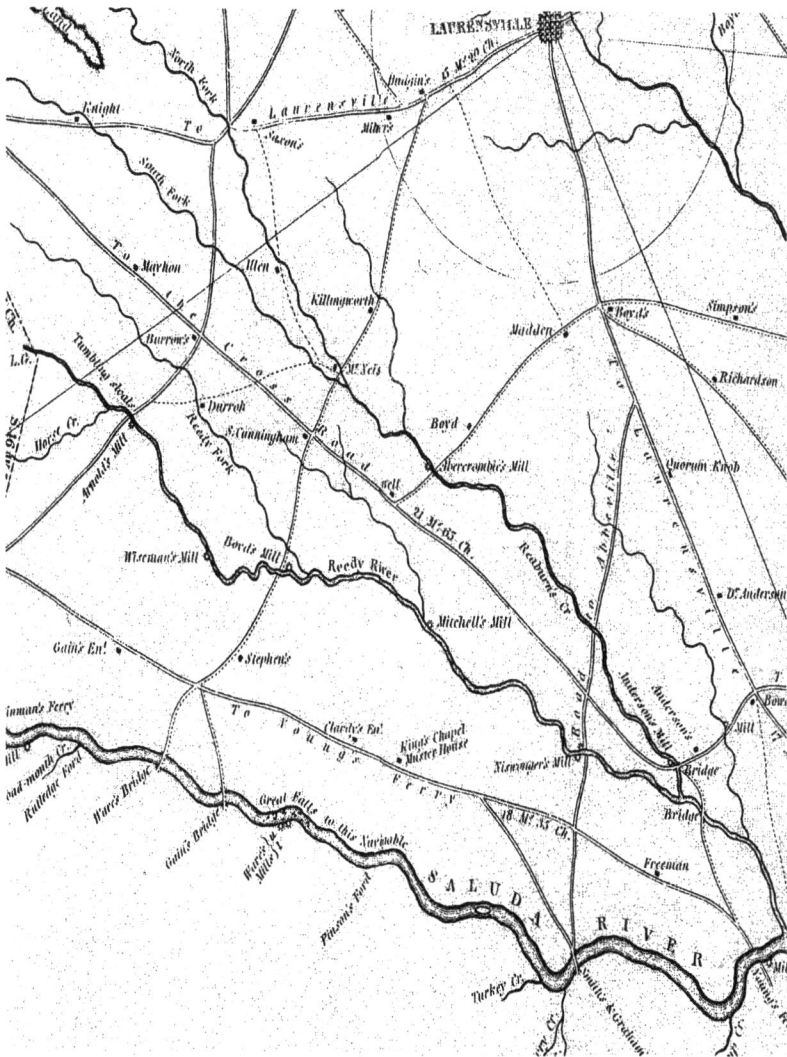

**Abercrombie's Mill, Anderson's Mill and unnamed Mills on Reaburns
Creek. Section of the map of Laurens County in Mills Atlas.**

1883 Kyzer & Hellans Map of Laurens County, showing the upper part of Rabun Creek.

The old burnt fort appears on S. Rabun Creek by S. Bolt's Shoals.

1883 Kyzer & Hellans Map showing where Rabun Creek joins the Reedy River.

On the 1883 Kyzer & Hellans map many of the names of the early settlers are still found in the area of Rabun Creek.

INTRODUCTION

Rabun Creek is located about five miles west of the City of Laurens in Laurens County, SC. The creek starts near the Greenville County border, runs into the Reedy River, and into the larger Saluda River at the Abbeville County line.

This area of South Carolina, known as the up-country or back-country became home to settlers from Virginia, Maryland, and North Carolina, many who were Scotch-Irish. There are notes in the early surveys stating "Bounty" or "Irish" in the margins. Some of the settlers who migrated into South Carolina had slaves or indentured servants in their household. These petitioners for land received acreage upon the total number of persons in their household including these indentured servants or slaves.

This area of South Carolina was Indian Territory, the home of the Cherokees. It was an area well known to trappers, hunters and those trading with the Indians. In 1755 Governor James Glen made a treaty with the Cherokees, which ceded areas of the Indian Territory to the crown of England. This treaty was the beginning of the large migration and settlements along the creeks and rivers in Berkley County, a portion of which would later become Laurens County.

The earliest record of a settler on Rabun Creek is John Turk's Petition in December 5, 1752 for 150 acres of land. It is thought that John Turk came from Augusta County Virginia. In 1746 petitions has been read for John and Thomas Turk and Michael Taylor of Augusta County, Virginia. "They had examined the lands of Ninety Six, which according to 'the Inhabitants dwelling there abouts', were claimed by the Indians. They asked that the government purchase the lands and serve them for new settlers ...of Virginia and Pennsylvania ...."[1] There were others from the area that may have followed the Turks into South Carolina. Eight years after John Turk made his petition, the news of an uprising on Raburn Creek was sent to Charleston.

In the 1760 letter from John Pearson to Excellency, Wm. Henry Lyttleton, Esq., Pearson writes "that 27 people had been killed on Rayburns Creek." His letter gives a historic and realistic view of the problems which the settlers were having with the Indian attacks in the Rabuns Creek settlement and other settlements in the up-country. The letter is in its entirety if found on page 5.

The area around Rabuns Creek had problems with Indian raids and the Loyalists. During this hostile period, the Loyalists took the opportunity to join with the Indians for revenge against their Whig neighbors. Life was difficult for the people in the up-country during this early settlement period, but the area continued to grow with the influx of settlers.

---

[1] Meriwether, Robert L., The Expansion of South Carolina 1729-1765, Kingsport, TN, 1940, pg.123-124.

A safe haven from the Indians was needed and these early settlers built stockades for their safety from attacks. A fortification had been built by John Goudy in the Ninety-Six District of Berkley County prior to the letter of 1760. James Lyndley's colonial survey for 200 acres on the Raburn Creek was dated 1 March 1768. The fort known as Lyndley's fort was built after 1768, the date of his survey. Though the builders of this fort are unknown, it was probably built by the settlers in the community as a place to seek shelter during raids. Lindley's Fort was located on Rabun Creek and during the Revolution known as an "old fort." There is a notation on the *Kyzer & Hellams, 1883* map showing an "old burnt fort." This could possible be the site of Lindley's fort.

In 1762 the other settlers appear in the South Carolina Colonial Records petitioning for land on Rabun Creek. The petitions were for John Mahaffey in March 1762, Able Thomas, Zebulon Gaunt and Israel Gaunt, all three Quakers, in April 1762; William Allison in Aug. 1762 and for Robert Box in October 1762.

James Abercrombie, another early settler on the creek, had a mill near the junction of Raburns and Dirty Creek in the 1780's. Other mills were located on the North Fork and South Fork creeks which fed into Rayburns Creek.

In 1768 the *"inhabitants, living and residing in the fork of Broad and Saluda rivers, and Bush and Rayburn's creeks, in this province, by their humble petition to the general assembly, have represented many inconveniences which they labour under, for want of having a road established and made public, to lead from Orangeburgh to Saluda, and from thence to Bush and Rayburn's creeks; and also, for the want of a ferry to be established and made public, over Saluda river: Therefore be it enacted, That shall be, and are herby nominated and appointed commissioners for laying out, and making, and keeping in repair, a road to lead from Orangeburgh to Saluda; and from thence to Bush and Rayburn's creeks."* [2]

"And all male inhabitants, from the age of sixteen to sixty years of age, within ten miles of the said road, shall be, and they are herby obliged to make the said road, and keep the same in repair." [3]

Researching early families has led to the discovery of the large migration out of South Carolina in the early 1800 and 1820's into Georgia, Alabama, and Tennessee as the Indian Land and bounty lands came available.

During the early 1800's the Quaker community left this SC area for Georgia, moving later to settle in the area of Miami County, Ohio.

I hope that these records of the early settlers in the Rabun Creek Settlement will help those researchers with their work in this area of Laurens County.

---

[2] Brevard, Joseph, An Alphabetical Digest of the Public Statue Law of South Carolina, Volume 3, Charleston, SC, 1814, pg. 346.

[3] Ibid,, pg. 142.

PETITIONS FOR LAND
FROM
SOUTH CAROLINA COUNCIL JOURNALS:
VOL IV 1754-1756[1]

Petition for Warrants of Survey for those who had lands on Raburns Creek, date of Council Meeting and the page listed.

I Certify that pursuant to his Excellency's Warrant dated Dec'r the 5th 1752 for the Survey of 150 acres of Land on the South Fork of Santee I caused the same to be executed by John Hamilton, Deputy Surv'r on the 20th day of August 1753 on Raburns Creek a Branch of Reedy River. The Plat thereof was returned into the office on the 15th January 1754 where it now remains, this March 32nd 1754. George Hunter, Surv'r Genl.

Ye prayer thereof was granted."

Meeting of Saturday A.M. 22 March 1754, pg. 43
"Pages 152-154: The Petition of John Turk humbly setting forth that the Petitioner obtained a warrant the 5 of December 1752 for 150 acres of land which was duly executed and the plat returned into the Surveyor General's office the 15th January last the time being Elapsed by accidental Sickness. The Petitioner humbly prays to Certifie the said Plat in order to his having the grant for the same. Char's Town, y'e 21st March 1754. John Turk. [N. B. John Turk's last will and testament was proved November 1755. M. Motes.]

§§§

[1] Holcomb, Brent H., Petitions for Land from South Carolina Council Journals: Vol. IV 1754-1756, SCMAR, Columbia, SC, 1998, pg. 43

PETITIONS FOR LAND
FROM
SOUTH CAROLINA COUNCIL JOURNALS:
VOL V 1757-1765[2]

Petition for Warrants of Survey for those who had lands on Rayborn Creek, date of Council Meeting and the page listed.

Meeting of Tuesday A.M. 6 August 1762, pg. 79
William Allison 150 acres Rayburns Creek

Meeting of Tuesday A.M. 5 October 1762, pg. 92.
To certify elapsed Platts
Robert Box 150 acres on Reaburn's Creek

Meeting of Tuesday 3 September 1765, pg. 262, 263
Richard Owens 150 acres Rayburns Creek
James Harvey 200 acres Rayburns Creek and Reedy Creek
Benjamin Brown 150 acres Rayburns Creek

§§§

PETITIONS FOR LAND
FROM
SOUTH CAROLINA COUNCIL JOURNALS:
VOL VI 1766-1770[3]

Petition for Warrants of Survey for those who had lands on Rayborn Creek, and other names in the area. Date of Council Meeting and the page listed.

Meeting of Tuesday 3 February 1767, pg. 55
John Shirley 200 acres Raburns Creek, Reedy River

Meeting of Wednesday 4 February 1767, pg. 58, 59
George Hollinsworth 100 acres Rayburns Creek
Daniel Allen 500 acres Rayburns Creek

---

[2] Holcomb, Brent H., Petitions for Land from South Carolina Council Journals: Vol. V. 1757-1765, SCMAR, Columbia, SC, 1998, pgs. 79, 92, 262, 263.
[3] Holcomb, Brent H., Petitions for Land from the South Carolina Council Journals, Vol Vi: 1766-1770, SCMAR, Columbia, SC, 1999, pgs. 55, 58, 59, 87, 108, 119, 124-125.

Meeting of Monday 22 June 1767, pg. 87
William Turk 200 acres
John Turk 100 acres

Meeting of Tuesday 1 September 1767, pg. 108
Joseph Waites 200 acres or Rayburns Creek

Meeting of Tuesday 3 November 1767, pg. 119
John Mahafy 150 acres on Rayburns Creek

Meeting of Tuesday 1 December 1767, pg. 124-125
William Hellum 200 acres North fork Rayburns Creek including his own
improvement
Richard Owens, Senr. 100 acres North fork Rayburns Creek.

Meeting of Tuesday 2 February 1768, pg. 156
John Abercrombie 200 acres Rayburnes Creek where he lives.

Meeting of Tuesday 23 February 1768, pg. 167
John Copland 100 acres Rayburns Creek

Meeting of Tuesday 1 March 1768, pg. 174
Benjamin Brown 100 acres on Rayburns Creek

Meeting of Tuesday 7 June 1768, pg. 188
Thomas Cahoun [Calhoun] 200 acres Rayburns Creek
John Holmes 100 acres Rayburns Creek

Meeting of Tuesday 7 June 1768, pg. 190
William Bough 150 acres in Craven County
William Waite 150 acres in Craven County
Ralph Humphreys 100 acres in Craven County

Meeting of Tuesday 2 August 1768, pg. 194
Robert Shirley 300 acres Rayburns Creek
Richard Shirley 500 acres Rayburns Creek

Meeting of Tuesday 1 November 1768, pg. 209
Thomas Lantrip 200 acres on Rayburns Creek

Meeting of Tuesday 7 February 1769, pg. 220
William Vaughn 200 acres Rayburn Creek

Meeting of Wednesday 8 February 1769, pg. 223
George Hollinsworth 100 acres Rayburns Creek

Meeting of Tuesday 7 March 1769, pg. 224
Wm. Burrows 200 acres Rayburns Creek

Meeting of Tuesday 1 August 1769, pg. 237, 238
Abram Ryley 100 acres waters Rayburns Creek
Joseph Waite 200 acres Rayburns Creek
Owen Reed 250 acres Rayburns Creek

Meeting of Tuesday 7 November 1769, pg. 253
John Mayhard 250 acres Rayburns Creek

Meeting of Tuesday 5 June 1770, to certify plats, pg. 287
Thomas Landrip 200 acres Rayburn's Creek
Abram Ryley 100 acres Rayburn Creek

Meeting of Tuesday 7 August 1770, pg. 293
Theodous Turk To certify plat. 50 acres on Reedy River Surveyed for James
Edes.

§§§
PETITIONS FOR LAND
FROM
SOUTH CAROLINA COUNCIL JOURNALS:
VOL VII 1771-1774 [4]

Petition for Warrants of Survey for those who had lands on Rayborn Creek,
date of Council Meeting and page number.

Meeting of Tuesday 6 April 1773, pg. 247
Wm. Savage & Ja's Simpson Esq'rs 500 acres on the waters or Rayburns
Creek

Wm. Savage & Ja's Simpson Esq'rs 500 acres on the waters of Rayburns
Creek

§§§

---

[4] Holcomb, Brent H., Petitions for Land from the South Carolina Council
Journals, Vol. VII: 171-1774, SCMAR, Columbia, SC, 1999, pg. 247.

Letter from John Pearson
to his Excellency, Wm. Henry Lyttleton, Esq.

8 February 1760: A letter from John Pearson to his Excellency, Wm. Henry Lyttleton, Esq. [56]
May it please your Excellency, The Result of this is to inform you in Brief of the deplorable State of our back Inhabitants, they being chiefly killed, taken Prisoners and drove into small Forts, only some who hath made their Escape by Flight and that as low as to Saxegotha Township, and we are now building places of safety in my District as well as we can. How long we may continue in Safety in them I know not for the Tourrant hath been so great they have a burnt all Goundy's House except the little Fort you built round his Barn, where he and Capt. Francis and some few more are penned up. They have likeways endeavoured a Fort (at) William Turner's where they have had a smart Engagement, and as I hear they killed some of the Indians notwithstand the went away down to old Thomas Haverds and got into his Barn, and there they, the old Man and what few Men he had in House a considerable Time *sic*, but in short they have burnt and destroyed all up Bush River, except Jacob Brooks where there is some People gathered together to stand in their own Defence. All up Saludy, Little River, *Rabourns Creek*, Long Cane and Stevens Creek, are all destroyed. *I am informed they have killed 27 persons on Rabourns Creek*, and out of 200 persons that were settled on the Long Canes and Steven's Creek not above 4_ to 50 to be found, so that the Case is very desperate, and all the People that move down, hardly one stops at the Congarees, so that I may say we are now the back Inhabitants, and unless there is about 2 or 300 Men raise in scouting Parties and an Officer over 50 to scour the woods and stop the Tourrant, I don't doubt that they will destroy chiefs of the Country.

So soon as I have finished my Fort I shall endeavor all I can for the common Good. I know of several stout Men, who with proper Encouragement, that is to say, so much certain per Month, and so much per Scalp, would make it their entire Business to pursue and kill and destroy those merciless Villains wherever they went. If your Excellency in your most wise Consideration should think proper to appoint Captains for Scouts and would send up Commissions for that Purpose with Orders to raise Men, and

---

3McDowell, William, Jr., Colonial, *Colonial Records of South Carolina*, Documents relating to Indian Affairs 1754 -1776, Columbia, SC 1992, pgs. 495-496.

on what Encouragement, I don't doubt but there may be a good many Men got here directly. And I am with humble Submission,

Your Excellency's most humble and most obedient Servant,
Jno. Pearson

Note:
"John Pearson wrote on February 8 that the Indians were reported to have killed twenty-seven on Rayburns Creek, but this was not confirmed. On Bush River Pearson said all the settlers had fled save a group with Jacob Brooks; these were doubtless the builders of Brooks' or Hall's fort, which appears to have been on the middle course of that stream. [fnote 27.JC, Feb 11, March 19, 21, Apr 1, 30, 1760. For approximate location of Brooks Fort, see P, VI, 333 and index to plats from which adjoining plats may be located. [7]

---

[7] Meriwether, Robert L.; The Expansion of South Carolina 1727-1763, Southern Publishers, Inc., Kingsport, TN, 1940, pg. 223.

MEETING HOUSES, MINISTERS, PLACES
OF PUBLIC WORSHIP, GRAVEYARDS
AND BURYING GROUNDS

Rocky Springs Presbyterian Church,[8] 1780: The Scotch-Irish came to the new colonies "escaping religious or economic oppression, while others moved south from Pennsylvania, Virginia, and North Carolina to a less crowded land." The Rev. John McCosh came to America from Ireland in 1772, preaching throughout South Carolina. About 1780, he was known to have preached to the "budding" congregation at a stand in the woods near the "Rocky Spring" from whence the church took its name. "The first elders of the "Rocky Spring Church, as it was first known, there William Taylor, William Hannah, William Cunningham and Robert Speers, who may have been ordained in Ireland or Scotland, for most emigrated to the Colonies as grown men."

Rev. John McCosh: About 1780: McCosh came to South Carolina and preached in the area.

Rev. Robert McClintock: An Irish minister and friend of Rev. McCosh, served the church from 1785 until his death in 1803.

Drury Sims, minister: 8 November 1792:[9]

Durham, Arthur: 1 March 1817: Moses Myers, Laurens Dist., S.C., *to the Church of the Poplar Springs District for $2.50; 104 Rood [sic] on waters of Reedy River. [meets and bounds given.] Originally granted to Arthur Durham in the year (blank)* and from said Durham to William South and since said South conveyed to sundry but lastly to the above Moses Myers. The said church land being purchased by the Babtist *sic* profession but the meeting house to be free to all Christians proffers preaching there in or on said land. Moses Myers (LS). Wit: E. Powell, John Walker. Proved by John Walker 7 April 1817 before J. Hitch, J.P. [10]

Rev. Robert Smith: 3 April 1798[11]

---

[8] *The Scrapbook, A Compilation of Historical Facts About Places and Events of Laurens County, South Carolina*, published by Laurens County Historical Society & Laurens County Arts Council 1982, pg. 486.
[9] LCDBK G: 679. See Samuel Bolling.
[10] LCDBK K: 168. See Arthur Durham.
[11] LCBK A: 187. See Patrick Cunningham.

Martin, Rodgers, Millner, heirs of Andrew Rodgers: 15 August 1811: We Robert McNees, Esq., Daniel Martin, Senr., Susannah Rodgers and Arnold Millner, of Laurens Dist., S.C., to Lewis Saxon, Charles Allen, Benjamin Nabors, of same place, for $3.00; 2 ½ acres in trust for the *purpose of building a meeting house thereon as a place of public worship and for a graveyard or burying ground,* at a spring thence nearly west to a post oak thence S to a black oak, thence to said spring. The said tract lying in the said district on the waters of Dirty Creek. The Meeting house intended to be brick on premises hereby conveyed Robert McNees (Seal), Daniel (X) Martin (Seal), Susannah (X) Rodgers (Seal), A. Millner (Seal). Wit: Robert Allison, Collyer Barksdale. Proved by Robert Allison 14 March 1812 before John Garlington, J.Q.[12] [LCDBK J: 257-258]

[Family: Susannah Rodgers, Sarah Rodgers and Arnold Millner, heirs of Andrew Rodgers.]

Hollingsworth: 16 April 1811: State of S.C., Laurens Dist.: I John Madden, of said place, to Thomas Norris, Junr., of same place, for $200; 50 acres on Raburns Creek, being *part of 150 acres formerly the property of Hollingsworth,* Thomas Madden and where James Green now lives. Bounded by said Norris's house; SW by James Boyd; N by John Simmons; E by Marmaduke Pinson. 50 acres except a *meeting house called the Quaker meeting house and 2 acres of land round the said assigned for public worship.* John Norris.16 April 1811. Wit. James Wier, E. S. Roland; Dower of Iby (X) Madden. Proved by E.S. Roland 16 April 1811 before Gabriel Jowell, J.P.[13]

Irwin, Capt. John: 13 March 1813: Estate administered 13 March 1813 by Humphrey Klugh, Robt. Roman bound to Taliaferro Livingston, Ord. Abbeville Dist., S.C., sum of $1000.00. Cit. Published at *Tabernacle Meeting House.* Sale 2 April 1813. Buyers: Rachel, James Irwin. Sale: Jno. Irwin made 9 August 1796. Byers: Jno., Martha, James Irwin. Box 50, Package 1151.[14]

Mitchell, Nimrod: 13 November 1837, Estate of Nimrod Mitchell administered: by John Weatherall, James H. Kay, Noah Reeves, bound to Moses Taggart Ord. Abbeville Dist. Sum of $1,000.00. Citations Published at *Turkey Creek Church.* Espend: October 28, 1842. Legatees, John Mitchell

---

[12] LCDBK J: 157-158. See Martin, Rodgers, Millner, heirs of Andrew Rodgers.
[13] LCDBK J: 213-214. See John Madden.
[14] Young, Pauline; Abstracts of Old Ninety-Six and Abbeville District, Wills and Bonds, Southern Historical Press, Easley, SC, 1977, pg. 161.

$17.74, Mathew Bell $17.74, Alason (Alanson) Lord $17.74, Wm. Mitchell $19.00, A.W. Mitchell $17.74, A.W. Mitchell guardian for minors, George and Dicey Mitchell $35.00. Sale held 38 November 1837. Box 58, Package 1382.[15]

Pinson, Duke [Marmaduke]: 14 March 1812: Mary Henderson, of Laurens Dist., S.C., to Levi Hill, of same place, for consideration of her lifetime maintenance conveys a tract of 53 acres less one half acres for a burying place. *Originally granted to Duke Pinson by Wm. Bull, and conveyed by said Pinson to David Morgan and from said Morgan to Nathan Austin and by said Austin to John Henderson and by John Henderson to Mary Henderson to Levi Hill.* The said tract of land on the waters of Reedy River. The land being part of a tract of 100 acres *originally granted to Duke Pinson* . Mary Henderson (mark). Wit: Isaac Moseley, James Henderson. Proved by James Henderson 28 May 1812 before Gabriel Jowell, J.P. [16]

Saxon, Lewis [?]: 7 March 1799: Elisha Casey, of Laurens Co., S.C., to Samuel Nesbit, of same place, for £23, 6 shillings, 8 p; 100 acres on a branch of Rabourns Creek called the Bullett Branch. Bounded N by land laid out unknown, S on Thos. Hooker, and on all other sides by vacant land, *except ½ acres around the graveyard.* Elisha Casey (LS). Wit: Drury Boyce, Edward Nash. Proved by Drury Boyce 13 March 1799 before Joseph Downs, J.P. [17]

Tweed, Eleanor: 6 March 1799: Elisha Casey, of Laurens Co., S.C., to Samuel Nesbit, of same place, for £23; 100 acres on a branch of Rabourns Creek called Bullett Branch, *except around the graveyard.* Bounded to the N by land laid out unknown, S on Thos. Hooker, all other sides vacant. Elisha Casey (LS) Wit: Drury Boyce, Edward Nash. Proved by Drury Boyce 12 March 1799 before Joseph Downs, J.P. [18]

MILLS AND HOUSE TRACTS

Dial, Isaac: 30 Sept. 1835: Survey for Garlington C. Dial, extr. of Isaac Dial, Dec'd. I have admeasured and laid off a tract of land containing 557 acres in Laurens Dist., S.C., on both sides of Dirty Creek, a branch of Rabens Creek, being a part of a tract of land belonging to said Dial known as the *House Tract* and having such shape and marks as plat represents. Alsey Fuller, D.S. [Plat, shows *House, and mill,* also bounding James Boyd, Isaac

---

[15] Ibid., pg. 194.
[16] LCDBK K: 259. See Mary Henderson.
[17] LCDBK G: 681. See Elisha Casey.
[18] LCDBK G: 781. See Elisha Casey.

Dial, Dec'd., David Helms, Hasting Dial, William Burton, Est. of Isaac Dial, sec'd, G. C. Dial, also on Shirrels Branch.] [19]

Anderson, William: 28 December 1792: William Anderson and Molly, his wife, of Laurens Co., S.C. David Anderson, of same place, for L75; 200 acres being part of one certain tract of land containing 200 acres in said county on Long Oak Creek of Reedy River. Bounded on a corner beach of Reaburns Creek, *at George Wrights old mill,* bounding on land granted to Foster, land sold by sd. William Anderson to Wm. Hughes. SW on Woods and William Mitchells land. Being land granted to said William Anderson by William Bull, Esq. In the year 1774. William Anderson (L.S), Molley (mark) Anderson (L.S.) Wit: James Middleton, George Anderson, Molly (M) Anderson. Proved by James Middleton 27 December 1792 before George Anderson, J.P. Meets and bounds. [20]

Niblett, Solomon: 16 & 17 January 1775: Solomon Niblett of 96 Dist., SC, planter, and Mary, his wife, to Abner Busship [Bishop], of said District, miller, for L500S.C., money; 200 acres in said district on a branch of Saludy called Rayburns Creek; being the lower half of a tract whereon said Solomon Niblett lives, *including the mill with* all the appurtences hereto belonging. Granted to said Niblet by George III. Solomon Niblett (X), Mary Niblet (mark). Wit: W. Paine, Mary Paine. Proved 96 District 18 Jan 1775 by oath of Wm. Paine before James Linle[y], J.P. Rec. 12 November 1787. [21]

O'Neall, Hugh: 3 October 1787: State of S.C. Know by these presents that I, Hugh Oneall, miller, of the said state and county of Laurens and District of Ninety Six, being of perfect mind and memory and knowledge that it is appointed son to a men once to die of calling to mind the present mortality of men do make this to be my last will and testament. First I commit my soul to God who gave it and my body to be decently buried at the d___ of my Ex[etors] to my son Hugh Oneall, that *tract of land lying on Little River above the mill granted to me for 150 acres and also a part in which the mill and dwelling house and mills.* I give unto Charles Neal the remaining part of said tract of land below the former on Little River in which the mill and house laid off as is above directed. To Thomas Neal that *tract of 270 acres of land on Raburns Creek bounded on Patrick Riley, Mary McDonald, Robert Sims.* To my daughter Elizabaeth McDaniel and her husband Thomas McDaniel, a cow and calf; my four young children to be well schooled; my movable effects to be divided among my four daughters: Patience, Ann,

---

[19] LCDBK N: 142.
[20] LCDBK E: 136.
[21] Holcomb, Brent H. South Carolina Deed Abstracts 1788-1788, SCMAR, Columbia, SC, 1996, p. 452.

Ruth, Rachel. Ex. Mercer Babb, Wm. Pinson, Elisha Ford. Wit: John Hunter, Thos. Wadsworth, Patk. McDowall.[22]

[Family: Sons Hugh Oneall, Charles O'Neal, Thomas O'Neal; daughter Elizabeth McDaniel, wife of Thomas McDaniel, daughters Patience, Ann, Ruth, Rachel.]

Bradey, Charles: 3 October 1793: LWT Charles Bradey. Laurens Co., S.C. I give and allow that they may dispose of in the following manner Viz.: That the plantation on which I now live be divided amongst my three eldest sons as follows [Viz.] That my son William shall have that part of it which lies on the east side of the Raburns Creek and that the W side shall be divided between John and Allexander. My old mill house and so to the creek aforesaid the N side to belong to my son John and the S side to Allex, but possession shall not be given to either of my sons until my wife tell when she shall enjoy possible possession of all the aforesaid plantation. I will and bequeath my *plantation on Reedy River to be equally divided between my two youngest sons at their mother's decease* (Viz.) Charles and George. I will and allow that my loving wife Eleanor Brady do remove as soon as may be covenant to the said plantation on Reedy river, the benefit for which sh shall enjoy during her life as a compensation for raising my young children, who shall be under her care during there maturity. I will and allow that my moveable effects be equally divided amongst my children, who are yet unmarried at their mother's decease, till which time she shall have the full use and benefit. I appoint my wife Eleaner Brady Executrix and my truly friend John Cocharn, executor. Charles Bradey (Seal). Wit: Ann (X) . Wadkins, Zuboriah (X) Barns, John Cockran. Date proved not available. [23]

[Family: Wife Eleaner, eldest sons: William, John, Allexander. Younger children Charles and George Bradey.]

Joseph Kershaw and Aaron Loocock, merchants: Joseph Kershaw, merchant, came to Frericksbeurg, in 1758 which made another evolution in the development of Camden, SC. "He found the county dotten with inhabitants along the riverside and creeks, but the area which is now Camden was unoccupied woods, except the spot in the SW corner where the Mathis family resided. Joseph Kershaw came up from Charlestown, S.C., with the purpose, it would appear, of establishing a country branch of the mercantile form of that city, composed of William Ancrum, Lambert Lance, and Aaron

Loocock." [Note: Many Laurens County Deeds have dealing with Kershaw

---

[22] LCDBK B: 302-304.
[23] LCWBK C-1: 167.

and Loocock, of Charlestown, SC.] [24] [Lucas, Silas Emmitt, *Quakers in South Carolina: Wateree and Bush River, Cane Creek, Piney Grove and Charlton Meetings, Southern Historical Press, 1991*, pgs. 26, 37, 38.]

ANCIENT BOUNDARY OR OLD INDIAN LINES

Sarah M. Nash wrote in her book, *Ancestors and Descendants*, that the "Ancient Boundary" or "Old Indian Line" was one of the most historic landmarks of the area. It was surveyed after 1761 by the agreement of 1755 between Governor Glen and the Cherokee Indians. It was the line separating the Cherokee lands from those of white settlers. It was an important line of defense which ran from an area near Tyron, North Carolina, down to Savannah River and had many forts and blockhouses for the soldiers during the Revolutionary War. One of these stations was knows as Kellett's Station and was most likely a blockhouse. There are references to this station in pension applications. Sarah Nash states the Kellett Station may have been near the old Babb-Kellett cemetery, which is said to have been first used as a burial place for some of the British soldiers killed in skirmishes in the area [25]

The Ancient boundary lines or Old Indian Lines are found in the deeds for Joseph Kellett, Robert Creswell, John Henderson, Patrick Cuningham, Daniel Ravenel, Wm. Simpson and James Savage.

Creswell land: 3 March 1806: We Robert Creswell, Elihu Creswell & James McCaa, of Laurens Dist., S.C., to Andrew McKnight, of same place, for $250; 105 acres lying on the *old Indian boundary line* and on a small branch of Reedy River. Bounding Raley's land and on Mary McDonalds. Robert Creswell (LS), Elihu Creswell (LS), Jas. McCaa (LS). Wit. Wm. McKnight, David Madden. Dower of Nancy [signed as Agness] Creswell and Phebe McCaa, wife of the within Robert Creswell and James McCaa made 3 March 1826 before Chas. Proved by David Madden 3 March 1806 before Chas. Allen, J.Q. [Plat][26]

Cuningham, Patrick: 12 June 1785: Patrick Cuningham of Ninety-Six Dist., S.C., planter, and Ann Cuningham, his wife, to David Green, [minister] of same place, for £30; 100 acres on N side of Reedy River, *below the old Indian Line* bounding on said river NE and NW on lands unknown.

---

[24] Lucas, Silas Emmett, Quakers, pg. 26, 37, 38.
[25] Nash, Sara M., *Ancestors and Descendants Nash, Gray, Fowler, King, Bailey, Mahaffey, Hopkins, Cureton and Others*" published privately, 1972, pg. 3.
[26] LCDBK H: 131-132.

Originally granted to said Patrick Cuningham 21 January 1785. Patrick Cuningham, Ann Cuningham. Wit: Wm. Harris, Edward Kemp. Benj. Turner. [27]

Henderson, John: 13 October 1788: John Henderson, of Ninety Six Dist., now Laurens Co., to Mary Henderson, of same place, for £20; 150 acres on Rabourns Creek below the ancient Boundary line. *Granted to John Henderson July 4, 1785.* Bounded on Nicholas Hill, vacant land. Wit: John Baugh, John Brodey. [28] [Poor microfilm copy. See Marmaduke Hollingsworth.]

Kellett Lands: 22 September 1820: Jennett Kellett, of Laurens Dist., S.C., James Kellett, my son, for $1 and divers other services which I have and am receiving from him; 200 acres on waters Raburns Creek. Bounded on the *old Indian boundary line*, Drury and William Boyce's land and McMahaus lands, except 14 acres on the S side of the road. . . . the tract of land I keep to live on during my natural life and at my death said James Killett to take it for him and his heirs forever. .Jennett Kellett (LS). Wit: Archable Owings, Micajah Berry. Proved by Archable Owings 19 February 1821 before Thos Wright J.Q. [29]

Ravenel, Daniel: Survey for Daniel Ravenel pursuant to precept 4 December, 1771; 500 acres in the District of Ninety Six, on the NW branch of Rabbins Creek, branch of Reedy River. Bounding Thos. Adamson and vacant land, S on Cornwell McMahon and Moses Kirkland, W on land belonging to the Indians and E on Isaac Huger's land. Certified 25 May 1772 by Moses Kirkland, D.S. [30]

Ravenel, Daniel: Memorial for Daniel Ravenel, Jr.; 500 acres on the SW fork of Rayburns Creek a branch of Reedy River in 96 Dist. Bound E on land of McMahon; W on Isaac Huger; S on said Daniel Ravenel, Jr. W by vacant land. Certified 15 December 1774. Also 500 acres in 96 Dist. on the NW branch of Rayburns Creek a branch of Reedy River. Bounded N on land of Thomas Adamson and vacant. S on Cornwell McMahon and Moses Kirkland, *W of land belonging to Indians*; E on Isaac Huger. Certified 2 February 1775. Granted 4 May 1775. 22 September 1775. Quit rent to commence in 2 years [Two tracts of 6 tracts listed] [31]

---

[27] LCDBK A: 123-127.
[28] LCDBK B: 395.
[29] LCDBK K: 318.
[30] [P20-19:1]
[31] [M2_364:2]

Simpson and Savage: Survey for William Savage and James Simpson, Esqrs. pursuant to precept 20 July 1772; 500 acres on waters of Rayborns Creek, Ninety Six Dist. Bounded N and S on land of Wm. Savage and James Simpson, Esqrs.; *W by Indian land.* Surveyed 3 March 1773. Ord. Co. 6 April 1773. Wm. Anderson, D.S. [32]

Weaver: 14 August 1789: [blank] Weaver is bounding on S side Reedy River below *Old Indian Line*, John Hall and Elizabeth Hall, his wife, deed of sale to Charles Smith. [33]

LOYALISTS NEAR RABURNS CREEK

"When the Cherokee Indians attacked the South Carolina frontier in July, 1776, some of the Loyalists took advantage of the opportunity for revenge again their Whig neighbours and joined the savages. A party attaching Lyndley's Fort was composed of 102 white men and 88 Indians. This fort, situated on Raburn's Creek, commanded the most strongly Loyalist settlements in South Carolina. Many of the assailants were from Raburn Creek neighborhood and it was believed by the Whigs that had the fort fallen a Loyalist insurrection would have follows." [David Fanning, who at that time lived on Raburn's Creek, led a party of twenty-five men from his neighborhood to make a juncture with the Indians at Pearls place [Parishes Place or plantation]
[Fanning's Journal, in N.C. St. Recs., XXII, 184.[34]

"Loyalism seemed strongest numerically in Robert Cunningham's and James Lyndley's companies, which comprised the settlements on Little River and Raburn's Creek. But even this area was not solidly Loyalist, for it was the home of a very prominent Whig, James Williams, and there evidently were a number of Whigs defending Lydley's Fort at the time it was attacked.[35]

Colonel John Boyd marched into Georgia back-county early in 1779 with a group of 600 loyalists to cooperate with the British invasion there. They were surprised and defeated by the Whigs commanded by Colonels Andrew Pickens, John Dooley, Elijah Clarke. James Lindley, John Anderson, Aquilla Hall, Samuel Clegg and Charles Draper were five, among those captured,

---

[32] [P19_325:1]
[33] LCDBK D: 146
[34] Barnwell, Robert W. Jr., *Loyalism in S.C. 1765-1785*, published as a thesis at Duke University, 1941, pg. 128.
[35] *Drayton's Memoirs*, I, pg. 342, 343; *Tennent's Journal*, in Gibbes, Doc. Hist., 1764-1776, pg. 231-232; Barnwell, pg. 130-131.

who were fined 86.4.0 each and sentenced to hang. Also tried at a special court held 22 February 1779 were others, including George Hollingsworth and William Lindley, probably the son of James. William Cunning (Bloody Bill) and James Cunningham, all probably neighbors of Lindley. The Sheriff of 96 Dist. compiled a list as part of his claim for money owned to him by S.C. State Government Audited Accounts #5335.

'To the goal fees on commitment of Jas. Linley, John Anderson, Aquilla Hall, Sm. Clegg and Charles Draper who were hanged &.C.£ 86; 4;0 each. . .
. . . ,,36

In the fall of 1973, Roy Christie, business man and historian in Laurens County read an article which mentioned Lindley's Fort, located in the area. Christie used Sara Nash's work, Kyzer-Helliam's map and questioned longtime residents of the area to see if he could locate the fort.

He called in Richard Carrillo, archaeologist from the University of South Carolina to come to inspect and document the site. "According to Christie, the fort was one of a number of fortified-type plantation homes in the area. A whole string of boundary forts ran in Greenville County. Laurens and Greenville county line served as a border between settlers and Cherokee Indian Nations. Whenever there was an Indian uprising, settlers would leave their home and take shelter in the fort."

Christie stated that when the fort was built, early records from 1776 refer to it as an "old fort; therefore, it likely served as a place of Defense in the colonial times that preceded the Revolution." The fort was most likely built prior to February 8, 1761, when 27 people on Raburn Creek had been killed during an Indian uprising. The property of Lindley, a Loyalist, the fort was taken over by the Patriots in 1775 for use as a defensive stronghold against Tory and Indian attacks."

The Laurens County Advertiser, December 4, 1979, states that "the fort has been found to be located as part of a cattle ranch owned by Raymond Williams of Mountville and is located on a knoll near Dirty Creek and Rabun Creek. A slight indentation around the top of the knoll marks where the trench in which the stakes for the stockade were placed upright. Piles of stone in the area mark where the fort's corners once stood. . . . the area is on the National Register." [37]

---

[36] No author given, *James Lindley, Tory*, website.Lindley.ntml 6 March 2006.
[37] Website: members.tripod.com/~MearsM2/Lindley.html. March 6, 2006.

QUAKERS IN THE RAYBURNS CREEK AREA

The following information on the Quakers who were in the Rabun Creek area was abstracted from the work of Rev. Silas Emmett Lucas, Jr.[38]

Large groups of Quakers had arrived in South Carolina by 1750. They came from Pennsylvania, Virginia, Maryland, Delaware and North Carolina. Some first settled in the Camden, South Carolina area and later moved into Laurens and Newberry Counties. The Bush River Monthly Meeting, in Newberry was established in 1770. The following is a list of Quakers who moved into the area and settled in the area of Reaburns Creek. There was a later migration out of South Carolina into Wrightsboro, Georgia and later to the Miami area of Ohio.

Babb, Mercer: [non-Quaker] Mercer Babb's father Joseph Babb, had been a Quaker, but had been disowned by the Quakers for "Marrying out of unity" as his wife was not a Quaker. Joseph Babb became the minister of the Beaverdam Church and later of Poplar Springs Baptist Church.

Brock, Elias: 31st January 1789: George, son of Elias, recrq.

Brock, Elias: 13th September 1792: Elias deceased by 13 September 1792: George, son of Elias, Dec., and Ann, Dist. 96, SC married Charity Cook.[39]

English, Joshua: Listed as early resident of Camden, S.C. Information states that Joshua English Sr. died in 1795.

Gaunt [Gault]: 1780, 11th mo. 2nd day. Zebulon Gaunt late of Camden Dist. [SC] married Mary Kelly, daughter of Samuel Kelly. [Lucas, Quakers, Bush River Monthly Meeting Records, pg. 105.]
1790, 3rd mo. 4nd day Nebo, Newberry Co., SC married Elizabeth Brooks.
1802, 4th mo. 29th day: Gaunt, Nebo, son of Zebulon Gaunt December Newberry Dist., SC married Judith.
1805: 3rd mo. 30th day: Gaunt, Nebo and family remove to Miami Co., OH.

Hollingsworth: 1768, 6 mo. 4th day: Joseph, son of George and Hannah, Berkley Co., SC married Margaret Hammer.
1777, 11 mo. 29th day Abraham's [Hollingsworth] death reported (leaving wife Amey and children).

---

[38] Lucas, Silas Emmitt, Quakers in South Carolina; Wateree and Broad River, Cane Creek, Piney Grove and Charleston Meetings, Southern Historical Press, Greenville, SC, 1991.
[39] Ibid, pg. 97.

1786, 11 mo. 16th day: James, son of George, deceased and Jane Dist. 96, SC married Sarah Wright.

1789, 3 mo. 12th day John Hollingsworth, son of George, December and Jane, Laurence Co., SC married Rachel Wright.

Kelly, Samuel: 16th December 1785: Samuel Kelly, son of Samuel of Edgefield, Co., SC found listing his marriage to Elizabeth Milhouse. Samuel Kelly native of Kings County, Ireland, came to Newberry, SC from Camden, SC. [40]

Kelly, Samuel: 30th April 1785: Abigail Kelly, daughter of Samuel and Hannah, of Dist. 96, SC married Samuel Gaunt. [41]

McClure: The surname McClure appears in Quaker Records of Bush River.[42]

McDonald, Mary, daughter of Hugh O'Neal.

Millhouse, Robert: 1792, Union Co., SC, Robert Millhouse, son of Henry and Rebecca married Sally Nelson Compton.
1799, 2nd mo. 23 day: Robert Millhouse gect Wrightsboro MM, GA.

O'Neal, Hugh: 1791, 11th mo. 10 day: Hugh O'Neall, son of William, December Newberry Co., SC married Ann Kelly.

Pugh, [not listed]

Thomas, Able: 30th April 1774: Abel Thomas with Edward, John and Isaac recrq. of father, Isaac and mother.
27nd November 1779: Abel Thomas rocf New Garden MM, NC dated September 25, 1779.
29th April 1797 Abel rmt Ruth Pemberton. [43]

Vanhorn: Robert: 1798, 10th mo. 27 day: Robert, Raburns Creek, rpd. mou [Benjamin Vanhorn is on Raburns Creek.]

Wadsworth, Thomas: 1799, 11th mo. 30 day: Thomas death reported. [44]

---

[40] Ibid., pg. 46, 105.
[41] Ibid., pg. 105.
[42] Ibid., pg. 106.
[43] Ibid., pg. 111.
[44] Ibid., pg. 111.

Wright, George: 6 February 1804: There is an estate appraisal for a George Wright, deceased granted to Jacob Niswanger and Jno. Shirley, Sr. Both of these men also lived in the Raburns Creek area, this may be the George Wright who had also lived in the same area.

Wright, George: 1 May 1804: Sale of estate of George Wright, dec'd. Purchasers: Edy Wright, John Shirley, Jacob Niswanger, Wm. McFerson, John Roberson, Zachariah Arnold, John Creecy, Robert Shirley, Wm. Williams, David Caldwell, Betsy Curtis, Wm. More, Saml. Anderson. Adm. Jacob Niswanger. [Many of the Quakers lived in the Raburns Creek area.] [45]

[45] Elliott, Colleen, *Laurens County, South Carolina Wills 1784-1840*, Southern Historical Press, Easley, SC, 1988, pgs. 44, 51.

RABUN CREEK SETTLEMENT 1762 - 1848

Abercrombie, James: Survey for James Abercrombie pursuant to precept dated 5 June 1770; 150 acres in Berkley Co. on Reburns Creek. Bounding SW on land claimed by William Hellimbs [Hellums]; NW by Bounty land; other sides vacant. Certified 3 December 1770. Pat. Cunningham, D.S. Examined by Josiah Kilgore, Surveyor General. Ord. Co. 8 July 1774. [P13_1:1]

Abercrombie, James: Memorial by James Abercrombie; 150 acres in Berkley Co. of Reburns Creek. Bounding SW by Wm. Hillumbs [Hellums]; NW on Bounty land; other sides vacant. Certified 8 July 1774 and granted 6 September 1774. Quit rent to commence in 2 years. 11 March 1775. Charles Sullivant. Patk. Cunningham, D.S. [M13_372:5]

Abercrombie, James: 4 May 1787: Witness to the will of William Baugh. [Revill, pg. 138] [LCWBK A: 27]

Abercrombie, James: Abercrombie's Mill – located at the junction of Rabon Creek and Dirty Creek. The mill was built in the 1780's. Later known as the McDaniel's Mill. [The Scrapbook, inside cover, item 18.]

Abercrombie, James: 22 November 1783: James Abercrombie, Administrator of the Estate of William McDonald. Wm. Baugh, Richard Pugh bound to John Thomas 96 Dist. sum £2,000. Inv. made 7 February 1784 by Jno. Baugh, Wm. Baugh, Chas. Bradey. [Young, pg. 216. Box 64, Pkg. 1535]

Abercrombie, James: 15 July 1786: We the arbitrators chosen to determine and decide a controversy between Charity Parker, Executrix and Andrew Rodgers, Junr., of the one part, and James Abercrumbie of the other part, viz.: it is our opinion and award that the parties do Quit all amounts on an even footing, the said Parker and Rodgers giving the said Crumbie [Abercrumbie] a Bond of Indemnity against a certain Bond now given to Dr. John Parker for £200 old currency. John Richey, Marmaduke Pinson, Jonathan Downs. Extended on Record 15 July 1786 [Revill, pg. 134] [LCDBK A: 315]

Abercrombie, James: 11 January 1787: James Abercrombie, of Ninety Six Dist., to Elias Brook of same place, for £100 stg.; 170 acres, part of 230 acres, on the branch called the Mill branch, where the said Elizas Brook now liveth. *Originally granted 8 May 1786 to James Abercrombie.* Signed James Abercrombie, Elizabeth Abercrombie. Wit: Hastings Doyall [Dial], John Pinson. [LCDBK B: 148-149]

Abercrombie, James: 12 April 1796: William Hall, of Charleston, S.C., to Abraham Box, of Laurens Co., S.C., for £55; 100 acres on Reedy River, bounding S by said river, all other sides by vacant land at time of the original survey. *Originally granted [no date given] to James Abercrombie,* conveyed to Acquilla Hall, now by William Hall, oldest son and heir of said Acquilla Hall, dec'd to Abraham Box. William Hall (Seal). Wit: Lewis Saxon, Thomas Lindley. Proved by Lewis Saxon 9 January 1797 before Reuben Pyles, J.P. [LCDBK F: 159]

Abercrombie, James: 23 December 1796: Jacob Williams, of Laurens Co., S.C., planter and John Cornelison, of same place, for the sum of £30 sterling sold unto said John Cornelison 100 acres of land being on the waters of Raburns Creek granted to the said Jacob Williams by James Abercrombie by deed baring date of 2 January 1785. Bounded on Samuel Williams Sr., William Owings, and William Boyd. Signed Jacob Williams (L.S.), Mary (X) Williams L.S. Wit. Saml. Cunningham, Jonathan Cox. Proved 18 February 1797 before Reuben Pyles, J.P. Wit: Saml. Cuningham, Jonathan Cox. Reuben Pyles, J.P. [The deed between James Abercrombie and Jacob Williams was not located.] [LCDBK F: 173]

Abercrombie, James: 23 December 1796: Jacob Williams, of Laurens Co., S.C., planter, to John Cornelison, of same place, for £30 stg; 100 acres on waters of Raburns Creek. Land granted to the said Jacob Williams by James Abercrombie by deed 3 January 1785. Bounded on land laid out for Samuel Williams Senr., William Owings, and Wm. Boyd. Jacob Williams (L.S.), Mary (X) Williams (L.S.) Wit: Saml. Cuningham, Jonathan Cox. Proved by Jonathan Cox 18 February 1797 before Reuben Pyles, J.P. [LCDBK F: 173-174]

Abercrombie, James: 1 February 1799: James Abercrombie, Laurens Co., SC to Elisha Casey, of same place. Whereas in and by a certain grant dated 15 November 1792; for £6, *part of 200 acres of land being granted to Lewis Saxon* and made from him to the said James Abercrombie, I the said James Abercrombie bargain, sell and deliver a part of the above mentioned the sum of 12 acres of land lying on the south side of Rabourns Creek in Laurens Co. and the south fork of said creek. Bounding N to the Creek and to Owing Reids. Bounding on Owing Reid. Wit: Wm. Camp. Thomas May. Signed James Abercrombie (L.S.) Proved by William Camp 18 February 1979 before Reuben Pyles, J.P. See Lewis Saxon. [LCDBK F: 422-423]

Abercrombie, James: 4 August 1793: I Moses Pinson of Laurens Dist., S.C., in consideration of the sum of $120 to me paid by James Huggins, of same place, have granted and released unto the said James Huggins a tract of land contain 100 acres more or less, being the *west part of 200 acres granted* *to James Abercrombie.* Bounding Samuel Williams and Wm. Owens and Wm. Boyd, on the waters of Rabourns Creek, conveyed from James Abercrombie to Jacob Williams and from Jacob Williams to John Cornelison. Set my hand Moses Pinson. Wit: Moses Pinson, Senr., John (X) Har[r]y. Proved by Moses Pinson, Senr. 30 February 1807 before Josiah Blackwell, J.P. [LCDBK J: 37]

Abercrombie, James: 27 November 1817: John Blackstock, of Laurens Dist., S.C., to Joseph McCullough, of Greenville Dist., S.C., for $1200; 300 acres in two tracts: 1) 100 acres purchased from David Smith, bounded S by Reedy River, other sides vacant at time of original survey and which was *originally granted to James Abercrombie* and by him conveyed to Acquilla Hall and by William Hall, heir at law to the said Acquilla Hall sold to Abraham Box, by him conveyed to David Smith 2) the other supposed to contain 100 acres on the N side of Reedy River, beginning on the river at the mount of the first branch above Peachlins old field or creek lying a small branch frequently dry, near the old Road above Peaching old field, to Halls old post to the river. John (B) Blackstock (Seal) Wit: C. Saxon, Ira Arnold. Dower of Jane Blackstock, give of the within named John Blackstock 27 November 1817 before Wm. Arnold, J.Q. Proved by Charles Saxon 27 November 1817 before Wm. Arnold, J.Q.[LCDBK K: 194]

Abercrombie [Abercromey], John: Survey for John Abercromey pursuant to precept dated 2 February 1768: 200 acres in Craven Co. on Raiburns Creek. Bounded S by land held by James Abercromey; all other sides by vacant land. Certified 27 April 1768. Ralph Humphreys, D.S. [P11_122:1]

Abercrombie, John: Memorial for John Abercrombie; 200 acres in Craven Co., S.C., on Rayburns Creek. Bounding S on land of James Abercrombie; other sides vacant. Certified 8 November 1769 and granted 21 December 1769. Quit rent to commence in 2 years. 24 January 1770. Jno. Lindly. Ralph Humphreys, D.S. [M10_34:5]

Abercrombie, James: 4 August 1803: I Moses Pinson, of Laurens Dist., S.C., to James Huggans, of same place, for $120; 100 acres being the West part of 200 acres granted to James Abercrombie. Bounding on Samuel Williams, Wm. Owens and Wm. Boyd, on waters of Rabourns Creek, conveyed from James Abercrombie to Jacob Williams and from Jacob Williams to John Cornelison. Moses Pinson (Seal). Wit: Moses Pinson Senr., John Harry. Proved by Moses Pinson, Senr. 20 February 1807 before Joshua Blackwell, J.P. [LCDBK J: 37]

Abercrombie, James: 29 November 1819: LWT of James Abercrombie. Daughter Marey Odonial $100, wife of William Odonial; daughter Isabella

Blackwell $30; daughter Rebecca Goswell, wife of Gabril Gowell [Gabriel Jowell,] a negro girl named Jane; daughter Suzanah Mathews, daughter Hannah Brook, daughter Margret Blackwell, daughter Elizabeth Andrews, grandson James Acrumbie; to my son James Acrumbie all the land I now possess estimated at about 800 acres with mills, building of all kinds, smith and other working tools, etc. To my step son Archibald McDaniel, Junr. 12 acres of land lying at the point joining lines below the point hills. Appoint son James Abrumbie and Elias Brook executors. James (X) Acrumbie (Seal). Wit. E.L. Rowling, David Bell, John Neel. [LCWBK E: 56]

[Family: Wife unnamed, daughters Mary O'Donial, wife of William O'Donial; Isabella Blackwell, Rebecca Goswell, wife of Gabriel Gowell [Gabriel Jowell,], Suzanah Mathews, Hannah Brook, Margaret Blackwell, Elizabeth Andrews, grandson James Acrumbie, son James Abercrombie, step son Archibald McDaniel, Junr.]

Abercromby, James: 2 April 1825: Hall County, Georgia: James Kirkpatrick, of Hall County, GA and John Kennedy of Laurens Dist., S.C., for $800; 300 acres, one supposed to contain 100 acres. Bounded S by Reedy River, on all other sides by vacant land at time of the original survey and which was *originally granted to James Abercromby* and by him sold, the other 100 acres supposed, on the first branch above Peaching old field or creek. Jas. Kirkpatrick (LS). Wit: James Brown, William Curry J.J.C. Proved State of Georgia, Decalb *sic* County. Dower of Elizabeth Kirkpatrick, wife of James Kirkpatrick 20 May 1825. Proved by James Brown 20 May 1825 before Ruben Cone, J.J.C. [LCDBK L: 196-197]

Abercrombie, John or Smith, Job: 20 September 1799: John Abercrombie, of Laurens Co., S.C., to Jonathan Abercrombie for $500; 150 acres on the waters of Rabourns Creek. Bounded on the W and NW by Lewis Saxon, W by Thomas Johnson, S by William Johnson, conveyed by indenture from Job Smith to John Abercrombie in 1 December 1788. Wit: Johna. and Margaret Cochran. Charles Smith, J.P. [Note: Poor microfilm] [LCDBK F: 471]

Abercrombie John: 3 June 1797: Robert Coker of Laurens Co., S.C. and Philip Coker, of same place, for £40; 100 acres *being part of a tract of land granted to John Abercrombie 1 December 1769*. On the N side of Rabourn Creek, E on James Abercrombie, N to a black oak and W to said creek. Robert (R) Coker. Wit. Robert Coker Jr. William Hellums. Proved by Robert Coker Junr. on 18 July 1787 before Jno. Coker, J.P. [LCDBK F: 229]

Adams, David: 18 June 1805: David Adams, of Laurens Dist., S.C., to William Mitchell, of same place, for $300; 48 and a half acres on Tumbling Shoals on Reedy River. David (X) Adams (LS) Jeremiah Hollingsworth, Elizabeth (X) Mitchell. Proved by Jeremiah Hollingsworth 10 August 1805 before Jonthan. Downs, J.Q. [Plat shows bounding on Abraham Box, Lewis Saxon, John Arnold, Samuel Nabours, and on the Waggon Road. [LCDBK H: 109]

Adams, David: 28 October 1805: William Mitchell, of Laurens Dist., S.C., to William Arnold and Benjamin Arnold, of same place, for $400; 50 acres known by the name of Tumbling Shoals, lying on both sides of Reedy River. Being a tract of land conveyed by David Adams to William Mitchell by a deed dated 18 June 1805. Wm. Mitchell (LS). Wit: Jeremiah Hollingsworth, Arthur Taylor. Dower of Mary (X) Mitchell, wife of the within named William Mitchell given 5 November 1805 before Jonthan. Downs, J.Q. Proved that Jeremiah Hollingsworth 5 November 1805 before. Jonthan. Downs, J.Q. [H: 112]

Adams, John: 26 December 1795: John Adams, of Laurens Co., S.C., planter, in consideration of the love, good will and affection I bear to my loving son Abraham Adams, of same place, give 150 acres on the N prong of Reaburns creek. Wit: Richard Childress, Jesse Childress. Signed John Adams. Proved by oath of Abraham Adams 2 January 1796 before Joseph Downs, J.P. [LCDBK F: 69]

Adamson, Thomas: Bounding Daniel Ravenel in 1775. No memorial found for Thomas Adamson.

Alexander, Joseph: No survey or Memorial located for Joseph Alexander.

Alexander, Joseph: 18 February 1814: Fleming Hatcher to James Delong for $30; 80 acres *originally granted to Joseph Alexander,* conveyed from Joseph Alexander to said Fleming Hatcher to James Delong. The 80 acres being on the S Fork Rabourns Creek. Bounded by John Nash, Edward Nash. Flannon (X) Hatcher (LS), Flemmin (X) Hatcher (LS) *sic.* Wit: John Harris, George Crowder, Burr Harriss. Proved by John Harriss on 13 April 1814 before Jesse Childress, J.P. [LCDBK K: 72]

Alexander, Samuel: Survey for Samuel Alexander pursuant to precept dated 2 September 1767; 100 acres in Craven Co. on Raiburn's Creek. Bounded N by Moses Coppock; W by James McCain. Certified 10 March 1768. R. Humphreys, D.S. [P13_30:3]

Alexander, Samuel: Memorial for Samuel Alexander; 100 acres in Craven Co. on Reyburns Creek. Bounded N on Moses Cappock; W on James McCain; other sides vacant. Certified 10 March 1768 and granted 4 October 1768. Quit rent to commence in 10 years. 27 February 1769. Samuel Alexander. Ralph Humphreys, D.S. [M8_341:4]

Allen, Daniel: Survey for Daniel Allen pursuant to precept dated 20 July 1765; 500 acres west side Raburns Creek a branch of Santee River. Bounded E on said creek; other sides vacant. Certified 24 August 1765. Jno. Pearson, D.S. Ord. Co. 4 February 1767. [P9_70:1]

Allen, Daniel: Memorial for Daniel Allen; 500 acres in Berkley Co. on the W side of Reyburns Creek on a branch of Santee River. Bounded E by said Creek; other sides vacant. Certified 4 February 1767 and granted 1 February 1768. Quit rent to commence in 2 years. 5 March 1768. For the Memorialist James (X his mark) Ryan. John Pearson, D.S.[M9_444:4]

Allen, Daniel, Sr.: 30 April & 1 May 1768: Daniel Allen, blacksmith and yeoman, to James McCain, yeoman, both of Craven Co., S.C., for £100; 150 acres in Craven Co., S.C., bounding SE on Daniel Allen, Jr.; SW on James Ryan; NE on Raiburns Creek, other sides on vacant land, *being a tract of land granted Daniel Allen, Sr.* Plat certified by Ralph Humphreys, D.S. Wit: Ralph Humphreys, James Lindley. Recorded 8 April 1771 by Henry Rugeley, Reg. [See Memorial for James McCain] [Langley, Vol. IV, pg. 165]

Allen, Daniel: 22 August 1799: I Joseph Holmes, of Laurens Co., S.C., to Jonathan Cox for consideration of $165; 50 acres on Rabourns Creek. Bounded on SE on Jane Holingsworth, dec'd., now Nathan Hollingsworth, W John Hollingsworth; NE by said Creek. Being part of a tract of land *originally granted to Daniel Allen* and by him conveyed to James McCain by lease and release dated 1 May 1768 and by the said James McCain bequeathed by his last well and testament, the said 50 acres unto his daughter Elizabeth McCain, alias, Elizabeth McGill, and by the said Elizabeth McGill and her husband Barnabas McGill sold and conveyed to the above mentioned Joseph Holmes by lease and release dated 3 September 1791. Joseph Holmes. Wit: Jonathn. Downs, Henry Buckner. Dower of Ann Holmes wife of the within names Joseph Holmes. Proved by Jonathan Downs, J.P. [LCDBK F: 530]

[Family: James McCain, daughter Elizabeth, wife of Barnabas McGill.]

Allen, Daniel: 13 January 1800: John Galbreath and James Galbreath, of Newberry Co., S.C., to Benjamin Vanhorn, of Laurens Co., S.C., for £70, 250 acres being half of 500 acres on Reaburns Creek. *Originally granted to Daniel Allen.* Bounded E by said Creek; other sides vacant. Which half was conveyed by said Daniel Allen to Samuel Kelly and conveyed by said Samuel Kelly to William Ancrum and Aaron Loocock and conveyed by said William Ancrum and Aaron Loocock to said John Galbreath and James Gilbert. Signed John Galbreath, James Galbreath. Wit. Joseph Furnas, Ephraim Owen. Release of Dower 21 February 1800 by Susanna Galbreath, wife of James Galbreath. Proved by Joseph Furnas before Thos. Brooks, J.P. [LCDBK G: 155-157]

Allen, Daniel: 28 April 1800: Benjamin Vanhorn, of Laurens Dist., to David Cox, of same place, for £28; 57 acres on W side of Reaburns Creek waters of Saluda, being part of 500 acres. *Originally granted to Daniel Allen* ½ moiety of which was conveyed to Samuel Kelley, and said Kelley conveyed to Wm. Ancrum and Aaron Loocock and by said Ancrum and Loocock conveyed to John Galbreath and said Galbreath conveyed the said Vanhorn. Signed Benjamin Vanhorn. Wit: Jonathan Downs, Wm. Downs. Proved 7 April 1800 by William Downs before Jonathan Downs, J.P. Release of Dower by Joanne Vanhorn, wife of Benjamin Vanhorn 26 April 1800. [See Benjamin Vanhorn] [LCDBK G: 28-29]

Allen, Daniel: 13 August 1805: We George Hollingsworth, James Hollingsworth, John Hollingsworth, Henry Hollingsworth and Susanna Hollingsworth, of Laurens Co., S.C., to Nathan Hollingsworth, of same place, relinquish to Nathan Hollingsworth all right and claim in 110 acres on Rabourn Creek. Bounded on Daniel Allen, Senr., N on said creek, NW on James McCain, SW on James Ryan. It being a *part of grant to said Danl. Allen, Senr.* conveyed to Daniel Allen Jr. then to James Hollingsworth, dec'd., by lease and release dated 21 August 1778 & by the said Jane Hollingsworth bequeathed to the said Nathan Hollingsworth by a verbal will which the said George Hollingsworth, Jane Hollingsworth, John Hollingsworth, Henry Hollingsworth and Susannah Hollingsworth submits to. George Hollingsworth (Seal), James Hollingsworth (Seal), John Hollingworth (Seal), Henry Hollingsworth (Seal), Susannah Hollingsworth (Seal). Wit: Evan Thomas, Josiah Cook, Joab Brooks. Proved by Evan Thomas 11 February 1806 before Jonthn. Downs, J.Q. [LCDBK H: 127-128]

Allen, Daniel: Proved 5 January 1807: Nathan Hollingsworth, of Laurens Co., S.C., to Henry Buckner, of same place, for $400; 110 acres on Reaburns Creek. being part of a tract of land *original granted to Daniel Allen, Senr.* and conveyed to Daniel Allen, Jurn. and by him to Jane Hollingsworth by a verbal will which the other heirs of the said Jane Hollingsworth, dec'd. have confirmed by a formal relinquishment of title 30 August 1805. Nathan Hollingsworth, (LS). Wit: Clarissa Saxon, Lewis Saxon. Proved by Lewis Saxon 5 January 1807 before Samuel Cunningham J.P. [Plat: At the instance and request of Daniel Allen, Senior. I have admeasured and laid off from his plantation unto Daniel Allen Junr., a parcel or tract of land containing 110 acres. Certified per by Ralph Humphreys, D.S. Plat shows 110 acres bounded on Daniel Allen Senr., Jno. Ryan, and James McCain.] [LCDBK H: 188]

Allen, Daniel: 24 April 1800: Benjamin Vanhorn, of Laurens Dist., S.C., to David Cox, of same place, for £28; 57 acres on the W side of Reaburns Creek waters of Saluda. *Being part of 500 acres originally granted to Daniel Allen* and being ½ moiety of said 500 acres of which was conveyed to Samuel Kelley 21 October [torn] and by Samuel Kelly conveyed to Wm. Ancrum and Aaron Loocock and by Ancrum & Loocock to John Galbreath, then by John Galbreath and Jane Gailbreath to Benjamin Vanhorn. Benjamin Vanhorn (LS) Wit: Jonthan. Downs, [torn] Downs. Proved by William Downs 7 April 18[torn] before Jonthan. Down, J.P. Dower of Joanna Vanhorn, wife of Benjamin Vanhorn given 26 April 1800 before [torn]. [See Daniel Allen] [LCDBK G: 28-30]

Allen, Daniel: 31 October 1820: John Belton, of Laurens Dist., S.C., to William Belton, of Newberry, for $376; 100 acres on waters of Rabourns Creek. *Originally granted to Dan[iel Allen?]* and from him by divers transferences conveyed to me by John Belton. Bounded by William Holliday, Junr., David Bell, Gabriel Joel [Jowell?], David Parks. John Belton. Wit. John Coates, Dolly Coates. Dower of Charity Belton, wife of the within named John Belton made 21 March 1821 before S. Cunningham, J.Q. [LCDBK K: 322]

Allen, Lydall: 6 January 1837: Laurens Dist., S.C.,: We Wiley Hill, Jonathan Allen, Charles Allen, William D. Allen, Frances Allen, William Atkins and Sarah his wife and Lucy of Laurens *being heirs and distributes of Lidall [Lydall] Allen*, in consideration of $1400 to Joseph Goodwyn of said place; all that tract containing 200 acres on Rabourns Creek bounded by Ezekiel Mathews, William Henderson, William F. Downs, Lewis Allen, and Milly Allen. Hereunto annexed the said part of the real estate of Lydall Allen, deceased and sold by consent, for partition and distribution to heirs. Wiley Hill (LS), Wiley Hill attorney for Charles Allen (LS), Lewis B. Allen (LS), Frances D. Allen (LS), Wm. Atkins (LS), Sally Atkins (LS). Wit: Lewis L. Allen, William F. Downs. Plat made 17 April 1834 shows bounding Wm. Henderson, L. Allen, W.F. Downs, Mrs. Allen's spring, Ezekiel Matthews. [LCDBK: N: 214]

[Heirs of Lydall Allen: Wiley Hill, Jonathan Allen, Charles Allen, Wm. D. Allen, Frances Allen, William Atkins and wife Sarah, Lucy Allen.]

Allen, Lydall: 22 March 1819: William Atkins, Laurens Dist., S.C., to William F. Downs, of same place, for $400; 84 acres on waters of Raybans Creek. Bounded on Lydall Allen, Lucy Smith, heirs of Thomas Lindley, said William F. Downs. William Atkins. Wit: Robert Dunlap, Nat. Day. Proved by Nat. Day 26 March 1819 before John Garlington, Clk. & J.P. [See LWT of Thomas Lindley] [LCDBK K: 240]

Allen, Peter: No survey for 100 acres found. Allen conveyed land 26 & 27 December 1768 to Richard Pugh. [See below] [See Pugh, Richard]

Allen, Peter: Memorial by Richard Pugh for 100 acres in Berkley Co. on a small branch of Reedy River, called the Reedy fork, bounded on all sides at the time of the survey on vacant land. *Originally granted 1 July 1768 to Peter Allen.* Quit rent to commence in two years. And conveyed by him to the memorialist by lease and release bearing date 26 and 27 December 1768. Set his hand 30 October 1769. James Loosk. Certified by R.L. [M8:530-2]

Allison, David: 2 April 1791: Whereas certain disputes and controversies have arisen between Charles Braudway [Charles Brody], of Ninety Six Dist., Laurens Co., S.C., and David Allison, of same place, concerning the boundaries and division lines between the said David Allison and the said Charles Braudy *sic*, the lines is not to be found corresponding with the plat or courses of the same. Settlement (meets and bounds). To acknowledge a sufficient right and title of the land lying to the Westward side of a line running S 45 W from a Wahoo[?] William Allisons old line bounding on Joseph Pinsons land. To be vested in the said Charles Brawdy until it intersects the true lines of the land contained with in the lines of the said Charles Brawdy's grant. Signed David Allison (L.S.) (A his mark). Wit. Joseph Pinson, John Woody. Proved 2 April 1791 by Joseph Pinson before John. John Hunter, J.P. [Also see Charles Broadway/Broady/Brody] [LCDBK D: 29-30]

Allison, David: 15 October 1788: David Allison, named as husband of Dorcas Cunningham in the LWT of her father John Cunningham. See LWT of John Cunningham. [Revill, pg. 143] [LCWBK A-1: 17]

Allison, Robert (also see Bize): 3 April 1805: Robert Allison, of Laurens Dist., S.C., to Mary McDaniel (widow of the late William McDaniel, Dec'd) and to Sarah and William McDaniel, children and heirs at law of the said dec'd. for $100; 150 acres on waters of Rabourns Creek. Bounded on land of Thomas Burton, W. Manley, J. Cochran, and Thos. Johnson, being a part of 500 acres granted to H.D. Bize and by sundry conveyances to me the said Robert Allison. Robert Allison (Seal). Wit: Hastings Dial, John Cochran. Proved by John Cochran 5 March 1806 before J. Blackwell, J.P. [LCDBK J: 29]

Allison, Robert: 5 January 1791: LWT of Robert Allison. I give unto my beloved wife Frances Allison, all horses, cattle, sheep, hogs, and household furniture; to my beloved son James Allison or his heirs 1 shilling sterling; to my daughter Margaret 1 shilling sterling, Mary 1 shilling sterling, son Robert Allison one shilling stg., daughter Janie 1 shilling stg, son Wm Allison 1 shilling stg. To my son Joseph Allison, I leave and bequeath 150 acres of land whereon he now lives, lying on the S side of Beaverdam Creek, to my son Samuel Allison one shilling sterling. To my son Francis Allison 50 acres whereon Wm. Stone now lies. To my daughter Ann, one black walnut chest during her lifetime and after her death to revert to her son Wm. Hellams. To my son Watson Allison, 1 shilling sterling. To my son Moses Allison one shilling sterling, to my daughter Bettey one black walnut chest after her mothers decease. Son Lewis Allison land whereon I now live, lying on the N side of Beaverdam Creek. Also that if the said Lewis Allison should neglect to maintain his mother at the discretion of my executors the said land to be sold to maintain his mother thereby to be judged by my son Joseph Allison and my grandson James Allison, whether or not she be used well. I ordain my wife Francis Allison executrix and my son Joseph Allison Executor. Robert Allison (Seal). Wit: William Turner, Emanuel York, Wm. Higgens. [LCWBK A: 53.]

[Family: Wife Francis, sons, James, Robert, Joseph, William, Francis, Moses, Joseph, Samuel, Lewis, Watson, daughters; Margaret, Mary, Janie, Ann's son is Wm. Hellams, Bettey, grandson James Allison; not mention of Watson Allison in will of William Hellams, Watson married to daughter of William Hellams.]

Allison, Thomas: Survey *originally for Hans Jurig Mars.* [See Hans Jurig Mars]

Allison, Thomas: Memorial for Thomas Allison; 100 acres in Berkley County, on Allisons Creek, in the fork between Broad and Saludy River. Bounded at the time of the survey by vacant land. *Originally granted 22 January 1759 to Hans Jurig Mars,* quit rent to commence in 10 years (being on Bounty); and conveyed by him to Thos. Allison the memorialist by Lease and release 10 November 1757. 6 April 1771. Thomas Allison. [See Hans Jurig Mars 1759 grant.] [M10_376:5]

Allison, Thomas: 11 March 1788: Thomas Allison, blacksmith, and Catherine, his wife, of Laurens Co., S.C., to James Adair, planter, of same place, for £57; 100 acres on Broad and Saluday Rivers on Allisons Creek. *Originally granted 22 January 1759 to Hans Jorgman [Hans Jurig Mars]* and by him to Thomas Allison on 9 & 10 November [_]. Bounded by vacant land at time of survey. Thomas Allison. Wit: Robert Hanna, Robert McCrarey, John Jones. [See Hans Jurig Mars] [LCDBK B: 328-300]

Allison, Thomas: Thomas Allison's records in same pack as William Allison. [Young, pg. 10; Box 2 Pack 24]

Allison (Ellison), Thomas: 3 October 1806: Thomas Ellison *sic*, of Laurens Dist., S.C., to William Ford, of same place, for $200; _ acres all that tract whereon I now live, only a spring that is in the said bounds, of this tract I except for the use of William Brody, which I gave him before the sealing for his use and the said land being on the S side of Reedy River. Bounded on lands of William Brody, William Simmons, John Pringle and Rebecca Elliott. Thomas Ellison (LS). Wit: William Simmons, Leannah (X) Powell. Proved by William Simmons 8 October 1806 before Jas. Powell, J.P. [LCDBK H: 223-224]

Allison, Thomas: 15 December 1780: LWT Thomas Allison – Ninety Six Dist., S.C. Executors: Wm. Pugh, Thos. Richardson. Wit: Richard Pugh, Thomas Richardson, Charles Brody. Wife: Margaret. Children: Thos, David, Ellenor, Nancy, Margaret Allison. Son-in-law Charles Brody. Inventory made January 9, 1783 by Wm. Baugh, Saml. Scott, Richard Owings, Sr. Thomas Allison's records in same packet: Benjamin Kilgore, Esq. of Duncans Creek. 96 Dist., Admr. of estate of Thomas Allison late of Reaburns Creek. Inventory made 26 April, 1783 by Basil Holland, Thos. Murphy, Robt. Hanna. [Young,. Box 3, Pack 24, pp 9 & 10.]

[Family: Wife Margaret, sons, Thomas, David, daughters, Ellenor, Nancy, Margaret, son-in-law Charles Brody.]

Allison, Watson: 3 December 1795: Land grant for 288 acres recorded in Grant Book F. No. 5 pg. 296. [LCDBK K: 187]

Allison, Watson: 5 January 1791: Watson Allison named as the son of Robert Allison in his will dated 5 January 1791 [See Robert Allison]. [LCWBK A-1: 54]

Allison, Watson: 28 March 1794: Watson Allison, of Laurens County, S.C., to Joseph Allison, of same place, for 35 shillings; 130 acres on a branch of Raburns Creek, it *being a part of a track of a creek of land granted to the*

30

said Watson Allison by the Honorable Charles Pinckney. Bounded SW on William Hed's [Head's] land, N on vacant land, SE by Watson Allison, SW by Watson Allison. Watson (A) Allison (Seal). Wit: Wm. Roundtree, John Wallace. Proved by Wm. Roundtree 21 March 1803 before Jonthn. Downs, J.Q. [LCDBK G: 602-603]

Allison, Watson: 2 August 1796: Joseph Allison, of Laurens Dist., S.C., planter, to Jacob Manord, of same place, planter, for $100; 130 acres bounded E by Mark Hanna, N on Solomon Niblet, SW on land belonging to William Hed [Head] at the time of original survey, down the branch on Jacob Morard to John Woody's line. On the waters of Raburns Creek and is the NE *part of 288 acres originally granted to Watson Allison 3 December 1795.* Joseph (a his mark) Allison (LS). Wit: Archd. Young, Thos. McCrary. Dower of Elizabeth Allison, wife of the within named Joseph Allison given 3 October 1806 before Danl. Wright, Q.M. Proved by Archd. Young 4 November 1806 before Daniel Wright, Q.M. [LCDBK H: 179-180]

Allison, Watson: 18 September 1815: Jacob Manord [Mayner?], of Laurens Dist., S.C., to Robert Thompson, of same place, for $200; 130 acres on the waters or Rayburns Creek. Bounding on E on Mack Hamonds [Hanna?] Line, N on Solomon Niblet, SW on William Head at the time or the original survey. thence down the branch to Jacob Manard's land, to John Woodies line when surveyed. *Original grant to Watson Allison 3 December 1795.* Jacob (A) Manard (LS) Wit: Flanders Thompson, Thomas Childress. Proved by Flanders Thompson 15 September 1815 before Jesse Childress, J.P. [LCDBK K: 187]

Allison, Watson: 13 November 1795: Watson Allison, of Laurens Co., S.C., planter to Jacob Mayner [Manard?], of same place, planter for £40; 152 acres on waters of Raiborns Creek, waters of Reedy River. *Being part of a grant of 288 acres dated 3 December 1792 to Watson Allison.* Including the tract where of Samuel Allison now lives, it being the N and W part of the above mention tract. Watson (A) Allison (Seal) Wit: Israel (I) Eastwood, Joel (X) Johnston, Elizabeth (E) Eastwood. Proved by Israel Eastwood 13 October 1795 before Hudson Berry, J.P. [LCDBK F: 341]

Allison, Watson: 21 October 1808: Watson Allison, of Anderson County, S.C. Deed Book I pg. 277, is mentioned in the deeds of William Stantion. [Revill, pg. 34]

Allison, William: Survey for William Allison pursuant to precept dated 6 April 1762; 150 in the fork between Broad and Saludy Rivers on a branch of Saludy River called Reyburns Creek. Bounded NE part on land laid out to Robert Box and part vacant; other sides vacant land. Certified 15 July 1762.

Edwd. Musgrove, D.S. [P7_277:1]

Allison, William: Memorial for William Allison; 150 acres in Berkley Co. in the fork between Broad and Saludy Rivers on a branch of Saludy river called Reaburns Creek. Bounded NW on land laid out to Robt. Box; other sides vacant. Certified 15 July 1762 and granted 4 November 1762. Quit rent to commence in 2 years. 20 November 1762. Edward Musgrove, D.S. William (A his mark) Allison. [M6_14:2]

Allison, William: Survey for William Allison pursuant to precept dated 3 February 1767; 50 acres between Broad and Saludy Rivers near Raburns Creek. Bounded NE on land surveyed for Charles Broady; SE vacant; SW land surveyed for Edward Box; NW vacant. Certified 18 March 1767. Richd. Winn, D.S. [P10_136:1]

Allison, William: Memorial for William Allison; 50 acres in Berkley Co. between Broad and Saludy rivers near Reyburns Creek. Bounded NE by land surveyed for Charles Broady; SE vacant land; SW by Edward Box; NW vacant. Certified 18 March 1767 and granted 28 August 1767. Quit rent to commence in 2 years. 1 October 1767. For the Memorialist Richard Winn. Richard Winn, D.S. [M9_328:1]

Allison, William: 1 March 1790: John Baugh, Jr. son of William Baugh, deceased, freeholder, of Laurens Co., to Joseph Pinson of same place, for £25 stg., 50 acres on Raborns Creek, land *granted to William Allison 26 August 1767,* bounded by Edward Box and Charles Bardy (Broady, Broadway). Wit: John Pinson, Moses Pinson. Proved 28 April 1790. [LCDBK C: 161-162]

Allison, William: Survey for William Allison pursuant to percept dated 30 February 1773; 200 acres in Craven Co. on waters of Raburn's Creek. Bounding NE on said Allison; NW by Robert Boxe; SE on William Williamson; all other sides by vacant land. Certified 11 February 1773. Pat. Cunningham, D.S. [P13_39:1]

Allison, William: Memorial by William Allison; 200 acres in Craven Co. on the waters of Rayburnes Creek. Bounding NE on said Allison; NW on Robert Box; SE on Wm. Williamson; other sides vacant. Certified 11 February 1773 and granted 23 June 1774. Quit rent to commence in 2 years. 11 June 1774. Chas. Suillvant. Pat. Cunningham, D.S. [M13_94:3]

Allison, William: 22 July 1791: David Allison and wife Dorcas to George Hollingsworth for £80, stg.; 100 acres, *part of 200 acres granted to William Allison,* my father bequested to me, where I now live on Reaburns Creek.

Bounded on other half of tact and on Robert Box. Wit: John Hutson, Charles England. Jonathan Down, J.P; [Information from Sarah Nash Deeds, pg. 129 Poor microfilm] [LCDBK F: 105]

Allison [Ellison], William: 2 June 1788: William Baugh, Exer., of William Ellison, dec'd, of Ninety Six Dist., S.C., last will and testament dated 23 December 1780 to Thomas Cuningham, for £54; 150 acres in Berkley Co. in the fork between Saluda and Broad River on a branch of Saluda River called and known by the name Rabourns Creek. Bounded on NE on land laid out for Robert Box; all other sides vacant. *Originally granted said William Ellison 4 November 1762.* Wit: John Cuningham, Wm. McDavid, Joseph Downs, J.P. [Poor microfilm] [LCDBK C: 55-57]

Allison, William: 1 March 1790: John Baugh, Jr., son of William Baugh, deceased, of Laurens Co. to Joseph Pinson, of same place, for £75, 20 acres being on E side of Rabourn Creek, *it being part of 150 acres originally granted Wm. Allison 4 November 1762.* Bounded by NE by land surveyed for Charles Broady (Broadway); E when surveyed by vacant land; SW by land surveyed for Edward Box. Signed John Baugh. Wit: John Pinson, Moses Pinson. Sworn by John Pinson before Joseph Downs, J.P. 8 March 1790. [Note: lease stated 50 acres; release 20] [LCDBK C: 161-162]

Allison, William: 8 January, 1816: Jeremiah Collins, of Laurens Co., S.C., to John Burton, of same place, for $200, 50 acres E side of Raybourns Creek. Bounded on the N by Edward Box; W by William Allison; S by Chas. Broadway. *Originally granted to [Moses Pinson]?* Also a tract of 20 acres on the E side of Raybourns Creek, *being part of land granted to Wm. Allison, being part of land granted to Moses Pinson.* Jeremiah Collins. Wit: Archid. McDaniel, William Burton. Proved by William Burton 19 March 1816 before Gabriel Jowel, J.P. [LCDBK K: 130]

Allwidice (Allirdin), John: No Survey located.

Allwidice [Alliordin], John: Memorial for John Allwidice [Alliordin]; 100 acres in Berkley Co. N side of Saludy River, on a branch of Rayburns Creek. Bounded on all sides by vacant land. Certified 14 October 1768 and granted 12 December 1768. Quit rent to commence in 10 years. 2 May 1769. Wm. Gist, D.S. David Merrell. [B in margin]. [M8_427:2]

Allwedice (Alliordin), John: 9 November 1770, conveyed 100 acres of land to David Maull.

Allwedice [Alliordin], John: 2 February 1804: James Maull, heir and son of David Maull dec'd., of Jacksonborough, S.C. to Abraham Bolt, of Laurens

Dist., for $200; 100 acres on the N side of Saluda River on a branch of Raburns Creek. Bounded on SW on land of John Alwidice [Allurdin]; other sides vacant. *Originally granted to Gilbert Chalmers 12 December 1768,* and conveyed by him to said David Maull 9 November 1770 to said David Maull. Also 100 acres on N side of Saluda River on a branch of Raybourns Creek bounding at time of survey by vacant land. *Originally granted to John Allwedice 12 December 1768* and him conveyed to said David Maull 9 November 1770. Signed James Maull. Wit: Isaac Underwood, P. G. Wharton. Proved by Pleasant Wharton 20 March 1804 before Joseph Downs, J.P. [See Gilbert Chalmers] [LCDBK H: 24]

Anderson, William: Survey for William Anderson pursuant to precept dated 5 November 1771; 400 acres on a branch of Saludy called Reedy River. Bounded E on Richard Lang, John Crotia[?] Foster, James Long and John Caldwell, N on Aaron Pinson, W on George Wright and the said Reedy River. Certified 11 March 1772. Jno. Caldwell. [P13-60:1]

Anderson, William: Memorial for William Anderson; 400 acres in Craven Co., S.C., on a branch of Saludy called Reedy river. Bounding E on Richd. Longs, Jno. Crotia?, Foster and James Longs and John Caldwell, N on Aaron Pinson; W on Geo. Wright, and said Reedy River. Certified 2 March 1773 and granted 8 July 1774. Quit rent to commence in 2 years. 19 December 1774. Delivered 2 June 1775 to John McNees. Jno. Caldwell, D.S. [M13_1543:1]

Anderson, William: 28 December 1792: William Anderson of Laurens Co., S.C. of the one part and David Anderson, of same place, Witnessseth that the said William Anderson, Molly, his wife, for the consideration of the full sum of £75 sell unto the said David Anderson one tract of land containing 200 acres in the County of Laurens, situated on Long Lick Creek a branch of Reedy River, beginning on a corner beach of Reaburns Creek at George Wrights old Mill. Bounded by said George Wright, land granted to Foster, land sold by said William Anderson to Wm. Hughes, also bounding Stephen Woods land and William Mitchell. *Originally granted to the said William Anderson* by William Bull in the year 1774. Wit: James Middleton, George Anderson and Molly (M) Anderson. Signed by William Anderson L.S., Molly (her mark) Anderson, L.S. Proved 27 December 1792 before George Anderson, J.P. [LCDBK E: 136-137]

Anderson, William: 9 January 1794: William Anderson and Mary, his wife, both of the county of Laurens, S.C., planter to Lewis Banton, of same place, planter. For £92 stg; 208 acres on the branches of Long Lick Creek, waters of Reedy River. *Being part of 500 acres granted to the said William Anderson 1 October 1784* and conveyed by the said William Anderson to

Lewis Banton by Deed. William Anderson (Seal), Moly (X) Anderson (Seal). Wit: George Anderson, John Rodgers, Stephen Wood. Proved by Stephen Wood 9 January 1794 before George Anderson. [LCDBK E: 393-394]

Anderson, William: 7 March 1795: William Anderson, of Laurens Co., S.C., to John Middleton, of same place, for £50; 100 acres on waters of Reedy River being on the said Long Lick Creek. Bounded on John Fosters' corner, Lewis Banton's corner, Long Lick and David Anderson. Granted to William Anderson in 1774. Signed Wm. Anderson (Seal), Molley Anderson (Seal). Wit: James Raines, Wm. McCall, Luke Demency[?] Proved by Luke Demcey 3 August 1799 before Lewis Graves, J.P. [Poor microfilm copy.] [LCDBK F: 465]

Anderson, William: [No Date]: Estate for William Anderson. Purchasers were John Middleton, Andrew Anderson, James Anderson, James Rains, Ambrose Anderson, John Dunlap, Molley Anderson, Samuel and Geo Anderson. George Morgan. Randolph Mitchell, Robert Young, James Clemons, Lewis Graves, Henry Hazel, James Anderson. [Some of these names are in the deeds of William Anderson. [LCWBK A: 190]

Andrews, Ezekiel: 4 February 1804: Jesse Pugh and wife Lydia Pugh, his wife, of Laurens Dist., S.C., to John Creecy, of same place, for $250; 75 acres on S side of Reedy River on Black Creek on the said river. In the original plat adjoining lands belonging to *Ezekiel Andrews*, and John Wait. Jesse Pugh (X) (LS) Wit: Joel Sims, John Sims, Geo. Wharton. Dower of Lyda Pugh (X) given 29 December 1805 before David Anderson J.Q. Proved by John Sims 29 December 1805 before DD. Anderson, J.Q. [LCDBK H: 139]

Armstrong, John: Found bounding land owners on Rayburns Creek.

Armstrong, John: Memorial by John Armstrong for 100 acres in Craven Co., S.C., Bounded on all sides by vacant land. Certified 15 April 1767 and granted 20 August 1767 to the memorialist. Quit rent to commence in 2 years from date. Set his hand 12 September 1767. For the memorialist James Armstrong. Francis Buttett, D.S. [M9-306:2]

Babb, Joseph: 1769 in South Carolina and is found bounding in 1769 William Burrows; 1772 James McLinto, 1773 Rachel Humble, who are on Rayburns Creek. Joseph Babb, Quaker roots and a brother of Mercer Babb who settled in Newberry, SC.

Ballard, Richard: 1778 land granted. [See Bowman]

Ballard, Richard: 21 March 1771: Pertinent to an order of Council I hereby certify for Richard Ballard a tract of 150 acres surveyed for him the 21 May 1771 in Berkley Co., on the Reedy River. Bounding NE on Robert Box, NW on Jacob Wright, all other sides on vacant land. [Plat of 150 acres survey for Richard Ballard]. [LCDBK F: 404]

Ballard to Bowman: No deed has been located for the sale of lands to Jacob Bowman from Richard Ballard.

Ballard, Richard: 19 November 1787: Jacob Bowman, son and heir to Jacob Bowman, deceased, of Laurens Co., S.C., to John Bowman, of same place, for £10; 150 acres on both sides of Reedy River. Being land *originally granted to Richard Ballard in 1778* and conveyed by him to Jacob Bowman, deceased. Bounded on Robert Box, now David Alexander, Jacob Wright. Jacob Bowman. Wit: Geo. Anderson, Saml. Wharton, Sarah Wright. [See Bowman] [LCDBK B: 267-268]

Ballard, Richard: 19 March 1796: John Bowman, of Laurens Co., S.C., to Reuben Arnold, of same place, for £23 stg.; 50 acres on NE side of Reedy River, it being a *part of 150 acres granted to Richard Ballard on 2 March 1773.* John Bowman (LS). Wit: John Hinton [Kinton?], John Shurley, Wm. Moore. Proved by John Shurley 18 August 1776 before George Anderson, J.P. [LCDBK F: 151-152]

Ballard, Richard: 6 December 1798: John Bowman, of Mercer Co., Caintucky [Kentucky], to Zechariah Arnold, of Laurens Dist., S.C., for £50 stg.; 100 acres S side of Reedy River, being part of 150 acres granted to Richard Ballard 2 April 1773 by Bull. John Bowman (LS) Wit: Lewis Graves, John (X) Willard, George (mark) Morgan. Proved by Lewis Graves 18 February 1797 before James Abercrombie, J.P. [LCDBK F: 429]

Ballard, Richard: 4 January 1803: Reuben Arnold, of Laurens Dist., S.C., to William Moore, of same place, for $200; 50 acres on E side Reedy River, *being part of original granted to Richard Ballard.* Reuben Arnold, Elizabeth (S) Arnold (LS). Wit: James Clardy, Robert Franks, Michael Swindle. Proved by Michael Swindle 4 January 1803 before James Powell, J.P. [LCDBK G: 588]

Banton, Lewis: Survey for Lewis Banton pursuant to precept dated 5 June 1771; 300 acres in Craven Co., on Long Lick Branch, waters of Saludy. Bounded on all sides by Patent land. [Plat] shows bounded by Ebenezer Stern; Thomas Wood; John Caldwell; Enos Simson. Certified 16 September

1771. John Armstrong, D.S. [P13_128:1]

Banton, Lewis: Memorial by Lewis Banton for 300 acres in Craven Co., on the Long Lick branch the waters of Saludy bounded by vacant land. Certified 16 September 1771 and granted 22 November 1771 to the memorialist. Quit rent to commence in two years. Set his hand 13 January 1772 John Armstrong, D.S. [M11-104:3]

Banton, Lewis: 11 September 1786: Lewis Banton, of Laurens Co., S.C., to Wm. Goodman of same place for £47; 200 acres on a branch of Reedy River called Long Lick, *being part of 300 acres granted to Lewis Banton 22 November 1771.* Bounding S on Wm. Caldwell, E on Enos Stinson, N on E on Ebenezer Starns. Lewis Banton, Jedida Banton. Wit: Joshua Arnoll [Arnold], Thomas Boyce. [LCDBK B: 60-62]

Banton, Lewis: 5 March 1790: Lewis Banton, of Laurens Co., S.C., to Wm. Goodman, of same place for £27; 55 acres on a branch of Reedy River called Long Lick. Bounding on lands of said William Goodman, David Caldwell, Lewis Banton and Aaron Starnes. The 50 acres being part of a tract of land containing 300 acres that was *granted unto the said Lewis Banton in 22 November 1771.* Lewis Banton (Seal), Jedidah (J) Banton (Seal). Wit. John Carter, Clabourn Goodman, Mary (M) Banton. Proved by Clabourn Goodman 12 May 1794 before Jonathan Downs, J.P. [LCDBK E: 241-243]

Baugh, John: Meeting of Monday 25 April 1774: Read the Petition of the persons under named praying to have their Elapsed platts certified. [Holcomb, Brent H., *Petitions for Land From South Carolina Council Journals, Vol. VII,* SCMAR, Columbia, SC, 1999, pg. 264.]

Baugh, John: Survey for John Baugh pursuant to precept dated 5 December 1767; 100 acres in Berkley Co. on the waters of Reedy River. Bounded on all sides on vacant land. Certified 20 December 1769. Pat. Cuningham, D.S. [P13-150:3].

Baugh, John: Memorial for John Baugh, in Berkley Co., for 100 acres on waters of Reedy River. Bounded on all sides by vacant land. Certified 25 April 1774 and granted 17 May 1774 to the memorialist. Quit rent to comment in two years from date. Set his hand 25 October 1774. Pat. Cunningham, D.S. [M13-64:3]

Baugh, John, son of William Baugh: 13 August 1788: John Baugh, witnessed deed from John Henderson to Mary Henderson for 150 acres on Rabourns Creek. [LCDBK B: 395]

Baugh, William: Survey for William Baugh pursuant to precept dated 6 February 1767; 150 acres lying on Reedy Creek, and the S fork, it being nine feet wide and seven inches deep. Bounded on all sides by vacant land. Certified October 22, 1767. Richd. Winn, D.S. [P10-156:1]

Baugh, William: Memorial for John Baugh, in Craven Co., S.C., for 150 acres on the S fork of Reedy River. Bounded on all sides by vacant land. Certified 7 June 1768 and granted 15 July 1768 to the memorialist. Quit rent to commence in ten years from date. Set his hand 28 September 1768. R. Winn, D.S. Delivered 8 October 1772 to William (A) Alliston. [M8-242:3]

Baugh, William: Wit for land deed of Richard Owen, land on Reedy River on 2 September 1786. [LCDBK B: 300]

Baugh, William and John: 22 November 1783: Witness will of William McDonald, 22 November 1783: Estate Admr. by James Abercrombie, Wm. Baugh, Richard Pugh bound to John Thomas 96 Dist. sum £2,000. Inv. made Feb 7 1784 by Jno. Baugh, Wm. Baugh, Chas. Bradey. [Young, pg. 216]

Baugh, William: 4 May 1787: LWT of Wm. Baugh, of Laurens Co., S.C., freeholder . . . .to my beloved wife Agness the third of my land whosesoever she chooses as long as she lives and also the third of all my movable property. I give to my sons John, William an David to each of them a part of my land; to my son John I give all between the creek and river above the old fence. to my son William I give, beginning at the lower corner of my improvement at the river straight by the E side of my old apple orchard. To my son David I give the remainder. The middle part after my wife Agness deceases. to daughter Elizabeth I give one cow and her bed and bedding; all the rest of my effects to be equally divided among the rest of my children (Viz.) Daughter Margaret, Mary and Agness, Jonathan. .Ordain my wife Agness Baugh and my son John Baugh to be my Executors. Signed Wm. Baugh (Seal). Wit: James Abercrombie, Wm. Obannon, John Pinson. [Ingmire, pp 13-14] [LCWBK A: 21]

[Family: Wife Agness, sons John, William, David, daughters Margaret, Mary and Agness, Elizabeth.]

Baugh, William: 4 May 1787: LWT of William Baugh, freeholder, to my wife Agness Baugh, the third of my land whosesoever she chooses as long as she lives and also the third of all my movable property. To my sons John, William and David to each of them a part of my land: to son John I give all between the creek and river above the old fence; to my son William I give beginning at the lower corner of my improvement at the river straight by the E side of my old apple orchard to my back line. Also to my son David I give the remainder. The middle part after my wife Agness deceased. To my daughter Elizabeth I give one cow and calf and her bed and bedding; and the rest of my effect to be equally divided amongst the rest of my children (Viz: Margaret, Jonathan, Mary and Agness after the reduction of my debts expenses of burial. Ordain my wife Agness Baugh and my son John Baugh Executors. Wm. Baugh (LS). Wit: James Abercrombie, Wm. Obannon, John Pinson. [Ingmire, pg. 14] [LCWBK A: 21].

[Family: Wife, Agness (called Nancy in deed), sons: John, William, David; daughters: Elizabeth, Mary Agness, Margaret.]

Baugh, John: 1 March 1790: Between John Baugh, Junr., son of William Baugh, deceased, of Laurens Co., S.C., to Joseph Pinson, of same place, for £7; 10 sh.; 20 acres on E side of Rabourns Creek, being part of 150 acres granted to Wm. Allison on 4 November 1762 and lies upon or next to the creek on the S side. John Baugh (LS) Wit: John Pinson, Moses Pinson. Proved by John Pinson 3 March 1790 before Joseph Downs, J.P. [LCDBK C: 162]

Baugh, John: 10 September 1796: John Baugh and Rosanna Baugh, of Ninety-Six Dist., Laurens Co., S.C., to George Cuningham, of same place, for £80; 100 acres on waters of Reedy River bounded on all sides by vacant land. The same being land laid out for John Baugh. John Baugh (LS) Rosanna (X) Baugh (LS). Wit: Philip Malkey [Mulkey], John Cuningham. Proved by John Cuningham before Joseph Downs, J.P. [LCDBK F: 123]

Baugh, John, Jr.: 2 June 1796: John Baugh, Junr., of Laurens Co., S.C., to Thomas Hood for £30 stg.; 84 acres between Reedy River and Reedy River, *being part of 150 acres granted to William Baugh, deceased* and by him willed to the said John Baugh. Bounded on Patrick Cuningham. John Baugh, Junr. (LS). Wit: John Cochran, Wm. Baugh. Dower of Dorcas Baugh, wife of the within named John Baugh, Junr., 18 July 1796 before be Jonathan Downs, J.L.C. Proved by John Cochran 19 July 1796 before James Saxon, J.P. [Plat At the request of John Baugh, Junr. I have laid off to Thomas Hood a tract of land containing 84 acres on the waters of Reedy River, having such form and marks as the plat shows . Plat for 84 acres on Reedy River, bounding Pat. Cuningham and on Reedy fork. 2 June 1796 John Cochran. [LCDBK F: 115]

[Family: Son of William Baugh; Dorcas, wife of John Baugh, Jr.]

Baugh, William Sr. and Jr., deceased: Before 14 November 1798: [See below LCDBK F: 421]

Baugh, William: 14 November 1798: We Nancy Baugh, widow of William Baugh, Senr., deceased, and mother of William Baugh, Junr, deceased, and David Baugh, of Laurens Co., S.C., to David Culbertson, of same place, for £30; 100 acres, being part of 150 acres of land *originally granted to William Baugh, deceased.* Bounding on the river along the lines of the said original survey until it intersect a creek called Reedy River, down said creek where it empties into Reedy River. Survey of 150 acres that lyes below the Reedy fork creek which said part of said survey was by William Baugh, Senr, decease in his LWT willed unto William Baugh, Junr, deceased and the above mentioned David Baugh. Nancy Baugh, (LS) David Baugh (LS). Wit. Thomas Hood, Abel Thomas, John Hill. Proved by Thomas Hood 19 February 1799 before James Abercrombie, J.P. [LCDBK F: 421]

Beard, Hugh: *Originally granted to Hugh Beard.* [no date given] He is in area by February 1786.

Beard, Hugh: 27 May 1820: I James Dorroh, Junior, of Laurens Dist., S.C., to John B. Simson, for $100; all my part of that undivided tract of 113 acres of land, *originally granted to Hugh Beard* and by divers transferences conveyed to William Dorroh, deceased, and transferred to me as one of the heirs of the said William Dorroh, deceased. Bounding James Smith, Robert Nickels, John McClanahan and lying of Reedy River. James Dorroh. Wit: John Cunningham, Junr. John Dorroh. Proved by John Cunningham, saddler, 3 April 1821 before James Dorroh, J.P. [LCDBK K: 322]

Blackley, John: 23 September 1812: John Blackley, Laurens Dist., S.C., to William Holliday, Junior, for $50; 36 acres on branch of Rabourns Creek. Bounded E on James Boyd, N on Widow Cunningham, W on Charles Miller. John Blackly (LS). Wit: Thomas Lewers, Robert Holliday, Matthew Holliday. Proved by Thomas Lewers 13 April 1813 before Saml. Cunningham, J.P. [LCDBK K: 17]

Blake, George: 1771 George Blake is bounding James Smith.

Bocquett, Peter: Survey for Peter Bocquett, Jr. pursuant to precept dated 4 May 1773; 616 acres in Ninety Six Dist. to the N side of Beaver Dam Creek. Bounded S by Samuel Simpson; SE by Thomas Hambie; NW land laid out; W by Samuel Hambie. Certified 12 May 1773. Jonathan Downs, D.S. [P13_256:2]

Bocquett, Peter: Memorial for Peter Bocquett; 616 acres in Ninety Six, the N side of Beaver Dam Creek. Bounding S by Samuel Simpson, SE on Thomas Hambie, NW of land laid and W on Samuel Hambie. Certified 12 May 1773 and granted 19 August 1774 to the memorialist. Quit rent to commence in 2 years from date. Set his hand 24 Jan 1775. Delivered to the memorialist 10 February 1778 by C. J. L. Jonathan Downs, D.S. [M13-257:2]

Bocquett, Peter: Survey for Peter Bocquett, Jr. being residue part of said precept in Craven Co., S.C., Ninety Six Dist. on NE side of Reyburn's Creek on a branch called Mountain Creek. Bounded on land claimed by Thomas Waring; all other sides vacant. Certified 14 May 1773, Jonathn. Downs, D.S. [P13_156:1]

Bocquett, Peter: Memorial by Peter Bocquett; 250 acres in 96 Dist. on Western branch of Rayburns Creek. Bounding SE on Thomas Waring; other sides vacant. Certified 14 May 1773 and granted 31 August 1774. Quit rent to commence in 2 years. Delivered 21 March 1775 to the Memorialist by Wm. Patri[d]ge. Jonathan Downs, D.S. [M13_319:2]

Bolt, Abraham, Senior: 4 January 1834: I Abraham Bolt, Senior, of Laurens Dist., S.C., to Edward Bolt, of same place, for $500; 246 1/4 acres on the branches of Raburns Creek. Meets and bounds given. Signed Abraham (A his mark) Bolt. Wit: William Bolt, William Manly. Proved by William Manly 18 February 1834 before____, J.P. [LCDBK M: 50]

Bolt, John: 29 August 1817: John Bolt, of Laurens Dist., S.C., to Samuel Bolt, of same place, for $64; 44 acres on waters of Rabens Creek. Bounded on lands of John Bolt and said Samuel Bolt. John Bolt (LS). Wit: George Peck, Wm. Milner. Proved by Wm. Milner 1 February 1810 before S. Cunningham., Q.M. [LCDBK K: 274]

Bolt, Wm. P.: 12 April 1817: Wm. P. Bolt, of Laurens Dist., S.C., to Samuel Bolt, of same place, for $265; 112 acres on waters of Raborns Creek, waters of Saludy. Bounded on lands of David Garry, John Bolt, Jonathan Vaughan, Samuel Franks, Thomas Parker and John Mathews. Wm. P. Bolt (LS). Wit: B. Nabers, E.S. Roland. Proved by E.S. Roland 7 February 1820 before S. Cunningham, J.Q. [LCDBK K: 274]

Bolling, Samuel: 1 January 1787: Grant for 250 acres on Reaburns Creek.

Bolling, Samuel: 2 January 1790: Samuel Boling, of Ninety Six Dist., S.C., planter to Drury Sims, of same place, for £55 stg; 150 acres on both sides of Reaburns Creek, *being part of 250 acres granted to Samuel Boling 1 January 1787,* whereon said Drury Sims now lives. Beginning on the NE side of the South fork of said creek near corner on Patrick Reylie [Riley] line, and Tully Choice's line. Samuel Boling (LS) Wit; Thomas Baskitt, John (J) Willson, Robert Boling. Jonathan Cries. Proved by John Willson 6

March 1790 before Daniel Wright, J.P. [LCDBK D: 50-51]

Bolling, Samuel: 8 November 1792: Drury Sims, Laurens Co., S.C., minister, to Samuel Nesbit, of same place, planter, for £16; 40 acres on both sides of Rabourns Creek. Beginning on Edward Nash's line opposite to the corner of the said Drury Sims fence and up the same near to the mouth of a branch, up hill to corner of John Wilson's' line, on Patrick Riley's line. *It being part of a tract of land originally granted to Samuel Boling* and conveyed to a deed unto Drury Sims. Drury Sims (LS) Wit: Elisha Hunt, Edward Nash. Proved by Edward Nash 17 October 1803 before Jonthan. Downs, J.P. [LCBDK G: 679]

Bolling, Samuel: 9 May 1808: LWT of Samuel Bolling, of Laurance sic Dist., S.C., living on Readi River, planter, to my beloved wife Abi Bolling, the house and plantation where I now live. . . . at her death the land is to be divided equally between my two youngest sons Samuel Bolling and Thornberry Bolling. . . . to my son John Bolling feather bed and furniture. . . debts is to be paid the remainder of my estate to remain in my wife Abi Bolling hands till death. Then to be divided equally between all my children Viz., Robert Bolling, Nancy Sullivant and Elizabeth Dunklin, Tully Bolling, John Bolling, Lucinda Bolling, Samuel Bolling, Polly Bolling and Thornberry Bolling. I appoint my beloved wife Abi Bolling Executrix and my son Robert Bolling, Tully Bolling, John Bolling and Samuel Bolling Executors. Signed Samuel. Bolling. (Seal). Wit: William Choice, Mary Choice, Tully Choice. [LCWBK C-1: 318]

[Family: Wife Abi, children: Robert Bolling, Nancy Sullivant, Elizabeth Dunklin, Tully Bolling, John Bolling, Lucinda Bolling, Samuel Bolling, Polly Bolling, Thornberry Bolling.]

Bowman, Jacob: Survey for Jacob Bowman pursuant to precept dated 4 December 1764; 100 acres in Berkley Co., on Reedy River (or rather creek). Bounded SE by Geo. Wright; other sides vacant. [no D.S. or date] [P8_211:1]

Bowman, Jacob: Memorial by Jacob Bowman 100 acres in Berkley Co., bounding on waters of Reedy River, about 2 chains wide and one foot deep. Bounded SE on land laid out to George Wright, other sides vacant. Certified 28 December 1796 and granted 16 July 1765 to the memorials. Quit rent to commence in two years. Delivered 9 August 1765. For Jacob Bowman, Pat. Calhoun, D.S. [M8-8:2]

Bowman [Bohman], Jacob: Memorial by Jacob Bohman for 100 acres in Berkley Co., on a branch of Saludy called Reedy River bounded NE by the said river, all other sides by vacant land. *Originally granted 15 July 1765 to David Haig* and by conveyed to Jacob Bohman the memorialist by lease and release dated 16 and 17 August 1769; also a tract of 100 acres as above bounded SE on land of Robt. Long, deceased, SW on land laid out to Jacob Bohman, all other sides by vacant land. *Granted 16 July 1765 to George Wright* and by him and Sarah, his wife, sold and conveyed to Jacob Bohman the memorialist by lease and release dated 1 and 2 September 1769; also 100 acres as above bounding SE on lands said to be an old survey, SW on an unpassable swamp and waters and lands belonging to the estate of Robert Long, deceased, NW on vacant land and NE part on vacant and part on land laid out to James Killpatrick. *Originally granted to John Bryan* the 8 August 1767 and conveyed by him and Mary, his wife, by lease and release dated 16 and 17 November 1767 to Jacob Bohman the memorialist; also a tract of 200 acres of land as above on the [torn] side of Reedy River bounded SW on said river, N on land of Richard Shurley, all other sides on vacant land. granted 25 June 1772 to John Kilters [?] and by him conveyed to Jacob Bohman by lease and release dated 15 and 16 July 1772. Set his hand 1 June 177(torn). Jacob Bohman. [See surveys for David Haig and John Bryan] [M12-210-1]

Bowman, Jacob: 3 April 1796: Jacob Bowman listed in the Appraisal of estate of Patrick Cunningham, dec'd 3 April 1796. [LDWBK: A: 187]

Bowman, Jacob: 26 May 1769: Jacob Bowman witness to deed from Richard Long,"deceased" to Daniel Williams. [See John Reed].

Bowman, Jacob, deceased: 11 September 1788: Sarah Right, *sic* of Laurens Co., S.C., do constitute appoints and ordain Jacob Bowman, my lawful attorney, to settle all matters relative to my part of my father, George Bowman' estate and all other of my business of what ever nature it may be in the State of Virginia and to bring suits in my name receiving money and give receipts and to pay money in all affairs of that of my deceased father George Bowman. Sarah Wright. In Open Court. Wit: Lewis Saxon, Clerk. [LCDBK B: 364]

Bowman, Jacob: 24 March 1795: Sarah Bowman is dis. mou. Bush River Monthly Meeting. This may be the Sarah Bowman Right [Wright] listed above, daughter of Jacob Bowman. [Lucas, *Quakers*, pg. 97.]

Bowman, Jacob: 2 October 1782: Estate Administrator by Sarah Bowman, Saml. Rosemond, Saml. Wharton, yeoman, bound, to Jno. Ewing Calhoun Ord. 96 Dist. S.C., sum £2,000. Sarah Bowman was of Reedy River in 96 Dist. S.C. [Young, pg. 30, Box 10, Pack 176.]

Bowman, Jacob: 11 September 1788: Sarah Bowman, Administrator of Jacob Bowman, deceased, of Laurens Co., S.C., appoints her son Jacob Bowman, her attorney relative to her part of her father Laurens Stephens' Estate. Signed Sarah Bowman. In Open Court. Wit: Lewis Saxon, C.C. [Poor microfilm] [LCDBK B: 365]

[Family, Daughter, Sarah Bowman, her son, Jacob Bowman.]

Box, Abraham: 10 June 1788: Samuel Neighbours to Abraham Box for £100 Stg; 114 acres on Reedy River, *part of 640 acres grant May 9, 1785.* Bounding John Box. Samuel Neighbours. Wit: Lewis Saxon, C.C. [Poor microfilm] [LCDBK B: 390]

Box, Edward: Survey for Edward Box pursuant to precept dated 3 February 1767; 150 acres in Craven Co. on Raiburns Creek. Bounding W on land held by Robert Box; S on land held by Wm. Ellison [Allison]; other sides vacant. Certified 23 February 1767. Ralph Humphreys, D.S. Ord. Co. 2 April 1771. [P13_290:2]

Box, Edward: Memorial for Edward Box; 150 acres in Craven Co., S.C., on Rayburns Creek. Bounding W on land held by Robert Box; S on land held by William Ellison; other sides vacant. Certified 2 April 1771 and granted 10 April 1771. Quit rent to commence in 2 years. 2 May 1771. Delivered 2 March 1773 to Jas. Lindly. Ralph Humphreys, D.S. [M10_425:2]

Box, Edward: 1 April 1775: Edward Box, freeholder and planter of Craven Co., S.C., to Matthew Love, of same place, for £200; 150 acres on Reaburns Creek. Bounded on W on lands held by Robert Box, S on land held by Wm. Allison. *Originally granted to Edward Box 10 April 1771.* Signed Edward (E) Box, Lydia (X her mark) Box, [wife of Edward Box]. Wit: James Lindly, William Boyd. Proved by William Boyd 6 April 1775 before James Lindly, J.P. [LCDBK D: 221-222]

Box, Edward: 2 February 1776: Matthew Love, of Ninety Six Dist., to George Neily, of same place, for £200; 150 acres on Reaburns Creek. *Originally granted 10 April 1771 to Edward Box.* Bounded on W by Robert Box, S by land held by William Allison, other sides vacant. Signed Mathew Love, Agnes (X her mark) Love. Wit: Sarah Terry, Jno. Beel. Proved 3 February 1776 by John Beel before Champness Terry, Esq. [LCDBK D: 224-225]

Box, Edward: 2 February 1792: George Neily, of Laurens Co., Ninety Six Dist., S.C. and Archibald McDonald, of same place, for £75; 100 acres a tract of land on the waters of Reaburns creek. Bounded W on land of Robert Box, S on William Allison, the other sides vacant. Signed George Neily (O his mark), Agnes (+) Neily. Wit. James Abercrombie, Mathew (+) McDonald. Proved by James Abercrumbie 6 January 1792 before George Anderson, J.P. (See land above. *Originally granted to Edward Box.* [LCDBK D: 225-227]

Box, Edward and Henry: 15 February, 1815: We Henry Box and Edward Box, of said Laurens Dist., S.C., to James South, of same place, for $320; 150 acres on Rabourns Creek, *being part of a tract of land originally granted to James[?] Williams,* the original line bounding S on Henderson and Sim[?], N with Hurnes[?] Brocks line, mouth of Burris Creek to Rabourns Creek. Edward (X mark) Box (Seal), Henry Box (Seal). Wit: James Powell, Joseph South. Proved by Joseph South 15 April 1815 before Joseph Bolton, J.P. [LCDBK K: 100-101]

Box, Henry: 22 August 1810: John Clark, sheriff, to Samuel Todd for $181; 350 acres on Reedy River, waters, *formerly property of Henry Box.* Bounded on William Moore, Wm. McPherson, James Roberts, Robert Box and the widow Moore. Sold by writ of Fascias issued from the Court of Common Please made the sum of $3.12 unto which Erwin Patten and Jones lately in the court of Common Please recovered against the said Henry Box as debt also the sum of $14.50. John Clark (Seal) Wit: John Garlington, John Dunlap. Proved by John Dunlap 23 February 1811 before John Garlington, Clk. [LCDBK J: 196]

Box, Henry: 27 February 1826: Jacob Niswanger, of Laurens Dist., S.C., to John Burton, for $400; 142 acres lying on the branches of Rabons Creek. Bounded S on lands of Pat. Spierin [Spieren?] and James Henderson, E and N on James South, W on Robert Shurley. *Being a tract originally owned by Henry Box.* Jacob Niswanger (LS). Wit; James Crocker, James Wait. Proved by James Crocker 4 February 1828. [LCDBK M: 27]

Box, James: 4 February 1793: land grant on Long Lick Creek.

Box, James: 11 November 1794: William Norris and Anna, his wife, all of Laurens Co., S.C., planter, to Rodger Murphy Senr., of same place, for £7, 10 shillings.; 100 acres on Long Lick Creek, being *part of tract granted to James Box,* by his Excellency., Wm. Moultrie, Esq., Lieut. Governor on 4 February 1793. Bounded on James Wills, Long Lick branch. William (his mark) Norris (L.S.) Anna (a her mark) (L.S.). Wit: Wm. (X) Cannon, Isaac (his mark) Bailey, Wm. (his mark) Sims. Proved by William Cannon 21 December 1794 before Thomas Wadsworth, J.L.C. [LCDBK F: 29-30] **Box, James**: 8 January 1795: William Norris and wife Anna Norris, his wife, of

Laurens Co., S.C., Joel Hughes, of same place, for £50; 100 acres bounded on Roger Murphy, Senr.'s line, on a watery branch, along said James Wells line to Burris's stake corner, to Wm. Crisp, Wm. Osbourn, Reedy Road, Daniel Osbourn, *being part of grant to James Box 30 January 1793* and conveyed to said Norris. William (mark(Norris (LS) Anna (A) Norris (LS) Wit: Thos. Hughes. John Osbourn, Danl. Osborne. Proved 17 July 1795 by Thos. Hughes before Zech. Bailey, J.P. [LCDBK F: 41-42]

Box, James and Henry: 13 June 1795: Purchaser at estate sale of Aaron Pinson, Deceased. [Elliott, pg. 12]

Box, John: 20 April 1791: Personally came Abraham Box, of Laurens Co., S.C., this day before me a Justice of said county and said that about six years ago [about 1785] from the date of this or something better that he heard Henry Box tell him the said Departed father John Box that he gave up to him all the right and title of a certain land lying an being on Reedy River in the county said which tract of land being then occupied by David Alexander who at that time lived on said land and further saith not, Sworn. Abrm. Box before Joseph Downs, J.P. [LCDBK F: 428]

Box, John: 19 April 1810: John Box, of Laurens Dist., S.C., to William Williams, of same place, for $140; 169 acres on waters of Rabourns Creek. Bounded on Benjamin Williams, Solomon Cole, John Henry, Wm. Boyd. John Box. Wit: Martin Graves, John Shurley [Shirley], Robert Shurley [Shirley]. Proved by John (X) Shirley 31 August 1810 before Larkin Gaines, J.P. [LCDBK J: 168-169]

Box, John, [bounding Mitchell]: 9 February 1813: Macklin Mitchell, of Laurens Dist., S.C., to William Rutledge, of same place, for $300; 108 acres on branches of Reedy River. Bounded on Thomas Allison, John Box, Fleet Nabers, John Johnson, Joseph Mahon. McLin Mitchell. Wit: Ira Arnold, Allen Mitchell. Dower of Polly Mitchell, the wife of the within named Machlin Mitchell given 21 February 1813 before Wm. Arnold, J.Q. Proved by Ira Arnold 9 February 1813 before Wm. Arnold, J.Q. [LCDBK K: 12]

Box, John: 2 November 1815: LWT of John Box: To my wife Rachel Box all my estate, both real and personal, during the term of her natural life and after her decease I give the tract of land whereon I now live to my two granddaughters Rachel Box and Luisa Box, daughter of Jemima Box, in perpetuity, it being 100 acres binding on lands belonging to Samuel Nabors, Jane Moore and Reedy River. I give or allow my daughter Jemema Snead the privilege of living on part of the said 100 acres during her lifetime. I give $50 to my grandson Elisha Williamson. To my son Shadrack Box $5; to my son Robert $5; and the balance of the money arising from the sale of said negro girl Charity I give to be equally divided between my son Abraham Box, Benjamin Box, Molly South, Rachel Banks, and Jemima Snead [Sneed]. Appoint my friend Elisha Williamson executor. John (mark) Box. Wit: William Arnold, Robert Nabors, Joseph M. Even. Recorded 5 February 1821. [LCWBK E:.173]

[Family: Wife Rachel, daughter Jemima Snead, Molly South, Rachel Banks; sons, Shadrack, Robert, Abraham, Benjamin; granddaughters: Rachel Box and Luisa Box, daughter of Jemima Box, grandson Elisha Williamson.]

Box, John: 24 August 1830: Whereas John Box, late of Laurens Dist., S.C., in his last will and testament bequeathed to his two granddaughters Rachel Box and Luisa Box, daughters of Jeremiah Box upon the death of his wife, the tract of land on which he lived containing 100 acres. Bounded by lands then belonging to Samuel Nabors, Saml. Moore and Reedy River in fee simple, and whereas Rachel Box, one of the devisees in the above will for the tract of land aforesaid has sold and conveyed to John Williamson, of said place, in fee simple, all her interest in the said tract of land and joined her sister Louisa in a general power of attorney authorizing James Walden, of Jackson Co., Alabama, to sell and convey the said tract of land. Know all that I James Walden of the County of Jackson in the State of Alabama, attorney in fact and deed for the said Rachel Box and Louisa Box, of Franklin Co., Tennessee, for $100; to Elisha Williamson of Laurens Dist., have by virtue of the authority granted sell unto the said Elisha Williamson; 100 acres in Laurens Dist., on Reedy River. Bounded by Jane Moore and others. James Walden, Attorney for Rachel and Luisa Box (Seal). Wit: William F. Down, Hugh Brewster. Proved by Hugh Brewster 11 December 1830 before Alfred Perritt, J.Q. [LCDBK M: 176]

Box, Robert: Survey for Robert Box pursuant to precept dated 3 August 1755; 150 lying and being on a branch of Saludy called Reaburns Creek. Bounded on all sides by vacant land. Certified 22 October 1755. John Hamelton, D.S. [P7_282:1]

Box, Robert: Memorial for Robert Box; 150 acres in Berkley Co., on a branch of Saludy River called Reaborns Creek. Bounded by vacant land. Certified 5 October 1762 and granted 4 November 1762. Quit rent to commence in 2 years. Jno. Hamilton, D.S. Robert ® his mark) Box, Jr. [M6_15:1]

Box, Robert: 17 August 1786: Robert Box and Robert Box, Jr. and Samuel Neighbours witness deed of John Goodwin to Elizabeth Jones 20 acres of land joining to where she now lives containing 70 acres. Grant dated 1 August 1785. [Another card says 20 acres]. [LCDBK A: 340]

Box, Robert: Land conveyed by Robert Box to James Ryan and from James Ryan to James Boyd - [No deed found.]

Box, Robert: 6 September 1797: Laird B. Boyd, of the State of Tennessee, Co., of Davidson (by his attorney John Boyd], to Matthew McDaniel, of Laurens Co., S.C., for £100 Stg; 150 acres on Rabourns Creek of Saluda River, bounded on all sides by vacant land at the time of survey. *Originally granted 14 November 1762 to Robert Box* and by said Robert Box conveyed unto James Ryan and by the said James Ryan unto James Boyd, of the State of South Carolina. John Boyd, attorney for Laird B. Boyd (Seal). Wit: Joseph Downs, William Hunter. Proved by William Hunter 18 July 1797 before Jas. Dillard, J.P. [LCDBK F: 238-139]

Box, Robert: 31 October 1807: John Box, Senr, of Laurens Dist., S.C., to Zechariah Arnold, of same place, for $400; 75 acres on the W side of Reedy River. *Originally granted to Robert Box.* John (mark) Box. Wit: W. Downs, Wm. Moore. Dower of Rachel Box, wife of John Box, Senr. Given 31 October 1807 before Jothan. Downs, J.Q. Proved by Wm. Moore 1807 before Jothan. Downs, J.Q. [LCDBK J: 41]

Box, Robert: 11 August 1810: John Clark, Sheriff, of Laurens Dist., S.C., to Samuel Todd [see below]. Whereas Henry Box of the said place was seized in fee simple and possessed a plantation of land containing 330 on waters of Reedy River. Bounded on lands of William Moore, William McPherson, James Roberts, Robert Box and widow Moore, and whereas a writ of fieri facias issued from the Court of Common Please held dated 3 Monday after the fourth Monday in October 1808 commanding that the goods, chattels, houses, land and tenements of said Henry Box should be levied and made the sum of $23.50 unto which Erwin Patten and Jones, recovered against said Henry Box' debt. Also the sum of $14.50 for their costs and charges. Sell and dispose of the said tract of land with the premises unto Samuel Todd for $180; 150 acres. John Clark, S.L. (Seal). Wit: John Garlington, John Dunlap. Proved by John Dunlap. February 1811 before John Garlington, Clk. Laurens Dist. [LCDBK J: 196]

Boyd, James: Survey for James Boyd pursuant to precept dated 7 April 1772; 300 acres in Craven Co., on the north side Saluda, small branch of Reburns Creek. Bounded NW by John Maharys; NE vacant; other sides vacant. Certified 18 July 1772. John Armstong, D.S. [P13_293:2]

Boyd, James: Memorial for James Boyd; 300 acres in Craven Co., on the N side of Saludy on small branches of Reburns Creek. Bounded NW by John Mahary; NE vacant; other sides by larger surveys. Certified 18 July 1772 and granted 30 October 1772. Quit rent to commence in 2 years. 13 January 1773. Delivered 28 March 1775 to Jacob _____. John Armstrong, D.S. [M12_64:5]

Boyd, James - LWT of James Boyd: [before 15 March 1787] Will dated August 10, 1784 in Craven Co., 96 Dist., S.C. Proved October 26, 1784 before Andrew Foster and Jas. Barnes, of Camden Dist., S.C., Executors: Wife, Martha;. Son, Saml. Boyd. Wit: Wm. Barnett Sr., Wm. Barnett Jr., Jas. Barnett. Children Mary, Jno., Saml., Abraham Boyd, son-in-law Robt. Barnes. "Bequeath to Saml. Horse Creek Mill and plantation on Reburns Creek."[See James Harvey] [See land conveyed from Martha Boyd and Samuel Boyd to Vincent Glass [LCDBK B: 144] [Young, pg. 33, *Box* 10, Pack 193]

[Family: Wife Martha, sons Samuel, Abraham, Jno.; daughter, Mary; son-in-law Robert Barnes.]

Boyd, James: 17 September 1794: Robert Barnet, of Cumberland on the Western Territory, to Robert Bolt, Junr., of Laurens Co., S.C., for £50 Stg; 300 acres originally *granted to James Boyd* and by his last will and testament conveyed to said Robert Barnet containing 300 acres on the N side of Saluda on a small branch of Rayburns Creek. Bounding NW on John McHarg, NE by vacant land, all other sides by larger surveys. Robert Barnet (LS) Wit: B.H. Saxon, Andw. Rodgers, Junr. Proved by Andw. Rodgers Junr., 18 September 1794 before Joseph Downs, J.P. [LCDBK E: 281-282]

Boyd, James: 8 May 1795: Robert Bolt, Junr., of Laurens Co., S.C., to Charles Henderson, of same place, for £10; *65 acres being part of a tract originally granted to James Boyd* and by him, in his LWT, conveyed to Robert Barnett and by Robt. Barnett conveyed to Robt. Bolt, Junr., by deed dated 17 September 1794. The tract located on the N side of Saluda, on a small branch of Reaburns Creek. Plat shows bounded by Wm. Fountain, Chas. Henderson, Widow McHurg's and A. Bolt. Robert (X) Bolt. Wit. Ezek. (X) Matthews, Saml. Downs. Proved by Ezekiel Matthews, 8 May 1795 before Jonthan. Downs., J. P. [Plat] [LCDBK F: 68]

Boyd, William: Survey for William Boyd pursuant to precept dated 6 January 1773; 222 acres in Craven Co., S.C., to the NE side of Rayburn's Creek. Bounded NE on land laid out to Samuel Williams; NW on land laid out to Philip Sherrill; SW on land laid out on Bounty; SE on land laid out. Certified 3 February 1773. Jonathn. Downs, D.S. [P13_327:2]

Boyd, William: Memorial by William Boyd; 222 acres in Craven Co., S.C., NE of Rayburns Creek. Bounding NE on Samuel Williams; NW on Philip

Sherril; SW on Bounty land; SE on said laid out. Certified 30 September 1774 and granted 9 November 1774. Quit rent to commence in 2 years. Delivered last August 23, 1775 to John Boyd. Jonathan Downs, D.S. [M13_471:3]

Bratcher, William: 5 March 1792: State Grant.

Bratcher, William: 10 May 1793: William Bratcher, Senr., of Ninety Six Dist. and Laurens Co., S.C., to William Bratcher, Junr., of same place, for £20 Stg.; 150 acres on both sides of a branch of Reaburns Creek, including place where said Junior now lives. Bounding W on an agreed on line between William Bratcher Senr. And William [Bratcher] Junr. *Being part of a grant of land originally granted to William Bratcher, Senr. 5 March 1792.* William Bratcher (W his mark). Wit: Elisha Hunt, John Gutrey. Proved by Elisha Hunt 11 May 1793 before Joseph Downs, J.P. [LCDBK D: 446-447]

Bratcher, William: 23 January 1796: William Bratcher, of Ninety Six Dist., Laurens Co., S.C., farmer, to Drury Boyce, (Miller), of same place, for £19 Stg.; 50 acres on both sides of a small branch called Bullets Branch. Bounding E on William Bratcher Jr's line N on the original line. *Originally granted to said William Bratcher, Senr.,* by his Excellency Charles Pinckney 5 March 1792. William (his mark) Bratcher (LS) Wit: Thomas Graydon, Thomas Gregory. Proved by Thomas Grayden 18 March 1805 before Jonathn. Downs, J.P. [LCDBK H: 74-75]

Bratcher, William: 13 October 1804: William Bratcher, Junior, of Laurens Dist., S.C., to Drury Boyce, of same place, for $300; 140 acres, *being part of an original grant to William Bratcher, Senr., bearing date 5 March 1792.* The 140 acres on the S fork of Reaburns Creek called Bullets Branch. Bounded on E adjoining Drury Boyce, W Samuel Nisbett. William Bratcher. Wit: Abner Babb, Levi Faris. Proved by Abner Babb 6 September 1806 before John Rowland, J.P. [LCDBK J: 215]

Brauday [Broadway/Brody], Charles: Survey for Charles Brauday pursuant to survey dated 3 February 1767; 150 acres on Raiburns Creek NE of Saludy. Bounded SE on land surveyed for William Allison; NW on land surveyed for Thomas Williams. Certified 18 May 1767. Richd. Winn, D.S. Ord. Co. 3 May 1768. [P10_184:1]

Brawdy, Charles: Memorial for Charles Brawdy; 150 acres in Berkley Co., on Raybournes Creek, NE of Saludy river. Bounded SE on Wm. Allison; NW on Thomas Williams. Certified 3 May 1768 and granted 19 August 1768. Quit rent to commence in 2 years. 13 October 1768. Richd. Winn, D.S. For the memorialist George Hollingsworth. [M8_262:4]

Brawdy, Charles: 15 December 1780: Listed as the son-in-law of William Allison's will dated 15 December 1780. [Young, pg. 9] [See William Allison.]

Brawdy/Brady: Charles: 3 October 1793: LWT, Laurens Co., S.C. Plantation on which I now live be divided amongst my three eldest sons - Viz. William that part which lies on the E side of the Raburns Creek and that the west side be divided between John and Alexander; lands to sons John. Charles, George. Wife. Eleanor. [LCWBK C: 167]

Brawdy {Brody], Charles: 20 May 1796: William Bradey [Brody/ Broadway] to John Brodey, both of Laurens Co., S.C. for £10 stg., 120 acres on waters of Raiborns Creek, being part of sundry grants to Charles Brodey [probably Broadway] dec'd. Plat shows bounding by Alex. Brodey, Watkins. William Brodey (L.S.) Wit: John Cochran, Henry Box. Proved by oath of John Cochran 21 April 1798 before Chas. Smith, J.P. [Plat] [LCDBK F: 299-300]

Bradey [Brody], Charles: 3 October 1793: LWT Charles Bradey. Laurens Co., S.C. I give and allow that they may dispose of in the following manner Viz: That the plantation on which I now live be divided amongst my three eldest sons as follows (Viz.) That my son William shall have that part of it which lies on the east side of the Raburns Creek and that the W side shall be divided between John and Allexander. My old mill house and so to the creek aforesaid the north side to belong to my son John and the South to Allex, but possession shall not be given to either of my sons until my wife tell when she shall enjoy possible possession of all the aforesaid plantation. I will and bequeath my plantation on Reedy River to be equally divided between my two youngest sons at their mother's decease (Viz.) Charles and George. I will and allow that my loving wife Eleanor Brody do remove as soon as may be covenant to the said plantation on Reedy river, the benefit for which she shall enjoy during her life as a compensation for raisin my young children, who shall be under her care during there maturity. I will and allow that my moveable effects be equally divided amongst my children, who are yet unmarried at their mother's decease, till which time she shall have the full use and benefit. I appoint my wife Eleaner Brody Executrix and my truly friend John Cocharn executor. Charles Bradey (Seal). Wit: Ann (X) Wadkins, Zuboriah (X) Barns, John Cochran. Date proved not available. [LCWBK C-1: 167]

[Family: Wife Eleaner, eldest sons: William, John, Allexander. Younger children Charles and George Brodey.]

Bradey/Brody, William: 27 February 1798–17 August 1802: William Brodey, of Laurens Co., S.C., planter to Thomas Lewis, of same place, for $235; 110 acres on Rabourns Creek in Laurens Co., being part land *originally granted to Charles Brodey* and conveyed by said Charles Brodey to William Brodey. William Brodey (Seal) Margaret (X) Brodey (Seal). Wit: George Brock, John Coats, John Brodey. Proved by John Coate on 8 June 1798 that he saw William Brodey and Margaret Brodey, his wife, seal and deliver deed before James Abercrombie, J.P. Proved by John Coate. [LCDBK G: 460-461]

Briggs, Robert: Survey for Robert Briggs pursuant to precept dated 30 May 1768; 100 acres on a branch of Raiburns Creek. Bounding NE on John Turk and part vacant; other sides vacant. Certified 30 June 1768. R. Humphreys, D.S. [P13_336:2]

Briggs, Robert: Memorial for Robert Briggs; 100 acres in Craven Co., on a branch of Raybournes Creek. Bounded NW part on John Turk and part vacant; other sides vacant. Certified 20 June 1768 and granted 12 September 1768. Quit rent to commence in 10 years. 15 October 1768. Ralph Humphreys, D.S. For the memorialist Ralph Humphreys. [B in margin]. [M8_279_3]

Briggs, Robert: Archives Department Spartanburg. file. Vol. 8, Book 279. 100 acres on a branch of Raybourns Creek. Bounded NE on John Turk. Certified 30 June 1768. Granted 12 September 1768. Men. 15 October 1768. [Revill, pg. 338]

Briggs, Robert: Conveyed land to Ralph Humphreys. No deed located.

Briggs, Robert: 7 & 8 September 1772: James Lindley, Esqr., of Craven Co., S.C., and Mary, his wife, to John Williams, merchant, of same place, for £112 S.C. money, *land granted 12 Sept 1768 to Robert Briggs,* on a branch of Rabins Creek. Bounding John Turk and said Robert Briggs did convey to Ralph Humphries and said Ralph Humphreys did on 31 January 1772 to James Lindley, Esqr. James Lindley (LS) Mary Lindley (LS). Wit: Thos. Cohune, Randal Hennessey. Recorded 15 January 1774. [Charleston DD Bk. G_4, pp 464_467; Holcomb, Bk. F_4_X_4, pg. 34]

Brooks, Jacob: Survey for Jacob Brooks pursuant to precept dated 7 May 1765; 100 acres on Rabourns Creek a branch of Saludy River. Bounded SE on land belonging to Robert Box; other sides vacant. Certified 26 August 1765. Jno. Pearson, D.S. Ord. Co. 4 February 1767 for G. Hollingsworth. [See memorial for George Hollingsworth.] [P10_126:2]

Brooks, Roger: No memorial found.

Brooks, Roger: 1 June 1789: Lewis Saxon, Clerk of Laurens Co., S.C., to James Tweedy, of same place, planter, for £20 Stg.; 200 acres on Reedy River bounding NE and SE on Hugh Beards land, NE on William Norris, all other sides vacant. *Originally being first granted to Roger Brooks* (and since conveyed by lease and release to the above mentioned Lewis Saxon bearing date [blank], now conveyed by said Lewis Saxon by way of lease and release unto the said James Tweedy. The said Lewis Saxon and Salley, his wife, have set their hands. Lewis Saxon (Seal) Sally Saxon (Seal). Wit: Lydall Allen, Samuel Nelson. Proved by Lydall Allen 8 April 1797 before Joseph Downs, J.P. [Brooks to Saxon to Tweedy] [LCDBK F: 191-192]

Broughton, Andrew: Survey for Andrew Broughton pursuant to precept dated 29 September 1772; 1000 acres on branch of Little River. Bounded NW by William Allison; NE unknown; thence after different courses Surveyed by Robert Allison; all other sides vacant. Certified 20 November 1772 by Richd. Winn, D.S. [P13_353:1]

Broughton, Andrew: See survey for James Tweed.

Broughton, Andrew: Memorial for Andrew Broughton; 250 acres in Craven Co., the NE side of Reedy River on a branch thereof called Rayburns Creek bounding SW on Mary Richie; other sides vacant land. Jonathan Downes, D.S. 21 July 1775. Delivered 31 July 1775 to Philip Henry. [One of 6 tracks] See survey for James Tweed. [M2_253:1]

Broughton, Andrew: __ March 1775: Andrew Broughton, Senr., of Charles Town, to Philip Henry, of same place, for £1000 [4 properties, one being]; 250 acres in Craven Co., on the north east side of Reedy River on Reybourns Creek. Bounding land of Mary Riche. Wit: William Next, Francis BreMarch Recorded 7 October 1775. [Charleston DD Bk V-4; Bk. F_4 through X_4] [Brent H. Holcomb, *South Carolina Deed Abstracts 1773-1778*, SCMAR, Columbia, SC, pg.199.]

Brown, Bartlett: Granted 11 May 1753: Not located.

Brown, Bartlett: 14 October 1785: Benjamin Brown, legal and real heir of Bartlett Brown, Deceased, of Berk Co., Georgia, to Abraham Gray, of Ninety Six Dist., Laurens Co., S.C., for £60 Stg.; 40 acres on S side of Enoree River, formerly called Kings River. *Being part of 600 acres patent granted 11 May 1753 to Bartlett Brown.* Bounding on N side of said river and W by a 40 acres tract of land of John Lindsey, purchased of said Brown, being a part of said *original grant and E by 100 acres belonging to Andrew*

Cuningham; also a part of said grant, S by the line of the old tract *being 160 acres it being land originally granted 11 May 1753* and enrolled in the auditor Genl. Office 12 May 1753. Benjamin Brown. Wit: Andrew Cunningham, John Lindsay, Henry Hamilton. [This may be the same Benjamin Brown named above as the Cunningham and Lindsay's are also in the same area of SC] [LCDBK A: 298]

Brown, Benjamin: Survey for Benjamin Brown pursuant to precept dated 3 September 1765; 150 acres in Craven Co., on the south fork Raibourns Creek commonly called Brown's Branch. Bounded on all sides by vacant land. Certified 18 February 1766. Ord. Co. 29 September 1772. Wm. Wofford, D.S. [P13_359:2]

Brown, Benjamin: Memorial for Benjamin Brown; 150 acres in Craven Co., on the S fork of Rayburns Creek, commonly called Browns branch. Bounded on all sides by vacant land. Certified 29 September 1772 and granted 19 November 1772. Quit rent to commence in 2 years. 17 February 1773. Delivered 1 September 1774 to A. Rodgers. Wm. Wofford, D.S. [M12_103:4]

Brown, Benjamin: 26 September 1773: Benjamin Brown, planter, of Craven Co., SC, to William Martin, merchant, of same place, for £150; 150 acres on Reaburns Creek. Bounded on all sides by vacant land. *Originally granted 19 November 1772 to Benjamin Brown.* Signed Benjamin Brown, Sarah (X her mark) [wife of Benjamin Brown]. Wit: Jonathan Downs, Acquilla Hall. Sworn 26 September 1773 by Jonathan Downs before William Arthur, J.P. [LCDBK C: 325-327]

Brown, Hugh: Survey and memorial not found.

Brown, Hugh: 8 & 9 July 1783: John Berwick, Thomas Waring and John Ewing Calhoun, Commissioners of forfeited estates, to David Dickson, for £737, 2p 10 Sterling, several adjoining plantations *late the property of Hugh Brown* in Ninety Six Dist., the two tracts 350 acres in the general plat of said land No. 1 and 2 adj. Hanah Hendricks [plats showing Saluda River, adj. land owner John Willard]. Thomas Waring, Senr. (LS), Jno. Ewing Calhoun (LS), Wit: Daniel Smith, James OHear. Oath of Daniel Smith 10 November 1785 before IL. Mazyck, J.P. [N-5, 464-466] [Holcomb, Brent H., *South Carolina Deed Abstract 1783-1788*, SCMAR, Columbia, SC, pg. 126]

Brown, Hugh: 11 July 1783: David Dickson, of Ninety Six Dist., S.C., to William Parker and Edward Blake, Commissioners of the Treasury, by bond date 8 July 1783 for 1475£ for the payment of £737 Stg. mortgage of two tracts late the property of Hugh Brown in Ninety Six Dist., containing 250 acres and No. 2 containing 150 acres lands adj. lands of Hanah Hendric[k]s, land *said to be late the property of Patrick Cunningham* on Saludy River and Reedy River. David Dickson (LS). Wit: Thomas Waring, Senr., Daniel Smith. Oath of Thomas Waring, Senr. 5 October 1784 before DL. Mazyck. J.P. [Holcomb, Brent H., *South Carolina Deed Abstract 1783-1788*, SCMAR, Columbia, SC, pg. 59] [M-5, 150-153]

Brown, Hugh: 10 & 11 November 1785: David Dickson, of Tyger River, Spartanburg, Co., S.C., planter, to Patrick Cuningham, of Ninety Six Dist., S.C., planter, for £30 stg., money of Great Britain ; 150 acres on the N side of Saluda River. bound S on Saluda River, W on Reedy River, E on said Patrick Cuningham, N on lands heretofore property of John Williard, and that tract of land containing 200 acres formerly property of John Willard, but late the property of Hugh Brown. on E side of Reedy River, bound W on Reedy River, N on Hans Hendrix, E partly of said Patrick Cuningham and part of land owner unknown S on land *formerly the property of Hugh Brown,* which tracts were sold in fee simple and conveyed by John Berwick, Thomas Waring, Senr. and John Ewing Calhoun, Commissioners of Forfeited Estates, 8 & 9 July 1783. David Dickson. Wit: Isaac Mitchell, John Elmore, Robt. Brown, Sarah Cuningham. [LCDBK A: 161-167]

Brown, Roger: Survey for Roger Brown pursuant to survey dated 2 September 1767; 100 acres in Berkley Co., on branch of Raiburns Creek. Bounded NW on land laid out to John Lawson; SE on land laid out to John Helms; other sides vacant. Certified 9 February 1768. Jno. Caldwell, D.S. [P13_381:1]

Brown, Roger: Memorial for Roger Brown; 100 acres in Berkley Co., on a branch of Raybornes Creek. Bounded NW on land of John Lawson; SE on John Helmes; other sides vacant. Survey 9 February 1768 and granted 13 May 1768. Quit rent to commence in 10 years. 1 September 1768. John Caldwell, D.S. James Abernathy [B in margin]. [M8_182:1]

Bryan, John: Survey for John Bryan pursuant to precept dated 6 April 1773; 150 acres in Ninety Six Dist. on Rayburns Creek. Bounded on all sides by land laid out [plat shows bounding land claimed by John Irvin, Alexr. Mazyck, laid claimed by William Martin]. Certified 14 May 1773. Jonth. Downs, D.S. [P13_397:1]

Bryan, John: Memorial for John Bryan for 150 acres in 96 Dist., on Rayburn's Creek. Bounded on all sides by land laid out. Certified 15 may 1773 and granted 6 September 1774 to the memorialist Quit rent to commence 2 years from date. Set his hand 13 march 1774. Delivered 14

June 1775 to Thomas Cohune. Jonathan Downs, D.S. [M13-374:2]

Bryan/t, John: 15 October 1800: James Irwin of Cumberland Co., Pennsylvania to James Hamilton Lowry and Robert Lowrey, of Laurens Dist., S.C., for 100£ stg.; 150 acres on waters of Reaburns Creek *originally granted to John Bryant 6 September 1774* and by him conveyed to James Lindley, Esq., and by James Lindley to Alexander Irwin of the state of Pennsylvania and by Ann Brewster (heir at law to the said Alexd. Irwin) conveyed to the above named James Irwin 4 February 1792. James Irwin. Wit: N. Franks, John Lynch. Proved by Nehemiah Franks before Q. A. Elmore, J.Q. [Plat shows bounded by Robert Cooper, Major Butler, James Irwin, Alex. Mazyck,]. See below. [LCDBK G: 223]

Bryan, John: 10 January 1787: Alexander Irwin, late of the Township of West Pennsborough, in the Co., of Cumberland in the Commonwealth of Pennsylvania, died intestate without issue, leaving Annie Brewster his only sister in the division of several plantations and tracts of land, situate in Berkley Count, S.C., containing 700 acres. .I Anne Brewster, appoint James Irwin, of the Co., of Cumberland by lawful attorney. Set my hand Anne Brewster. Wit; Thomas Lee, John Lee before Saml. Irwin. [LCDBK B: 128-129]

Bryan, John: Survey for 100 acres not found.

Bryan, John: Memorial for John Bryan for 100 acres in Craven Co., on a branch of Saludy River called Reedy Creek, waters of Santee river. Bounded SE on an old survey, SW on an unpassable swamp and water and lands belonging to estate of Robert Long, Dec'd.; NW on vacant land, NE on part of James Kilpatrick's land. Certified 4 August 1767 and granted 28 August 1767 to the Memorialist. Quit rent to commence 2 years from date. Set his hand 1 October 1767 Pat. Calhoun, D.S. For the memorialist James (X) Rind his mark. [See memorial for Jacob Bowman [Bohman]. [M9-329:1]

Bryan, John: 5 December 1796: We Jacob Bowman and Sarah Bowman, his mother, of Laurens Co., S.C., to Jacob Niswanger, of same place, for £100 stg.; *100 acres on Reedy River granted to John Bryan 28 August 1767* and was conveyed by indenture of lease and release to Jacob Bowman, Senr. Jacob Bowman (LS) Sarah (S) Bowman (LS). Wit: Lewis Graves, Geo. Anderson. W.C. Wood. Memorandum: Jacob Bowman and Sarah Bowman, his mother. [See Memorial for Jacob Bowman.] [LCDBK F: 121]

Bryan, John: 12 May 1796: We Jacob Bowman and Sarah Bowman, of Co. of Laurens, S.C., to Jacob Niswanger, of same place, for £100; 100 acres on Reedy River. Being land *granted to John Bryan 20 August 1767* and conveyed by lease and release to Jacob Bowman, Senr. Jacob Bowman (LS) Sarah Bowman (LS) Wit: Lewis Graves, George Anderson. Memorandum that the within named Jacob Bowman and Sarah Bowman, his mother delivered title unto Jacob Niswanger. Proved by Lewis Graves 8 May 1797 before Zach Bailey, J.P. [See memorial by Jacob Bowman.] [LCDBK F: 199]

Bumpass, James: 19 September 1810: James Bumpass, of Laurens Dist., S.C., to Nehemiah Franks, of same place, for $500; *250 acres on waters of Rabourns Creek where he now lives.* Bounded W by James Cunningham, S by James Dial, E by John Rodgers, W by Nehemiah Franks. James Bumpass (LS) Wit: John Rodgers, David Craddock. Proved by John Rodgers 1 March 1811 before Chas. Allen, Q.M. Dower of Sally Bumpass, wife of the within named James Bumpass given 1 Marcy 1811 before Chas. Allen, Q.M. [LCDBK K: 16]

Burton, Stephen: 4 February 1805: Thomas Land, of Laurens Dist., S.C., to Robert Allison, of same place, for $86.29; 135 acres on waters of Dirty Creek bounding lands of said Robert Allison, Hastings Dial, estate of Dr. Frazure. The said tract of land being conveyed to Thomas Land by *Stephen Burton 1804.* Thomas Land. Wit: R. Creswell, Joseph Strange. Proved by Robt. Creswell 3 June 1805 before J. Blackwell, J.P. Dower of Elizabeth Land, wife of the within Thomas Land given 3 June 1806 before B.H. Saxon, J.Q. [LCDBK J: 97]

Butler, Pierce: Pierce Butler was born 11 July 1744, County Carlow, Ireland and died 15 February 1822, Philadelphia, Pennsylvania. When the war between England and America broke out in 1775, Butler joined former British officers in supporting the American cause. He came to South Carolina and married Mary Middleton, daughter of Henry Middleton, wealthy planter in South Carolina and a colonial leader. Butler's father-in-law became the president of the First Continental which was held in Philadelphia. In 1787 Butler represented South Carolina at the Constitutional Convention.

In 1773, Butler upon being order to return to Great Britain decided to leave the army. He sold his commission and purchased a plantation on the coast of South Carolina. With his skills in management and his military experience his land holding grew to into the thousands of acres, many being in South Carolina's upcountry and Georgia. [Wright, Robert K. & Gregory, Morris J. Mac, *Soldier-Statesmen of the Constitution*, Center of Military History, United States Army, Washington, D.C., 2004.] May 5, 1772 – grant.

Butler, Pierce: Memorial for Major Pierce Butler for 500 acres in Craven Co., in the fork of Broad and Saludy rivers bounding NE and NW by Pierce Butlers land, W by James Lindley, SW by James Lindley and Grants land,

SE and S by surveyed land. Certified 6 September 1772, also 500 acres as above in the fork of Broad and Saludy river bounding NW by Benjamin Elliott and Samuel Elliott, SW and NW by Pady Cunningham, S by Gant, E and W by James Lindley, SE by Pierce Butler. Certified 6 September 1772; also 500 acres as above in the fork of Broad and Saludy rivers bounding SW by Benjn. Elliott and Pierce Butler, NW and NE by John Helms and Roger Brown, NW by Benjamin Williamson. Certified 8 September 1772; also 500 acres as above in the fork of Broad and Saludy rivers bounding NE by Pierce Butler, SW and SE by Richd. Winn, NW by Benjn. Williamson, NE and NW by Benjn. Elliott and Saml. Elliotts and NE by Kite Shote. Certified 5 September 1772. .All above tracts granted 29 September 1772 to the memorialist. [Note: This memorial above consisted of 9 tracks of 500 acres each and only those which are pertinent to this area have been used.] [M12-36:2]

Butler, Pierce: 20 & 21 February 1786: Hon. Pierce Butler of Charleston, and Mary, his wife, to Jan Gabriel Tegclaar, of Amsterdam in Holland, merchant, trustee and director, of a certain lease made to said Pierce Butler by sundry persons, whereas Pierce Butler did lately at Amsterdam in Holland negotiate a loan for the sum of 150,000 guilders Dutch current money and for securing the payment thereon entered into a bond, mortgage of [Note: as many transactions are listed here - I am only abstracting the items dealing with the lands on Reedy River, for full text see Charleston Deed Book $-5, pages 1 to 14]. (9). 500 acres in the fork of Broad and Saluda Rivers in Craven Co., adj. lands of Benjamin Elliott, Pierce Butler, John Holmes, Roger Brown, Benjamin Williamson and tract of 500 acres in the fork of Broad and Saluda Rivers in Craven Co., adj. Lands of Benjamin Elliott, Samuel Elliott, Paddy Cunningham, James Lindsay; also tract of 500 acres in the fork of Broad and Saluda Rivers in Craven Co., adj. Lands of said Pierce Butler, Richard Winn, Benjamin Williamson, Benjamin Elliott, Samuel Elliott, also tract of 500 acres in the for of Broad and Saluda River in Craven Co., adj. Land of said Pierce Butler, James Lindsay. (21) 500 acres on north side of Reedy River in Craven Co., adj. Land of Hugh Beard, James Read, Richard Pew, Elias Brock, Paddy Cunningham, and tract of 500 acres on branches of Little Saluda river in Craven Co., adj. land of Thomas Woodward, John Rodgers, Robert Tweedy. Pierce Butler (LS) Mary Butler (LS). Wit: J. Boomen Graves, Consul from the United Netherlands, Peter LePoole, Thomas Fingery. [Holcomb, Brent H., *South Carolina Deed Abstracts 1783-1788*, pg. 197-198.]

Butler, Pierce: 7 July 1792: Honorable Pierce Butler, Esq., of the State of S.C., to Hercules Daniel Bize, Esq., of same place, for sum of [blank]; 10,267 acres; Several plantations, parcels, tracts and lots of land. Being 500 acres in Craven Co., between Broad and Saluda Rivers on a small branch of

Reedy River called Beaver Dam Branch. Bounded S and SW by land laid out to Elias Brock and James Pew; NW by Jonathan Downes; other sides vacant land. Also 500 acres below the said rivers. Bounded NE by lands of said Pierce Butler, SW and SE by land laid out by Richard Winn; NW by Benjamin Williamson; NE and NW by Benjamin Elliott and Samuel Elliott; NW by Kitt Shoats. Also 500 acres between the rivers aforesaid. Bounded NW by Benjamin Elliott and Samuel Elliott; SW and NW by Paddy Cuningham; S by Gants; E, S and W by James Lindsay; SE by said Pierce Butler. Also 500 acres between the rivers aforesaid. Bounded NE and NW by land of said Pierce Butler; W by James Lindley and grants; SE and S by surveyed lands. Also 500 acres on the branches of Browns Creek. Bounded SW and E by Daniel Huger; N and E by Phillip Waters; N by William Gant, NW _____; other sides vacant. Also 300 on the branches of Tyger River called Dutchmans Creek. Bounded SE on Isaac Paten; Also 300 acres on Fergusons Creek a branch of Tyger River. Bounded SW on David Brenton; Also 500 acres on branches of Little River of Saluda. Bounded NE on Thomas Woodward; NW on John Rogers, and vacant land; SE on Robert Tweedy. Also 500 acres on the branches of Bufflew Creek. Bounded SE and SW on Jonathan Parker; W by Hillery Gees; other sides vacant. Also 500 acres on a branch of Enoree called Dry Branch. Bounded N and W by Alexander Fraser; W by Robert Goodwins; other sides vacant. Also 200 acres on branch of Elisha Creek. Bounded NW, SW, SE and NE on William Dod; NE on Whitaker. Also 200 acres on a Branch of Fergusons Creek. Bounded SE by Daniel Huger; SW by James Brewton; NW and SW by James Wofford. Also 500 in the Forks of Broad and Saluda Rivers. Bounded SW by Benjamin Elliott; Pierce Butler; NW and NE by John Helms, Elliott and Pierce Butler; NW by Benjamin Williamson.
Also 500 acres on the N side of Reedy River. Bounded NE and NW on Hugh Beard; NE on James Read; SW and NE by Richard Pew; SW and SE by Elias Brock; NW by Paddy Cunningham. Also 200 acres on a branch of Fair Forrest. Bounded when granted by vacant land. Also 500 acres between Great Saluda and Broad Rivers on Buffelow a branch of Camping Creek, waters of Saluda. Bounded NW on Michael _____; other sides vacant. Also 500 acres in the fork of Broad and Saluda Rivers. Bounded NE and NW by James Boyd; NW and SW by land laid out to Richard Winn; SW by Kitt Shoats; NW and SW by Paddy Cuningham; SW by James Lindsay. Also 500 acres on a branch of Little River. Bounded SE by John Caldwell; SW unknown; W and W by John Hunter; SW by Dick Neiley; NW by Lowery; NE and NW by Williamson; NE by George Ankerhorn; other sides vacant. Also 200 acres on the widow Stewarts Branch, Wateree River, said in the grant to have been surveyed 6 July 1775. Also 200 acres surveyed for him the said Pierce Butler on the 27 June 1775 on Beaver Dam Creek on the NE side of Wateree River. Also 4 town Lots in the city of Charleston; also a tract of land containing 1167 acres in Parish of St. Andrew. Set his hand. Pierce

Butler (LS). Wit: Thomas Marshall, Edward Rutledge. Proved by Edward Rutledge of the City of Charleston 21 March 1793 before D. Mazyck, J.P.Q.M. [LCDBK E: 353-359]

Butler, Pierce: 10 September 1793: John Hunter, Esqr., of Laurens Co., S.C., to David Ross, of same place. For £6, .6 sh.; indenture made 138 acres on Reedy River. Bounding lands of David Greene and John Rodgers and Reedy River. *Being part of a grant of land originally granted to Pierce Butler* and by him conveyed to Hercules Danl. Bize on 9 July 1792 and now conveyed by the said John Hunter by virtue of a power of attorney from said Hercules Danl. Bize, bearing date 1 June 1793. John Hunter, (LS) Attorney for Hercules Danl. Bize. Wit. Francis Foss, Sal. Cooper. Proved by Francis Ross 12 March 1794 before Joseph Downs, J.P. [Plat shows bounding David Green, David Ross, Reedy River, John Rodgers]. [LCDBK F: 135]

Butler, Pierce: 11 September 1793: John Hunter, Esq., of Laurens Co., S.C., attorney for H.D. Bize *to* Richard Pugh, of same place, for £15 Stg.; 100 acres on waters of Shirrels Branch, waters of Reaburns Creek. Bounded on land laid out or sold to John Manly and Oliver Matthews, being *part of 500 acres originally granted to Pierce Butler* conveyed by him on 9 July 1792 to Hercules Danl. Bize and now conveyed by the said John Hunter by virtue of power of attorney. John Hunter, (LS) Attorney for Hercules Danl. Bize. Wit: David Green, Jno. Cochran. Reuben. Proved by John Cockran 21 January 1796 before Reuben Pyles, J.P. [Plat] [LCDBK F: 71-72]

Butler, Pierce: 8 September 1793: Hercules Daniel Bize by his attorney John Hunter, of Laurens Co., S.C., to Ambrose Hudgins. Jr., of same place, for £35 stg.; 148 acres in Laurens Co., waters of Reaburns Creek, being part of 500 acres. [Plat shows bounded by John Rodgers, part of orig. survey, Saml. Elliott, and vacant land. *Originally granted to Pierce Butler,* and by him conveyed to Hercules Daniel Bize the 9 July 1792. Said tract is conveyed by the said John Hunter, by Power of Attorney, from the said Hercules Daniel Bize, dated 1 June 1793. Set his hand John Hunter, (LS) Attorney for Hercules Danl. Bize. Wit: Margaret Hunter, Alexander McNary. Bond received 8 October 1793. Proved by Alexander McNary 14 October 1794 before Joseph Downs, J.P. [plat] [Nash. deeds, pg. 106] [LCDBK E: 328-330]

Butler, Pierce: 11 September 1793: John Hunter, Est., of Laurens Co., S.C., Attorney for H.D. Bize to Richard Pugh, of same place, for £7 Stg.; 42 acres, *being part of 500 acres originally granted to Pierce Butler, on 5 May 1772* and by him conveyed to Hercules Danl. Bize on 9 July 1792 and now conveyed by said John Hunter by virtue of a Power of attorney from said Hercules Danl. Bize 1 June 1793. Situated in Laurens Co., on the waters of

Reedy river, bounding on land held by said Richd. Pugh, James Dorah and part of said survey. John Hunter, [LS] Attorney for Hercules Danl. Bize. Wit: David Green, John Cocharn. Proved by John Cochran 21 January 1796 before Reuben Pyles, J.P. [Plat 8 September 1793 shows bounding Richard Pugh, Jas. Dorroh and surveyed land.] [LCDBK F: 72]

Butler, Pierce: 9 & 10 September 1793: John Hunter, Esq., of Laurens Co., S.C., to William Dorough [Dorroh], of same place, for £27, 6 shillings; 182 acres on the waters of Reedy River, being *part of 500 acres granted to Pierce Butler on May 5, 1772* and conveyed to Hercules Danl. Bize 1 June 1793. Bounded on land of Arthur Taylor, Samuel Cooper, James Dorough, Samuel Cooper, Townsend lands and part of said survey. John Hunter (LS) Attorney for Hercules Danl. Bize. Wit: William Norris, John Dorough. Joseph Downs, J.P. [LCDBK E: 97-99]

Butler, Pierce: 10 September 1793: Hercules Daniel Bize by his attorney John Hunter, of Laurens Co., S.C., to James Green, of same place, for £48 stg. 1 shilling; 93 acres in Laurens Co., on Reedy River. Bounding on lands held by David Dunlap, John Rodgers, Beard and Reedy River. *Originally granted to Pierce Butler,* and by him conveyed to Hercules Daniel Bize the 9 July 1792. Said tract is conveyed by the said John Hunter by power of Attorney from the said Hercules Daniel Bize dated 1 June 1793. Set his hand John Hunter, Attorney for Hercules Danl. Bize. Wit: David Green, Samuel Green. Bond received 15 October 1793. Proved by Samuel Green 23 August 1794 before Danl. Wright, J.P. [Plat] [LCDBK E: 274-276]

Butler, Pierce: 15 October 1793: Hercules Daniel Bize by his attorney John Hunter, of Laurens Co., S.C., to John Manley, of same place, for £20 stg.; 100 acres in Laurens Co., on the waters of Reaburns Creek. Bounding land of Berry Harvey, John Cammoch, part of said Survey. *Originally granted to Pierce Butler,* and by him conveyed to Hercules Daniel Bize the 9 July 1792. Said tract is conveyed by the said John Hunter by power of Attorney from the said Hercules Daniel Bize dated 1 June 1793. Set his hand John Hunter, Attorney for Hercules Danl. Bize. Wit: Lewis Saxon, Little Berry Harvey. Bond received 15 October 1793. Proved by Little Berry Harvey 2 April 1794 before Joseph Downs, J.P. [Plat] [LCDBK E: 228-229]

Butler, Pierce: 15 October 1793: Hercules Daniel Bize by his attorney John Hunter, of Laurens Co., S.C. to Berry Harvey, of same place, for £32, 10 shilling Stg.; 200 acres in Laurens Co., on the waters of Reaburans Creek. Bounding land of James Cuningham, part of said Survey, John Manly, John Cammoch, Samuel Elliott. *Originally granted to Pierce Butler,* and by him conveyed to Hercules Daniel Bize the 9 July 1792. Said tract is conveyed by the said John Hunter by power of Attorney from the said Hercules Daniel

Bize dated 1 June 1793. Set his hand John Hunter, Attorney for Hercules Danl. Bize. Wit: Joseph Mathis, Robert McNees. Bond received 15 October 1793. Proved by Robert McNees 2 March 1794 before Joseph Downs, J.P. [plat, shows bounding Carnmoch, James Cuningham, John Manly, Saml. Elliott, part of said survey]. [LCDBK E: 192]

Butler, Pierce: 16 October 1793: Hercules Daniel Bize, by his attorney John Hunter, of Laurens Co., S.C., to Benjamin Williams, of same place, for £8, 7 shilling 6 pns; 67 acres on the water of Reaburns Creek. Bounded on lands of the said Benjamin Williams, Lewis Saxon, John Cockran and part of said survey it *being part of a tract of 500 acres originally granted to Pierce Butler,* and by him conveyed to Hercules Daniel Bize the 9 July 1792. Said tract is sold by the said John Hunter by power of Attorney from the said Hercules Daniel Bize dated 1 June 1793. Set his hand John Hunter, Attorney for Hercules Danl. Bize. Wit: Jonathan Williams, Benjamin Williams. Bond received 17 October 1793. Proved by Benjamin Williams, Jr. 2 March 1794 before Joseph Downs, J.P. [Plat, shows bounding Benj. Williams, Lewis Saxon, John Cockran, part of said survey] . [LCDBK E: 178]

Butler, Pierce: 16 October 1793: Hercules Daniel Bize, by his attorney John Hunter, of Laurens Co., S.C., to John Mathis, of same place, for £11, 5sh Sterling; 100 acres, *part of 500 acres originally granted to Pierce Butler,* Esq., and conveyed by him to Hercules Daniel Bize 9 July 1792. Bounded by Robert McNees, Robert Bolt, John King, the Waggon Road and part of said survey. The tract of 100 acres lies on the branches of Reaburns creek, waters of Reedy River. Wit: Lewis Saxon, Benjn. Williams. Signed by John Hunter, Atty. for Hercules D. Bize. Oath made by Lewis Saxon 18 February 1794 before Joseph Downs, J.P. [LCDBK E: 161-162].

Butler, Pierce: 17 October 1793: Hercules Daniel Bize, by his attorney John Hunter, of Laurens Co., S.C. to Lewis Saxon, of same place, for £15 Sterling; 225 acres on waters of Raburns Creek. Bounded on John Manley, James Cuninghan, James Irwin, Lewis Saxon, Benjamin Williams, Berry Harvey. *Part of 500 acres originally granted to Pierce Butler*, Esq. And conveyed by him to Hercules Daniel Bize 9 July 1792 and by said John Hunter by Power of Attorney from said Bize 1 June 1793. Signed John Hunter, Attorney for Hercules Danl. Bize. Wit: Lydall Allen, Thomas Holmes. Proved by oath of Lydall Allen 2 February 1797 before Chas. Allen, J.P. [LCDBK F: 397]

Butler, Pierce: 7 September 1793: John Hunter, Esq., of Laurens Co., S.C. to John Cammeck [Cammoch], of same place, for £22 16 sh Sterling; 176 acres [plat show 276 acres] part of 500 acres granted to Pierce Butler and by him conveyed to Hercules D. Bize. Bounded by Saml. Elliott, Jeaen?, John

Camack, James Cuningham, part sold to L [Little] B. [Berry]. Harvey. Also 144 acres bounding Benjn Eliot, John Manley, being part of survey. These different *tracts originally granted to Pierce Butler* and conveyed by him to Hercules Daniel Bize 9 July 1792 and now by John Hunter, by Power of Attorney from Hercules Danl. Bize 1 Jun 1793. Wit: Jonthan. Downs, David Gary. Signed John Hunter, Attorney for Hercules Danl. Bize. Both tracts of land on the waters of Raburns Creek. Proved b oath of David Gary 20 February 1798 before Reuben Pyles, J.P. [Plats] [LCDBK F: 278-279]

Butler, Pierce: 10 September 1793: John Hunter, Esqr. of the County of Laurens, S.C., to Arthur Taylor, of same place, for £51; Stg.; 232 acres on Reedy River. Bounded on David Dunlap, Samuel Cooper, Richard Pugh, William Dorough. Being part of a tract of 500 acres *originally granted to Pierce Butler 5 May 1772* and by him conveyed to Hercules Daniel Bize on 9 July 1792 and now conveyed by the said John Hunter by virtue of a Power of Attorney from the said Hercules Daniel Bize. John Hunter, Attorney for Hercules Danl. Bize. (LS). Wit: William Norris, John Dorough. Joseph Downs, J.P. Received from Arthur Taylor, Wm. Dorough and James Dorough a bond payable to Hercules Daniel Bize for the sum of £ 51, 14 shillings in full. 9 September 1794. Proved by John Dorough 14 February 1794 before Joseph Downs, J.P. [LCDBK E: 206-209]

Butler, Pierce: 25 August 1795: Arthur Taylor, of Laurens Co., S.C., to Richard Pugh, of same place for £20; 105 acres on the waters of Reedy River. *Being part of a tract of land originally granted to Pierce Butler, Esqr.* And by him conveyed to Hercules Danl. Bize and by his Attorney John Hunter, Esqr. Conveyed to said Arthur Taylor and now by said Arthur Taylor conveyed to Richd Pugh. Arthur Taylor (Seal), Margaret (X) Taylor (Seal). Wit: Benjamin Box, Wm. McClanahan. Proved by Wm. McClanahan 26 December 1795 before John Cochran.[Plat Bounded by Arthur Taylor, Unknown, R. Pugh, William Donah's (Dorrah). [LCDBK F: 71]

Butler, Pierce: 11 September 1793: John Hunter Esqr., of Laurens Co., S.C., to Richd. (Richard) Pugh, of same place for £15; 100 acres on the waters of Shirrels Branch, waters of Reaburns Creek. Bounded on the land laid out or told to John Manly and Oliver Matthews. *Being part of a tract of 500 acres granted to Pierce Butler* and conveyed by him on the 9 July 1792 to Hercules Danl. Bize and now conveyed by the said John Hunter by virtue of a power of attorney from Hercules Danl. Bize. [Plat shows bounded by Ben Williamson, John Manly, land laid out. John Hunter, Atty for Hercules Danl. Bize (Seal). Wit: David Greene, Jno. Cockran. Proved by John Cochran 21 January 1796 before Reuben Pyles, J.P. [LCDBK F: 71-72]

Butler, Pierce: 15 October 1793: Hercules Daniel Bize, by his attorney John Hunter, Esqr., of Laurens Co., Ninety Six Dist., S.C., and Berry Harvey, of same place, for £32, 10 sh; 200 acres on the waters of Reaburns Creek. Bounding lands of James Cuningham, part of said survey, John Manly, John Cammock and Samuel Elliott. *Being part of a tract of 500 acres granted to Pierce Butler* and by him conveyed to Hercules Daniel Bize on 9 July 1792 and now conveyed by the said John Hunter, by virtue of a power of attorney from the said Hercules Daniel Bize bearing date 1 June 1792. John Hunter, attorney for Hercules *sic* Danl. Bize. Wit: Joseph Mathis, Robert McNees. [Plat shows bounding James Cuningham, Cammock, Saml. Elliott, John Manly.] [LCDBK E: 192-194]

Butler, Pierce (Bize lands): 7 May 1794: Little Berry Harvey, of Laurens Co., S.C., to Samuel Saxon. Whereas the said Samuel Saxon stand bound as security for the said Little Berry Harvey in the sum of £30 18 sh, 4 p. Payable to Hercules Daniel Bize: one third of which payment is to be paid 1 January 1795; another the 1 January 1796 and 3 payment on 1 January 1791. . . . convey unto the said Samuel Saxon one tract of 200 acres on waters of Reaburns Creek being *part of a tract of land granted to the said Bize* and whereon the said Little Berry Harvey now lives. Also one horse, one black are, 5 head of cattle, 2 feather beds and furniture, 2 iron pots, one Dutch oven, one frying pan and all my plantation and working tools. Little Berry Harvey (LS) Wit: Stain Willson, Joshua Downs. [LCDBK E: 211-212]

Butler, Pierce: 6 October 1795: Littleberry Harvey and Nancy, his wife, of Laurens Co., S.C., to John Cargill, of same, for £38 Stg.; 200 acres on the waters of Reaburn's Creek, joining of James Cuningham, part on said Harvey, John Manly, John Cammoch and Samuel Elliot. Part of a tract of 400 acres *originally granted to Pierce Butler* and by him conveyed to Hercules Daniel Bize, and by John Hunter, Esq. Atty for said Bize, conveyed to said Harvey on 9 July 1793 and now conveyed by Littleberry Harvey and Nancy, his wife, to John Cargill. Littleberry Harvey (L.S.) Nancy Harvey L.S. Wit. John Martin, John Dendy. Proved by John Martin and John Dendy 6 October 1795 before Thomas Wadsworth, J.L.C. [LCDBK F: 78]

Butler, Pierce: 28 October 1799: John Cargill, (VA), of Laurens Co., S.C., to James Cunningham, of same place, for $180; 200 acres on waters of Rabourns Creek. Land adjoining lands of said James Cunningham, John Manly, John Cammock and Samuel Elliott. *It being part of 400 acres grant to Pierce Butler* conveyed to Hercules David Bize and by John Hunter, Esq., his attorney, for Bize to Little Berry Harvey then to me said John Cargill. John Cargill (Va) (LS). Wit: Gallanus Winn, Elizabeth Lester. Proved by Gallanus Winn 28 October 1799 before Wm. Mitchell, J.L.C. Dower of Rachel Cargill, wife of the within John Cargill given 28 October 1799 before

Wm. Mitchell, J.L.C. [LCDBK H: 155-156]

Butler, Pierce: 19 August 1797: John Hunter, Esqr., of Laurens Co., S.C., Attorney, for Hercules Danl. Bize, to Ambrose Hudgens, for £7 10 sh; 55 acres on waters of Reaburns Creek, *being part of 500 acres granted to Pierce Butler,* and now conveyed by virtue of a power of attorney from the said Bize. John Hunter, Attorney for Hercules Danl. Bize. (Seal) [Plat shows bounded on said Ambr. Hudgens, John Rodgers, Part of survey, Saml. Eliot. Wit: Saml. Henderson, Robert McNees. Proved by Robert McNees 17 October 1803 before Chas. Allen, J.P. [LCDBK G: 683-684]

Butler, Pierce: 19 August 1797: John Hunter, Esqr., of Laurens Co., S.C., attorney for Hercules Danl. Bize, to Robert McNees, for £7, 10 sh; 100 acres on waters of Reaburns Creek, *being part of 500 acres granted to Pierce Butler* and conveyed by him to said Hercules Danl. Bize and now by said John Hunter by virtue of a power of attorney. John Hunter, Attorney for Hercules Danl. Bize (LS). Wit: Saml. Henderson, Ambrose Hudgens. Proved by Ambrose Hudgens 17 October 1803 before Charles Allen, J.Q. [Plat made 3 September 1799 by Jno. Hunter, D.S. shows bounded by Robert McNees, John King, John Rodgers, Saml. Elliot]. [LCDBK G: 689]

Butler, Pierce: 27 May 1799: Lewis Saxon, of Laurens Co., S.C., to Walter Matthews, of same place, for $150; 175 acres on waters of Rabourns Creek. Bounded N on James Cuningham, S on John Cochran, W on Thomas Johnston, SW on James H. Lowery and said Lewis Saxon. *Being part land originally granted to Pierce Butler,* conveyed to H.D. Bize and by his attorney John Hunter to Lewis Saxon. Lewis Saxon (LS). Wit: Robt. Matthews. Wm. Neighbors. Chas. Smith, J.P. [Plat shows bounded by James Cuningham, Jno. Cochran, Thos. Johnston, Lewis Saxon, Lowry's land]. [LCDBK F: 464]

Butler, Pierce: 3 January 1800: I Hercules Danl. Bize, by my attorney, John Hunter, Esq., of Laurens Co., to William McDaniel, of same place, for £23; 150 acres on waters of Reaburns Creek. *Being part of a tract of 500 acres of land granted to Pierce Butler, Esq.* And by him conveyed to the said Hercules Danl. Bize, and now by the said Bize by his attorney John Hunter, Esq. Hercules D. Bize, by his attorney Jno. Hunter. Wit: James Hollingsworth, Jacob Williams. Proved by James Hollingsworth 15 October 1800 before James Abercrombie, J.P. [Plat made 10 October 1800 shows tract of 150 acres bounded by James McClanahan, John Crumby (Abercrombie), Ben Williams, John Achion, W. Manly. [LCDBK G:75-76].

Butler, Pierce: 5 October 1801: I John Hunter, Esqr., of Laurens Co., S.C., attorney, for Hercules Danl. Bize, to Ambrose Hudgens, of Laurens Co., S.C., for £25; 100 acres on the waters of Reaburns Creek. John Hunter,

Attorney for Hercules Danl. Bize. (LS) Wit: William Hunter, Samuel Henderson. Proved 18 October 1803 before Josiah Blackwell, J.P. [Plat made 5 October 1793 by Jno. Hunter, D.S. Shows bounded on Hastings Dial, Benjamin Williams, Saml. Elliot, and part of survey sold to Abner Hudgens. Also states 100 acres being *part of a grant of 500 acres originally granted to Pierce Butler* and by him conveyed to Hercules Danl. Bize on the 9 July 1792.] [LCDBK G: 685]

Butler, Pierce: 25 August 1801: Walter Matthews, of Laurens Dist., S.C., to David Burris, of same place, for $400; 161 acres on the waters of Reaburns Creek. Bounded on N on James Cuningham, E on John Cochran, S on Thos. Johnson, SW on Lewis Saxon and Lowrey. *Being part of original grant to Pierce Butler Esqr.,* and by him conveyed to Hercules Danl. Bize by his attorney John Hunter to Lewis Saxon, then by said Saxon to Walter Matthews. Walter Matthews (LS). Wit: John Cochran, Alexr. Calder. Dower of Jane Matthew, wife of the within Walter Matthews given 7 September 1801 before Q. A. Elmore, J.P. Proved by Alexander Calder 31 August 1801 before Q. A. Elmore, J.Q. [Plat shows bounding Jno. Cochran, Thos. Johnson, Lewis Saxon and Lowry's land, James Cunningham]. [LCDBK G: 286-287]

Butler, Pierce: 4 January 1802: John Hunter, attorney for Hercules Danl. Bize to Thomas Parker, of Laurens Dist., S.C., for $200; 141 acres on the branches of Reaburns Creek adjoining lands of Robert McNees, John Matthews, Randal Cook, *being part of a grant of 500 acres belonging to Pierce Butler, Esqr.,* and by him conveyed to the above Hercules Dl. Bize by John Hunter, Esq. Attorney for the said Bize and conveyed to the said James *sic* Parker. [Thomas Parker in other parts of doc.]. Hercules Dl. Bize by his attorney Jno. Hunter (LS). Wit: Robt. Creswell, James Taggart. Proved by Robert Creswell 23 February 1804 before Joseph Downs, J.P. [Plat shows bounded by Robert McNeese, John Matthews, and land laid out to Jas. Boyd] [LCDBK H: 12]

Butler, Pierce: 20 January 1803: David Burris, of Laurens Dist., S.C., to Thaddeus Sims and William Osbourn, of same place, for $400; 197 3/4 acres on waters of Rabourns Creek. *Being part of a tract of an original grant to Pierce Butler, Esq.,* and by said Butler to D. Bize and by sundry legal conveyances to the said David Burris. [Plat shows bounding Lewis Saxon, Thos. Johnson, James Cunningham, A. Calder, John Cochran]. David Burris (LS) Wit: James Hunter, John Cochran. Proved by John Cochran 20 January 1804 before Josiah Blackwell, J.P. Dower of Mary Burris, wife of the within named David Burris given 31 March 1804 before Charles Allen, J.Q. [LCDBK H: 57]

Butler, Pierce: May 3 1803: Wm. McDaniel, of Laurens Dist., S.C., to Robert Allison, of same place, for $100; 150 acres on waters of Raburns Creek. Bounded on Thomas Burton, M. Manley, J. Cochran, Thomas Johnson. Being part of 500 acres *formerly granted to Hercules D. Bize by his Atty, John Hunter, Esq.*, to me the said Wm. McDaniel. Wm. McDaniel (LS) Wit: Hastings Dial, John Cochran. Proved by Hastings Dial 22 March 1803 before J. Blackwell, J.P. [LCDBK H: 2]

Butler, Pierce: 11 February 1818: James Cunningham, of Laurens Dist., S.C., to William Hudgens, of same place, for $650; 140 acres on waters of Reabourns Creek on a branch called Shirrell's Branch. *Originally granted to Pierce Butler* and the balance of that part conveyed unto John Cargill to the said James Cunningham. Bounded on S on Mark Killingsworth, W on Cunningham, N on Nehemiah Franks, E on said William Hudgins. Being the other part too acres tract conveyed by the said John Cargill as aforesaid. Jas. Cuningham (LS). Wit; James Prim, Samuel Cuningham. Dower of Mary (x) Cuningham, wife of the within named James Cunningham given 11 February 1818 before Charles Allen, Q.M. (LS). Proved by James Prim 11 February 1818 before Chas. Allen, Q.M. [LCDBK K: 223-224]

Burrows, William: Survey for William Burrows pursuant to precept dated 7 March 1769; 200 acres on waters of Rayburns Creek in Craven Co., . Bounding SW land belonging to Joseph Babb; [Plat shows land laid out to Oliver Mathews now property of Joseph Babb.] Certified 10 April 1769. Ord. Co. 28 October 1774. Jno. Caldwell, D.S. [P13_447:1]

Burrows, William: Memorial by William Burrows; 200 acres in Craven Co., on the waters of Rayburns Creek. Bounding SW on Joseph Babb; other sides vacant. Certified 28 October 1774 and granted 8 December 1774. Quit rent to commence in 2 years. 29 May 1775. Delivered 18 July 1775 to Memorialist by C.J. Lindsfors. Jno. Caldwell, D.S. [M13_492:2]

Burrows, William: 12 December 1786: Laurens Co., S.C. Came into Open Court Jonathan Downs, Esq. and David Allison made oath that they have known *Wm. Burrows* to possess a certain tract of land containing 200 acres on Williams Creek, this 18 or 20 years and no ways interrupted, in accordance with *his grant of 5 December 1774,* (by warrant directed by Egerton Leigh, Esq. Surveyor General, dated 7 March 1769 for this land, on waters of Reaburns Creek in Craven Co., certified 10 April 1769 by John Caldwell, SC). Lewis Saxon, CC. [LCDBK B: 69]

Burrows [Burris], William: 10 September 1795: William Burris *sic* (Burrows), of Laurens Co., S.C., to John Blackwell, of same place, for £100 stg.; 200 acres in said county on a branch of Raiborns Creek. Bounded on

SW by Joseph Babb; other sides vacant land. Hereunto said William Burrows and Rachel Burrows, his wife, have set their seals. Signed William (W his mark) Burrows, Rachel (her mark) Burrows. Wit: James Abercrombie, John Pinson. Proved by John Pinson on 18 July 1797 before Joseph Downs, J.P. Recorded 18 July 1797. [LCDBK F: 247]

Burrows, William: 1 May 1800: I John Blackwell, of Laurens Dist., S.C., to John Harry, of same place, for $300; 100 acres on a branch of Raburns Creek, formerly called Williams, now Burrisses Creek. Being a part of a tract of 200 acres *originally granted to William Burrows 8 December 1774* and by him sold and conveyed unto the above named John Blackwell and now said 100 acres is by the said Blackwell sold and conveyed to John Harry. John (B) Blackwell (LS) Mary (X) Blackwell. Wit: John Pinson, Solomon Cole. Proved by Solomon Cole 24 October 1803 before Josiah Blackwell, J.P. [Plat shows bounding part on original survey, vacant land, and land laid out to Oliver Matthews.] [LCDBK H: 144]

Burrows [Burris], William: 21 January 1802: John Blackwell, of Laurence *sic* Dist., S.C., to Isaac Pinson, of same for $300; 100 acres on branch of Raburn Creek formerly called Williams, (now called Burris Creek), being part of a tract of 200 acres on Raburns Creek, formerly called Williams Creek (now Burris Creek) *originally granted to William Burris [Burrows] on 8 December 1774* and by him conveyed to the above named John Blackwell and now said 100 acres is sold and conveyed into said Isaac Pinson. Signed John (B) Blackwell. Wit: Josiah Blackwell, Isabella (J her mark) Blackwell. Proved by Josiah Blackwell 17 April 1810 before Z. Bailey, J.P. [LCDBK K: 120]

Caldwell, James: March 1826: I David Caldwell, Senr, of the State of Alabama, Sinclair Co. to John Robertson, of Laurens Dist., S.C., for $100; 20 acres a certain quantity or part of my Madden track of land, *where James Caldwell formerly lived.* Bounded by lands of Wm. Ritchey, Martin Shaw and Jno. Findley. David Caldwell (LS) Wit: James Rowland, Wm. T. Burnside. Proved by William Burnside 17 April 1726 before Jas. Neely, J.Q. [LCDBK L: 237]

Caldwell, John: 1773: Bounding Hastings Dial and Nathan Hampton.

Caldwell, William: 17 March 1786: William Caldwell, of Ninety-Six Dist., S.C., to Roger Murphey, of same place, for £10; 300 acres on a branch of Saluda River called Long Lick Creek. Bounded at the time of the original survey N and NW by Robert Woods, and Robert Gills, SE by Ebenezer Starns, SE by Patrick Cunningham. Granted 21 August 1774. William Caldwell (LS) Wit: Samuel Scott, John Ritchey, Robt. Ritchey.

Calhoun, Thomas: Survey for Thomas Calhoun pursuant to precept dated 7 June 1768; 200 acres in Craven Co., on a small branch of Raburn's Creek. Bounded E part on Ben. Brown and part vacant; other sides vacant. Certified 2 August 1768. R. Humphreys, D.S. Ord. Co. 25 November 1774 for Thomas Elliott.[See Thomas Elliott for memorial.] [P15_17:1]

Calhoun lands: 22 June 1826: John Calhoun of Laurens Dist., S.C., to Squire Calhoun; for $500; 126 acres on Rabons Creek and a large branch known by the name of Calhouns Branch. Bounded NE by W.F. Downs, E by Barrington Avry[?], S by James Johnston, SW by John Calhoun. John Calhoun (LS). Wit; James Brewster, Hugh Brewster, Proved by Hugh Brewster 24 March 1829 before A. Milner, J.Q. [LCDBK M: 89]

Cammeron, Alexander: Survey for Alexander Cammeron pursuant to precept dated 7 April 1772; 100 acres on Small branch of Little River in Craven Co. Bounded NW by Thomas Halsey; all other sides vacant. Certified 1 May 1772. Robt. Ellison, D.S. Ord. Co. 11 January 1773. [P13_497:2]

Cammeron, Alexander: Memorial for Alexander Cameron for 100 acres in Craven Co., on a S[small] branch of Little River. Bounding NW on Thomas Halsey's all other sides on vacant land. Certified 11 January 1773 and granted 6 February 1773 to the memorialist. Quit rent to commence 10 years from the date. Set his had 21 July 1773 Rt. Ellison, D.S. Delivered 4 September 1773 to John Ellison. [M12-309:6]

Camp, William: 225 acres granted --No date for grant given.

Camp, William: 2 February 1799: William Camp, of Laurens Co., S.C., to Elisha Casey, of same place; 155 acres, being part of 225 acres *originally granted to said William Camp.* On the waters of Raburns Creek, waters of Reedy River. Bounded by Henry Morgin, Raburns Creek, Thomas Camp, Eli Cashaw. Signed Wm. Camp. Wit: Thomas (C) Camp, Starling Camp. Proved by oath of Thos. Camp 18 February 1799 before Reuben Pyles, J.P. [LCDBK F: 422]

Camp, William: 2 September 1816: Elisha Casey, of Laurens Dist., S.C., to Mathew Landers, of same place for $125; 350 acres, *being a tract of land granted to William Camp and part of a tract granted to the said Elisha Casey.* The land being on the waters of Rabourns Creek. Bounding Henry Morgan, Raburns Creek, Thomas Camp, Joseph Avary, Bailey Mahon. Elisha Casey. Wit: Richard (X) Landers, James McKnight. Dower of Esther

Casey, wife of the within Elisha Casey given 11 October 1816 before Wm. Arnold, J.Q. Proved by James McKnight 11 October 1815 before Wm. Arnold, J.Q. [LCDBK L: 8]

Cargill, Cornelius: Survey for Cornelius Cargill pursuant to precept dated 7 April 1772; 100 acres in Craven Co., on waters of Reaburns Creek. Bounded by vacant land. Certified 10 September 1772. Pat. Cunningham, D.S. [P13_529:3]

Cargill, Cornelius: Memorial by Cornelius Cargill; 100 acres in Craven Co., on the waters of Rayburnes Creek. Bounding on all sides on land not known. Certified 7 June 1774 and granted 8 July 1774. Quit rent to commence in 2 years. Delivered 6 March 1775 to P. Cunningham. Pat. Cunningham, D.S. [M13_157:4]

Cargill, Daniel of VA: 17 February 1796: We Little Berry Harvey and Nancy, his wife, formerly Nancy Cargill, daughter of Daniel Cargile, deceased, of Laurens Co., S.C., do nominate and appoint our brother and friend John Cargill our attorney to settle our part of our said father, Danl. Cargile, decd. Estate, in the Commonwealth of Virginia. Littleberry Harvey (L.S.) Nancy Harvey (L.S.) Wit: Sl. Saxon, Whitfield Wilson. Proved by Whitfield Wilson 12 October 1795 before Wm. Hunter, J.P. [LCDBK F: 78]

[Note: Daniel Cargill, Dec'd, last will and testament found in Charlotte Co., Virginia. Apparently Nancy Cargill was married 1st to ____ Dendy, and 2nd marriage to Littleberry Harvey. Called Nancy Dandy *sic* in father's LWT accounting dated 1783.]

Chalmer, Gilbert: Survey for Gilbert Chalmer pursuant to precept dated 30 May 1768; 100 acres on north side Saludy on a branch of Reabins Creek. Bounded SW on land laid out to John Alliordin [Allwidice]; other sides vacant. Certified 14 October 1768. W. Gist, D.S. [P14_46:2]

Chalmer, Gilbert: Memorial for Gilbert Chalmer; 100 acres in Berkley Co., on N side of Saludy River, on a branch of Rabburn's Creek. Bounding SW on land of John Aldwidin; other sides vacant. Certified 14 October 1768 and granted 12 December 1768. Quit rent to commence in 10 years. 2 May 1769. Wm. Gist, D.S. David Marell. [B in margin]. [M8-430:4]

Chalmers, Gilbert: 9 November 1770 conveyed lands to David Maull. No deed located.

Chalmers, Gilbert: 2 February 1804: James Maull, heir and son of David Maull dec'd., of Jacksonborough, in the State aforesaid, to Abraham Bolt, of

Laurens Dist., for $200; 100 acres on the N side of Saluda River on a branch of Raburns Creek. Bounded on SW on land of John Alwidice [Allurdin]; other sides vacant. *Originally granted to Gilbert Chalmers 12 December 1768*, and conveyed by him to said David Maull 9 November 1770 to said David Maull. Also 100 acres on N side of Saluda River on a branch of Raybourns Creek bounding at time of survey by vacant land. *Originally granted to John Allwedice 12 December 1768* and him conveyed to said David Maull 9 November 1770. Signed James Maull. Wit: Isaac Underwood, P. G. Wharton. Proved by Pleasant Wharton 20 March 1804 before Joseph Downs, J.P. [LCDBK H: 24]

Childress, Thomas: 5 February 1813: Thomas Childress, of Laurens Dist., S.C., to William Curry, of same place, for $120; 100 acres on N Fork Rabornes Creek at the head of Peachlans Branch and the head of Durban Branch belonging to Rabarnes and Durbans Creeks. Bounded on Nathan Curry. Thomas Childress (LS). Wit: Nathan Curry, Junr., Richard Childress. Proved by Nathan Curry, Jurn. 15 June 1816 before Thos. Wright, J.Q. Dower of Polly Childress, wife of the within named Thomas Childress given 15 June 1816 before Thos. Wright, Q.M. [LCDBK K: 87]

Choice, Tully: 5 December 1785: 605 acres granted.

Choice, Tully: 8 November 1791: Tully Choice, of Laurens Co., S.C., planter to James McKnight, of same, farmer, for £86 stg.; 173 acres on small branch of Reedy River, *originally granted to Tully Choice 5 December 1785*. Tully Choice (LS). Wit: Edward Nash, Thomas Baskett. Proved by Edmond Nash before Joseph Downs, J.P. [Plat shows bounding on lands of Samuel Boling, Tully Choice, George Martin, and Mary____ [LCDBK D: 134-136]

Choice, Tully: 12 February 1792: Tully Choice, of Laurens Co., S.C., to Solomon Hopkins, of same place, for £125 Stg.; 387 acres *being part of 605 acres grant originally granted 5 December 1785*. Bounded by Samuel Boling, Thomas Graden, John Miller, bounded on lands unknown, Thomas Mathis, James McKnight. Wit: Edward Scarborough, Samuel Boling, Thomas (X) Mathis. Proved by Samuel Boling 16 February 1793 before Joseph Downs, J.P. [LCDBK D: 349-350]

Christian, Thomas: Survey for Thomas Christian pursuant to precept dated 5 July 1763; 150 acres in Berkley Co., on a branch of Saludy called Reyburns Creek. Bounded on all sides by vacant land. Certified 16 August 1762 for John Williams. Jo. Curry, D.S. [See memorial for John Williams] [P7_453:3]

Cochran, John: 21 February 1814: John Cochran, of Abbeville Dist., S.C., to Mark Killingworth, of Laurens Dist., S.C., for $70; 200 acres on E side of Reaburns Creek. Plat shows bounded on Thos. Johnson and John Martin, Ben. Nabers and Kitt Hardy, Heirs of W. McDaniel, on the road to court house. John Cochran (LS) Wit: Saml. Cunningham, Jonthn. Downs. Proved by Samuel Cunningham 5 August 1816 before John Garlington. Dower of Margaret Cochran, wife of the within John Cochran given 23 July 1816 before John Garlington. Q.M. [LCDBK K: 138]

Cogdell, John: Survey for 600 acres not found.

Cogdell, John: Memorial for John Cogdell; 600 acres in 96 Dist. on the ridge between Rayburns Creek and Reedy River. Bounded on all sides by vacant land. Certified 4 March 1773 and granted 2 April 1773. Quit rent to commence in 2 years. 4 August 1773. Delivered 17 September 1773 to John Cogdell. Wm. Anderson, D.S. [M12_343:3]

Cogell, John: Deceased before 21 May 1807.

Cogdell, John: 21 May 1807: We John S. Cogdell, Clement S. Cogdell and Richard W. Cogdell of Charleston, S.C., to Bailey Mahon, of Laurens Dist., S.C., for $350, 600 acres on the ridge between Rabourns Creek and Reedy River. Bounded on all sides by vacant land at the time or the original grant [n.d.]. John S. Cogdell (LS), Clement S. Cogdell (LS) Richard W. Cogdell (LS). Wit: Lionel H. Kennedy, A. Circide(?). Dowers of Mary Cogdell, and Cecile Cogdell. the wives of the within John S. Cogdell and Richard W. Cogdell on 22 May 1811 before Lionel H. Kennedy, Q.M. Proved by Lionel H. Kennedy before Jas. Nelson, Q.M. [Plat for 600 cares shows bounded by vacant lands. [LCDBK K: 13]

Cohun, Thomas: Survey for Thomas Cohun pursuant to precept dated 5 May 1772; 100 acres in Craven Co., on waters of Saludy River. Bounded SE by Richard Griffith, W and S on William Thomas; SW by John Smith; other sides vacant. Certified 24 May 1772. Dd. Cunningham, D.S. Ord. Co. 2 February 1772. [P14_121:7]

Cohune, Thomas: Memorial by Thos. Cohune for 100 acres in Craven Co., on the waters of Saludy river. Bounding SE on Richard Griffith, W and S on Wm. Thomas, SW on John Smith, all over sides vacant land. Certified 1 February 1773 and granted 25 February 1773 to the memorialist. Quit rent to commence in two years from date. Set his hand 5 July 1773. D. Cunningham, D.S. Delivered 7 October 1773 to David Cunningham. [M12-281:3]

Cole, William: 10 October 1808: I William Coll *sic*, of Laurens Dist., S.C., to Robert Culbertson, of same place, for $300; 128 acres being part of a tract of land containing 100 acres, being part of a tract of land *originally granted to Patrick Cuningham* and conveyed by him to Thomas Richardson, being the place whereon the said William Coal sic now lives, also one other tract of land containing 28 acres adjoining the above described tract. *Originally granted to Thomas Richardson*, bounded on lands of Thos. Cunningham, deceased, James Hall, land unknown. William Cole (LS) Wit: Samuel Weir, John Blackley. Proved by Samuel Weir 10 October 1808 before Jonthan. Downs, J.Q. Dower of Patsy Cole, wife of the said William Coal *sic* given 10 October 1808 before Jonathan. Downs, J.Q. [Note; no creek mentioned] [LCDBK J: 126]

Cole, William 16 July 1817: William Cole, Of Laurens Dist., S.C., to Philip Wait, of same place, for $1000; 250 acres on Walnut Creek on the road from the fish dam ford by the Poplar Spring Meeting House by Wm. South, by Mary Howell to Walnut Creek near mouth of a branch by land of William Howell, land of James Clardy. William Cole (LS) Wit: John Chism, John Wait. Proved by John Wait 17 July 1817 before James Powell, J.P. [LCDBK K: 191]

Cole, William: 2 January 1821: Samuel Downs, Sheriff, of Laurens Dist., S.C., to John Lindley, Jr., of same place. Whereas by virtue of a writ of fieri facias, which issued from the court of common Please of Laurens Dist., at *the suit of William Cole against John Lindley*, directed to all and singular the sheriff of the state aforesaid, which execution was duly entered in the office of the sheriff, of said district, the said Samuel Downs did enter and seize under the execution a certain tract of land herein after described and after notice of the said intended sale of said land, did no the day and year above mentioned openly and publickly expose the same to sale to the highest bidder, for ready money at Laurens Court House. The said land being struck off to the said John Hutson, Jr. for the sum of $3000 at the price being the highest and last bidder for the same. And whereas John Hutson has by his order dated 12 January 1820 authorized me to execute title for the said land to John Lindley. The land containing 100 acres lying and being on the waters of Reedy river bounded on lands of Crain Jones, William South, and Elijah Smith. Samuel Downs (LS) Sheriff. Laurens Dist. Wit: J.H. Irby, John B. Griffin. Proved by James H. Irby 14 February 1821 before John Garlington, J.Q. [LCDBK K: 316]

Coker, Robert, Senr.: 24 July 1797: Robert Coker, Senr., of Laurens Co., S.C., to James Coker, of same place, for 20 shillings; 100 acres on the S side of Raiborn Creek, waters of Saluda River. Bounded S by James Abercrombie and when laid out by Big Surveys and Richard Owens.

Granted 21 December 1769 [to who not named] Memorial dated 24 January 1770. Wit: Robert Coker, Thomas Coker. Signed Robert (R) Coker. Proved by the oath of Robert Coker 14 May 1798 before John Coker, J.P. [LCDBK F: 303]

Cooper, Samuel: 500 acres granted--no date given.

Cooper, Samuel: 18 August 1815: Samuel Cooper, of the State of Tennessee, Giles Co., to Joseph Downs, of Laurens Dist., S.C., for $300; 225 acres on Rabourns Creek and Reedy River, *being one half of 250 acres originally granted to Samuel Cooper.* Saml. Cooper (LS) Wit; J.P. Cunningham, Wm. Cunningham. Proved by John P. Cuningham 23 October 1815 before J. Hitch, J.P. [LCDBK K: 106]

Copeland, John: 6 April 1768 grant date--not located.

Copeland, John: 2 August 1769: John Copeland, of Berkley Co., S.C., weaver to Isaac Abercrombie, of same place, planter for £150; 100 acres in Berkley Co., on Raiborns Creek, a branch of Saluda. *Originally granted to John Copeland.* Wit: John Abercrombie, James Abercrombie. Signed John (J) Copeland . Proved by oath of John Abercrombie 27 February 1798 before James Abercrombie, J.P. [LCDBK F: 294]

Copeland, John: 8 November 1797: Isaac Abercrombie, of Anson Co., N. C., free holder, to James Abercrombie, of Laurens Co., S.C. for $250; 100 acres on a branch of Rabourns Creek in Laurens Co. *Originally grated to John Copland 6 April 1768* and from said Copeland to Isaac Abercrombie 2 August 1769. Wit: Hastings Dial, William Johnson. Signed Isaac Abercrombie. Proved by oath of William Johnson 8 November 1797 before James Abercrombie, J.P. [LCDBK F: 295-296]

Copeland, John: 22 February 1798: James Abercrombie, of Laurens Co., S.C., to Anderson Arnold, of same place, for $365; 100 acres on the N fork of Rabourns Creek of Reedy River. *Originally granted to John Copeland 6 April 1768.* Bounded by Anderson Arnold, John Thomason, Samuel Evans, John Frances Wolff. Proved by oath of William Thomason 28 February 1798 before Joseph Downs, J.P. Dower by Ann (I) Abercrombie wife of James Abercrombie made 22 February 1798 before Jonathan Downs, J.L.C. [LCDBK F: 295-196].

Coppock, Moses: 1767 bounding Samuel Alexander. No survey or memorial located.

Coppock, Moses: 30 December 1771: Moses Coppock, listed as deceased by 30 December 1771,this being the date of the marriage of his daughter, Marther to William Tomlinson. [Lucas; *Quakers*, pg. 98]

Cormack, Alexander: Certified for Alexander Cormack pursuant to precept dated 1 September 1772; 200 acres in Craven Count NE side of Saludy, branch of Reaburns Creek. Bounded N on land laid out person unknown; SE on land of John Williams and Samuel Williams; SW land claimed by Philip Sherrel; other sides vacant. Certified 17 October 1772. Jonth. Downs, D.S. [P14_196:2]

Cormack, Alexander: Memorial for Alexander Cormack; 200 acres in Craven Co., NE of Saludy on a branch of Rayburns Creek. Bounding N on land laid out; S and SE on John and Samuel Williams; SW on Philip Shearel [Sherrel]; other sides vacant. Certified 17 October 1772 and granted 2 April 1773. Quit rent to commence in 2 years. 5 August 1773. Delivered 14 August 1773 to Alexander Cormack. Jno. Downs, D.S. [M12_345:1]

Cormack, Alexander: 18 March 1801: That we Mary Donaldson, Executer and Mary Brailsford, daughter of Alexander Cormack, dec'd., to Isaac Dial, of Laurens Co., for $200, 200 acres on a branch of Rabourns Creek. *Originally granted to said Alexander Cormack 2 April 1773*. Signed Mary Donaldson, Mary Brailsford. Wit: Jonathan Abercrombie, Arch. McDaniel. Proved by Arch. McDaniel 24 March 1801 before James Abercrumbie, J.P. [LCDBK G: 214-215]

Copland, John: Survey for John Copland pursuant to precept dated 22 June 1767; 100 acres, tract of vacate land (on bounty) on a branch of Reburns Creek which empty into Saludy River. Bounded on all sides by vacant land. Certified 1 October 1767. Pat. Calhoun, D.S. [P14_182:2]

Copland, John: Memorial for John Copland; 100 acres in Berkley Co., on a branch of Reburns Creek waters of Saludy River. Bounded on all sides by vacant land. Certified 1 October 1767 and granted 6 April 1768. Quit rent to commence in 10 years. 27 July 1768. Pat. Calhoun, D.S. For the Mem. James Abercrombie. [B certified in Margin] [M2_537:2]

Copland, John: 2 August 1769: John Copeland, of Berkley Co., S.C., weaver, to, to Isaac Abercrombie, of same place, planter, for £150 lawful money of the province; 100 acres on a branch of Saluda called Raiborns Creek bounded on all sides by vacant lands. *Being land originally granted to John Copeland*. John (J his mark) Copland. Wit: John Abercrombie, James Abercrombie. Proved by John Abercrombie 27 February 1778 before James Abercrombie, J.P. [LCDBK F: 294]

Copland, John: 8 November 1795: Isaac Abercrombie, Anson Co., North Carolina, free holder, to James Abercrombie, of Laurens Co., S.C., for $250.; 100 acres on a branch of Rabourns Creek. *Originally granted to John Copland* by Hon. Granville Montague by patent dated 6 April 1768 and conveyed from said John Copland to the said Isaac Abercrombie by indenture dated 2 August 1769. Isaac Abercrombie, (L.S.) Wit: Hastings Dial, William Johnson. Proved 8 November 1797 by William Johnson before James Abercrombie, J.P. [LCDBK F: 295]

Copland, John: 22 February 1798: : James Abercrombie, planter of Laurens Co., to Anderson Arnold, of same place, for $365, 100 acres on N fork Rabourns Creek of Reedy River. Bounding S on Anderson Arnold; John Thomason; Samuel Evans, John Francis Wolff. *Originally granted to John Copland 6 April 1768,* conveyed by said Copeland to Isaac Abercrombie by lease and release, from Isaac Abercrombie to James Abercrombie by Deed 8 November 1797. Signed James Abercrombie. Wit: William Thomason, Joseph Camp. 2 February 1798; Dower of Mrs. Ann Abercrombie, wife of James Abercrombie. Proved by William Thompson 28 February 1798 before Joseph Downs, J.P. [LCDBK F: 295-296]

Copeland [Copland], John: Died 1826, age about 78. Born 1748 in Ireland. [Family: Wife: Margaret Blakely, born Ireland. Children: George, John Jr., William, James, Samuel, Rachel and Nancy.] Buried Duncan creek Presbyterian Church, organized in 1764. [Burying Grounds, Graveyards and Cemeteries, Vol. 1, pg. 4.]

Cox, William: 1809: Will dated 7 March 1809 Abbeville Dist., S.C. Recorded 17 August 1809: Executers: son-in-law James Young. Major David Anderson of Laurens Dist. Wit: Geo., Elender Shotwell, Alexr. W. Adams. Wife: Margaret Cox. Children: Rhoda, wife of James Young. Albert Walker my said daughters son. [Young, pgs. 390-191]

[Another book mentioned the children of James Young of Laurens Dist. Viz: Gallatin, Wm. A., Keturah, Phebe, Susannah C., Rhoda E.C. Young.]

Crackel, James:. July 1771 James Crackel, Esq. bounding Martha Goodwyn. No survey of memorial found for James Crackel.

Craddock, David: 13 August 1799: Pursuant to orders from the Executors of Adkinson, Decd., I have admeasured and laid out for Joseph Cox 103 acres on W side of Little River, *it being part of a tract originally granted to David Craddock, Dec'd.* Surveyed 13 August 1799 [Plat shows bounding Bridget McLancy, John Davidson, Joseph Cox, W [William] Glass, Little River area. John Rodgers, D.S.] [LCDBK F: 533-534]

Craddock, David: 19 March 1800: We the executors of Henry Adkinson, decd., of Laurens Co., S.C., to Joseph Cox, Senr. of said place, for $309 Sterling; 103 acres being part of a tract of land *originally granted to David Craddock, Dec'd* and conveyed by said Craddock to James McDowel and by said McDowall to Henry Adkinson, dec'd. Bounded as plat here represents. Mary (x) Adkinson (LS) Drury (x) Dupress (LS), John Dacey (LS). Wit: Joseph Cox, Thomas Cox, Jesse Cox. Dower of Mary Adkinson given 19 March 1800 before Wm. Mitchell, J.Q. Proved by Thomas Cox 19 March 1800 before Wm. Mitchell, J.Q. [LCDBK F: 533-534]

Creecy, John: 15 January 1812: LWT – I John Creecy, Doctor, of Laurens Dist., S.C. To my beloved wife Elizabeth a life estate in all my lands. . . . at the death of my wife, I do hereby give unto her children by Zacheriah Sims, deceased the aforesaid negroes and there increase. One equal part Fanney Clemmans, wife of Jacob Clemmans and her son Zachariah Simpson the other half of one equal share. . . to John Wait for said Zachariah Simpson. Should he not be of age at the death of his grandmother and to her son Joel Sims, I give $125. At the death of my wife Elizabeth Creecy, I give to her son James Sims the addition of one equal share of said negroes, all that land lying on the W side of Reedy River. I do give unto David Anderson all the remainder of my lands where I now live, lying on the E side of said River. .Appoint my friends David Anderson and Robert Cunningham, Executors. . Signed John Creecy (Seal). Wit: John Wait, John Middleton, Frances Wait (X) her mark. [LCWBK D: 64]

Creswell land: 3 March 1806: We Robert Creswell, Elihu Creswell & James McCaa, of Laurens Dist., S.C., to Andrew McKnight, of same place, for $250; 105 acres lying on the old Indian boundary line and on a small branch of Reedy River. Bounding Raley's land and on Mary McDonalds. Robert Creswell (LS), Elihu Creswell (LS), Jas. McCaa (LS). Wit. Wm. McKnight, David Madden. Dower of Nancy [signed as Agness] Creswell and Phebe McCaa, wife of the within Robert Creswell and James McCaa made 3 March 1826. Proved by David Madden 3 March 1806 before Chas. Allen, J.Q. [Plat] [LCDBK H: 131-132]

Creswell land: 18 August 1817: Robert Creswell and Elihu Creswell, of Laurens Dist., S.C., to William Atkins for $80; 84 acres on Rabourns Creek Bounding N on Lydall Allen, S on the Heirs of Thomas Lindley, dec'd., W on Widow Lucy Smith, E on vacant land. Robert Creswell (LS), Elihu Creswell (LS) Wit: Lydall Gordon, Jonathan Allen. Proved by Lydall Gordon 8 December 1817 before Chas. Allen, J.P. [LCDBK K: 193]

Creswell land: 22 March 1819: William Atkins, Laurens Dist., S.C., to William F. Downs, of same place, for $400; 84 acres on waters of Raybans

77

Creek. Bounded on Lydall Allen, Lucy Smith, heirs of Thomas Lindley, said William F. Downs. William Atkins. Wit: Robert Dunlap, Nat. Day. Proved by Nat. Day 26 March 1819 before John Garlington, Clk. & J.P. [See LWT of Thomas Lindley] [LCDBK K: 240]

Creswell land: 9 February 1821: Samuel Downs, Sheriff of Laurens Dist., S.C., and Thomas Spierin (by the directions of Robert Creswell), of the same place. By virtue of a writ of fieri facias issued from the court of common Please of Laurens Dist. at the suit of Peter Lavain[?] against Patrick Spierin, directed to seize a certain tract of land for public sale. The said land was struck to Robert Creswell for the sum of $200, being the highest bidder. Tract containing 212 acres on the waters of Rabourns Creek. Bounding land of James Burton, James South and Patrick Spierin. Samuel Downs (LS). Wit: R. Creswell, W.F. Downs. Proved by William F. Downs 28 May 1820 before John Garlington Clk and J.Q. [LCDBK L: 12]

Crisp, William: 16 August 1794: William Crisp, of S.C., and Elizabeth, his wife, to Charles Parks, of same place, for £70; 100 acres of land on both sides of Rockey branch of Burrises creek, being part of 155 acres granted to said William Crisp by Gov. Charles Pinckney Wit: Thomas Babb, Elisha Mitchell. Signed William (W) Crisp, Elizabeth (x) Crisp. Proved by oath of Thomas Babb 18 February 1795 before Zachariah Bailey, J.P. [LCDBK E: 396-397]

Crotia, Jno.: 1774 bounding William Anderson. No survey or memorial located.

Cunningham, John: Survey for John Cunningham pursuant to precept date [blank]; 850 acres in Craven Co., on waters of Saludy. Bounded SE and SW on land laid out to Josiah Furgild[?]; SE by James Boyle; SE, SW, NW by Alexander Killpatrick; NE and NW by John Brown; SE by John Willard; E and N by Richard Carter [plat shows Richard Carson]; SW and SE by William Turk; part SW on James Baird; N unknown; SW by Saludy River; other sides vacant. Certified 3 November 1772. Pat. Cunningham, D.S. [P14_290:0]

Cunningham, John: Memorial by John Cunningham for 850 acres in Craven Co., on waters of Saludy river. Bounding NE, SE, NW on Josiah Furgild?; SE on James Boyle, SE and SW Alexander Killpatrick, NE and NW on John Brown, NE on John Willard, E and N on Richard Carter, SW and SE on Wm. Terks [Turk], part of the SW on James Beard [Baird], part of the N on land the name not known, SW by Saludy river, all other sides on vacant land. Certified 3 November 1772 and granted 24 December 1772 to the memorialist. Quit rent to commence in two years. Set his and 20

78

May11773 Pat. Cunningham, D.S. Delivered 1 November 1773 to Pat. Cunningham. [M12-189:5]

Cuningham, John: 15 October 1788: LWT of John Cuningham, of Ninety Six Dist., S.C., now called Cambridge Dist. in Laurens Co., planter. I give and bequeath unto my son Thomas Cuningham, my son James Cuningham, daughter Dorcus and David Allison 5 shillings sterling; unto my son John Cuningham, William Cuningham and George Cuningham I bequeath one horse and saddled. The colt that the mare has now to my grandson Samuel Allison. To my daughter Catherine and Joseph Dean 5 shilling sterling; I bequeath unto my well beloved wife my house and as much cleared property to be at her disposal her lifetime, only if an of my sons marry that she may give them what property she shall think fit by the advise of the other executors. At my wife's death what property she has then to be equally divided between John, William and George Cuningham. I give and bequeath unto my son Samuel Cuningham the fourth part of the land I now possess and his part to be laid out where he now lives by the executors and the quantity shall be by the quality. Also I give and bequeath unto my sons John Cuningham, William Cuningham and George Cuningham the rest of my land to be equally divided between them by my executors. Also my well beloved wife and Thomas Cuningham and John Cuningham, whom I likewise constitute and ordain as sole executors. John Cuningham (LS). Wit: David Dunlap, James Dorroh. Date recorded not available. [LCWBK A: 17]

[Family: Wife - unnamed, sons: Thomas, James, John, William, George; daughter Dorcus Allison, wife of David Allison, Catherine, wife of Joseph Dean, grandson Samuel Allison.]

Cuningham, Patrick: 21 January 1785: Land grant 100 acres.

Cuningham, Patrick: 12 June 1785: Patrick Cuningham of Ninety-Six Dist., S.C., planter, and Ann Cuningham, his wife, to David Green, [minister] of same place, for £30; 100 acres on N side of Reedy River, below the old Indian Line bounding on said river NE and NW on lands unknown. *Originally granted to said Patrick Cuningham 21 January 1785.* Patrick Cuningham, Ann Cuningham. Wit: Wm. Harris, Edward Kemp. Benj. Turner. [LCDBK A: 123-127]

Cuningham, Patrick: 25 December 1794: David Green, of Laurens Co., S.C., to Nebo Gant, of same place, for £50 Stg.; 55 acres being a tract of land on the NE side of Reedy River. Bounding SE on David McGladery, SW and NW of Reedy River, NW on Saml. Green. *Originally granted to Patrick Cuningham, on 20 July 1785* and from said Pat. Cuningham conveyed to the said David Green. David Greene (LS) his wife Leannah Greene (LS) Wit:

79

Jonathan Cox, Wm. Norris, Nathl. Greene. Proved by Jonathan. Cox 20 July 1795 before Joseph Downs, J.P. [Plat shows bounding David McGladdry, Saml. Green and David Green, Reedy River and Old Mill place.] [LCDBK F: 46-47]

Cuningham, Patrick: 2 October 1796: LWT of Patrick Cuningham. To son William Cuningham £300 for this years schooling in order to complete his schooling and studies. All negroes, and stock to be equally divided into four equal parts between my beloved wife Ann Cuningham and my three sons, John Cuningham, William Cuningham and Robert Cuningham. After the decease of wife the above land to Robert Cuningham. My tract of land on Saluda and Reedy River be divided by a line beginning at a plant patch on Saluda and running to a branch Calo. To son William Cuningham the lower tract whereon my house it. To my son Robert Cuningham my tract of land lying on the Beaverdam Creek. P. Cuningham. Wit: Lewis Graves, Menn. Walker, Sarah (S her mark) Clarey. No recorded date. [LCWBK A: 153]

[Family: Wife Ann, sons: John, William and Robert Cuningham.]

Cuningham, Patrick: 3 April 1798: Appraisal of estate of Patrick Cuningham by Lewis Graves, Wm. Harris, James Nickels. List of lands on Reedy and Saluda River, Turkey, Cain, Walnut, Raburns Creek conveyed by Rev. Robert Smith, J. B. Holmes, Edward Rutledge, David Madden, Danl. McCallister, Isaac Hayne, Thomas Shirley, Jacob Bowman, Lewis Saxon, Mabra Madden, et al. [LCWBK A: 187]

Cuningham, Patrick and wife Ann: Buried in Rosemont Cemetery, Laurens Co., S.C.
"Below this monument lies the body of Patrick Cunningham, Esq., who died in the 54th year of his age on the morning of the 25th of October 1796."
"Mrs. Ann Cunningham, wife of Patrick Cunningham Esq., deceased, in Charleston in the 52nd year of age, 17th September 1799. She fell a victim to a fever then raging in that place." [*The Scrapbook*, Laurens County Historical Society and Laurens County Arts Council 1982; pg. 147]

Cunningham, Patrick: 30 March 1803: David Madden to Moses Pinson for $332; 133 acres on a branch of Burrises Creek, *part of a grant to Patrick Cunningham, dec'd.* conveyed to said David Madden. Wit: Thomas Hunter, Isaac Pinson. Josiah Blackwell, J.P. Dower of Sarah Madden. D. Anderson, J.Q. [LCDBK H: 202]

Cunningham, Patrick: 4 February 1806: David Madden, of Laurens Dist., to John Harry, of same place, for $145; 48 acres, being a part of 116 acres, on a branch of Raburns Creek, called Burrises Branch. [Plat] shows bounded by John Harry, Moses Pinson; David Madden. Signed David Madden. Wit: Ann Pinson, Solomon Cole. Proved by Solomon Cole 9 May 1806 before Josiah Blackwell, J.P. [Elliott, pg. 14 and 19. Son William, wife Ann, sons John and Robert] [LCDBK H: 145]

Cunningham, Patrick: 6 April 1805: David Madden to John Harry for the sum of $113; 43 1/3 acres in Laurens Dist. on a branch of Burress Creek, [plat shows bounding Moses Pinson, John Harry, Park, and David Madden. *Originally granted to Patrick Cunningham* and by said Cunningham sold unto me the said David Madden and now by me to the above named John Harry. Signed David Madden, Wit: Solomon Cole, John Cochran. Sworn by Solomon Cole 9 May 1806. [LCDBK H: 144]

Cunningham, Patrick: 26 April 1805: David Madden, of Laurens Dist., to John Harry, of same place, for $100; 43 ½ acres on a branch of Burreses Creek, being part of a tract. *Originally granted to Patrick Cunningham* and by said Cunningham conveyed to said David Madden. Signed David Madden. Wit: Solomon Cole, John Cochran. Probed by Solomon Cole 9 May 1806 before Josiah Blackwell, J.P. [LCDBK H: 145]

Cunningham, Patrick: 10 October 1808: William Coll *sic* [Cole], of Laurens Dist., S.C., to Robert Culbertson, of same place, for $300; 128 acres being part of a tract of land containing 100 acres, *being part of a tract of land originally granted to Patrick Cuningham* and conveyed by him to Thomas Richardson, being the place whereon the said William Coal *sic* now lives, also one other tract of land containing 28 acres adjoining the above described tract. *Originally granted to Thomas Richardson*, bounded on lands of Thos. Cunningham, deceased, James Hall, land unknown. William Cole (LS) Wit: Samuel Weir, John Blackley. Proved by Samuel Weir 10 October 1808 before Jonthan. Downs, J.Q. Dower of Patsy Cole, wife of the said William Coal *sic* given 10 October 1808 before Jonathan. Downs, J.Q. [Note; no creek mentioned] [LCDBK J: 126]

Cuningham, Patrick: 4 October 1820: Laurens Dist., S.C.: I Moses Pinson, of said place, to James Watkins, of same, for $600; 177 ½ acres *being part of a tract of land granted to Patric Cuningham* on the waters of Rabourns Creek called Burris. Bounded by land belonging to John Hary, Park land called Joseph Martins, also Mr. Doyals and conveyed by John Cuningham, David Madden and by David Madden unto Moses Pinson and by Moses Pinson unto James Watkins. John (H) Hary. Wit. James Huggins, John Harry, Proved by John Harry 7 January 1822 before John Madden, J.P. [LCDBK L: 35]

Cuningham, Matthew: No colonial survey or memorial located.

Cunningham, Mathew: 7 January 1811: Mathew Cunningham, deceased. Letters of administration to Widow, Susannah Cunningham, Sec: Benjamin Nabours, Robert Allen. [LCWBK D: 27]

Cunningham, Mathew: 14 March 1811: Sale bill for goods and chattels. Purchasers: Mrs. Cunningham, David Cowen, Benj. Strange, John Rodgers, Wm. Osburn, Robert Allison, Benjamin Nabours, William Hudgens. Administrator Susannah Cunningham [LCWBK D-1: 50]

Cunningham, Matthew; widow Susannah now wife of James Clardey [Clardy]: 28 February 1817: Matthew Cunningham, deceased. Return of James Clardey, administrator succeeding Susannah Cunningham, now his wife, mother of eight children of said Mathew Cunningham deceased. Paid Wm. Hudgens ad. of Zach Cunningham one of the legatees; pd. Wm. Hudgens guardian of Jane Cunningham. Now in my hands $188 as guardian of six children. Ad. James Clardey [LCWBK D-1: 356]

[Family: Widow Susannah Cunningham married by 1817 to James Clardy - 2nd husband. She had eight children by her first husband Matthew Cunningham.]

Cunningham, Matthew: 6 November 1818: James Clardy, of Laurens Dist., to William Hudgens, of same place, for $1020; 204 acres on Dirty Creek, *being part of a tract formerly the property of Matthew Cunningham, deceased.* Bounded S by W.P. Bolt,; W by John Dunlap; N by Susanna Rodgers; E by John Woody. Signed James Clardy. Wit: Robt. Allison, James Word. Proved by Robert Allison 3 May 1819 before Chas. Allen, Q.M. [LCDBK K: 249]

Daniel, John: 1800–Bounding land of William South in 1800.

Daniel, John: 29 December 1804: John Daniel, Junr, of Laurens Dist., S.C., to Elijah Walker, of same place, for $55; 55 acres on Reedy River bounding lands of James Powell and John Rains and lands of said Elijah Walker, Sarah Pugh and Rebecca Elliott. Jno. Daniel (LS) Wit: John Pringle, Samuel Meglaney[?]. Proved by John Pringle 4 May 1805 before J.J. Powell, J.P. [LCDBK H: 89]

Davenport, Thomas: 22 May 1816: LWT of Thomas Davenport: I will and bequeath all my estate real and personal to my present wife Latice. Second, with respect to a legacy bequeathed to my first wife, Salley Davenport by John Partlow of the State of Virginia, Spotsylvania Co, I give and bequeath to my wife Latice Davenport one half of all of said legacy and C___. The other half I give and bequeath to my son Burket; children of first wife Salley to receive legacy of Jno. Partlow. Daughter Lucy Harress [Harris] five shillings. Thomas Davenport (LS). Wit. William Nelson, Nathan Sims, Stephen Wharton. Will proved 23 May 1816. [LCWBK D-1: 295]

[Family, Present wife, Latice, Sally Davenport, 1st wife; son Burket, son of 1st wife, daughter Lucy Harress.]

Denner, Peter: Survey for Peter Denner pursuant to precept dated 3 September 1765; 250 acres in Berkley Co., on south fork of Rabourns Creek, waters of Santee. Bounded on all sides by vacant land. Certified 3 October 1765. W. Wofford, D.S. [P14_402:3]

Denner, Peter: Memorial for Peter Denner; 250 acres in Berkley Co., on the S fork of Raybornes Creek, waters of Santee. Bounded on all sides by vacant land. Certified 3 October 1765 and granted 13 May 1768. Quit rent to commence in 10 years. 2 September 1768. Wm. Wofford, D.S. For the memorialist James Dunn. [B in margin]. [M8_190:3]

Denner, Peter: Land conveyed to William Galaspy, deceased and by heirship to Moses Lawson. [See LCDBK E: 435-536 below.]

Denner, Peter: 24 August 1794: Moses Lawson, of Mecklinbough Co., N.C., to James Downen, planter, of Laurens Co., Ninety Six Dist., S.C., for £275; 250 acres on S Fork of Reaburns Creek. *Originally granted to Peter Denner 13 May 1769* and conveyed to William Galaspy, dec'd. and by heirship to said Moses Lawson. Bounded on all sides by vacant land at time of survey. Signed Moses Lawson, Catrrne (X her mark) or other ways Catrin Harris. Wit: Elisha Hunt, Wm. Kellett. Proved by Elisha Hunt that he did see Moses Lawson and Catren Galaspy, otherwise called Catrin Harris, sign release. 19 February 1795 before Joseph Downs, J.P. [Note: William Galaspy deceased before sale of land in 1794.] [LCDBK E: 435-436]

Dial, Isaac: 2 December 1833: Isaac Dial, of Laurens Dist., S.C., to Charlotte Lowrey, Mary L. Lowrey, Margaret W. Lowrey, James J. Lowrey and Benjamin L. Lowrey, of same place, for $260; 116 acres on the waters of Rayburns Creek; sold by the power in Equity as the properties of Matthew G. _____, deceased. . Set is hand Isaac Dial (Seal). Wit: James McDaniel, Matthew McDaniel, Thomas McDaniel. Dowers of Mary Dial, wife of Isaac Dial was given 29 April 1834 before Charles Allen, J.P. Proved by Matthew McDaniel 5 May 1834 before John Garlington, R.W. [LCDBK N: 52]

Dial, Isaac: 3 April 1834: Isaac Dial, Senr. of Laurens Dist. SC, for Love good will and natural affection I bear to my son Garlington C. Dial, of same place, to give and bequeath unto said Garlington C. Dial 163 acres of land in said District on the N side of Dirty Creek. Bounded at this time by lands belonging to James Boyd, Marmaduke Pinson, Hamilton Lowry, and the said Isaac Dial, Senr. Signed Isaac Dial Wit: Hastings Dial, Jr., Thos. Wright. Dower by Mary, wife of Isaac Dial 3 April 1834. Sworn by Hastings Dial, Jr. Recorded 16 November 1835. [LCDBK N: 116]

Dial, Isaac: 3 April 1834: Isaac Dial, Senr., of Laurens Dist., S.C., for and in consideration of the love good will and natural affection I bear to my son Hasting Dial of same place, have bequeathed to Hasting' Dial a tract of land containing 179 acres on the waters of Raburns Creek. Bounded at this time by lands of Wm. Henderson, Jno. Henderson, said Isaac Dial and Abner Putnam. . Set my hand Isaac Dial (Seal). Wit: G.C. Dial, Thos. Wright. Dower of Mary Dial, wife of Isaac Dial made 3 April 1834. Before Thomas Wright, J.Q. Proved by G.C. Dial 9 February 1836. [LCDBK N: 125]

Dial, Isaac: 16 November 1835: Garlington C. Dial of Laurens Dist., S.C., for $1630. paid by William Irby release unto said Wm. Irby all that 163 acres of land on the N side of Dirty Creek. Bounding Marmaduke Pinson, H. Lowry and lands of Isaac Dial, Senr, dec'd. Signed Garlington C. Dial. Wit: W.R. Farley, Jno. W. Simpson, Jr. Sworn by Jno. W. Simpson 16 November 1835. Recorded 16 November 1835. [LCDBK N: 116]

Dial, Isaac: 30 September 1835: Survey for Garlington C. Dial, Exer. of Isaac Dial, Dec'd., I have admeasured and laid off a tract of land containing 228 ½ acres in Laurens Dist., S.C., on both sides of Raberns Creek *being a part of a tract of land belonging to said Dec'd*. And having such shape and marks as plat represents. Alsey Fuller, D.S. Plat, shows bounding Wm. Boyd, David Helms, Jno. Woody, J. Johnsey[?], Mabry Madden.] [LCDBK N: 188]

Dial, Isaac: 30 September 1835: Survey for Garlington C. Dial, Exer. of Isaac Dial, Dec'd., I have admeasured and laid off a tract of land containing 557 acres in Laurens Dist., S.C., on both sides of Dirty Creek, a branch of Rabens Creek, *being a part of a tract of land belonging to said Dial* known as the House Tract and having such shape and marks as plat represents. Alsey Fuller, D.S. [Plat, shows House, and mill, also bounding James Boyd, Isaac Dial Dec'd., David Helms, Hastings Dial, William Burton, Est. of Isaac Dial, Dec'd, G. C. Dial, also on Shirrels Branch. [LCDBK N: 142]
Dial, Isaac: 16 November 1835: Garlington C. Dial of Laurens Dist., S.C., for $1630. paid by William Irby, release unto said Wm. Irby all that 163 acres of land on the N side of Dirty Creek. Bounding Marmaduke Pinson, H.

Lowry and lands of Isaac Dial, Senr., dec'd. Signed Garlington C. Dial. Wit: W.R. Farley, Jno. W. Simpson, Jr. Sworn by Jno. W. Simpson 16 November 1835. Recorded 16 November 1835. [LCDBK N: 116]

Dial, Isaac: 30 September 1835: Survey for Garlington C. Dial, executor of Isaac Dial, dec'd., I have admeasured and laid off a tract of land containing 228 ½ acres in Laurens Dist., S.C. on both sides of Raberns Creek *being a part of a tract of land belonging to said deceased* and having such shape and marks as plat represents. Alsey Fuller, D.S. [Plat, shows bounding Wm. Boyd, David Helms, Jno. Woody, J. Johnsey, Mabry Madden. [LCDBK N: 188]

Dial, Isaac: 30 September 1835: Survey for Garlington C. Dial, executor of Isaac Dial, deceased, I have admeasured and laid off a tract of land containing 557 acres in Laurens Dist., S.C., on both sides of Dirty Creek, a branch of Rabens Creek, *being a part of a tract of land belonging to said Dial* known as the House Tract and having such shape and marks as plat represents. Alsey Fuller, D.S. [Plat, shows House, and mill, also bounding James Boyd, Isaac Dial Dec'd., David Helms, Hastings Dial, William Burton, Est. of Isaac Dial, dec'd, G. C. Dial, also on Shirrels Branch. [LCDBK N: 142]

Dial, Hastings: Survey for Hastings Dial pursuant to precept 6 April 1773; 250 acres on waters of Little River. Bounded S land laid out to Hastings Dial; SE by Wm. Neeley; NE by Jean O'Neal and John Caldwell and vacant land; SE by John O'Neal. Certified 21 May 1772. Thos. Caldwell, D.S. [P14_385:1]

Dial, Hastings: Memorial for Hastin *sic* Doyill *sic* for 250 acres in Craven Co., on Waters of Little River bounding S on Hastings Dial, SE on Wm. Neely, NE on John Oneal, Jno. Caldwell and vacant land. Certified 21 May 1773 and granted 8 July 1774. Quit rent to commence 2 years from date. Set his hand 22 December 1774. 5 May 1775 to Wm. O'Neall. [M13-160:3]

Dial, Hasting: 2 October 1785, grant for 570 acres.

Dial, Hasting: 12 March 1790: John Swering, of Laurens Co., S.C. and Ann, his wife, freeholder, to William Hobbs, of same place, for £30 Sterling; 100 acres on Muddy Branch, waters of Dirty Creek and Reaburns Creek, being part of 147 acres conveyed to said John Swering by L & R in 1788 by Hasting Dial. Part of 570 acres granted to Hasting Dial 2 October 1785. Bounded by John Swering, Thos. Allison. Wit: Joel Hart, Robert Todd. Signed John Swering (LS) Anna (x) Swering. Proved by oath of Robt. Todd 11 April 1796 before John Cochran, D.C. [LCDBK F: 106]

Dial, Hastings: 24 December 1792: Hastings Dial to David Hellams, both of Laurens Co., S.C., for £10 stg., 91 acres being a tract of land situated on the branches of Dirty Creek, waters of Raiborns Creek, *being a part of a larger tract granted [not named]* Plat shows bounded by Maj. Butler, Hastings Dial, Saml. Williams, Jno. Owens. Hastings Dial (L.S.) Rebecca (D her mark) Dial. Wit: Samuel Williams, Isaac Dial, Rebecca (R) Dial. Proved by Samuel Williams 3 February. 1795 before Joseph Downs, J.P.
[LCDBK F: 169]

Dial, Hastings: 2 June 1788: 240 acres granted on Rayburns Creek.

Dial, Hastings: 4 August 1798: Hastings Dial of Laurens Co., S.C., planter to John Woody, of same place, planter, for £50; 159 acres on Raybourns Creek, *being part of a tract 240 acres of land granted 2 June 1788 to said Hastings Dial.* Bounding William Hellum's land, NE by land laid out to James Abercrombie, SE by vacant land at time of original survey. W by an old survey to land belonging to Joseph Hammond. Hastings Dial. Wit: Richard Owings, William Fowler. Proved by Richard Owings 19 February 1799 before Joseph Downs, J.P. [LCDBK F: 415-416]

Dial, Hastings: 2 June 1788: Grant for 100 acres on Raiborns Creek.

Dial, Hastings: 25 November 1795: Watson Allison, of Laurens Co., S.C., planter, to Joseph Hammond, of same place, planter for £35; 100 acres on Raiborns Creek. Where as in and by a *certain granted dated 2 June 1788 unto Hastings Dial* a tract of land on the waters of Raiborns Creek then by lawful titles from said Dial to Watson Allison, a part of the said tract of land, now this indenture that the said Watson Allison for £35; 100 acres on waters of Rayborns Creek being a part of the above mentioned tract. Bounding an old line supposed to be run for Jane McClurkin. Watson Allison (LS). Wit: John Childers, Jacob Manord. Proved by Jacob Mayner 18 July 1798 before Chas. Smith, J.P. [LCDBK F: 340-341]

Dial, Hastings: 2 June 1786 grant for 117 acres.

Dial, Hastings: 17 October 1797: Joel Hart, of Laurens Co., S.C., to Henry Box, of same place, for £37; 117 acres on waters of Rabourns Creek. *Originally granted to Hastings Dial 2 June 1786.* Bounded at the time of survey S on John Henderson, E on James Williams, N on Charles Bradey, W on William Watkins. Joel Hart (LS) Beththiah (X) Hart (LS) Wit: John Moore, Benjamin Sooter. Proved by John Moor 17 October 1797 before James Abercrombie, J.P. [Plat for 117 acres certified 15 August 1791 be John Rodgers, D.S. [See Hastings Dial] [LCDBK F: 414-415]

Dial, Hastings: 4 August 1798: Hastings Dial, of Laurens Co., planter, S.C., to Richard Owings, of same place, planter for £50; stg.; 217 acres on Peachland branch, waters of Raburns Creek and is the south part of a tract *granted 2 March 1795 to the said Hastings Dial.* Bounded by N by James Abercrombie, E by land not know; SE by Joseph Downs, said Hastings Dial. Hastings Dial. Wit: John Woody, William Fowler. Proved by William Fowler 19 February 1799 before Joseph Downs, J.P. [LCDBK F: 430]

Dial, Hastings: 7 August 1808: Richard Owings of Lawrence Dist., S.C., to Nathan Curry, of same place, for £28; 130 acres on the N fork of Raburns Creek on the S side of Peaching branch. Bounding William George, William Hellams. Richard Owings (LS). Wit: William Hellams, John Owings. Dower of Nancy Owins, wife of the within named Richard Owings given 6 January 1810 before Jonthan. Downs, J.Q. Proved by William Hellums 6 July 1809 before Jesse Childress, J.P. [LCDBK J: 151-152]

Dial, Hastings: 15 March 1806: Richard Owings, of Lawrence Dist., S.C., to Nathan Curry, of same place, for £75; 150 acres on N. Fork of Raburns Creek, on the N and E side of Peaching Branch. Bounded on NW on a conditional line between said Nathan Curry and William Owings, W along William Owings line, S along a condition line between Richard Owing and said tract up the N fork of said branch bounding on William Hellum's land. Richard Owings (SL) Wit: William Owings, James Dunlap. Dower of Nancy Owings, wife of the within named Richard Owings given 10 April 1807 before Daniel Wright, J.Q. Proved by William Owings 9 March 1807 before Stephen Garrett, J.P. [Question as to if this is Dials land] [LCDBK J: 152]

Dial, Hastings: 21 June 1801: Francis Nabors, of Laurens Co. to Benjamin Nabors for $150, 100 acres on the head of Dirty Creek; *being part of 570 acres originally granted to Hastings Dial* and by said Hastings Dial to said Benjamin Nabors. Signed Francis Nabors. Wit: Nathan Nabors, Benjamin Nabors. Proved by Nathan Nabors before Robt. Creswell, J.P. Recorded 18 December 1801. [LCDBK G: 335-336]

Dial, Hastings: 3 June 1805: Benjn. Nabers, of Laurens Dist., S.C., to Robert Allison, of same place, for $220; 110 acres on W side of Dirty Creek waters of Reaburns Creek, *being part of a tract of 570 acres originally granted to Hastings Dial* and by the said Dial conveyed to Andrew Rodgers and by Rodgers conveyed to the above named Nabors. Bounding lands of Stephen Plant, Stephen Burnet, John Woody and Hastings Dial. Benjn. Nabers (LS) Wit: Ambrose Hudgens, John Rodgers. J. Blackwell, J.P. Dower of Anne Nabours, wife of the within Benjamin Nabers given 1 February 1809 before Chas. Allen, J.P. Proved by Ambrose Hudgens 1 June 1805 before J. Blackwell, J.P. [LCDBK J: 97]

Dial, Hastings: 3 January 1805: Isaac Cook, of Laurens Dist., S.C., to Elias Brock, of same place, for $310; 129 acres, being part of a tract *originally granted to Thomas Shurbrick* and by sundry conveyances to Isaac Cook. One other tract containing 43 *acres originally granted to Hastings Dial* and by sundry conveyances to Isaac Cook the tract on waters of Rabourn Creek and Reedy River where said Isaac Cook now lives. Isaac (X) Cook (LS) Wit: John Coats, Charles Watkins. Proved by Charles Watkins 1 June 1805 before J. Blackwell, J.P. Dower of Charity Cook, wife of the within named Isaac Cook given 9 January 1805 before Dd. Anderson, J.Q. [LCDBK H: 94]

Dial, Hastings: 25 January1805: Hastings Dial, Senior, of Laurens Dist., S.C., Robert Ellison, of same place, for $467, 195 acres on lying and being on Dirty Creek. Plat shows bounded on Robert Ellison, Wm. Hubbs, said Hastings Dial. Hastings Dial. Wit: John Bolt, John Godfred. Dower of Rebecca Dial, wife of said Hastings Dial, Senior given on 1 February 1809. Proved by John Bolt 1 February 1809 before Chas. Allen, J.P. Plat. [LCDBK J: 98]

Dial, Hastings: 15 May 1805: Hastings Dial, of Laurens Dist., S.C., planter, to John Woody, of same place, planter, for $56; 56 acres on the waters of Dirty Creek a branch of Rabourns Creek. *Granted 2 March. 1795 to said Hastings Dial.* Bounded SW by John Woody; NE by Hastings Dial; NE by Robert Allison. Signed Hastings Dial, Senr. Wit: Robt. Allison, Robert Anderson. Proved by Robert Allison 3 June 1805 before J. Blackwell, J.P. [LCDBK H: 96]

[Note: Daughter of Hastings Dial marries John Woody. See will of Hastings Dial]

Dial, Hastings: LWT 17 April 1809: To my dearly beloved wife Rebecca, all my estate, both real and personal, during her natural life and after her decease to be disposed of as shall be herein afterwards directed, To my son Hastings Dial all the property already willed to my wife Rebekah at her decease, I will and allow, that after my wife's decease my four negro men be sold at public sale on a credit of 18 months and the money arising from said sale be equally divided between my son Isaac Dial and my two sons-in-law Mabra and Abraham Madden, I give an bequeath to my son-in-law John Woody my negro woman and her two children. So my son Isaac Dial $200, to my son James Dial the plantation on which he now lives containing 400 acres, except the 100 acres I give a bequeath to Hastings Dial, eldest son of *said James Dial.* To said James Dial and Elizabeth, his wife, negroes (named); I also will all my surplus land not adjoining the plantation whereon I now reside, after the decease of my wife Rebekah, to be equally divided between son Isaac Dial and my two sons-in-law Mabra and Abraham

Madden. Appoint my wife Rebekah and my two sons Isaac and Hastings Dial Executrix and Executors. Hastings Dial, Senr. (LS); Wit: John Godfrey, Asa (X) Turner. John Cockram. Proved 15 June 1809. [LCWBK C-1: 349]

[Family: Wife Rebekah, sons Isaac, James, Hastings, sons-in-law: Mabra Madden- wife Mary Dial, Abraham Madden - wife Jane Dial, John Woody, Rebecca Dial wife of James Johnson.]

Dial, Hastings, Senr.: Hastings, Dial, Senr. of Laurens. Will Laurens Equity 1811-5. Rebecca, Isaac, and Hastings Dial. Executor's. vs. John Rodgers over land he surveyed for deceased. [Revill, pg. 145]

Dial, Martin: 23 April 1825: Martin Dial of Laurens Dist., S.C., to John Dorroh, of same place, for $176; 42 acres on the waters of Raburns Creek. Bounding on Barnett Smith, said creek, Martin Dial. Martin Dial. (LS). Wit. Barnet Smith, Martin (X) Armstrong. Proved by Barnet Smith 9 November 1827 before A. Milner, J.Q. [LCDBK M: 19]

Dial, Hastings: 16 April 1825 – 18 July 1825: LWT wife of Hastings Dial, Senr, 16 April 1825: To son Hastings Dial five shillings. To son James Dial, 5 shillings, to my son-in-law Mabry Madden 5 shillings, to my son-in-law John Woodie, 5 shillings, to my son-in-law James Johnson and his lawful issue by Rebecca Johnson, formerly Rebecca Dial 5 shillings. To my granddaughter Rebeccah Johnson one negro woman named Rachel and her youngest child, Eliza. To my son Isaac Dial and his heirs the negro boy named Abraham. Also so my son Isaac Dial one negro girl named Mary and one negro boy named Andrew. Appoint my son Isaac Dial and Robert McNeese, executers. Rebecah (X) Dial. (LS). Wit. Samuel H. Lochart, David Hellums. [LCWBK E: 511]

[Family: Son Hastings Dial, James Dial, Isaac Dial; son- in- law Mabury Madden, John Woodie, James Johnson. Daughters: Rebecca Johnson, granddaughter Rebeccah Johnson.]

Dial, Hastings: 4 June 1823: Isaac Dial, Junr., of Laurens Dist., S.C., for $55; to Hastings [Dial] all my share, right, title, interest to a certain tract of land containing 300 acres which was devised by Hastings Dial, Senr., by his LWT dated 17 April 1809 to James [or Isaac?] Dial and after his death and that of his wife, to be equally divided among his children except Hastings and Joseph. It being the tract where on James Dial now lives, lying on the water of Raburns Creek. Bounding land of Widow Rodgers, William Hudgens, Nehemiah Franks. Isaac Dial, Junior (LS) Wit: Jas. S. Rodgers, Wm. Hudgens. Proved by James S. Rodgers 5 January 1824 before John

Garlington, Clk and J.Q. [See LWT of Hastings and Rebecca Dial]
[LCDBK: L: 134]

Dial, Hastings: 4 June 1823: Whereas John Douglass and his wife, Rebecca
Douglass, of Laurens Dist., S.C., have this day sold and conveyed to
Hastings Dial, Junr all their share, right and title to a certain tract of land
which was devised by Hastings Dial Senr to James Dial during life and after
his death and that of his wife, the same to be equally divided among his
children, except Hastings and Joseph, as will more fully appear by referring
to their deed of conveyance, for the sum of $55; their share of the said tract
of land (to which the said John and Rebecca were entitled) at the time
specified by the division by the will. [no acres given]. John Douglass (LS)
Rebecca (X) Douglas (LS). Wit. Jas. S. Rodgers, Wm. Hudgens. Proved by
Jas. S. Rodgers 5 January 1824 before John Garlington, Clk. and J.Q.
[LCDBK L: 135].

Dial, Hastings: 25 January 1825: James Dial, Junr and his wife, Luttuce
Dial, of Laurens Dist., S.C., have this day sold and conveyed to Hastings
Dial, Junr., their share, right and title to a certain tract of land [300 acres]
which was devised by Hastings Dial, Senr.[by his LWT dated 17 April
1809.] To James Dial during life and after his death and that of his wife, the
same to be equally divided among his children except Hastings and Joseph
as will more fully appear by referring to their deed of conveyance bearing
the same date with this. For the sum of $55; we do grant the said James Dial
and his heirs the said tract of land which the said James and Lettuce were
entitled, at the time specified for its division by the will. James Dial, Lettuce
(X) Dial. Wit: James S. Rodgers, Wm. Hudgens. Proved by William
Hudgens 6 June 1825. [LCDBK L: 197 also see L: 198]

Dial, Hastings: 9 February 1827: Settlement with Lewis Dial, of Laurens
Dist., S.C., for the funds belonging to him which now in my hands as his
guardian and find that I am indebted to him in the sum of $200 and whereas I
have an interest in certain property which my father James Dial by two deed
executed 8 August 1811 conveyed to Hastings Dial in trust for the use of my
mother Elizabeth Dial during her life and at her death to be divided among
their children. This therefore is to share that I have transferred and assigned
to the said Lewis Dial some of my interest in said property as will pay and
satisfy to him the said sum of $200. Joseph Dial. Wit. P. Farrow. Proved by
Pallitto Farrow 28 December 1829 before John G. Rinck[?]. Q.M. [See LWT
of John Dial] [LCDBK M: 125]

Dial, Hastings: 15 April 1829: I John Dial, of Laurens Dist., S.C., to Lewis
Dial, of same place, for $60; 300 acres, all my interest in a tract of land

90

whereon my father and mother now live containing 300 acres, on the waters of Dirty Creek. Bounded on Wm. Hudgens, John Douglass, Susanna Rodgers, Hastings Dial and Arnold Milner. John Dial (LS) Wit. A. Milner, Wm. (X) Vaughn. Proved by A. Milner 7 Set. 1829 before W.E. Lynch, J.P. [LCDBK M: 125]

Dial, Isaac, Senr.: 3 April 1834: Isaac Dial, Senr. of Laurens Dist., S.C., for Love good will and natural affection I bear to my son Garlington C. Dial, of same place, to give and bequeath unto said Garlington C. Dial 163 acres of land in said District on the N side of Dirty Creek [boundings given] Bounded at this time by lands belonging to James Boyd, Marmaduke Pinson, Hamilton Lowry, and the said Isaac Dial, Senr. Signed Isaac Dial Wit: Hastings Dial, Jr., Thos. Wright. Dower by Mary, wife of Isaac Dial 3 April 1834. Sworn by Hastings Dial, Jr. Recorded 16 November 1835. [LCDBK N: 116]

Dial, Isaac, Senr.: __ January 1836: I Garlington C. Dial, executor of the LWT of Isaac Dial, Senr., deceased, to Salethiel Shockley for $592; 148 acres lying near the Greenville Road 10 miles above Laurens Court. Bounding land of George Cook, Mary Dial, Elizabeth Coker and others, having such shape as the plat represents made by Alsey Fuller 9 January 1833. Set his hand Garlington C. Dial (LS). Wit: George M. Moore, Austin Moore. Proved by Austin Moore 11 June 1836 before M.P. Erins, J.Q. [LCDBK N: 229]

Dial: Mary: 21 December 1843: I Mary Dial, of Laurens Dist., S.C., to Nathaniel Barksdale, of same place, for $2,000; 168 acres lying on both sides of the road leading from Laurens to Greenville Court House. Bounded by lands of G.W. Conners, George Vaughan, Geo. Cook and others; also another tract adjoining containing 164 acres bounded by Abner Putman, Jeremiah Glenn, Salathiel Shockley and others. The first *being part of the tract devised to me by Isaac Dial* and the last being part of tract purchased by me from Hastings Dial. Set my hand Mary Dial (LS). Wit: V. Harrow, C.D. Kennedy. Proved by C.M. Kennedy 7 June 1844 before W.R. Farley, M.L.D. [LCDBK O: 229]

Dial, Rebecca, widow of Hastings Dial, deceased : 6 November 1819: Abraham Madden, of Laurens Dist., S.C., to Hastings Dial, Sr. for $600; sell and release unto the said Hastings Dial all my right, title or interest of or in the estate of Hastings Dial, deceased, to which I may be entitled at this time at the death or at the death of Rebecka Dial, who now hold a life estate of the said property under the will of Hastings Dial, deceased, and to hold the said right of interest to which I may be entitled at the death of the said Rebecka

Dial into the said Hastings Dial, Sr. A. Madden. Wit: H.H. Irby, Elias Brock Proved by James H. Irby 2 February 1821 before John Garlington, Clerk and J.Q. [LCDBK K: 318]

Dial, Rebecah: 16 April 1825: LWT of Rebecah Dial. To my son Hastings Dial 5 shillings, to my son James Dial 5 shillings, to my son-in-law Mabury Madden 5 shillings, to my son-in-law Abraham Madden 5 shillings, to my son-in-law John Moodie five shilling, to my son-in-law James Johnson and his lawful issue by Rebecca Johnson, formerly Rebecca Dial 5 shilling. To my granddaughter Rebeccah Johnson one negro woman named Rachel and her youngest child Elisa, to my son Isaac Dial negro boy named Abraham. So my son Isaac Dial a negro girl Mary and boy Andrew. Appoint my son, Isaac Dial and Robert McNees executors. Rebecah (X) Dial. (LS) Wit: Samuel H. Lockhart, David Hellums. [LCWBK E: 511]

[Family: Sons: Hastings, James, Isaac, sons-in-law: Abraham Madden, Mabury Madden, John Woodie, James Johnson. Daughters Rebeccah Johnson, _____Madden,_____ Madden. Granddaughter Rebeccah Johnson. [James Dial's wife Elizabeth] See LWT of Hastings Dial . Dial: daughters unnamed above: Madden, Abraham: wife Jean.] [LCDBK K: 55-56]

Dial, Rebeccah: Estate Protest: 18 July 1825: Protest by heirs of Rebecca Dial, deceased: Isaac Dial and Robert McKees, Executers. For probate. Robert McKees renounces executorship. 16 April 1825. [Elliot pg. 171]

Dorrah Family: James Dorrah came to South Carolina from Antrim, Ireland. In 1772. [The Scrapbook, pg. 171]

Dorrah, James: 25 January 1840: LWT of James Dorrah, Laurens Dist., S.C. To my son William M. Dorrah all the land that I hold on the S side of the S fork of Raiburns Creek above and below Mahaffeys bridge containing a number of acres, perhaps 300. The land is bounded by Horse McHaffeys land and Raiburns creek on one side and Crumbias [Abercrombie?], McMahon, Osa [Asa] Garrett and other. Sons, David and John, daughters: Margaret, Nancy, Martha, Mary. To my beloved wife Sarah the land that my father willed to me, whereon we now live together. At the death of my beloved wife, my son Lewis C. Dorrah is to have the tract that we now occupy and the Pugh and Tyner tracts together. Wife Sarah Dorrah and son David Dorrah my executrix and executor. James Dorrah, (LS). Wit: John B. Simpson, Daniel Todd, Samuel R. Todd. [LCWBK E: 94]

[Family: Wife, Sarah, sons: David, William M., John. Daughters: Margaret, Nancy, Martha and Mary. James Dorrah, son of William Dorrah, deceased.]

Dorrah, James: [no date] Wife Sarah, Laurens Probate Book 2, 1825/6. See card for David Ross. [Revell, pg. 146.]

Dorrah, James: Wife, Sarah, daughter of David Ross, deceased. David Ross, deceased. Settlement Robert Gray and wife, Jean vs. Francis Ross, John F. Simpson and wife, Mary, James Dorough and wife Sarah, David Boyd and wife Margaret. [Laurens Probate Book, pg. 2, 1825/6]

Dorrah, William: 16 March 1811: I David Hellums, Laurens Dist., SC., to James Dorrah, Senr., Admr., of William Dorroh, dec'd, of same place, one bay horse, three cows and calves, three feather beds and furniture, by cupboard and its furniture, together with plantation tools, kitchen and household furniture, one loom and womans saddle, my sheep and hogs, which said property to the James Dorrah, Senr, Admr., of Wm. Dorrah dec'd. (mortgage). D. David Helms (LS). James Dorrah, Junr, one of the subscribing witnesses to the within mortgage saith that he was present and saw David Helms sign seal and deliver the within mortgage to the within named James Dorrah, Senr. [LCDBK J: 207]

Dorrah, William, dec'd, lands : 27 May 1820: James Dorroh, Junior, of Laurens Dist., S.C., to John B. Simson, for $100; all my part of that undivided tract of 113 acres of land, *originally granted to Hugh Beard* and by divers transferences conveyed to William Dorroh, deceased, and transferred to me as one of the heirs of the said William Dorroh, deceased. Bounding James Smith, Robert Nickels, John McClanahan and lying of Reedy River. James Dorroh. Wit: John Cunningham, Jurn., John Dorroh. Proved by John Cunningham, saddler, 3 April 1821 before James Dorroh, J.P. [LCDBK K: 322]

Downen, James: 10 November 1791: Land grant for ___ acres.

Downen, James: : 11 January 1796: James Downen, of Ninety Six Dist., and Laurens Co., S.C., to Sampson Babb, of same place, for £60 Stg.; 222 acres on waters of Raborns Creek waters of Reedy River, and is *part of a tract of land granted to James Downen 10 November 1791*. James Downen (LS) Jane Downen (LS) Wit: Edward Scarborough *sic*, Andrew McKnight. Proved by Andw. McKnight 15 July 1797 before Jno. Coker, J.P. [LCDBK F: 234-235]

Downs, Joseph: 4 April 1785: Grant for 300 acres.

Downs, Joseph: 1 October 1790: Between Joseph Downs & Jean his wife of the Co., of Laurens, S.C. to John King, of same place, for £50; 150 acres on a branch of Reaburns Creek called long branch below the ancient boundary line. Bounded SE on lands unknown, NE of land laid out to Wm. Williamson, Esq. NW on sd. Williamson, SW on Major. Butlers land and being part of land containing 300 acres granted to Joseph Downs 4 April 1785. Signed Joseph Downs (LS) Jane Downs (LS). Wit: John Cammock, Robert (s) Bolt. Proved 3 October 1790 by John Commock before Jonathan Downs, J.P. [LCDBK C: 139-140]

Downs, Joseph: 26 December 1818: LWT of Joseph Downs of Laurens Dist., S.C. . To my beloved wife Jane the land whereon I now live, containing when consolidated 580 acres. .The above mentioned 580 acres to be divided equally between my two sons Samuel and Jonathan [after the death of my wife]. .to my son Jonathan Downs that the death of my wife the balance of the said tracts of land supposed to contain 295 acres. to seel *sic* and dispose of the best advantage. Land conveyed to me by Mily Jennings, being my part of what was commonly called T__ tract on the waters of Reaborn Creek. . to purchase a negro girl for my daughter Mary L. Downs. .I desire my executor to seel a tract of land in the fork between Reaburn Creek and Reedy River, *originally granted to Samuel Cooper* and by him conveyed to me. .to my daughters Annabella Lewis the balance of the money arising from the sale to be equally divided between my daughters Rebeckah Alexander, Sarah Gary, Annabella Lewis and Nancy Barkesdale. Appoint my son Samuel Downs, my nephew William T. Downs and my son Jonathan Downs executors. . Signed Joseph Downs, (Seal). Wit: E.A. Saxon, G.F. Wolff, J. Allen. [LCWBK E: 32]

Downs, William: 4 May 1812: William Downs, of Laurens Dist., S.C., to Jonathan Vaughan, of same place, for $100; 100 acres on Rabourns Creek having such shaped and mark as plat represents. Williams Downs (LS). Wit: Robert Coker, Mary Saxon. Dower of Clarrisa Downs, wife of the within names William Downs made 7 February 1814 before Dd. Anderson, J.Q.M Proved by Robert Coker 4 February 1814.[Plat shows bounded by Ball land, Kemp, John Johnson and Hawkins.] [Note: Clarissa, wife of William Downs, is the daughter of Lewis Saxon.] [LCDBK K: 44-45]

Dunlap, Samuel: Survey for Samuel Dunlap pursuant to precept dated 6 January 1773; 250 acres in Craven Co., NE side of Reyburns Creek, on a small branch thereof. Bounded on vacant land. Certified 3 February 1773. Jonah. Downes, D.S. Ord. Co. 1 March 1775 for Peter Leger. *See Peter Leger.* [P16_317:2]

Dunlap, Samuel: 3 June 1789: Appraiser of the estate of William Hellams, [See William Hellams LWT].

Dunlap, Samuel: 14 December 1785: Eliner Ritchey, Laurens Co., Dist., of Ninety Six, S.C., to Samuel Dunlap, of same place, planter, for £20 stg., 100 acres on SW side of Rayburns Creek on a branch called ODaniels Branch. Bounded by NE on Benjn. Jones; SE on William Daniels [O'Daniel in survey and memorial]. *Land granted to Elenor Richey 4 May 1775.* Elener Richey (L.S.) Wit. Lewis Saxon, CC [LCDBK A: 135 - 138]

Dunlap, Samuel: LWT dated 5 February 1791: To my son John Dunlap 100 acres of land lying on Raburns Creek surveyed by a warrant of Ellen [Eliner] Richey with the privilege of the spring on the other 65 acres with one more claims with one cow and one yew. To my son James Dunlap 165 acres of land joining the other land on Raburns Creek with one cow, one yew and the colt that is raised out of the estate. To my sun Samuel Dunlap 250 acres on which I now live, to my daughter Cathern Dunlap and Suzanna Dunlap 200 acres on Laurel Creek joining McDavids land to be equally divided to each with three shows each. To my dearly beloved wife Nancy and my three youngest daughters Sarah, Nancy and Mary my two work beasts with the remainder of my stock an of all kind. Make my trusty friends Martin Dial, John Dunlap and William Hellums sole executors. Samuel Dunlap (LS). Wit: Martin Dial, John Dunlap, Wm. Hellams. [LCWBK A: 43]

[Family: Wife Nancy, sons: James, John, Samuel; daughters, Cathern, Suzanna, Sarah, Nancy, Mary.]

Dunlap lands on Reaburns Creek: _____2 November 1809: Jacob Gary, Laurens Dist., S.C., to Samuel Dunlap, of same place, for $53; 120 acres on the N fork of Reaburns Creek on the waters of Mountain Creek. Bounded on land Jacob Gary and said Dunlap NE corner bound lands of Wolff, E on Braddock, lands of John Pots and William Hill. Jacob Gary (LS) Wit: William Matthews, James Dunlap. Dower of Sarah Gary, *sic* wife of the within named Jacob Gary given 13 February 1809 before Jonthn. Downs, J.Q. Proved by James Dunlap 14 February 1809 before Jonathan Downs, J.Q. [LCDBK J: 94]

_____ 2 July 1811: John Pels of Laurens Dist., S.C., to Susanna Dunlap, of same place, for $200; 100 acres on a branch of Raburns Creek. Bounded on land of Archabald[?] Young and Gideon Thomason. Sarah Parker, John Pels, Junr. William Hill. John (J) Pels (LS) Wit: James Dunlap, Poley Dunlap. Proved by James Dunlap 12 November 1811 before Jesse Childress, J.P. [LCDBK J: 241]

_____14 April 1813: Jacob Gary, of Laurens Dist., S.C., to Susannah Dunlap, of same place, for $50; 100 acres on waters of Rabourns Creek. Bounded on George Thomason and William Garey, where said Gary now lives. Jacob Gary (LS). Wit: Samuel Dunlap, Nathan Curry, Junr. Proved by Nathan Curry 3 September 1813 before Jesse Childress, J.P. [LCDBK K: 24]

Durham, Arthur: 1 March 1817: Moses Myers, Laurens Dist., S.C., to the Church of the Poplar Springs District for $2.50; 104 Rood [*sic*] on waters of Reedy River. [meets and bounds given.] *Originally granted to Arthur Durham* in the year (blank) and from said Durham to William South and since said South conveyed to sundry but lastly to the above Moses Myers. The said church land being purchased by the Babtist *sic* profession but the meeting house to be free to all Christians proffers preaching there in or on said land. Moses Myers (LS). Wit: E. Powell, John Walker. Proved by John Walker 7 April 1817 before J. Hitch, J.P. [LCDBK K: 168]

Edes, James: Survey for James Edes pursuant to precept dated 5 August 1755. 50 acres in Craven Co., on the NE side of Saludie on a branch thereof known by the name of Reedie River. Bounding SW and NE by said River, SE and SW by vacant land. Certified 18 October 1767. John Hamilton, D.S.[See petition for James Edes in Holcomb's Petition and Theodosius Turk's memorial.] [P11-376:4]

Edes, James: No memorial listed for James Edes.

Eddins, William: 1 January 1807: William Eddins and wife Rebecca, of Laurens Dist., S.C., to David Anderson, of same place, for $425; 147 acres on Reaburns Creek. Bounded on George Wright, said David Anderson, Silvanus Walker, and John Roberson. Wm. (X) Eddins (LS) Rebecca (x her mark) Eddins Wit: Silvanus Walker, Junr., John Creecy. Proved by Silvanus Walker 6 February 1807 before John Rowland, J.P. [LCDBK H: 208]

Elfe, Thomas: Survey for Thomas Elfe pursuant to precept dated 5 May 1772; 900 acres in C. County on the branch of Raburn's and Warrior Creek and round the Raburn's Creek Mount. Bounded on all sides by vacant land. Certified 23 May 1772. Richard Winn, D.S. [P15-1:2]

Elfe, Thomas: Memorial for Thomas Elfe; 900 acres in Craven Co., on the branches of Rayburns and Warriors Creeks and round the Rayburns Creek Mount. Bounded on all sides by vacant land. Certified 23 May 1772 and granted 17 December 1772. Quit rent to commence in 2 years. 24 April 1773. Delivered to the Memorialist by C.J.L. Richard Winn, D.S. [M12_162:3]

Elfe, Thomas: 25 & 26 November 1776: Rachel Elfe, of Charlestown, S.C., widow, qualified and acting executrix, and Thomas Hutchinson and Benjamin Baker, of same place, executers of the will of Thomas Elfe, late of Charlestown, cabinet maker, deceased to Philip Hawkins of Charlestown, merchant, £461 stg. S.C. money, *land granted 17 December 1772 to Thomas Elfe,* 900 acres in Craven Co., of Raibourn Creek and by his will dated 7 July 1775 mentioned that this land should be put to sale. Rachel Elfe (LS), Thomas Hutchison (LS), Benjamin Baker (LS). Wit: Christ'r. Hart, John Wagner. Recorded 13 December 1777. [Charleston DD Bk. T_4, pp 467_471; Holcomb, Bk. F_4_X_4, pg.193]

Elliott, Benjamin: Survey for Benjamin Elliott pursuant to precept dated 6 November 1771; 500 acres in Berkley Co., waters of Raburns Creek. Bounded NE by Samuel Elliotts; SW, SW, and SE by Benjamin Williams; other sides vacant. Certified 24 January 1772. Pat. Cunningham, D.S. Ord. Co. 8 July 1774 for Samuel Elliott. [P15_7:2]

Elliott, Benjamin: Memorial by Benjamin Elliott; 500 acres in Berkley Co., on the waters of Rayburns Creek. Bounded NE by Saml. Elliott; NW; SW and SE by Benjn. Williams; other sides vacant. Certified 8 July 1774 and granted 6 September 1774. Quit rent to commence in 2 years. 14 March 1775. Pat. Cunningham, D.S. [M13_376:5]

Elliott, Benjamin: Henry C. Young, of the State of S.C., Attorney for E.B. Luving, Executor of the last will and testament of Samuel P. Elliott, late of Charleston Dist., S.C., to Susannah Rodgers, Arnold Milner and Sarah Rodgers, the legal heirs of Andrew Rodgers, of Laurens Dist. S.C.; all that tract of land on the waters of Dirty Creek, containing 75 acres, being part of a tract containing 500 acres. *Originally granted to Benjamin Elliott,* and lately recovered in several actions of law by the heirs of the said Benjamin Elliott and presented by a survey and plan. Bounded N by land belonging to the said heirs; W by Hastings Dial, Jr. other sides belonging to the said Elliott. Dated 9 May 1826. Henry C. Young (LS) Atty. for E.B. Luving, Executor of Samuel P. Elliott. Wit: Thos. F. Jones, W.B. Jones. Proved by Thomas F. Jones 9 May 1826 before John Q. Klinck. Q.M. [LCDBK L: 238]

[Family: Andrew Rodger's heirs are Arnold Milner, Susannah Rodgers and Sarah Rodgers.]

Elliott, Samuel: Survey for Samuel Elliott pursuant to precept 5 November 17__ [year missing]; 600 acres in Berkley Co. Bounded SW on Kitt Shotes and vacant land. Certified 2 ____ [date missing] Ord. Co. 2 February 1773. [no D.S. listed] [P15_13:3]

Elliott, Samuel: Memorial for Samuel Elliott; 600 acres on the waters of Rayburns Creek. Bounded part SW by Kitt Shotes; other sides vacant. Certified 2 February 1773 and granted 17 February 1773. Quit rent to commence in 2 years. 6 July 1773. Delivered 24 July 1773 to Saml. Elliott. P. Cunningham, D.S. *See Henry Hunter.* [M12_282:4]

Elliott, Samuel: 13 December 1799: William Hunter, Esq., sheriff of Laurens Co., to Robert Franks, of same place, for £80; 600 acres sold at the courthouse of County of Laurens as the property of Col. Henry Hunter. The tract of land on the branches of Raburns Creek Bounding when surveyed on land held by Kitt Shote, other sides vacant. *Originally Granted to Samuel Elliott* and by him conveyed to the Col. Henry Hunter. Sold at Fairfield Co. suit of John Smith vs. Kemp T. Stother and Henry Hunter William Hunter, S.L.C. *Certified for Samuel Elliott 2 Jan 1792.* [Plat made 24 January 1792 by Pat. Cuningham, D.S.] Wit: Lewis Saxon, Saml. E. Stedman. Proved by Samuel E. Stedman 13 December 1799 before Charles Smith. Wit: Jno. Davis, Lewis Saxon, Sal. C. Stedman. Charles Smith, J.P. [Plat] [See Samuel Elliott.] [LCDBK F: 490-491]

Elliott, Thomas: Memorial by Thomas Elliott; 200 acres as above (96 Dist.) on a small branch of Rayborns Creek. Bounding SE on Benjn. Brown; and vacant; other sides vacant. Certified 25 November 1774 and granted 8 December 1774. Quit rent to commence in 2 years. 16 June 1775. Delivered this day to the memorialist by C.J. Lindsfors. (1 of 14 tracts) [See survey for Thomas Calhoun.] [M13_514:5]

Elliott, Thomas: 1 & 2 September 1777: Thomas Elliott, Esqr., of Charlestown, S.C., to Philip Henry, of same place, planter, 300 acres surveyed 28 January 1767 in Craven Co., of a fork of Rayburns Creek a branch of Saludy River. Wit: Zach. Cantey, Robt. Lithgow. Recorded 25 June 1778. [Charleston DD Bk. X_4, pp 76_82; Holcomb, Bk. F_4_X_4, pg.238]

Elliott, Thomas: 8 June 1789: Thomas Elliott, Sr., of Reaburns Creek Settlement, freeholder and planter, for the love and affection I have toward my loving son Thos. Elliott, Junr., of the same place aforesaid, bachelor, have given and grant unto said Thos. Elliott, Junr. all my lands and Tenements, all my estate real and personal. Thos. Elliott. Wit: Jonathn. Downs, J.P. Wm. Simmons. Proved by Wm. Simmons 20 June 1789 before Joseph Downs, J.P. [LCDBK B: 419]

Elliott, Thomas: 27 October 1789: Thomas Elliott, Junior, of Laurens Co., S.C., Reaburns Creek Settlement, freeholder and planter for and in consideration of the love and goodwill and affection which I have and do bare towards my loving father Thomas Elliott, Senior, of the same place and settlement, have given and granted and do freely give and grant unto the said Thomas Elliott, Senior, all my lands, tenements, and all my estate real and personal in the aforesaid state and county. Thomas Elliott Junr. Memorandum that on the 27 October 1789 Wm. Simmons personally appeared before me and made oath that he saw Thomas Elliott Junr sign, seal and deliver the above deed to Thomas Elliott, Senior. Wm. Simmons, David McCaa before Angus Campbell, J.P. [LCDBK C: 180]

Elliott, Thomas: 21 November 1795: Thomas Elliott, Senr. and Lucy Elliott, his wife, of Laurens Co., S.C., to Lewis Saxon, of same place for £66 Sterling; 110 acres on Reaburns Creek *originally granted to Thomas Elliott 6 November 1789.* Bounded by said Lewis Saxon, Mazyck, John McCain, James Findley and Reaburns Creek. Signed Thomas Elliott (LS) Lucey Elliott (LS). Wit: Wm. Simmons, Thos. (x) Elliott, John(o) Simmons. Proved by oath of Wm. Simmons 21 March 1796 before Joseph Downs, J.P. [LCDBK F: 97]

Elliott, William: See Survey for John Weatherspoon.

Elliott, William: Memorial for William Elliott; 300 acres in Craven Co., on Browns fork of Rayburns Creek a branch of Saludy bounded on all sides by vacant land. Certified 9 January 1775 and granted 1 March 1775. Quit rent 2 years. 25 July 1775. Ralph Humphrey, D.S. Delivered 16 August 1775 to Thos. Elliott by C.J. Lindfors. [one of eight tracts] [See survey for John Weatherspoon] [M2_258:1]

Elliott, William: 3 & 4 April 1775: William Elliott to Thomas Elliott of Charleston, merchant, [8 tracts of land, one being]; 300 acres on a fork of Reaburns Creek called Browns fork a branch of Saluda River. Wit: Geo. Chateris, John Bush. Recorded 10 may 1777. [Bk. F_4_X_4, pg.137; Brent H. Holcomb, *Charleston Deed Book P_4*, pp 476_479; SCMAR, Columbia, SC, pg._?]

Ellison, Robert: Memorial by Robert Ellison; 300 acres in Craven Co., on Lick Creek of Wateree. Bounded on all sides by vacant land,[one of 3 tracts]. Certified 1 June 1775 and granted 15 September 1775. Quit rent to commence in 2 years. 24 November 1775. John Ellison, D.S. Delivered 20 February 1776 to the memorialist. [M2_470:1]

Ellison, William: 2 June 1788: Wm. Baugh, Exer., of Wm. Ellison, Dec'd, of Ninety Six Dist., Laurens Co., S.C., to Thos. Cuningham, of same place, for £54; 150 acres in the fork between Saluda and Broad Rivers on

Reaburns Creek. Except 17 acres laid out for Charles Braudey. Bounded NE on Robert Box, other sides by vacant land. Granted 4 November 1762.Signed William Baugh. Wit: John Cuningham, William McDavid. [Poor microfilm] [LCDBK C: 55-57]

Ellison, Thomas: 3 October 1803– 5 May 1807: Thomas Ellison, of Laurens Dist., S.C., to William Ford, of same place, for $200; 70 acres all that tract whereon I now lives, only a spring that is in the said bounds, of this tract I except for the use of William Brody, on the S side of Reedy River. Bounded by land laid out by Jonathan Downs, Esquire, bounded on lands of William Brody, William Simmons, John Pringle and Rebecca Elliott. Thomas Ellison (LS). Wit: William Simmons, Leannah (X) Powell. Proved by William Simmons 8 October 1806 before Jas., J.P. [Note: This could be Thomas Allison.] [LCDBK H: 223]

Eslar, William: 30 September 1774: Council Meeting of Friday 30 September 1774: William Eslar petitioned for 150 acres in Craven Co. [Brent H. Holcomb; *Petitions for Land from South Carolina Council Journals,* SCMAR, Columbia, SC, 1999, pg. 313.]

Eslar, Wm. : Survey for William Eslar pursuant to precept dated 11 December 1772;200 acres in Craven Co. on waters of Reedy River. Bounding NE of James Ryan, SE and SW on, other sides vacant. Certified 13 March 1772. Pat. Cuningham, D.S. [P15-55:3]

Eslar, William: Memorial by Wm. Eslar in Craven Co., for 200 acres on the waters of Reedy River. Bounded NE on James Ryan, SE and SW on John Baugh's. Certified 13 March 1773 and granted 23 June 1774. Quit rent to commence in 2 years from date. Set his hand 16 November 1774. Delivered. 29 November 1774 to Pat. Cunningham. [M: 13-107:3]

Elser, William: 8 February 1791: Between Thomas Richardson of Ninety Six Dist., Laurens Co., S.C., and Thomas Norris, of same place, for the sum of £30; 100 acres of the south end of a tract of land containing 200 acres on the waters of Reedy River. Bounding N E on Jams Ryan, SE and SW on John Baugh, as a platt annexed to the original grant represents, which land [*was granted] unto William Elser 23 June 1774* and from then conveyed unto Patrick Cuningham, Esquire and further to Thomas McClurkin, and further to Thomas Richardson and now 100 acres of the S end of said tract to Thomas Richkerson, (LS) Keothern (X) Rikerson. Wit: Thomas Cuningham, John Cuningham, David Dunlap Proved by David Dunlap 26 March 1791 before Joseph Downs, J.P. [LCDBK E: 95-96]

Fash, John: Survey for John Fash [Task?] pursuant to precept 6 April 1773; 200 in Ninety Six District on the waters of Reaburns Creek. Bounded NW on James Williams, NE on Charles Broadway and William Elsons, SW on Nicholas Hill, all other sides vacant. Certified 4 May 1773. Ord Co. 9 December 1774 for Edmund Petrie. Thos. Clark, D.S [See memorial for Edmund Petrie] [P19-148:2]

Fields, John: 5 June 1786. 125 acres granted to John Field/s.

Field, John: 4 November 1786. John Field a witness to the last will and testament of Ebenezer Starnes

Field/s, John: 20 October 1788: John Fields and Bettyann, his wife, of Laurens Co., S.C., to Roger Murphy, of same place, for £29 stg. 19 shillings; 125 acres on a branch of Reaburns Creek called Ritcheys Branch. *Originally granted to John Fields 5 June 1786.* John Fields, Bettyann (+) Fields. Wit: Ebenezer Murphy, George Madden. [LCDBK C: 55]

Field/s, John: 4 November 1789: Witnesses LWT of Ebenezer Starnes. [See Ebenezer Starnes.] [LCWBK A: 23]

Field/s, John: 12 February 1796: John Fields, of Laurens Co., S.C., to Anna Starns, of same place, for 10£ Stg.; *25* acres on waters of Reedy River. *Being part of a tract of 196 acres granted in 1786 to [blank].* Bounding on Anna Starns [Starnes], Roger Murphy, and said John Fields. John Fields, (LS) Wit: John Starns, Jacob Paulk, John Creecy (mark). Proved by John Creecy 18 February 1796 before Reuben Pyles, J.P. [Plat shows bounding John Fields, Roger Murphey, Ann Starnes] [LCDBK F: 97-98]

Field, John: 1799: John Fields, witness to the will of William Richey [Ritchey]. Will dated 1779 in Ninety-Six Dist. Recorded 16 May 1783. Exr. Sister, Mary Ritchey. Wit: Ebenezer, Aaron Starns, John Field. Parents, Robert, Margaret Richey. One paper mentioned Mary Goodman Exr. Inventory made by Samuel Wharton, Saml. Weathers, John Carter. [Abstracts of Old Ninety-Six and Abbeville Dist., Wills and Bond, by Pauline Young, pg. 269. Box 79, Pack 1927]

Field/s, John: 8 March 1800: I William Runnolds (Reynolds),1799:Laurens Co., S.C., to Henry Fuller, of same place, for £80 Stg.; 171 acres, *being part of 196 acres of land originally granted to John Fields,* on the waters of Rabourns Creek or Starnes branch. William (W) Reynolds. Wit: Benjn. Carter, S. Adams. Dower of Alsey Runolds [Reynolds], wife of Wm. Runnolds given 17 March 1800 before Charles Allen, J.Q. Proved by

Silvanus Adams 17 March 1800 before Chas. Allen, J.Q. [LCDBK F: 534]
Foster, John: Survey for John Foster pursuant to precept 5 April 1767; 150
acres in Craven Co. in the fork between Reedy Creek and Long Lick Creek.
Bounded E by Long Lick Creek; S by Reedy Creek, all other sides vacant
land. Certified 30 May 1767. Ralph Humphreys, D.S. [P9-147:2]

Foster, John: Memorial by John Foster; 150 acres in Craven Co., in the fork
between Reedy Creek and Long Lick Creek. Bounded E by Long Lick
Creek, S by Reedy Creek. Bounded by vacant lands. Certified 2 December
1767 and granted 15 July 1765. Quit rent to commence in two years from
date. Signed 29 September 1768 for the memorialist Will Davis. Ralph
Humphreys, D.S. [M8-246:3]

Foster, John: Deed from John Foster to John Savage not found.

Foster, John: __ November 1797: Robert Carter and Elizabeth Carter, his
wife, of Laurens Co., S.C., to John Pinson, of same place, for $35; 35 acres
on Cain Creek, *being part of a tract originally granted to John Foster,* and
conveyed by him to John Savage and by William and Mary Conner, heirs of
the said Savage conveyed to said Robert Carter. Beginning in the middle of
Cane Creek a little below the Fish Trap Shole running down said creek to
Jonathan Johnson, on said Pinson and Robert Carter. Robert Carter (LS)
Elizth. (O) Carter (LS) Wit: Jonthn. Johnston, Richd. Duty. Proved 14
November 1797 by Jonan. Johnston before Angus Campbell, J.P.
[LCDBK F: 273-274]

Foster, John:: 5 August 1797: William Conner and wife Mary Conner, of
Abbeville Co., S.C., to John Middleton, of Laurens Co., S.C., for £50; 150
acres on waters of Reedy River called Long Lick Creek. Being land
originally granted to John Foster 15 July 1768 and conveyed to John
Savage. William Conner (LS) Mary Conner (LS) Wit: Jonathan Johnson,
Ste. C. Wood. Zech. Bailey, J.P. Dower of wife Mary Conner before Charles
T. Colcock, J.Q. Proved by Stephen Wood 13 January 1798 before Zach.
Bailey, J.P. [LCDBK F: 465]

Franks, Nehemiah: 5 June 1786: Grant for 340 acres on McHerg's creek, a
branch of Reaburns Creek.

Franks, Nehemiah: 28 September 1793: Archabald McHurgh, of Laurens
Co., S.C., to Salatheil Shockley, of place, for £50; 150 acres on Mchurgs
creek a branch of Reaburns creek, which Salathiel Shockley now possesses,
part of a tract granted to Nehemiah Franks. Bounded by Charles Garey,
Stephen Potter, vacant land. Wit: James Floyd, Drew Coker, Thomas Coker,
Signed Archibel (A) Mchurg. Proved by Drury Coker 29 August 1794 before

Jonthn. Downs, J.P. [Also see Archabald McHurgh] [LCDBK E: 277-278]

Franks, Nehemiah: 25 November 1793: Stephen Potter, of Laurens Co., S.C., freeholder, to Jonathan Skeen, of same place, for £40 Sterling; one tract of 100 acres on McHerg's Creek, a branch of Reaburns Creek, being part of an *originally granted to Nehemiah Franks 5 June 1786* of 340 acres. Wit: Benjamin Jones, John Potter. Signed Stephen Potter. Proved by Benjamin Jones 6 December 1793 before Joseph Downs, J.P. [LCDBK F: 116].

Franks, Samuel: 1 March 1811: Samuel Franks, of Laurens Dist., S.C., to Nehemiah Franks, of same place, for $250; 121 acres on waters of Rabourns Creek. Bounded N by Joseph Downs, E by S. Jennings, W by Nancy Sullivan, W by James Johnson. Samuel Franks (LS) Wit: Francis Sims, Joshua Franks. Proved by Frances Sims 1 March 1811 before Chas. Allen, Q.M. Dower of Polly Franks, wife of the within names Samuel Franks given 1 March 1811 before Chas. Allen, Q.M. [LCDBK K: 16]

Freer, William: Survey for William Freer pursuant to precept dated 6 April 1773; 750 acres in Dist. of Ninety Six on Raiburns Creek. Bounded SE by Solomon Niblet; NE unknown; SW by land claimed by one Crumbey. Certified 4 May 1773. Robert Long, D.S. [See Memorial for John Freer] [P15_217:0]

Freer, John: Survey for John Freer pursuant to precept dated 6 April 1773; 750 acres in Dist. of Ninety Six waters of Reedy River and Raiburns Creek. Bounded NW by Wm. Anderson, Esq.; NE unknown; SW by James Parson. Certified 9 May 1773. Robert Long, D.S. [P15_216:2]

Freer, John: Memorial for John Freer; 750 acres in Ninety Six Dist., on Rayburns Creek. Bounded SE on Solomon Nesbitt; NE on land owner unknown; SW on land claimed by one Crumby; other sides vacant. Certified 3 May 1773. Also 750 acres on the waters of Reedy River and Raybournes Creek. Bounding NW on Wm. Anderson; NE owner unknown; SW on Jas. Parson; other sides vacant. Certified 7 May 1774 and granted 7 May 1774. 16 September 1774. Delivered 13 October 1774 to the Memorialist by order of Mr. Carsen. Robert Long, D.S. [M13_2:5]

Gaillard [Gaullard], Tacitus: Survey for Tacitus Gaullard pursuant to precept dated 6 February 1771; 124 acres sic in the fork of Reedy River and Raborns Creek. Bounded NW on old purchased land; SW on Reedy River; SE on Raborns Creek. Certified 15 February 1771. Isaac Gaillard, D.S. [P16_7:1]

Gaillard, Tacitus: Memorial for Tacitus Gaillard; 120 acres in Craven Co., in the fork of Reedy River and Rayburns Creek. Bounding NW on old purchased lands; SW on Reedy River; SE on Rayburns Creek. Certified 15 February 1771 and granted 4 May 1771. Quit rent to commence in 2 years. 10 June 1771. Isaac Gaillard. Isaac Gaillard, D.S. [M10_464:4]

Gill, Robert: 1775 bounding Edmond Petrie.

Galaspy [Gallispie], William: 5 June 1786, land granted.

Gillispie, William: 3 December 1788: Patrick Reiley and Ann Reiley, of Ninety Six Dist., Laurens Co., S.C., to William Kellet, of same place, for £100 stg.; 100 acres on S fork of Reaburns Creek, formerly Craven now Laurens Co. *Originally granted to John Riley on 27 March 1775.* Bounded by vacant land at time of survey. Bounded by Thomas McDaniel (McDonald), Robert Sims, James Downing, also *part of a tract of land granted 5 June 1786 to William Galaspy [see Gillispie]* on the S fork of Reaburns Creek, containing 10 acres. Patrick Ryley, Ann Ryley. Wit: William Faris, John Kellet, Nathan (N) Camp. Proved by John Kellet 8 June 1789 before John Rodgers, J.P. [LCDBK C: 107-109]

_____5 December 1776: William Gillespie and held and firmly bound unto James Downen, yeoman, in the just and full sum of £500 and make a firm and proper title by lease and release of 25 acres on the waters of Reaburns Creek. Surveyed by a warrant of [blank.] Titles to be made at the last payment which is to be in the year 1780. The condition of the above obligation is such that said Downen is to pay said Gillispie a cost of £25 and £50 for 2 years. William Gillispie. Wit: Jena Downen. Proved by Margaret (X) Bracher before Joseph Downs, J.P. [LCDBK C: 347]

Gaunt, Israel: Survey for Israel Gaunt pursuant to precept dated 6 April 1762; 350 in the fork between Broad and Saludy Rivers on a branch of Saludy River commonly called Reaburns Creek. Bounded on all sides by vacant land. Certified 16 July 1762. Edwd. Musgrove, D.S. [P7_268:2]

Gaunt, Israel: Memorial by Israel Gaunt; 350 acres in Berkley Count in the fork between Broad and Saludy Rivers on a creek called Reaburns Creek, a branch of Saludy River, the waters of Santee. Bounded by vacant land. Certified 16 July 1762 and granted 7 October 1762. Quit rent to commence in 2 years. 18 November 1762. For the Memorialist William Ancrum. Edwd. Musgrove, D.S. [M14_264:1]

Gaunt, Israel: 22 February 1769: Israel Gaunt, (and Hannah Gaunt), of Berkley Co., S.C., to John Ervin [Irwin], saddler, of Greenville Co., S.C., for

£250; 350 acres in Berkley Co. between Broad and Saludy Rivers, on Rayburns Creek, a branch of Saludy River. *Granted 7 October 1761* by Gov. Thomas Boone. Wit: Joseph (his mark) White, Joseph Wright. Recorded 27 August 1770 by Henry Rugeley, Register. [Charleston DD Bk. R_3, pp. 99_105; Langley, Vol. IV, pg. 139]

Gaunt, Israel: 4 February 1792: Ann Brewster, widow, of the Township of West Pensborough, Cumberland Co., Pennsylvania, to James Irwin [Ervin], of same. Whereas a certain Alexander Irwin, late of the County and State aforesaid, deceased, was in his lifetime and at the time of his death seized of land in Laurens Co., S.C., and being so thereof seized died intestate and without issue, leaving a widow and one sister of full blood to wit, Ann Brewster, above named, but no full brothers or brothers children. This land became vested solely in the said Ann Brewster as heir at law, saving to his widow her right of dower, which she hath heretofore released to the said James Irwin. For a fee of £500; 724 acres in three tracts in S.C. One of these on Reaburn Creek, waters of Salauda River. 1) 374 acres on Reaburns Creek. *Originally granted to Israel Gant* who conveyed same to John Irwin, who conveyed same to said Alexander Irwin.; 2) 150 acres on Reyburns Creek, bounded by lands of Thomas Woodward, Major. Butler, and Robert Cooper, Alexand. Mazyck. Bounded on Casper Bayerly, Thomas Elliott, John Abercrombie, Thomas Woodward, Dec'd., conveyed to John Irwin and by him to said Alexr. Irwin. 3) 200 acres in Laurens Co bounded by the respective land of Joseph Downs. *Originally granted to Thomas Austin* who conveyed to Alexander Irwin. Signed, Ann (her mark) Brewster. Wit: Samuel Irwin, John Jordan. Probed 4 February 1792 by John Gordan, Esq. Before William Lyon, of Cumberland Co., at Carlisle Pennsylvania. [LCDBK D: 190-192]

Gaunt, Israel: 8 January 1793: Silvanus Walker, Senr. (Attorney for James Irwin) of Laurens Co., S.C., to Lewis Saxon, planter for £175; 350 acres, but by a resurvey to be 374 acres, on Reaburns Creek waters, waters of Saluda River, called and known by the name of Coppunks [Coppocks] place. Bounded on said Irwin, Gasper Bayerly, Thomas Elliott, John Abercrombie and Thomas Woodward, dec'd. and said James Irwin. *Originally granted to Israel Gaunt 17 October 1762,* conveyed to John Irwin and by him to Alexander Irwin, late of Pensylvania *sic* and by Ann Brewster, heir at law to the said Alexander Irwin conveyed to James Irwin 4 February 1792, and now by the said Silvanus Walker by Power of Attorney from the said James Irwin 14 July 1792 to the said Lewis Saxon. Wit: S. Saxon, James Saxon, John Rodgers. Proved by John Rodgers 8 June 1793 before Joseph Downs, J.P. [LCDBK D: 437-439]

Gaunt, Israel: 22 February 1793: I hereby certify that some time in the year 1773 (before the War), I did, together with Mary my wife, sign, seal and deliver unto Alexander Irwin (my brother) a lease and release for 360 acres of land lying on Reaburns Creek. *Originally granted to Israel Gaunt.* John Irwin. Wit: Silvanus Walker, Robert Swanzy. Proved by Silvanus Walker 22 February 1793 before Joseph Downs, J.P. [LCDBK D: 440]

Gaunt, Israel: 25 December 1798 : LWT of Israel Gaunt, Proved 24 March 1800. James and Jacob Gaunt, Executors. Wife: Hannah, sons; James, Joseph, Jacob: Daughters; Hannah Mooney, Rebecca Gilbert, Mary Coates. [Bundrick, Newberry Estates Box 8 Pkg. 5]

Gaunt, Israel: 15 August 1813: LWT of Hannah Gaunt, widow of Israel Gaunt, deceased, James Gaunt, Jacob Gaunt Executors. To: Eldest daughter: Susannah Coate, which I had by my first husband. Son: Jacob Gaunt, granddaughter Patsy Abernathy, grandson Grigsey Appleton; remainder to be equally divided among my six children: James Gauntt, Joseph Gauntt, Jacob Gauntt, Hannah Mooney, Rebecca Gilbert, Mary Coate. [Thomas Gilbert husband of Rebecca Gaunt]. [Bundrick, Newberry Est Box 9, Pkg. 3]

Gaunt, Zebulon: Survey for Zebulon Gaunt pursuant to precept dated 6 April 1762; 400 in the fork between Broad and Saludy Rivers on a branch of Saludy River commonly called Reaburns Creek. Bounded on all sides by vacant land. Certified 16 July 1762. Edwd. Musgrove, D.S. [P7_268:1]

Gaunt, Zebulon: Memorial for Zebulon Gaunt; 400 in the fork between Broad and Saludy Rivers on a branch of Saludy River, waters of Santee, commonly called Reaburns Creek. Bounded on all sides by vacant land. Certified 16 July 1762 and granted 7 October 1762. Quit rent to commence in 2 years. 18 November 1762. For the Memorialist William Ancrum. Edwd. Musgrove, D.S. [M14_264:2]

Gaunt, Zebulon: 22 December 1773: Bounding 200 acres on Reaburns Creek at time of sale from Thomas Hairston to Alexander Irwin. [LCDBK B:131]

Gaunt, Zebulon: 28 February 1788: Nebo Gaunt, of the Dist., of Camden, S.C., son and heir at law of Zebulon Gaunt, deceased, of same place, to Jonathan Downs, of the Dist. of Ninety Six, Laurens Co., for £42; 400 acres in the fork between Broad and Saludy Rivers on the waters of Santee commonly called or known by the name of Raburns Creek. Bounded on all round by vacant land at the time of the *survey granted 7 October 1762.* [See P & M for Zebulon Gaunt]. Nebo Gaunt. Wit: Robt. Cooper, John Calhoun. Proved by Robert Cooper before John Hunter, J.P. [LCDBK B: 335-337]

Gess, William: Survey for Wm. Gess pursuant to precept dated 3 February 1756; 150 acres in Craven Co. on Polks Branch. Bounded on all sides by vacant land. Certified 29 March 1756. Jas. Thomson, D.S. [P6_195:2]

Gess, William: Memorial by William Gess for 150 acres in Craven Co., on Polks Branch. Bounded on all sides by vacant land. Granted 8 May 1758 to the memorialist. 4 January 1759 William (mark) Gess. [M7-198:2]

Gibson, Jacob: 4 October 1792: Jacob Gibson, of Laurens Co., S.C., to Wm. Moore, same, for £40; 100 acres on W side of Reaburns Creek. Bounding NE John Ewing Calhoun, SW Wm. McPherson. Wit John Moore, Jno. Henderson, Hugh Henderson. Signed Jacob Gibson. Proved by John Henderson 10 March 1794 before Geo. Anderson, J.P. [LCDBK F: 21-22]

Gilbert, Anna Barbara: Survey for Anna Barbara Gilbert pursuant to precept dated 17 October 1766; 250 acres in Craven Co., on a small branch of Reborns Creek. Bounded NE by land surveyed for Wm. Sutter; other sides vacant. Certified 20 July 1772. Alexr. Kennedy, D.S. [P16_82:1]

Gilbert, Ann Barbara: Memorial for Ann Barbara Gilbert; 250 acres in Craven Co., on a small branch of Rayburns Creek. Bounding NE by Wm. Sulter; other sides vacant. Certified 11 Jan 1773 and granted 6 February 1773. Quit rent to commence in 10 years. 22 July 1773. A. Kennedy, D.S. [B in margin] [M12_313:3]

Goggans, William: 1770 bounding Thomas Jones. [P16-127:1]

Goodman, James: 7 June 1790. Grant for 193 acres.

Goodman, James: 2 May 1791: James Goodman, of Newbury Dist., S.C., to Ann Scurlock, of Laurens Co., S.C., for £20 Stg.; 193 acres on Reedy River. Bounded on NE on Thomas Carter, NW on George Anderson, SE on an old survey, SW on Lewis Banton and George Anderson. The 193 acres *granted to said James Goodman 7 June 1790.* James Goodman (LS). Wit: Wm. Caldwell, John Ritchey, Lewis Banton. Proved by Lewis Banton 18 February 1795 before George Anderson, J.P. [LCDBK E: 408-409]

Goodman, James: 29 February 1794: Ann Scurlock and John Scurlock, of Laurens Co., S.C., planter, to Lewis Banton, of same place, for £10 Stg.; 97 acres on Henrdicks Branch waters of Reedy River being *of 197 acres granted to James Goodman* and conveyed by James Goodman to the said Ann Scurlock by lease and release dates [blank] and conveyed by the said Ann Scurlock and John Scurlock to the said Lewis Banton. Ann (X)

Scurlock (LS) John (mark) Scurlock. Wit: William Hughes, Lazarus Wood, Margaret Hendrick. Proved by William Hughes 29 March 1794 before George Anderson, J.P. [LCDBK E: 394-395]

Goodman, James: 20 April 1801: Frances Scurlock, of Laurens Dist., S.C., to Archibald McKay, of same place, planter for £10, 10 sh.; 50 acres on Hendricks Branch the waters of Reedy River. Being *part of a tract of 197 acres of land granted to James Goodman* and conveyed by said James Goodman to the said Ann Scurlock and by her by lease and release to said Frances Scurlock. Frances Scurlock (LS).Wit: Jno. Middleton, Lewis Banton, Glover Banton. Proved by Lewis Banton 21 September 1801 before David Anderson, J.Q. [LCDBK G: 350-351]

Goodman, James: 6 December 1797: Frances Scurlock of Laurens Co., S.C., to James Pinson, of same for $57; 58 acres on waters of Reedy River, *being part of a tract of land that was originally granted to James Goodman containing 58 acres,* conveyed from Goodman to Ann Scurlock. Frances (her mark) Scurlock (LS). Wit: Thomas Davenport, J.W. Swancy, Thomas Withers. Proved by Thomas Davenport 17 March 1798 before Zechr. Bailey, J.P. [LCDBK F: 491]

Goodwyn, Jesse: No survey located for 50 acres for Jesse Goodwyn.

Goodwyn [Goodwin], Martha (Mrs.): Survey for Mrs. Martha Goodwyn pursuant to precept dated 3 June 1771; 50 acres in Craven Co., near Raifords Creek. Bounded SW on land granted to James Crackel, Esq. and part granted to Philip Raiford, dec'd.; other land granted to Jesse Goodwyn, dec'd. Certified 9 July 1771. Philip Pearson, D.S. [P16_141:2]

Goodwyn [Goodwin], Martha: Memorial for Martha Goodwin for 50 acres in Craven Co., near Raifords Creek. Bounding SW part on land granted to James Crockath, Esqr. And part of Philip Raiford deceased; all other sides granted to Jesse Goodwyn deceased. Survey certified 9 July 1771 and Granted 4 December 1771 to the memorialist. Quit rent to commence two years from date. Set his hand 9 March 1772 Philip Pearson, D.S. Del'd. 4 May 1772 to John Hopkins. [M11-151:5]

Goodwyn [Goodwin], Martha (Mrs.): Survey for Mrs. Martha Goodwyn pursuant to precept dated 5 June 1771; 200 acres in Craven Co. Bounded NE part on James Bell and part vacant; NW part vacant and part on Richard Bell; SW part vacant and part on Richard Bell; SE part on Philip Pearson and part on Henry Pritchard. Certified 12 July 1771. Philip Pearson, D.S. [P16_140:1]

Goodwyn [Goodwin], Martha Howell: 29 & 30 November 1771, Martha Goodwyn, of Craven Co., S.C., widow and executrix of Jesse Goodwyn, deceased, to Timothy Dargan, of Berkley Co., S.C., planter, by grant dated 22 January 1759 to Martha Howell; 250 acres on N side Santee River and said *Martha Howell hath since entered into an estate of Holy Matrimony with Jesse Goodwyn, and said Jesse Goodwyn* by his bond dated 15 September 1766 bound to said Timothy Dargan in the sum of £[blank]. To make sufficient title to said tract of 250 acres and by his will did appoint his wife, Martha Goodwyn, Executrix, now said Martha for £500 S.C. money. Martha Goodwyn (LS). Wit: William Pearson, Sarah Sims. Proved by oath of William Pearson 3 December 1771 before Philip Pearson, J.P. [S-5, 64-67; Brent H. Holcomb, *South Carolina Deed Abstract 1783-1788*, SCMAR, Columbia, SC, pg. 220]

Goodwyn [Goodwin], Martha Howell: 19 & 20 December 1771: Timothy Dargan, of Berkley Co., planter, to Isaac Huger of Charles Town, gentleman, for £1300 S.C. money, *250 acres granted to Martha Howell 22 Jan 1759 who intermarried with Jesse Goodwyn.* Timothy Dargan (LS). Wit: A. Belin, Junr. Richard Singleton before John Troup, J.P. [S-5, 67-69; Brent H. Holcomb, *South Carolina Deed Abstract 1783-1788*, SCMAR, Columbia, SC, pg. 220]

Goucher, John:. Land granted by Excellency William Moultree.

Goucher, John: 6 August 1792: John Gocher, of Pendleton, S.C., to John Dunkin, of Laurens Co., S.C., for £4; 36 acres on W side Rabourns Creek, *being land granted to John Goucher* by his Excellency William Moultrie. Bounded on said NE on John Dunklin, SE land held by Patrick Cuningham. John (mark) Gocher (LS). Wit: William Wright, Jacob Gibson, James (M) McFearson. Proved by William Wright 15 September 1792 before George Anderson, J.P. [LCDBK D: 276-277]

Goucher, John: 30 October 1794: John Dunklin, of Laurens Co., S.C., to Joseph Dunklin, of Greenville Co., S.C., for £4 Sterling; 36 acres on the W side of Reaburns creek, being part of land *originally granted to John Gocher.* Bounded NE by land *originally granted to John Richey*, SE on Patrick Cuningham. Wit: Nathaniel Sullivant, Hewlett Sullivant, Charles Sullivant. Signed John Dunklin. Sworn by Hewlet Sullivant 24 November 1794 before Joseph Downs, J.P. [LCDBK E: 307-308]

Granaker [Gramaker], Adam: No survey located.

Granaker, Adam: Memorial by Adam Granaker for 50 acres [one of two tracks] in Craven Co., N of Reedy River bounding NE on Hans Hendricks, N on land unknown S on Reedy River, the other sides by John Fosters lands. Certified 3 April 1775 and granted 4 May 1775 to the memorialist. Quit rent to commence in 10 years from date. Set his hand 3 October 1775 Pat. Cunningham, D.S. [M 2-389:3]

Granaker, Adam: 9 July 1775: Adam Granaker, planter, to Patrick Cuningham, for £50; 50 acres on N side of Reedy River. Bounding NE on lands of Hans Hendricks, N unknown, S on Reedy River, other sides claimed by John Foster. Being part of 200 acres *originally granted 4 May 1775 to Adam Granaker.* Adam Granaker. Wit: John Brown, J. Edward, D.S. [LCDBK A: 153-156]

Granaker, Adam: 29 January 1785. Patrick Cunningham to George Anderson for £20 stg.; 50 acres in Craven Co., on Reedy River. *Granted unto Adam Granaker 4 May 1775.* Bounded NE on Hans Hendricks, N on lands unknown, S on Reedy River, other sides claimed by John Foster. Patrick Cuningham, Ann Cuningham. Wit: Jonathan Johnston, Joshua Saxon. [LCDBK A: 157-160]

Green, Henry: Survey 9 March 1768- not located.

Green, Henry: Memorial by Henry Green for 150 acres in Craven Co., on Reedy Creek, waters of Saludy river. Bounded SE and SW on Danl. McLean [McClain?]; NE on Reedy Creek, other sides vacant. Certified 9 March 1768 and granted 1 September 1768. Quit rent to commence in ten years from date. 16 October 1766 For the memorialist Samuel Goode.[M8-288:4]

Green, Henry: 15 November 1792: Ninety Six Dist., S.C. Elizabeth Green, of the Town of Cambridge, S.C. to Charles Braudy, of Laurens Co., S.C. Whereas in and by a certain grant bearing the date 1 September 1768 under the hand of his Excellency William Bull, Esq., *granted to Henry Green* a plantation or tract of land containing 150 acres on the waters of Reedy River. This indenture Witnessseth that the aforesaid Elizabeth Green, as lawful heir to said Henry Green, for an in consideration of 30£ sterling, paid by the said Charles Braudy have release to the said Charles Braudy (in his actual possession now by virtue of a bargain), all that tract of 150 acres, being lawful heir of Henry Green of town of Cambridge, to Chas. Braudy, planter for 30£ stg.; 150 acres. *Originally granted 9 January 1768 by Gov. Bull to said Henry Green on Reedy River.* Elizabeth (X) Greene (L.S.) Wit: Jane (X) Dixon, Thomas Dixon, Thomas Richardson. Proved by Thomas Richardson 20 November 1793 before Jas. Mayson, J.N.C. Newberry Co. [LCDBK E: 172-175]

Green, Henry: 6 November 1807: Laurens Dist., S.C.: I Charles Brodey, of the said place, to George Brodey for $200; 75 acres of land, a certain piece, parcel or dividend of land (it being a legacy left to me by my father, deceased) containing 75 acres, *it being part of a tract originally granted to Henry Green* on the W side of Reedy River. Charles Brodey, (LS). Wit: John Watkins, Samuel Phifer. Proved by Samuel Phifer10 October. 1808 before Josiah Blackwell, J.P. [LCDBK J: 35]

Green, Henry: 30 September 1808: We Elender Brodey (widow) and George Brodey, her son, of Laurens Dist., S.C., to Terriel Andrews, of same place, for $450; 150 acres where we now live *granted unto Henry Green*, on the S side of Reedy River. Ellinder (mark) Brady (LS) George (X) Brody (LS). Wit: R. Powell, Ezekiel Andrews (A his mark), Jas. Powell. Proved by Ezekiel Andrews 10 October 1808 before Josiah Blackwell, J.P. [LCDBK J: 36]

Haig, David: No survey or memorial found for David Haig. In the memorial of Jacob Bohman [Bowman] is the following "*Originally granted 15 July 1765 to David Haig* and by conveyed to Jacob Bohman the memorialist by lease and release dated 16 and 17 August 1769." [See memorial by Jacob Bowman/ Bohman.]

Hairston, Thomas: Survey for James Lindley pursuant to precept dated 1 March 1768; 200 acres in Berkley Co. waters of Rayburns Creek. Bounded W on land laid out to Zebulon Gaunt; other sides vacant. Certified 1 April 1868. Jno. Caldwell, D.S. *Ord. Co. 5 January 1773 for Thomas Hairstone.* [See James Lindley] [P15_248:1]

Hairston, Thomas: Memorial for Thomas Hairston; 200 acres in Berkley Co., on the waters of Rayburns Creek. Bounding W on Zachariah Gaunt; other sides vacant. Certified 5 January 1773 and granted 23 Jan 1773. Quit rent to commence in 2 years. 8 June 1773. Delivered 29 June 1773 to John Irwin. John Caldwell, D.S. [M12_236:6]

Hairston, Thomas: 22 December 1787: Thomas Hairston, of Colleton Co., SC, freeholder, to Alexander Irwin, now of Laurens Co., for £210; 200 acres in Berkeley Co. in the fork between head of Saluda Rivers on the waters of a creek called and known by the name of Reaburns Creek. Bounded on land laid out to Zebulon Gaunt, other sides vacant. *Originally granted 23 January 1773.* Thomas Hairston. Wit: John Smith, Alexdr. Moore. [LCDBK B: 131-133]

Halsey, Thomas: 1772 bounding Alexander Cammeron. No survey found.

Hampton, Nathan: Certified 23 December 1771. Survey not located.

Hampton, Nathan: Memorial by Nathan Hampton for 200 acres in Berkley Co., on the waters of Reedy River bounding N on Lewis Bantons land, SW on Joseph Pinsons land, SE on William Andersons land, and to the E on John Caldwells land, other sides vacant land. Certified 23 December 1771 and granted 21 May 1772 to the memorialist. Quit Rent to commence in 2 years from date. Set his hand 7 August 1772 Patrick Cunningham, D.S. delivered 31 August 1772 Pat. Cunningham. [M11-328:2]

Hampton, Nathan: 9 & 10 December 1772: Nathan Hampton, of Greenville Co., S.C., and Sarah, his wife, to Joseph Pinson, of Berkley Co., S.C., for £100; 200 acres on Reedy River. Bounded on N on Lewis Banton, SW on said Joseph Pinson, SE on William Anderson, E on John Caldwell, other sides vacant at the time it was laid out. *Originally granted to Nathan Hampton 21 May 1772.* Nathan Hampton, Sarah Hampton. Wit: John Hughs, Robt. Middleton, Joseph Doolittle. [LCDBK A: 246-250]

Hampton, Nathan: 5 December 1786: Joseph Pinson and wife Mary, his wife, of Laurens Co., S.C., to Stephen Wood, of same place, for £28; 200 acres on the waters of Ready River. Bounding N on Lewis Banton, SW on said Joseph Pinson, SE on William Anderson, E on Caldwell, all other sides vacant at time of original survey. *Land granted unto Nathan Hampton 21 May 1772* [see LCDBK A; 246]. Joseph Pinson, (LS) Mary Pinson (LS). Wit: Jonathn. Downs, Geo. Anderson, Joseph Downs. [LCDBK A: 251-255]

Hampton, Nathan: 22 September 1797: Stephen Wood and Sarah, his wife, of Laurens Co., S. C. to David Anderson, of same place, for £40; 50 acres on the waters of Reedy River. Bounding on a certain old road on Wm. Mitchells' line, and said David Andersons land, on old road formerly known by George Wrights Road, said road crosses Raborns Creek at said George Wrights old mill on said Reaborns Creek, along the said road on the said William Mitchells line, the said land was *granted to Nathan Hampton* and by him conveyed by lease and release to Joseph Pinson and by him conveyed by lease and release to Stephen Wood and conveyed by the said Stephen Wood to David Anderson. Stephen C. Wood, Sarah Wood. Wit: John Middleton, Jonathan (X) Forgay, Jacob Niswanger. Proved by John Middleton 12 October 1794 before Wm. Burnside, J.P. [LCDBK G: 188-189]

Hampton, Nathan: 2 September 1797: Stephen C. Wood and Sarah, his wife, to John Davenport, of same place, for $300; 150 acres on waters of Ready River on Long Lick Creek. *Granted to Nathan Hampton* by his Excellency Rt. Hond. Lt. Chas. Greenville Montage, Capt. Governor Commander in Chief in and for the province of S.C. for the time being. Bounded on a new corner between David Anderson and said [Stephen] Wood, on George Wrights old Road, Lewis Bantons line, William Mitchell's line to said David Anderson's new corner. Ste. C. Wood (LS), Sarah Wood (LS). Wit: Thomas Davenport, Thomas Davenport, Junr. Lewis Banton. Proved by Lewis Banton 16 December 1797 before Zachariah Bailey, Esqr, J.P. [LCDBK F: 523-524]

Harris, Thomas: 12 March 1832: Whereas Thomas Harris (late of Laurens Dist., S.C.) departed this life intestate sometime in the year 1800 and possessed in fee simple a tract of land containing 145 acres on the branch waters of Raburns Creek and the said tract of land at present occupied by Mary Harris (widow of said Thomas Harris) bounded by lands at present owned by Turner Richardson, Asa Forgy, James Scott and Charles Brock at the time of his death, as wife Mary Harris and five daughters, to Wit: Sarah, Nancy, Pamela, Catherine and Elizabeth, all of whom are still living - And whereas Robert Wilson of said place, hath since the death of the intestate intermarried with Pamela, daughter of the said Thomas Harris. Know all men that I Robert Wilson for the sum of $75; sell unto Thomas F. Jones and J. Cunningham of Laurens Village, all my undivided right, title and interest which I have acquires (in right of my wife, in the above described tract of 140 acres of land. Robert Wilson (LS). Wit: M.B. Jones, Thos. Cunningham. Proved by W.B. James 21 March 1832 before Thos. B. Lockhart, J.P. [LCDBK M: 226]

Hart, Joel: 17 October 1797: Joel Hart, of Laurens Co., S.C., to Henry Box, of same place, for £37; 117 acres on waters of Rabourns Creek. *Originally granted to Hastings Dial 2 June 1786.* Bounded at the time of survey S on John Henderson, E on James Williams, N on Charles Bradey, W on William Watkins. Joel Hart (LS) Beththiah (X) Hart (LS) Wit: John Moore, Benjamin Sooter. Proved by John Moor 17 October 1797 before James Abercrombie, J.P. [Plat for 117 acres certified 15 August 1791 be John Rodgers, D.S. [See Hastings Dial]. [LCDBK F: 414-415].

Hart, Joel: 30 October 1809: Edward Box, of Laurence Dist. *sic*, S.C., to James Lee, of same place, for $235; 117 acres bounded on Wm. Watkins, Andrew Henderson, Edward Box, Sern., James McCain. Edward Box. Wit: Wm. Moore, Robert Box. Proved by Robt. Box 23 July 1811 before Larkin Gaines, J.P. [LCDBK K: 163]

Hart, Joel: 117 Acres *originally granted to Joel Hart,* no date given.

Hart, Joel: [blank] November 1816: James Lee, of Lawrence Dist., S.C., to Jacob Niswanger, of same place, for $320; 117 acres on waters of Rabon Creek. Bounded on lands of Wm. Wadkins, Andrew Henderson, James South, Jacob Niswanger, *Originally granted to Joel Hart,* conveyed to Henry Box, sold and conveyed to Jacob Niswanger. James Lee (LS) Wit: James

Crocker, Junr., William Anderson. By James Crocker 6 March 1817 before Gabriel Jowell, J.P. [believe this is land of Hastings Dial, see 117 acres sale of lands from Dial to Hart to Box - M. Motes.] [LCDBK K: 163]

Harvey, James: 6 November 1771: Petitions for 200 acres of land. [Brent H. Holcomb, *Petitions for Land from South Carolina Council Journals. Vol, II, 1771-1774*, SCMAR, 1999, pg. 64]

Harvey, James - 3 September 1765: Petitioned for 200 acres on Rayburns Creek. No survey found.

Harvey, James: 1772: No memorial found for James Harvey for 200 acres on Rayburns creek. 1772

Harvey, James: [blank] April 1773: Captain James Harvey, of Berkley Co., S.C., to James Boyd, of same place, planter, for £500; 150 acres on Little River *granted 15 May 1772 to Capt. James Harvey.* Bounded on all sides on vacant land at time or the original grant. James Harvey (LS) Wit: John Cargill, John Harvey, Wetenhall Warner. Proved on 31 July 1786 by Samuel Felder, J.P., Orange Co. S.C. *sic.* [LCDBK D: 434-435]

Harvey, James : 15 March 1787: Martha Boyd, of Chester Co., S.C., widow, and Samuel Boyd, Planter, of same place, executrix and executor of last will and testament of James Boyd, planter, deceased, of 96 Dist., to Vincent Glass the elder, planter, of Campbell Co., in the state of Virginia, planter, for £204; 150 acres on Little River in the county of Laurens, S.C. and also all that other tract of land containing 150 acres adjoining the said last mentioned tract bounded E by Martin Martin, N by lands of James McNeese, W of land now or late of [blank] Yarborough, NW by lands of John Boyd, which said two tracts of land was *formerly granted to James Harvey in 1772* and by him sold unto said James Boyd, deceased. Saml. Boyd. Martha Boyd by her attorney. Wit: Charles Goodwin, Charles Simmons. John Boyd, (oldest son and heir of James Boyd, deceased). Said James Boyd had contracted to sell said W. Glass this land in 1778, but died. His will dated August 10, 1781. [Note: This land transfer is not for lands on Raburns Creek, but does place where James Boyd's wife was in 1787 and that he was deceased by 15 March 1787. [Also see James Boyd.] [LCDBK B: 144-147]

Hatcher, Plemon [Fleming]: 20 July 1804: Plemon [Fleming] Hatcher, of Laurens Co., S.C., to Sampson Babb, of same, for $150; 70 acres on S fork Rabourns Creek. Bounded on Andw. McKnight. Flemon (X) Hatcher (LS). Janet (X) Hatcher. Wit: Thomas Childres, George Grizzel. Proved by Thomas Childres 20 July 1804 before John Childress, J.P. [LCDBK J: 199]

Hatcher, Plemon [Fleming]: 13 September 1804: Plemon [Fleming] Hatcher, of Laurens Dist., S.C., to Sampson Babb, of same place, for $150; 112 acres on S Fork Rabourns Creek and spring branch. Bounded on Mezrahs line to McMahan to Kellett's line. Flemmon (mark) Hatcher. Wit: Samuel Nisbett, John Nash. Proved by Samuel Nisbett 17 March 1810 before Hudson Berry, J.Q. Dower of Jean Hatcher, wife of the within Plemon Hatcher given 17 March 1810 before Hudson Berry, J.Q. [LCDBK J: 199]

Hayne, Isaac: 5 June 1771: Petitioned for 500 acres in S.C. [Holcomb, *Petitions for Land from S.C. Council Journals. Vol, II, 1771-1774*, SCMAR, 1999, pg. 31]

Hayne, Isaac: 3 December 1771: Read petitions for Warrants of Survey for Isaac Hayne for 500 acres. [Holcomb, *Petitions for Land from S.C. Council Journals. Vol, II*, 1771-1774, SCMAR, 1999, pg. 64]

Hayne, Isaac: Survey certified 19 March 1773. Survey not found.

Hayne, Isaac: Memorial by Isaac Hayne for 500 acres in Craven Co., on SE side of Reedy river bounding SE and SE on John Baws [Baugh's], NE on vacant land SW by said river. Also an other tract of 250 acres of land on the waters of Saludy river bounding SE on John Shurley's, NW on James Burnside, SE and SW on Robt. Woods, other sides on land name not know. Also a tract of 250 acres of land as above on the waters of Saludy and Reedy Rivers bounding SE and NE by Wm. Anderson, SW and SE on Robert Long, NW on land name not know, other sides vacant. Certified 19 March 1773 and granted 2 April 1773 to the memorialist. Quit rent to commence in two years from date. Set his hand 7 April 1773 Pat. Cunningham, D.S. Delivered 9 August 1773 to J.C. Lindfors, to the memorialist. [M12-352:3]

Hayne, Isaac: Memorial for Isaac Hayne for 250 acres in Craven Co., on Buckhead Creek the waters of Enoree. Bounded SW and SE on Joseph Halls, SW on Jas. Goulsby, other side Gideson land not known to who. Certified 16 February 1773. Also one other tract of 250 acres of land as above on the waters of Reedy River bounding S and E on land name not know the other sides on vacant land. Certified 17 April 1773 and both granted 19 August 1774 to the memorialist. Quit rent to commence in two years from date. Sit his hand 1 February 1775. Pat. Cunningham, D.S. [M13-268:1]

Hayne, Isaac: 3 April 1796: Isaac Hayne mentioned in the Appraisal of Patrick Cunningham's estate. [LCWBK A: 187]

Helum [Hellum], John: Survey for John Helum pursuant to precept dated 5 March 1767; 500 acres in Berkley Co., in the fork between Broad and Saludy Rivers and is on a small branch of Raborns Creek [plat states: small branch of Raborns called Williams Creek]. Bounded NE by laid out to Thomas Allison, other sides by vacant land. Certified 16 May 1765. Edwd. Musgrove, D.S. [P8_82:1]

Hellum, John: Memorial for John Hellum; 500 acres in Berkley Co., on the waters of Saludy on a small branch of Rabens Creek called Williamses branch. Bounded NE on land laid out for Thomas Allison; other sides vacant. Certified 16 May 1765 and granted 25 September. 1766. Quit rent in 2 years. 28 October 1766. Edward Musgrove, D.S. For the Mem, Jno. Woodin. [M9_136:3]

Hellum, William: Survey for William Hellum pursuant to precept dated 1 December 1767; 200 acres in Berkley Co., on the N fork of Rayburns Creek, waters of Saludy river bounded on all sides by vacant land. Certified 19 December 1767 Pr. Wm. Anderson. [P11-315:3]

Hellum, William: Memorial for William Hellum; 200 acres in Berkley Co., on the N fork of Rayburns Creek, waters of Saludy River. Bounded on all sides by vacant land. Certified 5 June 1770 and granted 13 July 1770. Quit rent in 2 years. 21 August 1770. Richd. Owing. Wm. Anderson, D.S. [M10_196:5]

Helum, William, Senr.: 7 September 1787: William Hellams, Senr, of Laurens Co., S.C., to John Hellams, planter, of same place, for £30, stg. 103 acres on both sides of Reaburns Creek *being part of a tract originally granted to William Hellams* by letters of patent [no date given]. Bounding on Richard Owings, Hasten Dial, Isaac Huger. William Hellams, Constant Hellams. Wit: John Coker, Samuel Williams. [LCDBK B: 190-193]

Hellams, William: 2 July 1788: LWT of William Hellams. Bequeath unto my dearly beloved wife Constant Hellams my land and stock and all my household good and chattels so long as she doth live and after her decease to be divided as follows: I give unto my beloved grandson Jonathan Hellams, son of Jonathan Hellams, 100 acres of land whereon I now live; bequeath to my dearly beloved grand children, sons and daughters of Wm. Hellams, Jonathan and Wm., Nancy and Rachael, 35 £ stg. To be equally divided amongst them; I give and bequeath to my dearly beloved daughter Rachel Allison and her son all the rest of my estate to be equally divided between them. William Hellams (LS). Wit: John Childress, Richard Owings, John Hellams. [Ingmire, pg. 5-6] [LCWBK A: 8]

[Family: Wife Constant, son Jonathan Hellams, William Hellams, daughter Rachel Allison, John Parker, son of Rachel Allison (most likely Parker before marriage to possibly Watson Allison, see land transfer), grandson Jonathan Hellams, son of Jonathan Hellams, grandchildren Jonathan, William, Nancy and Rachel, children of Wm. Hellams.]

Hellams, William: 3 June 1789 Estate appraised by Robert Coker, Samuel Dunlap and John Coker. [LCWBK A: 9]

Hellams, William: 5 February 1791: Wm. Hellams, Martin Dial and John Dunlap witnesses LWT of Samuel Dunlap [See Samuel Dunlap].

Hellums, William: 2 February 1795: John Hellums of Laurens Co., SC, to Watson Allison, of same place, for £50; 103 acres *being part of a tract of land originally granted to William Hellums* [no date given] lying and being on both sides of Raiborns Creek. Bounding E along Richard Owens line, W on Hastings Dials line, S along Isaac Hugars line. John Hellums (L.S.) Wit. Richard Owings, John Woody. Proved by Richard Owings 22 September 1795 before Hudson Berry, J.P. Meets and bounds. [LCDBK F: 152-153]

Helum, William: 9 September 1796: Watson Allison, of Laurens Co., S.C., to John Childers, of same place, for £50 Sterling; *103 acres being part of a tract of land granted to William Hellems* on both sides of Raburns Creek. Bounded on Richard Owings, Hastings Dial, Isaac Huger. Watson (A) Allison (LS). Wit: Richard Owings, Thomas Childres. Proved by Richd. Owings 22 September 1796 before Hudson Berry, J.P. [LCDBK F: 147-148]

Helum (Hallum), William: 21 February 1799: John Coker to Archabel Owings for £70 Stg.; 100 acres on Rabourns Creek *where William Hellams, dec'd. use to live,* which was willed to Jonathan Hellams by his grandfather William Hellams, Sr. Bounded by Joseph Hammons, John Woody, John Childress, Richard Owings Sr. and Big Survey. Wit: Thomas Childress, Samuel Nesbit. John Coker, J.P. [Poor microfilm] [LCDBK F: 454]

Helum (Hallum), William: 23 February 1799: Constant Hellums to Archey Owings for £10; or her maintenance during her natural life; 100 acres on Rabourns Creek where William Hellams dec'd. formerly lived, *part of 200 acres granted to said William Hellams.* Bounded E by Joseph Hammons; N by John Woody; W by John Childers and Richard Owings Sr; S by Big Survey. Signed Constant (J) Hellums. Wit: Thomas Childress, Samuel Nesbit. Proved by oath of Thomas Childress 23 February 1799 before John Coker, J.P. [Poor microfilm] [LCDBK F: 454]

117

Hellum, William: Memorial for William Hellum: 200 acres in Berkley Co., on the N fork of Rayburns Creek, waters of Saludy river. Bounded on all sides by vacant land. Certified 5 June 1770 and granted 13 July 1770. Quit rent to commence in 2 years. 21 August 1770. Richd. Owing. Wm. Anderson, D.S. [M10_196:5]

Helum (Hallum), William: 10 December 1807: Jonathan Hellams, of Laurens Dist., S.C., to Archable Owings, of same place, for £60; 100 a on Raburn Creek where Wm. Hellams dec'd, formerly use to live, which tract of land was willed to the said Jonthn Hellam, by his grandfather William Hellams, deceased, it being a part of a tract of land *granted to the said William Hellams, Senior deceased* containing 200 acres which lands are bounded E by Joseph Hammons, N by Woody, W by John Childress and Richard Owing, Senr., S by Big Survey. Jonthn. (J) Hellams (LS). Wit: William Owings, John Owings. Proved by William Owings 15 October 1807 before Danl. Wright, J.P. [See LWT of William Hellams and land transfers] [LCDBK H: 252]

Hellum [Hellams], William: 13 February 1808: Dower of Nancy Coker given to Archibald Owens. I Nancy Coker have this day received full satisfaction for my dower or part of a tract of land 100 acres on Rabourns Creek, where William Hellams, Senr., deceased formerly lived and which land are bounded E by Joseph Harmon, N by John Wooley [Woody], W by John Childress and Richard Owens, Senr, S by survey from Archibald Owings. Nancy (X) Cokiere (LS). Wit: Robert Bariet, Ethld. Wood. Proved by Robert Barrett 5 September 1808 before John Garlington, J.P. [LCDBK J: 29]

Hen, Elizabeth: 6 May 1774; 100 acres on waters of Reedy River, bounty land.

Hen, Elizabeth: 9 November 1795: David Ragsdale and Alse Ragsdale, his wife, of Laurens Co., S.C., Planter to John Watson, of same place; for £26; 100 acres of waters of Reedy River. *Originally granted to Elizabeth Ken____, Bounty on 6 Mary 1774* from King George the Third, then granted to her the 25 of May by the Honorable William Bull, Esq. David (X) Ragsdal (LS), Alsey (mark) Ragsdale (LS). Wit. Wm. Washington, George Gothard. Proved by George Gothard 23 April 1796 before George Anderson, J.P. [LCDBK F: 170]

Henderson, John: 4 July 1785, land grant.

Henderson, John: 13 October 1788: John Henderson to Mary Henderson

118

for £20; 150 acres on Rabourns Creek below the ancient Boundary line. *Granted to John Henderson July 4, 1785.* Bounded on Nicholas Hill. Wit: John Baugh, John Brodey. [See Marmaduke Hollingsworth] [Poor microfilm copy; LCDBK B: 395]

Hendrick, Hans: Survey for Hans Hendrix pursuant to precept dated 4 March 1775; 300 acres in Craven Co. on the NE sides of Reedy River. Bounded on land name not known, other sides vacant lands. Certified 28 April 1773. Pat. Cuningham, D.S. [P15-399:3]

Hendrix, Hans: Memorial for Hans Hendrick; 300 acres in Craven County, NE of Reedy river. Bounding NW and NE on land unknown, SE on said river, other sides vacant land. Survey certified 28 April 1773 and Granted 23 June 1774. Quit rent to commence Two years from date. Set his hand 22 November 1774. Pat. Cunningham, D.S. Del'd. 6 March 1775 to Pat. Cunningham, D.S. [M13-116:4]

Hendrix, Hans: No survey for Hans Hendrix found.

Hendrix [Hendrick], Hans: Memorial for Hans Hendrix for 150 acres in Berkley Co., on the SW of Reedy River. Bounding NW and NE on Jacob Bohman [Bowman], SW and NW on Theodosia Turk, SE and SW on Robert Long, other sides vacant land. Certified 2 February 1773 and granted 11 February 1773 to the Memorialist. Quit rent to commence in 2 years from date. Set his hand 22 June 1773 P. Cunningham, D.S. Delivered 5 November 1773 to P. Cunningham. [M12-257:2]

Hendrix [Hendrick], Hans: [blank] September 1784 – Deceased. [See Margaret Hendrix' estate below.]

Hendrix, Hans: 10 September 1784: Micajah Hendrix, planter of County of Pitsylvania and Parish of Camden, to my mother, Margaret, widow of Hans Hendrix, planter of 96 Dist., SC, deed of gift of 450 acres in two tracts on N side of Reedy River. Bounding on Patrick Cuningham, Thos. Carter, Richard Lanyard, Henry Parker, Mary Adkins, Sarah Bowman. Adjacent the river at a branch below the shoals. For and during her natural life and to whom she pleaseth forever. Micajah Hendrix. Wit: Lewis Banton, Edward Ware, Michael Lawless. Proved by Edward Ware 12 March 1785 before Geo. Anderson, J.P. [LCDBK B: 223]

Hendrix, Hans: 6 & 7 June 1791: Margaret Hendrick and McCajah Hendrick and Magdilin, his wife, of Laurens Co., S.C., to John Willard for £20 Stg.; 150 acres on Reedy River. Bounded at the time of the original survey SW side of Reedy River bounding NW and NE on Jacob Bowman,

SW and NW on Theodosia Turk SE and SW on Robert Long, other sides part on vacant land and by said Rover, which said tract of land was *granted to Hans Hendrick on 24 November 1771. (*And now sold by widow and oldest son of Hans Hendrick.) Margaret (X) Hendrick (LS), MyCajak (X) Hendrick, Magdilin (X) Hendrick. Wit: David Anderson, Peter Wood, Wm. Win. Hendrick. Proved by David Anderson and Peter Wood 28 August 1792 before George Anderson, J.P. [LCDBK D: 43-47]

Hendrix, Margaret: 2 January 1797: LWT of Margret Hendrick *sic*: That the land on which I now live shall be equally divided quantity and quality between by two sons Micajah Hendrick and Wm. Win Hendrick ; to my daughters Fanny Turner a girl named Leller, to my daughter Peggy Forgy one negro woman named any and child Tom; to daughter Rachael Hendrick one negro girl named Juda, to daughter May Burgess one negro girl Fil; to daughter Elizabeth Wright £40, to my daughter Martha Willard £5. I appoint my friend Lewis Graves sole Executor. Margret (mark) Hendrick (LS). Wit: John Middleton, Jacob (mark) Clemons, Elizabeth Sims. [LCWBK A: 158]

[Family: Margret Hendrick, widow of Hans Hendrix, daughters: Elizabeth Wright, Ma[r]tha Willard, Fanny Turner, Peggy Forgy, Rachael Hendrick, May Burgess, sons: Macajah Hendrick and Wm. Win Hendrick.]

Hendrick, Margaret, dec'd.: 6 February 1797: Appraisal of estate by D. Anderson, Jno. Middleton, Robert Freeman. [LCWBK A: 168]

Hendrix, Hans: 17 November 1798: Elizabeth Wright, of Pittsylvania Co., Virginia, has made ordained constituted and appointed my husband Wright, my true lawful attorney for me in my name and for my use to receive of Lewis Graves, executor, of Margaret Hendrick, deceased, of the County of Laurens State of S.C., administrix, of Hance Hendricks, decd, who was my father, and all and every goods and chattels due me by the last will and testament of the said Margaret Hendrick. Eliza. (mark) Wright (LS). At the court held for Pittsylavania Co. 19 November 1798. Will. Turnstall, C.P.C. [LCDBK F: 400-401]

Hendrix, Hans: 13 February 1800: Micajah Hendrix, of Laurens Co., S.C., to Wm. Win Hendrix, of same place, for £50; 300 acres on Reedy River. *Originally granted to Hans Hendrick 23 June 1774* and descended to the above Micajah Hendrick being his lawful heir and now conveyed by the said Micajah Hendrick to Wm. Win Hendrick. Micajah (his mark) Hendrick. Wit: John Wait, Elijah Burgess, Jacob Niswanger. Proved by Elijah Burgess 13 February 1800 before Lewis Graves, J.P. [LCDBK F: 522-523]

Hill, Nicholas: Survey for Nicholas Hill pursuant to precept dated 30*sic* February 1767; 200 acres in Craven Co., on a small branch of Raburns Creek, south side thereof. Bounded by vacant land. Certified 19 February 1767. Ralph Humphreys, D.S. [P10_48:1]

Hill, Nicholas: Memorial for Nicholas Hill; 200 acres in Craven Co., on a branch of Rayburnes Creek. Bounded on all sides by vacant land. Certified 19 February 1767 and granted 25 August 1769. Quit rent to commence in 2 years. 12. October 1769. Ralph Humphreys, D.S. Jacob Bowman. [M8_522:4]

Hill, Nicholas: Survey for Nicholas Hill pursuant to precept dated 5 November 1771; 250 acres in Berkley Co., waters of Reedy River and Raburns Creek. Bounded on all sides by vacant land. Certified 14 January 1772. Pat. Cunningham, D.S. [P15_443:1]

Hill, Nicholas: Memorial for Nicholas Hill; 250 acres in Berkley Co., on the waters of Reedy river and Rayburns Creek. Bounding on all sides by vacant land. Certified 14 Jan 1772 and granted 3 April 1772. Quit rent to commence in 2 years. 15 June 1772. Delivered 1 March 1773 to Patk. Cunningham. Patrick Cunningham, D.S. [M11_258:3]

Hill, Nicholas: 9 November 1803 *sic* Aaron Pinson, of Laurens Dist., S.C., to James Henderson, of same for $100; 60 acres on the waters of Rabourns Creek bounded at the time of surveying on all sides by vacant land. *Originally granted to the aforesaid Nicholas Hill* and now by his heirs to Aaron Pinson and now by Aaron Pinson to James Henderson. Aaron Pinson (LS) Wit: John Wells, William O'Daniel. Proved by John Wells 1 July 1842 before John Garlington, R.M.Q. [LCDBK O: 120]

Hill, Nicholas: 3 November 1812: Aaron Pinson, of Laurens Dist., S.C., to James Crocker, of same place, for $83; 140 acres part of *original grant to Nicholas Hill* on waters or Raborns Creek. Bounded at time of survey on all sides vacant land. *Originally granted to Nicholas Hill;* and now belonging to Aaron Pinson; sold and conveyed to the said James Crocker. Aaron Pinson. Wit. Martin Shaw, Moses Pinson. Dower of Salley Pinson given 3 February 1816 before John Garlington, Q.M. Proved by Martin Shaw 8 February 1816 before Dd. Anderson, J.Q. [LCDBK K: 122]

Hill, Nicholas: 9 November 1816: Whereas Nicklas [Nicholas] Hill did by deed of conveyance made 20 November 1799 convey unto William Wadkins [Watkins] a tract of land containing 250 acres; there know all men that I William Wadkins [Watkins], of Laurens Co., S.C., to Wm. Wadkins [Watkins], of same place, for $200; 125 acres being half of the said 150

121

acres of land sold by the said Nicklus Hill to said William Wadkins [Watkins]. William Watkins. Wit. Dd. Anderson, Wm. (X) Fleming. Proved by David Anderson 17 February 1718 before Robert McNees, J.P. [LCDBK K: 161]

Hill, Nicholas: 10 April 1820: I William Watkins, of Laurens Dist., S.C., for and in consideration of love and affection towards James Watkins, my beloved son, of same place, have granted, conveyed (reserving unto myself and Anna Watkins, my wife, life estate, or enjoyment) unto the said James Watkins; 125 acres of land being part of a tract conveyed by Nicholas Hill unto the said William Watkins, on the waters of Reedy and Raiburns Creek. Bounded by on Matthew McDaniel, James Boyd, Patrick Speiring, and on said James Watkins and James Burton. William Watkins (LS). Wit: John H. Henderson, Gabriel Jowell. Proved by Gabriel Jowell 10 April 1820 before Chas. Allen, Q.M. [LCDBK K: 292]

Hix [Hicks], William: 3 April 1786 land grant.

Hix [Hicks], William: 10 September 1790: William Hicks, of Laurens Co., S.C., to William Suter, of same place, for £22 ; 126 acres on a branch of Reaburns Creek called Burris Creek, the waters of Saluda river. Bounding SW on John Maden's [Madden] line. *Originally granted to said William Hix 3 April 1786.* William (x) Hix Edy (x her mark) Hix. Wit: David Maden, John Rodgers. Proved by John Rodgers 14 September 1790 before Charles Saxon, J.P. [LCDBK D: 115]

Hix, William: 16 October 1794: William Hix, of Laurens Co., S.C., planter to John Martin, of same place, planter, for £500; 640 acres on a branch called Burrises Creek and other streams. Bounded N by Duncan O'Bryant and Hastings Doyal (Dial), E land not known, all over sides on land not known. William Hix (X) (LS). Wit: Martin (mark) Martin, James Sullivant. Proved by James Sullivant, Junr. 3 January 1795 before Charles Saxon, J.P. [LCDBK E: 319-320]

Hix, William: 18 August 1794: John Martin, of Laurens Co., S.C., planter, to Frederick Sullivant, of same place, shoemaker, for £100; 233 acres *being part of 640 acres granted* by his Excellency (blank) [no date given]. John Martin, (LS) Wit: Ezekiel Roland, John Godfrey. Proved by Ezekiel Stephen Roland 30 September 1794 before Charles Saxon, J.P.[Plat certified 18 August 1794 by John Rodgers, D.S.] [LCDBK E: 322-323]

Hoge, Jacob: Survey for Jacob Hoge pursuant to precept dated 4 October 1768: 100 acres in Craven Co., on the waters of Rayburns Creek. Bounded on all sides by vacant land. Certified 4 February 1769. Jno. Caldwell, D.S.

Hoge, Jacob: Memorial for Jacob Hoge; 100 acres in Craven Co., on the waters of Rayburns Creek. Bounded by vacant land. Certified 1 August 1769 and granted 22 February 1771. Quit rent to commence in 2 years. 18 April 1771. Jno. Caldwell, J.D. Delivered 1 February 1772 to Philip (P his mark) Sherrell. [M10_378:2]

Hoge, Jacob: 21 March 1772: Indenture made 21 March 1772 in the 12 year of the Reign of our Sovereign Lord George the Third by the Grace of God of Great Britain, France and Ireland King Defender of the faith. Between Jacob Hogg (Hoge), of Laurens Co., S.C., planter and Ezekiel Mathews, of same place, for £100; 100 acres on a branch of Saluda, Reaburns Creek. *Originally granted which was to the said Jacob Hogg (Hoge).* Signed Jacob Hoge (L.S.) Wit. Richard Owings, James Abercrombie, Wm. Downs. Proved 21 March 1772 before James Lindley, J.P. [LCDBK D: 231-232]

Holcomb, Ruben: 22 July 1808: Ruben Holcomb, of Laurens Dist., S.C., to Lewis Cargill, of same place, £46, 13sh; 100 acres on N Fork of Raborns Creek on N side Peach lands Branch. Bounded W on a conditional line between Lewis Cargill and John Parker, SW on Archable Owings, SE on Richard Owings, E on William Owings, N on David Studdard. Ruben (X) Halcom (LS) Wit: William Owings, Nathan Curry. Proved by Nathan Curry 6 January 1810 before Jonthan. Downs. J.P. Dower of Mary Holcomb, wife of the within Ruben Holcomb given 6 January 1810 before Jonthan. Downs, J.P. [LCDBK K: 151]

Hollingsworth Family: Quaker. Many of the Hollingsworth families removed to Miami Monthly Meeting in Ohio in the early 1800's.

Hollingsworth, James: 2 February 1805: I James Hollingsworth, of Laurens Dist., S.C., to Thomas Madden, of same place, for $300, *50* acres on W side of Raburns Creek. *Originally grated to Isaac Lewis.* Bounding at the said original grant SE on William Turk, NE on Said creek, all other sides vacant, on a plat there of annexed to the said grant and conveyed by the said Isaac Lewis and Ralph Humphrey's and by him unto Samuel Kelley and by him unto the said William Ancrum and Aaron Loocock and from them to James Hollingsworth and from him to Thomas Madden. Likewise another plantation of 100 acres being part of a tract containing 152 acres granted to the said James Hollingsworth on Raburns Creek, the said land lying on the S side of said creek, bounded on NE by land laid out formerly to Daniel Allen, SE on land laid out to Wm. Williamson, S side of Turks land. James Hollingsworth (LS). Wit: George Brock, George Hollingsworth. Dower of Sarah Hollingsworth, wife of the within named James Hollingsworth given 2

March 1805 before Jonthn. Downes. Proved by George Brock 2 February 1805 before Samuel Cunningham J.P. [LCDBK H: 165]

Hollingsworth, James: 1787 Land Grant.

Hollingsworth, James: 2 January 1807: George Hollingsworth, of Laurens Dist., to Marmaduke Pinson, of same place, for $50; 50 acres, part of a tract of 152 acres, on a branch of Reedy River called Reabourns Creek. *Granted to James Hollingsworth* by Thomas Pinckney 1787. Bounded [none given]. Signed George Hollingsworth, Wit: Ezz. Hollingsworth, Polly Lindley. Dower by Lidid Hollingsworth 4 February 1807 before Jonathan Downs, J.Q. Proved 4 February 1807 by Ezekle Hollingsworth before Jonthn. Downs, J.Q. Rec. 27 April 1808. [LCDBK J: 12-13]

Hollingsworth, James: 15 February 1821: John Coates, of Laurens Dist., S.C., to Thomas Coates, of same place, for $400; 100 acres on Rabourns Creek. Bounding land of James Abercrumbie, David Bibb, Charles Parks, William Strain. It being part of 150 acres *originally granted to James Hollingsworth* and by divers transferences conveyed to me the said John Coates by Samuel Green. John Coates (LS) Wit: James Powell, William Cooper. Dower of Dolly Coates, the wife of the within named John Coates, given 21 March 1821 before S. Cuningham. J.Q. Proved by James Jowell 24 March 1824 before S. Cuningham, J.Q. [LCDBK L: 4]

Hollingsworth, James: 2 February 1805: I James Hollingsworth, of Laurens Dist., S.C., to Thomas Madden, of same place, for $300; 50 acres on W side of Raburns Creek. *Originally granted to Isaac Lewis.* Bounding on said original grant, SE on William Turk, NE on said Creek other sides vacant land. On a plat thereof annexed to the said grant and conveyed by the said Isaac Lewis and Ralph Humphreys and by him unto Samuel Kelley and by him unto the said William Ancrum and Aaron Loocock and from them to James Hollingsworth and from him to Thomas Madden. Likewise another tract of land containing *100 acres being part of a tract of 150 acres granted to the said James Hollingsworth,* lying on Raburns Creek, being on the S side of said creek, bounded on the NE by laid out formerly to Daniel Allen, SE on land laid out to Wm. Williamson, S side of Turk's land. James Hollingsworth (LS). George Brock, George Hollingsworth. Dower of Sarah Hollingsworth wife of the within named James Hollingsworth given 2 March 1805 before Jothan. Downs, J.Q. Proved by George Brock 2 February 1805 before Samuel Cunningham, J.P. [LCDBK H: 165-166]

Hollingsworth, James: 1 April 1809: John McCann, of Laurens Dist., S.C., to John Madden, of same place, for $400; 50 acres on the W side of Rabourns Creek. *Originally granted to Isaac Lewis.* Bounded SE on Wm.

Turk, NE of said Creek all other sides vacant at time of survey. The *original grant by the said Lewis* conveyed to Ralph Humphries and by him conveyed to Samuel Kelley to Wm. Ancrum and Aaron Locket [Loocook] from them to James Hollingsworth, from said Hollingsworth to Thomas Madden and from said Madden to said John McCan and now from the McCan to said John Madden. Likewise one other tract of land containing 100 acres being part of that tract of land containing 152 acres *granted to the said James Hollingsworth* lying on the S side of Raburns Creek Bounded NW on land laid out for Daniel Allen SW on William Williamson S by Tuckland [Turks land?]and the original sold and conveyed to said Thomas Madden bearing equal date with the other from the said Madden to the said John McCan and now by the said McCan to the said Madden. John McCan (LS). Wit: William McClanahan, George Madden. Proved by George Madden 4 September 1809 before John Boyd, J.P. [LCDBK J: 104-105]

Hollingsworth [blank]: 16 April 1811: John Madden, of Laurens Dist., S.C., to Thomas Norris, of same place, for $200; 50 acres, except a meeting house called the Quaker meeting house and 2 acres of land round the said assigned for public worship. The land being on Raburns Creek, *being part of a tract of 150 acres formerly the property of Hollingsworth, Thomas Madden and land where James Green now lives* (on the other part). Bounded by said Norris's house on a dividing line between him and said Green; SW on James Boyd; N on John Simmons; E on Marmaduke Pinson. John Madden. Wit. James Weir, E. S. Roland. Dower of Iby Madden 16 April 1811 before W. Burnside. Proved by E.S. Roland 16 April 1811 before Gabriel Jowell, J.P. [LCDBK J: 213-214]

Hollingsworth, Abraham: 29 November 1777: Abraham's death reported leaving wife Amey and children. [*Quakers*]

Hollingsworth, George: Memorial for George Hollingsworth; 100 acres in Berkley Co., on Reyburns Creek, a branch of Saludy River. Bounded SE by land of Robert Box; other sides vacant. Certified 4 February 1767 and granted 12 February 1769. Quit rent to commence in 2 years. 24 April 1769. George Hollingsworth. Jno. Pearson, D.S. [See Jacob Brooks] [M8_409:4]

Hollingsworth, George, eldest son of Abraham Hollingsworth of VA: 8 September 1788: George Hollingsworth, of Laurens Co., S.C., eldest son of Abraham Hollingsworth, deceased, late of Laurens, S.C., and formerly of Virginia, appoints Benjamin Grubb, of the State of S.C., my true and lawful attorney for me and to ask demand sue for and recover all debts monies lands or other property whatsoever due unto me by right of my grandfather, father or any other in the State of Virginia. George Hollingsworth. In Open Court. Wit: Lewis Saxon, J.P. [LCDBK: B: 363]

Hollingsworth, George: 2 January 1807: George Hollingsworth, of Laurens Dist., to Marmaduke Pinson, of same place, for $50; 50 acres, part of a tract of 152 acres, on a branch of Reedy River called Reabourns Creek. *Granted to James Hollingsworth by Thomas Pinckney 1787.* Bounded [none given]. Signed George Hollingsworth, Wit: Ezz. Hollingsworth, Polly Lindley. Dower by Lidid Hollingsworth 4 February 1807 before Jonathan Downs, J.Q. Proved 4 February 1807 by Ezekle Hollingsworth before Jonthn. Downs, J.Q. Rec. 27 April 1808. [LCDBK J: 12-13]

Holmes, James: Survey for James Holmes pursuant to precept dated 2 February 1768; 100 acres in Craven Co., on Raybons Creek, a fork of Saludy River. Bounded E on land laid out to Isaac Ditland [Isaac Pitts land? See memorial]; other sides vacant. Certified 2 April 1768. Wm. Gist, D.S. Ord. Co. 23 June 1774. [P17_45:2]

Holmes, James: Memorial by James Holmes; 100 acres on Rayburns Creek a fork of Saludy river. Bounding E on Isaac Pitt; other sides vacant. Certified 23 June 1774 and granted 26 July 1774. Quit rent to commence in 2 years. 3 January 1775. 5 May 1775 to Wm. Oneall. Wm. Gist, D.S. [M13_207:3]

Holmes, John: 7 June 1768, listed in petitions to receive 100 acres on Rayburns Creek. No survey or memorial located in the area of Rayburns Creek or Reedy River.

Hood, Elizabeth: Survey for Elizabeth Hood pursuant to precept dated 11 December 1772; 100 acres in Craven Co., on waters of Raburns Creek. Bounded SW on old survey; SW by James McClinto; other sides vacant. Certified 30 December 1772. Wm. Thos. Caldwell, D.S. [P5_79:2]

Hood, Elizabeth: Memorial for Elizabeth Hood; 100 acres on the waters of Rayburns Creek. Bounded on an old survey; SW on James McClinto. Certified 20 September 1774 and granted 4 May 1775. Quit rent to commence in 2 years. 15 September 1775. William Thomas Caldwell, D.S. [M2_350:4]

Hooker, Thomas: 1773 Thomas Hooker bounding Elenor Tweed. No survey or memorial found for Thomas Hooker.

Horry, Daniel: Survey for Daniel Horry pursuant to precept dated 2 February 1773; 500 acres in Craven Co. on the S fork of Reyburns Creek. Bounded W on land of Alexr. Cameron, N on Isaac Horry, other sides by vacant land. Certified 3 November 1774 for William Simpson. [P19-469:2]

Howell, Martha: No survey found. See Martha Goodwyn.

Howell, Martha: 22 January 1759: 250 acres granted to Martha Howell who intermarried with Jesse Goodwyn. [See Martha Goodwyn.]

Hubbs [Hobbs] lands on Rayburns:

Hubbs [Hobbs], Charles: 29 April 1817: Whereas Charles Hubbs, late of Laurens Dist., S.C., intermarried with Mary Taylor, daughter of John Taylor, of the said place, and whereas the said Charles Hubbs departed this life on or about 28 September 1817, intestate and without issue and whereas under the Act of the Legislatures of this State the Estate of the said Charles Hubbs is liable to equal distribution between Mary Hubbs (the widow of the said Charles), and William Hubbs his father. And whereas the said Mary and William in order to settle the estate of the said Charles equally voluntarily enter into the following agreements: That they will proceed to sell the whole of the estate of the said Charles Hubbs on a credit until the 16 March 1819 (except the tract of land and negro girl Julian) and the money arising from said sale to be divided equally between them. And whereas the said Mary and William agreed to divide between them the land and negro as follows: the said Mary to take the negro girl Julian and the said William the tract of land containing 75 acres and to leave the valuation of the same to William McClanahan, Robt. Taylor, Maxwell McCormick. Land valued $375 and the negro girl $400. Mary (mark) Hubbs, (LS), William (mark) Hubbs (LS). Wit. John Garlington, William McClanahan. Proved by Wm. McClanahan 3 February 1818 before John Garlington, Q.M. [Note: John Taylor's daughter Mary wife of Charles Hubbs] [LCDBK K: 197-198]

Hubbs [Hobbs], Charles: 8 December 1817: Hubbs, Charles, deceased: Laurens Dist., S.C.: Whereas my husband Charles Hubbs dec'd, of said place, departed this life intestate and whereas under an Act of the Legislature of this state, the estate of the said Charles Hubbs is liable between William Hubbs, the father of intestate and his widow, Mary Hubbs, share and share alike and whereas the said William Hubbs and myself in order to dispense with an administration of the estate of the said Charles have entered into an agreement to divide the land of the said Charles Hubbs and a negro girl at proper valuation, the said William Hubbs taking the said tract of land and said Mary Hubbs negro girl and in and by the said agreement dated 29 October that I Mary Hubbs (widow of said Charles Hubbs) in consideration of the sum of $175; sell to William Hubbs all my undivided one half share in the tract of land containing 75 acres, the place whereon the said Charles Hubbs formerly lived adjoining lands of James Todd, Ann Faysaux (or the Big Survey) and land belonging to the said William Hubbs. Mary (W) Hubbs (LS).[See K:197 Charles Hubbs dec'd.] Wit. John Garlington, Nat. Day. Proved by Nathaniel Day 3 January 1818 before John Garlington, Q.M. [LCDBK K: 197-198]

Hubbs [Hobbs], William: 28 June 1823: William McClanahan, of Laurens Dist., S.C., to Thomas F. Jones and Samuel Dorrus, of said place; 260 acres on the branches of Dirty Creek, a fork of Rabourns Creek, bounded E by land of James Todd and Charles Hobbs; NW William Hobbs [Hubbs] and Hastin Dial; SW by M. Madden; S by Robert Todd, with the exception of 33 3/4 acres lying immediately in the fork of the two branches which intersect above James Bates [Motes] spring (formerly William Hobbs). Wm. McClanahan (LS). Wit. R.F. Simpson, John Blakeley. Proved by R. J. Simpson 28 June 1823. [John Garlington, Clk. & J.Q. Plat made 24 July 1815 by John Cochran, D.S. shows bounding M. Madden, Has. Dial, Robt. Todd, William Hobbs, James Todd, Chas. Hobb. [LCDBK L: 112-113]

Hubbs [Hobbs], William: 11 March 1824: William Hubbs, Laurens Co., S.C., to Jonathan Motes and James Motes, both of said Dist., for $600; 125 acres on the waters of Raburns Creek, known by the name of Dirty Creek, bounding W on Hastings Dial and Robert Allison; E by James Prim and John Hobbs; S by James Todd, Robert Carter. Now know ye that we the said Jonathan and James Motes for the sum of $600 have bargained and agreed to a mortgage to the same William Hubbs. Jonathan Motes (LS), James (mark) Motes (LS). Wit. Thos. Porter, John Bolt. Proved by N. Franks 11 March 1824. [LCDBK L: 146]

Hudgens, Ambrose: 4 May 1836: Ambrose Hudgens, Senr., of Laurens Dist. SC, for Love good will and natural affection I bear to my son Samuel Hudgens, of same place, to give and bequeath unto said Samuel Hudgens, all that tract whereon I now live; 104 acres of land in said Dist. on the waters of Dirty Creek. Bounded S by John Woody, Senr. E by Jas. S. Rodgers, N and W by John Hudgens. A. Hudgens Wit: W.R. Farley, Wm. Mills, Jr. Sworn by William Mills, Jr. Recorded 14 May 1836. [LCDBK N: 141]

Hudgens, Ambrose: 14 April 1804: Ambrose Hudgens, of Laurens Dist., S.C., to Robert Anderson, of same place, for $200; 100 acres on waters of Reaburns Creek [Plat shows bounding Benjn. Williams and Thos. J. Dial, vacant land, Ambrose Hudgens, Samuel Elliott]. Ambrose Hudgens (LS) Wit: Mansil Craig, William M. Crisp. Proved by Mansil Crisp 12 September 1804 before Charles Allen, J.Q. Dower of Elizabeth Hudgens, wife of the within named Ambrose Hudgens given 12 September 1804 before Chas. Allen, J.P. [LCDBK H: 52]

Hudson, John: 1 November 1818: John Hudson, of Laurence Dist., S.C., to Thomas Adams, of Edgefield, S.C., for $2000; 250 acres on Reedy River on the W side of Reedy River, waters of Saluda. Bounding on Terrell Andrews, on Allens' land to Reedy River. John (x) Hudson (LS) Wit: Rush Hudson, Phillip Dillard. Proved by Phillip Dillard 3 October 1818 before S.

Cunningham, J.Q. Dower of Mary Hudson, wife of the within named John Hudson given 3 October 1818 before S. Cunningham, J.Q. [LCDBK K: 227]

Huger, Isaac: Survey for Isaac Huger pursuant to precept dated 31 August 1774; 500 acres in Ninety Six District, on the NE branch of Rabens Creek, branch of Reedy River. Bounded N on William McDaniel and Bounty land, E on William Helms and Richard Owens, W on Daniel Ravenel, Junr and Moses Kirkland, S on Isaac Huger. Certified 5 October 1774. Moses Kirkland, D.S. [P17-131:0]

Huger, Isaac: Survey for Isaac Huger pursuant to precept dated 31 August 1774; 500 acres in the District of Ninety Six on the NE branch of Rabens Creek, branch of Reedy River. Bounded N and W on land owner not known, W by land of Isaac Huger, S on Moses Kirkland. Certified 7 October 1774. Moses Kirkland, D.S. [P17-141:2]

Huger, Isaac: Survey for Isaac Huger pursuant to precept dated 3 December 1771; 500 acres in Craven Co. on a branch of Reyburns Creek called Browns. Bounded N on land laid out to Abram Reyley; NW land claimed by William Gess; SE on Bounty land; other sides vacant. Certified 10 April 1772. Jonthn Downs, D.S. [P17_149:1] or 17-147:1

Huger, Isaac: Memorial for Isaac Huger; 500 acres in Craven Co., on a branch of Rayburns Creek on Browns Creek. Bounding N on Abraham Ryley; NW by William Gess; SE on Bounty land; other sides vacant. Certified 10 April 1772 and granted 19 June 177(?). Quit rent to commence in 2 years. 24 August 1772. Jonathan Downes, D.S. [M11_369:2]

Huger, Isaac: Survey for Isaac Huger pursuant to precept dated 3 December 1771; 500 acres in Craven Co. on a branch of Reyburns Creek called Browns. Bounded N on land laid out to Abram Reyley; NY land claimed by William Giss; SE on Bounty land; other sides vacant. Certified 10 April 1772. Jonthn Downs, D.S. [P17_149:1]

Huger, Isaac: Memorial for Isaac Huger; 500 acres in Craven Co., on a branch of Rayburns Creek on Browns Creek. Bounding N on Abraham Ryley; NW by William Giss; SE on Bounty land; other sides vacant. Certified 10 April 1772 and granted 19 June 177(?). Quit rent to commence in 2 years. 24 August 1772. Jonathan Downes, D.S. [M11_369:2]

Huggins, James: 5 September 1816: James Huggins, of Laurens Dist., S.C., to Isaac Dial, of same place, for [blank]; 100 acres on S side of Dirty Creek. Bounded N on Saml. Williams, W by said Isaac Dial, S on William Boyd, E on John Lumkin. James Huggins (LS). Wit: William Bruce, Garlington

Coker. Proved by William Bruce 4 September 1816 before Chas. Allen, J.P. Dower of Biddy Huggins, wife of the within names James Huggins given 4 September 1816 before Chas Allen, J.P. [LCDBK K: 143]

Humbel, Rachel: Survey for Rachel Humbel pursuant to precept dated 2 March 1773; 100 acres in Craven Co., on the waters of Reaburns Creek; Bounded SE and NE on Joseph Babb; NW on Nicholas Hills; other sides vacant. Certified 10 March 1773. Pat. Cunningham, D.S. [P17_162:1]

Humble, Rachel: Memorial by Rachel Humble; 100 acres in Craven Co., on the waters of Rayburns Creek. Bounding SE and NE on Joseph Babb; NW on Nich[olis] Hill; other sides vacant. Certified 10 March 1773 and granted 25 May 1774. Quit rent to commence in 10 years. 30 September 1774. Delivered 20 November 1774 to Pat. Cunningham. Pat.Cunningham, D.S. [B in margin] [M13_31:4]

Hume, John: Survey for John Hume pursuant to precept dated 9 April 1772; 1000 acres in Craven Co., on a branch of Saludy called Reyburns Creek. Bounded as plat doth represent. [plat shows bounding James Abercrombie, John Abercrombie, Richard Owens, Will Helmes; other sides vacant]. Certified 15 May 1772. Jonathn. Downes, D.S. [P17_162:2]

Hume, John: Memorial for John Hume; 1000 acres in Craven Co., on a branch of Saludy called Reyburns Creek. Certified 15 May 1772 and granted 3 July 1772. Quit rent to commence in 2 years. 8 September 1772. 6 November 1772 sent to Georgia by R.L. per order. Jonathan Downes, D.S. [M11_400:1]

Hunter, Henry: Survey for Henry Hunter pursuant to precept dated 17 June 1758; 300 acres in Craven Co., in the province of S.C., on the N side of Santee River. Bounding SW on said River; W on land of James McKelvey, Jr.; NW on an old line laid out to person unknown; E vacant. Certified 3 August 1758. Wm. Jameson, D.S. [P6_266:3]

Hunter, Henry: Memorial for Henry Hunter 300 acres on the N side of Santee River in Craven Co., . Bounding S on said River, W on lands of James McKelvey, Junr., N on an old line of land laid out to an unknown person and E on vacant land. Granted 19 November 1769 to the memorialist. Set his land 9 May 1761. [M14-71:2]

Hunter, Henry: 13 December 1799: William Hunter, Esq., sheriff of Laurens Co., to Robert Franks, of same place, for £80; 600 acres sold at the courthouse of County of Laurens as the property of Col. Henry Hunter. The tract of land on the branches of Raburns Creek. Bounding when surveyed on land held by Kitt Shote, other sides vacant. *Originally Granted to Samuel Elliott* and by him conveyed to the Col. Henry Hunter. Sold at Fairfield Co. suit of John Smith vs. Kemp T. Stother and Henry Hunter. William Hunter, S.L.C. *Certified for Samuel Elliott 2 Jan 1792.* [Plat made 24 January 1792 by Pat. Cuningham, D.S.] Wit: Lewis Saxon, Saml. E. Stedman. Proved by Samuel E. Stedman 13 December 1799 before Charles Smith. Wit: Jno. Davis, Lewis Saxon, Sal. C. Stedman. Charles Smith, J.P. Plat. [See Samuel Elliott.] [LCDBK F: 490-491]

Hunter, John: 4 March 1801: We Robert Coker, Junr. and Wm. Helms, of Laurens Dist. S.C., to James Downey, of the State of North Carolina, for $300; 165 acres on a branch of Rabourns Creek called Mountain Creek. *Being part of two tracts originally one being originally granted to John Hunter, the other originally granted to Archibald McHurge.* Robert Coker, Junr. (LS) Wm. Hellems (LS).Wit: Wm. Owings, Aaron Moore. Proved by Wm. Owings on 4 March 1801 before Jonathan Downs, J.Q. [Two Plats shown by Jonthan Downs, D.S. Plat 1) for 100 acres shows bounded by owner unknown, Jonathan Downs, Benj. Camp, William Hellems, road to Wolffs store, land claimed by Calvin Coker. Plat 2) 65 acres shows bounded by David Gibson, John Armstrong, James Downey, on Road to Wolffs store [See Archibald McHurge] [LCDBK G: 190-191]

Hunter, John: 17 July 1793: John Hunter, Esq., of Laurens Co., S.C., to Benjamin Camp, of same place, for £80 Stg.; 407 acres on Reaburns and Mountain creek, being *part of 500 acres grant by Moultrie to John Hunter Esq.* Bounded on David Morgan, William Gary, Benj. Camp and unknown owner. John Hunter (LS) Wit: S. Saxon, John Cormack. Proved by Samuel Saxon 19 May 1796 before John Cochran, D.C. [Plat shows bounding William Gary, Benj. Camp., owner unknown, David Morgan. [Poor film copy] [LCDBK F: 102-103]

Hunter, John: 29 October 1796: Benjamin Camp, of Laurens Co., S.C. to George Thomason, of same place, for £30 Sterling; 100 acres, part of 500 acres, where on said George Thomason now lives on the middle fork of Mountain Creek, waters of Rabourns Creek. Being 500 acres granted 15 July 1793 [John Hunter] and conveyed from John Hunter to Benjamin Camp. Signed Benjamin (xx) Camp. Wit: Robert Atkins, Wm. Arnold. Proved by Robert Atkins 22 March 1797 before Joseph Downs, J.P. [See John Hunter to Benjamin Camp LCDBK F: 102-103] [LCDBK F: 345-346]

Hutson [Hudson?], Richard: Survey for Richard Hutson pursuant to precept dated 1 March 1775; 400 acres in Craven Co., on the waters of Reedy River. Bounding S part on Daniel Williams, part of Joseph Boxes land, NE and NW part on William Wallises land, part on Daniel McClains land, part on Henry Green, other sides laid out to said Richard Hutson. Certified 29 March 1775. Pat. Cuningham, D.S. [P17-201:0]

Hutson, Richard: Memorial for Richard Hutson for 500 acres in Craven County SW of Reedy River. Bounding of Samuel Weaver and land unknown; SW on Daniel Williams's; E on Henry Green. Survey certified 29 March 1775; of one other tract of 400 acres as above bounding S on Daniel Williams's and Joseph Box's, NE and NW on Wm. Wallis and Daniel McClain and Henry Green, other sides on Richard Watson. Also one other tract of 100 acres as above Waters of Saludy bounding E on Robert Box's and N on land owner unknown. Survey certified 3 March 1775 and granted 9 June 1775 to the Memorialist. Quit rent to commence two years from the date. Set his hand 9 October 1775. P. Cunningham, L.S. Del'd this day to Mr. Tennant by C.J. Lindfors. [M2-400:2]

Hutson [Hudson], Richard: _____ 1800: Charles Tennant, Laurens Dist., S.C., to Michael Swindle, of Dist. of Ninety Six, for $400; 400 acres on waters of Reedy River. *Originally granted to Richard Hutson [Hudson]*. Bounded at time of the *original survey S on Daniel Williams*, Joseph Box, NE and NW on William Willis? and Daniel McClain and Henry Green, other side on Richard Watson. Chas. Tennant. Wit: Patsey Tennant, Wm. Tennant. Proved by Wm. Tennent 2 June 1800 before Hugh Middleton, J.P. [LCDBK G: 229-230]

Hutson, Richard: 1800: Charles Tennant, Laurens Dist., S.C., to Michael Swindle, of Dist. of Ninety Six, for $400; 400 acres on waters of Reedy River. *Originally granted to Richard Hutson*. Bounded at time of the original survey S on Daniel Williams, Joseph Box, NE and NW on William Willis and Daniel McClain and Henry Green, other side on Richard Watson. Chas. Tennant. Wit: Patsey Tennant, Wm. Tennant. Proved by Wm. Tennent 2 June 1800 before Hugh Middleton, J.P. [LCDBK G: 229-230]

Irwin, Alexander: No survey or memorial located for 700 acres.

Irwin, Alexander: [No date], Proved 11 April 1787: Alexander Irwin, late of Township of West Pennsborough, Cumberland Co., in the Commonwealth of Pennsylvania, died intestates without issue, leaving Anne Brewster, his only sister and heir at law. And whereas the said Alexander Irwin at the time of his death was seized in his demesne as of fee of several plantations or tracts of land in Berkley Co., S.C., containing 700 acres. I the said Anne Brewster, do appoint James Irwin, of Cumberland Co., my attorney to look after comminute suits for the possession of the said lands and then to sell as he think fit and proper. I grant unto the said James Irwin full ample and complete power of attorney. Anne Brewster. Wit: Thomas Lee, John Lee.

Proved by Saml. Irwin, J.P., Cumberland Co., P. [LCDBK B: 128].

Irwin, Alexander: 4 January 1787: Proved 11 April 1787: Whereas a Certain Alexander Irwin, late of the Township of West Pennsborough, in the County of Cumberland in the Commonwealth of Pennsylvania, died intestate and without issue leaving his widow named Agness Irwin. And whereas the said Alexander at the time of his death was seized in his demesne as of fee and in several plantations and tracts of land in Berkley Co., S.C., containing 700 acres. Know all that I the said Agness Irwin by these present, to appoint my friend James Irwin of the County of Cumberland aforesaid, my true and lawful attorney to sell, release and convey all my right of title of tower and all my estate, interest, property, claim . Agness Irwin. Wit: William Brewster, Saml. Weakley. Proved 10 January 1787 John Jordon. [LCDBK B: 129-130]

Irwin, Alexander: 11 January 1787: Cumberland Co., [PA]. Depositions of John Lusk and David Ralston stated that they were acquainted with Alexander Irwin, now deceased, of Ann Irwin now Anne Brewster widow, children of William Irwin of West Pennsborough Township, Dec'd from their youth and always heard and understood that said Alexander Irwin of the said Ann, were full brother and sister and that the said Alexander Irwin had not a full brother of sister, only the said Ann. Sworn 11 January 1787 before John Jordan. David Ralston, John Lusk. [LCDBK B: 130]

Irwin, Alexander: 10 March 1788: Personally came before me Benjamin Smith, of Abbeville Co., S.C., deposeth that about 1782 Capt. John Irwin came to said Smith's house and demanded a lease and release made by James Lindley to Alexr. Irwin for 150 acres on Reaburns Creek from said Smith's mother-in-law then living at his house, widow of James Lindley decd. Benjamin Smith had been shown the land by James Lindley who said it was sold to Alexr. Irwin, brother of Capt. John Irwin, who lived northward. He (John Irwin) expected it to come by heirship to his oldest son. Signed Benjamin Smith. Wit. A. Blackburn, J.P. and Robert Maxwell, J.P., Greenville Co. [LCDBK D: 185]

Irwin, Alexander: 21 March 1788: Laurens Co., S.C.: Personally came and appeared Mary Lindley before us Jonathan Downs and Joseph Downs, two of the Justices for said County. That sometime about the 1782 came to the house of Benjamin Smith where the said deponent then lived Captain John Irwin and asked her for a sett of leases which she gave to him the said Irwin, with the plat and grant of a certain tract of land which she the deponent believes lies on Reaburns creek, and further says she remembers very well that Alexander Irwin came to the house of her deceased husband many years ago and was bargaining with her said husband for a certain tract of land which she belies to be the same land she delivered the titles for to *Capt. John Irwin*. Signed Mary (mark). Jonathan Downs, J.P. Joseph Downs, J.P. [LCDBK D:186]

Irwin, Alexander: 2 April 1792: Ann Brewster, of the Township of Pensborough, Cumberland Co., State of Pennsylvania, widow, to James Irwin, of same place, Esq., for £500; 724 acres in three tracts. Whereas a certain Alexander Irwin, late of the County and state aforesaid, decease, was in his lifetime and at the time of his death seized in Fee of and in Divers lands. Testament to hereditaments. Situate lying and being in Laurens Co., in the State of S.C.; Particularly the three tracts of land herein after mentioned and described and being so thereof seized died intestate and without issue leaving a widow and one only sister of the full book, to wit, Ann Brewster, above named. But no full brothers or brothers children. Whereupon all his lands and tenements descended to and became vested solidly in the said Ann Brewster as heir at law, saving to his widow her right of dower which she hath heretofore receded to the said James Irwin.; In consideration of the sum of £500 lawful money of Pensylvania to her in hand hath granted to James Irwin all three tracts of land herein after described. One of them on Reaburn Creek, waters of Saluda River, bounded by Casper Boyerly and lands of Thomas Elliott, John Abercrombie and land late of Thomas Woodward, deceased, *Originally granted for 350 acres 1) 374 acres on Reaburns Creek, originally granted to Israel Gaunt,* bounded on Caspar Boyerly, Thos. Elliott, John Abercrombie, Thos. Woodward, dec'd, conveyed to John Irwin and my him to said Alexr. Irwin; 2) 150 acres bounded on No. 1, also on Major Butler, Robert Cooper, Alexr. Mazyck; 3) 200 acres *originally granted to Thos. Austin,* conveyed to said A[lexander].I[rwin]. bounded on Joseph Downs, and Jonathan Downs, Esq. Ann (mark) Brewster, (LS) Wit: Samuel Irwin, John Jordan. Wm. Lyon of Cumberland Co., Pa. [LCDBK D: 190-191]

[Family: Alexander Irwin, brother of Ann Brewster of Pennsylvania.]

Irwin, Alexander: Deposition of John Lusk and David Ralston. . . acquainted with Alexander Irwin from their youth and his sister Anne Irwin, now Anne Brewster, widow, children of Wm. Irwin of West Pennsborough Township. .full brother and sister. .said Alexander had not any full brother or sister only the said Anne. [LCDBK B: 130]

Irwin, James: 9 March 1797: State of S.C., Laurens Co., I James Irwin of _____ Co., Pennsylvania to James Lowry and James Hamilton Lowry, both of Laurens Co., S.C., for £150 Stg.; 150 acres on Reaburns Creek where said Lowry's now live. *Granted 6 September 1774*_____. James Irwin (LS). Wit:

B.H. Saxon, John Hughes. Proved by John Hughes 14 June 1800 before Joseph Downs, J.P. [LCDBK G: 40-41]

Irwin, Capt. John: 13 March 1813: Estate administered 13 March 1813 by Humphrey Klugh, Robt. Roman bound to Taliaferro Livingston, Ord. Abbeville Dist., S.C., sum of $1000.00. Cit. Published at Tabernacle Meeting House. Sale 2 April 1813. Buyers: Rachel, James Irwin. Sale Jno. Irwin made 9 August 17996. Byers No, Martha, James Irwin [Pauline Young: *Abstracts of Old Ninety-Six and Abbeville District Wills and Bonds* pg. 161. Box 50, Pack 1151]

Jennings, Philip: Survey for Philip Jennings pursuant to precept dated 3 December 1771; 200 acres on Reburns Creek, waters of Saluda River. Bounded SE on Kitt Shotes; SW on Samuel Elliott; other sides vacant. Certified 21 February 1772. Pat. Cunningham, D.S. [P17_251:1]

Jennings, Philip: Memorial for Philip Jennings; 200 acres in Berkley Co., on Reyburns Creek, waters of Saludy river. Bounding SE on Kitt Shotes; SW on Samuel Elliott; other sides vacant. Certified 21 February 1772 and granted 19 June 1772. Quit rent to commence in 2 years. 24 August 1772. Delivered 2 March 1773 to Philip Jennings. Patrick Cunningham, D.S. [M11_369:4]

Jennings, Philip: 15 February 1810: We John Jennings, Jacob and Rebekah Culler, Margaret, Rachel and Elizabeth Jennings, of Orangeburgh Dist., SC, heirs of John Jennings, Senr., decreased, to Philip Samuel Jennings, of Laurens Dist., S.C., for $400; 200 acres on Raburns Creek, waters of Saluda River, all the land *granted Philip Jennings* (200 acres) in Laurens Dist. on Raburns Creek, the waters of Saluda River. Bounded SE on Kitt Shotes; SW on Samuel Elliot; other sides vacant when surveyed. Signed John Jennings, Jacob Culler, Rebekah Culler, Margaret Jennings, Rachel Jennings. Wit: John Murrow, Junr., James Hutts. Orangeburgh Dist., SC: Release of Dower by Rebekah Culler, wife of Jacob Culler before John M. Felder, Q.M. Proved by John Murrow 24 December 1811 before Sam. P. Jones, J.Q. Dower of Rebekah Culler. John M. Felder. Q.M. [LCDBK K: 88]

Jennings, Philip: 28 May 1816: Philip S. Jennings, of Orangeburg Dist., S.C., to John Lowe, of Newberry Dist., S.C., for $600; 200 acres on Raburns Creek the waters of Saluda River. Being all that tract *granted to Philip Jennings 21 June 1772*. Bounded on SE on Kitt Shote, SW on Samuel Elliott, all other sides vacant when laid out. P.S. Jennings (LS) Wit: David Pearson, Artemas Jennings. Dower of Elizabeth Jennings, wife of the within named Philip S. Jennings made 28 May 1816 before Saml. P. Jones. J.Q.

Proved by David Wm. Pearson 28 May 1816 before Saml. P. Jones, J.Q.
[Plat certified 21 July 1772 by John Bremar, D.S. Gen'l.] [LCDBK K: 152]

Jennings, Philip: 7 October 1825: John Heller and wife Sarah Heller, of
Newberry Dist., S.C., to Arnold Milner, of Laurens Dist., S.C., for $1034;
200 acres on Raburns Creek waters of Saluda. *Land granted to Philip
Jennings on the 21 June 1772.* Bounded when surveyed on lands of Kitt
Shotes., SW on Samuel Elliott, all other sides vacant when surveyed. *And
conveyed from Philip Jennings to John Low and from John Low to Sarah
Heller, wife of the aforesaid John Heller.* John Heller (LS) Sarah Heller (LS)
Wit: Lewis Hogg, Uriah Suber, John Suber. Dower of Sarah Heller, wife of
the within names John Heller given 25 Oc6ober 1835 before Lewis Hogg,
J.Q. Proved by John Suber, 7 October 1825 before Lewis Hogg, J.Q.
[LCDBK M: 126]

Jennings, Miles [Myles Gennings]: 13 December 1785: Witness deed of
James Cook of Newberry Co., S.C. to Robert Tate. [Z-5, 85; Brent H.
Holcomb, *South Carolina Deed Abstract 1783-1788,* SCMAR, Columbia,
SC, pg. 429]

Jennings, Miles: 1 May 1786: Grant of 1630 acres.

Jennings, Miles, dec'd: Died before 4 February 1817.

Jennings, Miles: 16 November 1813: Miles Jennings, of Greenville Dist.,
S.C., to Benjamin H. Saxon of Abbeville Dist.; for $350; 400 acres on
Middle Creek and other branches of Raburns Creek on the waters of Saluda
River containing by the *original grant 1630 acres originally granted to
Miles Jennings, deceased.* Miles (X) Jennings. Wit: Geo. Bowie, H. Cobb.
Proved by Geo. Bowie 16 November 1813 before Jonathn. Downs, J.Q.
[LCDBK K: 31]

Jennings, Miles: 4 February 1817: Benjamin H. Saxon, of Abbeville Dist.,
S.C., to Nathan Curry, Junior, of Laurens Dist., S.C., for $69; 46 acres part
of *1630 acres granted to Miles Jennings 1 May 1786* on Middle Creek,
waters of Raborns Creek. Bounded on Joseph Downs, said Nathan Curry, Jr.
B.H. Saxon. Wit. John Saxon, Oswald Saxon. Dower of Mary W. Saxon,
wife of the within Benjamin H. Saxon given 4 February 1817 before Andrew
Norris, J.Q. Proved by John Saxon 4 February 1817 before Andrew Norris,
J.Q. [Plat shows bounding B.H. Saxon to Thomason, Joseph Downs, Nathan
Curry, Junr. Plat made 5 April 1817 by B.H. Saxon shows 46 acres run off
for Nathan Curry, Junior by Joseph Downs and Samuel Moore, and
conveyed to the said Nathan Curry, Junior by B.H. Saxon. *It being part of a*

tract of 1630 acres originally granted to Miles Jennings 1 May 1786 on middle Creek, waters of Rabourns] [LCDBK K: 181]

Jennings, Miles: 16 December 1813: Miles Jennings, of Greenville Dist., S.C., and Samuel Tate, of Franklin Co., Georgia, to Hiram Sims, of Laurens Dist., S.C., for $157; 134 acres on branches of Peaching Creek a branch of Reedy River being part of a tract of land *originally granted to Miles Jennings, Senr.,* containing 1630 acres. Miles (mark) Gennings *sic.* Saml. Tate. Wit: Bailey Mahon, Elisha Casey. Proved by Elisha Casey 1 August 1814 before Chas. Allen, Q.M. [LCDBK K: 67]

Jennings, Miles [1814]. William Tate vs. Miles Jennings, Jr. - son and heir of Miles Jennings Sr. agreement concerning lands made with the senior Jennings in 1786. Laurens Equity 1814-2 [Revill, pg. 178]

Jennings land[?]: 1st Monday in November 1814: Benjamin Nabers, Sheriff of Laurens Dist., S.C., at the suit of B.H. Saxon against Miles Jennings, Saxon Vs. Miles Jennings in Greenville Dist did sell to David Anderson, of same place, as highest bidder $130; 130 acres on Rabourns Creek. Bounded on Genl. J.F. Wolff, Joseph Downs, Esq., and William Owens. Benjamin Nabers, S.L.D. (SL) Wit: S.B. Lewers, S. Downs. Proved by Samuel Downs 13 December 1816 before John Garlington, Q.M. [LCDBK K: 152]

Johnston, Elizabeth: Survey for Elizabeth Johnston Pursuant to Precept dated 3 December 1771; 200 acres in Berkley Co., on waters of Little River at the fork of Broad and Saluda Rivers. Bounded NW by Wm. Gillaland, Wm. Anderson and John Pitts; NE by Timothy Griffin; SE by David Richardson, James Waldrup and John Monk. Certified 14 May 1772. Joseph Wright, D.S. [P17_284:1]

Johnson, Elizabeth: Memorial by Elizabeth Johnston; 200 acres [no County given] on the waters of Little River in the fork of Broad and Saludy Rivers. Bounded NW by William Gillaland, William Anderson and John Pitts; NE by Timothy Griffeth; SE by David Richardson, James Waldrup and John Monk. Certified 14 May 1772 and granted 19 June 1772. Quit rent 3/ Stg., or 4/ proclamation money per 100 acres to commence 2 years from date. Signed 25 August 1772 by Joseph Wright, D.S. Delivered 5 November 1772 to James Johnston. [M11_370:1]

Johnston, Elizabeth: 6 & 7 August 1779: Joseph Hays, Blacksmith, of Ninety Six Dist., S.C., to John Mangrum, planter, of same place, for £200 S.C. money; 100 acres in Berkley Co., Ninety Six Dist., on waters of Little River, *half of 200 acres granted 19 June 1772 to Elizabeth Johnston* and conveyed by Elizabeth Johnston to Joseph Hays 23 & 24 February 1773, on the S side of the Main Country Road from Rebourns Creek to Charleston, adj. Land of John Pitts, David Richardson. Jos. Hays (LS). Wit. Daniel Williams, Samuel Goodman, James Goodman. Proved in Newberry Co. by the oat of James Goodman 4 October 1790 before William Caldwell, J.P. [Brent H. Holcomb, *Newberry County, South Carolina Deed Abstracts Volume I:* Deed Books AB, pg. 81] [Newberry DBK A, 236-238]

Johnston, Elizabeth: 13 December 1786: Thomas Pitts, planter, of Ninety Six Dist., to Berry Harris, carpenter, of same place, for £35 Stg.; tract on waters of Little River, one half of *200 acres granted to Elizabeth Johnston 19 June 1772* and conveyed by Elizabeth Johnston to Joseph Hays 23 and 24 February 1773, then conveyed by Joseph Hays to Thos. Pitts 8 & 9 December 1777 on N side of the main country road from Raburns Creek to Charleston, adj. Jas. Waldrop, John Monk, William Gilliland, William Anderson. Thos. Pitts (X) Pitts (LS), Sally Pitts (X) (LS). Wit. Samuel Harris, Reuben Holding, Harris Gillam. [Newberry DBK A, 236-238; Holcomb, Brent H., *Newberry County, South Carolina Deed Abstracts Volume I:* Deed Books AB, pg. 22]

Johnston, Elizabeth: 19 & 20 February 1797. David Motes, Newbury Co., S.C., planter, of County aforesaid, to William Anderson, Junr., of same place, carpenter, for £40 stg., 100 acres on waters of Little River, and *one half of 200 acres granted to Elizabeth Johnston 19 June 1773* and conveyed by said Elizabeth Johnston to Joseph Hayes, 23 February 1773 and conveyed by said Hayes to Thomas Pitts 8 & (December 1777, and from thence to Barry Harris 12 & 13 December 1786, and lies on the north side of the main Country road that leads from Raborn Creek to Charleston, adjacent land laid out to Jas Waldrop, John Monk, William Gilleland, William Anderson. David Motes (LS), Mary Motes (X) (LS). Wit. Ambrose Hudgens Senr., John Anderson, Joseph Pitts. Proved by Joseph Pitts 1 February 1806 before Charles Griffin, J.P. [Newberry DBK H: 305-308; Brent H. Holcomb, *Newberry County, South Carolina Deed Abstracts Volume III:* Deed Books E though H, pg. 211].

Johnson, [no name]: 28 February 1839: I Garlington C. Dial of Laurens Dist., S.C., to Abner Putman, of same place, for $567; 94 ½ acres on the waters of Raibons Creek, *being a part of a tract of land originally granted to Johnson* and from him to Lindley persons to the said Garlington C. Dial. Meets and bounds given. Bounding Mrs. Brown, Franklin Thompson, Thurman Coker and said Abner Putman. . .Set his hand G.C. Dial (LS). Wit: John Atwood, Hosea Garrett. Proved by John Atwood 11 December 1840 before George Cook, J.Q. [LCDBK O: 29]

_____: 16 & 17 April 1788: Jonathan Saragin, of Charleston, S.C., to William Johnson, for £40; [blank] acres, all that tract of land on waters of Reyburns Creek. Bounded S and SE by James Linley, NE by Philip Sherrill, N by David Reays land, W land laid out, over not known, other sides vacant. Jonathan Saragin. Wit: Mathew (X) McDaniel, Thomas (X) Johnson. Proved by Mathew McDaniel 9 March 1789 before Jonathan Downs, J.P. [no prior chain of title or acreage given] [LCDBK C: 7-9]

Johnson, William: 2_ March 1793: William Johnson, Laurens Co., Ninety Six Dist., planter, to Matthew Johnson, of same place for £40; 100 acres on waters of Rabourns Creek. Bounded on S by Thomas Lindley; SE by Merma Duke Pinson [Marmaduke Pinson]; NE by Philip Sherril; N by John Abercrombie; W by Thomas Elliot, rest by James McClanahan. William Johnson. Wit: James Johnson, Thomas Johnson. Proved by James Johnson 25 March 1793 before Joseph Downs, J.P. Plat. [LCDBK F: 493-494]

Jones, Mary: 5 October 1789. Land grant.

Jones, Mary: 17 September 1803: Sale of land from Mary Jones to David Darraugh [Darrough].

Jones, Mary: 12 January 1820: David Darraugh [Dorrah], of Fairfield Dist., S.C., to Alexander Pedin, Senr., of Greenville Dist., S.C., for $500; 167 acres on both sides of the N fork of Reburn Creek. *Originally granted to Mary Jones 5 October 1789 and Mary,* conveyed the said plantation to David Darraugh 17 September 1803. David Darraugh (LS). Wit: James Cannaday, Hugh Darraugh. Proved by Hugh Darraugh _ January 1820 before Jonathan Acrombie, J.P. [LCDBK L: 21]

Jones, Thomas: Survey for Thomas Jones pursuant to precept dated 3 April 1770; 150 acres in Berkley Co., on Reburns Creek, waters of Saludy. Bounded N by land claimed by James Linly [Lindley]; SE land laid out to William Goggans; other sides vacant. Certified 2 May 1770. Pat. Cunningham, D.S. Ord. Co. 29 September 1772. [P17_347:1]

Jones, Thomas (Capt.): Memorial for Capt. Thomas Jones; 150 acres in Berkley Co., on Rayburns Creek, waters of Saludy. Bounding N on James Lindley; SE on Wm. Goggans; other sides vacant. Certified 29 September 1772 and granted 19 November 1772. Quit rent to commence in 2 years. 25 February 1773. Delivered (_) September 1774 to A. Rodgers. Pat. Cunningham, D.S. [M12_118:3]

Jones, Jesse: Survey for Jesse Jones pursuant to precept dated 3 March 1769; 100 acres in Berkley Co., on one branch of Reedy River called Walnut

Branch. Bounded by vacant lands. Certified 18 June 1767 Jno. Caldwell, D.S. [P9-313:1]

Jones, Jesse: Memorial by Jesse Jones; 100 acres in Berkley Co., on a branch of Reedy River called Walnutt Branch. Bounded on all sides by vacant land. Certified 7 March 1764 and granted 22 March 1769. Quit rent to commence in 2 years from date. Set his hand 2 June 1769 Jacob Bowman, Jno. Caldwell, D.S. [M8-445:3]

Jones, Jesse: [No date] Jesse Jones and wife Ann [land granted] grant 1769 to Daniel Williams, Jr. 100 acres on Branch of Reedy River called Walnut Branch. 29 January 1774. C.T. Laurens File Deed 2-5-28 [Revill, pg. 158]

Jones, Jesse: Q-5, 24-26: 13 November 1784: Nimrod Williams, of Ninety Six Dist., S.C., attorney for Daniel Williams, Junr, a former residence, to Sarah Pugh for £28 Stg., 11sh.; 200 acres in 96 Dist. on a branch of Reedy River called Walnut Branch *granted to Jesse Jones 22 March 1769* and conveyed to Daniel Williams 29 January 1774, also another tract of 100 acres surveyed for Henry Sturm 20 May[?] 1773 and granted 23 June 1774. Nimrod Williams (LS). Wit: John Pugh, William Pugh. David Hunter. Proved by the oath of John Pugh 27 January 1785 before Geo. Anderson, J.P. Recorded 28 Jan 1786. [Brent H. Holcomb, *South Carolina Deed Abstracts 1783-1788*, SCMAR, Columbia, SC, pg. 173.].

Kellett, Joseph: No survey or memorial found for Kellett/Killett.

Kellett, Joseph: 9 October 1785: LWT Joseph Kellet, of Laurens Co., S.C. First I give an bequeath to Jennet my dearly beloved wife a horse saddle and med furniture, a negro wench Jenny at her disposal and the third part of all by personable estate, after my just debts is paid whilst she remains a widow and the land and the 3 negroes until the youngest child comes of age. I give unto Mary, well beloved daughter a mare and saddle; also to my beloved son John 100 acres of land where he lives along the Indian Line. Also I leave the 205 acres of land where Hugh McHaffey lies to be sold and divided amongst my four youngest children equally. I also give unto my well beloved daughter Martha one ewe and lamb. I give to my beloved daughter Esther?, one horse and saddle, bed and furniture, I give unto my beloved daughter Ann, one horse, saddle, bed and furniture. I give unto my beloved son James a horse and saddle; unto my beloved son Martin, a horse and saddle. I constitute and make my loving wife Jennet and my beloved son William to be the sole executors. Joseph Kellet (LS) Wit: Martin McHaffey, Cornelius McMahon, Andw. McKnit [McKnight] [LCWBK A: 4]

[Family: Wife, Jennet, daughter Mary, Martha, Ann, Esther, Sons: James, Martin, William.]

Kellett, Joseph: 30 July 1787: John Kellet (son and heir to Joseph Kellet, Deceased) and wife Hannah to Martin Mahaffey, planter, for £10, 80 acres on the ancient boundary line. Bounded on a small branch of Reedy river on Mary McDaniel, Patrick Riley. Part of grant to Joseph Kellett 5 December 1785. [Plat] Wit: Wm. Kellet, Andrew McNight. Nash book, [Poor microfilm] [LCDBK B: 230]

Kellett, William: 30 December 1794: William Kellett, of Laurens Co., S.C., to John Kellett, of same place, for £50 Stg.; 423 acres on Raborns Creek, waters of Saluda River. Including in the tract of 140 acres. Bounded by said creek, Cornelius McMahan, James Downen. And leaving out 3 acres at the Still. Signed William Kellet. Wit: Edwd. Scarbrough, Martin Kellet, James Ryley. Proved by oath of James Ryles 18 July 1798 before Jno. Coker, J.P. [LCDBK F: 356-357]

Kellett, William (son of Joseph): 13 August 1795: LWT of William Kellet, planter, of Laurens Co., S.C. First I give and bequeath to my dearly beloved wife Anna, all the land I hold in Greenville Co. up the still house bank to the Greenville line. Also horse, cow and calf, 1200 weight of tobacco, 100 bushels of corn, all the land I hold in Laurens Co. from the still house bank. I also give to my well beloved mother, Jennet Kellet all the land I hold in Laurens Co. from the still house branch. I also leave all the rest of my estate to my mother and she is to give my sister Jennet Kellet and Margaret Kellet their parts of the estate left them agreeable to my fathers will and dispose of the rest of the estate amongst my brothers and sisters, as she thinks proper, at her death, I appoint Martin Kellet and John Kellet, executors of my whole estate. William Kellet (LS). Wit: Edward Scarbrough, Hannah Kellet, Jane (mark) Kellet. [LCWBK A: 140]

[Family: Wife Anna, mother Jennet Kellet, sisters Jennet and Margaret Kellet; brothers and sister, not mentioned by name.]

Kellet, Martin: 6 February 1799: Martin Kellett, of Laurens Co., Ninety Six Dist., S.C., to Andw. McKnight, Senr., of same place, for £29, 3 sh, 4 p.; 100 acres on Rabourns Creek, waters of Reedy River. Bounded on Robert Sims' corner on the creek, up the creek to a branch to James McCaa's line up the original line to James McCaa's land to a corner on the waggon road to Drury Boyce line. *Being land granted [to whom not stated] 7 March 1776* by William Moultrie Esqr. Martin Kellet (LS) Wit. James McCaa, William McNt[?] Dixon. Proved by James McCaa before James Abercrombie, J.P.

[Martin is possibly the grandson of Joseph Kellet, and son of William
Kellett.] [LCDBK F: 426]

Kellet, Martin: 7 March 1803: I Thomas Matthews, administrator of the
estate of Martin Kellett, deceased, of Laurens Dist., S.C., to Andrew
McKnight, Senr., for $30; 50 acres on S side of Rabourns Creek. Bounded
W on Jean Kellett, on James McCaa's line and Andrew McKnight. Signed
Thomas (MC his mark) Matthews, (LS). Wit: John Garlington, John
Cochran. Proved by John Cochran on __ March 1809 before Charles Allen,
J.Q. [LCDBK G: 567-568]

Kellett lands: 11 September 1800: Jean Kellet, widow of Joseph Kellet,
deceased, James Kellet, Jean Kellet, widow of Joseph Kellet, deceased,
James Kellet, Thomas Babb and Mary his wife, Abner Babb and Pattey, his
wife, Ester Sims, widow of Wm. Sims, deceased, Sampson Babb and Ann
his wife, Archibald Owens and Jean his wife, Moses Kelley and Margaret his
wife and Hannah Kellet, widow of John Kellet, deceased, heirs and joint
heirs of the said J. Kellet deceased, heirs of Martin Mahaffee, deceased and
James Sullivan, Junr, on the other part. Witnessseth that the above named
James Kellet, Thomas Babb and other to James Sullivan, Junr. for £100; 105
acres on the old Indian Boundary line and on a small branch of Reedy River,
bounding on Riley land, on Mary McDaniel. Jennet (X) Kellet (LS), James
Kellet (LS), Ester (X) Sims, Moses Kelley, Margaret (X) Kelly, Hannah
Kellet, Jannet (X) Hatcher, Fleming (mark) Hatcher, Thomas Babb (LS).
Wit. Saml. Boling, Tully Boling, John Rodgers, Esqr. Proved by Samuel
Bolling before Zach. Bailey, J.P. [Plat for 105 acres made 22 October 1800.]
[LCDBK G: 130-131]

[Kellett and Babb families intermarried: daughters: Ann Kellett married
Sampson Babb, Pattey Kellett married Abner Babb, Mary Kellett married
Thomas Babb - Babb men are sons of Joseph Babb and his wife Mary; Ester
Kellett, widow of Wm. Sins; Jean Kellett, wife of Archibald Owen, Margaret
Kellett, wife of Moses Kelley, John Kellett, James Kellett.]

Kellett Lands: 22 September 1820: Jennett Kellett, of Laurens Dist., S.C.,
James Kellett, my son, for $1 and divers other services which I have and am
receiving from him; 200 acres on waters Raburns Creek. Bounded on the
old Indian boundary line, Drury and William Boyce's land and McMahaus
lands, except 14 acres on the S side of the road. The tract of land I keep to
live on during my natural life and at my death said James Killett to take it for
him and his heirs forever. Jennett Kellett (LS). Wit: Archable Owings,
Micajah Berry. Proved by Archable Owings 19 February 1821 before Thos.
Wright, J.Q. [LCDBK K: 318]

Kellett, Martin: 13 October 1800: Application of Thomas Mathis to administer estate of Martin Kellet, deceased. [LCWBK A: 248]

Kellett, Martin: Inventory of Martin Kellett made 1 November 1800. Includes notes and debts due by Joseph Avery, Solomon Hopkins, Samuel Bolling, Drury Boyce, James Kellet (paid), Joseph Reiley, James McKnight, Lard Burns, Danl. Corder, Garsham Kelley, James Gilland, John McKnight, Jane Kellet, Matthew Graydon, Abner and Samson Babb, Wm. Alexander, John Morton. Administrator, Thomas Mathis. [LCWBK A: 262]

Kellett, John: 29 March 1823: John Kellett of Laurens Dist., S.C., to Martin Babb, of same place; for $200; 100 acres whereon the said John Kellet, now lives, lying on the waters of Raburns Creek. Bounded W by Abner Babb, N and NE on Martin Babb, other sides by lands of Jonathan Abercrombie. John Kellet. Wit: Thomas Hay, S. Babb. Proved by Sampson Babb 6 February 1830 before Willis Bankam, J.Q. [LCDBK M: 140]

Kilpatrick, James: Survey for James Kilpatrick pursuant to precept dated 4 January 1763; 100 acres in Craven Co., at a place called Reburns Creek, a branch of Saludy River. Bounded on laid said to be an old survey. Certified 7 March 1763. Pat. Calhoun, D.S. [P8_280:2]

Kilpatrick, James: Memorial for James Kilpatrick; 100 acres in Craven Co., on the waters of Santee River, at a place called Rayburns Creek, a branch of Saludy River. Bounding SW on old survey; other sides vacant. Certified 7 August 1770 and granted 27 November 1770. Quit rent to commence in 2 years. 4 January 1771. John Field. Pat. Calhoun, D.S. [M10_304:3]

Survey for Moses Kirkland; 1000 acres, not located.

Kirkland, Moses: Memorial by Moses Kirkland; 1000 acres in 96 Dist. in the fork of Rayburns Creek a branch of Reedy River. Bounding NW on Isaac Huger and Herman Nuffer; NE on Irish and McGant; SE on Thomas Woodward, Jas. Linley and Gant; SW on Alexdr. Mazyck. Certified 13 January 1775 and granted 3 February 1775. Quit rent to commence in 2 years. 30 June 1775. Jno. Purves, D.S. [M13_533:6]

Kirkland, Moses: 1775: "Moses Kirkland was a prosperous planter owning a sawmill and many tracts of land by 1775, mostly in the Ninety-Six Judicial Dist. He was a Captain in the Royal Militia, serving under the overall command of Col. Thomas Fletchall; he actively participated in the Whig-Tory confrontations that took place in the summer of 1775. In September 1775, he and his son Moses, Jr. eluded Whig forces and reaches the house of the Royal Governor, Lord William Campbell in Charleston. From there he embarked for the British Province of East Florida. [Note: Moses Kirkland's estates were confiscated and sold at public auction during 1782-1786.]

"After the evacuation of South Carolina by the British, Moses Kirkland sought refute in Jamaica, where he settled in St. George's Parish. . His life was ended by drowning while on a voyage from the West Indies to England in December 1787. ." [Phil Norfleet, *Biographical Sketch of Moses Kirkland*, South Carolina Loyalists and Rebels - website sc_tories.com, September 24, 2003]

Kirkland, Moses: Benjamin Waller to Peter Bocquet and James Mitchell, Commissioners of the Treasury, by bond in the sum of £166 Stg. 10 d 10, mortgage of *tract late the property of Moses Kirkland;* 571 acres in the fork between Broad and Saluda Rivers on Indian Creek adj. land of Thomas Green, Crawford Lewis, Allen Wilson, Joseph Dean. Ben Waller (LS). Wit: Robt. Dewer, David Snetgar. Oath of Robert Dewar 8 February 1787 before DL. Mazyck, J.P. [W-5, 359-361; Holcomb, Brent H., *South Carolina Deed Abstract 1783-1788*, SCMAR, Columbia, SC, pg. 353]

Kirkland, Moses: 17 August 1797: John Dunlap, of Cambridge, S.C., to James Johnston. of Laurens Co. for £50; *all that part of a tract of land sold by the Commissioners of Confiscated Estates* to Robert Cooper containing 500 acres said tract originally containing 105 acres, the whole of which tract is hereby conveyed to said James Johnson except 100 acres laid out of said tract to Joseph Holmes by Jonathan Downs, Esq. Bounding on lands of Jonathan Downs, Esq., John Commock, Moses Kirkland and James Irwin. J. Dunlap. (LS). Wit: Taliaferro Livingston, David Smith. Proved by David Smith before Julius Nichols, T.R. [Plat for 605 acres.] [LCDBK F: 250]

Kirkland, Moses: 12 April 1792: Plat represents 605 acres in Laurens Co. in the fork of Raburns Creek a branch of Reedy River. It being all the land that is included within the lines and boundaries of a *tract of 1000 acres granted to Moses Kirkland* and sold by the Commissioners of Forfeited Estates to Robert Cooper (that is not included within the lines of bonding of lands granted of a prior date. The whole tract sold by the commissioners of confiscated estates to said cooper according to the original lines of boundaries containing by a resurvey 1224 acres, 605 acres only is not included within the lines and boundaries of the lands granted. Certified 12 April 1792. Jonthn. Downs, D.S. [Plat] shows bounding David McCaa, Hannan Nuffen, John Calhoun, on S fork of Raburns Creek, bounding James Irwin, Cunningham's corner, Moses Kirkland, Jonthn. Downs.
[LCDBK F: 250]

Kirkland, Moses: 4 April 1801: Joseph Holmes, of Laurens Dist., S.C., to Samuel Cooper, of same place, for $300; 100 acres on W fork of Raborns Creek. Being part of a track of land sold by Commissioners of Confiscated Estates unto Robert Cooper, late of this state. [Plat shows bounded on W. Wilson, Thos. Lindley, John Calhoun] Joseph (X) Holmes (LS). Wit: Jonathan Downs, George H. Owens. Proved by George H. Owens 18 April 1801 before Jonathan Downs, J.Q. Dower of Ann Holmes given 18 April 1801 before Jonathan Downs, J.Q. [See F: 250 Moses Kirkland lands] [LCDBK G: 276-277]

Kirkland, Moses: 5 August 1807: Samuel Cooper, of Laurens Dist., S.C., to Henry Burrow, of same place, for $350; 100 acres on the W fork of Reaburn Creek. Being part of track sold by the Commissioners of Confiscated Estates unto Robert Cooper, late of this State. [Plat shows bounded on Wilsons land, Thos. Lindley, John Calhoun.]. Samuel Cooper (LS) Wit: John Cochran, John McDavid. Proved by John Cochran 5 October 1807 before William Arnold, J.P. Dower of Caty Cooper, wife of the within named Samuel Cooper, given 17 February 1805 before by Jonthan. Downs, J.Q. [LCDBK H: 278-279]

Kirkland, Moses: 1 January 1801: James Johnson, of State of S.C., to John Calhoun, of Laurens Dist., S.C., for $60; 55 ½ acres on Raburn Creek being part of a tract of land sold by the Commissioners of Confiscated Estates to Robert Cooper. [Plat] shows bounded on James Johnson, Capt. John Calhoun, Joseph Holmes, Samuel Cooper. James Johnson, Rabek (X) Johnson. Wit: Jona. Hughes, Jon. Manley. Dower of Rebeckah Johnson, wife of the within named James Johnson given 2 March 1803 before Jonathn. Downs, J.Q. [See LCDBK G: 276-277 above] [LCDBK H: 36]

Kirkland, Moses: 15 November 1806: James Johnson, of Laurens Dist., S.C., to John P. Cunningham, of same place, for $100; 15 1/4 acres being on the mouth of Long Branch which flows __ into Rabourns Creek. Being part of land adjoining said Cunningham and being part of the said survey where said Johnson now lives. James Johnson. Wit: James Mc David, George Pope. Proved by James McDavid 11 July 1807 before Samuel Cunningham, J.P. [LCDBK J: 85]

Kirkland, Moses: 14 April 1836: Laurens Dist., S.C.: James Johnson, of said place, to Jonathan Johnson, of same place, for $5; 100 acres on Rabourns Creek bounding lands of John and James Williams, William Irby and other lands owned, being the parcel of land which I have laid off and entered for him for several years. James Johnson, (LS). Wit: James Cunningham, James Wilson. Proved by James Cunningham 30 March 1840 before John Garlington R.M.C. [LCDBK O: 5]

Kulmony, Jacob: Survey for Jacob Kulmony pursuant to precept dated 17 October 1766; 150 acres in Craven Co., on Reburns called the Lockest Fork. Bounded on all sides by vacant land. Certified 18 July 1772. Alexr. Kennedy, D.S. Ord. Co. 11 January 1773. [P17_530:2]

Kulmony, Jacob: Memorial for Jacob Kulmany; 150 acres in Craven Co., on a small branch of Reburns called the Locust fork. Bounded on all sides by vacant land. Certified 11 Jan 1773 and granted 6 February 1773. Quit rent to commence in 10 years. 26 July 1773. A. Kennedy, D.S. [B in margin]. [M12_320:3]

Lang [Long], James: 1 October 1799: Lewis Banton, of Laurens Co., S.C., to James Crocker, of same place, for $759; 253 acres on waters of Reedy River, being part of a tract whereon the said Banton now lives. *Granted to James Lang [no date given].* Lewis Banton (LS). Wit: Silvs. Walker, Junr., John Middleton, Robt. Pasley. Proved by Silvanus Walker 1 October 1799 before Wm. Mitchell, J.L.C. Dower of Jedidah (mark) Banton, wife Lewis Banton 1 October 1799 before L.S. Wm. Mitchell, J.F.C. [LCDBK F: 473-374]

Lantrip [Landtrip], Thomas: Survey for Thomas Lantrip pursuance to survey 2 February 1767 for 200 acres being on the N side of Saludy river on a branch called Raburns Creek. Bounding SE on land surveyed for Thomas Owens, other sides by vacant land. Certified 39 May 1767 by Richard Winn. D.S. [P11-319:2]

Landtrip, Thomas: Memorial for Thomas Landtrip; 200 acres in [blank] County, on the N side of Saludy River, on a branch called Rayburns Creek. Bounding SE on Thomas Owens; other sides vacant. Certified 5 June 1770 and granted 13 July 1770. Quit rent to commence in 2 years. 21 August 1770. John Mehany. Richd. Winn, D.S. [M10_201:1]

Landtrip, Thomas: before 1772: Land transferred to Thomas Woodward prior to 1772. Deeds not located.

Landtrip, Thomas: 7 & 8 July 1772: Thomas Woodward to William Williamson, Esq. for £300; [blank acres], on the N side Saludy River, on Reyburns Creek, *granted 13 July 1770 to Thomas Lantrip [Landtrip].* Bounded SE on Thomas Owen, other sides vacant. Wit: William Hasell Gibbes, Mary Jennet Boyd. Recorded 2 January 1773 by William Rugeley, Henry Rugeley, Reg. [Charleston DD Bk. A_4, pp. 299_305; Langley, Vol. IV, pg. 261] [Name is spelled Lantrip in other documents]

Landtrip, Thomas: 3 September 1796: Frederick Frasure, Esq., of the city of Charlestown, by his Attorney, John Hunter, Esqr. of Laurens Co., S.C., to Lydall Allen, of said County, for £83; 420 acres *(200 acres which was granted to Thomas Landtrip on 10 July 1770*; the other part of 220 acres being part of 950 acres *granted to Wm. Williamson* and conveyed by said Williamson to Frederick Frasure by lease and release 23 & 24 November 1777. Both tracts bounding each other and lying on Raburns Creek, waters of Reedy River. John Hunter Attorney for Frederick Freasure. Wit: Wm. Dunlap, Margaret Dunlap. Proved by William Dunlap 13 February 1799 before Joseph Downs, J.P. [Surveys - Plats]: Plat 1) Pursuant to a precept directed from John Troup, Esq. D.S Genl. dated 3 February 1767 I have *surveyed and laid out unto Thomas Landtrip a tract of land containing 200 acres on the N side of Saluda River on a branch called Raiborns Creek.* Bounding SE on land surveyed for Thomas Owens, other sides by vacant land. Certified 20 May 1767 by Richd. Winn, D.S. - True copy taken January 24 1792 from original. Plat 2) Survey for 220 acres on waters of Rabourns Creek, the same being part of a tract of 950 acres or *land originally granted to William Williamson* and by him conveyed to Fredrick Freasure. Certified 10 October 1793 John Hunter, S.D. Plat shows bounded on part of said survey, Dick Mathews land, Thos. Landtrip, and Widow Martins land. [Plats] [LCDBK F: 410-411]

Lang, James Myrick: 8 August 1772: 100 acres granted on a branch of Longlick Creek, waters of Reedy River.

Lang, James Myrick: W-5, 489-491: 10 October 1773: James Myrick Lang, of Ninety Six Dist., S.C., weaver, to Lewis Banton, carpenter, of same place, by *granted dated 8 Aug 1772 to James Myrick Lang,* tract of 100 acres in 96 Dist. on a branch of Longlick Creek, waters of Reedy River, adj. Land of John Foster, John Caldwell Lang, now for £100S.C. money. Jno. Mirah Lang (LS). Wit: John Caldwell, Jean Caldwell (X), Richard Goldin. Proved in Ninety Six Dist. before john Caldwell, J.P., by the oath of Richard Goldin 10 October 1773. Recorded 3 March 1787. [Charleston Deeds W-5, 489-491] [Holcomb, Brent H., *South Carolina Deed Abstract 1783-1788*, pg. 359]

Lawson, John: Survey for John Lawson pursuant to precept dated 24 November 1767; 100 acres in Berkley Co., on a branch of Rayburns Creek. Bounded by vacant land. Certified 8 February 1768. John Caldwell, D.S. [P16_292:2]

Lawson, John: Memorial for John Lawson; 100 acres in Berkley Co., on a branch of Reyburns Creek. Bounded on all sides by vacant land. Certified 8 February 1768 and granted 13 May 1768. Quit rent to commence in 10 years. 6 September 1768. Jno. Caldwell, D.S. For the memorialist James Lindley. [B in margin] [M8_208:4]

Leakron, Tobias: Survey for Tobias Leakron pursuant to precept dated 2 March 1773; 100 acres on the Bounty in Craven Co., on the waters of Reaburns Creek. Bounded South on Robert Milles land; W on James Williams; other sides vacant. Certified 23 March 1773. Pat. Cunningham, D.S. Ord. Co. 3 April 1773. [P16_298:1]

Leakron, Tobias: Memorial for Tobias Leakron; 100 acres in Craven Co., on the waters of Reyburns Creek. Bounding S on Robert Milles; W on James Williams; all other sides vacant. Certified 3 April 1775 and granted 4 May 1775. Quit rent to commence in 2 years. 5 October 1775. Pat. Cunningham, D.S. [M2_391:6]

Leger, Peter: Memorial for Peter Leger; 250 acres, as above on a small branch SE side of Rayburns Creek. Bounded on all sides by vacant land. Jonathan Downes, D.S. 1 of 16 memorials. Certified 1 March 1775 and granted 3 April 1775. Quit rent to commence in 2 years. 25 August 1775. Edward Musgrove, D.S. del. 2 September 1775 to Peter BreMarch [?] (See Plat for Samuel Dunlap) [M2_309_310:0]

Leger, Peter: Survey for John McHarg pursuant to precept dated 7 November 1769; 150 acres in Berkley Co., on the waters of Rebuns Creek. Bounded on vacant land. Certified 11 January 1770. Pat. Cunningham, D.S. *Ord. Co. 1 March 1775 for Peter Leger.* [P16_318:2]

Leger, Peter: Memorial for Peter Leger; 250 acres in Craven Co., on a small branch NE of side of Rayburns Creek. Bounded on all sides by vacant land. Jonathan Downs, D.S.; Also 200 acres as above waters of Rayburns Creek. Bounded S and SE by James Linley; NE by Philip Sherral; N by David Rey; SW by land owner unknown; other sides vacant. Pat. Cunningham, D.S.; also 200 acres as above on the waters of Rayburns Creek Bounded on all sides by vacant land. Certified 1 March 1775 and granted 2 April 1775. Quit Rent to commence in 2 years. 25 August 1775. Edward Musgrove, D.S. delivered 2 September 1775 to Peter BreMarch [part of 17 tracts for a total of 5000 acres] [M2_309:3]

Lewis, Isaac: Survey for Isaac Lewis pursuant to precept dated 7 April 1767; 50 acres in Craven Co., on Reaburns Creek. Bounded SE on land laid out to William Turk; NW of said Creek; other sides vacant. Certified 4 June 1767. Ralph Humphreys, D.S. [P16_343:1]

Lewis, Isaac: Memorial for Isaac Lewis; 50 acres in Berkley Co., on Rayburns Creek. Bounded SE on land of William Turk; NE of said Creek; other sides vacant. Certified 11 June 1767 and granted 29 July 1768. Quit rent to commence in 10 years. 7 September 1768. Ralph Humphreys, D.S. For the memorialist Ralph Humphreys. [B in margin] [M8_210:4]

Lewis, Isaac: 10 October 1773: Ralph Humphreys of Craven Co., S.C., to Samuel Kelley, Bush River, 96 Dist., merchant, for £100, 50 acres on W side of Rabourns Creek. Bounded by SE by William Turk, NE by said creek, all other parts by vacant land. *Originally granted to Isaac Lewis,* and from him conveyed to said Ralph Humphreys. Ralph Humphreys (LS), Agness Humphreys (LS). Wit: Daniel Allen, John Humphreys. Proved on 23 December 1773 by Daniel Allen he saw the within named Ralph Humphrey's and Agness, his wife, sign and seal the within release before Jno. Caldwell, J.P. [Recorded 15 October 1806] [LCDBK H: 163-164]

Lewis, Isaac: 1 October 1793: William Ancrum and Aaron Loocock, Esqrs., of the City of Charleston, to James Hollingsworth, of Raburns Creek, planter, for £25; 50 acres (see H:163) on W side of Raburns Creek. *Originally granted to Isaac Lewis,* bounded SW on William Turk, NE on said creek, all other sides vacant land. Annexed tract of said grant conveyed by said Isaac Lewis unto Ralph Humphreys and by him unto Samuel Kelley, and by said Samuel Kelley unto William Ancrum and Aaron Loocock. William Ancrum (LS), Aaron Loocock (LS). Wit. George Logan, W. M. Clarkson. Proved by William Clarkson 15 January 1793 before Peter Freneau, J.P.C.D. [LCDBK H: 164-165]

Lewis, Isaac: 2 February 1805: I James Hollingsworth, of Laurens Dist., S.C., to Thomas Madden, of same place, for $300; 50 acres on W side of Raburns Creek. *Originally granted to Isaac Lewis.* Bounding on said original grant, SE on William Turk, NE on said Creek other sides vacant land. On a plat thereof annexed to the said grant and conveyed by the said Isaac Lewis and Ralph Humphreys and by him unto Samuel Kelley and by him unto the said William Ancrum and Aaron Loocock and from them to James Hollingsworth and from him to Thomas Madden. Likewise another tract of land containing 100 acres *being part of a tract of 150 acres granted to the said James Hollingsworth,* lying on Raburns Creek, being on the S side of said creek, bounded on the NE by laid out formerly to Daniel Allen, SE on land laid out to Wm. Williamson, S side of Turk's land. James Hollingworth (LS). George Brock, George Hollingsworth. Dower of Sarah Hollingsworth wife of the within named James Hollingsworth given 2 March 1805 before Jothan. Downs, J.Q. Proved by George Brock 2 February 1805 before Samuel Cunningham, J.P. [Land granted to Isaac Lewis -See H: 164; 100 acres part of 152 acres granted to James Hollingsworth] [LCDBK H: 165-166]

Lewis, Isaac: 19 November 1806: Thomas Madden, of Laurens Dist., S.C., to John McCann, of same place, for $300; 50 acres on W side of Raburns Creek waters of Saluda. *Originally granted to Isaac Lewis,* bounded at the time of the original survey SE on William Parks land, NE on said Creek all other sides by vacant land, a plat thereof annexed to the original grant and by the said Lewis conveyed unto Ralph Humphreys and by him conveyed to Samuel Kelly by the said Kelley to William Ancrum and Aaron Loocock. And from them to James Hollingsworth and from said Hollingsworth sold and conveyed to me by indentured dated 2 February 1805. Likewise 100 acres being a part of a tract of land containing *152 acres granted to the said James Hollingsworth* being on Raburns Creek on the S side, bounded NW by land laid out to Daniel Allen, SW on land laid out for William Williamson, S by Turks. Thos. Madden (LS). Wit. Charles Madden, John Wills, Aaron Pinson. Dower of Ruth Madden, wife of Thomas Madden given 5 January 1807 before Jonthn. Downs, J.Q. Proved by Charles Madden 5 December 1807.[see land granted to James Hollingsworth] [LCDBK H: 191]

Lewis, Isaac: 1 April 1809: John McCann, of Laurens Dist., S.C., to John Madden, of same place, for $400; 50 acres on the W side of Rabourns Creek. *Originally granted to Isaac Lewis.* Bounded SE on Wm. Turk, NE of said Creek all other sides vacant at time of survey. The original grant by the said Lewis conveyed to Ralph Humphries and by him conveyed to Samuel Kelley to Wm. Ancrum and Aaron Locket [Loocook] from them to James Hollingsworth, from said Hollingsworth to Thomas Madden and from said Madden to said John McCan and now from the McCan to said John Madden. Likewise one other tract of land containing 100 acres being part of that tract of land containing 152 acres *granted to the said James Hollingsworth* lying on the S side of Raburns Creek Bounded NW on land laid out for Daniel Allen SW on William Williamson S by Tuckland [Turks land] and the original sold and conveyed to said Thomas Madden bearing equal date with the other from the said Madden to the said John McCan and now by the said McCan to the said Madden. John McCan (LS). Wit: William McClanahan, George Madden. Proved by George Madden 4 September 1809 before John Boyd, J.P. [LCDBK J: 104-105]

Lindley, James: Survey for James Lindley pursuant to precept dated 1 March 1768; 200 acres in Berkley Co. waters of Rayburns Creek. Bounded W on land laid out to Zebulon Gaunt; other sides vacant. Certified 1 April 1868. Jno. Caldwell, D.S. Ord. Co. 5 January 1773 for Thomas Hairstone. [See Hairstone, Thomas for memorial from James Lindley] [P15_248:1]

Lindley, James: L & R 1758 to Thomas Lindley, son of James Lindley.

Lindley, James: 15 May 1785: Thomas Lindley, oldest son of James Lindley, of Reighburns Creek Settlement, to Marmaduke Pinson, of same place, for £14; 100 acres *originally granted 15 July 1768 unto Charles Quails* and conveyed by said Charles Quails to Ralph Humphreys, and by said Humphreys to James Lindley, the father of said Thomas Lindley by lease and release dated 12 ____ 1758. . Bounded SW by George Hollingsworth; SE on John Williams; W on James Lindley; all other sides by vacant land. Thomas Lindley, Elizabeth Lindley (his wife).Wit: Richard Pugh, John Mitchell, Joseph Pinson. [See Charles Quail/s]
[LCDBK A: 348 - 351]

Lindley, James: No date: Appraisal of Estate of James Lindley, deceased. No date. By James Abercrombie, George Hollingsworth, Thomas Cunningham. Jno. Abercrombie. [Listed as these are surnames in the Rayburns Creek area. [LCWBK A: 16]

Lindley, James:: ___ December 1777: Administration of estate of James Lindley, deceased. List of debts December 1777, also 1 January 1778, Joseph Briton For diet, stabledge [stable lodging]. Above account pro before John Rodgers. 2 1784, Thos. Lindley, Adm. Added note: Found by me in the old papers and desired by Thomas Lindley ad. of James Lindley, dec'd., to be recorded 23 February 1801. [LCWBK A: 276]

Lindley, James: 12 January 1790: Sale of Estate of James Lindley. [LCWBK A: 17]

Lindley, James: 4 June 1803: Joseph Johnson, of Laurens Dist., S.C., to Matthew Johnson, of same place, for $220; 100 acres on the waters of Reaburns Creek, *being part of a tract of 200 acres originally granted to James Lindley Esq.,* and by Thomas Lindley, only son and heir of the said James Lindley, sold to the said Joseph Johnson. The 100 acres being bounded on part of the original survey by Reaburns Creek, and land of Lewis Saxon, Esqr., William Johnson and said Matthew Johnson. Signed Jos. Johnson. Wit: William Johnson, Jonathan Abercrombie. Proved by William Johnson 4 May 1807 before Saml. Cunningham, J.P. Dower of Mary Johnson, wife of the within Joseph Johnson made 20 February 1807 before Jonthan. Downs, Q. M [LCDBK H: 223]

Lindley, John, Harry, Jonathan. 9 April 1824: We John Lindley, Henry Lindley, Jonathan Lindley of Laurens Dist., S.C., to William J. David, Hugh Willson and William Bates for $650; 125 acres on Rabourns Creek. Known by the name of Lindleys Mill tract. John (X) Lindley (LS), Henry (X)

Lindley (LS), Jonathan (X) Lindley (LS). Wit. Jonathan Allen, John (mark) Anderson. Dower of Charity Lindley, wife of the within Henry Lindley, Francis, wife of the within named John Lindley, given 9 April 1824 before Saml. Cunningham. J.Q. Proved by John Henderson 9 April 1824 before Samuel Cunningham, J.Q. Plat by Jas. Bruster, D.S. 27 March 1823 shows bounded by Williams, Downs, H. Lindley, Burrows, Measley.[LCDBK L: 150-152]

Lindley, Thomas: [blank] October 1809: LWT made before October 1809: Will of Thomas Lindley, dec'd., proven by Charles Smith and Colville Abercrombie. Elizabeth, James and William Lindley qualified as executers. D. Anderson, Ord. 18 October 1809. Will of Thomas Lindley; sons: James and William; land mentioned of James Wilson, Charles Smith, Colville Abercrombie; daughters Mary Abercrombie and Nancy Bolt; wife Elizabeth; youngest sons Thomas, Aquilla, John, Jonathan and Henry Lindley; daughters Elizabeth, Hanna and Sarah. Exr.: wife and sons James and Wm. Wit: Chas. Smith, Colville Abercrombie and Jon Abercrombie. [LCWBK: D: 5]

[Family: Wife, Elizabeth, sons, James and William, Thomas, youngest son, John, Jonathan, Henry, Lindley Abercrombie, daughters Mary Abercrombie, Nancy Bolt, Elizabeth, Hanna and Sarah Abercrombie.]

Joseph Livingston [Levingston]: Survey for Joseph Levingston pursuant to precept dated 22 June 1767; 100 acres on a branch of Reaburns creek which empties into Saludy river. Bounded on all sides by vacant land. Certified 1 October 1767. Pat. Calhoun, D.S. also see [P16_381:1] [P16-336:3]

Livingston [Liveston], Joseph: 1 October 1767: Date survey was certified for 100 acres. [See below]

Livingston, Joseph: Memorial for Joseph Livingston; 100 acres in Berkley Co., on a branch of Saludy River, being a branch of Reybourns Creek. Bound ed on all sides by vacant land. Certified 1 October 1767 and granted 6 April 1768. Quit rent to commence in 10 years. 26 August 1768. Pat. Calhoun, D.S. For the memorialist James Abercrombie. [B in margin] [M8_170:4]

Livingston [Liveston], Joseph: 5 August 1783: David Liveston, of the State of Virginia, Co. of Orange, weaver, to Benjamin Rainy, of the State of S.C., Ninety Six Dist. . Whereas a certain *grant dated 6 April 1768 to Joseph Liveston,* a grant of 100 acres at the time of survey, track of land on a creek called Reaburns Creek being a branch of Saluda River. Bounded on all sides by vacant land. Now this indenture that the said David Lewiston, being eldest brother and heir to the estate of Joseph Liveston, Deceased release for the sum of £8 Stg. have sold all that plantation to Benjamin Rainey. David Liveston. Wit. Thomas (T) Cave, Sarah (V) her mark Cave. Proved Camden. by Thomas Cave 6 January 1784 before Phillip Walker, J.P. [LCDBK C: 321-323]

Livingston, Joseph: 9 November 1788: Benjamin Rainey, of Ninety Six Dist., Laurens Co., to Israel Eastwood, of same place, for £40, 100 acre on N fork Raiborns Creek bounded on all sides by vacant land at time of survey. *Originally granted to Joseph Livingston 6 April 1768* and conveyed by Lease and release to said Benjamin Rainey by David Livingston, brother and heir-at-law of Joseph Livingston, dec'd., bearing date 6 August 1783. Signed Benjn. Rainey. Wit. William Head, Thomas Head. Proved: Albert Co., Ga. by William Head 10 September 1796 before Saml. Woods, J.P. [LCDBK F: 321-322]

Livingston, Joseph: 20 November 1796: Israel Eastwood, of Laurens Co., S.C., to Jesse Childers, of same place, for £60; 100 acres on the waters of Rayborns Creek, *land granted to Joseph Livingston April 1768.* Being land which the said Israel Eastwood and Elizabeth his wife hath granted and sold to the said Jesse Childers. Israel (I) Eastwood (LS), Elizabeth (E) Eastwood (LS). Wit: Richard Childers, John Childers. Proved 11 April 1797 by Richard Childers, Junr. Before John Coker, J.P. [LCDBK F: 322]

Livingston [Liveston], Joseph: 1 October 1767: Survey was certified for 100 acres. [See below]

Livingston, Joseph: Memorial for Joseph Livingston; 100 acres in Berkley Co., on a branch of Saludy River, being a branch of Reybourns Creek. Bounded on all sides by vacant land. Certified 1 October 1767 and granted 6 April 1768. Quit rent to commence in 10 years. 26 August 1768. Pat. Calhoun, D.S. For the memorialist James Abercrombie. [B in margin] [M8_170:4]

Livingston [Liveston], Joseph: 5 August 1783: David Liveston, of the State of Virginia, Co. of Orange, weaver, to Benjamin Rainy of the State of S.C., Ninety Six Dist. *Whereas a certain grant dated 6 April 1768 to Joseph Liveston,* a grant of 100 acres at the time of survey, track of land on a creek called Reaburns Creek being a branch of Saluda River. Bounded on all sides by vacant land. Now this indenture that the said David Lewiston, being eldest brother and heir to the estate of Joseph Liveston, Deceased release for the sum of £8Stg., have sold all that plantation to Benjamin Rainey. David Liveston. Wit. Thomas (T) Cave, Sarah (V) her mark Cave. Proved Camden Dist. by Thomas Cave 6 January 1784 before Phillip Walker, J.P. [LCDBK C: 321-323]

Livingston, Joseph: 9 November 1788: Benjamin Rainey, of Ninety Six Dist., Laurens Co., S.C., to Israel Eastwood, of same place, £40; 100 acre on N fork Raiborns Creek bounded on all sides by vacant land at time of survey. *Originally granted to Joseph Livingston 6 April 1768* and conveyed by

Lease and release to said Benjamin Rainey by David Livingston, brother and heir-at-law of Joseph Livingston, dec'd., bearing date 6 August 1783. Signed Benjn. Rainey. Wit. William Head, Thomas Head. Proved: Albert Co., Ga. by William Head 10 September 1796 before Saml. Woods, J.P. [LCDBK F: 321-322]

Lewis, Isaac: 10 October 1773: Ralph Humphreys, of Craven Co., S.C., to Samuel Kelley, of Bush River, Ninety Six Dist., S.C., for £100; 50 acres on W side of Raburns Creek. Bounded SE by William Turk, NE by said Creek, all other parts by vacant land. *Originally granted to Isaac Lewis and from him conveyed to said Ralph Humphreys.* Ralph Humphrey (LS) Agness Humphreys (LS) Wit: Daniel Allen, John Humphreys. Proved by Daniel Allen he saw Ralph Humphreys and Agnes his wife sign seal and release the said deed. 34 December 1773 before Jno. Caldwell, J.P. [LCDBK H: 163-164]

Lewis, Isaac: 10 January 1793– 5 October 1806: Wm. Ancrum & Aaron Loocock, Esquires, of City of Charleston, S.C., to James Hollingsworth, of Raburns Creek, Laurens Co., S.C., for £25; 50 acres on west side of Raburns Creek, *Originally granted to Isaac Lewis* and conveyed by said Isaac Lewis to Ralph Humphreys and by him unto Samuel Kelley and by said Samuel Kelley unto William Ancrum and Aaron Loocock. Bounded SE on William Turk, NE on said creek other sides vacant land. William Ancrum (LS) Aaron Loocock (LS) Wit: George Logan, W. M. Clarkson. Proved by William Clarkson 15 January 1793 before Peter Freneau, J.P. [LCDBK H: 164-165]

Long, Robert: Memorial for John Reed/Read

Lowrey, James: 9 March 1797: Laurens Co., S.C.: James Lowry and James Hamilton Lowery, both of said place, to James Irwin, of the state of Pennsylvania, Co. [blank], for £75; 150 acres on Raiborns Creek. Bounded on the S on lands formerly belonging to said James Irwin; E by Maj. Butler; N & W on land laid out to Robert Cooper; SW on Alexr. Mazyck. James Lowry (L.S., James Hamilton Lowry (L.S.) Wit: B.H. Saxon, John Hughes. Proved by John Hughes 9 March 1797 before Chas. Smith, J.P. [See Irwin] [LCDBK F: 177 - 178]

Lowrey, _____ : 8 December 1799: Thomas Burton, of Laurens Co., S.C., to David Smith, of same place, for £25 Stg.; 133 acres on the branches of

Dirty Creek. [Plat shows bounded on Charles Lowery, Elliott, Oliver Matthis (Matthews)]. Wit: McNees Rodgers, Walter Matthews. Proved by Walter Matthews before Chas. Thomas Burton (LS). Wit: McNees, Rodgers, Walter Matthews. Proved by Walter Matthews 25 July 1799 before Chas. Smith, J.P. [plat shows bounding Oliver Mathews, Elliot, Charles Lowery, unknown owner]. [LCDBK F: 464]

Lowrey,____: 2 February 1801: Charles Lowry, Jr. to Charles Lowery, Sr., both of Laurens Co., for £70 Stg., 100 acres being on a branch of Dirty Creek, waters of Raburns Creek. Signed Charles Lowry. Wit: Thomas Burton, John Dedman. Proved by Thomas Burton this day before Joseph Downs, D.S. [LCDBK G: 564-565]

Lowrey, _____: 2 March 1801: Charles Lowry, Jr., planter, of Laurens Co., S.C., to Charles Lowery, Sr., of same place, for £13 Stg., 75 acres on a branch of Dirty Creek the waters of Raburns Creek. Signed Charles Lowry. Wit: Thomas Burton, John Dedman. Proved 20 March 1801 by Thomas Burton before Joseph Downs, J.P. [LCDBK G: 565-566]

Lowrey, _____:2 March 1801: Charles Lowry, Sr., to Hastings Dial, both of Laurens Dist., S.C., for $100; 175 acres in the waters of Dirty Creek. Bounded N on Capt. John Rodgers; W by Benjamin Neighbours; other sides vacant. Signed Charles Lowry, Sr. Wit: John Cockran, Charles Lowry. Proved 3 March 1803 by John Cockran before Joseph Downs, J.P. [LCDBK G: 566-567]

Lowrey, _____: 28 December 1802: Charles Lowery, Jr., to John Petterson, both of Laurens Co., S.C., for £60; 100 acres on a branch of Dirty Creek, waters of Rabourns Creek. Wit: Wm Burton, Thos. Burton. Proved 30 December 1802 by Wm. Burton before Charles Allen, J.Q. [LCDBK G: 537-538]

Lowrey, _____: 6 January 1832: I Charlotte Lowrey of Laurens S.C., in consideration of the sum of $300 paid by W.E. Lynch, of same place, release unto said John Garlington all that land tying in Laurens Dist. on the waters of Dirty Creek containing 193 acres. Bounding Isaac Dial, James Boyd, James Abercrombie and Marmaduke Pinson. [Plat]. Signed Charlotte (her mark) Lowry. Wit: Milton Pyles, Wm. Penny?. Sworn by Milton Pyles. Recorded 27 January 1832. [LCDBK M; 246-247]

Madden, John: 20 August 1795: Will of John Madden, freeholder. I give and bequeath all my effects whatsoever to my beloved wife Susannah Madden, while she remains a widow. But if any of her sons should marry which is now unmarried, I desire she may give them such necessaries as follows Viz: One feather bed and furniture for the same place, two cows and calves to each of them when married, and I her desire I give and bequeath unto my son Charles Madden the negro fellow Jim. Likewise, to my son Abraham Madden a negro wench Suse. I will and bequeath 152 acres to be his and his heirs forever. The said land lying upon the said side of what we call Burris's Branch. I give and bequeath to my son John Madden, the tract of land, houses and where I now dwell, supposed to contain 152 acres. If Marha [Martha?] Madden should be disappointed and not get the land which my son David and I bought lying over Reedy River, he is to have an equal share with Chas. And the rest aforementioned, deducting what he has received.£35 Stg. And after my wife's decease what property or effects of mine shall remain, my will is it shall be sold and divided equally among all my children. I appoint my loving wife Susannah Madden and son George Madden Executors and Executrix. John Madden. Wit: Richd. Pugh and Ann Madden. [LCWBK A: 142]

[Family: Wife Susannah, children: Charles, Abraham, John, Marbra, David, George.]

Madden, John: 20 August 1795: Legatees: Wife: Susannah, sons: Charles, Abraham, Wm. John, Mabra, elder sons already previously mention of son David, all my children. Ex. Wife Susannah, son George. (Land on Burris Creek). Wit: Richard Pugh, Anne Madden. [LCWBK A: 143]

Madden, John, deceased: [after 1795]: George Madden, Executors; vs. Moses, David, Mabry, Charles, William, Abraham, John Madden. [Laurens County Equity 1817-9] [Revill., pg. 161]

Madden: 16 January 1798: Charles Madden, of Laurens Co., S.C., to Robert Todd, of same place, for £60; 220 acres [see DBK F: 492] Bounded of on NW on Mabre Madden and John Blackwell; S on land laid out for David Burriss on Adams Garmans land. Charles Madden (LS). Wit: John Todd, Abraham Madden. Proved by John Todd 30 December 1799 before Joseph Down, J.P. [LCDBK F: 493]

Madden lands: 20 August 1789: George Madden and Ann Madden, his mother of Laurens Co., S.C., planter David Ragsdale, of same place, planter for 26£; 100 aces on waters of Reedy River. Bounded on SE on Jacob Wright, all other sides vacant. George Madden, Ann Madden. Wit: David Madden, Thomas Ragsdale. Proved by David Madden 11 October 1790 before George Anderson, J.P. [LCDBK: C 285-186]

[Family: Ann Madden, mother of George Madden.]

Madden: 5 July 1799: Charles Madden, of Laurens Co., S.C., to Robert Todd, of same place, for $100; 220 acres on a branch of Raborns Creek known as Todds Branch. [Plat shows bounding on Jacob Williams, Pat. Cuningham, John Todd, Benjn. Suter. Charles Madden. Wit: John (mark) Todd, David McCaa. Proved by John (X) Todd 27 December 1799 before Joseph Downs, J.P. Poor microfilm [LCDBK F: 492-493]

Madden, David: 4 February 1806: David Madden, of Laurens Dist., S.C., to Moses Pinson, of same place, for $332; 133 acres on a branch of Burrisses Creek, being land *granted to Patrick Cunningham, dec'd,* conveyed to said Davis *sic* Madden and now a part of said land conveyed said Madden to said Moses Pinson. David Madden (LS). Wit. Thomas Hunter, Isaac Pinson. Dower of Sarah (O) Madden given 24 February 1807 before David Anderson, J.Q. Proved by Isaac Pinson 20 February 1907. Before Josiah Blackwell, J.P. [LCDBK H: 202-203]

Madden, David: [No date]: David Madden of Laurens Dist., S.C., to Moses Pinson, of same place, for $200; 68 ½ acres being part of a tract of 116 acres, on a branch of Reaburns Creek called Burrises branch. David Madden. Wit. Aaron Pinson, Solomon Fole[?] [Cole] Dower of Sarah (mark) Madden, wife of David Madden made 14 February 1807 before David Anderson, J.Q. Proved by Aaron Pinson 20 February 1807 before Josiah Blackwell, J.P. Plat shows bounding by Moses Pinson, John Harry, W. Madden and R. Duty, Maddens land. [LCDBK H: 203]

Madden: 9 November 1811: John Madden, of Laurens Dist., S.C., to Samuel Green, of same place, for $200; 100 acres on Raburns Creek, bounding James Abercrombe, Robert Nichold's, Thomas Norris Junr., Marmaduke Pinson, *it being part of a tract of 150 acres originally granted to James Hollingsworth* and divers transferred to John Madden by John McCain. John Madden (LS). Wit. James McDowell, Elias Brock. Dower of Isbel Madden, wife of the within named John Madden 10 November 1811. Proved by Elias Brock 19 November 1811 before Samuel Cunningham, J.P. [See James Hollingsworth] [LCDBK J: 260]

Mahaffey, John: Survey for John Mahaffey pursuant to precept dated 3 November 1767; 150 acres in Berkley Co., on the south fork of Raybourns Creek. Bounded on all sides by vacant land. Certified 18 November 1767. Vidi Ord. 5 July 1768. Jno. Caldwell, D.S. [P17_542_1]

Mahaffey, John: Memorial for John Mahaffey; 150 acres in Berkley Co., on the S fork of Rayburnes Creek. Bounded on vacant land. Certified 5 July 1768 and granted 22 September 1769. Quit rent to commence in 2 years. 14 November 1769. John Caldwell, D.S. John Mehaffey. [M8_300:3]

Mahaffey, John: 27 March 1762: John Mahaffey, planter, and Elizabeth, his wife, to Thomas Mathews, Jr. both of Berkley Co., for £200; 150 acres on S fork of Rayburns Creek, a branch of Saludy River. Bounded on all sides by vacant land. Wit: Joseph Kellet, James Abercrombie. Recorded 20 January 1773 by Henry Rugerley, Reg. [Langley, Vol. IV, pg. 264.] [Charleston DD Bk. A_4, pp. 378_381]

Mahaffey, John: 30 June 1778: Will of John Richey, Province of S.C., Ninety Six Dist. 20 June 1778. Son, John; daughters, Mary and Ellinor, daughter, Martha Dunlap; son Robert to be raised and schooled. Mention of land which came from John Mehaffey.] [LCWBK A-1: 20]

[Family: Son John, Robert, daughters, Mary and Ellinor, Martha Dunlap.]

Mahaffey, John: The Mahaffey family information states that after John Mahaffey sold his land on Rabuns Creek that he moved to new land grants he had received which were on Rocky Creek of Enoree. [The Scrapbook, pg. 263.]

Manley, William: 1 June 1807: I Frederick Tavel, representative of the children of Hercules Daniel Bize, deceased, of Charleston Dist., S.C., to Elizabeth Manley, Joseph Manley and Washington Manley, of Laurens Dist., S.C., for £40; 230 acres bounding Hastings Dial, Benjamin Nabors, Mary Sawyer, Thomas Burton and Isaac Dial. Fredk. Tavel (LS) Representative of the late H.D Bize children. Wit: John Simpson, Isaac Underwood. Proved 28 September 1807 by John Simpson, Esquire before Josiah Blackwell, J.P. [LCDBK H: 247]

Manley, William: 11 September 1799: LWT of William Manly, of Laurens Co., S.C. First, I give my plantation, tools, household and stock of every king to my beloved wife Elizabeth Manly, during he r natural life. I give unto my beloved sons Joseph and Washington Manly at or after their mother's decease the aforesaid plantation containing 180 acres. I will and allow that all my horses, cows ad other stock with my plantation tools, household furniture be after y decease lawfully appraised and after my wife's decease that the said appraisement be paid in cash to my beloved children Jeremiah, Vincent, Joseph, Nancy and Washington Manly, with my granddaughter Dedamia Evans, in equal shares. After deducting $18 out of my sons Ephraims share for property already received by him. I appoint my beloved wife Elizabeth Manly my executrix and y trusty friend Joel Burgess my executor. William Manly (X) (LS) Wit: Joel Buress, Thomas Burton, John Cochran. Proved 1 January 1801. [LCWBK A: 265]

[Family: Wife: Elizabeth, sons: Ephraim, Joseph, Washington, Jeremiah, Vincent. Daughter: Nancy Evans [?], granddaughter Dedamia Evans]

Manley, William: 1 January 1801: Application of Elizabeth Manley and Joel Burgess, Executor and executrix of the will of Wm. Manley, deceased. Oath by John Cochran and Joel Burgess. [LCWBK A: 265]

Manley, William, dec'd: 2 June 1807: We Elizabeth Manly, Washing[ton] Manly and Joseph Manly, of Laurens Dist., S.C., to Hastings Dial, Senior, of same place, for $172.50; 115 acres, being one half of a certain tract of 230 acres belonging to the legatees of William Manley, deceased. The 115 acres lying on the waters of Reaborns Creek bounded on N by said Hastings Dial, W on Benjamin Nabors, S by Isaac Dial. Elizabeth (X) Manley (LS), Washington Manley (LS), Joseph Manley (LS). Wit: R. Creswell, Thos. Porter. Proved by Thos. Porter 31 January 1809 before John Garlington, C.C.P. [LCDBK J: 53]

Mars, Hans Jurig: Survey for Hans Jerg *sic* Mars, Pursuant to a precept dated 5 November 1756 for 100 acres in Berkley Co., on Allisons Creek, in the fork between Broad and Saludy Rivers. Bounding on vacant lands. Certified 20 May 1757 Jos. Curry, D.S. [P6-259:2]

Mars, Hans Jurig: Memorial for Hans Jorg Mars; 100 acres in Berkeley Co. on Allisons Creek in the fork between Broad and Saludy Rivers. Bounded on all sides by vacant land. Granted 22 January 1759 to the memorialist. Quit rent to commence in 10 years from the date. Set his hand 26 August 1765 Thomas Allison. Jos. Curry, D.S. [M8-40:4]

Martin, John: 6 March 1780: Grant for 640 acres part on head waters of Burris Creek.

Martin, John: Survey for John Martin, Pursuant to a precept dated 1 September 1767 I have laid out a tract of land to John Martin, containing 100 acres in Berkley Co., on the S side of Reedy Creek (formerly Reedy River). Bounding NW on land laid out to the Cherokee Indians NW by said Creek, all other sides vacant. Certified 28 October 1767 Jno. Caldwell, D.S. [Bounty] [P18-31:2]

Martin, John: Memorial for John Martin; 100 acres in Berkley Co. on the S side of Reedy Creek, formerly call'd Reedy River. Bounding NW on land laid out to the Cherokee Indians, NE by said Creek, all other sides vacant. Survey Certified 28 October 1767 and Granted 6 April 1766. Quit rent to commence 10 years from the date. Set his hand 26 August 1768 Jno. Caldwell, D.S. For the memorialist Oliver Towles. [M8-172:2]

159

Martin, John: 25 March 1795: John Martin, Laurens Co., S.C., planter, to William Wilson, planter, of same place, for £100 Stg.; 260 acres being part on the head waters of Burris's creek. *Being part of a tract of land granted to John Martin.* John Martin, (L.S.) Wit. Ezek. Roland. Alex. Grant. Proved 28 October 1795 by Ezel. Roland before James Saxon, J.P. [LCDBK F: 67-68]

Martin, John Junr.: 17 July 1793: John Martin and Elizabeth, his wife, to Thomas Wadsworth and Wm. Turpin, merchants, of Laurens Co., S.C.; £30 Stg.; 640 acres which was *originally granted to the said John Martin, Junr., 6 March 1780.* Said tract on a branch of Williams Creek, Reedy Lick, bounded at the time of the original survey by land held by Edmond Learwood, other sides vacant. John Martin (LS), Elizabeth (X) Martin (LS). Wit: Joseph Blackerby, Benjamin Blackerby. Proved by Benjamin Blackerby 17 July 1793 before Charles Saxon, J.P. [LCDBK D: 462-463]

Martin, John: 17 March 1795: John Martin, of Laurens Co., Ninety Six Dist., S.C., to Robert Todd, of same place, for £50 Stg.; a tract of 220 acres on Dirty Creek. Signed by John Martin, Elizabeth (X her mark). Wit: William Sooter, Benjamin Sooter. Proved 8 January 1796 by Benjamin Sooter before John Cockran, D.C., Jno. Cochran. Received of Robt. Todd the sum of 50L Stg., being the consideration money in full. Surveyed 14 March 1795 by Jno. Rodgers, (Plat). Recorded 8 January 1795. [LCDBK F: 67-68]

Martin, John: 25 March 1795: John Martin, of Laurens Co., S.C., planter, to William Wilson, planter, of same place, for £100 Stg.; 260 acres on head waters of Burriss Creek. Being a tract of land *granted to John Martin [no date].* John Martin (L.S.) Wit: Ezekl. Roland, Alexr. Grant. Proved by Ezl. Roland 28 October 1795 before James Saxon, J.P. [LCDBK F: 67]

Martin, John: 15 August 1795: Joseph Cole, of Laurens Co., S.C., to James Stinson, of same place, for $70; 60 acres on Chesnut Fork of Burrises Creek. Bounded on Robert Todds [Todds], John Madden. *Originally laid out for John Martin* and conveyed by him to Benjamin Suter and by several conveyances to John Jones unto Joseph Cole and now conveyed by Joseph Cole to James Stinson. Joseph (X) Cole (LS). Wit: Willie Beckham, Solomon Cole. Proved by Willey Beckham 16 August 180 before J. Blackwell, J.P. [LCDBK H: 246-247]

Martin, John: 15 September 1797: John Martin, of Laurens Co., S.C., to Thomas Burton, of same place, for $150; 210 acres on waters of Raburns Creek. [Plat shows bounded by unknown owner, Oliver Matthews, Elliott, Charles Lowry, Esq., Jno. Rodgers]. John Martin (LS) Wit: Ezekl. Roland,

John Rodgers. Proved by Ezekl. Roland 23 April 1798 before Chas. Smith, J.P. [LCDBK F: 300]

Martin, John: 21 May 1804: Charles Lowery, Junr., of Laurens Dist., S.C., to Matthew Cunningham, of same place, for $400; 75 acres on waters of Dirty Creek, being part of large survey *granted to John Martin.* Bounded by lands of Benjamin Nabours, John Rogers, David Craddock, and SE on Matthew Cunningham. Charles Lowery (LS). Wit: S. M. Henderson, Nathan Nabours. Proved by Samuel Henderson 21 May 1811 before Chas. Allen, J.Q. Dower of Sarah Lowery, wife of the within named Charles Lowery given 21 May 1804 before Chas. Allen, J.Q. [LCDBK H: 40-41]

Martin, William: 12 September 1796: John Martin and William Martin, of the County of Laurens, S.C., to William Hobb, of same place, planter, for £30 Stg.; 97 acres on Red Lick Branch of Little River. Bounded S on Horatio Walker E by Mrs. Barby, W on John Todd; N on Peter Faysaux. Being a *part of a tract of 640 acres bearing date 3 April 1786.* John Martin, William Martin. Wit: Mansil Crisp. Dower of Elizabeth Martin, wife of the within John Martin, and Sally Martin, wife of the within named William Martin. Jonathan Downs, J.L.C. Plat shows bounded by Horatio Walker, Mrs. Barby, Peter Faysaux, John Todd. [Plat] [LCDBK F: 505-506]

Matthews, Ezekiel: 6 January 1796: Ezekiel Matthews of Laurens Co., S.C., to John Frances Wolff, of same place, for £20 Stg.; 45 acres on Rabourns Creek. Being *part of a tract of 56 acres granted to said Ezekiel Matthews, 5 October 1789.* Ezekiel Matthews and his wife have set their hands. Ezekiel (X) Matthews (LS), Rebecka (X) Matthews. Wit: Jesse Garret, Isham (X) Histelo [?]. [Plat: shows bounded by John F. Wolff, William Gary, Ezekiel Matthews, Raburns Creek] [LCDBK F: 495]

Matthews, Ezekiel: 8 September 1802: Ezekiel Matthews, of Laurens Dist., S.C., to Joseph Downs, of same place, for $100; 118 acres on a small branch of Raburns Creek called the Hilly Branch. *Originally granted to Ezekiel Matthews* on Hilly Branch of Raburns Creek. Bounded by E by Robert Bolt, N on Boyd, W on said Joseph Downs, S on David Gary. Ezekiel (mark) Matthews (LS). Wit: Lydall Allen, Chas. Smith. Proved by Charles Smith 8 September 1802 before Jonathan Downs, J.P. Dower of Rebekah Matthews, wife of the within Ezekiel Matthews given 8 September 1802 before Jonthn. Downs, J.Q. [LCDBK G: 625]

Matthew, Oliver: Survey for Oliver Matthew pursuant to precept dated 2 December 1766; 200 acres in Craven Co., on a branch of Reaburns Creek. Bounded by vacant land. Certified 19 February 1767. Ralph Humphreys,

D.S. Ord. Co. 7 July 1767. [P9_114:1]

Matthew, Oliver: Memorial for Oliver Matthews; 200 acres in Craven Co., on Rayburns Creek. Bounded on all sides by vacant land. Certified 7 July 1767 and granted 24 November 1767. Quit rent to commence in 2 years. 15 February 1768. For the Memorialist John Cargill. Ralph Humphries, D.S. [M9_436:2]

Matthew, Oliver: See Oliver Mathess/Mathiss

Matthew, Oliver: 10 November 1790: Abner Babb, of Laurens Co., S.C., to John Blackwell, of same place, for £200 Stg.; 200 acres on Raiborns Creek, a branch of Saluda. Bounded on all sides by vacate land when surveyed. *Originally granted to Oliver Matthews* and conveyed to Joseph Babb including the plantation where said John Blackwell now lives. Wit: Richard Jowell, Thos. Babb. Signed Abner Babb (LS) Martha (x) Babb (LS). [Note: Whole deed was struck through] [LCBDK F: 137]

Matthew, Oliver: 10 November 1790: Abner Babb, of Laurens Co., S.C., to John Blackwell, of same place, for £200, Stg.; 200 acres on a branch of Saluda called Raiborns Creek. Bounded on all sides by vacant land when surveyed. *Granted to Oliver Mathews* and by him conveyed to Joseph Babb, including the plantation whereon the said John Blackwell now lives. In witness where of the said Abner Babb and Martha his wife set her seal. Abner Babb, Martha (X her mark) Babb. Wit: Richard Jowell, Thos. Babb. Proved 18 July 1798 by Thomas Babb that he saw Martha Babb, wife of the within Abner Babb sign and deliver deed. Zach. Bailey, J.P. [LCDBK F: 350]

Matthews, Oliver: 25 January 1802: John Blackwell, of the State of Georgia, to Gabriel Jowell, of Laurens Dist., S.C., for $500; 200 acres on the waters of Saluda River on a creek called on Burrisses Creek, *originally granted to Oliver Matthews [no date]*. Signed John (B) Blackwell. Wit: Joshua Blackwell, Thomas Hughes. Proved 25 Jan 1802 by Thomas Hughes before James Alexander, J.P. [LCDBK G: 439]

Matthews, William: Survey for William Matthews pursuant to survey dated 2 August 1768 in Berkley Co., on the waters of Rayburns Creek. Bounded on all sides by vacant land. Certified 12 August 1768 Jno. Caldwell, D.S. Ord. Co. 6 November 1771. NB. The branch represented is two feet width and one inch depth. [P18-57:1]

Matthews, William: Memorial for William Matthews for 200 acres in Berkley Co., on the waters of Rayburns Creek. Bounded by vacant lands.

Certified 6 November 1771 and granted 4 December 1711 to the memorialist. Quit rent to commence in two years. Sit his hand 11 March 1772 John Caldwell, D.S. Delivered 2 June 1772 to James (mark) Rind. [M11-157:1]

Mayhard, John: 7 November 1769: 250 acres Rayburns Creek recorded in South Carolina Council Meeting of Tuesday 7 November 1769, pg. 253.

Mayhard, John: No survey or memorials located.

Mahary [Maharg], John: 1772 bounding John Boyd. [See John Maharg]

Mathess [Mathews], Thomas: 1771 bounding Robert McKearmmy.

Matthews, Thomas: 22 September 1820: Thomas Matthews, of Laurens Dist., S.C., to Willis Benham of same place, for $1400; 325 acres on Rabourns Creek. Bounding lands of Martin Babb, Alexander Abercrumbie, William Choice and Geddes. [Plat - resurvey of land for Thomas Mathis Senr. by Tully Choice, D.S.] Thomas (TM) Matthews (LS). Wit: R. Creswell, Wm. Henderson. Dower of Elanor Matthews, wife of the within Thomas Matthews given 2 January 1821 before Jas. Bruster, J.Q. Proved by William Henderson 2 July 1821 before John Garlington, Clk. and J.Q. [LCDBK L: 19]

Mazyck, Alexander: Survey for Alexander Mazyck pursuant to survey dated 20 March 1772; 1000 acres on a branch of Saludy called Rayburn's Creek. And hath bounding as marks represent. [Plat shows bounding] Land claimed by John Irwin; land claimed by Jas. Lindley; land claimed by Wm. Martin; land claimed by Thos. Colman; land claimed by James N. Cain [McCain]; land claimed by James Ryan; land claimed by Joseph Wright; and vacant land. (no date) Jonathan Downes, D.S. Ord. Co. 6 May 1774. [P18_81:1]

Mazyck, Alexander: Memorial by Alexander Mazyck; 1000 acres in Craven Co., on a branch of Saludy called Reyburnes Creek. Certified 6 May 1774 and granted 17 May 1774. Quit rent to commence in 2 years. 29 October 1774. Delivered 23 November 1774. William Mazyck. Jno. Downs, D.S. [M13_72:4]

Mazyck, Alexander: 15 March 1817: We Alexander C. Mazyck, Paul D. Mazyck, Nathaniel B. Mazyck, Mary Mazyck and Catherine Mazyck, of Charleston Dist., S.C., to Henry Morgan, of Laurens Dist., S.C., for $3360; 1000 acres on Reybourns Creek. *Originally granted to Alexander Mazyck 17 May 1774.* Alex. B. Mazyck, Paul D. Mazyck, N.B. Mazyck, Mary Mazyck,

Catherine Mazyck. Wit: Morton W. Smith, Mahara Haig. Proved by Morton W. Smith before J.H. Mitchell, Q.M. Dower of Mrs. Catherine B. Mazyck, wife of the within names N.B. Mazyck given 18 March 1817 before Charles Sell, Q.M. [LCDBK K: 172]

McAffee [Mchaffey], Martin: [No date]. LWT of Martin McHaffey, Senr., of Laurens Co., S.C. I give unto my loving wife Mary, all my goods, chattels, lands and property, horse, east, cattle and hogs. I make my son Martin Mahaffey sole executor. Martin (mark) Mahaffey (LS) Wit: John McMahan, Elisha Hung. [LCWBK A: 69]

McAfee, Martin: 23 March 1793: Appraisal of estate of Martin Mahaffey, deceased by Samuel Bolling, William Choice, Alexr. Paden. [LCWBK A: 70]

McAfee, Martin: 23 March 1793: Sale of estate. Purchasers not named. [LCWBK A: 71]

McCain, James: [See survey for Daniel Allen.]

McCain, James: Memorial for James McCain; 150 acres in Craven Co., on the W side of Raibourns Creek a branch of Santee river. Bounding SE on Daniel Allen Jr.; SW by James Ryan; NW by said Creek; other sides vacant. *Being part of 500 acres originally granted 1 February 1768 to Daniel Allen* and convey by him to the memorialist by lease and release 20 April 1768. 2 June 1772, James Lindl[e]y. [See survey for Daniel Allen] [M11_242:3]

McCain, James: 5 August 1786: Will of James McCain, Ninety Six Dist., now called Oxford Dist. and Laurens Co., S.C., planter. I devise to my son John McCain the sum of 10 shillings. To my daughter Mary 5 shillings, .to my daughter [torn], executrix. . James McCain (seal).Wit: Richd. Pugh, John Hollingsworth, Henry Hollingworth. [LCWBK A: 3]

[Family: No wife named, son John McCain, daughters Mary, other name torn.]

McCain, James: No date: Inventory of Goods and Chattels of James McCain deceased. Appraisal by John Abercrombie, George Hollingworth, Marmaduke Pinson. [LCWBK A: 4]

McClintock [See McLinto]:

McClurkam, Samuel: Survey for Saml. McClurkam pursuant to precept dated 6 January 1773: 100 acres in Ninety Six Dist. on the waters of

Raiburn's Creek on the N side. Bounded NW on land laid out to Robt. Box and Edwd. Box; NE on James Williams; SW on Thomas McClurkam; all others sides by vacant land. Surveyed 20 March 1770. Thos. Clark, D.S. [Irish]. [P18_151:2]

McClurkam, Samuel: Memorial for Samuel McClurkam; 100 acres in 96 Dist. on the waters of Rayburns Creek on the north side. Bounding NW on Robert Box and Edward Box; NE on James Williams and SW on Thomas McClurkam. Certified 20 September 1774 and granted 4 May 1775. Quit rent to commence in 2 years. 18 September 1775. Thomas Clark, D.S. [M2_354:3]

McClurkam, Samuel: Survey for Samuel McClurkam pursuant to precept dated 6 January 1773: 100 acres in Ninety Six Dist. on the waters of Raiburn's Creek on the N side. Bounded NW on land laid out to Robt. Box and Edwd. Box; NE on James Williams; SW on Thomas McClurkam; all others sides by vacant land. Surveyed 20 March 1770. Thos. Clark, D.S. (Irish). [P18_151:2]

McClurkam, Samuel: Memorial for Samuel McClurkam; 100 acres in 96 Dist. on the waters of Rayburns Creek on the north side. Bounding NW on Robert Box and Edward Box; NE on James Williams and SW on Thomas McClurkam. Certified 20 September 1774 and granted 4 May 1775. Quit ret to commence in 2 years. 18 September 1775. Thomas Clark, D.S. [M2_354:3]

McClurkan, Samuel: 2 May 1795: Estate appraisal of Samuel McClurken, deceased by Archibald Owens, James Abercrombie, George Hollingsworth, Isaac Cook. [LCWBK A: 133]

McClurken, Samuel: 3 June 1797: Sale of estate of Samuel McClurken. Purchasers not names. Exr. Robert Haslet. John Cochran, Clerk. Ad. Nancy Haslet. [LCWBK A: 169]

McClurken, Samuel: 8 October 1816: James McClurkin and Samuel McClurkin, of Laurens Dist., S.C., to Ezekiel Andrews, of same place, for $454.50; *90 acres being part of a tract of land formerly the property of Samuel McClurken deceased,* and partitioned and divided amongst his heirs by Court of Equity District of Greenville, Laurens, and Newberry and being part of the two parcels of land containing 150 acres. James McClurkin (LS), Samuel McClurken (LS). Wit: John Garlington, Nathaniel Day. Proved by Nathaniel Day 11 October 1819 before John Garlington, Clk. And J.Q. [Plat made 26 September 1816 by L. Moore, D.S. [Plat shows bounding McClintin, Swindel and Washington and Howell].LCDBK: K 261]

McClurken, Samuel: 4 November 1818: Ezekiel Andrews, of Laurens Dist., S.C., to Susannah Hallums, of Abbeville Dist., S.C., for the sum of $2443; 349 acres on Reedy River, *part of three tracks originally granted to Daniel [Samuel] McClurkn?, one to Patrick Cunningham and the other to Samuel Rosamond,* being the whole of the tract of land whereon I now live. Ezekiel Andrews. (Mark) (LS) Wit: Henry Green, Aber. W. Adams. Dower of Elizabeth Andrews, the wife of the within named Ezekiel Andrews given 28 April 1819 before S. Cunningham, J.Q. Proved by Henry Gray 16 April 1819 before S. Cuningham, J.Q. [See Patrick Cuningham, Samuel Rosamond] [LCDBK K: 267]

McClurken, Samuel and James: minors: 26 March 1804: Samuel McClurkin, minor about 12 chose Wm. Wadkins as guardian, Security Ezekiel Andrews. On same date James McClurkin minor about 16 chose Wm. Wadkins as guardian, security Ezekiel Andrews. [LCWBK C-1: 107]

McClurkam, Jane: Survey for Jane McClurkam pursuant to precept dated 6 January 1773: 100 acres in Craven Co., on the waters of Raburn's Creek. Bounded on all sides by vacant land. Certified 13 April 1773. Pat. Cunningham, D.S. (Irish). [P18_149:2]

McClurkam, Jane: Memorial for Jane McClurkam ; 100 acres in Craven Co., on the waters of Rayburns Creek. Bounded on all sides by vacant land. Certified 20 September 1774 and granted 17 March 1775. Pat. Cunningham, D.S. delivered 14 August 1775 to George Norwood. [M2_291:2]

McClurkam, Jane: 2 February 1795: Jane McClurkam bounding Hastings Dial in land sale - land had been granted to Wm. Hellams. [See LCDBK F: 142]

McClurkam, Jane: 25 November 1795: Jane McClurkam bounding lands of Watson Allison, land granted to Hastings Dial in1788 [See LCDBK F: 340]

McCullock, James: Survey for James McCullock pursuant to precept dated 22 June 1767: 100 acres in Craven Co., on a branch of Raiborn's Creek; bounded on all sides by vacant land. Certified 10 December 1767. Ralph Humphreys, D.S. (Bounty). [P18_191:1]

McCullock, James: Memorial for James McCullock; 100 acres in Craven Co., S.C., on a branch of Reybornes Creek. Bounded on all sides by vacant land. Certified 10 December 1767 and granted 8 March 1768. Quit rent to commence in 2 years. Ralph Humphreys, D.S. 2 August 1768. [M8_134:3]

McDaniel, Mary: 2 April 1792: Laurens Co., S.C.: Personally came and appeared Mary McDaniel and under solemn affirmation says that sometime in the fall of 1781, there came to her home a company of men unknown to her this Deponent, one of which gave her a large paper said it belonged to one of her neighbours concerning his land which the paper was put in a box in her house. Sometime afterwards Shadrack Martin and others came to her said house and took said papers out of the box and the Martin said *that the paper belonged to Richard Carrel* and that he would take them and deliver them to the said Richard for he was his near neighbour and accordingly did take it. 2 April 1791. Mary (mark) McDaniel. Before Jonathan Downs, J.C. [LCDBK D: 31]

McDaniel, William: Survey for William McDaniel pursuant to precept dated 6 February 1771; 100 acres in Berkley Co., S.C., on Raburn's Creek; Butting and bounding to the NE on William O'Daniel; SW on Bounty land, name not known; all other sides on vacant land. Certified 27 March 1771. Pat. Cunningham, D.S. Ord. Co. 1 December 1772. [P18_202:1]

McDaniel, William: Memorial for William McDaniel; 100 acres in Berkley Co., S.C., on Rayburns Creek. Bounding NE on (torn) Daniel; SW on Bounty land name not known; other sides vacant. Certified 1 December 1772 and granted 24 December 1772. Quit rent to commence in 2 years. 24 May 1773. Delivered 9 October 1773 to Thomas McDonald. P. Cunningham, D.S. [M12_195:4]

McDaniel, William: 3 April 1805: Wm. McDaniel, deceased by 1805: 3 April 1805: Robert Allison, of Laurens Dist., S.C., to Mary McDaniel, of same place, widow of the late William McDaniel, deceased, and to Sarah and William McDaniel, children and heirs at law of the said deceased for $100; 150 acres on waters of Raborns Creek. Bounding on lands of Thomas Burton, W. Manley, J. Cochran, Thos. Johnston. *Being part of a tract of 500 acres formerly granted to H.D. Bize* and by sundry conveyances to me the said Robert Allison. Robert Allison (LS) Wit: Hastings Dial, John Cochran. Proved by John Cochran 5 March 1806 before J. Blackwell, J.P. [See Piece Butler to Bize to Allison] [LCDBK J: 29]

McDannld, *sic* **William:** 19 January 1804: Estate of William McDannel, dec'd. Administration of estate granted to wife Mary. Sec: Rowling, Thos. Davenport. [LCWBK C-1: 92]

McDaniel, William: [no date]: Sale of estate of William McDaniel [undated] purchasers Saml. Williams, Jr. Washington Manley, Jas. McCaine, Wm. Hill, Jas. Crumme (Abercrombie), Wm. Mathis, Wm. Williams, Edwd. Box, John Burton, Robert Allison, Mary McDaniel, Archibald McDaniel. Adm. Mary McDaniel [LCWBK C-1: 101]

McDaniel, William: Survey for William McDaniel pursuant to precept dated 6 February 1771; 100 acres in Berkley Co., on Raburn's Creek; Butting and bounding to the NE on William O'Daniel's; SW on Bounty land, name not known; other sides vacant. Certified 27 March 1771. Pat. Cunningham, D.S. Ord. Co. 1 December 1772. [P18_202:1]

McDaniel, William: Memorial for William McDaniel; 100 acres in Berkley Co., on Rayburns Creek. Bounding NE on (torn) Daniel; SW on Bounty land name not known; other sides vacant. Certified 1 December 1772 and granted 24 December 1772. Quit rent to commence in 2 years. 24 May 1773. Delivered 9 October 1773 to Thomas McDonald. P. Cunningham, D.S. [M12_195:4]

McDonald, William: 5 January 1795: Archibald McDonald, of Laurens Co. S.C., and Thomas Childers, of same place. Witnessseth that said Archibald McDonald for the sum of £35 Stg., 100 acres on the waters of Reaburns Creek, being *land granted to William McDonald* by Honorable Lord Charles Montague by patent December 1772. The above sold tract containing 100 acres all which the said Archabald McDaniel and Editha his wife hath granted and sold to him the said Thomas Childress. Archd. McDaniel (L.S.) Editha (her mark) McDaniel (L.S.) Wit: Isaac Norman, Samuel Green. Probed 16 March 1795 by Samuel Green before Jonathan Downs, J.P. [LCDBK E: 448-499]

McDonald, William: 27 July 1807: I Archibald McDaniel, Junr., of Dist. of Laurens, S.C., to William Johnson, of same place, for $150; 186 lying on the waters of Rabourns Creek, bounded by Duke Pinson, James Abercrombie, Archibald McDaniel, Senr., Moses Pinson, and Isaac Dial. Archd. McDaniel (LS) Wit: Jeremiah Manley, Thos. Wright. Proved by Thomas Wright 1 August 1807 before Josiah Blackwell, J.P. [See Rachel Turk's will - Archibald McDaniel brother] [LCDBK H: 241 - 242]

McDonald, William: 8 August 1809: Archibald McDaniel, Junior, of Laurens Dist., S.C., to James Boyd and William Boyd, Junr., of same place, for $400; 186 acres on Sandy Branch, waters of Reaburns Creek. [Plat shows] Bounded on Marmaduke Pinson, Abercrombie, Moses Pinson, A. McDonald, James and William Boyd, J. Dial. Archd. McDaniel (LS). Wit: Robert Lowry, John Cochran. Dower by Elizabeth McDaniel, wife of the within named Archbald McDaniel given 28 November 1809 (but signed as Editha (her mark) McDaniel. Proved by John Cochran __ December 1809. Before [torn] [LCDBK J: 123]

McDonald, William: 2 August 1809: William Boyd, of Laurens Dist., S.C., to James Boyd and William Boyd, Junior, of same place, for $100; 94 ½ acres on a branch of Reaburns Creek called Sandy Branch. Wm. Boyd. (LS). Wit: Thomas Cunningham, John Cochran. Proved by John Cochran 27 December 1809 before Chas. Allen, Q.M.[Plat shows bounded on Jno. Box, Pinson and McDaniel, J. Dial, William Boyd. [LCDBK J: 123]

McDonald, Williams: 7 September 1818: William Boyd, Senr, of Laurens Dist., S.C., to James Boyd, of same place, for $500; 300 acres on Sandy Branch, waters of Reaburns Creek. Wm. Boyd (LS). Wit: Asa Chandler, John Robertson. Proved by John Robertson 1 February 1819 before Chas. Allen, J.M. [LCDBK K: 236]

McHarg, John: Survey for John McHarg pursuant to precept dated 7 November 1769; 150 acres in Berkley Co., on the waters of Rebuns Creek. Bounded on vacant land. Certified 11 January 1770. Pat. Cunningham, D.S. Ord. Co. 1 March 1775 for Peter Leger. See Peter Leger for memorial. [P16_318:2]

McHarg, John: - See memorial for Peter Leger.

McHarg, John: 11 October 1792: Fredk. Freasure, of the City of Charleston, S.C., to Jacob Roberts, of Laurens Dist., S.C., for £73 Stg.; 436 acres on waters of Raburns Creek, *being part of 950 acres originally granted to William Williamson* and by him conveyed to Frederick Freasure; by said Frederick Freasure, by his attorney John Hunter, to sd Jacob Robert, which tract of 436 in two tracts joining each other. Frederick Freasure by his attorney John Hunter, (LS) Wit: Rodger Brown, John Cromton. [Plat of 128 acres shows land bounded by owner unknown, survey sold to John F. Wolff, John Mahony and Plat of 308 acres bounded by James Lindley, Jno. Maharg]. 1(308 acres of 950 acres granted to Wm. Williamson bounded on James Lindley and John McHarg; 2) part of *128 acres of same grant bounded on John McHarg and J.F. Wolff.* [LCDBK H: 178-179]

McHarg, John: 20 September 1783. Estate administered by Susannnah McHarg, Adam Goudalock [?]. Robert Bolt bound to Jno. Thomas, Jr. Ord. 96 Dist., S.C., sum £2,000. Inventory made November 1783 by Robt. Bolt, Robt., Jno. Woods. [Box 63, Pack 1509] [Young, pg. 213]

McHarg, Susannah: 20 October 1795: Susannah McHarg a witnesses with James Parker and Thomas Parker in the LWT of Robert Bolt, Jr. [LCWBK A: 143]

McHarg, Susannah: 5 June 1805: Susan McHarg, of Laurens Dist., S.C., widow, to my son John McHarg for $50; 110 acres on a branch of Reaburns

Creek called Lick Creek. *Being part of a tract originally granted to said Susannah McHarg.* Susannah McHarg (LS) Wit: William Kelley, Wm. H. Downs. Before Jonthan. Downs, J.Q. [Plat shows bounded on Charles Henderson, Jacob Roberts, William. McHarg, and heirs of R. Bolts.] [LCDBK J: 167]

McHarg, [McHurg], Archibald: 24 August 1793: Archibald Mchurg *sic*, of Laurens Co., S.C., to Benjamin Camp, of same place, planter, for £12 Stg. a tract of 100 acres on Mountain creek, a branch of Reaburns creek. Granted to said Mchurg 2 August 1790. Bounded by Jonathan Downs, not known, Benjamin Camp, Calvin Coker, Road to Wolff's store. Wit: Jonathan Downs, J.F. Wolff. Signed Archabald (A) Mchurg. Proved by J.F. Wolff 28 January 1794 before Joseph Downs, J.P. [LCDBK E: 126-128]

McHarg, [McHurg, McHurgh], Archibald: 28 September 1793: Archabald McHurgh, of Laurens Co., S.C., to Salatheil Shockley, of same place, for £50; 150 acres on Mchurgs creek a branch of Reaburns creek, which Salathiel Shockley now possesses, being part of a tract granted to Nehemiah Franks. Bounded by Charles Garey, Stephen Potter, and vacant land. Wit: James Floyd, Drew Coker, Thomas Coker, Signed Archibel (A) Mchurg. Proved by Drury Coker 29 August 1794 before Jonthn. Downs, J.P. [LCBDK E: 277-278]

McHarg, [McHurg], Archibald: 4 March 1801: We Robert Coker, Junr. and Wm. Helms, of Laurens Dist. S.C., to James Downey, of the State of N. C., for $300; 165 acres on a branch of Rabourns Creek called Mountain Creek. *Being part of two tracts originally one being originally granted to John Hunter, the other originally granted to Archibald McHurge.* Robert Coker, Junr. (LS) Wm. Hellems (LS).Wit: Wm. Owings, Aaron Moore. Proved by Wm. Owings on 4 March 1801 before Jonathan Downs, J.Q. [Two Plats shown by Jonthan Downs, D.S. Plat 1) for 100 acres shows bounded by owner unknown, Jonathan Downs, Benj. Camp, William Hellems, road to Wolffs store, land claimed by Calvin Coker. Plat 2) 65 acres shows bounded by David Gibson, John Armstrong, James Downey, on Road to Wolffs store]. [LCDBK G: 190-191]

McHarg, [McHurg], Archibald: 4 November 1805: Security for estate of William McHurg, deceased. Administration of estate granted to John McHarg and Susanna McHurg. [LCWBK C-1: 179]

[See Laurens Co. DD Bk. H: 145 for James McClintock to John Harry, land granted 17 March 1775; on Raburns Creek, also called James McLinto in document.]

McClennan [McLennan], John: Survey for John McLennan pursuant to Precept dated 6 Jan 1773; 220 acres in Craven Co., NE side of Reyburn's Creek, on a branch thereof called Bradshaw's Branch. Bounded S on Capt. James Lindley and Philip Sherrill; N and NE by land of John Owings and Alexr. Cormack; N and NW by land laid out unknown and David Rea. Certified 10 February 1773. [P18_294:1]

McClennan/McClanahan, John: Memorial by John McClennan; 220 acres in Craven Co., NE sides of Raburnes Creek, on Bradshaws Branch. Bounding S on land of Capt. James Lindly and Philip Sherrel; N and NE on Owings and Alexander Cormack; N and NW unknown and David Red(?). Certified 10 February 1773 and granted 19 August 1774. Quit rent to commence in 2 years. Jonathan Downs, D.S. [M13_289:6]

McClanahan/McClennan, John: 2 September 1799: James McClanahan, of Laurens Co., S.C., to Thomas Burton, of same place, for £40 Stg.; 151 acres on waters of Reaburns Creek. *Being part of a tract of 220 acres originally conveyed to John McClanaham 19 August 1774,* and by the said James McClanahan (son and heir of the aforesaid John McClanahan). James McClanahan. Wit: John Cochran, William Burton. Proved by William Burton 13 February 1801 before J. A. Elmore, J.Q. [Plat shows bounded by David Read, unknown survey, Alex Cormack, James Lindley]. [LCDBK G: 154-155]

McClanahan, William: 28 June 1823: I William McClanahan, of Laurens Dist., S.C., to Thomas F. Jones and Samuel Dorrus, of said place, for $252; 260 acres on the branches of Dirty Creek, a fork of Rabourns Creek. Bounded E by James Todd and Charles Hobbs, NW by William Hobbs and Hastin Dial, SW by M. Madden, S by Robert Todd. With the exception of 33 and 3/4 acres contained in said plat and lying in the fork of the two branches which intersect above James Bates [Motes] spring (formerly William Hobbs). Wm. McClanahan (LS). Wit. R.F. Simpson, John Blakeley. Proved by Richard F. Simpson 28 June 1823 before John Garlington, Clk. & J. Q. [Plat made 24 July 1816 by John Cochran, D.S. shows bounding Robert Todd, M. Madden, Has. Dial, William Hobbs, Charles Hobbs, Jas. Todd; survey made 24 July 1816 by John Cochran, D.S.] [LCDBK L: 112]

McClinto/McLinto, James: Survey for James McLinto pursuant to precept dated 11 December 1772; 100 acres in Craven Co., on the waters of Raburn's Creek. Bounding SE on land of Joseph Babb, NE on land of Wm. Burriss; NW on land of Elizabeth Hood. SW vacant. Certified 29 December 1772. Wm. Thos. Caldwell, D.S. [P18_292:3]

McClinto/McLinto, James: Memorial for James McLinto; 100 acres in Craven Co., waters of Rayburns Creek. Bounding SE on Joseph Babb; NE on Wm. Buriss; NW on Eliza. Hood; SW vacant. Certified 20 September 1774 and granted 17 March 1775. Quit rent 2 years. Wm. Thos. Caldwell. Delivered [?] December 1775 to Geo. Norwood. [Note "Irish" in margin]. [M2_293:6]

McClinto [McClintock], James: 15 July 1792: James McClintock of Laurens Co., Ninety Six Dist., to John Harry, of same for £15 Stg.; 100 acres on the waters of Raburns Creek. *Originally granted 17 March 1775 to James McLinto*. Signed James McClintock, Margaret McClintock (her mark). Wit: David Madden, Rodger Murphy 19 July 1791. Proved by David Madden 25 October 1803 before Josiah Blackwell, J.P. [LCDBK H: 144-145]

McClinto [McClintock], James: 23 January 1806: S.C., Laurens Dist. : I John Harry, of Laurens Dist., S.C., to James Huggins, of same place, for £100; 82 acres on waters of Rabourns Creek, part of *originally grant to James McClintock.* [Plat shows bounded on John Harry, Solomon Cole, J. Huggins. John Harry] Wit: Solomon Cole, Aaron Pinson. Proved by Solomon Cole 20 February 1807 before Josiah Blackwell, J.P. [Note: McClintock/McClinto appear to be same persons.] [LCDBK J: 37]

McClurkam, Mary: Survey for Mary McClurkam pursuant to precept dated 6 January 1773: 100 acres in Craven Co., on NE side of Rayburns Creek, on a small branch thereof called the Lick Branch. Bounded S and SW by William Williamson, Esq. and Thomas Weir, Jr.; NE by James Tweed; all other sides by vacant land. Certified 20 March 1773. Jona. Downs, D.S. [Irish] [P18_150:2]

McClurkam, Mary: Memorial for Mary McClurkam; 100 acres in Craven Co., NE of Rayburns Creek on Lick branch. Bounding S and SW on William Williamson and Thos. Weir Jr.; SE on James Tweed; other sides vacant. Certified 20 September 1774 and granted 17 March 1775. Quit rent 2 years. 14 August 1775. Jonathan Downes. D.S. [M2_291:3]

McKearmy (McKenney, McKemmey), Robert: Survey for Robert McKearmy pursuant to precept dated 5 November 1771: 100 acres in Berkley Co., on the waters of Raburn Creek. Bounding SW on land, name not known; NE on Thomas Mathess; all other sides on vacant land. Certified 21 December 1771. Pat. Cunningham, D.S. [P18_267:1]

McKenney, Robert: Memorial for Robert McKenney; 100 acres in Berkley Co., waters of Rayburn Creek. Bounding SW on land name not known. N on

Thomas Mathess; other sides vacant. Certified 21 December 1771 and granted 21 May 1772. Quit rent to commence in 2 years. 13 August 1772. Delivered 3 November 1772 to Hugh Brown. Patrick Cunningham, D.S. [M11_342:2]

McKenney, Robert: 12 March 1804: Thomas MacDonald, of Spartanburg Dist., S.C., planter, to Thomas Mathis, of Laurens Dist., S.C., for $200; 100 acres on the S fork Rabourns Creek as represented by a plat bearing date 5 November 1771 *annexed then from Robert McKenney* from him to Thomas McDaniel and from him to Thomas Mathis. Thomas McDonald (LS) Wit: Joseph Brown, John Spurgin. Proved by Joseph Brown 13 March 1804 before Danl. Wright, J.Q. [LCDBK H: 50]

McLean, James: No date: Grant of 100 acres.

McLean, James: 31 August 1792: Samuel McClurkin, of Laurens Co., S.C., to Edward Level, of same place, for £60 Stg., 60 acres on Reedy Creek. *Being part of 100 acres grant to James McLean by Wm. Bull [no date given].* Saml. McClurkin. Wit: E. Stonestreet Owings, Matthew Bolton. Proved by Edward Stonestreet Owings 17 March 1800 before James Abercrombie, J.P. [LCDBK G: 37]

McLean, Daniel: 3 February 1794: Aaron Steele, of Abbeville Co., S.C., am held and firmly bound and obligated unto Samuel McClurkin, of Laurens Co., S.C., in the full sum of £40 Stg. To be paid to the said Samuel McClarkin, his heirs, executors and administrations and truly to be made I bind myself, my heirs executers firmly by these presents this 3 February 1794. The conditions of the above obligations is such that if the above bond Aaron Starnes, his heirs, executors or administrators shall and will and truly make of cause to be made unto the above named Samuel McClarkin his heirs, executers a good and sufficient title and conveyance in law the tract of 50 acres on Reedy River it *being part of a tract of land laid out for Daniel McLean* and formerly possessed by Archible Owings. Bounded on the S by land now in the possession of the said Samuel McClarkin. Aaron Steele (LS) Wit: John Findly, Jane Steele. Proved by John Finley 16 October 1800 before Wm. Garrett, J.P. Edgefield Dist., S.C. [LCDBK G: 92]

McLennan, John: Survey for John McLennan pursuant to Precept dated 6 Jan 1773: 220 acres in Craven Co., NE side of Reyburn's Creek, on a branch thereof called Bradshaw's Branch. Bounded S on Capt. James Lindley and Philip Sherril; N and NE by land of John Owings and Alexr. Cormack; N and NW by land laid out unknown and David Rea. Certified 10 February 1773. Jon. Downs, D.S. [P18_294:1]

McLennan, John: Memorial for John McLennan; 220 acres in Craven Co., NE side of Reyburn's Creek, on Bradshaw's Branch. Bounded S on Capt. James Lindley and Philip Sherril; N and NE by land of Owings and Alexander Cormack; N and NW by land laid out unknown and David Rea. Certified 10 February 1773 and granted 19 August 1774. Quit rent to commence in 2 years. 7 February 1775. Jonathan Downs, D.S. [M13_289:6]

McKnight, Andrew: 8 February 1789: LWT of Andrew McKnight. I Andrew McNight, Senr., of Laurens Co., S.C. To Abigail my dearly beloved wife whom I constitute and ordain my Executor all the cleared land on the plantation whereon I now live during her life. .also I give to my well beloved daughter Abigail a sorrel mare. I will to my beloved daughter Jennet a sorrel colt. .to my son Archibald all the land on the west side of Reaburns Creek that I possess after my wifes decease. Andrew McNight, Senr. Wit: Martin Huey, Jno. Alexander, David Morton. [LCWBK A: 15]

[Family: Wife, Abigail, daughters, Abigail, Jennet, son Archibald McKnight.]

McKnight, John, land granted no date given [See below]

McKnight, John: 15 June 1811: John Stone, of Laurens Dist., S.C., to George Fowler, of same place, for $85; 100 acres on Raburn Creek, *part of a tract of land originally grant to John McKnight.* [Plat shows bounded on John McNight, John Harris, Polly Jone[s]. John Stone (x) (LS). Wit: Aaron Moore, Saml. S. Cammel. Proved by Aaron Moore 15 November 1811 before Jesse Childress, J.P. [LCDBK J: 242]

McKnight, John: 28 October 1818: Andrew McKnight, of Laurens Dist., S.C., to Richard Childress, of same place, for $100; *100 acres being part of a grant to John McKnight* on waters of Raburns Creek. Bounded on John McKnight's old line, Aberombies old line, Jesse Childress' line. Andrew McKnight. Wit: John Pels, Robert (X) Woods. Proved by Robert Woods 1 September 1819 before Jno. Abercrombie, J.P. [LCDBK K: 258]

McKnight, John: 15 December 1818: Richard Childress, of Laurens Dist., S.C., to Felt Hatcher, of same place, for $300; 123 acres *being part of a tract of land originally granted to John McKnight* and from John McKnight to John Stone and from John Stone to George Fowler and from said Fowler to John Hatcher and from Hatcher to William Hughs and from said Hughs to Richard Childress and from said Childress to Felt Hatcher. Being land on waters of Rabons Creek. Bounding John Harris, Polly Jones, John McKnight. Richard Childress. Wit: Robert (x) Woods. Jona. Abcrombie, J.P.

Probed by Robert Woods this day 1810. [LCDBK K: 258]

McKnight, John: 13 April 1821: John Terry [could be Berry], of Laurens Dist., S.C., to Micajah Berry of Greenville Dist., S.C.; for $133.75; 100 acres on the waters of the South fork of Raburns Creek. Bounding Wm. McMahan, Widow Sims. John Gerry, Senior, (LS). Wit; James Kellet, Rafe[?] (X) Cummel[?]. Proved by James Kellett 14 April 1821 before Jonathan Abrombie *sic*, J.P. [LCDBK L: 7]

McKnight, John: 16 December 1826: Easter Sims, of the State of Georgia [no County given], to Micajah Berry, of Laurens Dist., S.C., for $100; 71 acres in S.C., Laurens Dist., on the waters of the S fork of Raburns Creek. *Being part of a tract of land originally granted to John McKnight* and conveyed from him to the said Easter Sims. Bounding by William McMahan, SE on a branch, including land where James Sims lately lived. Easter (her mark) Sims. Wit: Thomas W. Alexander, Olly Ann (her mark) Sims. Proved by Thomas W. Alexander 5 January 1827 before Jonathan Acrombie, J.P. [LCDBK L: 262]

McNeese, Robert: 1785: 200 acres of land granted on Reedy River.

McNeese, Robert: 28 February 1805: Robert McNeese, of Laurens Dist., S.C., to Samuel Roseman, of Abbeville Dist., S.C., for $100; 200 acres on Reedy River. *Originally granted to said Robert McNeese 21 January 1785.* Robert McNeese (LS) Wit: Richard Owing, Senr., Frances Downs. Dower of Mary McNeese given 29 February 1804 before Jonathan Downs, J.Q. Proved by Richard Owings, Senr. 8 February 1804 before Jonthan Downs, J.Q. [LCDBK H: 11]

McNeese, Robert: 18 December 1804: Robert Hezlett, of Laurens Dist., S.C., to Ezekiel Andrews, of same place, for $500; 96 acres on Reedy River *being part of 200 acres originally granted to Robert McNeese on 25 January 1785* by his Excellency Benjn. Guerand and which said tract of land was made over from Samuel Rosamond to said Robert Hezlett by a deed bearing the data 17 March 1804. Robt. Hezlet (LS) Wit: Isaac Cook, James McClurkan. Dower of Nancy Hazlett (S) made 24 March 1804 before David Anderson, J.Q. Proved by James McClurken before David Anderson, J.Q. [LCDBK H: 67-68]

McNeese, Robert: 17 March 1804: Samuel Rosamond, of Abbeville Dist., S.C., to Robert Hazlett, of Laurens Dist., S.C., for $192; 96 acres on Reedy River, *being part of a 200 acres tract of land originally granted to Robert McNeese 24 January 1785.* Saml. Rosamond (LS). Wit: Isaac Cook, James McClurkin. Dower of Salley (X) Rosamond given 22 March 1804 before Adm. Cr. Jones, J.Q. Proved by Isaac Cook 23 February 1805 before J.

Blackwell, J.P. [Plat by A.C. Jones, D.S. shows bounded by Breen [?] dec'd. [LCDBK H: 77]

McPherson, Isaac: Survey for Isaac McPherson pursuant to precept dated 1 September 1772: 400 acres in Craven Co., on the waters of Reburn's Creek. Bounding NW part on Benj. Elliott; part on Samuel Elliott; other sides name not known. Certified 22 October 1772. Pat. Cunningham, D.S. [18_323:1]

McPherson, Isaac: Memorial for Isaac McPherson; 400 acres in Craven Co., on the waters of Rayburns Creek. Bounding NW on Benjamin Elliott; (torn) Saml. Elliott; other sides name not known. Certified 22 October 1772 and granted (torn) December 1772. (torn) April 1773. Delivered 19 May 1773 to W. Williamson. (?) Cunningham, D.S. [M12_171:1]

McPherson, Isaac: 28 & 29 December 1772: Isaac McPherson of St. Pauls Parish, Colleton Co., Esq. to William Williamson, Esq. of Charlestown [several parcels, one being]; 400 acres in Craven Co., on waters of Reyburns Creek. Bounding Benjamin Elliotts, Samuel Elliotts. *Originally granted on said day to Isaac McPherson.* Wit: Robt. Ladson, Edwd. Parry. Recorded 2 September 1773. [Charleston DD Bk. G_4, pp 50_55; Holcomb, Bk. F_4_X_4, pg. 23.]

McQueen, John: Memorial for John McQueen; 500 acres (1 of 11 tracts), on a branch of Saludy called Rayburns Creek. Bounding on all sides by vacant land. Certified 2 February 1773 and all granted 11 February 1773 to the memorialist. 23 June 1773 Wm. Anderson. Delivered 20 June 1773 to William Williamson, D.S. [See John Shirley for Survey] [M12_261:1]

Millhouse family: Quakers.

Millhouse, Robert: Survey for Robert Millhouse pursuant to precept dated 4 January 1763; 150 on the north side of Saludy River on Reaburns Creek in Berkley Co. Bounded on all sides by vacant land. Certified 17 February 1763. _____, D.S. [P7_335:3]

Millhouse, Robert: Memorial for Robert Millhouse; 150 acres in Berkley Co., on the N side of Saludy River, on Reaburns Creek. Bounded by vacant land. Certified 17 February 1763 and granted 18 May 1763. Quit rent to commence in 2 years. 13 July 1763. Jno. Belton, D.S. Jas. Hushaw [Henshaw?]. [M6_102:1]

Mitchell, Nimrod: Survey for Nimrod Mitchell pursuant to precept dated 5 March 1768; 200 acres on Long Branch of Raiburns Creek in Craven Co. Bounded on all sides by vacant land. Certified 29 April 1768. R. Humphreys,

D.S. [P9_241:2]

Mitchell, Nimrod: Memorial for Nimrod Mitchell; 200 acres in Craven Co., on Long branch of Rayburns Creek. Bounded on all sides by vacant land. Certified 29 April 1768 and granted 25 August 1769. Quit rent to commence in 2 years. 12 October 1769.For the memorialist James Currey. Ralph Humphreys, D.S. [M8_523:5]

Mitchell, Nimrod: 14 March 1789: Nimrod Mitchell, of Laurens Co., S.C., to Benjamin Smith, of same place, for £60 Stg.; 200 acres on Long Branch of Reaburns Creek. Bounded on all sides on vacant land at the time of survey. *Originally granted 20 August 1769 to [Nimrod Mitchell.]* Signed Nimrod Mitchell. Wit: William Mortimer, Aml. Arthur, J.P. Proved by Aml. Arthur *sic* 4 March 1789 before (blank). [LCDBK C: 105]

Mitchell, Nimrod: 14 March 1789: Benjamin Smith, Laurens Dist., S.C., to James Cuningham, of same place, for £75; 200 acres in the fork between Broad and Saluda River on Long branch of Raburns Creek. Bounded on all sides by vacant land at the time of survey. *Originally granted 20 August 1769 to [Nimrod Mitchell.]* Benjamin Smith (LS) Wit: John Pringle, Charles Garey. Proved by John Pringle 18 March 1789 before Jonathan Downs, J.P. [LCDBK C: 88-89]

Mitchell, Nimrod: 10 March 1821: Nimrod Mitchell, son of William Mitchell. Will of William Mitchell dated 10 March 1821, in Abbeville Dist. Proved 15 November 1821. Executers: Sons: John, Ephraim, Jas. Mitchell. Wit: James, Nimrod Mitchell. [Wife, Chole Mitchell. Children: Sarah, Nancy, John, Ephraim, William, James, Polly, Calous, Benjamin, Elizabeth Mitchell. Inventory made 13 December 1821 by Jas. Mitchell, Reuben Nash, Wm. Long. [Young, pg. 196- Box 59, Pack 1398]

[Family: Nimrod, son of William Mitchell. William Mitchell's family: Wife Chole, daughters Sarah, Nancy, Polly, Calous, Elizabeth, Sons; John Ephraim James, William, and Benjamin Mitchell.]

Mitchell, Nimrod: 13 November 1837: Estate of Nimrod Mitchell administered: by John Weatherall, James H. Kay, Noah Reeves, bound to Moses Taggart Ord. Abbeville Dist. Sum of $1,000.00. Citations Published at Turkey Creek Church. Espend: October 28, 1842. Legatees, John Mitchell $17.74, Mathew Bell $17.74, Alason (Alanson) Lord $17.74, Wm. Mitchell $19.00, A.W. Mitchell $17.74, A.W. Mitchell guardian for minors, George and Dicey Mitchell $35.00. Sale held 38 November 1837. [Young, pg. 194 - Box 58, Pack age 1382]

Mitchell, John, Appraiser: 3 January 1798: Appraisal of estate of David McGladery, dec'd by David Dunlap, John Mitchell, Wm. South. [LCWBK A: 184]

Mitchell, John, deceased: 13 October 1814: We David Michel, Isaac Mitchell, William Cole, David Robertson, John Lindley, Mary Michel [Mitchell] and John Baw [Baugh], legatees of John Michel, legatees of John Michel [Mitchell], deceased, of Laurens Dist., S.C., to James Hutson, of same, for $700; 200 aces on W side of Reedy River, being part of 500 acres *originally granted to Richard Hutson* and by him conveyed to Charles Tenant and by Tenant granted to John Mitchell. John Baugh (LS), John (x) Lindley (LS), Isaac Mitchell, William Cole, David Mitchell, David Robertson. Wit: James Bruster, Ezekiel Andrews, Daniel Ford. Dower of Mary Mitchell, wife of John Mitchell, deceased given 14 October 1814 before Jonthan Downs, J.Q. Mary (a her mark) Mitchell. Proved by James Bruster 14 October 1814 before Jonthn. Downs, J.Q. [LCDBK K: 200]

Mitchell, John, deceased: 18 October 1814: We the legatees of John Mitchell, deceased, namely John Findley, John Baugh, David Mitchell, Isaac Mitchell, David Robertson and Mary Mitchell, hath this day granted and sold unto William Cole for $395; 293 acres on waters of Reedy River. *It being a tract of land granted in the name of Richard Hudson* which we have sold. [Plat shows bounded on James Hudson, John Lindley, Mr. Fifer, Terrill Andrews, Wm. South.] John (X) Lindley (LS), John Baugh (LS), David Mitchell (LS), Mary (X) Mitchell (LS), Isaac Mitchell (LS). Wit: Robt. Allison, David Lindley. Proved by David Lindley 22 October 1814 before James Powell, J.P. [See K: 227 for John Hudson sale] [LCDBK K: 77]

Mitchell, John: 18 October 1814: We the legatees of John Mitchell, deceased namely John Lindley, John Baugh, David Mitchell, Isaac Mitchell, David Robertson and Mary Mitchell, to William Cole for $551; 160 acres on waters of Reedy River, which land has been sold as *confiscated property of Joshua Nims?, and part granted in name of Richard Hutson.* [Plat shows bounded on Jno. Lindley, James Hudson, Charles Smith. Wit: Robert Allison, David Lindley.] John (X) Lindley (LS), John Baugh (LS), David Mitchell (LS) Isaac Mitchell (LS) David Roberson (LS), Mary (a her mark) Mitchell (LS). Wit: Robt. Allison, David Lindley. Proved by David Lindley 22 October 1814 before James Powell, J.P. [LCDBK K: 76]

Mitchell, William: 18 June 1805: David Adams, of Laurens Dist., S.C., to William Mitchell, of same place, for $300; 48 and a half acres on Tumbling Shoals on Reedy River. David (X) Adams (LS) Jeremiah Hollingsworth, Elizabeth (X) Mitchell. Proved by Jeremiah Hollingsworth 10 August 1805 before Jonthan. Downs, J.Q. [Plat shows bounding on Abraham Box, Lewis Saxon, John Arnold, Samuel Nabours, and on the Waggon Road. [See David Adams] [LCDBK H: 109]

Mitchell, William: 28 October 1805: William Mitchell, of Laurens Dist., S.C., to William Arnold and Benjamin Arnold, of same place, for $400; 50 acres known by the name of Tumbling Shoals, lying on both sides of Reedy River. Being a tract of land conveyed by David Adams to William Mitchell by a deed dated 18 June 1805. Wm. Mitchell (LS). Wit: Jeremiah Hollingsworth, Arthur Taylor. Dower of Mary (X) Mitchell, wife of the within named William Mitchell given 5 November 1805 before Jonthan. Downs, J.Q. Proved that Jeremiah Hollingsworth 5 November 1805 before. Jonthan. Downs, J.Q [See David Adams] [LCDBK H: 112]

Monk, John: Survey for John Monk pursuant to precept [no date]: 300 acres in Ninety Six Dist. on Rayburns Creek. Bounding N on John Cunningham and James Williams; E on Ebenezer Stern and Lewis Banton; S on Joseph Pinson; W on Rayburns Creek, Richard Sherley [Shirley] and vacant land. Certified 25 December 1774. Jno. Caldwell, D.S. [P18_481:1]

Monk, John: Memorial by John Monk; 300 acres in 96 Dist. on Rayburns (Dist.) Creek. Bounding N by Jno. Cunningham and James Williams; E by Ebenezer Stern and Lewis Banton; S by Joseph Pinson; W by Richard Shelley and vacant land and Rayburns Creek. Certified 25 December 1774 and granted 10 February 1775. Quit rent to commence in 2 years. 12 July 1775. Delivered 21 March 1778 to John Caldwell. Jno. Caldwell, D.S. [M14_7:2]

Moore, William: 26 November 1792: William Moore, of Laurens Co., S.C., to Wiseman Box, of same place, for £41 Stg.; 300 acres on both sides of Reaburns creek, where William Moore, Edward Box and Henry Box now lives. Bounding lands of Charles Braidey and Millhouse. Wit: John Wadkins, John Moore, Henry Box. Signed William Moore. Proved by oath of Henry Box 18 February 1794 before Joseph Downs, J.P. [LCDBK E: 398-399]

Morgan, David: Survey for David Morgan pursuant to precept dated 7 November 1769: 200 acres in Berkley Co., on the waters of Reburn's Creek. Bounded on all sides by vacant land. Certified 11 January 1770. Pat. Cunningham, D.S. Ord. Co. 8 July 1774. [P18_535:2]

Morgan, David: Memorial by David Morgan; 200 acres in Berkley Co., on the waters of Reyburns Creek. Bounded on vacant land. Certified 8 July 1774 and granted 9 September 1774. Quit rent to commence in 2 years. 21

179

March 1775. Patrick Cunningham, D.S. [M13_401:6]

Morgan, David; 19 March 1804: Morgan Morgan, of Pendleton Dist., S.C., to J.F. Wolff, merchant, of Laurens Dist., S.C., for $300; 200 acres on waters of Raburns Creek. Bounded on said John F. Wolff, land *granted to David Morgan 9 September 1774.* Morgan Morgan [LS]. Wit: Jno. Pringle, Wm. Morgan. Proved by John Pringle 23 April 1804 before Joseph Downs, J.P. [LCDBK H: 32]

Motes [Moats], Jonathan: 30 December 1845: LWT Laurens Dist., S.C. In the name of God Amen. I Jonathan Moats of Laurens Dist., in the State aforesaid, being of sound and to make this to be my Last Will and Testament. bequeath unto my wife Susan one negro woman named Rachel. I will and desire that my wife Susan be comfortable and decently maintained. .by my son-in-law Benjamin Reynolds and my daughter Dicy Ann, his wife I will to my daughter Dicy Ann Reynolds the tract of land whereon I now reside and one negro boy named Joe and one woman named Lucy and her boy, .Jack. I will my daughter Betsey Moates, wife of Chesley Moates. I will to my daughter Mineva Pinson, wife of John Pinson $180. Appoint my son-in-law Benjamin Reynolds, Executor. Set his hand 30 December 1845. Jonathan (X) Moats Wilt G. Thomas, H. Finley, Sr., Reuben A. Griffin. [Bundle 104, Pkg. 7] [LCWBK A: 57]

[Family: Wife Susan, Son-in-law Benjamin Reynolds and my daughter Dicy Ann, his wife, daughter Betsey Moates, wife of Chesley Moates, daughter Mineva Pinson, wife of John Pinson.]

Motes, Jonathan: 15 May 1848: Benjamin Reynolds, of Laurens Dist., S.C., to Margaret Brown and R.C. Brown for $35.; 87 acres on Burris Creek bounded by land of William Madden, Hampton Finley and Elihu Madden. Ben Reynolds, (LS). Wit. J.E. Madden, W. Eppes. Dower of Dicy Ann Reynolds, wife of the within named Benjamin Reynolds 18 May 1858. Proved by John W. Eppes 2 October 1848 before John Garlington, Clk, L. Dist. [LCDDK P: 98]

[Family: Wife, Susan, daughters Dicy Ann Motes, wife of Benjamin Reynolds. Betsey, wife of Chesley Moates, Mineva, wife of John Pinson. Dicy Ann received land in her father's will. See Jonathan Motes, deceased LWT dated December 30, 1845.]

Nabours [Neighbors], Benjamin: 2 February 1804: Stephen Barnett, of Laurens Dist., S.C., to Thomas Land, of same place, for $100; 135 acres on the branches of Dirty Creek. *Being part of a survey originally granted and previously conveyed by Benjamin Nabours* to Francis Nabours and from

Roland, Menoah (M) Sullivan. Proved by Menoah (X) Sullivant, Senr 21 July 1804 before Jno. Davis, J.P. [LCDBK H: 51]

Neighbors, Samuel: *Original grant on 5 September 1785 for 248* acres on Reedy River.

Neighbors, Samuel: 17 August 1786: Robert Box and Robert Box, Jr. and Samuel Neighbours witness deed of John Goodwin to Elizabeth Jones 20 acres of land joining to where she now lives containing 70 acres. Grant dated 1 August 1785. [LCDBK A: 340]

Neighbors, Samuel: 14 September 1805: I Samuel Neighbors, of Greenville Dist., S.C., to John Alexander Jones, of Laurens Co., S.C., for $500; 248 acres on Reedy River. *Originally granted 5 September 1785 to said Samuel Neighbors.* Bounded on Abraham Box, Samuel Neighbors, James Riley and said John Alexander Jones, James Pool. Samuel Neighbors (LS). Wit: Henry Ridgeway, William Williams. Dower of Rebecca Neighbors, wife of the within named Samuel Neigbours given 16 September 1805 before Benja. Arnold, J.Q. Proved by Henry Ridgeway 20 November 1805 before William Arnold, J.P. [LCDBK H: 124-125]

Neeley/Neely: William: 1773 bounding Hastings Dial.

Niblet, Solomon: Certified Solomon Niblet pursuant to precept dated 1 March 1768; 400 acres in Craven Co., on north fork of Raibourns Creek, branch of Saludy River. Bounded by vacant land. Certified 31 March 1768. W. Gist., D.S. [P9_311:3]

Niblett, Solomon: Memorial for Solomon Niblett; 400 acres in Craven Co., on the W fork of Rayburns Creek, a branch of Saludy River. Bounded on all sides on vacant land. Certified 7 March 1769 and granted 22 March 1769. Quit rent to commence in 2 years. 2 June 1769. Wm. Gist, D.S. For the memorialist James Abercrombie. [M8_447:3]

Niblett, Solomon: 1 March 1787: Solomon Niblet and Mary his wife, of Laurens Co., S.C., to Joshua Saxon, of same for £200 Stg., 400 acres on Reighburns Creek waters of Saluda River. Bounded at time of the original survey on vacant land. *Originally granted to Solomon Niblet 22 March 1769.* Solomon (X) Niblet. Wit: Robert Cooper, Joshua Downs, Joseph Downs. [LCDBK B: 70-72]

Niblett, Solomon: 16 & 17 January 1775: Solomon Niblett of 96 Dist., SC, planter, and Mary, his wife to Abner Busship *sic* of said Dist., miller, for £500 S.C. money; 200 acres in said Dist. on a branch of Saludy called

Rayburns Creek; being the lower half of a tract whereon said Solomon
Niblett lives, including the mill with all the appurtences hereto belonging.
Granted to said Niblet by George III. Solomon Niblett (X), Mary Niblet
(mark). Wit: W. Paine, Mary Paine. Proved 96 Dist. 18 Jan 1775 by oath of
Wm. Paine before James Linle[y], J.P. Rec. 12 November 1787. [Brent H.
Holcomb; *South Carolina Deed Abstracts 1783_1788*, Charleston Deed
Book. Z_5, 300, 301, SCMAR Columbia, SC, 1996, p. 452]

Niblett, Solomon: 29 January 1789: Wm. Thomason, of Laurens Co., S.C.,
to Benjamin Camp, of Rutherford, North Carolina, for £250; 200 acres on
Rayburns creek, on the N fork of said creek & on both sides, including
Thomasons mill. Bounding Woolfs corner, Thomasons old field. . . . Niblets
old line to the mountain creek. .And *granted to Solomon Niblet 27 March
1769.* Conveyed from Niblet to Bishop and from Byshop [Bishop] to
Nathan Austin and from Nathan Austin to Wm. Thomason. Signed Wm.
Thomason, Mourning Thomason. Wit: Charles Sullivant. Nathan Camp
gave oath that he saw Wm. Thomason Senr. & Mourning his wife sign seal
and deliver the within deed. . Signed 4 February 1790 Nathan Camp, before,
Jonathan Downs, J.P. [LCDBK C: 208-209]

Niblet, Solomon: 15 August 1790: Benjamin Camp, of Laurens Co., S.C.,
planter, to John Francis Wolff, of same place, merchant, for £50 Stg.; 98 ½
acres on Reaburns Creek, *being part of originally grant to Solomon Niblet
22 March 1769 and conveyed to Abner Bisop [Bishop] from him to Nathan
Austin and from said Austin to William Thomason, from said Wm. Thomason
to Benjamin Camp.* Bounded on Ezekiel Mathews, William Thomason and
Sarah Morgan. Benjamin Camp (XX), Elizabeth (+) Camp. Wit: Lewis
Saxon, Robert Atkins, Joseph Camp. Plat shows bounded by Ezekiel
Mathews, Sarah Morgan, William Thomason, Benjn. Camp.
[LCDBK C: 231- 233]

Niblet, Solomon: 22 July 1790: John [and] Jennet Killett, of Ninety Six
Dist., and Laurens Co., S.C., farmer, to William Thomason, of same place,
carpenter, for £10 Stg.; 200 acres on Raborns creek waters of Saluda river
and being the upper part of a tract of 400 acres of land. Bounded on all sides
on vacant land, being part of a tract of land *originally granted unto Solomon
Niblet 22 March 1769.* In witness John and Jenet Kellet, his mother. John
Kellett, Jenet (her mark) Kellet. Wit: John F. Wolff, Elisha Hunt. Proved by
John F. Wolff 16 August 1790 before Jonathan Downs, J.P.
[LCDBK C: 234-235]

Niblet, Solomon: 21 April 1792: William Thomason, Senr., of Laurens Co.
SC, indebted to John Frances Wolf, merchant, of same place, for £28, 6 p
Stg., to be paid on a mortgage on or before 25 December 1792; 200 acres on

both sides of Reaburns Creek which said Wm. Thomason now possesses. If said Wm. Thomason, Senr., pays the sum this instrument is void. William (A) Thomason. Wit: John Pringle, Robt. J. David. Sworn by John Pringle 7 May 1792 before Joseph Downs, J.P. [Note: this most likely is part of the 22 July 1790 land sold to William Thomason] [LCDBK D: 164-165]

Niblet, Solomon: 23 October 1797: John F. Wolff, of Laurens Co., S. C., to William Thomason Second Jr., of same place, for $300; *200* acres, being part of a tract of land *originally granted to Solomon Niblet* (the original tract for 400 acres). and by the said Niblet conveyed to Joseph Kellet and by him conveyed to William Thomason, Sr. *Originally granted by his Excellency Charles Granville Montague, Gov. on 22 March 1769 to Solomon Niblet.* The land was taken and sold by executions subject to a mortgage and bought by John Frances Wolff, and now conveyed by him to the said William Thomason 2nd, Jr. Being in the N fork of Raborns Creek on the w/side of said Creek. Wit: Anderson Arnold, John Guttery, Joseph Downs, J.P. [Plat shows bounding John Williams, John Thomason, and Thomas Garner.] [LCDBK F: 293]

Niblett, Solomon: 28 January 1789: William Thomason, of Laurens Co., to John Francis Wolff, of same place, for £10, 300 acres on Raburns Creek, *being part of a tract granted to Solomon Niblet* 22 March 1769. Signed William Thomason, Mourning Thomason [wife of William Thomason]. Wit: Jonathan Downs, John Rodgers. Proved 28 Jan 1789 by John [torn] before Jonathan Downs, J.P. [LCDBK B: 441-442]

[Family: Wife, Mourning Thomason.]

Niblet, Solomon: 11 February 1793: Between John F. Wolff, merchant, of Laurens Co., S.C., to William Thomason, of same place, for £29, 13 shillings; 200 acres on Reaburns Creek, being the half part of a track of land *originally granted to Solomon Niblet 22 March 1769* and from Solomon Niblet to Joseph Kellet, from Joseph Kellet to William Thomason. William (mark) Thomason, *sic* (LS). Wit: James McCaa, James Floyd. Proved by James McCaa 7 March 1793 before Joseph Downs, J.P. [LCDBK D: 404-405]

Niblett, Solomon: 6 February 1796: John F. Wolff, Merchant, Laurens Co., S.C., to William Dunlap, of same place, for £24 Stg.; by virtue of sundry writs of Fieri Facias from the clerks office at the suits of Joseph Gallegly, Joshua Downs and John F. Wolff against the property of William Thomason, Senr. Directed to the sheriff of the County, said William Dunlap as sheriff did enter into sale of a certain tract of 200 acres on N fork Raiborns Creek [plat] Formerly property of William Thomason, Sr. sold for judgment in suit of Joseph Gallegly, Joshua Downs, J.F. Wolff. Part of 400 acres *granted to Solomon Niblett in 22 March 1769* by Montague and conveyed to Jos. Kellett, then to said Wm. Thomason. Wit: John Cargill of Va., James McCaa, Charles Smith, J. P. [LCDBK F: 257]

Niblett, Solomon: 13 October 1797: [Plat] Pursuant to orders to me given by Wm. Dunlap, Esq. Late Sheriff, of Laurens Co. I have resurveyed and laid out for John F. Wolff being 320 acres out of 400 *originally granted to Solomon Niblet* and conveyed and now sold by virtue of an execution obtained by John F. Wolff against William Thomason, Sr. Surveyed 6 September 1796. John Rodgers, D. Surveyor. Bounded by John Williams, John Thomason, Thomas Garner, John F. Wolff. Rayburns Creek runs through the tract. [LCDBK F: 256]

Niblett, Solomon: 23 October 1797: John F. Wolff, of Laurens Co., S.C., to William Thomason, Second Junr. *sic,* of same place, for $300; *200 acres* W side N fork of Raiborns Creek, *part of 400 acres originally granted to Solomon Niblet 1769* and by said Niblet to Joseph Kellett, then to William Thomason, Sr, and then granted by his Excellency Charles Granville Montague, Governour on 22 March 1769 the above parcel of land was taken and sold by execution subject to a mortgage and bought by John Frances Wolf and now conveyed by him to the said William Thomason 2nd, Junr. The tract being on the N fork of Raburns Creek. Plat shows bounding Thomas Garner, John Williams, John Thomason. John F. Wolfe, (L.S.) Wit: Anderson Arnold, John Guttery, Proved by Anderson Arnold 24 February 1798 before Joseph Downs, J.P. Plat. [LCDBK F: 293]

North, Richard: Survey for Richard North pursuant to precept dated 8 July 1774; 300 acres in Ninety Six Dist., waters of Long Lick and Rayburns Creek. Bounded N on land laid out owner unknown; W on Samuel Millhouse and vacant land; S on James Williams, John Cunningham, and Ebenezer Stems; other sides vacant. Certified 1 December 1774. Jno. Caldwell, D.S. [P12_117:2]

North, Richard: Memorial by Richard North; 300 acres in 96 Dist. waters of Long Lick and Rayburns Creek. Bounding NE owner unknown; NW on Saml. Millhouse and vacant; SW on James Williams, John Cunningham, and Ebenezer Stern; SE owner unknown. Certified 1 December 1774 and granted 10 February 1775. Quit rent to commence in 2 years. 13 July 1775. Delivered 21 March 1778 to John Caldwell. John Caldwell, D.S. [M15_9:1]

North, Richard: 19 August 1795: Richard North, of the state of Georgia, and Columbia Co., sell to Roger Murphey, of Laurens Co., S.C., for £6 Stg.; 50 acres *being part of a tract of 300 acres laid off for the said Richard North* and granted by his Excellency William Bull, Esq. Governor. Lying and being in Ninety Six Dist. on the waters of Long Lick on Reaburn Creek and granted 10 February 1775. Bounded on James Williams land, and John Cuningham on Reedy River. Granted by Gov. Bull. Richard (N) North. Wit: Joshua Noble, John Motes. Proved by Joshua Noble 20 August 1796 before Thomas Wadsworth. [LCDBK F: 120]

North, Richard: 5 April 1780: Richd. North, of Ninety Six Dist., S.C., planter, to Hamilton Murdock, of said Dist., planter for £6000 cur.; 250 acres being part of a tract of 300 acres, in the fork between Broad and Saluda rivers on the waters of Long Lick and Reaburns Creek. Bounding S on Ebenezer Starns and land laid out to John Cuningham and Jas. Williams; NE on land owner unknown; NW on Saml. Millhouse and vacant land W on the remaining *part of the original tract granted to Richard North 10 February 1775.* Richard (N) North, L.S.0. Wit: Jno. Caldwell, Jno. Thompson, A. Rodgers. Proved by Andrew Rodgers 4 January 1796 before John Hunter, J.P. [LCDBK F: 62]

North, Richard: 15 June 1784: Hamilton Murdock, planter of Ninety Six Dist., S.C., to John Sims, of said Dist., planter for £5000 old cur.; 250 acres on [see LCDBK F: 62 Richard North to Hamilton Murdock] being part of a tract of 300 acres, in the fork between Broad and Saluda rivers on the waters of Long Lick and Reaburns Creek. Bounded S on Ebenezer Starns and land laid out to John Cuningham and Jas. Williams; NE on land owner unknown; NW on Saml. Millhouse and vacant land W on the remaining *part of the original tract granted to Richard North 10 February 1775.* Hamilton Murdock. Wit: Henry (H) Butler, George Goggans, John Fletchall. Proved by Henry Butler 26 November 1795 before Thos. Wadsworth, J.P. [LCDBK F: 62]

Nuffer, Harman: Survey for Herman Nuffer pursuant to precept dated 29 September 1772; 500 acres in Craven Co., on the NE side of Reedy River on a branch called South fork of Raburns Creek. Bounded SW by Thomas Cahun, NW on Bounty land and Isaac Huger; NE by Thomas Landtrip; other sides vacant. Certified 22 November 1772. Jontha. Downes, D.S. [P16_527:1]

Nuffer, Ha[e]rman: Memorial for Herman Nuffer: 500 acres in Craven Co., NE of Reedy River on a branch called the S fork of Rayburns Creek. Bounding SW on Thos. Cohune; NW on Bounty land and Isaac Huger; NE on Thomas Landtrip and vacant; other sides vacant. Certified 23 November 1772 and granted 20 January 1773. Quit rent to commence in 2 years. 3 June 1773. John Downs, D.S. [M12_218:2]

Nuffer, Herman Senr. : 24 May 1800 Deceased before this date. [See below.]

Nuffer, Herman: 24 May 1800: Herman Nuffer, of Charleston, S.C., baker, to Jacob Bieller [Buller], of Newberry Dist., S.C., for $125; all that undivided moiety or third part of 500 acres *of land originally granted to Herman Nuffer, Senr. deceased.,* lying in Laurens Dist. on the S fork of Reaburns Creek and at the time of survey adjoined land of Thos. Lantrip, Thos. Cohan, Isaac Huger and vacant lands. Herman Nuffer (LS) Wit: Joseph Bieller, Michael Sailer. Dower of Mary Nuffer, wife of the within names Herman Nuffer given 26 May 1800 before Wm. Cunningham, Q.M. Proved by Michael Sailer before John Johnson, J.P. for Charleston Dist. . [LCDBK G: 164]

Nuffer, Herman: No date: I Jacob Bieller, of the Co. of Newberry, S.C., to Thomas Lindley, of Laurens Co., S.C., for $375.00; 500 acres *originally granted to Herman Neuffer dec'd. 23 November 1772* and conveyed to Jacob Bieller by his intermarriage with Mary, daughter of said Herman Nuffer. Jacob Bieller. Wit: James Copeland, William Abercrombie, Thomas Oneall. Proved by Wm. Abercrombie 13 August 1799 before Jonathan Downs, J.P. Dower of Mary Bieller before Jacob R. Brown, J.N.C. [LCDBK F: 473]

[Family: Mary Nuffer, daughter of Herman Nuffer married Jacob Bieller of Newberry, SC.]

O'Daniel, William: Survey for William O'Daniel pursuant to precept dated 7 February 1769: 200 acres on the waters of Saludy River on the North Fork of Raiburns Creek in Craven Co. Bounded on all sides by vacant land. Certified 24 February 1769. Jared Nelson, D.S. [Also listed as McDaniel] [P11_56:2]

O'Daniel, William: Memorial for William O'Daniel for 200 acres in Craven Co., on the waters of Saludy River, on the N. Fork of Rayburn's Creek. Bounded on all sides by vacant land. Certified 25 February 1769 and granted 31 October 1769 to the memorialist. Quit rent to commence two years. Set his hand 28 December 1769 Wm. McDaniel *sic.* Jared Nelson, D.S. [M-10-25:2]

O'Daniel, William: 26 December 1800: William O'Daniel, of Laurens Dist., S.C., to Douglass Johnson, of same place, for £96 Stg.; 200 acres *originally grated to my father William O'Daniel on the 31 September 1769* on Raburns Creek, having devolved to me by heirship. Bounded on all sides by vacant land at time of the original survey and now joined by John Jones on two sides, and by Childres Crandec on the other parts. William O'Daniel. Wit: Isaac Thomas, Archd. McDaniel. Proved by Isaac Thomas 26 December 1800 before James Abercrombe, J.P. Dower of Mary (X) O'Daniel, wife of the within named William O'Daniel given 17 March 1801 before David Anderson, J.Q. [LCDBK G: 669-670]

[Family: His father, William O'Daniel, wife Mary.]

O'Daniel, William: 25 December 1804: Douglass Johnson, Laurens Dist., S.C., to Aaron Moore, of same place, for $500; 200 acres on Raburns Creek bounded on vacant land when granted. *Originally granted to William O'Daniel 31 September 1769.* Now bounded on John Jones, Childres. Dougless Johnson. Wit: George Teague, John Drury Mitchesson. Dower of Jane Johnson, 25 February 1804 before Danl. Wright, J.Q. Proved by George Teague 23 February 1804 before Danl. Wright, J.Q. [LCDBK H: 63 - 64]

O'Neal [O'Neall]: Quaker.

O'Neall, Hugh: 3 October 1787: Hugh Oneall, miller, to my son Hugh Oneall, gift of 150 acres on Little River, above the mill; to my son Charles gift of 150 acres on Little River; to my son Thomas Oneall, 270 acres on Reaburns Creek. Bounded on Patrick Riley, Mary McDonald, Robert Sims. To my daughter Elizabeth McDaniel and her husband Thomas McDaniel, a cow and calf; my four young children to be well schooled; my movable effects to be divided among my four daughters: Patience, Ann, Ruth, Rachel. Ex. Mercer Babb, Wm. Pinson, Elisha Ford. Wit: John Hunter, Thomas Wadsworth, Patrick McDowall. [LCDBK B: 302]

[Family: Daughter Elizabeth McDaniel, wife of Thomas, daughters Patience, Ann, Ruth, Rachel. Sons, Charles, Hugh, Thomas O'Neall.]

O'Neall, Hugh: 3 October 1787: Laurens Co., S.C. Will of Hugh O'Neal, dated 3 October 1787. Sons Hugh O'Neal, Charles O'Neal, Thomas O'Neal; daughters Elizabeth McDanal (wife of Thomas McDanel), Patience, Ruth, Ann and Rachel O'Neil. [LCWBK A: 268].

O'Neall, Hugh: 9 April 1796: We the executors of the Estate of Hugh ONeal, deceased in complying with Hugh ONeall agreeable to the LWT of the said Hugh Oneall, deceased, have according to the best of our knowledge appraised or valued the three tracts of land that the said Hugh O'Neall deceased left to his three sons, Hugh, Charles and Thomas O'Neall. The Upper tract on Little River that was left to Hugh O'Neall valued to £150 ; the lower division of Little River that was left to Charles O'Neal was valued to £65; the other tract of 270 acres lying on the waters of Ready River was valued to £80 [to Thomas O'Neall]; also agreeable to the said will of the said Hugh O'Neall, deceased, we have admeasured of the lower tract of Little River 6 and a quarter of land which contained the Mill and Dam and dwelling house which will appear by a platt. Under our hands Mercer Babb, Elisha Ford, Hugh O'Neall. [Plat for 6 1/4 acres by John Hunter, D.S., shows bound lands of Thos. Wadsworth, waggon road, Little River] [LCDBK F: 186-187]

O'Neal Hugh: 1 September 1804: Thomas Oneale, of Newberry Dist., S.C., to Wm. Choice, of Greenville Dist., S.C., for $250; 252 acres on waters of Raburns Creek and Reedy River. Bounding the lines of Mary McDonald, Robert Sims, Patrick Riley, vacant land and William Choice at the time of original survey. *Originally granted to Hugh Oneal for 270 acres the 3 April 1786,* but since a small part taken of by an older right by the line of Robert Sims suppose to be 18 or 20 acres the balance now suppose to be 252 and willed to me by my father Hugh Oneal, deceased. Thomas Oneale (LS) Wit: Charles Oneall, John McDonald. Dower of Rachel Oneal given 1 September 1804 before J.R. Brown, J.Q.N.D. Proved by John McDonald 15 October 1804 before W. Burnside, J.P. [LCDBK H: 57]

O'Neal, Hugh: 3 February 1827: I William Choice, Senr., of Greenville Dist., S.C., to Drury Boyce, Senr., of Laurens Dist., S.C., for $50; 200 acres on the S side of the S fork of Raburns Creek, being part of a tract of land granted to Hugh Oneal in 1786, willed by the said Hugh Oneal to Thomas Oneal and by said Thomas Oneal conveyed to William Choice, of Greenville Dist., and now from the said William Choice to said Drury Boyce, Senr. A part of the said tract of land that was in possession of John McDonald containing 200 acres. Bounding land formerly Mary McDonald, now Nesbit, land that belongs to the estate of Samuel Nesbit, deceased. Drury Boyce and William Choice. William Choice (LS) Wit: John Armstrong, Senr., Nathan Nesbit. Proved by Nathan Nesbitt 26 February 1827 before Willis Benham, J.Q. [LCDBK L: 266-267]

O'Neal, Hugh: 3 October 1787. Will of Hugh Oneall, miller, Legatees: Sons, Hugh, Charles, Thomas. Mention of tract on Raborns Creek. "To my son Thomas Neal sic, the tract on Raburns Creek. Bounded by Patrick Riley, Robt. Sims and Mary McDonald, containing 270 acres. Daughter Eliz. McDonal and husband Thos. McDonal. Four younger children to be well schooled. Daughters, Patience, Ruth, Ann, Rachel. Ex. Mercer Babb, Wm. Person, Elisha Ford. Wit: John Hunter, Thos. Wadsworth, Patrick McDowell. [LCWBK A: 268]

[Family: Wife not named, Daughters: Elizabeth McDonal [McDonnal, wife of Thomas], Patience, Ruth, Ann, Rachel. Sons, Hugh, Charles, Thomas O'Neill.]

O'Neal, Hugh: 7 May 1788: Appraisal of Hugh O'Neall, deceased 7 May 1788 by Samuel Henderson, William Cason, James Henderson. Includes notes and book accounts on Thomas Carter, James Henderson, Mary Griffin, Wm. (?), William Millwee, Abraham Nabours, Joel Chandler, Saml. Akin, Martin Martin, James Mauldin, Willing Donnal, Dr. J.R. Brown, Wm. Watson, Wm. Dunlap. Ex. Mercer Babb, Elisha Ford. [LCWBK A: 269]

O'Neal, Hugh: 9 May 1788. Sale of estate of Hugh O'Neall, deceased. [LCWBK A: 271]

O'Neal, John: 1773 bounding Hastings Dial. Also see [P16-558:3 and P16-564:1]

O'Neal, Jean: 1773 bounding Hastings Dial.

Owen/s, John: 15 September 1771: Grant of 250 acres.

Owen/s, John: 2 September 1788: John Wells and Rebecca, his wife, of Laurens Co. & Ninety Six Dist., S.C., to Margaret Cuningham, of same place, for £100; 150 acres, part of 250 acres on the waters of Cain Creek. *Originally granted to John Owens 15 September 1771.* Bounded by vacant lands at time or original survey. Now bounding NE on Reaburns Creek by Sarah Hodges, SW by Richard Pinson, W by Jacob Bowman and NW by John Ritchy said deed conveyed by sd. John Owens to Wm. Oneal by L & R and 2 April 1775 and from him unto John Wells and Rebecca his wife 5 & 6 August 1785. Signed John Wells, Rebecca Wells (X her mark). Wit: John Hempens, Moses Wells, Clement Wells. [LCDBK C: 95-98]

Owen/s, John: 21 October 1798: William Owen, formerly of Laurens Co., S.C., to James Cammock for $500; 150 acres on a branch formerly called Hellams Branch of Raburns Creek. *Originally granted to John Williams 10 September 1765,* conveyed to Jno. Owens Aug 1772, now by Wm. Owen, lawful heir of John Owens. Wit: Jno. Hughes, Jno. Harris. Charles Saxon, J.P. [Poor microfilm] [See John Williams] [LCDBK F: 428]

Owen/s, Richard, Jr.: Survey for Richard Owens, Jr. pursuant to precept dated 1 December 1767; 100 acres on north fork of Rayburns Creek, waters of Saludy River, in Berkley Co. Bounded on all sides by vacant land. Certified 19 December 1767. Wm. Anderson, D.S. [P9_312:1]

Owen/s, Richard, Jr.: Memorial for Richard Owen, Jr.; 100 acres in Berkley Co., on the N fork of Rayburns Creek, waters of Saludy River. Bounded on all sides by vacant land. Certified 7 March 1769 and granted 22 March 1769. Quit rent to commence in 2 years. 2 June 1769. Wm.

Anderson, D.S. For the memorialist James Abercrombie. [M8-447:5]

Owen, Richard: Survey for Richard Owen pursuant to precept dated 8 September 1765; 150 acres in Craven Co., in the fork of Broad and Saludy Rivers. Bounded on sides by vacant land. Certified 16 September 1765. Js. Wofford, D.S. [P8_505:1]

Owen, Richard: Memorial for Richard Owen; 150 acres in Craven Co., in the fork of Broad and Saludy Rivers. Bounded on sides by vacant land. Certified 16 September 1766 and granted 16 December 1766. 20 February 1767 Richd. Owen, Jr. William Wofford, D.S. [M9_188:4]

Owen, Richard: 25 June 1771: Richard Owings [Owen] and wife Ann of Craven Co., Province of S.C., to Silvanus Walker, of same place, for £325; 150 acres lying on both sides of Reaburns Creek. Land *originally granted to said Richard Owings 25 June 1770.* Richard Owings (LS), Ann (+) Owings (LS) Wit: Wm. Downs, Zachary Phillips. Proved by William Downs 4 September 1771 before James Lindley, J.P. [LCDBK C: 327-329]

Owen/s, Richard: 7 October 1789: Richard Owens, of Laurens Co., S.C., to David McCaa, of same place, for £20 Stg.; 163 acres, *being part of 260 acres originally granted to Richard Owings sic 1 May 1786.* Bounded by Reaburn's Creek, Robert Cooper, Wm. Millwee, and an Old Survey. Wit. Jonathan Downs, William Owings. Signed Richard Owings and Sarah (x) Owing. Proved by Jonthn. Downs 19 December 1794 that he saw Richard Owings and Sarah his wife sign the deed before Joseph Downs, J.P. [LCDBK F: 55-56]

Owen/s, Richard: 20 December 1794: David McCaa, of Laurens Co., to Charles Wilson, of same place, for £31 Stg.; 163 acres, *part of 260 acres originally granted to Richard Owens 1 May 1786.* Wit: James Wilson, John (x) McCurly, William (x) Comer. Proved 24 February 1795 by other of James Wilson that he was David McCaa and his wife Polly, sign the deed to Charles Wilson. [LCDBK F: 56]

Owen, [Owings] Richard: 14 August 1812: James Hall, attorney for Rosanah Hall, Thomas Hall, William Hall, Samuel Hall and Jane Hughs, of the state of Kentucky, to William Holliday, Junior, of Laurens Dist., S.C., for $200; 100 acres on the waters of Reedy River and Rabourns Creek. Bounded by Mary Cunningham, Robert Culbertson, John Blackley and James Boyd. *Originally granted to Richard Owings* and by sundry conveyances to Samuel Hall, deceased, and now me, as attorney for his legatees. James Hall an attorney (LS). Wit: James Blackley, Robert Holliday. Proved by James Blackley 13 April 1813 before Saml. Cunningham, J.P. [LCDBK K: 17]

O'Daniel, William: Survey for William ODaniel pursuant to precept dated 7 February 1769: 200 acres on the waters of Saludy River on the North Fork of Raiburns Creek in Craven Co. Bounded on all sides by vacant land. Certified 24 February 1769. Jared Nelson, D.S. [P11_55:2]

O'Daniel, William: Memorial for William O'Daniel; 200 acres in Craven Co., on the waters of Saludy River; on the N fork of Rayburns Creek. Bounded on all sides by vacant land. Certified 24 February 1769 and granted 31 October 1769. Quit rent to commence in 2 years. 28 December 1769. Wm. McDaniel. Jared Nelson, D.S. [M10_25:2]

O'Daniel, William: 26 December 1800: William O'Daniel, of Laurens Dist., S.C., to Douglass Johnson, of same place, for £96 Stg.; 200 acres on Raburns Creek. *Originally granted to my father William O'Daniel 31 September 1769* and devolving to me by heirship. Bounded on all sides by vacant land at the time of the original survey and now joined by John Jones, Childres Crandel,. William O'Daniel Wit: Isaac Thomas, Archd. McDaniel. Dower of Mary O'Daniel, wife of the within named William O'Daniel given 17 March 1801 before David Anderson, J.Q. Proved by Isaac Thomas 6 December 1800 before James Abercrombe, J.P. [LCDBK G: 669-670]

Parker, John: 4 July 1809: John Parker, deceased. Letters of administration of estate of wife Sarah Parker. Security John Pitts, Theophilus Goodwin. [LCWBK C-1: 359]

Parker, John: 2 April 1810: David Cowan, of Laurens Co., S.C., to Francis Stuart, of same place, for $75; 100 acres on Raburns Creek. *Formerly property of John Parker sold* by execution. Bounding lands of Wm. Owens, Reuben Holcomb, and John Pitts and now conveyed by the said David Cowan unto Francis Stuart. David Cowart (LS). Wit: David Speers, John Ross. Proved by John Ross 2 March 1810 before William Cowan, J.P. [LCDBK J: 145]

Parker, Sarah: 8 February 1812: John Clark, sheriff of Laurens Co., S.C., to Archibald Young, of same place. Whereas Sarah Parker of the same place was seized in fee simple and possessed a tract of land containing 200 acres on the waters of Raburns Creek, bounded on lands of Lewis Cargil, Charles Smith, John Spelts, William Owens. Whereas a writ of fieri facias issued by the Court of Common Pleas under John Garlington, Esq. of the said court listed by the Hon. John F. Grimke, Esqr., Senior justice of said stated dated 3 Monday in November 1812 all items, goods and chattels, houses, lands and tenements of the said Sarah Parkers, should cause to be levied and made the sum of 448.05 which Archd. Young lately in the court of Common Pleas held for against the said Sarah Parker. John Clark, S.L. Dist. (LS) Wit: B.

Nabers, John Dendy. Proved by Benjamin Nabers 20 April 1812 before John Garlington, [LCDBK J: 264-265]

Parks, John: 15 December 1812: John Parks, Laurens Dist., S.C., to James Young, of same place, merchant for $350; 293 acres where I now live on the waters of Burris Creek of Rabourns Creek. Bounded at this time as follows Viz. N corner on land Isaac Pinson, SW on John Motes corner, SE on Gabriel Jowell, SE on Thos. Davenport, NW on Water Burgess, NE on Nathan Sims. John Parks (LS). Wit: Joel Walker, John Bowland. Dower of Isabella Parks, wife of the within named John Parks 25 March 1813 given before Z. Bailey, J.P. [LCDBK K: 21]

Parks, John: 8 March 1813: Thomas Davenport, of Laurens Dist., S.C., planter, to James Young, merchant, for $51; 17 acres where I now live. Joining said Young which he purchased from John Parks, bounded as follows: Viz. John Young corner, on my own line joining Motes, land part of tract where I now live. Thomas Davenport (LS).Wit: Joel Walker, Ursula Brooks. Dower of Letty Davenport made 13 April 1813 before W. Burnside, J.Q. Proved by Joel Walker 25 March 1813 before Z. Bailey, J.P. [LCDBK K: 20-21]

Parson, James: Survey for James Parsons Esq., pursuant to precept 6 April 1775; 500 acres on the waters of Reedy River on a small creek known in these parts by the names of Peachlings Creek. Bounded NE by Mr. John Freer, SE by land owners not known, all other sides vacant. Certified 9 May 1774 Robert Long, D.S. [P19-69:1]

Petrie, Edmund: Memorial for Edmund Petrie; 200 acres in Ninety Six Dist. on the waters of Rayburns Creek. Bounded NY by James Williams; NE by Charles Broadway and Wm. Elson; SE by Nicholas Hills; other sides vacant. Certified 9 December 1774 and granted 1 March 1775. 31 July 1775. Thos. Clark, D.S. Delivered 17 August 1775 to Edmund Petrie. [See survey for John Fash [Task?] [M2_266:1]

Petrie, Edmund: 18 November 1805: I John Kershaw, of Kershaw Dist., S.C., to Benjamin Williams, of Laurens Dist. S.C., for $200; 200 acres on waters of Raburns Creek. *Originally granted Edmund Petrie in 1775* and by sundry conveyances to John Kershaw and now to Benjamin Williams. John Kershaw (LS). Wit: Aaron Pinson, James Stinson. Sworn by Aaron Pinson 12 March 1807 before Josiah Blackwell. [Plat shows bounding Nicolas Hills, Wm. Caldwell, vacant land, Wm. Ellison, J. Williams, Peter Woods]. [LCDBK K: 131]

Petrie, Edmund: See survey of James Wells.

Petrie, Edmund: Memorial for Edmund Petrie for 300 acres in 96 Dist., on the waters of Rayburns Creek. Bounding NW by Nicholas Hill, NE by Jos. Babb, SW by Wm. Burrows, SE and SW by Robert Gill, owner un-known, other sides vacant. Thos. Clark, D.S. (1 of 6 tracts) [See James Wells] [M-13-537:3]

Petrie, Edmund: 1 November 1803: John Brannan, of Abbeville Dist., S.C., to Gabriel Joel [Jowell], of Laurens Dist., S.C., for $100; 170 acres on the waters of Reabourns Creek. [Plat] shows bounded by Ditney Hill, James Henderson, Wm. O'Donal. *Originally granted to Edmond Petrie in 1775* and by sundry other conveyances to the aforesaid John Brannan and now by him to Gabriel Joel [Jowell]. Signed John Brannan, Wit: John Chambers, George Jowell. Proved 21 March 1814 by George Jowell before Josiah Blackwell, J.P. [LCDBK H: 21]

Petrie, Edmund: 14 May 1814: Gabriel Jowell, of Laurens Dist., S.C., to Sarah Wright, of same place, for $150; 150 acres on waters of Reaburns Creek, *being part of a tract originally granted to Edmond Petrie in 1775,* and then to John Branner and then to said Gabriel Jowel. Gabriel Jowel (LS) Wit: Jacob Niswanger, Edward C. Harris. Proved by Jacob Niswanger 18 November 1815 before Joseph Bolton, J.P. [Plat shows bounded by James Huggens, James Wells, Isaac Pinson, George Madden.] [LCDBK K: 110]

Petrie, Edmund: 3 March 1819: Gabriel Jowell of Laurens Dist., S.C., to Jeremiah Collins, of same place, for $200; 112 acres on E side of Rabourns Creek. Bounded N on James Wells, W James Henderson, E on Stephen Wharton and John McCain. *Being part of a tract of land of 300 acres originally granted to Edmund Petrie in the year 1775* and by sundry other conveyances to said Gabrel Jowell. Gabriel Jowell (LS) Wit: David Bell, John H. Strange. Proved by David Bell 14 April 1819 before Chas. Allen, Q.M. [LCDBK K: 246]

Petrie, Edmund: 3 January 1818: I Gabriel Jowel, of Laurens Dist., S.C., to Isaac Pinson, of same place, for $550; 200 acres on the waters of Rabournes Creek. Bounding NE by George Madden, NW by Isaac Pinson; NW by James Huggens; SE and NE by James Wells; S by John McCain. Gabriel Jowel (LS). Wit: B. N. Williams, Jeremiah Cole, Jesse Pinson. Release of Dower by Rebecca Jowell, wife of Gabriel Jowell 11 March. Proved by Benjamin Williams 4 March 1816 before Chas. Allen, Q. M. Rec. 4 March 1816. [LCDBK K: 120]

Pinson, Aaron: Survey for Aaron Pinson pursuant to precept dated 5 May 1767; 250 acres on NE side of Saludy River and is supposed to be in Berkley Co. Bounded on the SE side on land laid out to Joshua Moor, SE on said river; other sides vacant. Certified 18 June 1767. Jno. Pickens, D.S. [P10-186:3]

Pinson, Aaron: Memorial by Aaron Pinson; 250 acres Craven Co., on the NE side of Saludy River. Bounded SE on land of Joshua Moore; SW by said river; other sides vacant land. Certified 3 May 1768 and granted 2 June 1769. Quit rent to commence in 2 years. 16 September 1769. For the memorialist Adam. Sony[?] [M8_504:3]

Pinson, Aaron: 12 November 1784: Aaron Pinson and Elizabeth his wife of Ninety Six Dist. S.C., to Joseph Chapman for £70 Stg., 250 acres in 96 Dist. on the NE side of Saludy River adjacent land of Joshua Moore, *granted to said Aaron Pinson 2 June 1769.* Aaron Pinson (LS) Elizabeth Pinson (X) (LS). Wit: Wm. Anderson, Thos Hallum, Moromodupe *sic*[Marmaduke?] Pinson. Proved by William Anderson 27 March 1785 before Geo. Anderson, J.P. [Holcomb, Brent H., *Charleston South Carolina Deeds*, Q-5, 22-24. South Carolina Deed Abstract 1783-1788, pg. 173]

Pinson lands: [Note: Indian Hutt branch, not located, but it may be useful to researchers working on Aaron Pinson.]

Pinson, Aaron: 11 & 12 August 1774: Nathan Fowler, of Enoree, S.C., to Richard King, of Turkey Creek, waters of Saludy River, planter, for £250 S.C. money, plantation now in the possession of Aaron Pinson, the younger, 100 acres, on a branch of Saludy known by the name of Indian Hutt Branch in Berkley Co. Nathan Fowler (LS). Wit: Samuel Neel, Richard Ratliff. Proved in 96 Dist., by the oath of Samuel Neal before Andrew Neel, Esqr. J.P., 20 August 1774. [Charleston South Carolina Deeds N-4, 144-184; Holcomb, Brent H., *South Carolina Deed Abstracts 1773-1778*, pg. 92.]

Pinson, Aaron: 21 February 1794. LWT I Aaron Pinson, Minister of the Gospel. Bequeath to Elizabeth, my dearly beloved wife all my estate together with all my household good debts and moveable effects all and singular my lands, I also give to my dearly and well beloved sons Moses Pinson and Isaac Pinson and my daughter Jemimah Kennery, each of them one cow and calf to be raised out of my estate at my wife's death, this performed and one I desire that one tenth part of my estate that shall remain be reserved to be equally divided amongst the heirs of my daughter Mary Cole, deceased as they shall come of age. Then the remainder of my estate I desire to be equally divided amongst the remainder of my children John Pinson and Moses Pinson, my well beloved sons, whom I likewise constitute and make and ordain the sole Executors of this my last will and testament. Dated 21 February 1794. Aaron Pinson (LS). Wit: John H. Kennery, Aaron (mark) Pinson, Jr. [LCWBK A: 159]

[Family: Wife: Elizabeth, sons: Moses Pinson, Isaac Pinson, John Pinson, daughter Jemimah Kennery, Mary Cole, dec'd.]

Pinson, Elizabeth, deceased, wife of Aaron Pinson: 3 September 1803: Aaron Pinson, Senr., deceased. Wife Elizabeth, now being deceased, his legatees chose Moses Pinson, named Executor of will to continue executor of said will. Signed Jno. Pinson, Jno. Hursey, James Byrum, Jas. Fowler, Joseph Pinson, John Pinson, Aaron Pinson, Thos Shurley, Isaac Pinson. Wit; Moses Pinson, Jr., Aaron Pinson. Proved by Joseph Blackwell, J.P.
[LCWBK C-1: 75]

Pinson, Aaron: 3 February 1829: Isaac J. Pinson, of Gwinnette Co., GA, to Marmaduke Pinson, of Laurens Dist., SC, for $325; 150 acres in Laurens Co., S.C., on a creek called Dirty Creek a branch of Rabourns Creek waters of Reedy River. Bounded E by land of Isaac Dial; W Marmaduke Pinson; S by James Abercrombie; SE James Boyd. *With the original grant annexed [?] left to me by my fathers will* and conveyed to him by a deed from James McClannahan which land I warrant and forever defend unto Marmaduke Pinson with special contract made between the said Marmaduke Pinson and myself about 20 February 1828. with the delivery of the above described land with other property for the assumption to pay all my just debts cost and interest then cost against me; on an estimate supposed to be $325.00. Signed Isaac J. Pinson. Wit: G.B. Waldrop, James (his mark) Wells. Proved by Green Berry Waldrop before James Wills, J.P., 3 February 1829.
[See will of Aaron Pinson] [LCDBK M:-114]

Pinson, Duke - [no date given] 100 acres granted by Wm. Bull.

Pinson, Duke: 21 March 1795: Nathan Austin, of Pendleton Co., S.C., to John Henderson, of Laurens Co., Dist., of Ninety Six, S.C., for £50 Stg.; 100 acres on the Reedy River. *Originally granted to Duke Pinson,* under the hand of the Honble. William Bull, Esq., and conveyed by said Pinson to David Morgan and conveyed by said Morgan to Nathan Austin. Bounded by SW on John Reed, SE on land of Joshua Saxon, and bounded by John Moore's lands. Nathan Austin (LS) Wit: Wm. Henderson, Saml. Burton. Proved by Wm. (Mark) Henderson 18 July 1795 before Wm. Hunter, J.P.
[LCDBK F: 14-15]

Pinson, Duke: 13 March 1805: John Henderson, of Franklin Co., Georgia, to Mary Henderson, of Laurens Dist., S.C., for $188; 47 acres on waters or Reedy River. *Being part of 100 acres originally granted to Duke Pinson* under the hand of his Excellency the Honorable Wm. Bull, Esquire and conveyed by said Pinson to David Morgan and conveyed by said Morgan to

Nathan Austin and conveyed by said Austin to John Henderson. Bounded on SW on John McGee. *Originally granted to Duke Pinson* and conveyed as before mentioned unto her the said Mary Henderson. John Henderson (LS) Wit: Wm. Henderson, Levi Hill. Proved by Levi Hill 17 March 1815 before Wm. Burnside, J.P. [See John Reed] [LCDBK H: 103]

Pinson, Isaac: 16 March 1857: I Sarah Madden, of Laurens Dist., S.C., for love and affection which I bear to my nephew Mabra Madden in consideration of $5; sell to the said Mabra Madden all that interest which I may be entitled to in the estate of Isaac Pinson, dec'd, formerly of Ripley Co., Tennessee, together with a buggy. Sarah (X) Madden (LS) Wit. R.W. Allison, Huldah Pinson. Proved by R.W. Allison 4 May 1857 before J. Wislar Simpson, N.P. [LCDBK Q: 163]

Pinson, John (Uncle to Sarah Henderson, widow): 20 July 1808: I Sarah Henderson of Laurens Dist., S.C., widow, for the tender love and affection I have for my two sons viz. Daniel and William Henderson to hereby and voluntarily give my two sons the following personal property, Viz. one sorrel mare, and colt, 2 cows and calves, beds, woman saddle and all my household and kitchen furniture and in case of my death or marriage I hereby request and appoint my uncle John Pinson as guardian of the said Daniel and William and to see that the same is carefully preserved for them. Should the said Daniel or William die that said property should altogether belong to the surviving brother and if both lives to marry or come to nature age the property be equally divided according to the true interest. Sarah (x) Henderson (LS). Wit: Solomon Cole, Moses Pinson. Proved By Solomon Cole 16 November 1808 before W. Burnside, J.Q. [LCDBK J: 45]

[Family: Mother, Sarah Henderson: sons Daniel and William Henderson, uncle, John Pinson.]

Pinson, John: 26 June 1811: LWT, I John Pinson, planter, of Laurens Dist., S.C., to my loving wife Betsey Pinson, three negroes, Nan, Fillis, and Naie?, to John Pinson, my son I give the tract of land where I formerly lived to be 130 acres bounded by the tract I now live on by Howard Pinson, Jonathan Johnson and the Mr. Cunninghams, lands at the death of my wife to him and his heirs. . one equal part of my personal estate to my son Howard Pinson. . . . to my son-in-law William Strain. . . . to my son-in-law Richard Duty $120. To my son-in-law Cornelius Pucket. . . . to my son-in-law Thomas Weathers. Appoint my two sons Howard and Thomas Pinson Executors. .Signed John (X his mark) Pinson. (Seal). Wit: Robert Carter, Senr. Richard Pucket, Robert Carter, Jr. [LCWBK D: 46]

[Family: Wife Betsey Pinson, Sons John, Howard, Thomas; sons-in-law

196

William Strain, Richard Duty, Cornelius Pucket, Thomas Weathers.]

Pinson, Joseph: 1762 bounding Nathan Hampton.

Pinson, Joseph: 13 June 1795: Sale of estate of Joseph Pinson, dec'd. Purchasers: Mrs. Mary Pinson, Marmaduke Pinson, Jr. Wm. Watkins, John Blackwell, Josiah Blackwell, James Box, Henry Box, Benj. Vaughn, Berry West, Colvel[?] Abercrombie, John Cochran, Stephen Potter, David Ross, Wm. McPherson, Isom Histeloe. Adm.: John Blackwell and Mary Pinson. [Elliott, pg. 12]

Pinson, Duke [Marmaduke]: 14 March 1812: Mary Henderson, of Laurens Dist., S.C., to Levi Hill, of same place, for consideration of her lifetime maintenance convey a tract of 53 acres less one half acres for a burying place. *Originally granted to Duke Pinson* by Wm. Bull, and conveyed by said Pinson to David Morgan and from said Morgan to Nathan Austin and by said Austin to John Henderson and by John Henderson to Mary Henderson to Levi Hill. The said tract of land on the waters of Reedy River. The land being *part of a tract of 100 acres originally granted to Duke Pinson,* Mary Henderson (mark). Wit: Isaac Moseley, James Henderson. Proved by James Henderson 28 May 1812 before Gabriel Jowell, J.P. [LCDBK K: 259]

Pinson, Marmaduke: 26 April 1820: LWT of Marmaduke Pinson, Senr. of Laurens Dist., S.C. To my beloved wife Molly Pinson to negros Named Jacob and Milly, together with all and singular the plantation whereon I now reside together with all stock and furniture during her natural life or widowhood, having portioned off my four daughters namely: Edes, Sally, Suckey and Ruth, that after their mother Molly's decease the above named two negros be equally divided between them. My eldest son Bejah Pinson the property already given namely the plantation he sold; to my son Isaac Pinson 150 acres on Dirty Creek, to daughter Huldsath Pinson one negro girl Hannah, daughter Polly Strain, youngest son Marmaduke Pinson all that plantation I now reside on after his mother death. Also *50 acres formerly granted to James Hollingsworth.* To my grandson Pinson McDaniel one negro boy named Bob. Appoint my son Bijah Pinson and William Madden my sold executors. Marmaduke Pinson (LS). Wit: Isaac Dial, James Boyd, S. Cuningham. Proved 6 October 1820. [LCWBK E: 100]

[Family: Wife, Molly, daughters: Edes, Sally, Ruckey, Ruth, Huldath, Polly Strain. Sons: eldest Bejah, Isaac, youngest son Marmaduke, grandson Pinson McDaniel.]

Pinson, Marmaduke: 1 March 1838: M.D. Pinson, of Laurens Dist., S.C. to

John W. Simpson, of same place, for $150; 20 acres on Raburns Creek. Bounded by lands of sd John W. Simpson, E and S, on the W by lands of Thomas Coats, N by said M.D. Pinson's land. Signed M.D. Pinson (Seal). Wit: Isaac P. Boyd, A.R. Simpson. Proved by A.R. Simpson 24 July 1839 before Jno. S. James. J. Q. [LCDBK N: 250-251]

Pinson, Moses: 13 September 1813: Moses Pinson, of Laurens Dist., S.C., to Thomas B. Williams, of same place, for $800; 105 acres on waters of Raburns Creek. Bounded by NW by Joseph Pinson; NE by Archabald McDaniel; NE and SE by William Boid [Boyd.] Signed Moses Pinson. Wit: Solomon Cole, Ben. Williams, Catharine (X her mark) Cole. Proved 26 February 1814 by Benjamin Williams before Gabriel Jowel, J.P. [LCDBK K: 120]

Pinson, Richard: 1774 bounding Daniel Williams on Rayburns Creek. No survey or memorial found for Richard Pinson.

Pitchlynn, Isaac: Survey for Isaac Pitchlynn pursuant to precept dated 3 September 1765; 200 acres in Berkley Co., on Raburns Creek between the forks of Broad and Saludy Rivers. Bounded on sides by vacant land. Certified 7 September 1765. Js. Wofford, D.S. [P8_423:2]

Pitchlynn, Isaac: Memorial for Isaac Pitchlynn; 200 acres in Berkley Count on Raburns Creek between the forks of Broad and Saludy Rivers. Bounded on all sides by vacant land. Certified 3 September 1765; also 50 acres in Berkley Co., in the fork between Broad and Saludy Rivers bounded on all sides by vacant land. Certified 19 September 1765 and both granted 29 October 1766. Quit rent to commence in 2 years. Set his hand 28 November 1766. W. Wofford, D.S. For the Memorialist Will. Brown. [M9_149:3]

Pitchlynn, Isaac: Memorial for John Spurgin; 150 acres in Berkley Co., on the waters of Enoree River between Broad and Saludy Rivers. Bounded at the time of the survey S by land laid out to John Gordon and part vacant. *Originally granted 12 March 1762 to Isaac Pitchlynn,* Quit rent to commence in 2 years. and conveyed by him and Jemma his wife by Lease and release 22 and 2[3] August 1765 to Samuel Chew who with (torn)er, his wife, conveyed same to John Spurgin by Lease and release 2[torn], October 1767. 27 December 1767. For the Memorialist William Allison. [M9_424:2]

Pitts, Isaac: 1770 bounding Edward Williams and James Holmes. No survey or memorial found for Isaac Pitts.

Pitts, William: 17 October 1829: I William Pitts, of Laurens Dist., S.C., to

Thomas Morgan, of same place, for $310; *119 acres on the waters of Rabourns Creek.* Bounded by lands of John Garlington, John Calhoun, William Morgan, Daniel Johnson and James Dorroh. Set my hand William Pitts (LS) Wit. James Morgan, Joseph Gaines. Dower of Francis Pitts, wife of the within named William Pitts 12 December 1829 before Saml. Cunningham, J.Q. Proved by James Morgan 28 December 1829 before S. Cunningham. [LCDBK M: 127]
Platt, John: No survey found.

Platt, John: Memorial by John Platt; 100 acres in Craven Co., S side of Wateree river on a branch of Rayburns Creek and the Great Road from McCords. Bounding NE and SE on Joshua English; SW on Henry Hunter and vacant land; NW on Robert Millhouse. Certified 8 July 1774 and granted 6 September 1774. Quit rent to commence in 2 years. 14 March 1775. Delivered 24 May 1775 to Aaron Loocock. Jno. Belton, D.S. [M13_379:2]

Powell, Benjamin: 1773 bounding William Savage and James Simpson's lands.

Powell, Henry: Survey for pursuant to precept dated 25 January 1764; 100 acres in Ninety Six Dist, waters of Rayburns Creek. Bounded SW laid surveyed for William Savage and James Simpson; E on Bounty land; N vacant. Certified 4 March 1773. Wm. Anderson, D.S. [Bounty] [P19_251:2]

Powell, Henry: Memorial for Henry Powell; 100 acres in Ninety Six Dist., waters of Rayburnes Creek. Bounded S and W by William Savage and James Simpson; E by Bounty; N by vacant land. Certified 4 March 1774 and granted 25 May 1774. Quit rent to commence in 10 years. 7 October 1774. Delivered 19 June 1774 to Thomas Hutchison. [B in margin]. [M13_44:4]

Powell, Henry: 25 May 1785: Henry Powell bounding lands granted to William Savage and James Simpson on waters of Raburns Creek. [See William Savage and James Simpson.] [LCDBK B: 92]

Powell, Henry: 13 February 1818: I John Adams, of Greenville Dist., S.C., to James Dunlap, of Laurens Dist., S.C., for $275; 100 acres on the waters of Rabons Creek. *Originally granted to Henry Powell 25 May 1774.* Bounded on land surveyed for Savage and Simpson, NW on Bounty land, SW on vacant land, S on Savage and Simpson and on the waters of Rabons Creek. John Adams (LS). Wit: John Harris, Thomas (X) Dagny? Proved by John Harris 9 October 1820 before Thos. Wright, J.Q. [LCDBK L: 22]

Pugh, Richard: Memorial by Richard Pugh for 100 acres in Berkley Co. on a small branch of Reedy River, called the Reedy fork, bounded on all sides at the time of the survey on vacant land. *Originally granted 1 July 1768 to Peter Allen.* Quit rent to commence in two years. And conveyed by him to the memorialist by lease and release bearing date 26 and 27 December 1768. Set his hand 30 October 1769. James Loosk. Certified by R.L. [See Peter Allen] [M8:530-2]

Pugh, Richard: 10 June 1796: LWT: Richard Pugh, of Laurens Co., S.C., to by beloved wife Mary Pugh all my land and other property during her natural life, except one cow which I give to my grand daughter Nancy Cochran. Except by said wife should marry after my decease then she shall have an equal third of my moveable property during her life time. At her decease the whole of my moveable property to be equally divided amongst my four step children Viz: John McClanahan, Margaret Cochran, William McClanahan, Samuel McClanahan. And also my lands to be divided amongst my three step sons, Viz: John, William and Samuel McClanahan. Appoint my wife Mary Pugh and my stepson John McClanahan my Executrix and executor. Richard Pugh. (LS). Wit. Wm. Boyd, Samuel Matthews, John Cochran. [See Pierce Butler sale of land to Richard Pugh.] [LCWBK A: 148]

[Family: Mary Pugh, previously married to John McClanahan, deceased, granddaughter Nancy Cochran, and three step sons: John McClanahan, William McClanahan and Samuel McClanahan; step-daughter Margaret Cochran, granddaughter Nancy Cochran.]

Pugh, Richard: 28 September 1822: William McClanaham, of Laurens Dist., S.C., convey unto James Dorrough, all my right, title, interest in land devised by Richard Pugh, deceased of said place to his three stepsons, John, William and Samuel McClanahan per Richard Pugh's' will. Wm. McClanahan. Wit: James Todd, S.B. Lewers. Dower of Catharine McClanahan, wife of the within names Wm. McClanahan, given 28 September 1822 before S.B. Lewers. Proved by Samuel B. Lewers 20 January 1823. [LCDBK L: 81-82]

[Family: Wife Catharine McClanahan, step-sons, John, William and Samuel McClanahan.]

Putnam, Abner: 25 November 1842: Mary Putman, of Laurens Co., S.C. and other to heirs of Wm. Putman, deceased. Agreement. I Mary Putman, wife of Wm. Putman deceased have this day made and entered into an agreement wit the heirs and legatees of Wm. Putman, deceased. The said Mary Putman shall have the use of two Negroes named Henry and Ellen and other property sufficient for her support during her natural lifetime and she the said Mary Putman is hereby bound not to waste nor squander any of said property or any of its effect and at her death said Negroes and their increase with the remainder of her effects is to be equally divided among said heirs and legatees. As follows: Abner Putman, James Putman, Daniel Putman, Elizabeth Owens, Lavina Thomas, Lucinda Franks, Nancy Garrett, and Polly Garrett, Michael Putman and Reuben Putman. Mary (X) Putman (LS), Abner Putman (LS), R. Thomas (LS), Gideon Owens (LS), Daniel Putman (LS), James (X) Putman (LS), N.G. Frank (LS), Osborn Garrett (LS), Seborn [Seaborn] Garrett (LS). Wit: John Putman, Harris (X) Owens. [LCDBK: O: 229]

Quail, Charles: Survey for Charles Quail pursuant to precept dated 5 January 1768; 100 acres in Craven Co., on a small branch of Raiburns Creek. Bounded SW by George Hollingsworth; SE by Jno. Williams; W by James Lindleys; other sides by vacant land. Certified 23 April 1768. Ralph Humphreys, D.S. [P9_246:2]

Quail, Charles: Memorial for Charles Quail; 100 acres in Berkley Co., on a small branch of Rayburnes Creek. Bounded SW by George Hollingsworth; SE on John Williams; W on James Lindley; other sides vacant. Certified 28 April 1768 and granted 15 July 1768. Quit rent to commence in 2 years. 30 September 1768. Ralph Humphreys, D.S. For the memorialist Ralph Humphreys. [M8_256:3]

Quail, Charles: prior to 1785: Charles Quail sold land to Ralph Humphrey, then by said Ralph Humphrey to James Lindley, father of Thomas Lindley. Deeds of sale were not found.

Quail, Charles: 15 May 1785: Thomas Lindley, oldest son of James Lindley of Reighburns Creek Settlement, to Marmaduke Pinson, of same place, for £14; 100 acres *originally granted 15 July 1768 unto Charles Quails* and conveyed by said Charles Quails to Ralph Humphreys, and by said Humphreys to James Lindley, the father of said Thomas Lindley by lease and release dated 12 [blank] 1785. Bounded SW by George Hollingsworth; SE on John Williams; W on James Lindley; all other sides by vacant land. Thomas Lindley, Elizabeth Lindley (his wife). Wit: Richard Pugh, John Mitchell, Joseph Pinson. [LCDBK A: 348 - 351]

Raburn, Richard: Survey for 150 acres not located.

Raiford, Philip: July 1771: Philip Raiford, deceased by July 1771, as he appears listed as deceased bounding land of Martha Goodwyn.

Rayburn, Richard: Memorial by Richd. Rayburn for 150 acres in Craven

Co., on a branch of Indian Creek bounded NE on Clement David, other sides vacant land. Certified 7 June 1774 and granted 8 July 1774 to the memorialist. Quit rent to commence in two years from date. Set his hand 27 December 1774. William Gist, D.S. Delivered 11 February 1775 to Charles Roberts [M13-183:3]

Ravenel, Daniel: Memorial for Daniel Ravenel, Jr.; 500 acres on the SW fork of Rayburns Creek a branch of Reedy River in 96 Dist. Bound E on land of McMahon; W on Isaac Huger; S on said Daniel Ravenel, Jr. W vacant. Certified 15 December 1774. Also 500 acres in 96 Dist. on the NW branch of Rayburns Creek a branch of Reedy River. Bounded N on land of Thomas Adamson and vacant. S on Cornwall [?] McMahon and Moses Kirkland, W of land belonging to Indians; E on Isaac Huger. Certified 2 February 1775. Granted 4 May 1775. 22 September 1775. Quit rent to commence in 2 years. [two tracts of 6 tracts listed] [M2_364:2]

Ravenel, Daniel: 15 May 1775: Daniel Ravenel, of Wantook, in St. John's Parish, Berkley Co., Province of S.C., planter, [note several land transactions, but only noting those dealing with Raburns Creek] to Paul Mazyck of Charleston, S.C. [Deeds for three tracts, only using those referencing Raburns Creek]. 2) 500 acres on SW fork of Rayburns creek of Reedy river in 96 Dist. bounded E on McMahan, W on Isaac Huger S on said Daniel Ravenel, W on vacant land; 3) 500 acres surveyed for him 25 May 1772 on NW branch of Reaburns Creek a branch of Reedy River. Bounding N on Thomas Adams and vacant land, S on Cornwall McMahan and Moses Kirkland, W on land belonging to the Indians and E on Isaac Huger. Daniel Ravenel (LS). Wit. Stephen Mazyck (Son of Benjamin) 3 November 1795 before Peter Freneau, J.P.Q. [LCDBK J: 70-72]

Ray, David: Survey for David Ray pursuant to precept dated 1 September 1767: 150 acres in Berkley Co., on the waters of Raburns Creek. Bounded NW on land laid out to Israel Gant [Gaunt]; all other sides on vacant land. Certified 12 September 1767. Jno. Caldwell, D.S. [P11_323:3]

Ray, David: Memorial for David Ray; 150 acres in Berkley Co., on the waters of Rayburns Creek. Bounding NW on Israel Gant [Gaunt]; other sides vacant. Certified 5 June 1770 and granted 13 July 1770. Quit rent to commence in 2 years. 22 August 1770. James Lindt (?). Jno. Caldwell, D.S. [M10_207:4]

Ray, David: 27 March 1802: David Ray listed is bounding property being mortgaged by Thomas & William Burton to James McClanahan on Rabourns Creek. Also *bounded at time of original survey by Alex. Cormack,* James Lindley, David Rea *sic* and land unknown. [LCBK G: 670]

Reed (Read), John: 5 November 1755: *Original grant made 5 November 1755 and conveyed 2 March 1756 to Robert Long.*

Reed, John: Survey for 250 acres not located.

Reed [Read], John: Memorial for Robt. Long, 250 acres in Berkley Co., on a branch of Saludy River called Reedy River, bounded at the time of the grant NE on the said River, all other sides by vacant land. *Originally granted the 5 November 1755 to John Read,* and by him conveyed by lease and release 1 & 2 March 1756 to Robert Long the memorialist. Set his hand for the memorialist Jacob Bowman. [M8-450:3]

Reed, John: 26 May 1769: Richard Lang, "deceased" to Daniel Williams, of Halifax Co., Va., for 10 shillings; 250 acres on a branch of Saludy River called Reedy River. *Originally granted to 5 November* 1755 and conveyed 1 and 2 March 1756 from John Reed to said Robert Long, deceased and has legally descended from said Robert [Lang], deceased to his eldest son Richard Lang. Wit: Jacob Bowman, George Wright, Junr. Hans Hendrick. Receipt for £60 signed by Jacob Bowman, 28 June 1770. Wit: Nimrod Williams. [Charleston Deeds K-4, 11-12] [Brent H. Holcomb, *South Carolina Deed Abstract 1773-1778,* pg. 58]

Reed, John: Robert Long and wife Millicent: Laurens C.T. Oldest son: Richard Long and wife Sarah to Daniel Williams of Halifax Co., Va. 250 acres on Reedy R. of Saluda. *Originally granted to John Reed 5 November 1755.* Conveyed to Robert Long 1 or 2 March 1756. [See Deed N4-357] [Revill, pg 160]

[Family: Wife Millicent, son Richard Long and wife Sarah.]

Reed, John: 13 March 1805: John Henderson, of Jackson Co., GA, to Mary Henderson, of Laurens Dist., S.C., for $34; 6 acres on the waters of Reedy river. *Being part of 150 acres of land laid out for John Reed* under the hand of his Excellence Honorable William Bull, Esquire. (Book CCC pg. 385) said 6 acres bounding a spring and said Henderson's line. John Henderson (LS) Wit: Wm. Henderson, Levi Hill. Proved by Levi Hill 19 March 1805 before Wm. Burnside, J.P. [LCDBK H: 103]

Reid, Owen: Survey for Owen Reid pursuant to precept dated 1 August 1769: 250 acres in Berkley Co., on Reburns Creek, waters of Saludy River. Bounded on all sides by vacant land. Certified 10 August 1769. Pat. Cunningham, D.S. [P11_33:2]

Reid, Owen: Memorial for Owen Reid; 250 acres in Berkley Co., on Rayburns Creek, waters of Saludy River. Bounded on all sides by vacant land. Certified 10 August 1769 and granted 22 September 1769. Quit rent to commence in 2 years. 15 November 1769. Patrick Cunningham. Patrick Cunningham, D.S. [M10_3:1]

Reed, Owen: No Date: Thomas Camp, of Laurens Co., S.C., to Joseph Camp, of same place, for £100; 150 acres on S Fork of Reburns Creek. Being part of the *original grant to Owen Reed* 22 September 1769, on Widow Reed's branch. Signed Thomas (C) Camp. Wit: Robt. Atkins, Benj. Camp. Joseph Downs, J.P. Proved by oath of Robert Atkins 17 July 1798 before Joseph Downs, J.P. [LCDBK F: 335]

Reed [Reid], Owen: 30 June 1797: George Vaughan, of the Co. of Franklin and State of Georgia to Thomas Camp, of Laurens Co., S.C., for £200; 250 acres on the S fork of Rabourns Creek, being a tract of land *originally granted to Owen Reed, dec'd. 22 September 1769,* conveyed by George Vaughan, attorney, for William Reed, heir of said Owen Reed to Thomas Camp, Jr. George Vaughn. Wit: Lydall Allen, Wm. Camp. Proved by Lydall Allen 20 October 1800 before Wm. Nibbs, J.Q.
[LCDBK G: 688-689]

Reed [Reid], Owen: 16 July 1797: Thomas Camp, of Ninety Six Dist., S.C., to Joseph Camp, of same place, for £100 Stg.; 150 acres in Laurens Co. on the S Fork of Rayborns Creek, *being part of a tract of land granted to Owen Reed bearing date 22 September 1769.* Bounding Widow Reeds branch. Thomas (C) Camp (L.S.) Wit: Robert Atkins, Benj. Camp. Proved by Robert Atkins 17 July 1798 before Joseph Downs, J.P. [LCDBK F: 335]

Reid [Read/Reed], Owen: 10 December 1797: Thomas Camp, Junior, of Laurens Co., S.C., to Martin Mchaffey, of same place, for $225; 100 acres on NE side S Fork of Raybourns Creek, being *part of a tract original granted to Owen Reid,* and conveyed by the heirs of said Owen Read conveyed unto said Thomas Camp, Junr. Plat shows bounded on Widow Reid's spring branch, Thos. Camp land, land sold to M. Mchaffee. Thomas Camp. (L.S.) Wit: B.H. Saxon, Solomon Hopkins. Proved by Solomon Hopkins before Jonathan Downs, J.P. Dower of Susannah, wife of Thomas Camp made 13 August 1798. Jonathan Down, J.P. [Plat shows land on widow Reeds spring branch, Thos Camp, land sold to M. Mchaffee]
[LCDBK F: 427]

Reed [Reed], Owen: 1 February 1798: Thomas Camp, of Laurens Co., S.C., to Elisha Casey, of same place, for £60; 100 acres on S Fork of Raburns Creek and on the S side of said creek. *Being part of a grant to Owen Reid*

22 September 1769, and conveyed by George Vaughn, attorney for William Reid, the lawful heir of the said of Owen Reid, deceased, to said Thomas Camp to said Elisha Casey. Thomas (C) his mark) Camp. Wit: Wm. Camp. Elizabeth (X) Camp. Proved by William Camp 18 February 1797 before Reuben Pyles, J.P. [LCDBK F: 423]

Reed [Reid], Owen: 14 June 1800: Joseph Camp of Laurens Dist., S.C., to Martin Mahaffey, of same place for $300; 150 acres on the S side of the S fork of Rabourns Creek. *Being part of a tract of land granted to Owen Reed dated 22 September 1799.* Bounding Widow Reeds branch. Joseph Camp (LS). Wit. William Morgan, Hugh Mahaffey. Proved by Hugh Mahaffey 6 August 1800 before Jonthn. Downs, J.Q. [LCDBK G: 687-688]

Reed [Reid], Owen [See land below for William Camp & Elijah Casey]: 10 September 1817: Laurens Dist., S.C., I Matthew Landers, of said place, to James Dorrough, Jr., of same place, for $550; 500 acres on the S Fork of Rabourns Creek and S side of said Creek waters of Reedy River. [Meets and bounds given]. *Originally granted 100 acres to Owen Reed* and from him conveyed to Thos. Camp and from him to Elisha Casey and from Casey to the aforesaid Matthew Landers and now from him to the said James Dorrough, Jr. and 225 acres of said land *granted to William Camp* and from him to Elijah Casey and from him to the said Mathew Landers and from him conveyed to the said James Dorrough Jr. Also *168 acres granted to Elisha Casey* and from him conveyed to said Mathew Landers and now conveyed to the said James Dorrough, Jr. Mathew Landers (LS). Wit: Samuel Moore, Wm. Arnold. Dower of Jane Landers, wife of the within named Mathew Landers given 10 September 1817 before Wm. Arnold. J.Q. [LCDBK L: 8-9]

Reed [Reid/Read], William: 12 February 1791: William Read, of S.C., appoints George Vaughan, of S.C., my Attorney to sell 250 acres on Reaburns Creek, by public or private sale. Wit: Silvanus Walker, Sen., John Cuningham. Signed William Read. Proved by oath of Silvanus Walker 18 February 1795 before John Davis, J.P. [LCDBK E: 406-407]

Reynolds, David: Survey for David Reynolds pursuant to precept dated 7 April 1772; 300 acres on waters of Rabourns Creek. Bounded SE land surveyed for Wm. Savage and James Simpson, Esqr.; other sides vacant. Certified 4 June 1774. Wm. Anderson, D.S. Ord. Co. 17 June 1774. [P20_75:2]

Reynolds, David: Memorial by David Reynolds; 300 acres on the waters of Rayburns Creek. Bounding SE on William Savage and James Simpson; other sides vacant. Certified 17 June 1774 and granted 23 June 1774. Delivered 14 January 1775 to David Reynolds. Wm. Anderson, D.S.

Reynolds, David: 2 November 1790: David Reynolds listed as bounding on land on Rayburns Creek in sale of lands by Richard Wild, Esq. of the Kingdom of Great Britain to Edward Penman, of Charleston, S.C. [1 deed of over 32 listed] [LCDBK C: 288-289]

Richardson, Thomas: 8 September 1787: Edmond Martin, Esquire, Sheriff, of Ninety Six Dist., S.C., and Aaron Steel, planter. Whereas Thomas Richardson, late of the Dist. and state, was seized in fees of a certain plantation or tract of land in Laurens county on the Reedy Ford of Reedy River containing 200 acres. Bounding S by Cuningham land, E by John Baughs N by Thomas Cuningham W by David Dunlap and Robert Hood. Where as the said Aaron Steel in November 1785 imprecated the said Thomas Richardson in the Court of Common please of said state in joint suit with Archibald Owins for the recovery of the sum of £65 Stg. - in which such proceedings was therefore had that the said Aaron Steel did obtain and recover judgment against the said Thomas Richardson as well for the debt as for the sum of £35, 8 shillings in as for his damage or cost of suit. Now this indenture witnessseth that the said Edmond Martin for the sum of $60 to him in hand paid by the said Aaron Steel hath granted and sold unto the said Aaron Steele all that tract of land containing 200 acres on the Reedy fork of Reedy River. Bounding S on Patrick Cuningham, E by John Baugh, N by Thos. Cuningham W by David Dunlap and Robert Hood. Edmond Martin. Wit: Jonathan Downs, Samuel Taylor. Proved by Jonathan Downs, 12 August 1789 before Joseph Downs, J.P. [LCDBK C: 71-72]

Richardson, Thomas: 8 September 1787: Edmond Martin, Esquire, Sheriff of Ninety Six Dist., S.C., and Aaron Steel, planter, of the same place. Whereas Archibald Owins [Owens], late of the Dist. and Sate aforesaid was seized of a certain tract of land in Laurens County on the S side of Reedy River containing 50 acres bounded N by the Reedy River, S and W by Daniel McLain, other lands laid out to one McAnulty, as appears by a plat. And whereas the said Aaron Steele in November term 1785 impleaded the said Archibald Owins in the Court of Common Please in the state aforesaid held at Ninety Six in a joint suit with Thomas Richardson for the recovery of the sum of £64 Stg. in which action such proceedings was there for had that the said Aaron Steel did obtain and recover judgment against the said Archibald Owins. Edmond Martin. Wit: Jonathan Downs, Samuel Taylor. Proved by Jonathan Downs 20 August 1789 before Joseph Downs, J.P [LCDBK C: 72-73]

Richardson, Thomas: 10 October 1808: I William Coll *sic [Cole]*, of Laurens Dist., S.C., to Robert Culbertson, of same place, for $300; 128 acres being part of a tract of land containing 100 acres, *being part of a tract of land originally granted to Patrick Cuningham* and conveyed by him to Thomas Richardson, being the place whereon the said William Coal *sic* now lives, also one other tract of land containing 28 acres adjoining the above described tract. *Originally granted to Thomas Richardson*, bounded on lands of Thos. Cunningham, deceased, James Hall, land unknown. William Cole (LS). Wit: Samuel Weir, John Blackley. Proved by Samuel Weir 10 October 1808 before Jonthan. Down, J.Q. Dower of Patsy Cole, wife of the said William Coal *sic* given 10 October 1808 before Jonathan. Downs, J.Q. [Note; no creek mentioned] [LCDBK J: 126]

Richie, Eleanor: Survey for Eleanor Richie pursuant to precept dated 11 December 1772; 100 acres in Craven Co., on NW side of Reyburns Creek on branch thereof called O'Daniel's Branch. Bounded NE on Benjn. Jones; SE by Wm. O'Daniels; other sides vacant. Certified 22 January 1773. Jonthn. Downs, D.S. [P20_122:1]

Richie, Eleanor: Memorial for Eleanor Richie; 100 acres in Craven Co., NW side of Rayburns Creek on a branch thereof called O'Daniels branch. Bounding NE on Benjamin Jones; SE of Wm. O'Daniel. Certified 20 September 1774 and granted 4 May 1775. Quit rent in 2 years. 22 September 1775. Jonathan Downes, D.S. [M2_365:4]

Richie, Eleanor: 14 December 1785: Eliner Ritchey, Laurens Co., Dist. of Ninety Six, S.C., to Samuel Dunlap, of same place, planter, for £20 Stg., 100 acres on SW side of Rayburns Creek on a branch called ODaniels Branch. Bounded by NE on Benjn. Jones; SE on William Daniels [O'Daniel in survey and memorial]. *Land granted to Elenor Richey 4 May1775*. Elener Richey (L.S.) Wit. . Lewis Saxon, CC [LCDBK A: 135 - 138]

Richie, John: Survey for John Richie pursuant to precept dated 11 December 1772; 100 acres in Craven Co., on south fork of Reyburns Creek. Bounded by vacant land. Certified 16 February 1773. Jonthn. Downs, D.S. [P20_122:2]

Richie, John (Jr.): Memorial for John Richie Jr.; 100 acres in Craven Co., S fork of Rayburns Creek. Bounded on all sides by vacant land. Certified 20 September 1774 and granted 17 March 1775. Quit rent to commence in 2 years. 17 August 1775. Jonathan Downes, D.S. [Irish in margin]. [M2_299:2]

Richie, John: Survey for John Richie, Senr. Pursuant to precept dated 11 December 1772; 250 acres in Craven Co., on NE side of Reyborns Creek, branch thereof called Reynolds Branch. Bounded SW laid out to William

Daniel; other sides vacant. Certified 16 January 1773. Jonthn. Downs, D.S.
[P20_121:3]

Richie, John: Memorial for John Richie; 250 acres in Craven Co., NE of
Rayburns Creek a branch of Reynolds. Bounding SW on Wm. O'Daniel;
other sides vacant. Certified 20 September 1774 and granted 1 March 1775.
31 July 1775. Jonathan Downes, D.S. [M2-267:1]

Ritchy [Richie], John: 28 July 1792: Thomas Elliott, of Laurens Co., S.C.,
to John Dunklin, of same place, for £140; 104 acres on W side Rabourns
Creek being *granted by Moultrie to John Ritchy and recorded in the
secretary office grant book 6 February 1736.* Bounded NW on land of John
Erwin Calhoun and SW on John Gocher. Signed Thomas Elliott (L.S.) Wit:
Jacob Bowman, Marmaduke Pinson, William Wright, Junr. Proved 15
September 1792 by Jacob Bowman before George Anderson, J.P.
[LCDBK D: 275 - 176]

Ritchey, John: 30 October 1794: John Dunklin, Ninety Six Dist., S.C., to
Joseph Dunklin, of Washington Dist., S.C., for £100; 137 acres on the W
side Reaburns Creek. *Granted on 6 February 1786 to John Richey.* Bounded
NW on lands of John Ewing Calhoun, SW on John Gocher. John Dunkin,
(LS). Wit: Nathaniel Sullivant, Hewlet Sullivant, Charles Sullivant. Proved
by Hewlet Sullivant 24 November 1794 before Joseph Downs, J.P.
[LCDBK E: 306-307]

Ritchey, John: 11 May 1796: John Dunklin, of Mercer Co., Canetuckey *sic
{Kentucky]* to John F. Wolff, Laurens Co., S.C., for £66 ; 133 acres on the W
side of Raibourns Creek. *Originally granted to John Ritchey and recorded 6
February 1786.* Bounding NW on John Ewen Calhoon, SW by John
Boucher. Signed John Dunklin. Wit: John Rodgers, Hewlet Sullivant. Proved
by Oath of John Rodgers 11 May 1796 before Joseph Downs, J.P. [Plat]
[LCDBK F: 447-448]

Ritchey, John: 13 October 1793: William Arnold Senr., of Reaburns Creek,
Laurens Co., S.C., Yeoman, for £100 Stg. by William Arnold, Jurn., of same
place, Yeoman, 100 acres of Reaburns creek. Bounded by said creek, the
plantation I bought of John Richey, Roger Murphey Senr., Patrick
Cuningham. Wit: Samuel Arnold, Reuben Arnold. Signed Wm. Arnold,
Mary (x) Arnold. Probed by Samuel Arnold 15 October 1793 before George
Anderson, J.P. [LCDBK: E: 132-133]

Ritchey, John: 21 October 1793: William Arnold, Junr., stands bound of
Thomas Wadsworth & William Turpin, Merchants, of S.C., for £112, 1sh 2
d Stg. William Arnold Junr. and Ann his wife sold a tract of land where they

now live containing 100 acres, *being part of a tract of land originally granted to John Richey 6 February 1786* and by said John Richey to William Arnold Senr. The tracing being on Reaburns Creek, bounded by said creek, Wm. Arnold Senr, Roger Murphey Sen., Patrick Cuningham. Wit: James Young, William Carson, William Arnold, Senr. Signed William (x) Arnold, Ann (x) Arnold. Oath by James Young 4 November 1793 before John Hunter. [LCBDK E: 109-112]

Ritchey, John: 4 March 1799: Between John Ritchey and Margaret Ritchey, his wife, both of Laurens Co., S.C. and Thomas Elliott, of same place, planter; £85 Stg.; 150 acres of land being on the NW side of Reaburns Creek, bounding at time of the original survey SE on said Creek NW on John Ewing Calhoun's, SW on John Gocher. *The said tract of 150 acres being part of a tract of land containing 630 acres granted to the said John Ritchey 6 February 1796.* John Ritchey, Margrit (mark) Ritchey. Wit. William Caldwell, Elisabeth Ann Caldwell, Clough Harris. Plat shows bounding John Gocher, John E. Calhoun, John Ritchey. Proved by Clough Harris 28 January 1791 before Angus Campbell, J.P. [LCDBK D: 76-77]

Ritchey, John: 4 November 1808: I William Moor of Laurens Dist., S.C., to Wm. Moore, of same place, for $500; 133 acres. *Originally granted to John Ritchey 6 February 1786* bounded NW on land of John Ewing Calhoun, SW on John Gocher. Also one tract of 38 acres on the W side of Rabourns Creek bounding lands of Wm. McPherson, land not know, and on the above mentioned tract of 133 acres of land. William Moor. Wit: Thomas Wood, Wm. Norman. Proved by Wm. Norman 4 November 1808 before J. Blackwell, J.P. [LCDBK J: 18-19]

Ritchey, John: 23 July 1790: John Ritchey and Margaret, his wife, to William Caldwell and Elizabeth, is wife, all of Ninety Six Dist., S.C., planters, to Lewis Banton, of same place, for £81 Stg.; 328 acres on waters of Reaburns Creek of Reedy River. *Being a part of 630 acres originally granted unto the said John Ritchey 15 October 1784.* John Ritchey (LS), Margret (M) Ritchey (LS), William Caldwell (LS). Wit: John Rodgers, John Carter, Sarah (X) Banton. Proved by John Carter 23 July 1790 before William Caldwell, J.P., Newberry, Co, S.C. [LCDBK: E 391-393]

Ritchey[Richie], John: 16 August 1790: John Ritchey, of Laurens Co., S.C., to William Arnold, of same place, planter, £200; 300 acres on Reaburans Creek Bounded NW by lands of John Ewing Calhouns and lands of Roger Murphy: to the SE of lands formerly sold by the said John Ritchey to Lewis Banton and lands of Mr. Hodges. *300 acres of land being all the remainder part of 637 acres granted to the said John Ritchey by Wm. Moultrie, Governor of said state 6 February 1786.* John Ritchey (L.S.)

Margaret (M her mark) Ritchey (L.S.) Wit: William Caldwell, Thomas
Boyce, William Arnold. Proved by Thomas Boyce 14 September 1792
before John Hunter, J.P. [LCDBK D: 289-290]

Richey, John: 8 July 1819: LWT of John Richey, of Laurens Co., S.C. I
direct that all my just debts should be paid out of the residue of my property
that my wife can best share to be sold. . . . give to my wife Margret Richey
all of my property both real and personal during her life to be freely
possessed and enjoyed. To my son William said Negro boy Billey, at the
death of his mother Margrett the tract of land where on I now live containing
220 acres. . . . to my daughter Jane Harris I give her at the death of her
mother the sum of $4. . . . at the death of my wife I desire that what property
I have not given as above be divided to my son-in-law Joseph Graves and
Samuel Richey. .I appoint my friend Martin Shaw and son Wm. Richey
Executors. . John (X) Richey (LS) Wit: David Caldwell, Jurn, Archibald
Scott, Aven Fuller. Proved 8 November 1819 [Ingmire, p. 13]
[LCWBK A: 20]

[Family: Wife Margaret, son William, daughter Jane Harris, son-in-law
Joseph Graves.]

Ritchey, Robert & Elener McCluer: 22 January 1791: This day came
Ellener McClure before me Charles Saxon, Esq., and made oath that she
bought of Elliott Monary two sow piggs which increased now to 14 heads
and as her brother Robert Ritchey is often disputing with her concerning the
increase of said Hoggs, they being marked of the same mark they formerly
gave on the plantation which is a crop and slitt in each ear, she is making
oath to said hoggs which she on her oath saith that the very hoggs now in her
possession is the increase of one of the sows she bought Elliot Monary and
they are her just and right property. Ellener (mark) McCluer) before Charles
Saxon, J.P. [LCDBK C: 321]

[Family: Elener McCluer, sister of Robert Ritchey.]

Ritchey, John: 22 January 1791: This day Elenor McClure, daughter of
John Ritchey, deceased, made oath that a certain branded cow 13 years old,
now in her possession which was willed to her by her deceased father as will
appear by the will to be her just right and property and also the following
cattle the increase of said cow which she now in her possession, is the same
and that she never, bargained, sold them to any person. Ellener (Mark)
McCluer. [LCDBK C: 321]

[Family: Father John Ritchey, deceased by 1791, daughter Elenor McClure,
son Robert Ritchey.]

Richey, John: LWT dated 3 July 1819: I direct that all my just debts should be paid out of the rediest of my property that my wife can best share to be sold by my Executors on a credit of 12 months. I give and bequeath to my wife Margaret Richey all of my property both real and personal during her life to be freely possessed, enjoy except one negro boy Billey. To my son William Richey the said negro boy Billey, at my death and at the death of his mother Margaret the tract of land where on I now live containing 220 acres; to my daughter Jane Harris, I give her at the death of her mother the sum of $4.00 it being all that I intend for her both out of real and personal estate. At the death of my wife I desire that what property I have not given as above be divided in the following manner, that is to say to my son-in-law Joseph Graves and Samuel Richey can divide the same equally betwixt them . Appoint my friend Martin Shaw and my son William Richey executors. John (X) Richey (LS). Wit: David Caldwell, Junr. Archibald Scott. Aven. Fuller. [LCWBK E: 41]

[Family: Wife Margaret, son William, daughter, Jane Harress [Harris], son-in-law Joseph Graves, Samuel Richey]. [Is Jane's husband Clough Harris who signs deed of John Richey?]

Richey lands: 18 January 1799: Robert Richey, of Laurens Co., S.C., to Richard Childress, of same place, for £40; 176 acres on waters of Rabourns Creek. Robert (R) his mark Richey (LS). Wit: John Woody, John Jones. Proved by John Woody 12 February 1799 before Danl. Wright, J.P. [LCDBK H: 111]

Richie, Mary: Survey for Mary Richie pursuant to precept dated 11 December 1772; 100 acres in Craven Co., on a small branch of Reyburns Creek called Jones's Branch. Bounded on all sides by vacant land. Certified 22 January 1773. Jonthn. Downs, D.S. [P20_125:1]

Richie, Mary: Memorial for Mary Richie; 100 acres in Craven Co., on a small branch of Rayburns Creek Jones's branch. Bounded on all sides by vacant land. Certified 20 September 1774 and granted 17 March 1775. Quit rent to commence in 2 years. 17 August 1775. Jonathan Downes, D.S. [Irish in margin]. [M2_299:1]

Richie, Mary: 13 December 1787: Adam Gordon, of Laurens Co., S.C., to Samuel Dunlap, of same place, for £80 Stg.; 100 acres on a branch of Reaburns Creek called Jones Branch. Bounded on all sides by vacant land when first surveyed. Originally *granted 17 March 1775 to Mary Ritchey.* [The deed states that Mary, his wife, hath hereunto set their hands. (No signature found for Mary]. Adam Gordon. Wit. Lewis Saxon, C.C. [LCDBK B: 284-286]

Richie, Mary [bounding]: W-5, 156-160: 1& 2 June 1786: Lease & release. Lewis Ogier, of St. Pauls Parish, S.C., Esquire, and Susannah, his wife, to Thomas Ogier, Esquire, of Charleston, for L265 Stg. tract in Craven Co., [listing only the one deed pertinent to Rayburns Creek]. On a branch thereof called Rayborns Creek, 250 acres adjacent land of Mary Richie. Lewis Ogier (LS), Susanna Ogier (LS). Wit: Dan Langford, Jno. Perry. Proved in Charles Town Dist. by the oath of Dan Lanford, 17 July 1786 before W. Dewitt, J.P. [Holcomb, Brent H., *South Carolina Deed Abstract 1783-1788*, SCMAR, Columbia, SC, pg. 344]

Rickenbaker, Henry: Survey for Henry Rickenbaker pursuant to precept dated 4 February 1772; 200 acres in Berkley Co., on a spring of Rebourns Creek, waters of Saludy. Bounded on all sides by vacant land. Certified 27 February 1772. Pat. Cunningham, D.S. [P20_96:3]

Rickenbaker, Henry: Memorial for Henry Rickenbacker; 200 acres in Berkley Co., on a spring of Raybons Creek, waters of Saludy river. Bounded on all sides by vacant land. Certified 27 February 1772 and granted 28 August 1772. Quit rent to commence in 2 years. 20 October 1772. Delivered 1 March 1772 to Thos. Wild. Patk. Cunningham, D.S. [M11_493:4]

Riley, Abraham: Survey for Abraham Riley pursuant to precept dated 1 August 1769: 100 acres on Rayburns Creek, waters of Saludy River. Bounded on all sides by vacant land. Certified 12 September 1769. Wm. Anderson, D.S. [P11_324:3]

Riley, Abraham: Memorial for Abraham Ryley; 100 acres in Berkley Co., on Rayburns Creek, waters of Saludy. Bounded on all sides by vacant land. Certified 5 June 1770 and granted 13 July 1770. Quit rent to commence in 2 years. 22 August 1770. Charles Sullivant. Wm. Anderson, D.S. [10_207:3]

Riley, Patrick: 9 March 1787: Patrick Riley, Ninety Six Dist., now Laurens Co., farmer, to Robert Sims, miller, of same place, for £20; 50 acres on S fork of Reaburns Creek. *Originally granted 5 June 1786 to Patrick Riley.* On the S fork of Reaburns creek. Bounded on lands laid out for Thos. McDaniel, Robert Sims, James McClanahan. Wit: Wm. Fariss, Andrew McKnight, Abraham Riley, Drury Boyce. [Nash, Abstracts of Early Records of Laurens Co., South Carolina, as this deed part of microfilm roll missing.] [LCDBK B: 19 & B: 156-158]

Riley, Patrick: 17 January 1785. Grant of 106 acres

Riley, Patrick: 9 & 10 June 1788: Patrick Riley, of Ninety Six Dist., and Laurens Co., to Martin Hughey, of same place, for £20; 106 acres on the S fork of Reaburns Creek. Bounded on Robert Sims, Thomas N. Daniel and James Downing. *Originally granted unto Patrick Riley 5 June 1786.* Signed Patrick Riley, Wit. Wm. Kellet, Wm. Sims. [LCDBK C: 50-52]

Riley, Patrick: 26 February 1807: Isaac Sharp, of Laurens Dist., S.C., to Drury Boyce, of same place, for $250; 106 acres on SE side of S Fork of Reaburns Creek. Bounded on lands of James Downen, Patrick Riley, Thomas McDonald, and Robert Sims at time of survey. *Originally granted to Patrick Riley 17 January 1785.* Isaac (T) Sharp (LS). Wit: Andrew (mark) McKnight, Bailey Mahon. Proved by Bailey Mahon before Jonthn. Downs, J.Q. Dower of Bettey Sharp, wife of the within named Isaac Sharp given 1 October 1808 before Jonathan Downs, J.Q. [See Tweedy land sales.] [LCDBK J: 214]

Riley, John: 3 December 1788: Patrick Reiley and Ann Riley, of Ninety Six Dist., Laurens Co., S.C., to William Kellet, of same place, for L100 Stg.; 100 acres on S fork of Reaburns Creek, formerly Craven now Laurens Co. *Originally granted to John Riley on 27 March 1775.* Bounded by vacant land at time of survey. Bounded by Thomas McDaniel (McDonald), Robert Sims, James Downing, also part of a tract of land granted 5 June 1786 to William Galaspy [see Gallispie] on the S fork of Reaburns Creek, containing 10 acres. Patrick Ryley, Ann Ryley. Wit: William Faris, John Kellet, Nathan (N) Camp. Proved by John Kellet 8 June 1789 before John Rodgers, J.P. [LCDBK C: 107-109]

Roberson, John: 17 November 1805: John Roberson, of Laurens Dist., S.C., to David Anderson, of same place, for $320; 177 acres on Robertson and James Crocker land, NW on a road known by the name of Swanseys, NW on a old road then along said road to said Andersons and Robertson land. [Plat shows on both sides Swansey's Road. Bounded on James Crocker, said John Robertson, said David Anderson, John Middleton.] John Roberson (LS) Wit: James Findley, Howell Mosely, David McCaa. Dower of Kinney Roberson, wife of the within named John Roberson given 4 July 1805 before B.H. Saxon, J.Q. Proved by 2 February 1807 before Lewis Graves, J.P. [LCDBK H: 208-209]

Rodgers, John: Memorial by John Rodgers for 600 acres in Craven Co., on a branch of Saludy river called Little River. Bounding N on land laid out to Charles Allen, William Linn? And Thomas Jones, W on Archibald Williamson, S on Major Williams, SE on Major Anderson. Certified May 1774 and granted 31 August 1774 to the memorialist. Quit rent to commence in two years from date. Set his hand 20 February 1774. Delivered 1 June 1775 to John McNees. [M13-340:5]

Rodgers, John: 29 October 1790: John Rodgers, of Laurens Co., S.C., to Elisha Mitchell, of same, for £50; 475 acres on branches of Reedy Fork and Dirty Creek, being part of 640 acres granted [no date given] to John Rodgers by his Excellency Wm. Moultrie Esqr. Governor Commander in Chief. Bounded N on John Brown, W by said Rodgers. John Rodgers Wit: Joshua Downs, Ezekiel Roland, Mansil Crisp. Proved by Joshua Downs 8 April 1793 before Charles Saxon, J.P. [Plat shows bounded by Doctor Faysaux, Mansil Crisp, Wm. T. Rodgers, John Brown.] [LCDBK D: 400-401]

Rodgers, John: 3 November 1791: Elisha Mitchell of Lauren Co., S.C., to Robert McNees, of same place, for £90; 475 acres on the branches of Reedy fork and Dirty Creek, *being a part of 640 acres granted to John Rodgers* bound N on land laid out to John Brown, W on land of said Rodgers. Elisha Mitchell, (LS). Wit: Boling (mark) Bishop, Andrew Rodgers, Uriel (mark) Nixon. Proved by Andrew Rodgers 6 April 1793 before Charles Saxon. [LCDBK D: 401-402]

Rodgers, John: [blank]1791: John Rodgers, of Laurens Co., S.C., to Mansil Crisp, of same place,.£50; 165 acres on the waters of Durty *sic* [Dirty] Creek of Reaburns Creek, *being part of 640 acres granted to said John Rodgers by his Excellency William Moultrie, Esq.* John Rodgers. Wit. Robert Culbertson, Ezekiel S. Roland, Joshua Downs. Plat shows bounded by Pierce Butler, Elisha Mitchell, Wm. Rodgers. Wit: Robert Culbertson, Ezekiel S. Roland, Joshua Downs. Joshua Saxon, J.P. [Plat] [LCDBK C: 362-363]

Rodgers, John: 29 October 1796: John Rodgers Esq., of Laurens Co., S.C., to John Francis Wolff, Esq., of same place, for £50 Stg.; 100 acres on the waters of Raiborns Creek. Bounded on the S by Isaac Abercrombie, N of said Rodgers, W on Raiborns Creek, being part of 333 acres. *Originally granted to said [John] Rodgers 2 March 1795.* Plat. John Rodgers, (LS). Wit. Charles Smith, James McCaa. Proved by James McCaa 18 January 1797 before Chas. Smith, J.P. Plat shows bounding John Rodgers, Isaac Crumby [Abercrombie]. Survey 6 September 1796 by John Rodgers, D. S. [LCDBK F: 160-161]

Rodgers, John: 15 November 1806: John F. Wolff, of Laurens Dist., S.C., to Anderson Arnold, of same place, for $120; 100 acres on Raburns Creek, waters of Reedy River. Bounding Anderson Arnold, Gideon Thomason, William Gray, *being part of a tract of 333 acres of land originally granted to John Rodgers 2 March 1795* and conveyed from the said John Rodgers to John H. Wolff by deed of conveyance dated 29 October 1796. J.F. Wolff (LS) Wit: Robert Matthews, James Thomason. Proved by James Thomason 18 November 1806 before William Arnold, J.P. [LCDBK H: 213-214]

Rodgers, John: November 18, 1806: John Rodgers, of Laurens Dist., S.C., to Anderson Arnold, of same place, for $20; 7 acres lying on Raburns Creek. Bounded on E on Anderson Arnold, NW on Gideon Thomason, S on Martin Dial. *Being part of 333 acres originally granted to said John Rodgers 2 March 1795.* John Rodgers (LS) Wit: J. F. Wolff, Thos. Wright. Proved by John F. Wolff 18 November 1806 before William Arnold, J.P. [LCDBK H: 214]

Rodgers, John: 19 February 1804: John Rodgers, of Laurens Dist., S.C., to David Studdard for $50; 50 acres on a branch of Reabourns Creek, it *being a part granted to John Rodgers* and now conveyed to David Studdard. John Rodgers (LS) Wit: Mansil Crisp, William M. Crisp. Proved by Mansel Crisp 19 November 1805 before Robert Hutchison, J.P. [Plat shows bounding lands of Martin Dial, Wm. Garey, and John F. Wolff. [LCDBK J: 25-26]

Rodgers, John: 27 October 1806: David Studdard, of Laurens Dist., S.C., to Gideon Thomason for $50; 50 acres on the branches of Rebourns Creek, *it being a part granted to John Rodgers* and now conveyed to Gideon Thomason. David (D his mark) Studdard, Junior. Wit: David Studdard, Senr., J.F. Wolff. Dower of Nancy Studdard, the wife of the within named David Studdard given 3 August 1808 before Jonathan Downs, J.Q. [Plat shows bounded by Martin Dial, Wm. Garry, John F. Wolf. [LCDBK J: 26]

Rodgers, John: 3 August 1808: Gideon Thomason, of Laurens Dist., S.C. to George Thomason, of same place; 50 acres for $115 in Laurens Dist., lying on Rabourns Creek waters of Reedy River. Bounding Anderson Arnold's, Martin Dial, William Garey and William Gary's land. Being part of a tract of 300 acres of land. *Originally granted to John Rodgers on the 6 March 1795* and conveyed from said John Rodgers to David Studdard by deed dated 19 February 1804 and conveyed from David Studdard to Gideon Thomason by deed 27 October 1806. Gideon Thomason. Wit: David Studdard, Anderson Arnold. Dower of Elenor Thomason, the wife of Gideon Thomason 3 August 1808. Elenor Thomason. Jonathan Downs, J.Q. [LCDBK J: 24]

Rodgers, John: 10 February 1812: John Rodgers, of Laurens Dist., S.C., to Doct[or] Samuel Todd, of same place, for $100; 125 acres, on a creek called Ready fork, the waters of Little River, *and being a part of 600 acres granted to John Rodgers Senr. 31 August 1774* and by the said John Rodgers, Senr. conveyed to the above named John Rodgers. Bounded on Jack Valk, Andrew Rodgers Junr, John Rodgers, Senr. John Rodgers (LS). Wit: R.A. Todd, Jas. L. Rodgers. Sally Rodgers, the wife of the within named John Rodgers, Junr. appears before me and upon being privately and separately examined by me did declare that she does fully voluntarily and without any compulsion dread or fear, renounce release and forever relinquish unto Samuel Todd. 28 October 1819. on presenting the above relinquishment of Dower to Mrs.

Sally Rodgers, she refused her signature before John Garlington. Proved by James S. Rodgers 28 October 1819 before John Garlington, Q. M. [LCDBK K: 262]

Rodgers, John: 12 December 1821: William C. Gary, of Laurens Dist., S.C., to John Dorough, of same place, for $300; 128 acres on the branches of Rabourns Creek, *it being a part of a tract of land originally granted to John Rogers.* Bounding on Red creek, W by Martin Armstrong and Martin Dial and S by Anderson Arnold, James G. Coker and William C. Gary. Wm. C. Gary (SL) Wit: Drury Coker, Mary Coker. Proved by Drury Coker 2 June 1822 before James Dorrah, J.P. [LCDBK L: 57]

Ross, David: 10 September 1793: John Hunter, Esqr., of Laurens Co., S.C., to David Ross, of same place., for £6, 6 sh.; 138 acres on Reedy River. Bounding lands of David Greene and John Rodgers and Reedy River. *Being part of a grant of land originally granted to Pierce Butler* and by him conveyed to Hercules Danl. Bize on 9 July 1792 and now conveyed by the said John Hunter by virtue of a power of attorney from said Hercules Danl. Bize, bearing date 1 June 1793. John Hunter, Attorney for Hercules Danl. Bize. (Seal). Wit. Francis Ross, Sal. Cooper. Proved by Francis Ross 12 March 1794 before Joseph Downs, J.P. [Plat shows bounding David Green, David Ross, Reedy River, John Rodgers] [See Pierce Butler] [LCDBK F: 135]

Ross, David, dec'd: No date [1825/6]. Daughter Sarah, wife of James Dorough [Dorroh]. David Ross, deceased. Settlement Robert Gray and wife, Jean vs. Francis Ross, John F. Simpson and wife, Mary, James Dorough [Dorroh] and wife Sarah, David Boyd and wife Margaret. Laurens Probate Book pg. 2, 1825/6] [Revill, pg. 173]

[Family: Daughters: Jane Gray, wife of Robert Gray, Mary Simpson, wife of John F. Simpson, Sarah Dorough/Dorroh wife of James Dorough, Margaret Boyd, wife of David Boyd.]

Ryan, James: 1768 bounding Daniel Allen, Senr.

Ryan, James: 19 October 1797: James Oliphant, of Laurens Co., S.C., to Joseph Cox, of same place, for 5sh. Stg.; 100 acres on the N side of Little River *part of original granted to James* Ryan, and conveyed by said Ryan to James Boyd and at said Boyd at his death left it to his daughter Polley, now wife of Ephraim McClain and conveyed by John Boyd, the attorney of the said Polley and Ephraim, to James Oliphant. James (O) Oliphant (LS) Wit: John Davis, Thomas Cox. Probed by Thomas Cox 19 October 1797 before John Davis, J.P. [LCDBK F: 320]

[Family: James Boyd's daughter Polly, wife of Ephraim McClain.]

Sarrazen, Jonathan: Z-5, 76-78: Lease & release. 23 & 24 January 1787: Jonathan Sarrazen, of Charleston, Esquire, to Richard Humphreys of same place, for £25 12sh 6d Stg. three tracts, in all 500 acres; [only listed the one pertinent to Rayburns Creek] 200 acres in Berkley Co., on waters of Rayburns Creek surveyed 1 March 1775. J. Sarrazin (LS). Proved by the oath of James Kennedy. [Charleston Deeds Z-5, 76-78] [Brent H. Holcomb, *South Carolina Deed Abstract 1783-1788*, pg. 429]

Saxon, Charles: 2 October 1786: 176 acres granted.

Saxon, Charles: 23 April 1791: Charles Saxon, Esquire, of the Co. of Laurens, S.C., of one part & Samuel Saxon, Batchelor, of same place, of the other part for £69; 176 acres on Reaburns creek, waters of Saluda River. Bounded SW on Samuel Scott, NE on lands unknown, and NW on James Williams's & Ratcliff Jowels lands. *Original grant containing 176 acres granted unto sd. Charles Saxon Esq. 2 October 1786.* Signed Charles Saxon (LS) Wit: Williams Barksdale, Ann Craddock, Mary (S) Barksdale. Proved by William Barksdale 16 August 1791 before George Anderson, J.P. [LCDBK D: 40]

Saxon, Lewis: 1 January 1785 and 23 January 1785 - land granted

Saxon, Lewis: 13 March 1786: Lewis Saxon, of Laurens Co., S.C., to Joel Burgess, of same place, for £43 11 sh.; 150 acres on S fork of Reaburns Creek. *Being part of land granted to the said Lewis Saxon 21 January 1785* by his Excellency Benjamin Guerand, Esq. *Tract of land originally granted January 23, 1785.* Bounded S by Alex. Mazyck and land laid out to Thomas Calhoun; NE on lands laid out to John McClanahan other sides on land laid out to Moses Kirkland, dec'd. Lewis Saxon (LS) [LCDBK A: 197-200]

Saxon, Lewis: 27 December1787: Joel Burgess, of Laurens Co., S.C., to Lewis Saxon, of same place, for £60; 150 acres on S fork of Reaburn Creek, bounding lands of Alexr. Mazick, Moses Kirkland, Thomas Cahoon, John McClanahan, being land *granted to said, Lewis Saxon 21 January 1785* and conveyed to said Joel Burgess by lease and release dated 3 March 1786. Joel Burgess. Wit: Joshua Downs. Wm. Rodgers. [LCCDK B: 366-267]

Saxon, Lewis: 30 December 1798: William Thomason, Junr., of Laurens Co., S.C., Dist. of Ninety Six, to Hugh Mahaffey, of same place, for $220; 100 acres on NE side of S. Fork of Rabourns Creek, being *part of a tract granted to Lewis Saxon*, and conveyed by him to James Abercrombie and from him to William Thomason, Junr. Bounded on W on Thomas Camp, to Sarah Jeffrey's line to said creek. William (mark) Thomason (LS) Wit: Robert Coker, Junr., Alexander Mahaffey. Proved by Alexr. Mchaffey 20 November 1799 before Joseph Downs, J.P. Dower of Sarah Thomason, wife of the within William Thomason given 20 September 1799 before Jonthn. Downs, J.L.C. [LCDBK F: 489-490]

Saxon, Lewis: 1 February 1799: James Abercrombie, of Laurens Co., S.C., to Elisha Casey, of same place, £6 Stg.; *12 acres part of original grant of 200 acres granted to Lewis Saxon 5 November 1792* on the S side of Rabourns Creek and the S fork of the said creek. Granted by said Saxon to James Abercrombie. Bounding Owing Reid's. James Abercrombie. Wit: William Camp. Thomas May. Proved by William Camp 18 February 1797 before Reuben Pyles, J.P. [LCDBK F: 422-423]

Saxon, Lewis: 7 March 1799: Elisha Casey, of Laurens Co., S.C., to Samuel Nesbit, of same place, for £23, 6 shillings, 8 p; 100 acres on a branch of Rabourns Creek called the Bullett Branch. Bounded N by land laid out unknown, S on Thos. Hooker, and on all other sides by vacant land, except ½ acres around the graveyard. Elisha Casey (LS). Wit: Drury Boyce, Edward Nash. Proved by Drury Boyce 13 March 1799 before Joseph Downs, J.P. [LCDBK G: 681]

Saxon, Lewis: 23 September 1816: Elisha Casey, of Laurens Dist., S.C., to Mathew Landers, of same place, for $200; 112 acres *being a part of a tract of land granted to Lewis Saxton and Owing Read* and made from James Abercrumby and Thomas Camp and made from said James Abercrumby and said Thomas Camp to the aforesaid Elisha Casey. Tract on the fork of Raborns Creek on the S side of the said creek. Elisha Casey (LS). Wit: Richard (X) Landers, James McKnight. Dower of Esther Casey, wife of the within Elisha Casey given 11 October 1816 before Wm. Arnold, J.Q. Proved by James McKnight 11 October 1816 before Wm. Arnold, J.Q. [LCDBK L: 8]

Saxon, Lewis: Grant for 200 acres in 1792 on W side of Raibourns Creek.

Saxon, Lewis: 29 January 1799: James Abercrombie, of Ninety Six Dist., S.C., to Sarah Jeffres, of same place, for £15 Stg.; 50 acres, being part of 200 acres on the W side of Raibourns Creek. *Originally granted to Lewis Saxon and recorded 5 November 1792.* Bounding the mouth of Rock House branch-original line, William Camp, and creek. Signed James Abercrombie. Wit: Joseph Dunklin, Sarah (x) Dunklin. Proved by oath of Joseph Dunklin 16 March 1799 before John McElroy, J.P. Greenville Co. [LCDBK F: 440]

Saxon, Lewis.: 18 July 1810 *sic*: We Lewis Saxon and Jeremiah Hollingsworth, otherwise L. Saxon and Co., Merchants, of Laurens Dist., S.C., to John Blackstock, of same place, for $300; 100 acres on the N side of Reedy River below the mouth of the first branch above Peaching old field or creek. Wit: W.F. Downs, C. Saxon. Dower of Sarah McNeese, widow of Lewis Saxon, dec'd. given 27 November 1817 before Wm. Arnold, J.Q. Proved by C. Saxon 27 November 1817 before Wm. Arnold, J.Q. [LCDBK K: 193-194]

Saxon, Lewis: October 21, 1813: Death. Rev. War Soldier, born December 10, 1761. Wife Sarah McNeese Saxon born August 19, 1769, died March 26, 1831. Both buried in Saxon, Cleveland Cemetery, Rt. 252, right side of Lake Rabon. [*Burying Grounds, Graveyards and Cemeteries, Laurens Co., South Carolina. Vol. One*, pg. 35.]

Saxon, Lewis: 18 November 1813: Whereas Lewis Saxon, late of Laurens Dist., S.C., departed this life intestate having a widow Sarah Saxon and twelve children: To wit: Clarissa, the wife of William F. Downes, Charles, David, Mary, Hugh, Allen, Joshua, Lydall, Tabitha, Susan, Samuel and Harriet all of who are infants under the age of twenty one except Clarissa and Charles being at the time of his death seized and possessed of a considerable real and personal estate and whereas the said Lewis Saxon in his lifetime intended to have made a will and to have disposed of his property in a manner that the same should be continued on his plantation for the support of the said Sarah and the maintenance and education of his children and to have directed that each child receive his or her distributive share of the estate as they arrive of age or married. And whereas he unfortunately departed this life before he made a will, by which his intentions could be carried unto execution and it now becomes necessary that administration should be granted on his estate and a take place a certain the distributive share to which each child shall be entitled and whereas the said Sarah Saxon is by law entitled to the administration on his estate, but is unwilling to take upon herself the trouble of the same and is desirous that her son-in-law William F. Downs and her son Charles Saxon should jointly administer thereon and begin the intentions of the intestate and execution as nearly as possible. Signed Sarah Saxon (LS). Wit: R. Creswell, Turner Richardson, Jonthan Downs, Proved by Turner Richardson 13 May 1816 before John Garlington, Q.M. [LCDBK K: 127-182]

[Family: Wife, Sarah; daughter Clarissa, wife of Wm. F. Downes, Mary, Tabitha, Susan, Harriet, sons Charles, David, Hugh, Allen, Joshua, Lydall, Samuel.]

Saxon, Lewis: 20 October 1816: William F. Downes and Clarrisa Downs, his wife, late Clarissa Saxon, daughter of Lewis Saxon, deceased to Charles A. Saxon, for $800; 215 acres on the waters of Raburns Creek, bounded N on the said Charles A. Saxon, W on land assigned to the widow of Lewis Saxon, deceased, S by William Johnson, E on land of Thomas Johnson, deceased, being part of the tract of land whereon Lewis Saxon, deceased formerly lived and which (by the commissioners appointed agreeable to the At of the Governor in such case made to made partition and division of the lands of the said Lewis Saxon, deceased) - and assigned to the said William F. Downs, in right of his wife Clarissa Downs aforesaid. William F. Downs, (LS) Clarissa Downs (LS). Wit: John Cunningham, James Word. Dower of Clarissa Downs, that she did actually join her husband in executing the within release and renounces all her estate interest and inheritance dated 20 March 1817 Clarissa Downs. before John Garlington, Clk. of Laurens Dist. . Proved by John Cunningham 20 March 1817 before John Garlington, Clk. of Laurens Dist. and Q.M. [LCDBK K: 164]

Schaufferburger, Johannes: Survey for Johannes Schaufferburger pursuant to precept dated 17 October 1766; 150 acres in Craven Co., on a small branch or Reborns Creek, called the Lokest [Locust] Fork. Bounded NE by Jacob Kuhmany; other sides vacant. Certified __ July 1772. Alexd. Kennedy, D.S. Ord. Co. 11 January 1773. [P19_332:3]

Schaufferburger, Johannes: Memorial for Johannes Schaufferberger; 150 acres in Craven Co., on a small branch of Reyburns Creek called Locust fork. Bounded NE by land surveyed for Jacob Kulmany; other sides vacant. Certified 11 Jan 1773 and granted 6 February 1773. Quit rent to commence in 10 years. 31 July 1773. A. Kennedy, D.S. [B in margin] [M12_331:6]

Scott, Samuel: Land *originally granted 21 January 1785.*

Scott, Samuel: 19 September 1794: Samuel Scott, of Laurens Co., S.C., to David McCaa, of same place, for £10 Stg.; 150 acres on waters of Rayburns Creek. Bounded W on Miss Millhouse, S James Williams, and all other sides by vacant land at time of original survey. *Land originally granted to Samuel Scott on 21 January 1785.* David McCaa to pay a certain Judgment now extent and by virtue of a Power of Attorney in possession of Hezekiah Alexander of Mecklenburg Co., N.C. Samuel Scott (LS) Wit: Litt. B. Wilson, William Harris. Proved by William Harris 20 September 1794 before Charles Saxon, J.P. [LCDBK E: 278-281]

Scott, Samuel: 4 April 1796: David McCaa, of Laurens Co., S.C., to Samuel Scott, of same place, for £100; 150 acres on waters of Reaburns Creek were Samuel Scott now lives. Bounded on W by Miss Millhouse, S by

James Williams, all other sides vacant. David McCaa. Wit: John Sims, John (mark) Manly. Proved by John Sims 5 April 1796 before John Cochran, D.C. [LCDBK F: 86]

Scott, Samuel: 5 April 1796: Samuel Scott, of Laurens Co., S.C., to John Sims, of same, for £100 Stg.; 50 acres part of 150 acres on waters of Reaburns Creek where Samuel Scott now lives. Bounded on the Dittany hill and Samuel Scott. Saml. Scott (LS) Wit: S. Saxon, Jno. Rowland. Proved by Saml. Saxon 5 April 1790 before John Cochran, D.C. [LCDBK F: 85-86]
Scott, Samuel: 28 March 1796: John Sims, of Laurens Co., S.C., to Samuel Scott, of same place, for 20 sh. to be paid annually during the term of 20 years, all that plantation, piece or *parcel of land on which the said Saml. Scott now lives belonging to him the said John Sims.* John Sims, (LS) Wit: Wm. Dunlap, John Cochran. Proved by John Cochran 14 September 1796 before Chas. Saxon, J.P. [LCDBK F: 136]

Scott: Samuel: 8 & 9 July 1792: Samuel Scott, of Laurens Co., Ninety Six Dist., S.C., to John Ritchey, of same place, for £50 Stg.; 150 acres on Reedy River. Bounded on SW on land of Ms. Millhouse, SE by James Williams, NE on vacant land. Samuel Scott (LS). Wit; Thos. Wadsworth, Thomas Meaid. Proved by Thomas Wadsworth 25 May 1797 before Zachr. Bailey, J.P. [See Deed J: 27 for *originally grantee Samuel Scott 1785.*] [LCDBK F: 219-22]

Scott, Samuel: 17 September 1805: John Ritchey, of Laurens Dist., S.C., to Robert McCurley, of same place, for $400; 150 acres on waters of Reaburns Creek, all that land whereon Samuel Scott formerly lived. *Originally granted to Samuel Scott in January 1785,* conveyed by him to John Richey by lease and release 8 July 1792. John Ritchey (LS) Wit: S. Adams, John Roberson. Proved by John Robinson 10 August 1808 before John Garlington, R.M.C. [LCDBK J: 27]

Scott, Samuel: 12 March 1807: Robert McCurley, of Laurens Dist., S.C., to Frederick Burtz, of same place, for $400; 150 acres on waters of Raburn Creek, all that land whereon Samuel Scott formerly lived. *Originally granted to Samuel Scott in January 1785*, conveyed by him to John Richey by lease and release 8 July 1792. Robert (R) McCurly (LS) Wit. P.G. Wharton, Wm. Moore, Andw. Burnside. Proved by Andrew Burnside 10 August 1808 before Dd. Anderson. [LCDBK J: 27]

Scott, Samuel: 1809: Samuel Scott vs. John Ricthey – money. Laurens Equity 1809-4. [Revill, pg. 175]

Shelley, Richard: 1775 bounding John Monk. No survey found for Richard Shelley/Shelly.

Sherrill, Philip: Survey for Philip Sherrill pursuant to precept 5 March 1768; 250 acres on a branch of Rabens creek called Helms Creek (waters of Saludy). Bounded NE part by John Williams and part vacant, SE by vacant land, NW by John Williams, N vacant land. Certified 7 March 1768 Wm. Wofford, D.S. [P19-422:1]

Sherrill, Philip: Memorial by Philip Sherrill; 250 acres in Craven Co., on a branch of Rayburns Creek called Hellems Creek, waters of Saludy bounded NE by John Williams and vacant land, NW by John Williams, SE and N by vacant land. Certified 6 April 1773 and granted 5 May 1773 to the memorialist. Quit rent to commence in two years from date. Set his hand 24 August 1773 Wm. Wofford, D.S. Delivered 14 August 1775 to George Norwood. [M12-400:5]

Sherrill, Philip: 18 October 1798: Philip Sherril, of Greenville Co., S.C., to Isaac Dial, of Laurens Co., S.C., for £100; 250 acres on waters of Rabourns Creek on a branch known by the name of Hellams Branch. Bounded NE by John Williams and vacant land, NW by John Williams SE and N by vacant land at the time of the survey. Philip (X) Sherril. Wit: Benjamin Holley, Briton (mark) Neal. Proved by Benjamin Holley 18 October 1798 before George Salmon. Dower given by [blank] Sherril, wife of Philip Sherril given 18 October 1798. [LCDBK F: 411-412]

Sherrall, Philip: Memorial by Philip Sherrall; 200 acres in Craven Co. on a branch of Rayburns Creek called Hellems Creek, waters of Saludy. Bounded NE on John Williams and vacant land; NW by John William; SE and N by vacant land. Certified 6 April 1773 and granted 5 May 1773. Quit rent to commence in 2 years. 24 August 1773. Delivered 14 August 1775 to George Norwood. Wm. Wofford, D.S. [M12_400:5]

Sherrall, Philip: 18 October 1798: Philip Sherril, of Greenville Co., S.C., to Isaac Dial, of Laurens Co., S.C., for £100; 250 acres on waters of Rabourns Creek (also known as Hellams Creek). Bounded by NE by John Williams and vacant land NW by John Williams; SE and N by vacant land at the time of the survey. *Originally granted to* [not named]. Philip (X) Sherril. Wit: Benjamin Holley, Briton Neal. Proved by Benjamin Holley 18 October 1798. Dower of ____ Sherril, wife of Philip Sherril before George Salmon, J.G.C. [LCDBK F: 411- 412]

Shirley, John: Survey for John Shirley pursuant to precept dated 3 February 1767; 200 acres in Craven Co., on Raiburns Creek. Bounded SW on land held by George Wright; other sides vacant. Certified 19 February 1767. Ralph Humphreys, D.S. [P9_21:2]

Shirley, John: Memorial for John Shirley; 200 acres in Craven Co., on Rayburns Creek. Bounded SW on land of George Wright; other sides vacant. Certified 19 February 1767 and granted 28 August 1767. Quit rent to commence in 2 years. 2 October 1767. For the Memorialist John Cargill. Ralph Humphreys, D.S. [M9-344:1]

Shirley, John: 31 January 1788: John Shirley and Rebecca, his wife, of Laurens Co. to Wm. Mitchell, of same place, for £70 Stg.; 200 acres on Raburns Creek. Bounded SW on George Wright; other sides vacant. *Originally granted 28 August 1767 to said John Shirley.* Signed John Shirley, Rebecca Shirley. Wit: Aaron Starnes, Wm. Goodman, Stephen Wood. [LCDBK B: 319-320]

Shirley, John: 20 February 1788: John Shirley, of Laurens Co., S.C., has sold, and firmly by these presents doth sell in open market unto my own son Aaron Shirley three horse kid of creatures. [Descriptions given with marks], also all my household furniture which I now posses and live stock [listed] for the sum of £60 Stg. John Shirley. Wit: George Hollingsworth, Marmaduke Pinson. Proved by Marmaduke Pinson 28 December 1789 before Silvanus Walker, J.P. [LCDBK C: 121]

[Family: Wife Rebecca, son Aaron Shirley.]

Shirley, John: 12 February 1792: John Williams, Laurens Co., S.C., to Anderson Arnold, of same for £7, 10 sh.; 100 acres on N fork of Rabourns Creek waters of Reedy River. Bounded SW on John Thomason, NE on William Anderson, SE on land not known, S on laid out for Isaac Abercrombie, *part of 1682 acres grant in 1786.* John Williams. Wit. William Thomason, Hastin Dial. Proved by John Williams before Joseph Downs, J.P. [LCDBK D: 248-249]

Shirley, Richard: Survey for Richard Shirley pursuant to precept dated 2 August 1768; 500 acres in Berkley Co., on a branch of Saludy called Rayburns Creek. Bounded by vacant land. Certified 11 August 1768. Jno. Caldwell, D.S. Ord. Co. for John McQueen 8 February 1773. [P10_236:1]

Shirly [Shirley], Richard: Memorial for Richard Shirly; 500 acres in Berkley Co., on a branch of Saludy called Rayburnes Creek. Bounded on all sides by vacant land. Certified 11 August 1768 and granted 15 February 1769. Quit rent to commence in 2 years. 26 April 1769. Jno. Caldwell, D.S. John Caldwell. [M8_423:2]

Shirley, Richard: Deceased before 10 Jan 1775.

Shirley, Richard: 10 January 1775: Robert Shirley, of Craven Co., S.C., planter and Jane, his wife, and Mary Shirley, his mother Mary Shirley, to Andrew Cuningham, of same place, for £450; *350 acres where we now live, part of 500 acres granted to Richard Shirley, deceased,* which was the said Robert Shirleys father and the said Mary Shirleys husband. Situated in Craven or Berkley Co., on Raborns Creek, the waters of Reedy River and Saluda River. Bounded all sides by vacant land at the time it was laid out. *Grant dated 15 February 1769.* Robert Shirley (LS), Jane (X) Shirley (LS), Mary (W) Shirley (LS). Wit: David Cuningham, Godfrey Jobell [Isbell?], Joseph (mark) Pinson. Proved by David Cunningham 4 September 1788 before William Moore, J.P. [LCDBK F: 212-213]

[Family Wife Mary, son Richard Shirley, Jane Shirley, daughter-in-law.]

Shirley, Richard: 18 May 1792: Margaret Cuningham, of Laurens Co., Ninety Six Dist., S.C., widow woman. That said Margaret Cuningham for consideration of the sum of £100 Stg., sold and released unto said Patrick Cuningham, (which is in his actual possession) for £100 Stg.; a tract of land containing 300 acres on S side of Reaburns Creek the waters of Reedy and Saluda Rivers, being part of 500 acres formerly in Berkley Co., but now in Laurens Co. *Originally granted unto Richard Shurley* by the Right Honorable Lord Charles Granville Montague, Capt. Genl. Governor and Commander in Chief in and over *S.C., by a grant bearing date the 15 February 1769* and bounded on all sides by vacant land at the time it was laid out., as a plat there of to the original grant annexed doth represent. Sold and conveyed away by Robert Shirley and Mary Shurley sic his mother unto Andrew Cuningham, now deceased by a lease and release dated 9 and 10 January 1775 the said Robert Shurley being the eldest son and lawful heir of the said Richard Shirley which land was confiscated by the assembly of the state aforesaid by an Act passed at Jacksonburough in the year 1780 on the account of the said Andrew Cuningham being a Bristish sic subject and the said tract of land was given and granted by the legislature of the state aforesaid unto the said Margaret Cuningham, relict of the said Andrew Cuningham and his children by the said Andrew Cuningham their heirs and assigns forever by an Act passed in Charleston 1783 and the said plantation or tract of land at this time is bounded NE on Reaburns Creek and Sarah Hodges; SW on Richard Pinson; W on Jacob Bowman; NW on land formerly John Ritchie. Margaret (her mark) Cuningham (L.S.) Wit. Isaac Gray, Charles Simmons, Wm. Cuningham. Proved by Charles Simmons 18 February 1795 before Daniel Wright, [LCDBK E: 425 - 427.]

Shirley, Richard: 5 October 1811: Robert Shirley, of Fairfield Co., S.C., planter, to Robert Shirley, son of John Shirley, of Laurens Dist., S.C., for £50 Stg.; 150 acres on Raburns Creek *part of 500 acres originally granted to Richard Shirley 15 February 1769* and conveyed to said Robert Shirley of Fairfield, heir of said Richard Shirley. Robert Shirley (LS). Wit: John Shurley, Elijah Shurley. Proved by John Shirley 6 February 1812 before James Powell, J.P. [Plat shows bounded by vacant land and land of Richard Shirley.] [LCDBK J: 253-254.]

Shirley, Richard: 29 April 1812: We John and Robert Cuningham, of Laurens Dist., S.C., to William More, of same place, for $200; 144 acres on Rabourns Creek, *being part of 500 acres granted to Richard Shirley 15 February 1769*. John Cunningham (LS), Robt. Cunningham (LS). Wit. Ursula Brooks, Dd. Anderson. Proved by Ursula Brooks 30 April 1812 before David Anderson, J.Q. [LCDBK K: 19]

Shirley, Robert: Petition 2 August 1768 for 300 acres on Rayburns Creek. No survey or memorial found.

Shote, Kitt: 1771 Kitt Shote bounding lands of Philip Jennings and in 1773 bounding lands of Samuel Elliott. No survey or memorial found.

Shote, Kitt: 1772: Kit Shote is bounding lands of Pierce Butler and Philip Jennings. No survey found for Kitt Shote.

Shote, Elizabeth: 6 April 1789: Grant for 300 on branches of Raburns Creek.

Shote, Elizabeth: 24 April 1790: Elizabeth Shote, of Laurens Co., S.C., to Bradford Camp, of Greenville Co., S.C., for £100; 296 acres on branches of Raburns Creek *being part of original grant of 300 acres granted to said Elizabeth Shote on 6 April 1789*. Elizabeth Shote (LS) Wit: Abraham (mark) Bolt, Joseph (Mark) Holms, Proved by Abram. Bolt 24 April 1790 before Jonathan Downs, J.P. [LCDBK C: 307-308]

Shote [Shoud/Stroud], Elizabeth: 10 May 1798: Bradford Camp, Laurens Co., S.C., planter, to Thomas May, of same place, merchant for £85 Stg.; 296 acres on branches of Reedy River and Reaburns Creek. *Originally granted to Elizabeth Shote* and conveyed to her by said Camp.*sic* [most likely should read conveyed by her to said Camp]. Bounding NW on Isaac Huger, S on William Tate, SE on Joseph Dorset, NE on Robert Coopers land formerly known by the name of Hickory Tavern, now New Market. Bradford Camp. Wit.: Robert Bolling, Wm. Camp. Proved by Robert Bolling 10 May 1800 before Reuben Pyles, J.P. [LCDBK G: 86-87]

225

Shote [Shoud/Stroud], Elizabeth: 14 June 1799: Thomas May, planter to Henry Burrow for $500; 296 acres on branches of Reedy River and Rabourns Creek. *Originally granted to Elizabeth Shote, conveyed to Camp,* then to said Thomas May. Bounded NW on Isaac Huger, S on Wm. Tait, SE on Jos. Dorset; NW on Robert Cooper. Formerly knows by name of Hickory Tavern, now New Market. T. May (LS). Wit: Hezekiah Dyer, Wm. (X) Adkins. Proved by Hezekial Dyer 17 February 1800 before Reuben Pyles, J.P. [LCDBK F: 503 - 504]

Shote: Elizabeth: The land which Elizabeth Shote sold to Bradford Camp was later conveyed to Thomas May. It consisted of 296 acres, being part of a 300 acres tract. It was on branches of Rabun Creek and known by the name Hickory Tavern. In 1796 Thomas May sold the property to Henry Burrow, it was described as "formerly known by the name of Hickory Tavern, now Newmarket." [The Scrapbook, pg. 50-51 and LCDBK G: 86]

Shote [Shode/Stroud], Elizabeth: 1 August 1800: Elizabeth Shroud, of Laurens Dist., S.C., for divers good causes and considerations have made and appointed my trusty friend William Penny, Power of Attorney to receive of Matthew McCawley, of Orange Co., North Carolina, $265; left me as a legacy by my two brothers, John Stroud and Latson Stroud. Elizabeth (X) Stroud. Wit: John Wiseman, John Hunter. Proved by John Wiseman 9 October 1800 before Zach. Bailey, J.P. [LCDBK G: 85]

Shubrick, Thomas - Survey for Thomas Shubrick pursuant to precept dated 5 February 1772; 1300 acres in the fork of Broad and Saludy river waters of a river called Reedy River. Bounded by Elias Brock, Daniel Allen, Nicholas Hill, John Baugh, Wm. Baugh, Ratcliff Joels *sic* [Jowell] Certified 6 March 1773. Wm. Gist., D.S. [P19-438:1]

Shubrick, Thomas: Memorial by Thomas Shubrick; 700 acres in Craven Co., in the N side of Enoree bounded NE and SE on John Deens, all other sides vacant. *Certified 26 February 1772.* Also a tract of land containing 1300 acres in the fork of Broad and Saludy Rivers on the waters of a river called Reedy River. *Certified 6 March 1772;* also a tract of land containing 3000 acres on the S side of Reedy River a branch of Saludy. Certified 11 March 1772 and all three granted 15 May 1772 to the memorialist. Quit rent to commence two years from date. Set his hand 26 June 1772. William Gist., D.S. Delivered to William Williamson by Charles Jacob Lindfors. [M11-275:1]

Shubrick, Thomas: 19 October 1792: John Hunter, Esq., attorney for John Rutledge, Junr., to Thomas Cook, of Newberry Co., S.C., for £42; 184 acres on waters of Reedy River. Bounding Elias Brock and *being part of 1300* *acres originally granted to Thomas Shubrick 15 May 1772,* conveyed by him to William Williamson, to John Rutledge, Esq., Junr and now conveyed by the said John Hunter by a Power of Attorney from said John Rutledge bearing date 31 January 1791. John Hunter (LS) attorney for John Rutledge, Junr. Wit: Thomas Wadsworth, Samuel Henderson. Joseph Downs, J.P. [Plat for 184 acres shows bounding on Part of said survey, Elias Brock. Certified 20 October 1792 by John Hunter, D.S.] [LCDBK D: 299-300]

Shubrick, Thomas: 19 October 1792: John Hunter, Esq., of Laurens Co., S.C., to Isaac Cook, of Newberry Co., S.C., for £63 Stg.; 315 acres on the [blank] side of Reedy River, *being part of 1300 acres granted to Thomas Shubrick 15 May 1772* and conveyed to William Williamson then to John Rutledge, Jr. Bounded on said Reedy river, widow Baugh and part of said survey. John Hunter, (LS) attorney for John Rutledge, Junr. Wit: Thomas Wadsworth, Samuel Henderson. Joseph Downs, J.P. [plat for 315 acres bounded by Widow Bough, Reedy River, Owins' land, said survey. Certified 20 October 1792 John Hunter, D.S. [LCDBK D: 303-304]

Shurbrick, Thomas: 5 September 1793: John Hunter, Esq., of Laurens Co., S.C., to Hugh Henderson, of same place. Witnessseth that the said John Hunter for the sum of £17 Stg.; 177 acres, *being part of a tract of 1300 acres of land originally granted to Thomas Shurbrick,* and by conveyance to Wm. Williamson and by the said Williamson to John Rutledge Junr., Esq. And from him by a power of attorney to the said John Hunter. John Hunter, (L.S.) Atty for John Rutledge, Junr. Wit. John Henderson, John Brodey. Proved 6 September 1793 by John Brodey before Joseph Downs. Plat for 177 acres. Plat shows bounding Wm. Allison, William Wadkins, part of said survey. [LCDBK E: 175- 178]

Shubrick, Thomas: 24 July 1797: John Rutledge, of Charleston, [S.C.] by my attorney, John Hunter, Esqr., to John Box, of Laurens Co., S.C., for £7; 50 acres on waters of Reedy River *being part of 3000 acres granted to Thomas Shubrick* and conveyed to Williamson then to John Rutledge. Bounded on said John Box, Big Survey. John Rutledge, by his attorney John Hunter. Wit: James Powell, Thomas Gaines. Proved by Thomas Gaines 8 December 1798 before Reuben Pyles, J.P. [Plat for 50 acres by my calculations is only 35 acres - shows bounding part of survey, part of Big survey, John Box]. [LCDBK F: 427-428]

Shubrick, Thomas: 20 April 1791: Deposition of Abraham Box made 20 April 1791 before Jonathan Downs, J.P. that about 6 years ago [1791], he heard his Uncle Henry Box tell the Deponent's father John Box that he gave up to him all the right and title of the above tract, then occupied by David Alexander, who at that time lived on said land. [See sale from Rutledge to

John Box above.] [LCDBK F: 428]

Shubrick, Thomas: 31 December 1799: Abel Thomas, of Laurens Co., S.C., to Nehemiah Thomas, of same place, for $94 and 1/4 dollars; 60 acres on waters of Reedy River, *part of 1300 acres granted to Thomas Shubrick.* Abel Thomas (LS). Wit: Edward Thomas, Evan Thomas, John Thomas. Plat by John Cochran made 9 March 1799 shows bounded by Edwd. Thomas, James Abercrombie, G. Brock, Abel Thomas, Robert Culbertson, on waggon Road to Brock's Store, part of survey for Isaac Thomas 14 November 1792 now to his son said Nehemiah Thomas. [LCDBK G: 89-90]

Shubrick, Thomas: 26 December 1799: Abel Thomas, of Laurens Co., S.C., to John Thomas, of same place, for $109; 68 acres on waters of Reedy River, *being part of 1300 grant to Thomas Shubrick.* Abel Thomas (LS). Wit: Edward Thomas, Thomas Hall, Nehemiah Thomas. Proved by Edward Thomas 17 March 1801 before James Abercombie, J.P. [LCDBK G: 182]

Shubrick, Thomas: 3 January 1805: Isaac Cook, of Laurens Dist., S.C., to Elias Brock, of same place, for $310; 129 acres, *being part of a tract originally granted to Thomas Shurbrick* and by sundry conveyances to Isaac Cook. *One other tract containing 43 acres originally granted to Hastings Dial* and by sundry conveyances to Isaac Cook the tract on waters of Rabourn Creek and Reedy River where said Isaac Cook now lives. Isaac (X) Cook (LS) Wit: John Coats, Charles Watkins. Proved by Charles Watkins 1 June 1805 before J. Blackwell, J.P. Dower of Charity Cook, wife of the within named Isaac Cook given 9 January 1805 before Dd. Anderson, J.Q. [LCDBK H: 94]

Shubrick, Thomas: 30 May 1807: Charles Miller, Laurens Co., S.C., to Elias Brock, of same, for $150; 60 acres on waters of Rabourn Creek, *the same being part of 1300 acres granted to Thomas Shubrick.* Charles Miller. Wit: John B. Simpson, James Dorrough, Junr. Proved by John B. Simpson 12 August 1807 before Samuel Cunningham, J.P. [LCDBK H: 245]

Shubrick, Thomas: 13 August 1808: Asa Mitchell, of Livingston Co., Kentucky, to John South, of Laurens Dist., S.C., for $150; 150 acres on waters of Reedy River, *it being part of a tract of 3000 acres granted to Thomas Shubrick* and conveyed to John Rutledge and by the said John Rutledge, by his attorney, John Hunter, conveyed to the above. [Plat shows land on waggon road, no bounding names listed]. Asa Mitchell. Wit: William (W) Macdavid, John (Dan his mark) Cunningham. Proved by John D. Cunningham 3 March 1817 before S. Cuningham, J.P. [LCDBK K: 227]

Shubrick, Thomas: 8 April 1811: Charles Madden and Abraham Madden, both of Laurens Dist., S.C., planters, to Lewis Mitchell, of Abbeville Dist., S.C., for $1000; 283 acres on E side of Reedy River, *being part of original grant to Thomas Shubrick* and conveyed to us by Thomas Lewis . Also 50 acres on W side of Reedy River *being part of a tract granted to Daniel McClain [McLain?]* and was to us by Thomas Lewis. Charles Madden (LS), Abraham Madden (LS) Wit: Samuel Cunningham, Margaret Cunningham. Dower of Keturah Madden, said wife of the within named Charles Madden, Jean Madden, said wife of the within named Abraham Madden. Proved by Samuel Cunningham 17 April 1814 before Chas. Allen. [LCDBK K: 55-56]

Shubrick, Thomas: 15 October 1793: John Rutledge Esq. Junr., of the City of Charleston, by his attorney John Hunter, Esqr., of Laurens Co., S.C., to David Green, of Laurens Co., S.C., £58 Stg., 8 p; 281 acres on Reedy River and Arthur Durham, William Simmons, Widow Swain, John Robinson and said river. Being part of a tract of 3000 acre, *originally granted to Thomas Shubrick on 15 May 1772,* and conveyed by him to William Williamson and by him to John Rutledge, Junr. and now conveyed by the said John Hunter by virtue of a Power of Attorney. John Hunter (LS) attorney for John Rutledge, Junr. Wit: John Pringle, Wm. Simmons. Proved by William Simmons 18 July 1794 before Danl. Wright, J.P. [LCDBDK E: 272-274]

Shubrick, Thomas: 21 April 1806: David Green, of Laurens Co., S.C., to Thomas Allison, of same place, for $250; 100 acres on the South side of Reedy River, *being part of grant to Thomas Shubrick* and by him conveyed to William Williamson and by him to John Rutledge and by him to John Hunter, by him to said David Green, now by said Green to Thomas Allison. David Green (LS).Wit: Jno. Pringle, Elijah Walker. Proved by Jno. Pringle 23 August 1806 before Jas. Powell, J.P. [LCDBK H: 253]

Simmons, Charles: No survey or memorial found.

Simmons, Charles: 13 March 1786: Charles Simmons, of Laurens Co., S.C., planter, to Samuel Bolling, of Ninety Six Dist., S.C., planter, for £60; 168 acres on a branch of Saluda River called Reedy River. Bounding N on Saluda River, NE on land laid out to George Martin, SW on John Milling. Charles Simmons, Elizabeth Simmons. Wit: Lewis Saxon, C.C. [LCDBK A: 201-205]

Simpson and Savage: Survey for William Savage and James Simpson, Esqrs. pursuant to precept 20 July 1772; 500 acres on waters of Rayborns Creek. Bounded N and S on land of Wm. Savage and James Simpson, Esqrs.; W by Indian land. Surveyed 3 March 1773. Ord. Co. 6 April 1773. Wm. Anderson, D.S. [P19_325:1]

Simpson and Savage: Survey for William Savage and James Simpson, Esqrs. pursuant to precept 20 July 1772; 500 acres waters of Rayburns Creek, Ninety Dist. S.C. Bounded by N by said Wm. Savage and James Simpson, Esqrs. and Henry Powell; E vacant land; W by Indian Line; S by Mr. Adamson and land surveyed for Moses Kirkland. Certified 3 March 1773. Ord. Co. 6 April 1773. Wm. Anderson, D.S. [P19_326:1]

Simpson and Savage: 26 May 1785: William Anderson, Esquire, of Ninety Six Dist., S.C. and Rachel, his wife, to Samuel Kelley, of same place, farmer, for £100; 500 acres. Whereas his Majesty King George the 3rd, by his letters of Patent bearing date 5 May 1773 did grant to Wm. Savage & James Simpson Esquires a certain plantation containing 500 acres on the waters of Reaburns Creek. Bounded at the time of survey, N & S by land surveyed for the sd. Savage & Simpson; W by the Indian Line, E by Henry Powell and vacant land. . Whereas the said Wm. Savage & John James Simpson did by lease and release dated 28 & 29 March 1776 conveyed all the said tract of 500 acres unto the aforesaid William Anderson. Now the sd. Wm. Anderson & Rachel his wife for the sum of £100 sell unto sd. Samuel Kelley. Signed William Anderson, Rachel Anderson. Wit: Samuel Kelley, Sen., James Daugherty. Received the day & year within mentioned of Samuel Kelly the sum of £100. Wm. Anderson. [LCDBK B: 92-93]

Simpson and Savage: Survey for William Savage and James Simpson, Esqrs. pursuant to precept 20 July 1772; 500 acres on waters of Rayburns Creek in Ninety Six Dist. . Bounded N and S by land surveyed for Savage and Simpkin *sic*; W by Indian Line; E by Benjamin Powell and vacant land. Survey 3 March 1773. Ord. Co. 6 April 1773. Wm. Anderson, D.S. [P19_324:1]

Simpson and Savage: Survey for William Savage and James Simpson, Esqrs. pursuant to precept 20 July 1772; 500 acres on waters of Rayborns Creek waters of Saludy River. Bounded NW on land surveyed for David Reynolds; other sides vacant. Surveyed 4 March 1773. Ord. Co. 6 April 1773. Wm. Anderson, D.S. [P19_324:2]

Simpson, William: Memorial by William Simpson; 500 acres in Craven Co., on a branch S Fork of Rayburns Creek; Bounding W on Alexdr. Cammeron; S on Danl. Horry; other sides vacant. Also 500 acres as above, S fork of Rayburns creek. Bounded W on Alexdr. Cameron; N on Danl. Horry; other sides vacant. Certified 9 November 1774 and granted 8 December 1774. Quit rent to commence in 2 years. 23 June 1775. Delivered 3 October 1775 to Wm. Simpson. [M13_521:3]

Simpson and Savage: Survey for William Savage and James Simpson, Esqrs. pursuant to precept 20 July 1772; 500 acres on waters of Rayborns Creek, Ninety Six Dist. Bounded by said Savage and Simpson; W on Cherokee Indian Line; other sides vacant. Surveyed 3 March 1773. Ord. Co. 6 April 1773. Wm. Anderson, D.S. [P19_325:2]

Simpson and Savage: Memorial by James Simpson and Wm. Savage; 500 acres on the branches of Rayburns Creek waters of Saludy rivers. Bounding NW by David Reynolds; other sides vacant. Also 500 acres, as above, on the waters of Rayburns and Dartons Creeks. Bounded S by said Savage and Simpson; W by Cherokee Indian Line; other sides vacant. Certified 6 April 1773 and granted 5 May 1773. Quit rent to commence in 2 years. Delivered 27 August 1773 to the Memorialist by C.J. Lindfors. William Anderson, D.S. [2 of 6 tracts of 500 acres each totaling 3000 acres for James Simpson and William Savage] [M12_397:3]

Sims, Drury and Bolling, Samuel: 3 August 1797: Drury Sims, of Laurens Co., S.C., to Thomas Matthews, of same place, for £70 Stg.; 160 acres on both sides of Raiborns Creek. Bounded on Tully Choice's land, near his corner, to Thomas McDonald, crossing Raiborns Creek to Mr. Anderson's, where Sarah McHaffee now lives, or to McDonalds corner, said Sims and Samuel Nesbits land near Edward Nashes line. Being land where Drury Sims now lives, contains by estimation 160 acres and was *granted to Samuel Bolling and Drury Sims* by his Excellency William Moultrie [no date]. Drury Sims (LS), Ruth Sims (LS) Wit: Solomon Hopkins, Henry Morgan. Proved by Henry Morgan 18 July 1798 before John Coker, J.P. [LCDBK F: 336]

Sims, John: 28 August 1792: Hastings Dial to John Madden, Laurens Co., S.C., for £1 Stg.; 59 acres on Burris Creek, waters of Reaborn Creek, *being part of 640 acres granted to John Sims* by Moultrie and conveyed by said Sims to Hastings Dial. Plat shows bounded on one side by John Sims. Hastings Dial. Wit: David Madden, John Rodgers. Proved by David Madden before Charles Saxon, J.P. Plat [LCDBK F: 95-96]

Sims, John: 7 December 1807: Robert Word, Sheriff, of Laurens Dist., S.C., to John Robeson, of same place. Whereas Ann Simons, John Lewis and Thomas Sims was seized and possessed of a tract of 150 acres on the waters of Reedy River, bounded on land of Thomas Davenport, John Sims, and William Sims, deceased. And whereas a writ of fieri facias was issued in the Court of Common Please held the in the said District, and State, under the hand and seal of John Garlington, Esq., clerk of said court and tested by the Honorable John F. Grimke, Esq., Judge of the said state dates 13 April 1807, directed to sell the foods and chattells, houses, land and tenements of the said Ann Sims, John Sims and Thomas Sims, they should cause to be and made as well the sum of $296 which Samuel Scott lately of the Court of Common Please recovered again the said Ann Sims, John Sims and Thomas Sims. The said tract sold to John Robeson, highest bigger. Robert Word (LS) L.S. Dist., Wit: B. Nabers, Jonthn. Downs. Proved by Benjamin Nabers 16 March 1814 before John Garlington, Q.M. [LCDBK K: 51]

Sims, John: Deceased before October 23, 1823.

Sims, John: 23 October 1823: We Thomas Sims, Joshua Nobly and heirs of John Sims, dec'd, of Abbeville Dist., S.C., to Solomon Cole, of Laurens Dist., S.C., for $60, 100 acres being *the balance of a tract of land granted to John Sims* which being in Laurens Dist. on Burris Creek. Bounding Joseph Martin, William Madden and estate of George Madden. Thos. Sims. (LS), Joshua Noble (LS). Wit. Jeremiah Cole, William (X) Sims. Proved by Jeremiah Cole 26 February 1822 before John Madden, J.P. [LCDBK L: 45]

Sims, John 9 April 1828: Laurens Dist., S.C. Solomon Cole of said place to Elihu Madden, *227 acres on Burris Creek, being part of 600 acres, originally granted to John Sims* and conveyed by the heirs of John Sims, deceased, to Solomon Cole and from Solomon Cole to Elihu Madden. Bounded by John Madden, William Madden, Phebe Madden, deceased, Robert Creswell, James Watkins and James Wright. Solomon Cole. Wit: David Madden, William Madden, Junr. Proved by William Madden, Junr 6 October 1828 before Charles Williams, J.P. [LCDBK M: 58]

Sims: Zachariah: Deceased before 24 August 1790: Appraisal of the estate of Zachariah Sims made by David Abercrombie, Lewis Banton, and Samuel Wharton. [LCWBK A: 26]

Sims re-marriage: 9 June 1810: I John Creecy have intermarried with Elizabeth Sims, widow of Zachariah Sims, deceased and as there has been a settlement with the said legatees of the said deceased by the administrator of the said deceased. As I would wish to assist the said children wit the consent of my wife Elizabeth I do hereby give unto the said children of the said deceased and my wife the negroes (to wit) to John Sims, Thomas Sims, to Jessie Pugh and his wife Lydia, to James Wait and Sarah is wife, to James Sims. Signed Jesse (X) Pugh, John Creecy (LS), James Wait (LS), James Sims (LS)l, John Sims (LS), Thos. Sims (LS). Wit: Dd. Anderson, John Wait. [LCDBK J: 253]

[Family: Wife Elizabeth, widow of Zachariah Sims, sons John, Thomas, James; daughters: Lydia wife of Jessie Pugh, Sarah, wife of James Wait.]

Sims, Zachariah: Widow Elizabeth married John Creecy: 15 January 1812: LWT of John Creecy. I John Creecy, Doctor of Laurens Dist., S.C. To my beloved wife Elizabeth a life estate in all my lands, for her to live on which land she is not to make any new settlement or improvement, nor allow any other person only her and her negros. I give her a life estate in all my negros and goods and chattels and to the following property to dispose of at her death as she shall see cause (to wit). At the death of my wife, I do here by give unto her children by Zachariah Sims, deceased the following: one equal part to Fanny Clemmans, wife of Jacob Clemmans, she is to have one half share and her son Zachariah Simpson [Sims?] the other half; to John Wait for said Zachariah Simpson [Sims?]. Should he not be of age at the death of his grandmother and to her son Joel Sims. To her son James Sims in addition to one equal share of said negros all that tract of land lying on the W side of Reedy River to him and his heirs; to David Anderson all the remainder of my lands lying in Laurens Dist., where I now live, on E side of said River. I constitute and ordain my good friend David Anderson and Robert Cunningham my executors. John Creecy (LS) Wit. John Wait, John Middleton. Estate appraisal made 15 February 1812. [LCWBK D: 64]

Smith, Benjamin: 1768 for land on Raburns Creek. No survey located for Benjamin Smith.

Smith, Charles: 4 February 1811: John Clark, Sheriff of Laurens Dist., S.C., to Thomas Childress, of same place, for $71; 140 acres on waters of Raborns Creek. Bounded on Nathan Curry, David Glenn, Jacob Maner. Being property *lately of Charles Smith* sold by Di-Fa at suit of James Mills. John Clark, S.L.D. Wit: James Strain, Thos Campbell. Proved by James Strain 23 July 1811 before John Garlington, Clk. [LCDBK J: 227]

Smith, Charles: 3 December 1811: Appraisal of estate of Charles Smith, dec'd, by Jonathan Downs, J.P. Wolf, Abraham Bolt and Colville Abercrombie [Elliott pg. 78] [See Lucy Smith, wife.]

Smith, Charles: 18 October 1809: Charles Smith witnesses LWT of Thomas Lindley dated 18 October 1809. Mention is said will as "give to my son William Lindley 100 acres joining land of Charles Smith, Colvil Acrumbie [Abercrombie]. [LCWBK D-1: 5]

Smith, Charles: 18 November 1811. Letters of administration of estate of Charles Smith, *dec'd to Widow Lucy Smith*; Security: Chas. and Lydall Allen [Elliot pg. 78]

Smith, Charles: 18 March 1813: Estate sale of Charles Smith, dec'd. Adm. Lucy Smith. [Elliott pg. 84]

Smith, Charles: 18 February 1817: Charles Smith, Senr., of Laurens Dist., S.C., in consideration of the natural love and affection I bear to by son, Charles Smith, Junr.; 119 acres where I now live on the SW side of Reedy River adjoining lands of Isaac Mitchell, John Lindley, Elijah Smith and Elijah Walker. Also one black mare, and one yearling colt, one sorrell mare, and six head of cattle together with my plantation tools. Charles (X) Smith (LS) Wit: Thomas Cunningham, Catey Cunningham. Proved by Thos. Cunningham 18 February 1817 before Samuel Cunningham, J.P. [LCDBK K: 162]

Smith, Lucy, wife of Charles: 28 June 1822: Laurens Dist., S.C., I Lucy Smith for and in consideration of the love and affection which I have for my daughter Mary Harris and her husband John L. Harris and for sum of $5. Paid by William F. Downs, I have granted unto the said William F. Downs all that plantation of 100 acres on the waters of Rayburns Creek Bound as the plat represents in trust to and for the following use and purposes and the sole use and benefit of the said Polly Harris and the said John L. Harris or the survivors of them and after their death to such persons or persons as the said Poly Harris may choose. Lucy Smith (LS). Wit: Jas. Bruster, A. Milner. Proved by A. Milner 2 September 1822 before John Garlington. Plat shows bounding Lucy Smith, Calvin Abercrombie, G. Wolff, Jesse Garrett. [LCDBK L: 63-64]

[Family: Lucy Smith, widow of Charles Smith, daughter Marry Harris, wife of John L. Harris.]

Smith, Lucy, wife of Charles: 28 June 1822: Whereas my mother Lucy Smith, late of Laurens Co., S.C., deceased bearing date 28 June 1822, did give to William F. Downs a certain negroes to wit: Charles, Martha and Eliza in trust to and for the use of myself and my husband John L. Harris or the survivors of us during our lives and by virtue of a power contained and empowered me understanding my conjure to convey and dispose of the said Negroes and their increase by deed or will to take effect after the death of myself and my husband J. L. Harris to such persons or persons s I might choose. I Polly Harris, of said place by virtue and in execution of the trust contained in the aforesaid deed of trust made by said Lucy Smith and consideration of the love and affection I bear to Dr. Hugh Saxon, John Saxon, son of Charles Saxon, dec'd. Sophia Downs, and Susan Downs, daughter of William F. Downs and also of $1. Paid by Dr. Hugh Saxon, have given granted and sold unto said Hugh Saxon the following Negroes. (Listed by name). Polly Harris (x) (LS). Wit. H.C. Young, William Mahon, Daily Mahon. Proved by H.C. Young 1 January 1839 [LCDBK N: 248]

Smith, David: 3 April 1786: Original grant date.

Smith, David: 18 July 1793: Randolph Cook and Stephen Potter, of Laurens Co., S.C., planters, to John Brown, Junr for £40; 50 acres being part of an *original grant to David Smith 3 April 1786* on Reedy Fork of Little River. conveyed to Potter and given to said Cook as a marriage dowry with Potter's daughter named Mary. Bounded on the lower side by land held by said John Brown, S by land held by John Rodgers. Deed certified 6 June 1793 by Jonathan Downs, D.S. Stephen Potter (LS), Randolf (his mark) Cook (LS). Wit: David Dunlap, Boland (mark) Bishop. Roger Brown, J.P. [LCDBK E: 92-93]

Smith, David: 7 October 1801: David Smith, of Laurens Dist., to Benjamin Nabours, of same place, for $300; 133 acres on branches of Dirty Creek. Being land conveyed by Thomas Burton to David Smith to Benjamin Nabours. Plat shows bounded by Samuel Matthews, Charles Lowery, David Cradock. Signed David Smith. Wit: Robt. Creswell, Wm. Franks, John Rodgers. Release of Dower by Mary Smith, wife of David Smith. 16 October 1801. Proved by Robert Creswell 2 January 1802 before Charles Allen, J.P. [LCDBK G: 341-343]

Smith, David: 29 February 1808: Benjn. Nabers, of Laurens Dist. S.C., to John Plant, of same place, for $250; 100 acres on the branches of Dirty Creek. Being part of a tract conveyed by David Smith to said Benj. Nabers. [Plat] shows bounded by Mattw. Cunningham, Christo. Hardy, Jas. Dial, and unknown. Signed Benj. Nabours. Wit: Robert NcNees, B. Strange. Release of dower by Ann Nabors, wife of Benjamin Nabours 18 July 1811 before Chas. Allen, J.Q. [LCDBK J: 243]

Smith, James: Survey for James Smith pursuant to a precept 22 June 1767; 100 acres in Berkley Co. on the S branch of Rayburns Creek. Bounded on all sides by vacant land. Certified 25 August 1767. Jno. Caldwell, D.S. [P19-528:3]

Smith, James: Memorial by James Smith; 100 acres in Berkley Co., on the S branch of Reybornes Creek. Bounded on all sides by vacant land. Certified 25 August 1767 and granted 13 May 1768. Quit rent to commence in ten years. Set his hand 15 September 1768. For the memorialist John Dalrymple. Jno. Caldwell, D.S. [B in side margin for Bounty land] [M8-227:2]

Smith, James: 12 September 1785: Robert Sims, of Ninety Six Dist., Laurens Co., SC, miller to Drury Boyce, of same, for £20 Sterling; part of a tract containing 100 acres on the S fork of Rayburns Creek. Bounded on vacant land at the time of survey on the NE side of said creek [bounding] the Griss Mill. *Originally granted to James Smith 13 May 1768.* Robert Sims. [LCDBK: A: 6-9]

Smith, James (and part Riley, Patrick): 11 September 1787: Robert Sims, of Ninety Six Dist., Laurens Co., S.C., miller, to Micajah Sims, of same place, for £40; 400 acres on S Fork of Reaburns Creek on S side. *Originally granted to James Smith by his majesty's letters patent dated 14 May 1768; Also 50 acres adjacent granted to Patrick Riley 5 June 1786.* Bounded SW by James McClanahan, W by Thomas McDaniel; N by said Robert Sims. Wit: Lewis Saxon, CC. [LCDBK B: 239]

Smith, James (and part Riley, Patrick): 18 March 1789: Micajah Sims, of Laurens Co., S.C, farmer, to Edmond [Edward] Nash, of same place, for £20; 100 acres on S Fork of Reaburns Creek. *Originally granted to James Smith 13 May 1768* bounded by vacant land at time of survey and *part granted to Patrick Riley 5 June 1786.* Bounded on Thomas McDonald, Robert Sims, James McClanahan. Micajah Sims. Wit: Andrew McKnight, Drury Boyce. Proved by Andrew McKnight 15 September 1789 before Joseph Downs, J.P. [LCDBK C: 74 -76]

Smith, James: 27 & 28 April 1789: Micajah Sims, of Ninety Six Dist., now Laurens Co., S.C., farmer, to Robert Filpot, of same place, for £20; 100 acres on the S fork of Raburns Creek. Bounded by vacant land at the time or the original survey. Granted to James Smith 13 May 1768. Singed Micajah Sims. Wit: Saml. Burton, Elias Walker. [Poor film] [LCDBK B: 414]

Smith, James: Survey for James Smith pursuant to precept dated 4 December 1771; 500 acres on branch of Little River and Rayburns Creek near Mount Warrior. Bounded NE by George Blake; other sides vacant. Certified 25 May 1772. Richd. Winn, D.S. [P19_534:3]

Smith, James: Memorial for James Smith; 500 acres on the branches of Little River and Rayburns Creek near Mount Warrior. Bounding NE on Geo. Blackies; other sides vacant. Certified 25 May 1772 and granted 3 July 1772. Quit rent to commence in 2 years. 11 September 1772. James Smith. Richard Winn, D.S. [M11_411:5]

Smith, James: 25 October 1783: Joseph Kellet, of Ninety Six Dist., planter, to Robert Sims, Sr., of same place, for £100 st.; 100 acres on S Fork of Reaburns Creek. *Originally granted to James Smith,* and from said Smith to Martin Mehaffey, and from said Martin Mahaffey to said Joseph Killet. Signed Joseph Killet, Jane Killet. Wit: Martin Mehaffey, Wm. Burton, Drury Boyce. Recorded 25 October 1783. [LCDBK B: 158-160]

South, William: 10 November 1800: William South, of Laurens Dist., S.C., to Elijah Walker, of same place, for $550; 240 acres on Reedy River. Bounding lands of David Green, John Rutledge, Esqr., Junior, John Daniel and adjoining the Poplar Spring Meeting. William South, Caty (x) South. Wit: Jno. Pringle, Wm. Simmons, William Pinson. Dower by Caty South 14 April 1801 before Jonthan Downs, J.P. Proved by William Simmons 16 June 1801 before James Powell, J.P. [LCDBK G: 231-232]

Spence, Sarah: 26 January 1793: David Spence and Sarah his wife, formerly Sarah Neilson, of Laurens Co., S.C., to Daniel Osborn, of same place, for £100; 400 acres on waters of Little River, *granted to Sarah Neilson (struck out) Spence in 1771* when she was Sarah Neilson and previous to her marriage to and with the said David Spence. David (x) Spence (LS) Sarah (O) Spence, formerly Sarah Neilson. Wit: Silvanus Walker, Thomas Norris, *Thomas Richardson*, Robert (R) Spence. Proved by Silvanus Walker, Esq. 3 February 1793 before John Hunter. [LCDBK D: 325-327]

Starne/Starnes, Ebenezer: No survey located.

Starne/Starnes, Ebenezer: Memorial for Ebenezer Starne; 300 acres in Craven Co., on the waters of Saludy a small branch thereof called Long Lick Creek. Bounding SE on Lewis Banton, all other sides vacant. Land Certified 10 December 1771 and granted 21 February 1772 to the memorialist. Quit rent to commence two years from date. Set his hand 7 May 1772. John Caldwell, D.S. Delivered 7 July 1772 to Pat. Cunningham. [M11-222:2]

Starnes, Ebenezer and Aaron: 1779: Witnesses LWT of William Richey - will dated 1779, Recorded 16 May 1783. [See William Richie]

Starnes, Ebenezer: 9 March 1786: Ebenezer Stearnes, of Laurens Co., S.C., planter, to Aaron Starnes, of same place, laborer, for £10; 300 acres on Long Lick Branch. *Originally granted 7 May 1772 to Ebenezer Starns.* Bounded at time or original survey SE on Lewis Banton, all other sides vacant. Ebenezer Starns. Wit: Thomas Scurry, Roger Murphy, Wm. Low. [LCDBK A: 346-348]

Starns, Ebenezer: 4 November 1786: LWT of Ebenezer Starns, 96 Dist., S.C. Son: Aaron Starnes, 100 acres of land on which he lives on the S end of my tract .and 5 shillings. To my eldest daughter Mary 5 shillings, with what she has had, to my daughter Anna 5 shillings Stg. with what she has had and to Rebekah 5 shillings Stg., with what she has had. To sons: Ebenezer and John Starnes the remainder of the land where I now live to be equally divided between then, allowing my beloved wife Anna her use of the farm land. . Set his hand Ebenezer (X) Starns (LS). Exrs. Wife Anna and son Aaron. 4 November 1786. Wit: Samuel Wharton, John Field, Roger Murphy, Sr. [LCWBK A: 23; Ingram, pgs. 15-16]

[Family: Wife Anna, daughters: Mary, Anna, Rebekah; sons, Aaron, Ebenezer and John Starnes.]

Starns, Ebenezer: 11 November 1793: Received of Anna Starnes, Esta[Executrix], of Ebenezer Starnes, dec'd. £15 Stg.; and for that sum of money I do hereby acknowledge myself fully satisfied, contented and paid for all legacies to me now arising from the estate of either my father or mother namely Ebenezer and Anna Starns. He will make no claim on lands of Jno. Starns should he die without issue. Ebenezer Starnes (LS) Wit: Wm. Mitchell, Geo. Wright, Saml. Anderson. Proved by William Mitchell 17 February 1796 before Danl. Wright, J.P. [LCDBK F: 92]

[Family: Wife, Anna. Sons: Aaron, Ebenezer, John. Daughter: Milly Murphey, Ann Jones, Rachel Hughs, Rebecah Sims.]

Starnes, Ann, wife of Ebenezer: 28 November 1800: LWT of Ann Starnes Legatees: sons: Aaron, Ebenezer, John; daughters, Milly Murphey, Ann Jones, Rachel Hughs, Rebecah Sims: Executor, son Aaron Starnes. Wit: Rachel Anderson, Peggy Middleton, David Anderson. Will proved 1 October 1802 by Peggy Middleton, Rachel Anderson. Sale of estate made 4 and 5 November 1802. [LCWBK C: 6]

Starnes lands bounding: 8 March 1792: Samuel Wharton, planter, of Laurens Co., S.C., to Aaron Starnes, planter, of same place, for £10 Stg.; 58 acres on Reedy River bounded SE by William Goodman, NW by Enos Stinson and John Fields, SW by Ebenezer Starnes. *Originally granted to said Samuel Wharton 4 April 1791.* Samuel Wharton (LS) Maudlin Wharton (his wife) (LS) Wit: John Findley Roger Murphy, Stephen Wood. Proved by Stephen Wood 17 July 192 before Joseph Downs, J.P. [LCDBK D: 208-210]

Stinson, Enos: 200 acres. Survey not found.

Stinson, Enos: Memorial by Enos Stinson; 200 acres in Berkley Co., on the waters of Reedy River. Bounding W on Lewis Banton, S on Evin Pinson, other sides vacant. Certified 16 August 1771 and granted 4 December 1771. Quit rent to commence 2 years from date. Wet his hand 13 March 1772. Patk. Cunningham, D.S. Delvd. 31 August 1772 to Pat. Cunningham. [M11-164:2]

Stinson, Enos: 7 July 1798: LWT. I Enos Stinson. Bequeath unto the girl that I brought in my house now known by the name of Mary Stinson all my estate, both real and personal, consisting of land, horses, cattle, hogs, household, kitchen furniture and plantation tools. I do appoint my friend and neighbors, Samuel Wharton Executor of my LWT and do revoke and renounce all other wills made by me. Enos Stinson (LS). Wit: Thomas Davenport, Jno. Davenport, Bena. (B) Watson. Proved December 8, 1800. [LCWBK A: 262]

Stinson, Enos: 21 June 1800: Samuel Wharton, Attorney for Enos Stinson, of Laurens Dist., S.C., to Paul Finley, of same place, for $200; 110 on waters of Long Lick Creek. *Being part of a tract granted to said Enos Stinson.* Bounded on James Finley. Enos Stinson (LS) Saml. Wharton (LS) Wit: Polly Fuller, John Ritchey. Proved by John Ritchey 17 March 1801 before John Davis, J.P. [LCDBK H: 91]

Stinson, Enos: 15 August 1807: Mary Stimpson [Stinson], of Laurens Dist., S.C., to John Findley, of same place, for $165; 100 acres on waters of Long Lick Creek of Reedy River. Being part of a tract of land which was left to the said Mary Stinson by Enos Stinson by his last will and testament. Bounded by Moses Madden, John Ritchey, on [James] Findleys land part of original tract then on James Findley. Mary (x) Stimpson (LS) Wit: Jones Fuller, Paul Findley, James (mark) Findley. Proved by Paul Findley 3 August 1812 before Chas. Allen, Q.M. [LCDBK J: 274]

Strum, Henry: Survey for Henry Strum pursuant to precept dated 2 March 1773; 150 acres in Craven Co., on the waters of Reaburns Creek. Bounded SE and SW on Cilvenis [Sylvanus] Walker; S on Ezebelin's land; E on James Lindley; N unknown. Certified 27 May 1773. Pat. Cunningham, D.S. [P21_181:1]

Strum, Henry: Memorial for Henry Strum; 150 acres in Craven Co., on the waters of Rayburnes Creek. Bounding SE and SW on Sullivaus Walker; S on Ezebelius; E on James Lindley; N unknown. Also 150 acres, as above, on the waters of Rayburnes Creek. Bounding on John Stitlius; SW on said Stitlius and Joseph Williams; SE of Saml. Williams; other sides unknown. Certified 23, 28 and 25 May 1773 and granted 23 June 1774. Quit rent to commence in 2 years. 3 December 1774. Delivered 6 March 1775 to Pat. Cunningham. Pat. Cunningham, D.S. [M13_136:1]

Strum, Henry: 2 October 1774: Henry Strum, of Ninety Six Dist., S.C. and Elizabeth, his wife, to Patrick Cuningham, Esq., of the said Dist., planter, for £100; 150 acres on waters of Reaburns Creek. Bounding SE and SW on Silvanus Walker, S on Ezeblins land[?], E on James Lindley, N unknown. *Originally granted unto Henry Strum by Wm. Bull 23 June 1774.* Henry Strum, Elizabeth (X) Strum. Wit: Peter Mehl, Christopher Humble, Mary (O) Meal. Proved by Peter Mehl 17 April 1775 before Robt. Cunningham, J.P. [LCDBK G: 76-78]

239

Strum, Henry: 29 April 1794: P. Cuningham, of Laurens Co., S.C., to Jonathan Downs, of same place, for £38, Stg.; 150 acres on waters of Reaburns Creek in Laurens Co. Bounded NE and SW on Silvanus Walker; S on Ez. ___ [Ezeblin] land; E on James Lindley; N unknown. *Originally granted to Henry Strum by Wm. Bull, Esquire 29 June 1774* and by him conveyed to P. Cunningham by lease and release dated 1 and 2 October 1774. P. Cuningham, Ann Cuningham [his wife]. Wit: Isaac Gray, Samuel Swancy. Proved by Samuel Swancy 18 April 1797 before Joseph Downs, J.P. [LCDBK G: 79-80]

Strum, Henry: 28 March 1797: We John and William Cunningham, executors to the estate of Patrick Cunningham, deceased of Ninety Six Dist., Laurens Co., to Mabra Madden, of same place, for £60 Stg.; 150 acres on the waters of Rayburns Creek bounding NW on John Hellum, SW part on John Hellum, Joseph Williams SE on Samuel Williams, other sides on lands owners not know at time of survey. *Granted to Henry Strum on 2 June 1774* and conveyed to Patrick Cunningham by lease and release 1 and 2 October 1774 by said Henry Strum and Elizabeth Strum, his wife. John Cunningham, William Cunningham. Wit. David Madden, William Rusk. Proved by David Maden 18 July 1798 before James Abercrombie, J.P. [LCDBK G: 18-19]

Sutter, (Suter?) William: 1766 bounding Barbara Ann Gilbert. No survey or memorial found.

Swindle, Michael: 14 July 1800: Michael Swindle, Laurens Co., S.C., to John Phillips, of Abbeville Dist., S.C., for $100; 200 acres on waters of Reedy River. Bounded on Michl. Swindel, Joseph Williams, Martin Norman. [Plat by John Rodgers, D.S. Shows Richard Swindle, Joseph Williams, Martin Norman]. Michael Swindle (LS). Wit: George Swindle, William Gafferd, Joseph Bolton. Proved by George Swindle 14 July 1810 before Joseph Bolton, J.P. [LCDBK K: 217-281]

Swindle, Michael: 9 September 1811: Michael Swindle [Swindel], of Laurens Dist., S.C., to James Clardy, of same place, for $464; 154 acres on Walnut Creek waters of Reedy River, bounded at the road on Wm. Coles line, Wm. Howell, Margaret Box, Michael Swindle, John Hudson, to the road. Michael Swindle (LS) Wit: Jesse E. Clardy, James Wright. Proved by James Wright 19 November 1811 before W. Burnside, J.Q. [LCDBK K: 318]

Swindle, Michael: 18 October 1809: Michael Swindell, of Laurens Dist., S.C., to William Cole, of same place, for $124; 62 acres on waters of Reedy River. [Plat shows bounded on William Cole, John Mitchell, Michael

Swindle and Fifer [Phifer?] and waggon road]. Michael Swindel (LS) Wit: David Braden, Henry Hall, Asa (X) Hall. Proved by David Braden 25 March 1809 before Joseph Bottom., J.P. [LCDBK K: 76]

Swindle, Michael: 3 July 1809: LWT of Michael Swindle, of Laurens Dist., S.C. To my well beloved son John Swindle one equal half of that tract of land whereon I now live. .to my well beloved son Daniel Swindle one half of that tract of land whereon I now live. To my beloved son George Swindle one bed and furniture also one waggon and team of horses. . . .I give to my beloved daughter Suzy Saxon one bed and furniture and $150. . .to my beloved daughter Delila Swindle $150. . . . I appoint my brother George Swindle and Aaron Cloar? Executors. Signed Michael Swindle (SL) Wit: Philip Waits, Wm. Washington, J___ Box. Proved 8 July 1815. [LCWBK D: 210]

[Family: Father, Michael Swindle; sons John, Daniel, George; daughters Suzy Saxon, Delila Swindle, brother George Swimdle.]

Thomas, Able: Quaker.

Thomas, Abel: Survey for Abel Thomas pursuant to precept dated 5 April 1762; 150 in Berkley Co., on the fork between Broad and Saludy Rivers on a branch of Saludy River called Reaburns Creek, waters of Santee. Bounded SW on land laid out to John Turk; other sides vacant. Certified 15 July 1762. Edwd. Musgrove, D.S. [P7_267:3]

Thomas, Abel: Memorial for Abel Thomas; 150 acres in Berkley Co., in the fork between Broad and Saludy Rivers on a branch of Saludy River known by the name of Reaburns Creek, waters of Santee. Bounded on SW on land laid out to John Turk; other sides vacant. Certified 15 July 1762 and granted 7 October 1762. Quit rent to commence in 2 years. 118 November 1762. E. Musgrove, D.S. For the memorialist. Wm. Ancrum. [M6_5:3]

Thomas, Abel: 12 June 1785: Abel Thomas, of Ninety Six Dist., to George Hollingsworth, of same place, for £17, 1 p.; 150 acres on a branch of Saluda River called Reaburns Creek. Bounding SW by land held by John Turk, over sides vacant. *Originally granted 7 October 1762 to Abel Thomas.* Signed Abel Thomas. Wit: John Hollingsworth, Elias Brock, Isaac Hollingsworth. Proved 13 June 1785 by John Hollingsworth before J. Rodgers, J.P. [LCDBK C: 118-120]

Thomas, Able: 30 March 1805: LWT of Abel Thomas dated 30 March 1805, Proved 16 March 1805. Brother Timothy's oldest daughter Sarah Thomas, bed. Elizabeth Coner; bed. Real and personal estate sold and

divided among children of Timothy Thomas, Isaac Thomas, Elizabeth
Rankin, Prudence Hawkins. Executors: Brother, Timothy Thomas, Samuel
Gaunt, Jacob Hawkins. Witnesses: Zach. Prater, David Jenkins, Archibald
Boyd. See Newberry Box 19-41 - March 1805 for complete list of sale and
items paid by estate. Legatees: Daniel Thomas, Wm. Thomas, Wm. Pugh,
Ann Thomas, Cassandra Thomas, Elizabeth Rankin, Timothy Thomas, Jr.
Wm. Hawkins, Peter Hawkins. [Bundrick; Suber, Vol. 2, pg. 590]

[Family: Abel Thomas, father, brother, Timothy, niece, Sarah Thomas,
Elizabeth Coner, Elizabeth Rankin, Prudence Hawkins, Nephew, Isaac,
Thomas; legatees: Daniel, William, Ann Cassandra, Timothy Thomas, Jr.;
Wm. Pugh, Wm. And Peter Hawkins.]

Thomas, Abel: 2 January 1807: George Hollingsworth, of Laurens Dist., to
Marmaduke Pinson, of same place, for $600; 150 acres on Reabours Creek.
Bounded SW on land laid out to John Turk, other sides vacant when
surveyed. *Originally granted to Abel Thomas,* which said Abel Thomas did
sell to said George Hollingsworth 13 June 1785. Signed George
Hollingsworth. Wit: Ez. Hollingsworth, Polly Lindly. Release of Dower by
Lidid (X her mark) Hollingsworth, wife of within names George
Hollingsworth 4 February 1807. Proved 4 February 1807 by Ezekle
Hollingsworth before Jonthn. Downs, JQ. Rec. 27 April 1808.
[LCDBK J: 12-13]

Thomas, Able: 13 May 1838: Marmaduke Pinson of Laurens Dist., S.C. to
Thomas Coats, for $100; 20 acres being part of a tract of land containing 150
acres *granted to Abel Thomas 16 July 1763* on a branch of Reedy River
called Raborns Creek. M.D. Pinson (LS). Wit. Joseph Cooper, David Boyd,
Junr. Proved by Joseph Cooper 8 October 1838 before J. Thomas, J.P.
[LCDBK N: 241]

Thomas, Able: 18 July 1820: Samuel Todd, of Laurens Dist., S.C. to
William Strain, of same place, for $100; 150 acres on Rabourns Creek,
granted to Able Thomas on Rabourns Creek. Bounding SW on land laid out
to John Turk, other sides vacant when surveyed. Signed Saml. Todd (LS).
Wit: Tho. F. Jones, S.B. Lewers. Proved by S.B. Lewers 20 March 1821
before John Garlington, Clk. and J.Q. [LCDBK K: 320]

Thomas, Able: 15 May 1838: Marmaduke Pinson, of Laurens Dist., S.C.,
have granted and released unto Thomas Coals a tract of land containing 20
acres, *being part of a tract containing 250 acres granted to Abel Thomas 16
July 1762.* Situate on a branch of Reedy River called Raborns Creek. No
bounding names given. Set his hand M.D. Pinson (Seal). Wit: Joseph
Cooper, David Boyd, Junr. Proved by Joseph Cooper 8 October 1803 before

Js. Thomas. J.P. [LCDBK N: 241]

Thomason, George: 100 acres granted in 1779.

Thomason, George: 23 October 1797: William Gilliland, of Laurens Co.,
S.C., to Henry Morgan, of same place, for £30 Stg.; 100 acres on the S fork
of Raiborns Creek. *Originally granted to George Thomason in 1779.*
Bounded by said Creek, and near the Sholes. Signed William Gilliland. (LS).
Wit: Thomas (TM) Matthews Robert, Gilliland. Proved by oath of Thomas
(TM) Matthews 18 July 179 before Jno. Coker, J.P. [LCDBK F: 356]

Thomson, George: Survey for George Thomson pursuant to precept dated 1
December 1772; 100 acres in Craven Co., waters of Rubens Creek. Bounded
on all sides by vacant land. Certified 17 February 1773. Pat. Cunningham,
D.S. [P20_313:3]

Thomson, George: Memorial by George Thomson; 100 acres in Craven
Co., on the waters of Rayburns Creek. Certified 17 February 1773 and
granted 25 May 1774. Quit rent to commence in 10 years. 17 October 1774.
Delivered 2 May 1775 to Thomas Clark. Pat. Cunningham, D.S.
[B in margin] [M13_56:3]

Toad [Todd], Margaret: Survey for Margaret Toad pursuant to precept
dated 6 January 1773; 100 acres in Craven Co., NE side of Reyburns Creek
on a small branch called Reyburns Branch. Bounded N by John Richie,
Senr.; other sides vacant. Certified 18 March 1773. Jonthn Downs, D.S.
[P20_362:2]

Toad [Todd], Margaret: Memorial for Margaret Toad; 100 acres in Craven
Co., on a small branch N of Rayburns Creek. Bounding NE on John Richie,
Senr.; other sides vacant. Certified 20 September 1774 and granted 17 March
1775. Quit rent to commence in 2 years. 19 August 1775. Jona. Downes,
D.S. [Irish in margin] [M2_302:3]

Toad [Todd], Margaret: 17 June 1779: Margaret Todd [Toad] of 96 Dist.,
S.C., to Frederick Little, of same place, labourer, for £40; 100 acres on small
branch on the NE side of Reaburns Creek. Bounding W by land laid out to
John Ritchey Senr., other sides on vacant land at time of survey. Margaret
(mark) Todd. Wit: Wittenhall Warrner, Tandy Walker, Elizabeth Warner.
Proved by Tandy Walker 14 April 1789 before John Hunter, J.P.
[LCDBK C: 22-23]

Toad [Todd], Margaret: 1 December 1787: Frederick Little, of Laurens
Co., S.C., to William Hubbs, of same place, for £20, 100 acres on a small

branch of Raburns Creek on the NE side. Bounding W on land laid out to John Richey, Sr.; other sides vacant. *Originally granted to Margaret Toad 17 March 1775* and by said Margaret Toad to said Frederick Little by Lease and release 17 June 1779. Signed Frederick Little. Wit: Alexander Hamilton, Robert Todd, Chas. Gaffy. [LCDBK B: 276-177]

Toad [Todd], Margaret: December 11 & 12, 1790: William Hubbs and Elizabeth Hubbs, his wife, of Laurens Co., S.C., planter, to George Fuller of said place, for £20; 100 acres on small branch of Raburns Creek on the North side. Bounding W on John Ritchie, Senr. Other sides when first surveyed on vacant land. *Originally granted to Margaret Todd 117 March 1775* and conveyed to Frederick Little by Lease and release 17 June 1779 and by said Frederick Little unto said Wm. Hubbs by deed 1 December 1787 and now by said William Hubbs and Elizabeth his wife unto said George Fuller. William (X) Hubbs, Elizabeth (mark) Hubbs. Wit. Mansil Crisp, James (mark) Wilson, George (mark) McVay. Jonathan Downs, J.P. proved by James Wilson before Jonathan Downs, J.P. [LCDBK C: 195-197]

Toad [Todd], Robert: Survey for Robert Toad pursuant to precept dated 6 January 1773; 100 acres in Ninety Six Dist., between Broad and Saludy on a small branch of Williamses Creek, waters of Reburns Creek, thence to Saluda. Bounded NE by Jno. Helms. E laid out for Patrick Cunningham, Esqr.; SW vacant. Certified 29 March 1773. John Rodgers, D.S. Ord. Co. 30 September 1774. [P20_357:1]

Toad [Todd], Robert: Memorial for Robert Toad; 100 acres in 96 Dist. between Broad and Saludy rivers on a small branch of Williams Creek waters of Rayburns Creek. Bounded NW on John Helem, Jr.; E by Pat. Cunningham. Certified 3 September 1774 and granted 4 May 1775. Quit rent in 2 years. 30 September 1775. John Rogers, D.S. [M2_379:1]

Todd, Robert: 27 August 1808: Robert Todd, of Laurens Dist., S.C., to James Todd, of same place, for $100; 187 acres on the waters of Reaburns Creek. Robert Todd (LS) Wit: Robert Bryson, John Cochran. Proved by Robert Bryson 16 February 1809 before John Garlington, CC P. [Plat shows bounded by Robert Todd, David Burress, Wm. Loyd, Mabra Madden]. [LCDBK J: 59]

Todd, Robert: 2 January 1830: I Robert Todd, Senr., of Laurens Dist., S.C., to Benjamin Yeargin, of Greenville Dist., S.C., for $372; 92 and 8/10 acres on the waters of Burresses Creek a branch of Rabourns Creek, waters of Saluda River. [Plat shows bounded by Robert Todd Senr., Widow Wilson, A [Albert] Madden, on Cumbia's Road.] Robert (R) his mark. Wit: Albert Madden, William Todd. Proved by Albert Madden 5 January 1832 before

Thos. P. Lockhart, J.P. [LCDBK M: 217-218]

Todd, James: 17 March 1828: James Todd, of Laurens Dist., State of S.C., to John Blakely, of same place, 100 acres, being the tract of land whereon I now live. Bounding lands of John Hobbs, James Motes, Also two Negroes, three head of horses being all I now own, together with all my stock, tools, and household furniture for the following use of my wife Polly Todd during her natural life and at her death for the use of my children William, Benjamin, Robert, John, Daniel, James, Betsey and Nancy and any others which may here after be born of the present marriage. James Todd (LS). Wit: P. Farrow, W.E. Lynch. Proved by Pattillo Farrow 17 March 1828 before Jno. S. James Q.M. [LCDBK M: 34-35]

[Family: Wife Polly Todd, sons William, Benjamin, Robert, John, Daniel, James; daughters Betsey, Nancy Todd.]

Turk, John: Survey for John Turk pursuant to precept dated 5 December 1752; 150 acres north side of Saludie on a branch called Raburns Creek. Bounded NE by said Creek; other sides vacant. Certified 20 August 1753. John Hamilton, D.S. [P5_407:2]

Turk, John: No memorial listed for John Turk for 150 acres. Deceased before 22 November 1755.

Turk, John: Settlement of John Turk, Will of John Turk Proven (22 November 1755) names wife Agnes all the articles that he was bound to deliver her by agreement before Capt. James Francis and the benefit of house for taking care of three children. The tract of land "where I now live" containing 400 acres, went to the eldest son William Turk. His son, John Turk, received the tract of 150 acres lying 10 miles from the mouth of Rebans (Reaburns) Creek. His daughter Neomy, was given a warrant for 100 acres to be cleared by eldest brother, William, and to his wife's son, Theodore (Theodocius), one gray mare, branded by Henry Fosters brand. Remainder was to be divided between sons, William, John and Thomas Turk. [Wills of Charleston County 1752-1756: Vol 7, pp. 441-442].

[Family: wife Agnes, sons William, John and Thomas. William's son John, his daughter Neomy and his wife's son Theodore.]

Turk, John (son of John): 30 June 1768: John Turk bounding Robert Briggs. [See Robert Briggs.]

Turk, John (son of John): 12 June 1785: John Turk bounding lands of Able Thomas when granted. [See Able Thomas].

Turk, John (son of John): 2 January 1807: John Turk bounding lands of Able Thomas when surveyed. [See Able Thomas].

Turk, Rachel: 16 July 1797: LWT of Rachel Turk, widow, of Laurens Co., S.C. I give to my beloved brother Archibald McDaniel and Matthew McDaniel whom I constitute made and ordain sole executors, two notes of hand of Richard Puckett to brother Archibald, one note payable 25 December 1799 which note demands $50. Also the third of my cattle, third of my pots. I also give to my beloved sister Margaret McDaniel one note upon Richard Puckett which demands $50 payable the 25 December 1797. Also my loom and my saddle, and all my wearing clothes, one cross bard sheet, nephew Matthew Odonal my mare and colt to be sold and the money arising with all the rest of my effects that is not heretofore mentioned. I give to the said Matthew O'Daniel at the time when he arrives at the years of 21. If it should please God to call him hence before that time I order that the mare and colt with the rest that I have mentioned, shall be equally divided between the three fir mentioned. Rachel (mark) Turk. Wit: Matthew Johnson, Archl. McDaniel. [LCWBK A: 171]

[Family: Brothers Archibald and Matthew McDaniel, sister Margaret McDaniel, nephew Matthew O'Donald (O'Daniel).]

Turk, Rachel: 6 October 1798: Received of Matthew McDaniel, the full sum of the cattle and potts *sic* and also the loom, and the saddle and with all the wearing chattel according to the will of my sister's will Rachel Turk deceased. Margaret (X) McDonald (LS) 6 October 1798: Received of Matthew McDonald, Executor of Estate of Rachel Turk, deceased my third of the cattle and the third of the potts according to the Will. Received by me Archibald (X) McDonald. [LCDBK F: 433]

Turk, Theodosius: Meeting of Tuesday 7 August 1770, pg. 293. Theodous Turk To certify plat. 50 acres on Reedy River [See James Edes' survey for 50 acres; See Petitions by Brent H. Holcomb.]

Turk, Theodosius: Memorial for Theodoius Turke *sic*; 50 acres in Craven Co., S.C., on the NE side of Saludy on a branch thereof called Reedy River. Bounding NE and NW on said river, other sides vacant land. Certified 7 August 1770 and granted 24 August 1770. Quit rent to commence in two years. Dated 19 September 1770 Pat. Cuningham. Jno. Hamelton, D.S. [M10-236:3] [See Survey for James Ede.]

Turk, Theodosius: 6 January 1790: Received of John Willard, of Laurens Co., S.C., the sum of £10 Georgia money and I hereby relinquish and confirm to him the said John Willard all right, title, interest, claim a certain tract of land containing 50 acres on the S side of Reedy River, opposite mouth of the Long Lick Creek. *Land that was granted to me [Theodosius Turk]* under the sanctions of the State of South Carolina. Theodosius Turk. Wit: Joseph Henry, Peter Edwards. Proved in Abbeville Co., S.C., by Peter Edwards 9 January 1790 before William Moon, J.P. [LCDBK D: 43]

Turk, Theodosius: (bounding) 18 September 1805: Wm. West, of Laurens Dist., S.C., to William Crocker, of same place, for $50; 20 acres on Reedy River. [Plat shows bounding of lands laid out to Theodashe *sic* Turk, Thomas Hendocks, on Reedy River. William (X) West. Wit: Lewis Graves, James (mark) Crocker, Ezekiel (mark) Andrews. Proved by James Crocker 25 June 1810 before Dd. Anderson, Q.M. [LCDBK J: 164-165]

Turk, William: No survey found.

Turk, William: Memorial by William Turk; 100 acres in Granville Co. on the SE branch of Calhouns creek branch of Long Cane Creek. Bounded NW by Lorry and Genard?; SE by Sammy McMurty other sides vacant land. Certified 24 April 1767 and granted 8 March 1768 to the memorialist. Quit rent to commence in 10 years from date. Set his hand 3 August 1768. For the Memorialist Jesse Campbell. Matt. Long, D.S. [B in margin] [M8-143:5]

Tweed, Elenor: Survey for Elenor Tweed pursuant to precept dated 6 January 1773; 100 acres in Ninety Six Dist. on a branch of Raburns Creek called the Bullet Branch. Bounded N on laid out owner unknown; S land claimed by Thos. Hooker; other sides vacant. Certified 5 March 1773. Jonthn. Downs, D.S. Ord. Co. 30 September 1774. (Irish) [P20_418:1]

Tweed, Elenor: Memorial for Eleanor Tweed; 100 acres on Bullet Branch of Rayburns Creek. Bounding N of land laid out to person unknown; S on Thomas Hooker; other sides vacant. Certified 20 September 1774 and granted 4 May 1775. Quit rent to commence in 2 years. 29 September 1775. Jonathan Downes, D.S. [M2_378:6]

Tweed, Eleanor: 6 March 1799: Elisha Casey, of Laurens Co., S.C., to Samuel Nesbit, of same place, for £23; 100 acres on a branch of Rabourns Creek called Bullett Branch, except around the graveyard. Bounded to the N by land laid out unknown, S on Thos. Hooker, all other sides vacant. Elisha Casey (LS) Wit: Drury Boyce, Edward Nash. Proved by Drury Boyce 12 March 1799 before Joseph Downs, J.P. [LCDBK G: 681]

Tweed, Ellenor [Eleanor]: 16 December 1784: Thos. Boyce and wife Elliner, of 96 Dist., S.C., to Zachariah Green for £15 Stg.; 100 acres on

Bullet Branch of Rabourns Creek. Bounded when surveyed on Thomas Hooker and *granted 3 April 1775 to Ellenor Tweed, now wife of said Thomas Boyce*. Signed Thomas Boyce, Alanor *sic* (x) Boyce. Wit: David Green, James Green. Jno. Duncan. Proved by oath of David Green, 17 [blank] 1784 before Geo. Anderson, J.P. [poor microfilm] [LCDBK F: 433]

Tweed, James: Survey for James Tweed, Sr. pursuant to precept dated 5 January 1773; 250 acres on NE side Reedy River, on a branch there of called Reaburns Creek. Bounded W on land laid out to Mary Riche; other sides vacant. Certified 2 March 1773. Jonth. Downs, D.S. Ord. Co. 10 February 1775 for Andw. Broughton. For memorial see Andrew Broughton [P9_366:3]

Tweed, James: 3 August 1787: Thomas Boyce, of Laurens Co., S.C., to John Adams, of same place, for £50 Stg.; 250 acres on both sides of Raborns Creek. Being a tract of land o*riginally granted to James Tweed by letter of Patent dated 1785.* Bounded on all sides by vacant land. Thomas Boyce (LS), Elenor Boyce (LS). Wit: Charles Willson, John Johnston, Elizabeth Dennel *sic*. [LCDBK B: 277-279]

Tweed, James: 12 August 1803: Paul Hamilton, of the City of Charleston, S.C., to Abraham Adams, of Laurens Dist., S.C., for the sum of $475; 150 acres on the N side of Reedy river, on a branch thereof called Rabourns creek. Surveyed by Jonathan Downs for James Teed [Tweed] Bounded SW by land laid out for Mary Riche and other sides vacant. (Except 100 acres of the said tract of land that was claimed and taken by an old right, and is not by these presents sold to the said Abraham Adams, but is deducted of the said 250 acres). Paul Hamilton (LS) by Thos. Moore Attorney for Paul Hamilton. Wit: Polly Moore, Douglass Johnson. Proved by Douglass Johnson 4 October 1803 before John Childres, J.P. [LCDBK G: 669]

Tweed, James: March 9, 1807: I William McClintock, of Laurens Dist., S.C., to Isaac Sharp, of same place, for $805; 450 acres on the N side of Reedy River on a branch called Raburns Creek; *250 acres of said land surveyed by Jonathan Downes for James Tweed,* bounded to the S by land laid out for Mary Richy [Ritchy], other sides vacant. And 162 acres of the late survey joining the said 250 surveyed by Jonathan Downs for *said Abraham Adams* bounded NE by William McClintock, other sides vacant. William McClintock (LS) Wit. Andrew McKnight, William McKnight. Proved by Andrew McKnight 17 April 1807 before Hudson Berry, J.Q. Dower of Susannah McClintock, wife of the within William McClintock given 9 March 1807 before Hudson Berry, J.P. [LCDBK H: 272-273]

Tweed, James: 27 March 1809: Isaac Sharp, of Laurens Dist., S.C., to Samuel Nisbett, of same place, for $350; 402 acres on Rabourns Creek, a branch of Reedy River, *250 acres of said land surveyed by Jonathan Downs, for James Tweed.* Bounded S by land laid out for Mary Rich[y], all other sides vacant; also 162 acres of a late survey joining the said 250 acres surveyed to the said Jonathan Downs for Abraham Adams. Bounded NE by said Abraham Adams, all other sides vacant. Isaac (X) Sharp. Wit: John Adams, David Dorrough, Andrew McKnight. Proved by David Dorrough 27 March 1809 before Jessee Childress, J.P. [LCDBK J: 63]

Tweed, James: Survey for James Tweed pursuant to precept 6 January 1773; 100 acres in Craven Co., NE side of Raibourns Creek, on a small branch called Lick Creek. Bounded on all sides by vacant land. Surveyed 21 March 1773. Jonathan Downs, D.S. [P20_419:1]

Tweed, James: Memorial for James Tweed; 100 acres in Craven Co., of Lick Creek NE of Rayburns Creek. Bounded on all sides by vacant land. Certified 20 September1774 and granted 17 March 1775. Quit rent to commence in 2 years. 19 August 1775. Jonathan Downes, D.S. delivered [___] September 1775. [Irish in margin]. [M2_302:2]

Tweed[y], James: 15 March 1792: James Tweedy, of Laurens Co. Dist., S.C., of Ninety-six, S.C., freeholder, to William Norris, of same place, planter for £35 Stg.; 100 acres being part of 200 acres on the waters or Reedy River. *The tract being laid out for Roger Brooks grant bearing date 3 September 1787.* Bounded NE side of the steep hollow branch; NE on William Norris and Hugh Beards; SE on Reedy River. James Tweedy (LS). Wit: Joshua Downs, William Nugent, Samuel Saxon. Proved by Joshua Downs before Charles Saxon, J.P. [Note: this area may be to far from Rabuns Creek] [LCDBK: D: 142-144]

Valk [Volk], Jacob: Survey for Jacob Valk pursuant to precept dated 1 December 1772; 250 acres in Ninety Six Dist. on a branch of Raburns Creek, waters of Saludy. Bounded NE on Wm. Williamson; SW on Cornelius Cargill [plat also shows NE by John Armstrong]. Certified 10 February 1775. Jno. Rogers, D.S. Ord. Co. 1 June 1775. [P20_438:1]

Valk, Jacob: Memorial for Jacob Valk; 250 acres in 96 Dist., S.C., on a branch of Rayburns Creek the waters of Saludy. Bounding SE on land of Wm. Williamson; W on Cornelius Cargil; NW unknown. Certified 1 June [no year] and granted 28 July 1775. Quit rent to commence in 2 years. 16 November 1775. Lewis Linder, D.S. Delivered to the memorialist. [1 of 3 tracks] [M2_459:4]

Valk, Jacob: 10 & 11 April 1781: Jacob Valk of Charles town, gentleman, to Julius Smith, of same place, merchant for £1000 money of Great Britain, ten tracts of land [only listing the one relevant to this work]. . .900 acres part of 100 acres *sic* in Ninety Six Dist. upon Reedy Fork Creek a branch of Little River the waters of Saludy River adj. land of Charles Allen, John Rogers, who also became entitled to the remaining 100 acres adj. John Armstrong, John Brown, *granted to Jacob Valk 21 April 1775.* Jacob Valk (LS). Wit: Jas. Cha Neal. William Rugge. Proved by Wm. Rugg 16 November 1781 before William Rugely. [D-5, 510-515; Brent H. Holcomb, *South Carolina Deed Abstracts 1776-1783*, Books Y-4 - H-5, SCMAR, Columbia, SC, pg. 159]

Valk, Jacob: 6 October 1800: David Wardlaw, Sheriff of Abbeville Dist., S.C., to John Brannon, agent for Wm. Bowen highest bidder for $22; 250 acres on Enoree River *sic.* Bounding at survey NE on John Boyd and James Moore, SE on John Wallace, W on William Williamson. *Granted to Jacob Valk 28 July 1775,* now sold for judgment at suit of Wm. Clarkson, executor, of Aaron Loocock, deceased and at suit of Joseph Hall Ramsey, Admr., of Salude Benefort[?], deceased, at the time of the sale. D. Wardlaw, Sheriff, assistant. Wit; Geo. Bowie, Wm. Hamilton, A? Sanders. Proved by Geo. Bowie 16 March 1802 before James Saxon, J.Q. [LCDBK G: 416-417]

Vanhorn Family: 1776-1804: (Quakers from Pennsylvania, to Maryland, North Carolina, to South Carolina)
27 January 1776 Benjamin Vanhorn received certificate from Pine Creek MM, Maryland dated 26 February 1774; endorsed to New Garden, NC.
11 July 1776: Benjamin Vanhorn, late of Pennsylvania married Jane Milhouse (widow)
13 November 1783: Benjamin, Dist 96, SC md. Joanna Demoss
26 February 1785, Benjamin Vanhorn dismissed
27 October 1798 Robert Vanhorn of Raburns' Creek, rpd mou.
27 February 1802 Benjamin's death reported (father of Jane and Rebecca)
25 August 1804, Roberts gc.
[Rev. Silas Emmett Lucas, Jr. Quakers in S.C., Southern Historical Press, Greenville, SC, 1991, pg. 111]

Vanhorn, Benjamin: No Colonial survey or memorial found for Benjamin Vanhorn.

Vanhorn, Benjamin: 13 June 1795: Benjamin Vanhorn one of the purchasers at the estate sale of Joseph Pinson. [LCWBK A: 138]

Vanhorn, Benjamin: 24 April 1800: Benjamin Vanhorn, of Laurens Dist., S.C., to David Cox, of same place, for £28; 57 acres on the W side of

Reaburns Creek waters of Saluda. *Being part of 500 acres originally granted to Daniel Allen* and being ½ moiety of said 500 acres of which was conveyed to Samuel Kelley 21 October [torn] and by Samuel Kelly conveyed to Wm. Ancrum and Aaron Loocock and by Ancrum & Loocock to John Galbreath, then by John Galbreath and Jane Galbreath to Benjamin Vanhorn. Benjamin Vanhorn (LS) Wit: Jonthan. Downs, [torn] Downs. Proved by William Downs 7 April 18[torn] before Jonthan. Downs, J.P. Dower of Joanna Vanhorn, wife of Benjamin Vanhorn given 26 April 1800 before [torn]. [See Daniel Allen] [LCDBK G: 28-30]

Vanhorn, Benjamin: 7 September 1804: Robert Vanhorn, of Laurens Dist., S.C., appoint Henry Buckner, of same place, my true and lawful attorney for me and in my name and to release unto my two sisters, Jane Buckner, wife of Philip and Rebecca Vanhorn a minor of 17, when she shall arrive at the age of desecration all by right and title, claim or demand to an undivided tract of land whereon Mrs. Joannah Vanhorn now resides. Supposed to contains 200 acres which said tract of 100 acres I have sold and conveyed unto the said Henry Buckner by deed dated 31 May 1804 and granting unto my said attorney Henry Buckner full power for me and in my name to convey to my said 2 sisters Jane Buckner and Rebecca Vanhorn all my right title claim or demand in the residue of my fathers real estate. Robert Vanhorn (LS) Wit: R. Creswell, E. Creswell. Proved by Elihu Creswell 24 September 1804 before B.H. Saxon, J.Q. [LCDBK H: 52-53]

Vanhorn, Benjamin: 13 September 1805: Affidavit by James Buckner: James Bucker gave oath that on the 30 August last the dwelling house of the deponent was consumed by fire and that a deed for the conveyance of 57 acres from Benjamin Vanhorn to David Cox with a part of the said land there unto annexed also and for the conveyance of the said 57 acres of land from the said David Cox to Jonathan Cox and a deed for the conveyance of the said 57 acres of land to the said Jonathan Cox to this deponent were all burned in the dwelling house of this deponent on the said 39 August last. James (x) Buckner. Samuel Cunningham, J.P. [See Benjamin Vanhorn] [LCDBK H: 119]

Vanhorn, Benjamin: 7 December 1805: Survey Request: At the request of James Buckner I have resurveyed the tract of land on which he now resides and find it to contain 52 and 3/4 acres and to have such form and marks butting and bounding as the above plat represents - Certified 7 December 1805 John Cochran. [Plat shows bounding Henry Buckner, M. Cunningham, James Boyds, Philip Buckner being on Rabourns Creek.] [LCDBK H: 119]

Vanhorn, Benjamin: 24 October 1808: Phillip Buckner and Jinney Buckner, of Buncombe Co., North Carolina, appoint Henry Buckner, of said county, our true and lawful attorney to sign, seal and deliver to John Simmons, of Laurens Dist., S.C., lands in Laurens Co., S.C., on Raburns Creek in which tract of land said Philip Buckner, Joanna Vanhorn and Rebecca Vanhorn each hold an equal third part. We therefore grant our attorney with full power to convey one third our undivided moiety of said tract to said John Simmons. Philip (mark) Buckner (LS) Jinney (mark) Buckner (LS). 25 October 1808: David Vance, Clerk of Buncombe Co., Asheville, North Carolina, certified that he witnessed saw Philip Buckner and Jinney Buckner, his wife, each make their mark. [LCDBK J: 49]

Vanhorn, Benjamin: 7 December 1808: Henry Buckner, of Buncombe Co., North Carolina, attorney for Philip and Jenny Buckner, to John Simmons, of Laurens Dist., S.C., for $216.60; undivided one third part of 200 acres on Reaburns Creek. Bounded on lands now held by Thomas Norris, James Boyd, Nathl. & Robert Nichols, John McCann and S on Reaburns Creek, being the place whereon John Simmons now lives. Hen. Buckner (LS) Attorney for Phillip and Jenney Buckner. Wit: Samuel Cunningham, Lewis Saxon. Proved by Samuel Cunningham 6 January 1809 before John Garlington, J.Q. [SCBDK J: 49-50]

Vanhorn, Benjamin: 5 April 1809: Rebecca Vanhorn, of Warren Co., Ohio, to John Simons [Simmons], of Laurens Co., S.C., for $216.66; one third part of the undivided tract of land on Raburns Creek, *this being her quota of that tract of landed deeded to her by Benjamin Vanhorn, deceased.* Rebecca (X) Vanhorn. Wit: Simon Cobb, Caleb Easterlin. Proved by Simon Cobb 19 July 1809 before Samuel Cunningham, J.P. [See LWT of Benjamin Vanhorn] [LCDBK J: 183]

Vanhorn, Robert: No survey or memorial located for Robert Vanhorn.

Vaughn, William: 7 February 1769. Petition for 200 acres on Rayburn Creek. [No survey or memorial located for 200 acres on Rayburns Creek.]

Waite [Wheaite], Joseph: Survey for Joseph Wheaite *sic* pursuant to precept dated 1 August 1769; 200 acres in Berkley Co., on the waters of Rabouns Creek. Bounded by vacant land. Certified 19 August 1769. Pat. Cunningham, D.S. Ord. Co. 3 November 1772. [P21_258:1]

Waite [Waites], Joseph: Memorial for Joseph Waite; 200 acres in Berkley Co., on the waters of Rayburns Creek. Bounded on all sides by vacant land. Certified 3 November 1772 and granted 19 November 1772. Quit rent to commence in 2 years. 24 March 1773. Delivered 5 April 1773 to John Baugh. P. Cunningham, D.S. [M12_140:1]

Waits, Joseph: 28 January 1780: Thomas McClurken, of Ninety Six Dist., S.C., merchant, to John Cuningham, of same place, planter, for $5,000; 200 acres on the waters of Reyburns Creek. Bounded on all sides by vacant land. *Originally granted 19 November 1772 to Joseph Waits,* and conveyed unto Radcliff Jowell and by said Jowell to said Thomas McClurken. Thomas McClurkin (LS). Wit: Thomas Richardson, James Cuningham, James McClerkin. [LCDBK A: 63-64]

Wallis, John: 11 December 1816: Patsy Holcomb, one of the heirs of Moses Holcomb, dec'd, of Laurens Dist., S.C., to John Gilbert, of same place, all my undivided part of two tracts of land containing 130 acres, viz. One part containing 125 acres *formerly willed to Jonathan Wallis by his father John Wallis* and by him conveyed to Moses Holcomb Bounding NW by Jesse Wallis, N by Thomas Parks, SE on Thomas Parks and William Roundtree, SW on Jones lands, the other part containing 5 acres which includes the cabin where Moses Holcomb deceased did live. Patsey (X) Holcomb. Wit: John Garlington, Nat. Day. Proved by Nathaniel Day 18 December 1816 before John Garlington, Q.M. [LCDBK K: 151-152]

Walker, William: 6 September 1804: Deed from William Walker to John Sims for 119 ½ acres on waters of Raybans Creek on a branch called Longlick. [LCDBK K: 21-22]

Walker, William: 10 November 1811: John Sims of Laurens Dist., S.C., to James Young, of same place, merchant, for $240; 119 ½ acres of land where I now lives on the waters of Raybans Creek on a branch called Longlick. Being a tract of land containing 119 ½ acres *which was conveyed to said John Sims by William Walker by lead dated 6 September 1804.* Reference being had to said deed will more fully appear the other tract of land containing 30 acres of land bounding Aaron Starns, John McCurley, John Sims, William Walker by deed dated 19 November 1811. John (X) Sims (LS). Wit. Joel Walker, F. Burtz. Dower of Elizabeth Sims, wife of the within John Sims given 3 June 1813. Before David Anderson, J.Q. Proved by Joel Walker August ----no date. Before Dd. Anderson, J.Q.M. [LCDBK K: 21-22]

Waring, Archer: Survey not found.

Waring, Archer: Memorial for Archer Waring; 500 acres in Craven Co., on the branch of Rayburns Creek and near the Mount Warrior. Bounded NE by Simon Tuft; SE by James Smith; other sides vacant. Certified 20 June 1772 and granted 19 November 1772. Quit rent to commence in 2 years. 26 March 1773. Delivered 13 July 1773 to Thos. Waring. Richd. Winn, D.S. [M12_141:1]

Weaver, Frederick: Survey for Frederick Weaver pursuant to precept dated 6 March 1770; 150 acres in Berkley Co., waters of Reedy River. Bounded N by land laid out to James Kilpatrick; W by Rebuons Creek; other sides vacant. Certified 28 May 1770. Pat. Cunningham, D.S. [P21_367:1]

Weaver, Frederick: Memorial for Frederick Weaver; 150 acres in Berkley Co., on the waters of Reedy River. Bounding N on land laid out to James Kilpatrick; W on Reburns Creek; other sides vacant. Certified 28 May 1770 and granted 22 February 1771. Quit rent to commence in 2 years. Pat. Cunningham. Pat. Cunningham, D.S. [M10_389:5]

Weaver, A[blank]: 14 August 1789: A [blank] Weaver is bounding on S side Reedy River below Old Indian Line, John Hall and Elizabeth Hall, his wife, deed of sale to Charles Smith. [LCDBK D: 146]

Weatherspoon, John: Survey for John Weatherspoon pursuant to precept dated 4 November 1766; 300 acres in Craven Co., in the fork on Raiburns Creek called Brown's Fork, a branch of Saludy River. Bounded on all sides by vacant land. Certified 28 January 1767. Ralph Humphreys, D.S. Ord. Co. 9 January 1775 for Wm. Elliott.[See memorial for William Elliott.] [P15_30:3]

Webb, David: Survey for David Webb pursuant to precept dated 5 August 1766; 600 acres on a branch of Reedy River and Rabuons Creek in Berkley Co. Bounded NW by land surveyed for Daniel Allen; other sides vacant. Certified 2 Sept. 1766. Wm. Anderson, D.S. Ord. Co. 7 May 1771. [P21_372:1]

Webb, David: Memorial for David Webb; 600 acres in Berkeley Co., on a branch of Reedy River and Reaburns Creek. Bounding NW part on land surveyed for Daniel Allen and vacant land; other sides vacant. Certified 1 May 1771 and granted 18 May 1771. Quit rent to commence in 2 years. 28 June 1771. Delivered 2 June 1772 to James Kind (J his mark). William Anderson, D.S. [M10_500:1]

Webb, David: before 1780: Land was conveyed to James Ryan and by him to Thomas McClerkin. [Deeds not found.]

Webb, David: 28 January 1780: Thomas McClurken, of Ninety Six Dist., S.C., merchant, to Thomas Cunningham, of same place, sadler, for £10,000; 600 acres on the branches of Reedy River of Reyburns Creek. Bounded N and W by Daniel Allen; other sides vacant. *Originally granted 8 May 1771 to David Webb,* and conveyed to James Ryan, by him to said Thos. McClerkin. Signed Thomas McClerkin. Wit: Thomas Richardson, James

Cuningham, James McClerkin. [LCDBK A: 60--61]

Webb, David: 11 September 1789: Thomas Cunningham, Ninety Six Dist., Laurens Co., S.C., freeholder, to James McDavid, of same place, for L39; 200 acres on a branch of Reedy River and Raburn Creek.; *part of 600 acres originally granted 18 May 1774 to David Webb* in Berkeley Co. Bounded on NW on land surveyed for Daniel Allen and vacant land. Which land David Webb had made a right or title unto James Ryan by lease 9, 10 October 1771 and the said James Ryan conveyed unto Thomas McClurkin by Lease 14, 15 April 1778 and said Thomas McClurkin conveyed said tract unto Thomas Cuningham by lease 26 and 28 January 1780. Thomas Cuningham, Mary (C) Cuningham (his wife). Wit: Richard Pugh, George (e) Cunningham. Proved by Thomas Cuningham. Jonathan Downs, J.P. Plat shows bounding on David Dunlap, Thos. Cuningham and land laid out. [LCDBK C: 292-294]

Webb, David: 5 April 1795: Thomas Cunningham, of the Dist. of Ninety Six, S.C., to Samuel Cuningham, of same place, for £30 Stg.; 139 acres on the waters of Reaburns Creek *Being part of 600 acres granted to David Webb.* Bounded on land laid out for said Thomas Cuningham, Jno. Hollingsworth, John Cuningham, Jonathan Cox. Thos. Cuningham. Wit. David Dunlap, Geo. Cuningham, Proved by David Dunlap 19 July 1749 before Joseph Downs, J.P. [LCDBK F: 124]

Webb, David: 9 December 1799: Jonathan Cox of Laurens Co., S.C., to Henry Buckner, of same place, for $300; 100 acres on waters of Reedy River, the said tract of 100 aces being part of a tract of 600 acres *originally granted to David Webb* and by the said David Webb conveyed to James Ryan and by said James Ryan conveyed to Thomas McClurken and from him to Thomas Cuningham and by said Thomas Cuningham conveyed the said 100 acres to James McDavid and by said James McDavid conveyed to the said Jonathan Cox. Jonathan Cox (LS) Wit: Lewis Saxon, William David? Dower of Mary Cox, wife of the within named Jonathan Cox given 9 December 1799 before Jonathan Downs, J.L.C. Proved by Lewis Saxon 6 February 1801 before Robert Creswell, C.C.C. [LCDBK G: 152-153]

Weir, John: 28 December 1786: Haisten Doyall [Hastings Dial], of Laurens Co., S.C., freeholder, to John Todd, of same for £30; 100 acres on waters of Reaburns Creek *originally granted to John Weir on 4 May 1775.* Bounded SW by John Hellams, all other sides vacant. The above land conveyed unto said Hasten Dyal [Dial] 12 October 1786. Hastings Dial, Rebeckah Dial [his wife] Wit: Robert Todd, David Hellams, William Hobbs. [LCDBK B: 166 - 167]

Weir, Thomas (Jr.): Memorial for Thomas Weir, Jr.; 100 acres in Craven Co., waters of Rayburns Creek. Bounding SW on John Hallem; other sides vacant. Certified 20 September 1774 and granted 4 May 1775. Quit rent in 2 years. 2 October 1775. Pat. Cunningham, D.S. [M2_384:3]

Weir, Thomas (Jr.): Memorial for Thomas Weir, Jr.; 100 acres in Craven Co., SE of Rayburns Creek on a small branch thereof. Bounding SW on William Williamson; all other sides vacant. Certified 30 September 1774 and granted 4 May 1775. Quit rent to commence in 2 years. 2 October 1775. Jonathan Downes, D.S. [M2_384:2]

Weir, Thomas: 9 May 1792: Thomas Weir is found *bounding lands originally granted to David Weir in 1774* on SW side of Durbins Creek. [LCDBK F: 157]

Weir, Thomas: before 23 January 1800, Thomas Weir sold land James Gary.

Weir, Thomas: 23 January 1800: James Gary, of Laurens Co., S.C., planter, to John Henderson, of same place, for $170; 100 acres on Lick Creek of Rabourns Creek. Bounded SW on land of Williamson, Esq., all over sides vacant. *Originally granted to Thomas Weir, Junior on 30 September 1774.* James Gary (LS). Wit: Jesse Garrett, Nathan (N his mark) Henderson, Lettey Skin *sic*. (LS). Elizabeth Gary (LS). Jonathan Downs. J.Q. Dower of Elizabeth Gary, wife of the within James Gary given 10 January 1802 before Jonathan Downs, Q.M. [LCDBK G: 535-356]

Wells, James: Survey for James Wells pursuant to precept 2 March 1773; 300 acres in Ninety six District, upon the waters of Reburns creek, on the N side bounded NW on Nicholas Hills, NE on Joseph Bobs sic [Babb] land, SW on William Bures, SE and SW owner not known and Robert Gill. Certified 24 March 1773 Thos. Clark, D.S. Ord Co. 9 Dec. 1774 for Edmund Petrie. [See memorial for Edmund Petrie] [P19-149:1]

Wells, James: Bounding lands of James Box [LCDBK F: 29]

Wells, James: 8 January 1795: Bounding lands of James Box. [LCDBK F: 41]

Wells, James: 18 November 1803: James Wells, was along the purchasers at estate sale of Aaron Pinson, Sr., deceased. Some others from the Raburns Creek area at the sale were Abel Thomas, Benjamin Williams, John Shurley, Thomas Hunter, Josiah Blackwell, John Sims, Jacob Niswanger. [See Aaron Pinson's estate for full text] [LCWBK C-1: 79]

Willard, John: Survey for John Willard 100 acres not found.

Willard, John: Memorial by John Willard for 100 acres in Craven Co., on the waters of Reedy River. Bounded SE by land name not known, SW by Patrick Cuningham, NW by John Willard, other sides vacant land. Certified 8 July 1774 and granted 6 September 1774 to the memorialist. Quit rent to commence 2 years from date. Set his hand 13 March 1774. Delivered 18 October 1775 to Geo. Norwood. [M13-381:1]

Willard, John: 3 February 1768: Grant for 250 acres.

Willard, John: 19 May 1774: John Willard, of the Dist., of Ninety Six and Parish of St. Mark, Province of S.C., [and Martha is wife] to Joseph Atkins, of same for £375; *179 acres part of 250 acres granted 30 February 1768* to said John Willard for a mill seat lying and being as aforesaid creek being the dividing line and extension to the middle or center of said creek. In Berkley Co., on both sides of Reedy Creek. Bounding SW on lands when surveyed the property of John Brown, NW on land laid out to John Cargill, SE on land laid out to Hans Hendrick, all other sides on vacant land at time of the original survey. John Willard (LS) Martha Willard (LS). Wit: John Cobb, William Burgess, Pat. Cuningham. Proved by John Cobbs that he saw John Willard and Martha his wife sign, seal and deliver this to Joseph Atkins. before P. Cuningham, J.P. Patrick Cuningham J.P. [Note: Martha Willard, daughter of Hans Hendricks, see LWT of Margaret Hendricks, wife of Hans Hendricks. Also see Hans Hendrick, Theodosius Turk deed to John Willard.] [LCDBK E: 438-441]

Willard, John: 5 February 1790: John Atkins, of Moore Co., North Carolina, and his wife to George Morgan, of Laurens Co., S.C., for £100; *179 acres being part of 250 acres granted to John Willard 3 February 1768* on both sides of Reedy River . Bounded SW on lands then surveyed and property of John Brown, NW on land laid out to John Cargill, SE on lands laid out to Hance [Hans] Hendrick, other sides vacant. John Atkins, Margaret Atkins (X her mark) Wit: Lewis Graves, Middleton Praytor, James Morgin. Proved by Midleton Praytor 25 May 1790 before George Anderson, J.P. [LCDBK C: 215-217]

Willard, John: 9 February 1815: John Willard, of Laurens Dist., S.C., to James Hathorn, of same place, for $400; 93 ½ acres. Bounding on Reedy River, John Willard, and George Morgans land, now James Hathorns. John Willard (X) (LS) Wit: Samuel Anderson, Shubel Starns. Dower of Patsy Willard wife of the within names John Willard made on 9 February 1815 before D.D. Anderson, J.Q. Patsey (her mark) Willard. [Plat for 93 ½ acres] [LCDBK K: 88]

Willard, John: 29 June 1816: LWT of John Willard. . . I leave to my dearly beloved wife Patty, her life time full possession of all my land. I give unto my son Macajah Willard all my land at his mothers death. I give unto all my children a equal portion of all my personal property. (Viz) Macajah, Polly, Elizabeth and Sarah a equal part after my funeral expenses and all my just debts are paid. I appoint my son Macajah Willard executor. John Willard (X). Wit: J. L. Neely, Walter Burgess, Elizabeth Davenport. Recorded 2 November 1816. Proven 2 November 1816. David Anderson, Ord. Laurens Dist. Bundle 76, Pkg. 10. [LCWBK D-1; 342]

[Family: Wife Patty, son Macajah, daughters, Elizabeth and Sarah Willard.]

Willard, John: 2 November 1816: John Willard, deceased. Will proved by Elizabeth Davenport. Micajah Willard qualified as executor.

Willard, John: deceased, 1816: We Melagah *sic* Willard and Patsey Willard, mother of said Melajah Willard are indebted to David Anderson by a note of land payable on demand dated 1 January 1819 for the sum of $182 part of which note was due the said David Anderson by John Willard of said Melajah. Therefore for the better securing the payment of the said note and interest we the said Melajah Williard and Patty Willard do hereby mortgage unto the said David Anderson all that tract of land of 210 acres will by John Willard to Patsey and at her death to sd Micajah Willard. Micaejah Willard, Pattey (X) Willard (LS). Wit: Jos. Neely, B.B. Cheshire.[LCDBK K: 251-252]

Willard, John: 24 March 1819: We Micajah Willard and Martha Willard, do owe and acknowledge ourselves indebted to Robert Campbell (all of Laurens Dist., S.C.,) in the following notes Viz: one for $42 dated 1 January 1817 due on demand and bearing interest from the date, the other for $65, dated March 1819 bearing interest from the 1 January in the same year and for better securing the payment of the said notes with legal interest we Micajah Willard and Martha Willard do grant and sell unto the said Robert Campbell 200 acres where we now live adjoining Joseph Neely, Mrs. Harthorn, William Crocker and Jas. Crocker. Also horses, wagon, 5 featherbeds, cattle, etc. Micajah Willard (LS) Martha (X) Willard (LS). Wit: Joseph Crocker, Samuel Hanna. Proved by Samuel Hanna 17 September 1819 before Howard Pinson, J.P. [LCDBK K: 262-263]

Williamson, Benjamin: Survey for Benjamin Williamson pursuant to precept dated 4 May 1772; 1400 acres in Craven Co., in the fork of Broad and Saludy Rivers on the branches of Reaburns Creek. Bounded SW on land laid out to Richard Winn; SE, SW and SE on land laid out to Pady Cunningham; NW and NE on Wilson; other sides vacant. Certified 5 June 1772. Wm. Gist, D.S. Ord. Co. 5 January 1773. [P21_494:1]

Williamson, Benjamin: Memorial for Benjamin Williamson; 1400 acres in Craven Co., in the fork of Broad and Saludy Rivers on the branches of Raibens Creek. Bounding SW by Richd. Winn; SE and SW by Paddy Cunningham; NE and NE by Wilson; other sides vacant. Certified 5 Jan 1773 and granted 23 January 1773. Quit rent to commence in 2 years. 8 June 1773. Delivered to Wm. Williamson as heir at law. Wm. Gist, D.S. [M12_232:1]

Williamson, Benjamin: 8 & 9 February 1773: Benjamin Williamson, Esq. of Stono, in St. Pauls Parish, [S.C.] to William Williamson, Esqr., of Charleston, for 10 sh. ; also 1400 acres in Craven Co., in the fork of Broad and Saludy Rivers, on the branches of Rebens Creek. Bounded OW *sic* on Richard Winn; SE and S on Paddy Cunningham; NW and NE on Wilson's land; other sides vacant. Which tract was *granted Benjamin Williamson 23 January 1773.* Wit: Francis Guirin, George Greenland, James Stanyarne. Recorded 7 April 1773 by William Rugeley, Henry Rugerley, Reg. [Langley, Vol. IV, pg. 298]

Williams, Benjamin: 14 February 1791: Benjamin Williams of Laurens Co., S.C., Reaburns Creek Settlement, freeholder and planter, for and in consideration of the Good will, love and affection which I have towards my loving son Jonathan Williams, of same place, bachelor, have given and granted unto said Jonathan Williams a tract of land lying bounding SW on the Reedy fork of Dirty Creek, extending up to the Little branch, and up that to the NW line. Benjamin (X) Williams Wit: James Parker, Thomas Elliott. Probed by Thomas Elliott, Junr. 15 March 1791 before Joseph Downs, J.P. [LCDBK C: 361]

Williams, Benjamin: 9 August 1794: Benjamin Williams, of Laurens Co., S.C., to Charles Lowry, Junr., of said place, for £60 Stg.; 100 acres on a branch of Dirty Creek waters of Reaburns Creek. Benjamin (X) Williams, Lucretia (+) Williams. Wit: Thos. Burton, Wm. Burton. Proved by Thomas Burton 25 June 1796 before John Cochran, D.C. Plat. [LCDBK F: 113]

Williamson, Benjamin: 4 June 1821: William Dunlap, Attorney for Bernard E. Bee, of Laurens Dist., S.C., to Thomas Brownlee, of same place; for $390; 195 acres on the waters of Raybourns Creek, part of a tract of land of 1100 acres granted to Benjamin Williamson in the year 1772. [Plat shows bounded by Charles Prim, on the Road to the C. [Court] House, John Rodgers, surveyed 9 April 1816 by Wm. Dunlap, D.S.] Bernard E. Bee (LS) by his Atty Wm. Dunlap. Wit: R. Simpson. D.P. Saxon. Proved by Richard F. Simpson 15 June 1821 before John Garlington, Q.M. [LCDBK L: 17]

Williams, Daniel: Survey for pursuant to precept dated 6 April 1773; 160 acres in Craven Co., waters of Reaburns Creek. Bounded SW and NW by Richard Pinson; SW by Jacob Bowman; part SE vacant; and part SE on Jacob Bowman. NE unknown and part by Geo. Wright; other sides by Reaburn's Creek. Certified 6 August 1773. Pat. Cunningham, D.S. [P21_470:1]

Williams, Daniel: Memorial by Daniel Williams; 160 acres in Craven Co., on the waters of Rayburns Creek. Bounding SW and NW on Richard Pinson; SW on Jacob Bowman; SE on vacant and Jacob Bowman; NE on Geo. Wright and unknown; other sides on Rayburnes Creek. Certified 6 August 1773 and granted 23 June 1774. Quit rent to commence in 2 years. Delivered 18 January 1775 to Charles King Chitty. Pat. Cunningham, D.S. [M13_150:4]

Williams, Daniel, deceased: Died by 6 October 1801. [See below LCDBK G: 285.]

Williams, Daniel: See Jesse Jones and Robert Long.

Williams, Daniel: 6 October 1801: Oliver Williams and Wright Williams, of Davidson Co., Tennessee to Lewis Banton for $10; 160 acres on Raybans Creek, bounding Richard Pinson, John Shearly [Shirley], Jacob Bowman (now Jacob Niswanger), George Wright. *Originally granted to Daniel Williams 23 June 1774,* now conveyed by legatees of said Daniel Williams, deceased. Wit: Nimrod Williams, Wm. Groggon, Thos. Edmonson, David Anderson, J.Q. [LCDBK G: 285]

Williams, Edward: Survey for Edward Williams pursuant to precept dated 5 June 1770: 350 acres in Berkley Co., on Reburns Creek. Bounding N and W on land laid out to John Abercrombie; S by land claimed by Isaac Pitts; all other sides by vacant land. Certified 12 June 1770. Pat.Cunningham, D.S. [P11_464:2]

Williams, Edward: Memorial for Edward Williams; 350 acres in Berkley Co., on Rayburns Creek. Bounding N and W on John Abercrombey; S on land claimed by Isaac Pitts; other sides vacant. Certified 12 June 1770 and granted 27 November 1771. Quit rent to commence in 2 years. 7 January 1771. Pat. Cunningham, D.S. [M10_320:3]

Williams, James: Survey for James Williams pursuant to precept dated 7 August 1755; 300 acres lying and being the NW side of Saludy on a branch called Reaburns Creek. Bounded by vacant land. Certified 21 November 1755. John Franellen?, D.S. [P6-176:2]

Williams, James: No memorial for 300 acres listed.

Williams, James: Survey for James Williams pursuant to precept dated 7 August 1770; 150 acres on Reyburn's Creek. Bounded N on land laid out to Saml. Millhouse; other sides vacant. Certified 25 August 1770. Jno. Caldwell, D.S. Ord. Co. 2 March 1773. [P21_478:2]

Williams, James: Memorial by James Williams; 150 acres in Craven Co., on Rayburns Creek. Bounding N on Samuel Millhouse; other sides vacant. Certified 2 March 1773 and granted 2 April 1773. Quit rent to commence in 2 years. 13 August 1773. Delivered 9 November 1773 to Joseph Williams. John Caldwell, D.S. [M12_373:2]

Williams, James: 4 March 1786: Deposition: Oath of Hester Williams that sometime in March 1782 her husband James Williams being on his death bed, *sayed that his desire was that his son-in-law Robert Box should inherit that tract of land that he and said James Williams then lived on,* and this deponent further sayeth that the said James Williams desired her the deponent to deliver up said land to said Robert Box. Signed Hester Williams. Wit: Joseph Downs, J.P. in the presence of John Goodwin. Recorded 31 March 1786. [LCDBK A: 207]

[Family: Wife Hester; son-in-law Robert Box.]

Williams, James: 14 March 1791: Laurens Co., S.C.: I Thomas Williams, grandson of James Williams, deceased, *being lawful heir of the said James Williams, deceased of a tract of land containing 300 acres,* have delivered unto William Moore for £25; 300 acres. Thomas (X) Williams (LS). Wit: Jesse Moore, James McClannahan. Proved 17 March 1791 by Jesse Moore before Joseph Downs, J.P. [LCDBK: E 362-363]

Williams, James: 26 November 1792: William Moore of Laurens Co., S.C., to Wiseman Box, of same place, for £41 Stg., a tract of 300 acres on both sides of Reaburns Creek including plantation where said Moore, Edward and Henry Box now lives. Bounded on Charles Bradey [Broadway], and land belonging to Millhouse. William Moore, (L.S.) Wit: John Wadkins, John Moore, Henry Box. Proved by Henry Box 18 February 1794 before Joseph Downs, J.P. [LCDBK E: 398-239]

Williams, James: 24 August 1794: Wiseman Box, of Laurens Co., Dist. of Ninety Six, S.C., and Hugh Henderson, of same for £26, *40 acres being part of 300 acres laid out for James Williams,* under the land of his Excellency the Honorable James Glenn. The land on the waters of Reaburns Creek, Said 40 acres on the N side of Raburns creek, lying on the NE corner of said tract and down Burrises creek unto the mouth, to William Bradey, then along Broadway's. Wiseman (X) Box. (L.S.) Wit: James Robinson, Jonathan (mark) Box. N.B. Hugh Henderson doth hereby grant the aforesaid Wiseman Box the privilege of lifting and carrying water from the spring. Jonathan (mark) Box. Proved by Jonathan Box 18 February 1795 before Zachariah Bailey, J.P. [LCDBK E: 399 - 400]

Williams, James: 24 March 1807: William Matthews and Avyrilar, his wife, of Lawrence *sic* Dist., S.C. to Edward Box for ___; the third part of that tract of land containing 150 aces of land being a part of 300 *originally granted to James Williams.* Beginning at the mouth of Burrows Creek. William Matthews (LS) Avyrilar (X) Wit: Henry Box, Jacob Box. Proved by Jacob Box that he saw Wm. Matthews and Eveviler *sic*, his wife, sign, seal and deliver unto Edward Box. Before Joseph Bolton, J.P. [LCDBK J: 249]

Williams, James A. [Atwood]: 17 February 1819: Daniel Williams, acting executor, of James A. Williams, deceased, of Edgefield Dist., S.C., to Nancy Mahaffey, of Laurens Dist., S.C., for $350; 341 ½ acres on Raburns Creek, being *part of a grant to said James A. Williams.* Daniel Williams (LS). Wit: Robert Coker, B.L. Bullock. Proved by Robert Coker 19 February 1819 before John Garlington, Clk Laurens Dist. And____, J.Q. [LCDBK K: 237]

Williams, John: Survey for John Williams pursuant to precept dated 2 September 1766; 150 acres in Berkley Co., on Helmns. Branch waters of Rabons Creek. Bounded on sides by vacant land. Certified 23 October 1766. William Anderson, D.S. [P8_580:2]

Williams, John: Memorial for John Williams for 150 acres in Berkley Co., on Helme's branch. Bounded on all sides by vacant land. Certified 23 October 1766 and granted 7 may 1767 to the memorialist. Quit rent to begin in two years. Set his hand 3 July 1767 Wm. Anderson, D.S. For the Memorialist David Ray. [M9-260:3].

Williams, John: 19 January 1773: John Williams, of Craven Co., S.C., planter, to Capt. James Lindley, Esq., planter, of same place, for £300 Stg.; *150 acres on Hallums Branch of Reaburns Creek, originally granted 7 May 1767 to John Williams.* John Williams (LS). Wit: Geo. Wright, Junr., John Madden, Benjn. Woods. Proved by John Madden 7 December 1784 before Jonathan Downs, J.P. [LCDBK F: 72-73]

Williams, John: 28 August 1778: James Lindley, of Ninety Six Dist., S.C., planter, to John McClanahan, of same place, planter for £800 cur; 150 acres on Hallums Branch being a branch of Reaburns Creek. Bounded on vacant land *when surveyed for John Williams.* Granted to John Williams 7 May 1767. Jas. Lindley (LS) Mary Lindley (LS). Wit: Thos. McClurkin, Robert (R) Jno. Wood, John AbCrombie *sic* [Abercromby]. Proved 14 January 1784 before Robert Hannah, J.P. [LCDBK F: 73-74]

Williams, John: 4 June 1795, 150 acres granted to John Williams on waters of Reaburns Creek.

Williams, John: 13 December 1791: Leanna Arnald, [Arnold] widow woman, Exor., of Joshua Arnall [Arnold] to Benjamin Jones, f same place, blacksmith, for £30 Stg.; 161 acres on Mchurgs creek, waters of Reaburns creek. *Originally grated 4 June 1787 to John Williams* and conveyed by said John Williams to Leanna Arnall Wit: Stephen Potter, William Franks. Proved by Stephen Potter 23 January 1795 before Joseph Downs, J.P. [LCDBK E: 325-327]

Williams, John: 10 February 1795: Benjamin Jones, of Laurens Co., S.C., to Charles Henderson, of same place for £60; 150 acres on McHurg's creek, waters of Reaburns Creek. Bounded S on Jas. Boyd, deceased, SW unknown, SE on Joshua Arnold. Granted to John Williams 4 June 1787. Wit: John (x) Henderson, Thos. (x) Henderson. Proved by oath of John Henderson 29 December 1795 before Joseph Downs, J.P. [LCDBK F: 70]

Williams, John: 6 April 1799: James McClanahan (son and heir of Jno. McClanahan, decd.), of Laurens Co., S.C. to Marmaduke Pinson, of same place, for £125 Stg.; 150 acres on waters of Reaburns Creek, viz. On a branch thereof called Dirty Creek (formerly Hallams's Branch). Bounding at the time of survey by vacant land. *Originally granted to John Williams on 7 May 1767,* and conveyed to said James Lindley 19 January 1773. In witness the said James McClanahan and Mary Pugh (formerly Mary McClanahan, and widow of John McClanahan, dec'd have set their hand. James McClanahan (L.S.), Mary (mark) Pugh. Wit: John Cochran, John McClanahan. Proved by John Cochran 3 June 1799 before James Abercrombie, J.P. [Plat for 150 acres]. [See will of Richard Pugh] [LCDBK F: 531]

Williams, John: 30 December 1795: William Fountain and Sarah, his wife, of Laurens Co., S.C. to Jesse Adams, of same place, for £40 Stg.; 137 acres on boundary of Reaburns Creek, part of a tract of land *formerly belonging to John Williams* and conveyed from John Williams to Stephen Potter and conveyed from Stephen Potter to Sarah Fountain and given to William Fountain by marriage. Bounded on Charles Henderson, Robert Bolt, John Lowry, Isom Histelow. Signed William Fountain. Wit: Isom Histelow, Chas. Miles. Joseph Downs, J.P. [LCDBK F: 126-127]

Williams, John: 23 December 1795: William Fountain, planter, and wife Sarah to Cornelius Hooker for £20 Stg.; 50 acres on branches of Reaburns Creek, being *part of land granted to John Williams,* and conveyed by him to Stephen Potter, by said Potter to Sarah Durham, then by said Sarah Durham given to Wm. Fountain in marriage. Bounded on James Smith's Big Survey line, Burgess Goolsby, Isham Histelow. Sarah Fountain (x) her mark, William Fountain (+) mark. Wit: James McCaa, John Cochran. Proved by John Cochran 14 September 1796 before Chas. Saxon, J.P. [LCDBK F: 135-136]

Williams, John.: 30 December 1795: William Fountain and his wife Sarah, of Laurens Co., S.C., to Jesse Adams, of same place, for £40 Stg.; 137 acres being on branches of Reaburns Creek being land *formerly belonging to John Williams* and conveyed from John Williams to Stephen Potter and from said Potter to Sarah Fountain and given to William Fountain by marriage. Bounded on Charles Henderson, Robert Bolt, John Lowry, Isom Histelow. William (+) Fountain, Sarah (+) Fountain. Wit: Isom Histelow, Charles Miles. Proved by Isom Histeloe 27 June 1790 before Joseph Downs, J.P. [LCDBK F: 126]

Williams, John: 10 November 1796: Jesse Adams of Laurens Co., S.C., to Charles Henderson, of same place, for £30 Stg.; 137 acres on a branch of Raiburns Creek, *being part of a tract of land formerly belonging to John Williams* and conveyed to Stephen Potter and conveyed from Stephen Potter to Sarah Fountain and given to William Fountain by marriage and is bounded by Charles Henderson, Bolts line, Isham Histelow. Jesse Adams (LS). Wit: Jesse Garrett, James Vines (mark). Proved by Jesse Garrett 11 November 1796 before Chas. Smith, J.P. [LCDBK F: 151-152]

Williams, John: 24 January 1796: Burgess Guldsby [Goolsbe], of Laurens Co., S.C., to John Lowry, of same place, for £30 Stg.; 50 acres on a branch of Raburns Creek. Bounded on W by Jas. Boyd, NE by David Smith, S by Pearce Butler, land being part of land *originally granted to John Williams dated 7 February 1791* by his Excellency Charles Pinckney, Governour. Conveyed from said John Williams to Stephen Potter. Birdgis Goolsbe (L.S.) Elazabeth (mark) Goolsbe (L.S.). Wit: Thos. Burton, Charles Lowry. Proved by Charles (C) Lowry 22 October 1798 before James Abercrombie, J.P. [LCDBK F: 380]

Williams, John: 28 December 1796: Cornelius Hooker, of Laurens Co., S.C., to Benjamin Couch, of same place, for £20 Stg.; 50 acres on branches of Raiborns Creek. *Being part of a tract granted to John Williams and conveyed by him to Stephen Potter and from Stephen Potter to Sarah Durham and from Sarah Duran given to William Fountain in marriage.*

264

Bounded on James Smiths' big survey line, S on Burgess Goldsby, to Isham Histelow's line. Cornelius (X) Hooker (LS) Wit: James (C) Couch, Anderson Arnold. Proved by James Couch 18 February 1997 before Jas. Dillard, J.P. [LCDBK F: 182]

Williams, John: 9 August 1772: John Williams, of Berkley Co., planter, and Elizabeth his wife, to John Owens, blacksmith, for £400; 150 acres on Reaburns Creek of Saluday River, called Reaburns Creek. Granted to said John Williams by patent dated 10 September 1765. Bounded on all sides by vacant land at the time or survey. John Williams, Elizabeth Williams. Wit: Henry Box, John Hellams. [LCDBK B: 185-186]

Williams, John: 21 October 1798: William Owen, formerly of State and Co., to John Cammock, of Laurens Dist., S.C., for $500; 150 acres on a branch formerly called Hellams Branch of Raburns Creek. *Originally granted to John Williams 10 September 1765,* conveyed to Jno. Owens Aug 1772, now by Wm. Owen, lawful heir of John Owens. Signed William Owens. Wit: Jno. Hughes, Jno. Harris. Signed William Owins. Proved by oath of John Harris 19 February 1799 before Charles Saxon, J.P. [Poor microfilm] [LCDBK F: 428]

Williams, John, Junr: 4 December 1780, land grant for 1682 acres.

Williams, John, Junr.: 5 August 1805: We John Griffin, James Williams, both of the Dist., of Newberry, and Washington Williams of the Dist. of Laurens, S.C., to James Atwood Williams, of the Dist. of Lawrence *sic*, S.C., for $600; 830 acres, all the following plantations or tracts of land that is to say each and all of our shares or parts of a certain tract of land in the District of Laurens on the head waters of Raburns Creek *originally granted to John Williams, Junr, now deceased, the 4 December 1780 for 1682 acres,* the above said shares, or dividends devolving on us by heirship, except the part sold off the NE corner by said John Williams in his lifetime to Arnold for 100 acres as appears by a dotted line in the original plat annexed to the grant and except for the part belonging to James Tinsley who intermarried with Elizabeth, the sister of the said, deceased John Williams, and also except that part belonging to said James Atwood Williams who also intermarried with Mary the sister of the said John Williams, deceased, the whole of these bargained supposes to be 830 acres. John Griffin (LS), James Williams (LS) Washington Williams (LS). Wit. J. Sproull, William Farrow, Jno. Leonard. Proved by John Leonard 23 October 1809 before James Williams, J.Q. [LCDBK J: 115-116]

[Family: John Williams, dec'd: His sister Elizabeth Williams married James Tinsley; sister Mary Williams, wife of James Atwood Williams.]

Williams, John: 23 February 1807: James A. Williams, of Laurens Co., S.C., to Hugh Mahaffey, of same place, for $150; 100 acres on the west fork of Raburns Creek Bounded on said Hugh Mahaffey hence north to the head of Schoolhouse Branch to Calvins Crumbie [Colvil Abercrombie], *being part of a granted to John Williams* and by his legatees conveyed to the said to James A. Williams. Jas. At. Williams (LS) Wit: Jonthn. Downs, Frances Downs. Dower of Mary Williams, the wife of the within named James Atwood Williams made 2 April 1807 before Jonthn. Downs, Q.M. Proved by Francis Downs 23 February 1807 before Jonthan. Downs. J.Q. [LCDBK H: 224-225]

Williams, John, Junr: 31 March 1807: James Tinsley, of Newberry Dist., S.C., to James Atwood Williams, of same place, for $75; all my part of above land left me and others by John Williams Junior, deceased, by his last will and testament. Lying on Rabourns Creek. Bounding land of Lydall Allen, Col. John F. Wolff, NE on Colvol A. Crumbie *sic*, ___ Mahaffey, SW other unknown said land *was granted to said John Williams, Junior, deceased. Originally containing 1500 acres (see deed J: 115-116 above for 1682 acres].* James Tinsley (LS) Wit: Elijah Watson, Daniel Williams, Junr., John Armstrong. Proved by John Armstrong 23 October 1809 before James Williams, J.Q.N.D. [LCDBK J: 115-116]

Williams, John: 29 August 1815: John Nash, of Laurens Dist., S.C., to John Hopkins, of same place, for $210; 137 acres on waters of Rabourns Creek. Bounded on Martin Mahaffey, said Williams, Guttery's branch. Being a part of land granted to John Williams, deceased and conveyed by one of his legatees to John Nash, from John Nash to John Hopkins. *Being part of grant to John Williams deceased, conveyed by one of his legatees to said John Nash.* John Nash, Junior (LS). Wit: Henry Morgan, Jeremiah Hopkins. Proved by Henry Morgan 29 September 1815 before Jonthn. Downs, J.Q. Dower of Hannah Nash, wife of the within names John Nash given 29 September 1815 before by Jonthan Downs, J.Q. [LCDBK K: 143]

Williams, John, Dec'd: 7 October 1819: Benjamin T. Guttery, of Laurens Dist., S.C., to James Brown, of same place, for $340; 137 acres on waters of Rabourns Creek. Bounded on Widow Savage, Martin Mahaffey, up Guttery's Branch to Nancy Mahaffey, *being part of grant to John Williams, dec'd and conveyed by one of his legatees to John N. Nash and from John N. Nash to John Hopkins and from said Hopkins B. T. Guttery and now to James Brown.* Benjamin T. Guttrey (x) (LS). Wit: Wm. Mahaffey, John N. Nash. Proved by William Mahaffey 1 May 1820 before John Garlington,

266

J.Q. [LCDBK K: 291]

Williams, John: No date: Colvill Abercrombie, of Laurens Dist., S.C., to Colvin Abercrombie for : 100 acres, *being part of a tract of land originally granted to John Williams* and by his heirs conveyed to the said Colvin Abercrumbie, Senr, and now by him conveyed to his son Colvin Abercrombie, land on the waters of Raborns Creek. Bounding Wm. Smith, Wm. Lindley, Colvin Abercrombie, Senr, down a hollow to the head of the still house branch. Colvill Acrombie *sic* (LS). Wit: J [Jesse] Garrett, Housley Garrett, Senr. Dower of Mary Abercrumbie, wife of the within named Colvill Abercrumbie made 5 November 1824. Proved by Jesse Garrett 5 November 1824 [LCDBK L: 233]

Williams, John: Memorial for John Williams; 150 acres in Berkley Co., on a branch of Saludy called Rayburns Creek. Bounded on all sides by vacant land. Certified 7 May 1765 and granted 10 September 1765. Quit rent to commence in 2 years. Jos. Curry, D.S. 12 October 1765. For the memorialist Richard Owings. [See survey for Thomas Christian] [M8_115:3]

Williams, John: 21 October 1798: Wm. Owens, formerly of State and Co. [Laurens Co., SC], to John Cammock for $500; 150 acres on Raburns Creek, on a branch of said Creek formerly called Hellams Branch. Bound at time on original survey by vacant land. *Originally granted to John Williams 10 September 1765* and conveyed by said Williams to John Owens by lease and release dated 9 and 10 August 1772 and is now conveyed by said Wm. Owens (lawful heir to the said John Owens) to John Cammock. William Owins (LS) Wit: John Hughes, John Harris. Proved by John Harris 19 February 1799 before Charles Saxon, J.P. [LCDBK F: 428-429]

Williams, John: 28 August 1778: James Lindley, Ninety Six Dist., S.C., planter, to John McClanahan, of same place, planter, for £800 cur; 150 acres on a branch of Reaburns Creek bounded on all sides by vacant land when surveyed for John Williams. *Originally granted 7 May 1767 to John Williams*. Jas. Lindley (L.S.), Mary Lindley (L.S.). Wit: Thos. McClurkin, Robert (R) Wood, John Abercrombie. Proved by John Abercrombie 14 January 1784 before Robert Hannah, J.P. [LCDBK F: 72]

Williams, John: 6 April 1799: James McClanahan (son and heir of the late John McClanahan, decd.), of Laurens Co., S.C., to Marmaduke Pinson, of same place, for £125 Stg.; 150 acres on Dirty Creek (formerly Hallams Branch of Reaburns Creek). Bounded at time of survey by vacant lands. *Originally granted to John Williams on 7 May 1767* and conveyed to James Lindley Esq. On 19 January 1773 and by said Js. Lindly unto the above named John McClanahan 28 August 1778 and now to said Marmaduke

Pinson. In witness the said James McClanahan and Mary Pugh (formerly Mary McClanahan, and widow of John McClanahan, dec'd.) have set their hand and seal. James McClanahan, Mary (X) Pugh (L.S.) Wit: John Cochran, John McClanahan. Proved by John Cochran before James Abercrombie, J.P. Plat. [See LWT of Richard Pugh] [LCDBK F: 531]

Williams, John: 12 February 1792: John Williams to Anderson Arnold for [?]; 100 acres on N. Fork of Rabourns Creek waters or Reedy River. Bounding John Thomason, William Anderson, Isaac Abercrombie. Being *part of 1682 acres grant in 1786. John Williams* (LS). Plat for 100 acres. Wit. William Thomson. [Poor microfilm] [LCDBK D: 248-249]

Williams, John: 3 February 1797: Benjamin Couch, of Laurens Co., S.C., to Charles Henderson, of same place, for $60; 50 acres on the branches of Raiborns Creek, *being a part of a tract of land granted to John Williams* and conveyed from him to Stephen Potter and from Stephen Potter to Sarah Durham and from Sarah Durham given unto William Fountain in marriage. Bounded on James Smiths big survey, Burgess Goldbergs line, on John Histelow. Benjamin (mark) Couch (LS). Wit: Wm. King, Rebecah Downs. Proved by William King 3 February 1797 before Joseph Downs, J.P. [LCDBK F: 171]

Williams, John: 1 March 1807: I James Tinsley of said State, Newberry Dist., S.C., to James Atwood Williams, for $25; 1500 acres which was left to me and others by John Williams, Junior, deceased, by his last well and testament laying on Rabourns Creek. Joining land of Lydall Allen, Col. John F. Wolff; NE Colven A. Crumbia, ____ Maheffey; SW other unknown. *Said land was granted to said John Williams, Junr, deceased, containing 1500 and some more acres.* James Tinsley (LS). Wit. Elijah Watson, Daniel Williams, Junr. John Armstrong. Proved by Elijah Watson 23 October 1809 before James Williams, J.Q. [LCDBK J: 115-116]

Williams, Joseph: Survey for Joseph Williams pursuant to precept 2 July 1765; 300 acres on head branches of a small creek called Flat Creek. Bounded SW by land laid out to Benjamin Williams; other sides vacant. Certified 15 August 1765. John Wade, D.S. Ord. Co. 3 February 1768. [P10_185:3]

Williams, Joseph: Memorial by Joseph Williams; 300 acres in Craven Co., on the head branches of a small creek called the Flat Rock. Bounding SW on land of Benjamin Williams, other sides vacant land. Certified 3 February 1768 and granted 2 August 1768. Quit rent to commence in 2 years from date. Set his had 31 September 1768. For the memorialist John Williams. Jno. Wade, D.S. [M8-260:1]

Williams, Joseph: No survey found.

Williams, Joseph: Memorial by Joseph Williams: 200 acres, being part of a tract of 500 acres. *Originally granted 25 September 1766 to John Hullum* [Hellam] and conveyed to the memorialist Joseph Williams by lease and release dated 20 and 21 January 1769. The tract of 200 acres in Berkley Co., on the N side of Saludy river bounded NE by land laid out for Thomas Allison, all other sides vacant. Set his hand 9 November 1773 Joseph Williams. [See John Hellam] [M12-445:1]

Williams, Joseph,: [No date]: Sale bill of estate of Joseph Williams: Purchasers: George and David Adams, John Yager, Wm. Smith, Wm. and Elizabeth Williams, Joseph Bolton, Stephen Gaines, Wm. Saxon, Gray Yager, Elizabeth Waldrop, Joseph South, Samuel Saxon, Daniel South, Wm. Powell, Elijah Howell, Elisha Williams, James South, Mary Howell, Margaret Braden, John McGee, Mikel Marlow, John Hutson, Terrell Andrews, Mathew Bolton, Lewis Watson, David Anderson, Thos. Adkins, John Roberson, Samuel Freeman, John Hazel, Wm. Williams, Martin Pugh, Henry Box. Administrator: Eliz. Williams. [LCWBK C-1: 337]

Williams, Samuel: Survey for Samuel Williams, pursuant to precept dated 30 February 1767; 150 acres in Craven Co., on Raeburns Creek called Helm's Creek. Bounded NE by John Williams, SE by Jno. Williams and part vacant, all over sides vacant. Certified 12 February 1767. Ralph Humphreys, D.S. [P10-92:2]

Williams, Samuel: Survey for Samuel Williams pursuant to precept dated 30 February 1767; 150 acres in Craven Co., on a branch of Raiburns Creek called Helms's Creek. Bounded NE on land laid out to Joseph Williams; SW part by land laid out to Jno. Williams and part vacant. Certified 12 February 1767. Ralph Humphreys, D.S. [this may be P10] [P17_92:2]

Williams, Samuel: Memorial for Samuel Williams; 150 acres in Craven on Reyburns Creek called Helms Creek. Bounded NE by land laid out to James Williams; W by John Williams and part vacant; other sides vacant. Certified 12 February 1767 and granted 28 August 1767. Quit rent to commence in 2 years. 2 October 1767. For the Memorialist Richard Owings. Ralph Humphries, D.S. [M9_347:1]

Williams Tract: 7 December 1829: Susannah Clardy, of Laurens Dist., SC, to William Hudgens, of same, for $102; 51 acres on waters of Dirty Creek, *being part of a tract of land where the said Mrs. Clardy now lived called the Williams tract.* Bounded on land of John Woody, Hasting Dial, Senr, Wm P. Bolt and sd Susannah Clardy. Signed Susannah (her mark) Clardy. Wit:

W.P. Bolt, John Douglass. Proved by John Douglass 5 July 1830. Recorded 5 July 1830. Not known how Susannah Clardy get this land. [LCDBK M_149]

Williams lands: 5 February 1815: William Williams, of Larrenc *sic* Dist., S.C., to John Fowler, of same place, for $300; 202 acres on waters of Raburn Creek. Bounded on Benja. Williams, Solomon Cole, John Henry, William Boyd. Wm. Williams (LS) Wit: Benja. Williams, Thomas B. Williams, John Pinson. Proved by Benja. Williams 3 June 1816 before John Garlington, J.P. [See John Box land, same bounding names.] [LCDBK K: 132]

Williamson, William: Survey for William Williamson, Esqr. pursuant to precept dated 7 April 1772; 100 acres, it being a balance of a warrant of 150 acres granted to said Williamson in Craven Co., on a small branch of Reyburn's Creek called Mol Kelley's Branch. Bounded by vacant land. Certified 15 May 1772. Jonthn. Downes, D.S. [P21_498:3]

Williamson, William: Survey for William Williamson pursuant to precept dated 7 April 1772; 950 acres in Craven Co., on Reyburn's Creek a branch of Great Saludy. Bounded as plat represents [plat shows bounding Thomas Landtrip, Wm. Martin, Jas. Lindley, Solomon Niblet, Thomas Maltren?]. Certified 15 July 1772. [P21_500:0]

Williamson, William: Memorial for William Williamson; 950 acres in Craven Co., on Rayburns Creek a branch of Great Saludy. Bounding as the plot represents. Certified 10 May 1772. Also 100 acres in Craven Co., on a branch of Rayburns Creek, called Moll Kelleys branch. Bounding as the plot represents. Certified 15 May 1772 and granted 20 July 1772. Quit rent to commence in 2 years. 16 September 1772. Delivered this day by C.J.L to Mr. Williamson. Jonathan Downes, D.S. [M11_424:2]

Williamson, William: 21 February 1793: John Hunter, Esq., of Laurens Co., S.C., to Ezekiel Mathews, of same place, for £14 8 shilling Stg. a tract of land containing 46 acres. Bounded by Mathews, Dunlap and Reaburns Creek. Also 60 acres, both being part of 950 acres on the N fork of Reaburns Creek. Bounded by Ezekiel Mathews, and the Waggon Road. *Granted to William Williamson on 20 July 1770* and conveyed to Fredrick Frasure by L & R 23 and 24 November 1779, now by Power of Attorney of John Hunter. 30 March 1793 plat made by John Hunter, D.S. Witness by John F. Wolff 14 August 1793. [Two plats are contained in this deed.] [LCDBK E: 79]

Williamson, William: 29 October 1794: John Woods, planter, of Laurens Co., S.C., to Jesse Garret, of same place, for £75 Stg.; 150 acres on the N fork of Reaburns creek, being part of 950 acres *granted to Wm. Williamson*

20 July 1772 and by him conveyed to Fredrick Freasure by L & R 23 and 24 November 1779, and by John Hunter, Esq. By Power of Attorney 30 March 1792 to John Woods. 17 and 18 July 1794. Wit: James McCaa, J.F. Wolff. Proved by John F. Wolff on 6 November 1794 before Daniel Wright, J.P. [LCDBK E: 292-95]

Williamson, William: 21 August 1794: Fredrick Freasure, of Charleston, S.C., Attorney for John Hunter to Henry Byram for £20 Stg.; 100 acres on waters of Reaburns Creek, on a branch called Moll Kelley's. Bounded at time or original survey by Robert Milhouse and James Williams. *Granted to Wm. Williamson* and by him conveyed to Fredrick Freasure by L & R 23 and 24 November 1779 and by said Freasure by John Hunter, his attorney by Power of Attorney 31 March 1792. Wit: Jos. Galligly, Mansd. Walker. Signed Fredrick Freasure by his Attorney John Hunter. Proved by Mansfield Walker 18 July 1796 before Jonthan. Downs, J.P. [LCDBK F: 132]

Williamson, William: 3 September 1796: Frederick Frasure, Esq., of the City of Charlestown, S.C., Attorney for John Hunter, Esqr. of Laurens Co., S.C., to Lydall Allen, of same place, for £83; 420 acres *(200 acres which was granted to Thomas Landtrip 10 July 1770; the other part of 220 acres being part of 950 acres granted to Wm. Williamson* and conveyed by said Williamson to Frederick Frasure by lease and release 23 & 24 November 1779. Both tracts bounding each other and lying on Raburns Creek, waters of Reedy River. John Hunter Attorney for Frederick Freasure. Wit: Wm. Dunlap, Margaret Dunlap. Proved by William Dunlap 13 February 1799 before Joseph Downs, J.P. [Surveys - Plats]: Plat 1) Pursuant to a precept directed from John Troup, Esq. D.S. Genl,. dated 3 February 1767 I have surveyed and laid out unto Thomas Landtrip a tract of land containing 200 acres on the N side of Saluda River on a branch called Raiborns Creek. Bounding SE on land surveyed for Thomas Owens, other sides by vacant land. Certified 20 May 1767 by Richd. Winn, D.S. - True copy taken January 24 1792 from original. Plat 2) Survey for 220 acres on waters of Rabourns Creek, the *same being part of a tract of 950 acres or land originally granted to William Williamson and by him conveyed to Fredrick Freasure.* Certified 10 October 1793 John Hunter, S.D. Plat shows bounded on part of said survey, Dick Mathews land, Thos. Landtrip, and Widow Martins land. [LCDBK F: 410-411]

Williamson, William: 11 October 1792: Fredk. Freasure, of the City of Charleston, S.C., to Jacob Roberts, of Laurens Dist., S.C., for £73 Stg.; 436 acres on waters of Raburns Creek, the same being part of 950 acres *originally granted to William Williamson* and by him conveyed to Frederick Freasure and by said Frederick Freasure, by his attorney John Hunter to the said Jacob Robert, which tract of 436 in two tracts joining each other.

271

Frederick Freasure by his attorney John Hunter, (LS) Wit: Rodger Brown, John Cromton. [Plat of 128 shows land bounded by owner unknown, survey sold to John F. Wolff, John Mahony and Plat of 308 acres bounded by James Lindley, Jno. Maharg]. 1(308 acres of 950 acres granted to Wm. Williamson bounded on James Lindley and John McHarg; 2) part of 128 acres of same grant bounded on John McHarg and J.F. Wolff. [LCDBK H: 178-179]

Williamson, William: 10 November 1792: The above plat represents the shape form marks buttings and bounding of a tract of 128 acres in Laurens Co. on the waters of Raburns Creek, it being part of a tract of 950 acres *originally granted to William Williamson* and by him conveyed to Frederick Freasure by John Hunter by virtue of a Power of Attorney from said Freasure. John Hunter, D.S. [Plat shows bounded by land unknown, part of said survey, John Mahony, part of said survey sold to John F. Wolff. [LCDBK G: 535]

Williamson, William: 28 August 1793: John Hunter, Esq., of Laurens Co., S.C., to John F. Wolff, merchant, of same place, for £50 Stg.; 300 acres on waters of Reaburns Creek, part of 950 acres *originally granted to William Williamson* and conveyed by said Williamson to Fredrick Freasure 23 and 24 November 1779, and then conveyed by said John Hunter by Power of Attorney 13 March 1792. Wit: Jonathan Downs, William Dunlap. Signed John Hunter, Attorney for Fredrick Freasure. Oath given by Wm. Dunlap 13 May 1794 before Joseph Downs, J.P. [LCDBK E: 224-226]

Williamson, William: 26 December 1812: Jacob Roberts, of Laurens Dist., S.C., to William Henderson, of same place, for $700; 308 acres on Raborns Creek, being part of a tract of land containing 900 acres. *Originally granted to William Williamson* and by him conveyed to Frederick Freasure, and by power of attorney by him to John Hunter, conveyed to Jacob Roberts, deceased. Jacob Roberts (LS) Wit: Thomas Porter, Wm. Irby. Proved by Thomas Porter 1 May 1813. Dower of Elizabeth Robert [signed Ctiycle [?] Roberts] given 31 December 1812 before Jonthn. Downs, J.Q. [LCDBK J: 13]

Williamson, William: 21 August 1794: Frederk Freasure, of the city of Charleston, by his Attorney John Hunter, of same place, to Henry Bryan, for £20 Stg.; 100 acres on waters of Reaburns Creek on a branch called Moll Kellys Branch. Bounded at the time or the original survey on Robert Millhouse and James Williams. *Originally granted to Wm. Williamson* and convey by him to Fredrick Freasure by lease and release 23 and 24 November 1772. Fredrick Freasure by his Attorney John Hunter (LS) Wit: Jos. Gallegly, Mansd. Walker. Proved by Mansfield Walker 18 July 1796 before Jonathan Downs, J.P. (Bond for £20 payment by David McCaa to Joseph Winthrop of Charleston.). [LCDBK F: 132]

Williamson, William and Lantrip, Thomas: 3 September 1796: Frederick Freasure, Esq., of the City of Charleston, by his attorney John Hunter, Esq., of Laurens Co., to Lydall Allen, of same place, for £83, *420 acres (200 acres which was granted to Thomas Lantrip 10 July 1770, the other part of 220 acres being part of 900 acres originally granted to Wm. Williamson* and conveyed by said Williamson to Frederick Freasure by Lease and release 23 and 24 November 1779. Bounding as plat represents both adjoining each other, lying on Rabourns Creek, waters of Reedy River. Signed John Hunter, Attorney for Frederick Frasure. Wit: Wm. Dunlap, Margaret Dunlap. Proved By Frederick Frasure on 19 February 1799 before Joseph Downs, J.P. [plat shown] 1) 200 acres on N side of Saluda River on a branch called Raiborns Creek. Bound SE by land surveyed for Thomas Owens; other sides vacant. Certified 20 May 1767 Richd. Winn., D.S.; 2) 220 acres on waters of Rabourns Creek, part of 900 acres. *Orig. granted William Williamson* and conveyed to Frederick Freasure. Certified 10 October 1793, John Hunter, SC. Plat shows bounding Widow Martin, Thos. Lantrip, Kirk Mathews. [LCDBK F: 410-411]

Williamson, William: 4 January 1810: John Meader, of Laurens Dist., S.C., to General John F. Wolff, of same place, for $259; 128 acres, a tract adjoining the land of said Wolff and others being part of a 950 acre tract *originally granted to William Williamson* and from said Williamson conveyed to Frederick Freasure and by said Frazer (by his attorney John Hunter to Jacob Roberts. now as part of the real estate of Jacob Roberts, deceased, by the said John Meddors the legal qualified Executor to the estate of the said Jacob Roberts, deceased. [meets and bounds]. John Meddor (LS). Arhd. Young. John Mehony. Proved by Archd. Young 15 April 1812 before J.A. Elmore, J.Q. [LCDBK J: 265]

Williams, Gainer: 4 December 1792: John Rodgers to Robert McNees, both of Laurens Co., S.C., for £80 Stg.; *300 acres being part of 400 acres granted to Gainer Williams* by his Excellency Benjamin Guirard and conveyed by the said Williams to John Rodgers. John Rodgers, (LS). Wit: Andrew Rodgers, James Rodgers. Proved by Andrew Rodgers 6 April 1793 before Charles Saxon, J.P. Plat shows bounded by Wm. Williamson, John Brown. [LCDBK D: 402-403]

Wilson, John: 15 November 1796: John Wilson, of Laurens Co., S.C., to Sampson Babb, of same place, for £40 Stg.; 80 acres on S Fork of Raiborns Creek. Bounded on Abner Babb, Joseph McNeely, where John Wilson now lives. John Wilson. Wit: Drury Sims, Joseph McNeely. Proved by Joseph McNeely 15 July 1797 before Jno. Coker, J.P. [LCDBK F: 246]

Wilson, John: 17 November 1796: John Wilson, of Laurens Co., S.C. to Joseph McNeeley, of same place, for £60 Stg.; 112 acres where Joseph McNeeley now lives. On the S fork of Rabourns Creek. Bounded on Mazyck, McMahan, Kellet branch. Wit: Drewry Sims, Samson (x) Babb. Signed John Wilson. Proved by oath of Sampson (x) Babb 15 April 1797 before Jno. Coker. J.P. [LCDBK F: 227]

Wolff, John F.: 3 February 1820: LWT of John F. Wolff. I give to my wife Mary Wolff and her heirs all the plantation of land whereon I now live, the mill and all other appurtenances there unto belonging, which said tract of land is formed by several different tracts which I have purchased at different time of different people. Also negros Jacob, Billy, Doroh, Joshua, Leroy, Matilda, Elza, George, Madison, Creswell, Emily and Polly. Son: George, to Hugh Saxon and son George Wolff, right title in trust for the benefit of Elizabeth Milner and Isabella Saxon, my two daughters the following negros Bunney, Henry, Harriett, Louisa and Charles. and son George Wolff, slaves [listed above] in trust, for the following uses. [LCWBK E.: 150]

[Family: Wife Mary, son George, two daughters Elizabeth Milner and Isabella Saxon, wife of Hugh Saxon.]

Woodward, Thomas: 1775 bounding Moses Kirkland.

Woody, John: [Son-in-law of Hastings and Rebecca Dial.]

Woody, John: 10 December 1800: I John Woody, of Laurens Co., S.C., planter, to Thomas Green, of same place, planter, for $170; 100 acres on Rabourns Creek. Bounded E by Will. Hellam, W by vacant land S land laid out to James Abercrumbie. John Woody (LS). Wit: Thomas Childress, John Childress. Proved by John Childress 11 July 1803 before John Childris, J.P. Dower of Isabella (mark) Woody, wife of the within John Woody, given 21 May 1805 before Jonthn. Downs. [LCDBK H: 124]

[Family: John Woody son-in-law of Hastings Dial. See Hastings and Rebecca Dial's LWT.]

Wright; George: Survey 100 acres, not located.

Wright, George: Memorial by George Wright for 100 acres in Berkley Co., bounding on a branch of Saludy River called Reedy River. Bounding SE on land of Robert Long, dec'd., NW on Jacob Bowman, all other sides vacant. Certified 29 December 1764 and granted 16 July 1765 to the memorialist. Quit rent to commence in two years. Set his hand 9 August 1765 for the memorialist Jacob Bowman. Pat. Calhoun, D.S. [M8-17:4]

Wright, George: [George Wright bounding]: Lease and release 23 & 24 March 1787, Augustus Merrick, of Charleston, S.C., merchant, to Thomas Wadsworth and William Turpin, of same place, merchants for £200 Stg.; 177 acre surveyed for Paul Findley 21 March 1785 in the Dist. of Ninety Six on branches of Cane Creek and Reedy River, adj. James Neely, George Dalrymple, George Wright, Patrick Cunningham [portion of deed.] [Charleston Deed, Deed Book Z-5, 23-28: Brent H. Holcomb, *South Carolina Deed Abstract 1783-1788*, pg. 423]

Wright, George: 7 February 1803: George Wright, deceased. Administration of estate to Jacob Niswanger and John Shurley, Senr. Security: Robert Freeman, Asa Turner. [LCWBK C-1: 98]

Wright, George: 17 February 1804: George Wright, deceased. Appraisal of estate by Silvs. Walker, Junr., Wm. Eddins, Jonathan Forgey. [LCWBK C-1: 98]

Wright, George: 1 May 1804: George Wright, deceased. Sale of estate: Amount those in the sale are Edy Wright, John Shirley, Jacob Niswanger, John Roberson, Robert Shirley, William Williams. [See estate package for full listing.] [LCWBK C-1: 159]

Wright, Jacob: Land grant 6 March 1786:

Wright, Jacob, deceased: Died before 10 March 1794: Appraisal of estate of Jacob Wright, deceased by John Henderson, John Baugh, Sr., Robert Freeman. [LCWBK A: 90; Elliott, pg. 9]

Wright, Jacob: 6 November 1795: Elizabeth Wright and George Wright, her son, of Laurens Co., S.C., to William Arnold, Senr., of same place, for £40; 78 acres on Beaverdam Branch of Reedy River, being land granted to Jacob Wright 12 November 1784 and from descended to his widow Elizabeth and son George and by them conveyed to the said William Arnolds, Senr. Elizabeth (X) Wright (LS) George Wright (LS). Wit: Jno. Bowman, Jacob Wright, Thos. Wright. Proved by Jno. Bowman 18 March 1796 before Geo. Anderson, J.P. [LCDBK F: 130-131]

[Family: Wife, Elizabeth, son George Wright.]

Wright, Jacob: 10 November 1795: William Arnold, Senr., of Lauren Co., S.C., to Thomas Wadsworth and William Turpin, otherwise called Wadsworth & Turpin, merchants. Whereas the said William Arnold Senr., in and by his Bond duly executed under his hand dated 5 November 1795 stands held and bound unto said Wadsworth & Turpin in the sum of £72; 78

acres on Beaverdam of Reedy River. Bounded SE on Widow Madden, SW on Widow Bowman. *Granted to Jacob Wright 6 March 1786* and from descended to Elizabeth his wife and George Wright his son and by them conveyed unto William Arnold Senr by deed dated 6 November 1795. William Arnold Senr. (LS) Wit: James Young. James Boyce. Proved by James Young 13 February 1796 before William Hunter, J.P.
[LCDBK F: 80-81]

Young, James: 5 June 1824: LWT of James Young, of Laurens Dist., S.C., to my beloved wife Mary Ann Young my small tract of land whereon Jonathan Motes now lives and also one adjoining tract which I lately purchased at Sheriffs sale as Walkers, formerly Medleys land. I also give to my said wife $1000 to be paid in equal installments. . . . two cows and calves, 2 sows and pigs, stem of glass for a side board, 2 feather beds, bedstead and furniture I received with her at the time of our marriage, and all her bed clothes, one sixth part of all the crop that will be last made on my said plantation. I further give and bequeath to my said wife all the negroes which belonged to her at the time of our intermarriage and every other article of every description of which she was then possessed and provided she pays of any balance that may be remaining due on my notes to the administrations of her mothers estate for purchases made at the sale thereof. I also give to my said beloved wife the three slaves which I bought of the said estate. .and where any two of my children want the same article they shall draw lots thereof upon the sale of my homestead, I devise that my stock of every kind shall be removed to my Abbeville plantation for the use and support of my children. Also all my slaves and other wise disposed of until my youngest daughter than living shall arrive to the age of 16 or marry. That the residue of the last crop made on the homestead plantation after taking but the overseers part and one sixth part for my wife, shall be removed to my Abbeville plantation for the use of my children or sold at the discretion of my executors. Nominate by two sons Gallaten and William Agustin and friend Turner Richardson, Esqr., Executers. James Young (LS). Wit: Benjamin James, Wm. Moore, Hugh Saxon. Proved date 16 October 1824.
[LCWBK E: 429]

[Note: This sounds like a 2nd marriage and most of the children are underage, except for sons Gallaten and Wm. Agustin Young.] [Young, pg. 391]

James Young Lands by executors of estate made in 1825/1826 to David Anderson.

Young, James: 26 January 1825: David Anderson, of Laurens Dist., S.C., to Turner Richardson, of the same place for $1220; 297 acres on Raiburns Creek. [Plat By request of T. Richardson and W.A. Young acting executor of the *Estate of James Young, dec'd.,* have re-surveyed a tract of land belonging to the said estate containing 297 acres on both sides of Rabons Creek. *Originally granted to [_____].* Surveyed 4 January 1825, Alsey Fuller, D.S. Plat shows bounding Henry Thompson, Mrs. Harris, James Croker, on Rabens Creek.]. David Anderson (LS). Wit: Henry Thompson, James Wait. Proved by Henry Thompson 2 September 1826 before David Mason, J.Q. [LCDBK L: 260]

Young, James: 12 December 1826: We Turner Richardson and W.A. Young, executors of James Young, Dec'd, of the Dist. of Laurens, S.C., to David Anderson, of same place, for $122; 297 acres. Plat shows land on *both sides of Rayburns Creek,* bounding land of Colcock, Samuel Millhouse, Thos. Ligon, Thos. Harris. Resurveyed by Wm. Dunlap 22 December 1813. Plat made out by James Young. T. Richardson (SL), Wm. A. Young (SL) acting executors of James Young, Dec'd. Wit: Martin Miller, Reuben Brownless. Proved by Reuben Brownless 7 August 1826 before Wm. Nelson, J.P. [LCDBK L: 260]

NAME INDEX

Unknown last names:
Mary, 71
Matthew, 83

A

Abercrombie, 92, 168,
174
Alexander, 163
Ann, wife of James,
74
Calvin, 233
Colvil, 197, 266
Colvill, 267
Colville, 152, 233
David, 232
Isaac, 74, 75, 76,
214, 223, 268
James, 20, 21, 22,
39, 45, 68, 73-
76, 86, 123, 130,
131, 151, 153, ,
155, 157, 158,
165, 168, 181,
189, 195, 217,
218, 227
Jas., 167
Jno., 151
John, 3, 22, 75, 105,
130, 131, 134,
139, 164, 260,
263, 267
Jonathan, 23, 143,
151
Mary, dau of T.
Lindley, 152
William, 186
Abercrombie, J.P.
James, 36, 40, 52,
65, 74-76, 87,
113, 141, 173,
186, 191, 228,
240, 263, 264,
268
Jno., 174
Abercrombie, Mrs. Ann,
wife of James, 76
Abercrumbie

James, 124, 274
Mary, wife of
Colvill, 267
Abercrumbie, Sr.
Colvin, 267
Abercrumby
James, 218
Abernathy
James, 55
Patsy, g-dau of H.
Gaunt, 106
Achion
John, 65
Acrombie, J.P.
Jonathan, 139, 175
Acrumbie
Colvil, 233
James, 23
Adair
James, 30
Adams
Aber. W., 166
Abraham, 24, 248,
249
Alexr. W., 76
David, 24, 178, 179,
269
George, 269
Jesse, 263, 264
John, 199, 248, 249
S., 101, 221
Silvanus, 101
Thomas, 128, 202
Adamson
Thomas, 24, 202
Thos., 13
Adkin/s
Wm., 226
Adkinson, 76
Henry, 77
Mary, 77
Mary, wife of Henry,
77
Thos., 269
Akin/s
Saml., 188
Aldwidin
John, 70

Alexander
David, 36, 46, 227
Hezekiah, 220
Jno., 174
Joseph, 24
Rebecka, dau. of J.
Downs, 94
Samuel, 25
Thomas W., 175
Wm., 143
Alexander, J.P.
James, 162
Allen
Charles, 8, 27, 213,
228, 233, 250
Daniel, 2, 3, 25, 26,
123, 124, 125,
149, 150, 154,
164, 226, 251,
254
Frances, 27
Frances D., 27
J., 94
Jonathan, 27, 77, 152
L., 27
Lewis, 27
Lewis B., 27
Lewis L., 27
Lucy, 78
Lydall, 27, 28, 53,
62, 77, 78, 147,
161, 204, 233,
266, 268, 272
Milly, 27
Peter, 28, 199
Robert, 82
William D., 27
Allen,
Charles, 27
Allen, J.M.
Chas., 169
Allen, J.P.
Charles, 62, 77, 88,
128, 130, 235
Allen, J.Q.
Charles, 12. 65, 67,
77, 101, 128,
142, 155,
161,235

Allen, Jr.
Daniel, 25, 27, 164
Allen, Mrs., 27
Allen, Q.M.
Charles, 57, 67, 103,
122, 137, 168,
193, 239
Allen, Sr.
Daniel, 25, 26, 27
Alliordin
John, 33
Allison
Ann, 29
Bettey, 29
Catherine, wife of
Thomas, 30
David, 28, 30, 32, 67
Dorcas, dau of James
Cuningham, 79
Dorcas, wife of
David, 32, 79
Elizabeth, wife of
Joseph, 31
Ellenor, 30
Frances, wife of
Robert, 29
James, 29
Janie, 29
Joseph, 30, 31
Lewis, 29
Margaret, 29, 30
Mary, 29
Moses, 29
Nancy, 30
Rachel, dau of W.
Hellams, 116
Robert, 8, 28, 29, 53,
57, 67, 82, 87,
88, 128, 167, 178
R.W., 196
Samuel, 29
Thomas, 29, 30, 46,
85, 100, 116,
159, 269
Watson, 30, 31, 86,
117, 166
William, 2, 28, 29,
30, 32, 33, 45,
50, 51, 53, 198

Wm., 39, 44, 227
Alliston
William, 38
Allurdin
John, 71
Allwedice
John, 34, 71
Allwidice
John, 33
Alwidice
John, 71
Ancrum
William, 11, 26, 104,
106, 123, 124,
149, 150, 154
Wm., 27, 125, 150,
154, 241, 251
Anderson, 213
Ambrose, 35
Andrew, 35
D., 120
David, 10, 34, 35,
77, 96, 112, 113,
120, 122, 137,
213, 233, 238,
258, 269, 276,
277
Dd., 122, 225, 232
George, 35, 56. 57,
107. 112
James, 35
John, 14, 138, 152
Mary, wife of Wm.,
34
Molley, 35
Molly, wife of Wm.,
34
Moly, 35
Rachel, 238
Robert, 88, 128
Samuel, 18, 35, 238,
257
William, 10, 34, 35,
78, 112, 114,
137, 138, 194,
223, 231, 268
Wm., 103, 115, 116,
137, 176, 194,
229

Anderson, D.S.
William, 14, 72,
116, 118, 189,
199, 205, 212,
229, 254, 262
Anderson, J.P.
Geo., 107, 140, 194,
248, 275
George, 10, 34, 36,
45, 107, 108,
109, 118, 156,
208, 217, 257
Anderson, J.Q.
D., 80
David, 35, 108, 157,
186, 191, 225,
253, 260
D.D., 35, 257
Dd., 88, 121, 228
Anderson, J.Q.M.
Dd., 94, 253
Anderson, Jr.
William, 138
Anderson, Maj., 213
Anderson, Major
David, 76
Anderson, Mr., 231
Anderson, Ord.
David, 258
Anderson, Q..M.
Dd., 247
Anderson, wife of Wm.
Molly, 10
Anderson, J.Q.
David, 175
Anderson
George, 110
Andrews
Elizabeth, 23
Elizabeth, wife of
Ezekiel, 166
Ezekiel, 35, 111,
165, 166, 175,
178, 247
Terrell, 111, 128,
178, 269
Ankerhorn
George, 59

279

Appleton
  Grigsey, g-son of H.
    Gaunt, 106
Armstrong
  John, 35, 131, 170,
    249, 250, 266
  Martin, 89, 216
Armstrong, D.S.
  John, 36, 37, 48, 49,
    268
Armstrong, Sr.
  John, 188
Arnal/Arnald/Arnall (See
    Arnold)
  Joshua, 263
  Leanna, widow, 263
  Leannah, 263
Arnold, 265
  Anderson, 74, 76,
    183, 184, 214-
    216, 223, 265,
    268
  Ann, wife of Wm.,
    208
  Benjamin, 178
  Elizabeth, 36
  Ira, 22, 46
  John, 24, 178
  Joshua, 263
  Leanna, widow, 263
  Mary, 208
  Reuben, 36, 208
  Samuel, 208
  William, 47, 178,
    209
  Wm., 131, 205, 208
  Zechariah, 36, 48
Arnold, J. P.
  William, 214
Arnold, J.P.
  William, 145, 181
Arnold, J.Q.
  Benja., 181
  William, 205
  Wm., 22, 46, 70, 218
Arnold, Jr.
  William, 208
Arnold, Sr.
  William, 275, 276

Arnoll (See Arnold)
  Joshua, 37
Arthur
  Am., 177
Arthur, J.P.
  William, 54
Atkins
  John, 257
  Joseph, 257
  Lucy, 27
  Margaret, 257
  Robert, 131, 182,
    204
  Sarah, wife of Wm.,
    27
  William, 27, 28, 77,
    78
Atwood
  John, 138
Austin
  Nathan, 9, 182, 195,
    197
  Thos., 134
Avary
  Joseph, 70
Avery
  Barrington, 69
  Joseph, 143

B
Babb
  Aber, 143
  Abner, 50, 142, 162,
    273
  Ann, wife of Abner,
    142
  Joseph, 16, 35, 67,
    68, 130, 171,
    192, 256
  Martha, wife of
    Abner, 162
  Martin, 163
  Mary, wife of
    Thomas, 142
  Mercer, 11, 16, 35,
    187, 188
  S., 143
  Sampson, 93, 114,
    115, 273

  Samson, 143, 274
  Thomas, 78, 142
  Thos., 162
Badden
  Sarah, wife of David,
    80
Bailey
  Isaac, 45
Bailey, J.P.
  Z., 192
  Zach., 57, 142, 162,
    226
  Zachariah, 78, 113,
    262
  Zachr., 221
  Zech., 46, 102
  Zechr., 108
Baird
  James, 78
Baker
  Benjamin, 97
Ball, 94
Ballard
  Richard, 36
Bandam, J.Q.
  Willis, 143
Banks
  Rachel, 47
Banton
  Glover, 108
  Jedida, 37
  Jedidah, wife of
    Lewis, 146
  Lewis, 34, 35, 36,
    37, 107, 112,
    113, 146, 147,
    179, 209, 232,
    237, 238, 260
  Mary, 37
  Sarah, 209
Barby, Mrs., 161
Bardy
  Charles, 32
Bariet
  Robert, 118
Barksdale
  Collyer, 8
  Mary, 217

Nancy, dau of J.
Downs, 94
Nathaniel, 91
William, 217
Barnes
Jas., 49
Robert, 49
Zuboriah, 51
Barnet/tt
Robert, 49
Stephen, 180
Barrett
Robert, 118
Baskett
Thomas, 71
Baskin
Thomas, 41
Bates
James, 128, 171
William, 151
Baton
Lewis, 108
Baugh
Agness, 38
Agness, wife of
Wm., 38, 39
David, 38
David, son of Wm.,
40
Dorcas, wife of John
Baugh, Jr., 39
Elizabeth, dau. of
Wm., 38, 39
Jno., 20
John, 13, 37, 38,
100, 115, 119,
178, 206
John, son of Wm., 37
Jonathan, 38
Jonathan, son of
Wm., 39
Margaret, 38
Margaret, dau of
Wm., 39
Mary, 38
Mary, dau of Wm.,
39
Nancy, widow of
Wm., 40

Rosannah, 39
William, 20, 32, 33,
38, 40, 100
Wm., 30, 99, 226
Baugh, Jr.
John, 33, 39
William, 40
Baugh, Sr.
John, 275
William, 40
Baugh, widow, 227
Baws
John, 115
Bayerly
Casper, 105
Beard, 61
Hugh, 40, 58, 59, 93
James, 78
Beards
Hugh, 53, 249
Beckham
Willie, 160
Bee
Bernard E., 259
Beel
Jno., 44
Belin, Jr.
A., 109
Bell
David, 23, 27, 193
James, 109
Mathew, 9, 177
Richard, 109
Belton
Charity, wife of
John, 27
John, 27
William, 27
Belton, D.S.
Jno., 176, 199
Benefort
Salude, 250
Benham
Willis, 163
Benham, J.Q.
Willis, 188
Berry
John, 174
Macajah, 13

Micajah, 142, 174,
175
Berry, J.P.
Hudson, 117, 248
Berry, J.Q.
Hudson, 115, 248
Berwick
John, 54, 55
Bibb
David, 124
Bieller
Jacob, 185
Joseph, 186
Mary, dau of H.
Neuffer, 186
Mary, wife of Jacob,
186
Bishop
Abner, 181
Boland, 235
Boling, 213
Bisop [Bishop], 182
Bize, 28
H.D., 29, 60, 167
H.D. children, 158
Hercules D., 63
Hercules Daniel, 61,
62, 63, 64, 158
Hercules Danl., 60,
61, 63, 65, 66,
216
Bize, Esq.
Hercules Daniel, 59
Blackburn, J.P.
A., 133
Blackerby
Benjamin, 160
Joseph, 160
Blackies
Geo., 236
Blackley
John, 40, 73, 81,
190, 206
Blackstock
Jane, wife of John,
22
John, 22, 218
Blackwell
Isabella, 68

281

John, 68, 156, 162
Joshua, 162
Josiah, 68, 192, 256
Margaret, 23
Blackwell, J.P.
Isabella, dau of
James
Abercrombie, 22
J., 29, 57, 67, 88,
160, 167, 175,
209, 228
John, 196
Joseph, 195
Josiah, 11, 22, 66,
80, 81, 111, 157,
158, 168, 172,
193, 197
Blake
George, 40, 236
Blakeley
John, 128, 171
Blakely
John, 245
Margaret, fie of John
Copland, 76
Bobs (Babb)
Joseph, 256
Bocquet
Peter, 144
Bocquett
Peter, 41
Bohman
Jacob, 43, 111, 119
Boid
William, 198
Boling
Robert, 41
Saml., 142
Samuel, 41, 71
Tully, 142
Bolling
Abi, wife of Samuel,
42
Lucinda, dau of
Samuel, 42
Nancy, dau of
Samuel, 42
Polly, dau of
Samuel, 42

Robert, 225
Robert, son of
Samuel, 42
Samuel, 41, 42, 142,
143, 164, 231
Samuel, son of
Samuel, 42
Thornberry, son of
Samuel, 42
Tully, son of
Samuel, 42
Bolt
A., 49
Abraham, 33, 34, 71,
225, 233
Abram., 225
Edward, 41
John, 41, 88, 128
Nancy, dau of T.
Lindley, 152
Robert, 62, 94, 161,
169, 263, 264
Samuel, 41
William, 41
Wm. P., 41, 269
W.P., 82, 269
Bolt, Jr.
Robert, 49, 169
Bolt, Sr.
Abraham, 41
Bolton
Joseph, 45, 240, 269
Mathew, 269
Matthew, 173
Bolton, J.P.
Joseph, 193, 240,
262
Bolts
R., 169
Boolsbe [See Goolsbee]
Burgess, 264
Boone, Gov.
Thomas, 105
Bottom, J.P.
Joseph, 241
Boucher
John, 208
Bough
William, 3

Bounty, 129, 167, 185,
199, 235
Bouquett
Peter, 40
Bouquett, Jr.
Peter, 40
Bowen
Wm., 250
Bowie
Geo., 136, 250
Bowland
John, 192
Bowman
Jacob, 36, 42, 43, 44,
56, 57, 80, 111,
119, 121, 140,
189, 203, 208,
224, 260, 274
Jacob, son of Sarah,
44
Jno., 275
John, 36
Sarah, 43
Sarah, mother of
Jacob, 56, 57
Sarah, wife of Jacob,
44
Bowman, widow, 275
Box
Abraham, 21, 22, 24,
44, 46, 47, 178,
181, 227
Abrm., 46
Benjamin, 47, 63
Edward, 32, 33, 45,
113, 165, 179
Edwd., 164, 167
Henry, 45, 46, 48,
51, 86, 113, 179,
197, 227, 261,
262, 265, 269
Jacob, 262
James, 45, 46, 197,
256
Jno., 168
John, 44, 46, 227
Jonathan, 262
Joseph, 132
Louisa, 47

282

Luisa, dau of
  Jemima, 46
Margaret, 240
Rachel, dau of
  Jemima, 46
Rachel, wife of John,
  46, 48
Robert, 2, 31, 32, 33,
  36, 44, 45, 47,
  48, 52, 100, 125,
  132, 165, 180,
  261
Robt., 164
Wiseman, 179, 261,
  262
Box, Jr.
  Robert, 47, 180
Box, Sr.
  Edward, 113
  John, 48
Boxes
  Joseph, 131
Boyce
  Alanor, 248
  Drury, 9, 13, 50,
    141, 142, 143,
    212, 218, 235,
    236, 247
  Elenor, 248
  Ellenor (See Tweed),
    wife of Thomas,
    248
  Elliner, 248
  James, 276
  Thomas, 37, 209,
    248
  William, 13, 142
Boyce, Sr.
  Drury, 188
Boyd, 161
  Abraham, son of
    James, 49
  Archibald, 242
  David, 216
  Isaac P., 197
  James, 8, 10, 40, 48,
    49, 59, 84, 85,
    91, 114, 122,
    125, 155, 168,

169, 190, 195,
  197, 216, 251,
  252
Jas., 66, 263, 264
Jno., son of James,
  49
John, 48, 163, 216,
  250
John, son of James,
  114
Laird B., 48
Margaret, wife of
  David, 216
Martha, widow, 114
Martha, wife of
  James, 49
Mary, dau of James,
  49
Mary Jennet, 146
Saml., 114
Saml., son of James,
  49
Samuel, 49
William, 21, 49, 129,
  168, 198
Wm., 22, 46, 84, 85,
  200
Boyd, Col.
  John, 14
Boyd, J.P.
  John, 125, 150
Boyd, Jr.
  David, 242, 243
  William, 168
Boyd, Sr.
  William, 169
Boyerly
  Casper, 134
Boyle
  James, 78
Bracher
  Margaret, 104
Bracher, Jr.
  William, 50
Braden
  David, 241
  Margaret, 269
Bradey
  Allex, 11

Allex, son of
  Charles, 51
Allexander, 11
Charles, 11, 86, 113,
  261
Chas., 20, 38
John, 11
William, 11, 262
Bradey/Brody, 51
Braidey
  Charles, 179
Brailsford
  Mary, daughter of
    Alexander
    Cormack, 75
Brannan
  John, 193
Branner
  John, 193
Brannon
  John, 250
Bratcher
  William, 50
Bratcher, Sr.
  William, 50
Brauday
  Charles, 50
Braudey
  Charles, 100
Braudway
  Charles, 28
Braudy
  Charles, 110
Brawdy
  Alexander, son of
    Charles, 51
  Charles, 28, 50
  Eleanor, wife of
    Charles, 51
  George, son of
    Charles, 51
  John, son of Charles,
    51
  William, son of
    Charles, 51
Breen, 175
Bremar, D.S.
  John, 136

283

BreMarch
  Francis, 53
  Peter, 148
Brenton
  David, 59
Brewster
  Ann, 56, 105
  Ann, widow, 134
  Anne, sister of A.
    Irwin, 132
  Anne, sister of J.
    Irwin, 132
  Anne, widow, 133
  Hugh, 69
  James, 69
  William, 133
Brewter
  Hugh, 47
Brewton
  James, 59
Briggs
  Robert, 52, 245
British soldiers, 12
Briton
  Joseph, 151
Broadway/Broady/Brody
    , 28, 262
  Charles, 33, 101,
    192, 261
Broady
  Charles, 32, 33
Brock
  Ann, 16
  Charles, 113
  Elias, 16
  elias, 58
  Elias, 59, 88, 157,
    226, 228, 241
  G., 227
  George, 52, 123,
    124, 149
  George, son of Elias,
    16
  Hurnes, 45
Brodey
  Alex., 51
  Charles, 52, 111
  Elender, widow, 111
  George, 110

George, son of
  Elender, 111
John, 13, 51, 119,
  227
Margaret, 52
Margaret, wife of
  William, 52
William, 52
Brody
  Charles, 28, 30
  William, 30, 100
Brook
  Elias, 23
Brooks
  Elizabeth, 16
  Hannah, 23
  Jacob, 5, 6, 52, 125
  Joab, 26
  Roger, 53, 249
  Ursula, 192, 225
Brooks, J.P.
  Thos., 26
Broughton
  Andrew, 53, 248
  Andw., 248
Broughton, Sr.
  Andrew, 53
Browlee
  Thomas, 259
Brown
  Bartlett, 53
  Ben., 69
  Benjamin, 2, 3, 53
  Hugh, 54, 55, 172
  James, 23, 266
  John, 78, 110, 213,
    235, 250, 257,
    273
  Joseph, 173
  Margaret, 180
  R.C., 180
  Robert, 55
  Rodger, 169, 271
  Roger, 58
  Sarah, wife of
    Benjamin, 54
  Will., 198
Brown, Dr.
  J.R., 188

Brown, J.N.C..
  Jacob R., 186
Brown, J.P.
  Roger, 235
Brown, J.Q.N.D.
  J.R., 188
Brown, Jr.
  John, 234
Brown, Mrs., 138
Brownless
  Reuben, 277
Bruce
  William, 129, 130
Bruster
  Jas., 233
Bruster, D.S.
  James, 178
  Jas., 152
Bruster, J.Q.
  Jas., 163
Bryan
  Henry, 272
  John, 43, 56, 57
  Mary, wife of John,
    43
Bryan/Bryant, 56
Bryant
  John, 56
Bryson
  Robert, 244
Buckner
  Henry, 26, 251, 255
  James, 251
  Jane, sister of R.
    Vanhorn, 251
  Jane, wife of Philip,
    251
  Jinney, 251
  Philip, 251, 252
Bull, 36
  Wm., 9, 173, 195,
    197, 239
Bull, Esq.
  William, 10, 110,
    184, 195, 203
Bull, Gov., 184
Bull, Hon.
  William, 118

Buller
 Jacob, 185
Bullett, D.S.
 Francis, 35
Bullock
 B.L., 262
Bumpass
 James, 57
 Sally, wife of James,
  57
Bures
 William, 256
Buress
 Joel, 158
Burgess
 Elijah, 120
 Joel, 159, 217
 May, dau of M.
  Hendrix, 120
 Walter, 258
 Water, 192
 William, 257
Burnett
 Stephen, 180
Burnside
 Andrew, 221,
 James, 115
 W., 125
 William, 68
 Wm. T., 68
Burnside, J.P.
 W., 188
 Wm., 112, 195, 203
Burnside, J.Q.
 W., 192, 196, 240
Burress
 David, 244
Burris, 46
 David, 66, 67
 Mary, wife of David,
  66
 William, 68
Burriss
 David, 156
 Wm., 171
Burrow/s, 152
 Henry, 145, 226
 Rachel, wife of
  Wm., 68

William, 4, 35, 67,
 68, 192
Burton
 Chas. Thomas, 155
 James, 78, 122
 John, 33, 45, 167
 Saml., 195, 236
 Stephen, 57
 Thomas, 67, 154,
  155, 158, 160,
  167, 171, 202,
  235, 259, 264
 William, 33, 84, 85,
  155, 171, 202,
  236, 259
Burton, Esq.
 Thomas, 28
 William, 10
Burtz
 F., 253
 Frederick, 221
Bush
 John, 99
Busship [See Bishop}
 Abner, 181
Butler
 Henry, 185
 Mary (Middleton),
  wife of Pierce,
  58
 Pearce, 264
 Pierce, 57, 60, 61,
  62, 63, 64, 65,
  66, 67, 167, 200,
  214, 216, 225
Butler, Esqr.
 Pierce, 63
Butler, Hon.
 Pierce, 58, 59
Butler, Maj., 86, 94, 105,
  134, 154
Butler, Major, 56
 Pierce, 58
Byram
 Henry, 271
Byrum
 James, 195

C
Cahoon/Calhoun
 Thomas, 3, 217
Cahun
 Thomas, 185
Cain
 James N., 163
Calder
 A., 66
 Alexr., 66
Caldwell, 112
 David, 18, 37
 Elisabeth Ann, 209
 Elizabeth, wife of
  William, 209
 James, 68
 Jean, 147
 Jno., 140, 185
 John, 34, 36, 59, 67,
  68, 85, 112, 147,
  179, 223
 William, 37, 68, 107,
  192, 209
Caldwell, D.S.
 Jno., 34, 55, 67, 111,
  122, 140, 150,
  157, 159, 162,
  179, 184, 202,
  223, 235, 261
 John, 147, 162
 Thos., 85
 William Thomas,
  126, 171
Caldwell, J.D.
 Jno., 123
Caldwell, J.P.
 Jno., 149, 154
 John, 147
 William, 138, 209
Caldwell, Jr.
 David, 210, 211
Caldwell, Sr.
 David, 68
Calhoon/Calhoun
 John, 69, 106, 144,
  145, 198
 John E., 209
 John Erwin, 208

285

John Ewing, 54, 107, 209
Thomas, 69, 217
Calhoun, Capt.
John, 145
Calhoun, commissioner
John Ewing, 55
Calhoun, D.S.
Jno. Ewing, 43
Pat., 42, 56, 75, 143, 152, 274
Thomas, 98
Camack
John, 63
Cameron
Alexdr., 229
Alexr., 126
Cammeck
John, 63
Cammel
Saml. S., 174
Cammeron
Alexander, 69, 111
Alexdr., 229
Cammoch
John, 61, 62, 64
Cammock
James, 189
John, 64, 94, 265, 267
Camp
Benj., 131, 170, 204
Benjamin, 131, 170
Bradford, 225, 226
Joseph, 76, 204, 205
Nathan, 182, 213
Starling, 69
Susannah, wife of Thomas, 204
Thomas, 69, 70, 204, 217, 205, 218
William, 21, 69, 204, 205, 218
Camp, Jr.
Thomas, 204
Campbell
Jesse, 247
Robert, 258
Thos., 233

Campbell, J.P.
Angus, 99, 102, 209
Campbell, Lord
William, 144
Cannaday
James, 139
Cannon
William, 45
Cantey
Zach., 98
Cappock
Moses, 25
Cargil
Lewis, 191
Cargile
Daniel, 70
Cargill
Cornelison, 70
Cornelius, 249
Daniel, 70
John, 64, 67, 114, 162, 183, 222, 257
Lewis, 123
Nancy, dau of Daniel, 70
Cargill, of VA
Daniel, 70
Carrel
Richard, 167
Carrillo
Richard, 15
Carsen, Mr., 103
Carson
Richard, 78
William, 208
Carter
Benjamin, 101
Elizabeth, wife of Robert, 102
John, 101, 209
Richard, 78
Robert, 102, 128
Thomas, 107, 188
Carter, Jr.
Robert, 196
Carter, Sr.
Robert, 196

Casey
Elijah, 205
Elisha, 9, 21, 69, 70, 137, 204, 205, 218, 247
Esther, wife of Elisha, 70, 218
Cashaw
Eli, 69
Cason
William, 188
Cave
Sarah, 153
Thomas, 153
Chalmer
Gilbert, 70
Chalmers
Gilbert, 34, 71
Chambers
John, 193
Chandler
Asa, 169
Joel, 188
Chapman
Joseph, 194
Chateris
Geo., 99
Cherokee Indian
Nations, 15
Cherokee Indians, 12, 14
Cheshire
B.B., 258
Chew
Samuel, 198
Childers
Jesse, 153
John, 86, 117, 153
Richard, 153
Thomas, 168
Childers, Jr.
Richard, 153
Childres, 187
Childres, J.P.
John, 248
Childress
Jesse, 24
John, 116, 117, 118, 274

286

Polly, wife of
    Thomas, 71
Richard, 24, 71, 174,
    211
Thomas, 31, 71, 114,
    117, 233, 274
Childress, J.P.
    Jesse, 24, 31, 87, 95,
      96, 114, 174
    Jessee, 249
Childris, J.P.
    John, 274
Chism
    John, 73
Chitty
    Charles King, 260
Choice
    Mary, 42
    Tully, 41, 42, 71,
      231
    William, 42, 163,
      164, 188
    Wm., 188
Choice, D.S.
    Tully, 163
Choice, Sr.
    William, 188
Christian
    Thomas, 71, 267
Christie
    Roy, 15
Clardey
    James, 82
    Susannah, wife of
      James, 82
Clardy
    James, 36, 73, 240
    Jesse E., 240
    Susannah, 269
Clardy, Mrs., 269
Clarey
    Sarah, 80
Clark
    John, 191, 233
    Thomas, 243
Clark, D.S.
    Thomas, 101, 164,
      165, 192, 256

Clark, S.L.
    John, 48, 191
Clark, S.L.D.
    John, 233
Clarke
    Elijah, 14
    John, 45, 48
Clarkson
    W. M., 149, 154
    William, 149, 250
Clegg
    Sm., 15
Clemmans
    Fanney, wife of
      Jacob, 77, 232
    Jacob, 232
Clemons
    Jacob, 120
    James, 35
Cloar?
    Aaron, 241
Coal
    William, 73, 81, 206
Coate
    Susannah, dau of H.
      Gaunt, 106
Coates
    Dolly, 27
    Dolly, wife of John,
      124
    John, 27, 52, 124
    Mary, dau of H.
      Gaunt, 106
    Mary, dau of I.
      Gaunt, 106
    Thomas, 124
Coats
    John, 52, 88, 228
    Thomas, 197, 242
Cobb/s
    H., 136
    John, 257
    Simon, 252
Cochran
    J., 28, 67, 167
    Jno., 60, 64, 65, 66,
      160
    John, 29, 39, 51, 66,
      72, 81, 142, 145,

      158, 159, 165,
      167, 168, 171,
      197, 200, 221,
      227, 244, 251,
      263, 264, 268
    Johna., 23
    Margaret, 23
    Margaret, step-dau
      of R. Pugh, 200
    Margaret, wife of
      John, 72
    Nancy, gr-dau of R.
      Pugh, 200
Cochran, D.C.
    John, 85, 131, 160,
      220, 259
Cochran, D.S.
    John, 128, 171
Cockran
    John, 62, 89, 155
Cogdell
    Cecile, wife of
      Richard W., 72
    Clement S., 72
    John, 72
    John S., 72
    Mary, wife of John
      S., 72
    Richard W., 72
Cogell
    John, 72
Cohan/Cohun/Cohune
    Thomas, 52, 56, 72,
      185, 186
Coker
    Calvin, 131, 170
    Drew, 102, 170
    Drury, 102, 216
    Elizabeth, 91
    Garlington, 129
    James, 73
    James G., 216
    John, 117
    Mary, 216
    Nancy, 118
    Philip, 23
    Robert, 23, 74, 94,
      117, 131, 262
    Thomas, 74, 170

Thurman, 138
Coker, J.P.
    Jno., 93, 141, 243,
        273, 274
    John, 74, 117, 153,
        231
Coker, Jr.
    Robert, 23, 131, 170,
        217
Coker, Sr.
    Robert, 73
Cokiere
    Nancy, 118
Colcock, 277
Cole/s [See Coll]
    Catharine, 198
    Jeremiah, 193, 232
    Joseph, 160
    Mary, dau of A.
        Pinson, 194
    Patsy, wife of
        William, 73, 81,
        207
    Solomon, 46, 68, 81,
        157, 160, 172,
        196, 198, 232
    William, 73, 81, 178,
        206, 240
Coll [See Cole]
    William, 73, 81, 206
Collins
    Jeremiah, 33, 193
Colman
    Thos., 163
Comer
    William, 190
Commock
    John, 144
Compton
    Sally Nelson, 17
Cone, J.J.C.
    Ruben, 23
Coner
    Elizabeth, 241
Conner/Connor
    G.W., 91
    Mary 102
    William, 102
Cook, 234

Charity, wife of
    George Brock,
    16
Charity, wife of
    Isaac, 88, 228
George, 91
Isaac, 88, 165, 175,
    227, 228
James, 136
Josiah, 26
Mary, dau of
    Stephen, 234
Mary, wife of
    Randolf, 234
Randolf, 235
Randolph, 234
Thomas, 226
Cook, J.Q.
    George, 138
Cooper
    Caty, wife of
        Samuel, 145
    Joseph, 242, 243
    Robert, 56, 105, 134,
        144, 154, 181,
        190, 225
    Robt., 106
    Sal., 60, 216
    Samuel, 61, 63, 74,
        145
    William, 124
Copeland
    George, son of John,
        76
    James, 186
    James, son of John,
        76
    John, 74
    Nancy, dau of John,
        76
    Rachel, dau of John,
        76
    Samuel, son of John,
        76
    William, son of
        John, 76
Copeland, Jr.
    John, son of John, 76

Copland
    John, 3, 75, 76
Coppock, 105
    Marther, daughter of
        Moses, 75
    Moses, 24, 74, 75
Coppunk, 105
Cormack
    Alex., 170, 171, 173,
        202
    Alexander, 75, 171
    John, 131
    Mary, dau of
        Alexander, 75
Cornelison
    John, 21, 22
Cornwall, 202
Couch
    Benjamin, 268
    James, 264
Cowan
    David, 191
Cowan, J.P.
    William, 191
Cowart
    David, 191
Cowen
    David, 82
Cox
    David, 26, 27, 250,
        251
    Jesse, 77
    Jonathan, 21, 25, 80,
        251, 255
    Joseph, 76, 77, 216
    Margaret, wife of
        William, 76
    Mary, wife of
        Jonathan, 255
    Thomas, 77, 216
    William, 76
Crackel
    James, 76
Crackel, Esq.
    James, 76, 108
Craddock
    Ann, 217
    David, 57, 76, 77,
        161

Cradock
David, 235
Craig
Mansil, 128
Crandec
Childres, 186
Crandel
Childres, 191
Crawdy
Charles, 51
Creecy
Elizabeth, wife of J.
Creecy, 232
Elizabeth, wife of
John, 77, 232
John, 35, 77, 96,
101, 232
Creecy, Dr.
John, 77, 232
Creswell, 78
E., 251
Elihu, 12, 77, 251
Nancy, wife of
Robert, 12, 77
R., 57, 159, 163,
219, 251
Robert, 12, 57, 66,
77, 78, 232, 235
Robt., 235
Creswell, C.C.C.
Robert, 255
Creswell, J.P.
Robt., 87
Cries
Jonathan, 41
Crisp
Mansil, 161, 213,
214, 215, 244
William, 46, 78
William M., 128,
215
Crockath, Esq.(Crackel)
James, 108
Crocker
James, 45, 121, 146,
213, 247
Jas., 258
William, 247, 258

Crocker, Jr.
James, 114
Croker
James, 276
Cromton
John, 169, 271
Crotia
Jno., 78
Crowder
George, 24
Crumbey [See
Abercrombie],
103
Crumbias [See
Abercrombie],
92
Colven A., 268
Crumbie [See
Abercrombie],
20
Calvin, 266
Colvol A., 266
Crumby [See
Abercrombie]
Isaac, 214
John, 65
Crumme [See
Abercrombie]
Jas., 167
Culbertson
Robert, 73, 81, 190,
206, 214, 227
Culler
Jacob, 135
Rebekah, wife of
Jacob, 135
Cummel
Raf?, 174
Cuningham, 206
Andrew, 54, 223,
224
Ann, 13, 110
Ann, wife of P., 240
Ann, wife of Patrick,
12, 79, 80
David, 224
George, 39
George, son of
James, 79

James, 62, 63, 64,
65, 66, 177, 255
James, son of John,
79
John, 28, 79, 100,
184, 185, 205,
225, 255
John P., 74
John, son of Patrick,
80
Margaret, 189
Margaret, relict of
Andrew, 224
Margaret, widow,
224
Mary, wife of James,
67
Mary, wife of
Thomas, 255
Matthew, 82, 161
P., 240
Paddy, 59
Pat., 100, 157, 246,
257
Patrick, 12, 13, 39,
73, 79, 80, 81,
109, 206, 208,
224, 257
Robert, 225
Robert, son of
Patrick, 80
S., 197
Samuel, 67, 255
Samuel, son of
James, 79
Sarah, 55
Thomas, 79, 100,
255
Thos., 99, 206, 255
Wife, unnamed, 79
William, son of
James, 79
William, son of
Patrick, 80
Cuningham, D.S.
Pat., 37, 119, 130,
132, 176
Cuningham, Esq.
Patrick, 100, 239

Cuningham, J.P.
P., 257
Cuningham, J.Q.
S., 124
Samuel, 198
Cunning (Bloody Bill)
William, 15
Cunningham
Catey, 233
David, 72
Dorcus, wife of
David Allison,
28
George, 255
J., 113
James, 57, 64, 66,
67, 145
Jno., 179
John, 78, 179, 184,
220, 228, 240
John D., 228
John P., 145
J.P., 74
M., 251
Margaret, 228
Mary, 190
Matthew, 82
Mattw., 235
Paddy, 58, 59, 258,
259
Pat., 112, 238, 254
Patrick, 43, 55, 69,
81, 115, 121,
165, 203, 240
Robert, 14, 77, 233
S., 198
Saml., 21, 72
Samuel, 228
Susannah, wife of
Mathew, 82
Thomas, 33, 113,
151, 168, 206,
233, 254
William, 7, 74, 240
Zach., 82
Cunningham, D.S., 176
Dd., 72
P., 98, 120

Pat., 32, 70, 78, 79,
97, 110, 115,
121, 135, 139,
148, 166, 167,
169, 172, 179,
203, 212, 239,
243, 252, 254,
256, 260
Patrick, 20, 112, 172,
203, 238
Cunningham, Esq.
Patrick, 80, 244
Cunningham, J.P.
Robt., 239
S., 228
Saml., 40, 151, 190
Samuel, 27, 123,
124, 145, 149,
157, 228, 233,
251, 252
Cunningham, J.Q.
S., 27, 41, 129, 166
Samuel, 152
Cunningham, Jr.
John, 40
Cunningham, L.S.
P., 132
Cunningham, Mr., 196
Cunningham, Mrs., 82
Ann, wife of Patrick,
80
Cunningham, Q.M.
S., 41
Wm., 186
Cunningham, Widow, 40
Cunningham, Susannah,
widow, 82
Curry
Nathan, 71, 87, 123
William, 71
Curry, D.S.
Jo., 71
Jos., 159, 267
Curry, J.J.C.
William, 23
Curry, Jr.
Nathan, 71, 96, 136,
233

Curtis
Betsy, 18

D
Dacey
John, 77
Dagny
Thomas, 199
Dalrymple
George, 275
John, 235
Dandy [Dendy]
Nancy, dau of Daniel
Cargill, 70
Daniel/s
John, 82, 236
Thomas N., 212
William, 95, 207
Daniel, Jr.
John, 82
Dargan
Timothy, 109
Darraugh/Darrough
David, 139
Hugh, 139
Davenport
Burket, son of
Thomas, 83
Elizabeth, 258
Jno., 239
John, 112
Latice, wife of
Thomas, 83
Letty, 192
Salley, 1st wife of
Thomas, 83
Thomas, 83, 108,
113, 167, 192,
231, 239
Davenport, Jr.
Thomas, 113
David
Clement, 201
Robt. J., 182
William J., 151
Davidson
John, 76
Davis
Jno., 131

John, 216
Will, 102
Davis, J.P.
Jno., 180
John, 205, 216, 239
Day
Nat., 28, 78, 127, 253
Nathaniel, 127, 165, 253
Dean
Catherine, dau of James Cuningham, 79
Catherine, wife of Joseph, 79
Joseph, 144
Dedman
John, 155
Deens
John, 226
Delong
James, 24
Demency?
Luke, 35
Demoss
Joanna, 250
Dendy
John, 64
Dennel
Elizabeth, 248
Denner
Peter, 83
Dewer
Robt., 144
Dewitt, J.P.
W., 212
Dial [See Doyll]
Elizabeth, 90
Elizabeth, wife of Hastings, 89
Garlington C., 9, 85, 91, 138
Garlington C., son of Isaac, 84
G.C., 10, 84, 138
Has., 128
Hasten, 116

Hastin, 128, 171, 223
Hasting, son in law of J. Woody, 274
Hasting/s, 10, 29, 57, 66, 67, 68, 74, 76, 84, 86, 88, 89, 90, 91, 92, 113, 114, 117, 122, 128, 155, 158, 166, 167, 181, 189, 228, 231, 255
Hastings, son of Hastings, 89
Hastings, son of Rebecca, 92
Isaac, 83, 84, 85, 129, 155, 158, 159, 168, 195, 197, 222
Isaac, son of Hastings, 88
Isaac, son of Rebecca, 92
J., 168
James, 57, 89
James, son of Hastings, 89
Jas., 235
Joseph, 89, 90
Lewis, 91
Lewis, son of James, 90
Luttuce, wife of James, 90
Martin, 89, 95, 117, 214, 215, 216
Mary, 91
Mary, wife of Isaac, 83, 84, 91
Rebecca, 86
Rebecca, dau of J. Woody, 274
Rebecca, dau of Rebecca, 92
Rebecca, wife of Hastings, 88, 91, 274

Rebecka, 91
Rebeckah, wife of Hastings, 255
Rebekah, wife of Hastings, 88
Thos. J., 128
Dial, dec'd.
Isaac, 10
Dial, est.
Isaac, 9
Dial, Jr.
Hastings, 84, 90, 91, 97
Isaac, 89, 90
James, 90
Dial, Sr.
Hasting/s, 88, 89, 159, 269
Isaac, 84, 85, 91
Dickson
David, 55
Dillard
Phillip, 128
Dillard, J.P.
Jas., 48, 265
Ditland
Isaac, 126
Dixon
Jane, 110
William McNt, 141
Dod
William, 59
Donaldson
Mary, 75
Donnal
Willing, 188
Dooley
John, 14
Doolittle
Joseph, 112
Dorah
James, 61
Dorough
James, 63, 216
John, 215
Sarah, dau of James, 216
Sarah, wife of James, 216

291

William, 61, 63
Wm., 63
Dorrah
  David, 139
  David, son of James,
    92
  James, 92, 93
  John, son of James,
    92
  Lewis C., son of
    James, 92
  Margaret, dau of
    James, 92
  Martha, dau of
    James, 92
  Mary, dau of James,
    92
  Nancy, dau of James,
    92
  Sarah, dau of David
    Ross, 93
  Sarah, wife of James,
    92, 93
  William, 40
  William M., 92
Dorrah, J.P.
  James, 216
Dorrah/Dorroh, Jr.
  James, 40, 93
Dorrah, Sr.
  James, 93
Dorroh
  James, 79, 198
  John, 89, 93
  William, 61, 93
Dorroh, J.P.
  James, 40
Dorrough
  David, 249
  James, 200
Dorrough, Jr.
  James, 205, 228
Dorrus
  Samuel, 128, 171
Dorset
  Jos., 226
  Joseph, 225
Dougherty
  James, 229

Douglass
  John, 90, 91, 269
  Rebecca, wife of
    John, 90
Downen
  James, 83, 93, 104,
    141, 212
  Jane, 93
  Jena, 104
Downes
  Clarissa, dau of L.
    Saxon, 219
  Clarissa, wife of
    William F., 219
  Jonathan, 59, 248
  Jonthan., 123
Downes, D.S.
  Jona., 243
  Jonah., 94
  Jonathan, 53, 129,
    130, 148, 163,
    207, 211, 247,
    249, 256
  Jonthan., 130, 131,
    185, 270
Downey
  James, 131, 170
Downing
  James, 104, 212, 213
Downs
  Annabella, 94
  Clarissa, 220
  Clarrisa, wife of
    William, 94
  Clarrisa, wife of
    William F., 219
  Frances, 175
  Francis, 266
  Jane, wife of Joseph,
    94
  Jean, wife of Joseph,
    94
  Jonathan, son of
    Joseph, 94
  Jonathan, 25, 26, 54,
    63, 95, 100, 106,
    133, 145, 170,
    190, 206, 240,
    248, 249, 272

Jonathan, son of
  Joseph, 94
Jonathn., 112, 144
Jonthan., 27, 72, 95,
  231, 251, 266.
  274
Joseph, 48, 74, 87,
  93, 94, 103, 105,
  133, 134, 136,
  161, 181, 227
Joshua, 64, 181, 183,
  213, 214, 217,
  249
Mary L., dau of
  Joseph, 94
Nancy, 94
Rebeccah, 268
Rebecka, 94
S., 137
Samuel, 73, 78, 137
Samuel, son of
  Joseph, 94
Sarah, 94
Sophia, dau of W.F.
  Downs, 234
Susan, dau of W.F.
  Downs, 234
W., 48
W.F., 27, 69, 218
William, 27, 152,
  190, 251
William F., 27, 28,
  47, 78, 233, 234
William T., nephew
  of J. Downs, 94
Wm., 26, 123, 190
Wm. H., 169
Downs, D.S.
  Jno., 163
  John, 185
  Jona., 172
  Jonathan, 40, 41, 49,
    56, 235
  Jonthan., 75, 129,
    207, 144,. 207,
    211, 243, 247.
    248
  Joseph, 155

Downs, Esq.
Jonathan, 67, 134, 144
Joseph, 137
Downs, J.C.
Jonathan, 167
Downs, J.L.C.
Jonathan, 39, 74, 161, 217
Downs, J.P.
Drury, 9
Jon., 173
Jonathan, 20, 26, 31, 32, 37, 42, 50, 94, 98, 102, 123, 134, 139, 161, 168, 170, 171, 173, 177, 182, 186, 225, 227, 233, 236, 244, 251, 255, 262, 271, 272
Joseph, 9, 24, 33, 34, 39, 46, 49, 50, 53, 60, 61, 62, 63, 66, 68, 71, 74, 76, 80, 83, 86, 87-100, 103-105, 109, 131, 134, 135, 139, 147, 155-157, 170, 179, 182-184, 190, 204, 206, 208, 216-218, 223, 226, 227, 236, 238, 240, 247, 255, 259, 261, 263, 264, 268, 271-273
Downs, J.Q.
Jonathan, 24, 48, 73, 81, 87, 124, 126, 131, 136, 145, 150, 169, 170, 178, 179, 207, 213, 215, 242, 256, 266, 272

Downs, Q.M.
Jonthan., 151, 266
Doyal [See Dial]
Hastings, 122
Doyal, Mr., 81
Doyall/Doyill [See Dial]
Haisten, 255
Hastings, 20, 85
Draper
Charles, 15
Duncan/Dunkin
Jno., 248
John, 109
Dunklin
Elizabeth, dau of S. Bolling, 42
John, 208
Joseph, 109, 208, 218
Sarah, 218
Dunlap, 270, 271
Cathern, dau of Samuel, 95
David, 61, 63, 79, 100, 177, 206, 235, 255
J., 144
James, 87, 199
James, son of Samuel, 95
John, 35, 45, 48, 82, 144
John, son of Samuel, 95
Margaret, 147, 271, 273
Martha, dau of J. Richey, 158
Mary, dau of Samuel, 95
Nancy, wife of Samuel, 95
Robert, 28, 78
Samuel, 94, 95, 117, 148, 207, 211
Sarah, dau of Samuel, 95
Susannah, 96

Suzanna, dau of Samuel, 95
William/Wm 147, 183, 188, 221, 259, 271, 272, 273
Dunlap, Esq.
Wm., 183
Dunn
James, 83
Dupress
Drury, 77
Durham
Arthur, 7, 96, 229
Sarah, 264, 268
Duty
Richard, 196
Richd., 102
Dyal [Dial]
Hasten, 255
Dyer
Hezekiah, 226

E
Easterlin
Caleb, 252
Eastwood
Elizabeth, 31
Elizabeth, wife of Israel, 153
Israel, 31, 153
Eddins
Rebecca, wife of William, 96
William, 96
Wm., 275
Edes
James, 4, 96, 246
Edmonson
Thos., 260
Edwards
Peter, 247
Edwards, D.S., 261
J., 110
Elfe
Rachel, wife of Thomas, 97
Thomas, 96, 97

Elliot/Elliott, 59, 154
 Benjamin, 58, 59,
  97, 176
 Lucy, wife of
  Thomas, 99
 Rebecca, 30, 82, 100
 Samuel P., 97
 Samuel, 58, 59, 60,
  62-66, 97, 98,
  99, 128, 131,
  135, 136, 176
 Thomas, 69, 98, 105,
  134, 139, 208,
  209, 259
 Thomas, son of
  Thomas, 99
 William, 99, 254
Elliott, Esq.
 Charles, 160
 Thomas, 98
Elliott, Jr.
 Thomas, 259
 Thomas, son of
  Thomas, 98
Elliott, Sr.
 Thomas, 98, 99
Ellison [See Allison]
 Robert, 88, 99
 Thomas, 30, 100
 William, 33, 99
 Wm., 44, 192
Ellison, D.S.
 John, 99
 Robt., 69
 Rt., 69
Elmore
 John, 55
Elmore, J.P.
 Q.A., 66
Elmore, J.Q.
 J.A., 171, 273
 Q.A., 56
Elson
 William, 101
 Wm., 192
England
 Charles, 32
English
 Joshua, 16, 199

Eppes
 John W., 180
Erins, J.Q.
 M.P., 91
Ervin/Erwin
 James, 105
 John, 104
Eslar
 William, 100
Evan/s
 Dedamia, gr-dau of
  Wm. Manley,
  158
 Joseph M., 47
 Samuel, 74, 76
Ezebelin/Ezeblin,
  239,240

F
Faris/Fariss
 Levi, 50
 William, 213, 212
Farley
 W.R., 84, 85, 128
Farley, M.L.D.
 W.R., 91
Farrow
 P., 90, 245
 Pallitto, 90
 Pattillo, 245
 William, 265
Fash
 John, 101, 192
Faysaux
 Ann, 127
 Peter, 161
Faysaux, Dr., 213
Felder, J.P.
 Samuel, 114
Felder, Q.M.
 John M., 135

Field/s
 Bettyann, wife of
  John, 101
 John, 101, 142, 237,
  238
Fifer, 241
Fifer, Mr., 178

Filpot
 Robert, 236
Findley/Findly
 James, 213, 239
 Jno., 68
 John, 173, 178, 238,
  239
 Paul, 239, 274
Fingery
 Thomas, 58
Finley
 Hampton, 180
 James, 239
 Paul, 239
Finley, Sr.
 H., 180
Fleming
 Wm., 122
Fletchall
 John, 185
Fletchall, Col.
 Thomas, 143
Floyd
 James, 102, 183
Ford
 Daniel, 178
 Elisha, 11, 187, 188
 William, 30, 100
Forgay/Forgey
 Jonathan, 112, 275
Forgy
 Asa, 113
 Peggy, dau of M.
  Hendrix, 120
Foss
 Francis, Capt., 60
Foster, 10
 Andrew, 49
 Henry, 245
 John, 102, 110, 147
 John Crotia?, 34
 Fountain
 Sarah, 263, 264
 Sarah, wife of Wm.,
  263, 264
 William, 263, 264,
  268
 Wm., 49

Fowler
  George, 174
  Jas., 195
  Nathan, 194
  William, 86, 87
Francis, Capt., 5
  James, 245
Franellen?
  John, 260
Franks
  Joshua, 103
  Lucinda, 200
  N., 56, 128
  Nehemiah, 56, 57,
    67, 90, 102, 103,
    170
  N.G., 200
  Polly, wife of
    Samuel, 103
  Robert, 36, 98, 130
  Samuel, 41, 103
  William, 263
  Wm., 235
Fraser
  Alexander, 59
Frasure/Freasure
  Frederick, 169, 270-
    273
Frasure, Esq.
  Frederick, 147, 271
Frazure, Dr., 57
  Fredrick, 270, 271
Freeman
  Robert, 120, 275
  Samuel, 269
Freer
  William, 103
  John, 192
Freneau, J.P.
  Peter, 154
Freneau, J.P.C.D.
  Peter, 149
Freneau, J.P.Q.
  Peter, 202
Fuller
  Alsey, 84, 276
  Aven., 211
  George, 244
  Henry, 101

Jones, 239
Polly, 239
Fuller, D.S.
  Alsey, 9, 10, 84, 85
  Aven, 210
Furgild
  Josiah, 78
Furnas
  Joseph, 26

G
Gafferd
  William, 240
Gaffy
  Chas., 244
Gailbreath
  Jane, 27
  John, 27
Gaillard
  Isaac, 104
  Tacitus, 103, 104
Gaillard, D.S.
  Isaac, 103
Gaines
  Joseph, 198
  Stephen, 269
  Thomas, 227
Gaines, J.P.
  Larkin, 46, 113
Galasby
  Catren [Harris], 83
  William, 83, 104,
    213
Galbreath
  James, 26
  John, 26, 251
  Susanna, wife of
    James, 26
Gallegly
  Jos., 272
  Joseph, 183, 271

Gallispie
  William, 213
Gant,/s 59, 143
  Israel, 202
  Nebo, 79
  William, 59

Garey
  Charles, 102, 177
  William, 96, 215
  Wm., 215
Garlington, R.W.
  John, 83
Garlington
  John, 45, 48, 72,
    127, 142, 155,
    165, 198, 215,
    233, 253
Garlington, C. L.D.
  John, 220
Garlington, C.C.P.
  John, 159, 244
Garlington, Clk
  John, 45, 48, 233,
    262
Garlington, Clk & J.P.
  John, 28, 78
Garlington, Clk & J.Q.
  John, 90, 128, 163,
    165, 171, 242
Garlington, Clk. L. Dist.
  John, 180
Garlington, Esq.
  John, 191, 231
Garlington, J.P.
  John, 118
Garlington, J.Q.
  John, 73, 252, 266
Garlington, Q.M.
  John, 8. 72, 121,
    127, 137, 215,
    219, 231, 253,
    259
Garlington, R.M.C.
  John, 146, 221
Garlington, R.M.Q.
  John, 121
Garlington
  John, 191
Garman
  Adams, 156
Garner
  Thomas, 183, 184
Garret/Garrett
  Hosea, 138
  J., 267

Jesse, 161, 233, 256, 264, 267, 270
Nancy, 200
Osa [Asa], 92
Osborn, 200
Polly, 200
Seaborn, 201
Seborn, 201
Garrett, J.P.
Stephen, 87
Wm., 173
Garrett, Sr.
Housley, 267
Garry/Gary
David, 41
David, 63
Elizabeth, 256
Elizabeth, wife of James, 256
Jacob, 95, 96
James, 256
Sarah, dau of J. Downs, 94
Sarah, wife of Jacob, 95
William, 131, 161, 215
William C., 215, 216
Gaullard [See Guillard]
Tacitus, 103
Gaunt [See Gauntt]
Hannah, widow of Israel, 106
Israel, 134, 202
Jacob, 106
Jacob, son of H. Gaunt, 106
Jacob, son of Israel, 106
James, 106
James, son of Israel, 106
Joseph, son of Israel, 106
Nebo, 106
Zebulon, 106, 111
Gaunt (Gault), 16
Hannah, 104
Israel, 104, 105, 106

Jacob, 106
James, 106
Judith, wife of Nebo, 16
Mary, wife of Israel, 106
Nebo, 16
Nebo, son of Zebulton, 16
Samuel, 17, 242
Zebulon, 16, 106, 150
Gauntt [See Gautl]
Jacob, son of H. Gaunt, 106
James, son of H. Gaunt, 106
Joseph, son of H. Gaunt, 106
Geddes, 163
Gees
Hillery, 59
Genard, 247
Gennings
Miles, 137
Myles, 136
George
William, 87
George, III, 10, 181
Gerry, Sr.
John, 174
Gess
William, 107, 129
Gibbes, 146
Gibson
David, 131, 170
Jacob, 107, 109
Gideson, 115
Gilbert
Anna Barbara, 107
Barbara Ann, 240
John, 253
Rebecca, dau of H. Gaunt, 106
Rebecca, dau of I. Gaunt, 106
Thomas, husband of Rebecca, 106
Gill

Robert, 69, 104, 256
Gillaland
Robert, 192
William, 137
Wm., 137
Gillam
Harris, 138
Gilleland
William, 138
Gilliland
Robert, 243
William, 138, 243
Gillispie
William, 104
Giss
William, 129
Gist, D.S.
W., 181
William, 201, 226
Wm., 70, 126, 181, 226, 258
Glass
Vincent, 49, 114
W., 114
William, 76
Glen, Gov., 12
Glenn
David, 233
Jeremiah, 91
Glenn, Hon.
James, 261
Gocher
John, 208, 209
Godfred
John, 88
Godfrey
John, 89, 122
Goggans
George, 185
William, 107, 139
Wm., 139
Goldberg
Burgess, 268
Goldin
Richard, 147
Goldsby
Burgess, 265
Goode
Samuel, 110

Goodman
  Clabourn, 37
  James, 107, 108, 138
  Mary, 101
  Samuel, 138
  William, 238
  Wm., 37, 223
Goodwin
  Charles, 114
  John, 47, 180, 261
  Robert, 59
  Theophilus, 191
Goodwyn
  Jesse, 108, 109, 127
  Martha, 76, 109, 201
  Martha, widow of
    Jesse, 109
Goodwyn, Mrs.
  Martha, 108
Goolsbe/Goolsby
  Birdgis, 264
  Burgess, 264
  Elazabeth, 264
Gordan, Esq.
  John, 105
Gordon
  Adam, 211
  John, 198
  Lydall, 77
Gorgans
  George, 257
Goswell [See Jowell]
  Gabril, 23
  Rebecca, Gabril, 23
Goswell [Jowell], 23
Gothard
  George, 118
Goucher
  John, 109
Goudalock
  Adam, 169
Goulsby
  Jas., 115
Graden
  Thomas, 71
Gramaker/Granaker
  Adam, 109
Grant, 58
  Alex., 160

Alexr., 160
Graves
  J. Booman, 58
  Joseph, 210, 211
  Lewis, 35, 36, 56,
    80, 120, 247, 257
Graves, J.P.
  Lewis, 35, 57, 120,
    213
  Martin, 46
Graydon
  Abraham, 53
  Henry, 166
  Isaac, 224, 240
  Jacob, 95
  Matthew, 143
  Thomas, 50
  William, 214
Green/Greene, 125
  David, 12, 60, 61,
    64, 80, 216, 229,
    236, 248
  Elizabeth, 110
  Henry, 110, 111,
    132, 166
  James, 8, 61, 125,
    248
  Leannah, wife of
    David, 80
  Nathl., 80
  Saml., 79, 80
  Samuel, 61, 124,
    157, 168
  Thomas, 144, 274
  Zachariah, 248
Green, minister
  David, 79
Greenland
  George, 259
Gregor
  Thomas, 50
Gregory
  Morris J. Mac, 57
Griffin
  John, 265
  Mary, 188
  Reuben A., 180
  Timothy, 137
Griffin, J.P.

  Charles, 138
Griffith
  Richard, 72
Grimke, Esq.
  John F., 231
Grimke, Hon.
  John F., 191
Grizzel
  George, 114
Groggon
  Wm., 260
Grubb
  Benjamin, 125
Guerand, Esq.
  Benjamin, 175, 217
Guirard, Excl.
  Benjamin, 273
Guirin
  Francis, 259
Gutrey/Guttery
  Benjamin T., 266
  John, 50, 183, 184

H
Haig
  David, 43, 111
  Mahara, 163
Hairston/e
  Thomas, 106, 111,
    150
Hall/s
  Acquilla, 14, 21, 22,
    54
  Asa, 241
  Elizabeth, wife of
    John, 254
  Elizabeth, wife of
    John, 14
  Henry, 241
  James, 73, 81, 190
  John, 14, 254
  Joseph, 115
  Rosanah, 190
  Samuel, 190
  Thomas, 190, 228
  William, 21, 190
Hallum/s
  Susannah, 165
  Thos., 194

Halsey
 Thomas, 69, 111
Hambie
 Samuel, 40
 Thomas, 40
Hamilton
 Alexander, 244
 Henry, 54
 Paul, 248
 Wm., 250
Hamilton, D.S.
 Jno., 246
 John, 1, 47, 245
Hammond/Hammons
 Joseph, 86, 117, 118
Hamonds
 Mack, 31
Hampton
 Nathan, 68, 111, 112
 Sarah, wife of
  Nathan, 112
Hanna
 Mark, 31
 Robert, 30
Hannah
 Samuel, 258
 William, 7
Hannah, J.P.
 Robert, 263, 267
Hardy
 Christo., 235
 Kitt, 72
Harmon
 Joseph, 118
Harress
 Lucy, daughter of
  Thomas
  Davenport, 83
Harris
 Barry, 138
 Berry, 138
 Catherine, dau of
  Thomas, 113
 Catrin, 83
 Clough, 209
 Edward C., 193
 Elizabeth, dau of
  Thomas, 113

Jane, dau of J.
 Richey, 210
J.L., 234
Jno., 189, 265
John, 24, 174, 199,
 267
John L., 233
Mary, dau of L.
 Smith, 233
Mary, widow of
 Thomas, 113
Mary, wife of John
 L., 233
Nancy, dau of
 Thomas, 113
Pamela, dau of
 Thomas, 113
Polly, 234
Polly, dau of L.
 Smith, 233
Polly (Mary), 233
Samuel, 138
Sarah, dau of
 Thomas, 113
Thomas, 113
Thos., 277
William, 13, 79, 80,
 220
Harris, Mrs., 276
Harriss
 Burr, 24
Harrow
 V., 91
Harry
 John, 22, 68, 81, 82,
  170, 172
Hart
 Beththiah, 87, 113
 Christr., 97
 Joel, 85, 86, 87, 113
Harthorn, Mrs., 258

Harvey
 Berry, 61, 62, 64
 James, 2, 49, 114
 John, 114
 Little Berry, 61, 63,
  64, 70
 Littleberry, 70

Nancy, wife of Little
 Berry, 70
Nancy, wife of
 Littleberry, 64
Harvey, Capt.
 James, 114
Hary
 John, 81
Hasell
 William, 146
Haslet
 Nancy, 165
 Robert, 165
Hatcher
 Felt, 174
 Flannon, 24
 Fleming, 24, 114,
  142
 Flemmin, 24
 Flemmon, 115
 Flemon, 114
 Janet, 114
 Jannet, 142
 Jean, wife of
  Plemon, 115
 Plemon [Fleming],
  115
Hathorn
 James, 257
Haverd
 Littleberry, 64
 Thomas, 5
Hawkins, 94
 Jacob, 242
 Peter, 242
 Philip, 97
 Prudence, dau of T.
 Thomas, 242
 Wm., 242
Hay/s/Hayes
 Joseph, 138
 Thomas, 143
Hayne
 Isaac, 80, 115
Hays
 Joseph, 137, 138
Hazel
 Henry, 35
 John, 269

Hazlett
  Nancy, 175
Head/Hed
  Thomas, 153
  William, 31, 153
Helem, Jr.
  John, 244
Hellam/s
  Ann, wife of Wm.,
    29
  Constant, 116
  Constant, wife of
    William, 116
  David, 86, 255
  John, 116, 255, 265,
    269
  Jonathan, 117, 118
  Jonathan, gr-son of
    William, 116
  Jonathan, son of
    Jonathan, 116
  Jonathan, son of
    Wm., 116
  Nancy, dau of
    William, 116
  Rachael, dau of
    William, 116
  William, 29, 87, 95,
    117, 166, 274
  Wm., son of Wm.,
    116
Hellams, Sr.
  William, 116, 117,
    118
Hellem/s
  John, 256
  William, 117, 131,
    170
Heller
  John, 136
Heller [Hellem]
  Sarah, wife of John,
    136
Hellimbs [Hellums]
  Wm., 20
Hellum/s
  Constant, 117
  David, 89, 92
  John, 116, 117, 240

William, 3, 23, 86, 5,
  118
Helmes
  Will, 130, 131
Helms
  David, 10, 84, 85
  D. David, 93
  Jno., 244
  John, 58, 59
  William, 129
  Wm., 131, 170
Helum/s
  John, 116
  William, 117, 118
Hempens
  John, 189
Hen
  Elizabeth, 118
Henderson, 45
  Andrew, 113
  Charles, 49, 169,
    263, 264, 268
  Daniel, son of Sarah,
    196
  Hugh, 107, 227, 261,
    262
  James, 9, 45, 121,
    188, 193, 197
  Jno., 84, 107
  John, 9, 12, 13, 37,
    86, 113, 118,
    119, 152, 195,
    197, 203, 256,
    275
  John H., 122
  Mary, 9, 13, 37, 197,
    203
  Mary, wife of John,
    118, 195
  Nathan, 256
  Samuel, 188, 226,
    227
  Sarah, widow, 196
  S.M., 161
  William, 27, 163,
    272
  William, son of
    Sarah, 196

Wm., 27, 84, 163,
  195, 203
Hendocks
  Thomas, 247
Hendrick/s [Hendrix]
  Hanah, 55
  Hance, 257
  Hance, father of E.
    Wright, 120
  Hans, 119, 120, 203,
    257
  Magdilin, wife of
    McCajah, 120
  Margaret, 107, 120
  Margaret, wife of
    Hans, 257
  McCajah, 120
  Micajah, son of M.
    Hendrix, 120
  Wm. Win, 120
Hendrix [Hendrick/s]
  Hans, 55
  Margaret, 120
  Micajah, 120
  Wm. Win, 120
  Wm. Win, son of M.
    Hendrix, 120
Hennessey
  Randal, 52
Henrick [Hendrick/s]
  Hanah, 54
  Hans, 109
Henry
  John, 46
  Joseph, 247
  Philip, 53, 98
Henshaw
  Jas., 176
Hezlett
  Robert, 175

Hicks
  William, 122
Higgens
  Wm., 29
Hill
  Ditney, 193
  John, 40

Levi, 9, 195, 197, 203
Nich, 130
Nicholas, 101, , 119, 120, 121, 122, 226
Nicklas, 121, 122, 130, 192, 256
Nicklus, 122
Wiley, 27
William, 95, 167
Hillinsworth [Hollingsworth]
Nicholas, 13
Hinton
John, 36
Histelo/Histeloe/ Histelow
Isham, 161, 263, 265, 264
Isom, 197, 263
John 268
Hitch, J.P.
J., 7, 74, 96
Hix
Edy, 122
William, 122
Hobb/s
Charles, 128, 171
Charles, son of Wm., 127
John, 128, 245
William, 85, 128, 161, 171, 255
Hodges
Sarah, 189, 224
Hodges, Mr., 209
Hoge/Hogg
Jacob, 122, 123
Lewis, 136
Hogg, J.Q.
Lewis, 136
Holcomb/Holcumb
Mary, wife of Ruben, 123
Moses, 253
Patsy, 253
Reuben, 123, 191

Holding
Reuben, 138
Holingsworth
Jane, 25
Holland
Basil, 30
Holley
Benjamin, 222
Holliday, Jr.
Matthew, 40
William, 27, 40, 190
Hollingsworth, 8, 123, 125
Abraham, 16, 125
Amey, wife of Abraham, 16, 125
December, 17
Ez., 242
Ezekle, 124, 126, 242
Ezz., 124, 126
G., 53
George, 15, 16, 17, 26, 32, 51, 53, 123, 124, 125, 126, 151, 164, 201, 223, 241, 242
George, son of Abraham, 125
Hannah, wife of George, 16
Henry, 26, 164
Isaac, 241
James, 17, 26, 65, 123, 124, 149, 150, 154, 157, 197
Jane, 17, 26, 27
Jeremiah, 24, 178, 218
Jno., 255
John, 17, 25, 26, 164, 241
Joseph, son of George, 16
Lidid, 124, 126

Lidid, wife of George, 242
Marmaduke, 119
Nathan, 25, 26, 27
Sarah, wife of James, 123, 124, 149
Susannah, 26
Hollingworth
Marmaduke, 13
Hollinsworth
George, 2, 3, 4
Holmes/Holms
Ann, 145
Ann, wife of Joseph, 25
James, 126, 198
J.B., 80
John, 3, 58, 126
Joseph, 25, 144, 145, 225
Thomas, 62
Hood
Elizabeth, 126, 171
Ralph, 206
Thomas, 39, 40
Hooker
Cornelius, 264
Thomas, 126, 248
Thos., 9, 218, 247
Hopkins
Jeremiah, 266
John, 109, 266
Solomon, 71, 143, 204, 231
Horry
Daniel, 126, 229
Isaac, 126
Howell, 165
Martha, 109, 126, 127
Mary, 73, 269
William, 73
Wm., 240
Hubb/s [See Hobb/s]
Wm., 88
Charles, 127
Elizabeth, wife of Wm., 244
William, 88, 244

William, father of
Charles, 127
Hudgens
A., 128
Abner, 65, 66
Ambrose, 65, 87, 88,
128
Elizabeth, wife of
Ambrose, 128
John, 128
Samuel, son of
Ambrose, 128
William, 67, 82, 90,
91, 269
Hudgens, Jr.
Ambrose, 60
Hudgens, Sr.
Ambrose, 138
Hudson
James, 178
John, 128, 240
Mary, wife of John,
129
Richard, 131, 178
Rush, 128
Huey
Martin, 174
Hugar/Huger
Daniel, 59
Isaac, 13, 109, 116,
117, 129, 143,
185, 186, 202,
225
Huges
John, 135
Huggans/Huggens/
Huggins
Biddy, wife of
James, 130
J., 172
James, 21, 22, 81,
129, 193

Hughes
Jno., 189, 265
Joel, 46
John, 154, 267
Jona., 145
Thomas, 46, 162

William, 10, 34, 107
Hughey
Martin, 212
Hughs
Jane, 190
John, 112
Rachel, dau of A.
Starnes, 238
William, 174
Hullum [See Hellam/s]
John, 269
Humbel/Humble
Christopher, 239
Rachel, 35, 130
Hume
John, 130, 131
Humphrey, D.S.
Ralph, 99
Humphrey/s
Agness, wife of
Ralph, 154
Agness, wife of
Wm., 149
John, 149, 154
Ralph, 3, 52, 99,
123, 124, 149,
150, 151, 154,
201, 222
Richard, 216
Humphreys, D.S.
R., 24, 52, 69, 176
Ralph, 22, 25, 27,
44, 102, 121,
149, 161, 166,
176, 201, 254,
269
Humphries
Ralph, 150
Humphries, D.S.
Ralph, 162, 269

Hunger
Elisha, 164
Hunt
Elisha, 42, 50, 83,
182
Hunter
David, 140

Henry, 98, 130, 131,
199
John, 11, 59, 60, 61,
62, 63, 169, 170,
188, 208, 216,
226-228, 237,
271-273
Margaret, 60
Thomas, 80, 157,
256
William, 48
Hunter, Col.
Henry, 98, 131
Hunter, D.S.
Jno., 65
John, 187, 226, 270-
272
Hunter, Esq.
John, 60, 63- 67,
147, 216, 226,
227, 229, 270
William, 98, 131
Hunter, J.P.
John, 28, 106, 185,
209, 243
William, 276
Wm., 70, 195
Hunter, S.L.C.
William, 98, 131
Hunter, Sur. Gen.
Elisha, 83
George, 1
Hursey
Jno., 195
Hushaw [Henshaw]
Jas., 176
Hutchinson
Thomas, 97, 199
Hutchinson, J.P..
Robert, 215
Hutson [See Hudson]
James, 178
John, 32, 73, 269
Richard, 131, 132,
178
Hutts
James, 135

I

Indians, 13, 202
Irby
  James H., 73
  William, 84, 85, 145
  Wm., 272
Irish, 143, 164, 171, 172, 207, 211, 243, 249
Irvin/Irwin
  Agness, widow of A. Irwin, 133
  Alex., 133, 134
  Alexander, 105, 106, 111, 132, 133, 134
  Ann, 133
  Anne, 134
  James, 8, 56, 62, 105, 132, 133, 134, 135, 144, 154
  Jno., 135
  John, 55, 104, 111, 163
  Martha, 135
  Martin, 8
  Rachel, 8, 135
  Samuel, 56, 105, 134
  William, 133, 134
Irwin, Capt.
  John, 8, 133, 134, 135
  John, bro of James, 133
Irwin, J.P.
  Saml., 132
Isbell
  Godfrey, 224

J

James
  Benjamin, 276
  W.B., 113
James, J.Q.
  Jno. S., 197
James, Q.M.
  Jno. S., 245
Jameson, D.S.

Wm., 131
Jeffres/Jeffrey
  Sarah, 217, 218
Jennings
  Artemas, 135
  Elizabeth, 135
  Elizabeth, wife of Phil S., 135
  John, 135
  Margaret, 135
  Miles, 136, 137
  Mily, 94
  Philip, 135, 136, 225
  Philip S., 135
  Philip Samuel, 135
  P.S., 135
  Rachel, 135
  S., 103
Jennings, Jr.
  Miles, son of Miles, 137
Jennings, Sr.
  John, 135
  Miles, 137
Jobell
  Godfrey, 224
Joel/s [See Jowell]
  Gabriel, 193
  Ratcliff, 226
Johnsey
  J., 84, 85
Johnson, 138
  Daniel, 198
  Douglass, 186, 187, 191, 248
  James, 89, 139, 144, 145
  James, son in law of H. Dial, 89
  Jane, wife of Douglass, 187
  John, 46, 94
  Jonathan, 102, 110, 145, 196
  Joseph, 151
  Mary, wife of Joseph, 151
  Matthew, 139, 151, 246

Rabek, 145
Rebecca, wife of James, 89, 92
Rebeckah, wife of James, 145
Thomas, 23, 28, 66, 67, 72, 139, 219
William, 23, 74, 76, 139, 151, 168, 219
Johnson, J.P.
  John, 186
Johnston
  Elizabeth, 137, 138
  James, 69, 137, 144
  John, 248
  Joel, 31
  Thomas, 65. 167
Jones, 45, 48, 253
  Ann, dau of A. Starnes, 238
  Ann, wife of Jesse, 140
  Benjamin, 103, 207, 263
  Benjn., 207
  Benjnj., 95
  Crain, 73
  Elizabeth, 47, 180
  Jesse, 139, 140, 260
  Jno., 211
  John, 30, 160, 186, 187, 191
  John Alexander, 181
  Mary, 139
  M.B., 113
  Polly, 174
  Thomas, 107, 139, 213
  Thomas F., 97, 107, 113, 128, 242, 171
  W.B., 97
Jones, Capt.
  Thomas, 139
Jones, D.S.
  A.C., 175
Jones, J.Q., 175
  Sam. P., 135

Saml. P., 135
Jordan/Jordon
John, 105, 133
Jorgman
Hans, 30
Jowel, J.P.
Gabriel, 33
Jowell [See Joel]
Gabriel, 23, 27, 122,
162, 192, 193
James, 124
Ratcliff, 226
Rebecca, wife of
Gabriel, 193
Richard, 162
Jowell, J.P.
Gabriel, 8, 9, 114,
125, 197, 198
George, 193
Ratcliff, 217

K
Kay
James H., 8, 177
Kellet/Kellett, 115
Ann, dau of Joseph,
140
Anna, wife of Wm.,
141
Esther, dau of
Joseph, 140
Hannah, 141, 142
Hannah, widow of
John, 142
Hannah, wife of
John, 141
J., 142
James, 13, 142, 143,
174
James, son of
Jennett, 142
James, son of
Joseph, 140
Jane, 141, 143
Jean, 142
Jean, widow of
Joseph, 142
Janet, mother of
John, 182

Jennet, 142
Jennet, mother of
Wm., 141
Jennet, wife of
Joseph, 140
Jennett, 13, 142
John, 141
John, son of Joseph,
140, 141
Joseph, 12, 140, 141,
142, 158, 183,
184, 236
Margaret, 141
Martha, dau of
Joseph, 140
Martin, 141-143
Martin, son of
Joseph, 140
Mary, dau of Joseph,
140
William, 104, 141,
212, 213
William, son of
Joseph, 140, 141
Wm., 83, 141
Kelley/Kelly
Abigail, 17
Ann, 17
Margaret, 142
Margaret, wife of
Moses, 142
Moses, 142
Mary, dau of
Samuel, 16
Samuel, 16, 17, 26,
27, 123-125,
124, 149, 150,
154, 229, 251
William, 169
Kemp, 94
Edward, 13, 79
Kennedy
C.D., 91
John, 23
Lionel H., 72
Kennedy, D.S.
A., 107, 146
Alexr., 107, 146, 220
James, 217

Kennery
Jemimah, dau of A.
Pinson, 194
John H., 194
Kershaw
John, 192
Joseph, 11
Kilgore, Esq.
Benjamin, 30
Killet/Killett
Jane, 236
Jennet, 182
John, 182
Killingsworth/
Killingsworth
Mark, 67
Killpatrick/Kilpatrick
Alexander, 78
James, 43, 56, 143,
254
Kilter
John, 43
Kind
James, 254
King
John, 62, 65, 94
Richard, 194
Wm., 268
King George III, 118
Kirkland
Moses, 13, 129, 143,
144, 145, 202,
217, 274
Kirkland, D.S.
Moses, 13, 129
Kirkland, Jr.
Moses, 143
Kirkpatrick
Elizabeth, wife of
James, 23
James, 23
Klinck, Q.M.
John Q., 97
Klugh
Humphrey, 8, 135
Kuhmany/Kulmony
Jacob, 146, 220

L

Ladson
  Robt., 176
Lance
  Lambert, 11
Land
  Eliabeth, wife of
    Thomas, 57
  Thomas, 180
Landers
  Jane, wife of
    Matthew, 205
  Mathew, 69, 218
  Matthew, 205
  Richard, 70, 218
Landrip'Landtrip
  Thomas, 3, 4, 57,
    146, 147, 185,
    186, 270, 271,
    273
Lang/Long
  James Myrick, 147
  Robert, 260
Langford
  Dan., 211
  Thos., 273
Lavain
  Peter, 78
Lawson
  John, 55, 147
  Moses, 83
Leakron
  Tobias, 148
Learwood
  Edmond, 160
Lee
  James, 113
  John, 56, 132
  Thomas, 56, 132
Leger
  Peter, 94, 148, 169
Leigh, Esq.
  Egerton, 67

Leonard
  Jno., 265
  John, 265
LePoole
  Peter, 58

Lester
  Elizabeth, 65
Level
  Edward, 173
Lewers
  Samuel B., 200
  S.B., 137, 200, 242
  Thomas, 40
Lewis
  Annabella, dau of J.
    Downs, 94
  Crawford, 144
  Isaac, 123, 124, 148,
    149, 150, 154
  John, 231
  Thomas, 52, 228
Lewiston
  David, 152, 154
Ligon
  Thos., 277
Linders, D.S.
  Lewis, 249
Lindfors
  Charles Jacob, 226
  C.J., 99, 132, 231
  J.C., 115
Lindley, 15, 138
  Aquilla, son of
    Thomas, 152
  Charity, wife of
    Henry, 152
  David, 178
  Elizabeth, 152
  Elizabeth, dau of
    Thomas, 152
  Elizabeth, wife of
    Thomas, 151,
    152
  Francis, wife of
    John, 152
  Hanna, dau of
    Thomas, 152
  Harry, 151, 152
  Henry, son of
    Thomas, 152
  James, 15, 25, 58,
    111, 139, 148,
    150, 151, 152,
    164, 169, 171,

201, 202, 239,
    240, 262
Lindley
  James, 44. 263. 267,
    271, 272
  James, bro of John,
    133
  James, son of
    Thomas, 152
  Jas., 163, 263, 270
  John, 73, 151, 152,
    178, 233
  John, son of Thomas,
    152
  Jonathan, 151
  Jonathan, son of
    Thomas, 152
  Mary, 133, 263, 267
  Mary, wife of James,
    52
  Polly, 124, 126
  Sarah, dau of
    Thomas, 152
  Thomas, 21, 28, 77,
    78, 139, 145,
    151, 186, 201,
    233
  Thomas, son of
    James, 151
  Thomas, son of
    Thomas, 145.
    151. 152
  William, 15, 152,
    233
  William J., 152
  William, son of
    Thomas, 152
  Wm., 267
Lindley, Capt.
  James, 170, 173, 262
Lindley, Esq.
  James, 52, 56, 151,
    267
Lindley, J.P.
  James, 123, 190
Lindley, Jr.
  John, 73
Lindly
  Jno., 22

Polly, 242
Lindly, Capt.
  James, 171
Lindsay/Lindsey
  James, 58, 59
  John, 54
Lindsfors
  C.J., 67, 98
Lindt
  James, 202
Lindly
  Jas., 44
Linley
  James, 139, 148
  Jas., 143
Linley, J.P.
  James, 10, 181
Linly
  James, 139
Linn?
  William, 213
Lithgow
  Robt., 98
Little Berry [See
  Littleberry]
  Frederick, 243
Liveston
  David, 152, 153
  Joseph, 153, 154
Livingston
  David, 154
  David, bro. of
    Joseph, 153
  Joseph, 152, 153
  Taliaferro, 135, 144
Livingston, Ord.
  Taliaferro, 8
Lochart/Lockhart
  Samuel H., 89, 92
Locket
  Aaron, 125, 150
Lockhart, J.P.
  Thos. B., 113
  Thos. P., 245
Logan
  George, 149, 154
Long [See Lang]
  James, 34, 146
  Jno. Mirah, 147

John Caldwell, 147
Millicent, wife of
  Robert, 203
Richard, 34, 43, 203
Richard, son of
  Richard, 203
Robert, 43, 56, 115,
  119, 154, 203,
  274
Wm., 177
Long, D.S.
  Matt., 247
  Robert, 103, 192
Loocock
  Aaron, 11, 26, 27,
    123, 124, 125,
    149, 150, 154,
    199, 250, 251
Loosk
  James, 28, 199
Lord
  Alason (Alanson), 9,
    177
Lorry, 247
Love
  Agnes, 44
  Matthew, 44
Low
  John, 136
  Wm., 237
Lowe
  John, 135
Lowery, 59
  Charles, 154, 235
  Charlotte, 83
  James H., 65
  James Hamilton, 154
  Sarah, wife of
    Charles, 161
Lowery, Jr.
  Charles, 161
Lowrey, 66
  Benjamin L., 83
  Charlotte, 155
  James, 154
  James J., 83
  Margaret W., 83
  Mary L., 83
  Robert, 56

Lowry
  Charles, 264
  H., 85
  Hamilton, 84, 91
  James Hamilton, 56,
    134
  John, 263, 264
  Robert, 168
Lowry, Jr.
  Charles, 155, 259
Lowry, Sr.
  Charles, 155
Loyalists, 14, 15
Loyd
  Wm., 244
Lumkin
  John, 129
Lusk
  John, 133, 134
Luving
  E.B., 97
Lynch
  John, 56
  W.E., 155, 245
Lynch, J.P.
  W.E., 91
Lyndley [See Lindley]
  James, 14
Lyon
  William, 105
  Wm., 134
Lyttleton, Esq.
  Wm. Henry, 5

M
Macdavid
  William, 228
MacDonald
  Thomas, 172
Madden/Maden, 68, 125
  A., 245
  Abraham, 91, 92,
    156, 228
  Abraham, son in law
    of H. Dial, 88
  Albert, 245
  Ann, mo. of George,
    156
  Anne, 156

Charles, 150, 156, 157, 228
David, 12, 77, 80, 81, 157, 172, 231, 232, 240
David, son of John, 156
Elihu, 180, 232
George, 101, 125, 156, 157, 193, 232
George, son of John, 156
Goodwyn, 150
Harry, 157
Iby, 125
Isbel, wife of John, 157
Jean, wife of Abraham, 228
John, 8, 122,, 124, 150, 155, 157, 160, 231, 232, 262
John, son of John, 156
Keturah, wife of Charles, 228
M., 128, 171
Mabra, 196, 240, 244
Mabra, son in law of H. Dial, 88
Mabra, son of John, 156
Mabre, 80
Mabry, 84, 85, 92, 156
Mabry, son in law of H. Dial, 89
Martha, dau of John, 156
Moses, 156, 239
Phebe, 232
Ruth, wife of Thomas, 150
Sarah, 157
Sarah, widow, 196

Sarah, wife of David, 157
Susannah, wife of John, 155
Thomas, 123, 124, 125, 149, 150
W., 157
William, 180, 197, 232
Madden, J.P.
John, 82, 232
Madden, Jr.
William, 232
Madden, widow, 275
Madden, wife of John
Iby, 8
Mahaffee/Mahaffey, 266
Alexander, 217
Elizabeth, wife of John, 158
Hugh, 205, 217, 266
John, 157
Martin, 142, 205, 266
Martin, son of Martin, 164
Nancy, 266
Mahafy
John, 3
Maharg
Jno., 272
John, 163
Mahary
John, 48, 163
Mahon/Mahony
Bailey, 70, 72, 137, 213
Daily, 234
John, 169, 271, 272
Joseph, 46
William, 234
Malkey
Philip, 39
Maltren?
Thomas, 270
Maner
Jacob, 233
Mangrum

John, 137
Manly/Manley
Elizabeth, 158, 159
Elizabeth, wife of William, 158
Jeremiah, 168
Jeremiah, son of William, 158
John, 60-64, 220
Jon, 145
Joseph, 158, 159
Joseph, son of William, 158
M., 67
Nancy, dau of William, 158
Vincent, son of William, 158
W., 28, 65, 167
Washington, 158, 159
Washington, son of William, 158
William, 41, 158, 159
Manord
Jacob, 31, 86
Marell [Maull]
David, 70
Marlow
Mikel, 269
Mars
Hans Jorg, 159
Hans Jurig, 29, 30, 159
Marshall
Thomas, 60
Martin, 8
Daniel, 8
Elizabeth, wife of John, 160, 161
George, 71
John, 64, 72, 122, 159, 160, 161
Joseph, 81, 232
Martin, 114, 122, 188
Sally, wife of William, 161

306

Shadrack, 166
William, 54, 55, 161
Wm., 163, 270
Martin, Esq.
  Edmond, 206
Martin, Jr.
  John, 160
Martin, Sr.
  Daniel, 8
Martin, widow, 147, 271,
  273
Mason, J.Q.
  David, 277
Mathess
  Thomas, 163, 172
Mathews, 270
  Dick, 147, 271
  Ezekiel, 27, 123,
    182, 270
  John, 41
  Kirk, 273
  Suzanah, 23
  Thomas, 163
Mathews, Jr.
  Thomas, 158
Mathis
  John, 62
  Joseph, 62, 64
  Thomas, 71, 143,
    172
  Wm., 167
Mathis family, 11
Mathis, Sr.
  Thomas, 163
Matthew/s
  Avyrilar, wife of
    Wm., 262
  Elanor, wife of
    Thomas, 163
  Eveviler, 262
  Ezekiel, 161
  Jane, wife of Walter,
    66
  John, 66
  Oliver, 60, 63, 68,
    154, 160-162
  Rebecka, wife of
    Ezekiel, 161
  Robert, 214

Robt., 65
Samuel, 200, 235
Thomas, 142, 231,
  243
Walter, 65, 66, 155
William, 95, 162,
  262
Matthis [Mathew/s]
  Oliver, 154
Mauldin
  James, 188
Maull
  David, 33, 70, 71
  James, 33, 34, 71
  James, son of James,
    33
Maxwell, J.P.
  Robert, 133
May
  T., 226
  Thomas, 225, 281
Mayhard
  John, 4, 163
  Thomas, 21
Mayner
  Jacob, 31
Mayson, J.N.C.
  Jas., 110
Mazyck, 99, 274
  Alex., 55, 56, 134,
    154, 217
  Alex. B., 163
  Alexand., 105
  Alexander, 163
  Alexdr., 143
  Catherine, 163
  Mary, 163
  Nathaniel B., 163
  N.B., 163
  Paul D., 163
  Stephen, son of
    Benjamin, 202
  William, 163
Mazyck, J.P.
  Dl., 55
  DL., 144
  Il., 54
Mazyck, J.P.Q.M.
  D., 60

Mazyck, Mrs.
  Catherine B., wife of
    N.B., 163
McAfee/McAffee
  Martin, 164
McAnulty, 206
McCaa
  David, 99, 144, 157,
    190, 213, 220,
    272
  James, 12, 77, 142,
    183, 264, 270
  Phebe, wife of
    James, 12, 77
  Polly, wife of David,
    190
McCain/Mccain/McCain
  James, 24, 25, 26,
    27, 113, 164, 214
  James N., 163
  John, 99
  John, 157, 193
  John, son of James,
    164
  Mary, dau of James,
    164
McCain, alias
  Elizabeth, 25
McCain [See McGill],
  25
McCaine
  Jas., 167
McCall
  Wm., 35
McCallister
  Danl., 80
McCan/McCann
  John, 124, 125,
    150, 252
McCass
  James, 141
McCawley
  Matthew, 226
McClain
  Daniel, 110, 132,
    228
  Polley, dau of J.
  Ryan, 216

307

Polley, wife of
  Ephraim, 216
McClanahan
  Catharine, wife of
    Wm., 200
  James, 65, 139, 202,
    212, 236
  James, son of Jno.,
    263
  James, son of John,
    267
  Jno., 263
  John, 40, 171, 217,
    262, 263, 267
  John, step-son of R.
    Pugh, 200
  Mary, widow of
    John, 263, 267
  Samuel, step-son of
    R. Pugh, 200
  William, 125, 127,
    128, 150, 200
  William, step-son of
    R. Pugh, 200
  Wm., 63, 128, 171
McClanahan, Jr.
  John, 93
McClannahan
  James, 195, 261
McClans
  Daniel, 131
McClennan
  John, 170, 171
McClerkin
  James, 255
  Thomas, 254, 255
McClintin, 165
McClinto
  James, 126, 171, 172
McClintock, 164
  James, 170, 172
  Margaret, 172
  Susannah, wife of
    Wm., 248
  William, 248
McCluer/McClure, 17
  Elener, sister of R.
    Ritchey, 210
  Ellener, 210

Elenor, dau of J.
  Ritchey, 210
McClurkam/McClurkan/
  McClurken
  Jane, 166
  James, 165, 166, 175
  Mary, 172
  Samuel, 165, 166,
    173
  Thomas, 100, 164,
    165, 255
McClurkin
  James, 165, 175
  Jane, 86
  Samuel, 164, 173
  Thomas, 100
  Thos., 263, 267
McCords, 199
McCormick
  Maxwell, 127
McCosh, 7
McCosh, Rev.
  John, 7
McCrarey/McCrary
  Robert, 30
  Thos., 31
McCullock
  James, 166
McCullouogh
  Joseph, 22
McCurley
  John, 253
  Robert, 221
McCurly
  John, 190
  Robert, 221
McDaniel, 186
  Arch., 75
  Archabald, 198
  Archd., 186, 191
  Archibald, 23, 167
  Archibald, bro of R.
    Turk, 168, 246
  Archid., 33
  Archl., 246
  Editha, 168
  Editha, wife of
    Archabald, 168

Elizabeth, dau of H.
  O'Neall, 187
Elizabeth, wife of
  Archbald, 168
Elizabeth, wife of
  Thomas, 187
James, 83
Margaret, 246
Mary, 141, 142, 166,
  167, 188
Mary, widow of
  Wm., 28, 167
Matthew, 48, 122,
  139
Matthew, bro of R.
  Turk, 246
Pinson, grandson of
  M. Pinson, 197
Sarah, 167
Thomas, 10, 83, 104,
  173, 212. 213,
  236
W., 72
William, 28, 65, 67,
  129, 167, 186,
  191
William, son of
  Wm., 167
McDaniel, Jr.
  Archibald, 168
McDaniel, Sr.
  Archibald, 168
McDaniel, wife of
  Thomas
  Elizabeth, 10
McDannel
  Mary, wife of Wm.,
    167
  William, 167
McDavid, 95
  James, 145, 255
  John, 145
  William, 100
  Wm., 33
McDonal
  Eliz, dau of H. Oneall,
    188
  Eliz, wife of
    Thomas, 188

308

Thomas, 188
McDonald
  A., 168
  Archibald, 44, 168
  John, 188
  Mary, 10, 12, 77,
    187, 188
  Mary, dau of Hugh
    O'Neal, 17
  Matthew, 45
  Thomas, 104, 167,
    168, 212, 213,
    231, 236
  William, 20, 38, 168,
    169
McDonald, 231
McDowall/McDowel/
  McDowell
  James, 77, 157
  Patrick, 11, 188
McElroy, J. P..
  John, 218
McFearson/McFerson
  James, 109
  Wm., 18
McGant, 143
McGee
  John, 195, 269
McGill
  Barnabas, 25
  Elizabeth, 25
McGill [See McCain],
  25
McGladery
  David, 79, 177
Mchaffee/McHaffee/
  McHaffey/ Hchaffey
  Horse, 92
  Hugh, 140
  M., 204
  Martin, 141, 164,
    204. 236
  Mary, wife of
    Martin, 164
  Sarah, 231
McHaffey, Sr.
  Martin, 164
McHan
  John, 164

Mchany
  John, 146
McHarg
  Archibald, 170
  Jno., 169
  John, 49, 148, 169,
    170, 272
  John, son of Susan,
    169
  Susan, 169
  Susannah, 169
McHarg/McHurg/
  McHargh, 170
  Archabald, 103, 170
  Susanna, 170
  William, 170
McHurg, widow, 49
McHurge/McHurgh
  Archibald, 102, 108,
    131
McKay
  Archabald, 108
McKearmmy/McKearmy
  Robert, 163, 172
McKees
  Robert, 92
McKelvey, Jr.
  James, 130, 131
McKemmey/McKenney
  Robert, 172, 173
McKnight
  Abigail, wife of
    Andrew, 174
  Andrew, 77, 93, 142,
    174, 212, 213,
    114, 140, 236,
    248, 249
  Archibald, son of
    Andrew, 174
  James, 70, 71, 143,
    218
  Jennet, dau of
    Andrew, 174
  John, 174, 175
  William, 248
  Wm., 12
McKnight, Sr.
  Andrew, 142
  Andw., 141

McKnit
  Andw., 140
McLain
  Daniel, 206, 228
McLancy
  Bridget, 76
McLean
  Daniel, 173
  Danl., 110
  James, 173
McLennan
  John, 170
McLinto, 164
  James, 35, 170, 171,
    172
McMahan, 115, 274
  Cornelius, 141
  Cornwall, 202
  William, 175
  Wm., 174
McMahans, 13, 142
McMahon, 13, 92, 202
  Cornelus, 140
  Cornwell, 13
McMurty
  Sammy, 247
McNary
  Alexander, 60
McNeeley
  Joseph, 273
McNeely
  Joseph, 273
McNees/McNeese
  James, 114
  John, 34, 213
  Mary, 175
  Robert, 8, 62, 64, 65,
    66, 89, 92, 175,
    213, 235, 273
  Sarah, widow of
    L. Saxon., 218
McNees, J.P.
  Robert, 122
McNight
  Andrew, 141
  John, 174
McNight, Jr.
  Andrew, 174
McPherson

309

Isaac, 176
William, 48
Wm., 45, 107, 197,
   209
McQueen
   John, 176, 223
McVay
   George, 244
Meader
   John, 273
Mead
   Thomas, 221
Meal
   Mary, 239
Measley, 152
Meddor
   John, 273
Medley, 276
Meglaney
   Samuel, 82
Mehl
   Peter, 239
Merrick
   Augustus, 274
Mezhar, 115
Michel
   David, 178
   Mary, 178
Middleton
   Henry, 57
   James, 10
   Jno., 108, 120
   John, 35, 77, 102,
      112, 120, 146,
      213, 233
   Mary, daughter of
      Henry, 57
   Peggy, 238
   Robt., 112
Middleton, J.P.
   Hugh, 132
Miles
   Charles, 263, 264
Milhouse/Millhouse, 179
   Henry, 17
   Elizabeth, 17
   Jane, widow, 250
   Jane, wife of B.
      Vanhorn, 250

Rebecca, wife of
   Henry, 17
Robert, 17, 176, 199,
   271, 277
Samuel, 185, 261,
   184, 277
Millhouse, Miss,
   220, 221
Miller
   Charles, 40, 228
   John, 71
   Martin, 277
Milles
   Robert, 147
Millner
   A., 8
   Arnold, 8
Mills
   James, 233
Mills, Jr.
   William, 128
Millwee
   William, 188
   Wm., 190
Milner
   A., 233
   Arnold, 91, 97, 136
   Elizabeth, dau of J.F.
      Wolff, 274
   Wm., 41
Milner, J.Q.
   A., 69, 89
Minister, 12
Mitchell
   Allen, 46
   Asa, 228
   A.W., 9, 177
   Calous, dau of Wm.,
      177
   Chole, wife of Wm.,
      177
   David, 178
   Dicey, 9, 177
   Elisha, 78, 213, 214
   Elizabeth, 178
   Elizabeth, dau of
      Wm., 177
   Ephraim, son of
      Wm., 177

George, 9, 177
Isaac, 55, 178, 233
James, 144
John, 9, 151, 177,
   178, 201, 240
John, son of Wm.,
   177
Lewis, 228
Macklin, 46
Mary, 178
Mary, wife of John,
   178
Mary, wife of Wm.,
   24, 178
McLin, 46
Nancy, dau of Wm.,
   177
Nimrod, 8, 176, 177
Nimrod, son of Wm.,
   177
Polly, dau of Wm.,
   177
Polly, wife of
   Macklin, 46
Randolph, 35
Sarah, dau of Wm.,
   177
William, 9, 10, 24,
   34, 112, 177,
   178, 223, 238
Mitchell, J..L. C.
   Wm., 65, 146
Mitchell, J.Q.
   Wm., 77
Mitchell, Q.M.
   J.H., 163
Mitchesson
   John Drury, 187
Moates [See Motes]
   Betsey, wife of
      Chesley, 180
   Chesley, 180
Moats [Motes]
   Jonathan, 180
Monary
   Elliott, 210
Monk
   John, 137, 138, 179,
      221

Montage, Hon.
Chas. Greenville,
112
Montague, 183
Montague, Excl.
Charles Granville,
184
Montague, Gov.
Charles Granville,
183
Montague, Hon.
Charles, 168
Charles Granville,
224
Granville, 76
Moodie
John, 92
Moon, J. P.
William, 247
Mooney
Hannah, dau of H.
Gaunt, 106
Moony
Hannah, dau of I.
Gaunt, 106
Moor/Moore, 261
Aaron, 131, 170,
174, 187
Alexdr., 111
Austin, 91
George M, 91
James, 250
Jane, 46
Jesse, 261
John, 87, 107, 113,
195
Joshua, 193, 194
Polly, 248
Samuel, 136, 205
Thos., 248
William, 45, 48, 179,
209, 261
Wm., 36, 48, 107,
221, 276
Moore, D.S.
L., 165
Moore, J.P.
William, 224
Moore, widow, 48

More
William, 225
Wm., 18
Morgan/Morgin
David, 9, 131, 179,
195, 197
George, 35, 36, 257
Henry, 69, 70, 163,
231, 243, 266
James, 257
Morgan, 179
Sarah, 182
Thomas, 198
William, 198, 205
Wm., 179
Mortimer
William, 177
Morton
David, 174
John, 143
Moseley/Mosely
Isaac, 9, 197
Howell, 213
Motes,[See Moates},
192
Betsy, dau of J.
Motes, 180
David, 138
Dicy Ann, dau of J.
Motes, 180
James, 128, 171, 245
John, 184, 192
Jonathan, 128, 180,
276
Mary, 138
Mineva, dau of
J. Motes, 180
Susan, wife of
Jonathan, 180
Moultrie, 131, 208
William, 109
Moultrie, Esq.
William, 214
Wm., 45, 213
Moultrie, Exc.
William, 141, 231
Moultrie, Gov
Wm., 209

Murdock
Hamilton, 185
Murphy/Murphey
Ebenezer, 101
Milly, dau of A.
Starnes, 238
Rodger, 172
Roger, 68, 101, 184,
209, 237, 238
Thos., 30
Murphy, Sr.
Rodgers, 45
Roger, 46, 208
Murrow, Jr.
John, 135
Musgrove, D.S.
E., 241
Edward, 32, 148
Edwd., 104, 106,
116, 241
Myers
Moses, 7, 96
N
Nabers
Nabers, S.L.D.
Benjamin, 137
Nabors/Nabers
Ann, wife of
Benjamin, 235
B., 41, 191, 231
Ben., 72
Benjamin, 88, 137,
231
Benjn., 235
Benjamin, 8, 87,
158, 159
Fleet, 46
Francis, 87
Nathan, 87
Robert, 47
Nabours
Abraham, 188
Anne, wife of
Benjamin, 88
Benjamin, 82, 161,
180, 235
Francis, 180
Samuel, 24, 178

Nash
  Edmond, 236
  Edward, 9, 24, 42,
    71, 218, 231,
    236, 247
  Hannah, wife of
    John, 266
  John, 24, 115, 266
  John N., 266
  Reuben, 177
  Sarah, 12
Neal/Neel
  Briton, 222
  Charles, 10
  Jas. Cha., 250
  John, 23
  Samuel, 194
  Thomas, 10
Neel, Esq.
  Andrew, 194
Neeley/Neely
  James, 275
  J.L., 258
  Jos., 258
  Joseph, 258
  William, 85, 181
Neely, J.Q.
  Jas., 68
Negroes, [See Slave],
    89, 94, 196, 232,
    233, 245, 276
  Abraham, 89, 92
  Andrew, 89, 92
  Billey, 210
  Billy, 273
  Bob, 197
  Charity, 47
  Charles, 234
  Creswell, 273
  Doroh, 273
  Elisa, child of
    Rachel, 92
  Eliza., 273
  Eliza, dau of Rachel,
    89
  Elizabeth, 234
  Ellen, 200
  Emily, 273
  Fil, 120

Fillis, 196
George, 273
Hannah, 197
Henry, 200
Jack, son of Lucy,
  180
Jacob, 197, 273
Jane, 23
Jenny, 140
Jim, 156
Joel, 180
Joshua, 273
Juda, 120
Julian, 127
Leller, 120
Leroy, 273
Lucy, 180
Madison, 273
Martha, 234
Mary, 92
Matilda, 273
Milly, 197
Naie?, 196
Nancy, 196
Polly, 273
Rachel, 89, 92, 180
Suse, 156
Tom, 120
Woman and child
  Tom, 120
Neighbors/Neighbours
  Benjamin, 155, 180
  Rebecca, wife of
    Samuel, 180, 181
  Samuel, 44, 47,
  Wm., 65
Neiley/Neily
  Agnes, 45
  Dick, 59
  George, 44, 45
Neilson
  Sarah, 237
Nelson
  Jared, 186
  Samuel, 53
  William, 83
Nelson, D.S.
  Jared, 186, 190, 191
Nelson, J.P.

Wm., 277
Nelson, Q.M.
  Jas., 72
Nesbit/Nesbitt
  Solomon, 103
Mary, 188
  Nathan, 188
  Samuel, 9, 42, 117,
    218, 231, 247
  Solomon, 103
Neuffer
  Herman, 186
Next
  William, 53
Nibbs, J.Q.
  Wm., 204
Niblet/Niblett
  Mary, wife of
    Solomon, 10,
    181
  Solomon, 10, 31,
    103, 181, 182,
    183, 184, 270
Nicholas/Nichold
  Robert, 157, 252
Nichols, T.R.
  Julius, 144
  Nathl., 252
Nickels
  James, 80
  Robert, 40, 93
Nims
  Joshua, 178
Nisbett [See Nesbit/tt]
  Samuel, 115, 249
Niswanger
  Jacob, 18, 45, 56, 57,
    112, 113, 120,
    193, 256, 275
  Jacob, previously
    Bowman, 260
Nixon
  Uriel, 213
Noble
  Joshua, 184, 232
Nobly
  Joshua, 232
Norman
  Isaac, 168

Martin, 240
Wm., 209
Norris
  Anna, wife of Wm.,
    45, 46
  Thomas, 100, 125,
    237, 252
  William, 45, 46, 53,
    63, 249
  Wm., 80
Norris, J.Q.
  Andrew, 136
Norris, Jr.
  Thomas, 8, 157
North
  Richard, 184, 185
Norwood
  Geo., 257
  George, 166, 222
Nufer, Sr.
  Herman, 185
Nuffen/Nuffer
  Hannan, 144
Nuffer
  Harman, 144, 185
  Herman, 143, 186
  Mary, wife of
    Herman, 186
Nugent
  William, 249

O

Obannon
  Wm., 38, 39
O'Bryant
  Duncan, 122
O'Daniel/s
  Mary, wife of Wm.,
    186, 191
  William, 95, 121,
    167, 186, 187,
    190, 191, 207
O'Donal/Odonal
  Matthew, nephew of
    R. Turk, 246
  Wm., 193
Odonial
  Marey, wife of
    William, 22

William, 22
Ogier
  Lewis, 211
  Susannah, wife of
    Lewis, 211
Ogier, Esq.
  Thomas, 211
OHear
  James, 54
Oliphant
  James, 216
O'Neal/Oneal/ Oneale
  Hugh, 188, 189
  Jean, 189
  Thomas, 188
  Wm., 189
O'Neall
  Ann, 11
  Ann, dau of H.
    O'Neall, 187
  Charles, 187
  Hugh, 10, 17, 187,
    188
  Hugh, son of Hugh,
    187
  Jean, 85
  John, 85
  Patience, 11
  Patience, dau of H.
    O'Neall, 187
  Rachel, 11
  Rachel, dau of H.
    O'Neall, 187
  Ruth, 11
  Ruth, dau of H.
    O'Neall, 187
  William, 17, 85
Oneall
  Ann, dau of H.
    O'Neall, 188
  Charles, son of
    Hugh, 187, 188
  Hugh, son of Hugh,
    188
  Patience, dau of H.
    O'Neall, 188
  Rachel, 188
  Rachel, dau of H.
    O'Neall, 188

Ruth, dau of H.
  O'Neall, 188
Thomas, 186
Thomas, son of
  Hugh, 187, 188
Wm., 126
Osborn/Osbourn/Osburn
  Daniel, 46, 237
  William, 66
  Wm., 46, 82
Owen, Jr.
  Richd., 190
Owen, Sr.
  Richard, 118
Owen/s
  Ann, wife of
    Richard, 190
  Archibald, 142, 165
  Elizabeth, 200
  Ephraim, 26
  George H., 145
  Gideon, 200
  Harris, 201
  Jean, wife of
    Archibald, 142
  Jno., 189
  John, 189, 265

  Richard, 2, 28, 73,
    117, 129, 130,
    131, 189, 190
  Thomas, 146, 271,
    273
  William, 189, 191
  Wm., 22, 191, 265,
    267
Owens, Jr.
  Richard, 189
Owens, Sr.
  Richard, 3
Owing, Sr.
  Richard, 118, 175
Owing/s, 171
  Ann, wife of
    Richard, 190
  Archabel, 117
  Archable, 13, 118,
    123, 142
  Archey, 117

313

Archibald, 118
Archible, 173
E. Stonestreet, 173
Edward Stonestreet,
173
John, 118, 170, 173
Richard, 86, 87, 116,
117, 118, 123,
190, 267, 269
Sarah, 190
William, 21, 118,
123, 131, 170,
190
Owings, Sr.
Richard, 30, 117
Owins/Owens, 227
Archibald, 206
Jno. 86
John, 265
Nancy, wife of
Richard, 87
Richard, 190
William, 137, 265

P
Paden
Alexr., 164
Paine
Mary, 10, 181
W., 10, 181
Wm., 10
Park, 81
Parker
Charity, 20
James, 66, 169, 259
John, 123, 191
Jonathan, 59
Sarah, 95, 191
Sarah, wife of John,
191
Thomas, 41, 66
William, 55
Parker, Dr.
John, 20
Thomas, 41
Parks
Charles, 78, 124
David, 27

Isabella, wife of
John, 192
John, 191
Thomas, 253
William, 150
Parry
Edwd., 176
Parson
Jas., 103
Parsons, Esq.
James, 192
Partlow
John, 83
Partridge
Wm., 41
Pasley
Robt., 146
Patten
Erwin, 45, 48
Paulk
Jacob, 101
Pearson
David, 135
David Wm., 136
Jno., 6
John, 5, 6
William, 109
Pearson, D.S.
Jno., 25, 52, 125
Philip, 108, 109
Peck
George, 41
Pedin, Sr.
Alexander, 139
Pels
John, 95, 174
Pels, Jr.
John, 95
Pemberton
Ruth, 17
Penman
Edward, 205
Penny
William, 226
Wm., 155
Perritt, J.Q.
Alfred, 47
Perry
Jno., 211

Person
Wm., 188
Petrie
Edmund, 101, 104,
192, 193, 256
Petterson
John, 155
Pew
James, 59
Richard, 58, 59
Phifer, 241
Samuel, 111
Phillips
John, 240
Zachary, 190
Pickens, Col.
Andrew, 14
Pickens, D.S.
Jno., 193
Pinckney
Thomas, 124, 126
Pinckney, Gov.
Charles, 78, 264
Pinckney, Honlb.
Charles, 31
Pinson, 102
Aaron, 34, 46, 121,
150, 157, 172,
192, 193, 194,
195
Ann, 81
Bejah, son of
Marmaduke, 197
Betsey, wife of John,
196
Duke, 168, 195, 197
Duke (Marmaduke, 9
Edes, dau of
Marmaduke, 197
Elizabeth, wife of
Aaron, 194
Evin, 238
Howard, 196
Howard, son of John,
196
Huldah, 196
Huldsath, dau of
Marmaduke, 197

Isaac, 192, 193, 195,
196
Isaac J., 195
Isaac, son of Aaron,
194
Isaac, son of
Marmaduke, 197
James, 108
Jesse, 193
Jno., 195
John, 32, 33, 38, 39,
68, 102, 180,
195, 196
John, son of Aaron,
194
John, son of John,
196
Joseph, 28, 32, 39,
112, 151, 179,
195, 196, 198,
201, 224, 250
Marmaduke, 8, 20,
84, 85, 91, 124,
125, 126, 139,
151, 155, 157,
164, 168, 195,
197, 201, 208,
223, 242, 263,
267
Marmaduke, son of
Marmaduke, 197
Mary, wife of
Joseph, 112
M.D., 197, 242
Merma Duke, 139
Mineva, 180
Mineva, wife of
John, 180
Molly, wife of
Marmaduke, 197
Moromodupe
[Marmaduke],
194
Moses, 21, 22, 32,
33, 39, 80, 81,
121, 157, 168,
195, 196, 198
Moses, son of Aaron,
194

Richard, 189, 198,
224, 260
Ruth, dau of
Marmaduke, 197
Salley, 121
Sally, dau of
Marmaduke, 197
Suckey, dau of
Marmaduke, 197
Thomas, son of John,
196
William, 236
Wm., 11
Pinson, J.P.
Howard, 258
Pinson, Jr.
Aaron, 194
Marmaduke, 196
Moses, 195
Pinson, Mrs.
Mary, 196
Pinson, Sr.
Aaron, 194, 256
Marmaduke, 197
Moses, 22
Pinson, the younger
Aaron, 194
Pitchlynn
Isaac, 198
Jemma, wife of
Isaac, 198
Pitts
Francis, wife of
Wm., 198
Isaac, 126, 198, 260
John, 137, 138, 191
Joseph, 138
Sally, 138
Thomas, 138
Thos., 138
William, 198
Plant/Platt
John, 199, 235
Stephen, 87
Pool
James, 181
Pope
George, 145

Porter
Thomas, 272
Thos., 128, 159
Potter, 234
John, 103
Mary, dau of
Stephen, 234
Stephen, 102, 103,
197, 234, 235,
263, 264, 268
Powell
Benjamin, 199, 229
E., 7, 96
Elijah, 269
James, 45, 82, 124,
227
Jas., 111
Leannah, 30, 100
R., 111
Wm., 269
Powell, J.P.
James, 36, 73, 178,
224, 237
Jas., 30
J.J., 82
Prater
Zach., 242
Praytor
Middleton, 257
Prim
Charles, 259
James, 67, 128
Pringle
Jno., 179, 236
John, 30, 82, 100,
177, 179, 182
Pritchard
Henry, 109
Pucket/Puckett
Cornelius, 196
Richard, 196, 246
Pugh, 17
Jesse, 35, 232
Jessie, 232
John, 140
Lydia, dau of E.
Sims, 232
Lydia, wife of Jesse,
35, 232

Martin, 269
Mary, formerly
   McClanahan,
   263, 267
Mary, wife of
   Richard, 200
Richard, 20, 28, 38,
   60, 61, 63, 151,
   156, 164, 199,
   200, 201, 255,
   263
Sarah, 82, 140
William, 30, 140
Wm., 242
Purves, D.S.
   Jno., 143
Putman/Putnam
   Abner, 84,91, 138,
   200
Daniel, 200
James, 200
Mary, wife of Abner,
   200
Michael, 200
Reuben, 200
Pyles
   Milton, 155
   Reuben, 60
Pyles, J.P
   Reuben, 69
Pyles, J.P.
   Reuben, 21, 60, 61,
   63, 64, 101, 204,
   218, 225, 227

Q
Quail/s
   Charles, 151, 201
Quakers, 15, 16, 17

R
Raburn
   Richard, 201
Ragsdale
   Alse, wife of David,
   118
   David, 118, 156
Raiford
   Philip, 108, 109, 201
Raines/Rains

James, 35
John, 82
Rainey/Rainy
   Benjamin, 152-154
Raley, 12, 77
Ralston
   David, 133, 134
Ramsey
   Joseph Hall, 250
Rankin
   Elizabeth, 242
   Elizabeth, dau of T.
   Thomas, 242
Ratliff
   Richard, 194
Ravenel
   Daniel, 12, 13, 24,
   202
Ravenel, Jr.
   Daniel, 13, 129, 202
Ray/Rea/Reays
   David, 139, 170,,
   173, 202, 262
Read
   David, 171
   James, 58, 59
   John, 203
   William, 205
Red/Reed [See Reid]
   David, 171
   John, 195, 202, 203
   Owen, 4, 204, 205
   William, 204
Reeves
   Noah, 8, 177
Reid [See Red/Read]
   Owen, 203, 204, 205
   Owing, 21, 218
Reiley
   Ann, wife of Patrick,
   104
   Joseph, 143
   Patrick, 104, 213
Rey [See Ray]
   David, 148
Reyley/Reylie
   Abram, 129
   Patrick, 41
Reynolds

Alsey, wife of Wm.,
   101
Ben., 180
Benjamin, 180
David, 205, 229, 231
Dicy Ann, wife of
   Benjamin, 180
William, 101
Richardson
   David, 137, 138
   T., 276, 277
   Thomas, 30, 73, 81,
   100, 110, 206,
   237, 255
   Turner, 113, 219,
   276, 277
Richardson, Esq.
   Turner, 276
Riche/Richey
   Elener, 95
   Elenor, 207
   Ellen, 95
   Ellinor, dau of John,
   158
   John, 20, 109, 158,
   208, 209, 210,
   221
   John, son of John,
   158
   Margaret, wife of
   John, 209, 210
   Mary, 53, 248
   Mary, dau of John,
   158
   Robert, 211
   Robert, son of John,
   158
   Samuel, 210, 211
   William, 101, 211
   William, son of
   John, 210
Richey, Sr.
   John, 244
Richie [See Richey]
   Eleanor, 207
   John, 207, 209
   Mary, 53, 211
Richie, Jr.
   John, 207

Richie, Sr.
  John, 207, 243
Richkerson
  Thomas, 100
Richy
  Mary, 248, 249
Rickenbacker
  Henry, 212
Ridgeway
  Henry, 181
Right [See Wright]
  Sarah, 43
Rikerson
  Keothern, 100
Riley, 142
  Abraham, 212
  Ann, wife of Patrick,
    213
  James, 181
  John, 104, 213
  Patrick, 10, 42, 141,
    187, 188, 212,
    213, 236
Rinck
  John G., 90
Rind
  James, 56, 162
Ritchey [See
    Richie/Richey]
  Eliner, 95, 207
  John, 69, 107, 189,
    208, 209, 221,
    239
  Margaret, 101
  Margaret, wife of
    John, 209
  Mary, 211
  Mary, sister of
    William, 101
  Robert, 101
  Robert, bro. of E.
    McCluer, 210
  Robt., 69
  William, 101
  Wm., 68
Ritchey, Sr.
  John, 243
Ritchie/Richy
  John, 208, 224

Mary, 248
Ritchie, Sr.
  John, 244
Roberson
  John, 96, 213, 221,
    269, 275
  Kinney, wife of
    John, 213
Roberts
  Charles, 201
  Elizabeth, 272
  Jacob, 169, 271, 272,
    273
  James, 45, 48
Robertson, 213
  David, 178
  John, 68, 169, 213,
    231
Robinson
  James, 262
  John, 229
Rodgers, 8, 214
  A., 139, 185
  Andrew, 8, 87, 97,
    185, 213, 273
  James, 273
  James S., 90, 215
  Jas. L., 215
  Jas. S., 90, 128
  Jno., 160
  John, 35, 57, 58, 60,
    61, 65, 82, 87,
    89, 105, 122,
    151, 208, 209,
    213, 214, 215,
    216, 231, 235,
    259, 273
  McNees, 155
  Sally, wife of J.
    Rodgers, Jr., 215
  Sarah, 97
  Susanna, 91
  Susannah, 8, 97
  Wm., 214, 217
  Wm. T., 213
Rodgers, Capt.
  John, 155
Rodgers, D.S.

John, 76, 87, 113,
    122, 184, 214,
    240, 244
Rodgers, Esq.
  John, 142
Rodgers, Esq.
  John, 214
Rodgers, J.P.
  J., 241
  John, 104, 213
Rodgers, Jr.
  Andrew, 20, 215
  Andw., 49
Rodgers, Sr.
  John, 215
Rodgers, widow, 90
Rogers
  John, 59, 161, 250
Rogers, D.S.
  Jno., 249
  John, 244
Roland
  E.S., 8, 41, 125, 180
  Ezek., 160
  Ezekiel, 122, 213
  Ezekiel S., 214
  Ezekiel Stephen, 122
Roman
  Robt., 8, 135
Rosamond/Roseman/
Rosemond
  Salley, 175
  Samuel, 43, 166, 175
Ross
  David, 60, 93, 197,
    216
  Francis, 216
  Jean, 216
  John, 191
  Sarah, dau of David
    Ross, 93
Roundtree
  William, 253
  Wm., 31
Rowings/Rowling, 167
  E.L., 23
  Richard, 123
Rowland
  James, 68

Rowland, J.P.
  Jno., 220
  John, 50, 96
Rugeley/Rugely
  William, 146, 250
Rugeley, Ord.
  William, 259
Rugeley, Reg.
  Henry, 146
Rugeley, Register
  Henry, 25, 105
Rugge
  William, 250
Runnolds/Runolds
  Alsey, wife of Wm.,
    101
  William, 101
Rusk
  William, 240
Rutledge
  Edward, 60, 80
  John, 227, 228
  William, 46
Rutledge, Esq., Jr.
  John, 226, 229, 236
Rutledge, Jr.
  John, 226, 227
Ryan
  James, 25, 26, 48,
    100, 163, 164,
    216, 254, 255
  Jno., 27

Ryley
  Abraham, 129, 212
  Abram, 4
  Ann, wife of Patrick,
    104
  James, 141
  Patrick, 104

S
Sailer
  Michael, 186
Salmon
  George, 222
Sanders
  A., 250
Saragin

Jonathan, 139
Sarrazen/Sarrazin
  J., 216
  Jonathan, 216
Savage, 231
  James, 12
  John, 102
  William, 14, 199
  Wm., 4, 229
Savage, Esq.
  William, 229
  Wm., 205
Savage, widow, 266
Sawyer
  Mary, 158
Saxon
  Benjamin H., 136
  B.H., 49, 135, 136,
    154, 204
  C., 22, 218
  Charles, 22, 213, 234
  Charles A., 219
  Charles, decd., 219
  Charles, son of
    Lewis, 219
  Clarissa, 27
  Clarissa, decd., 219
  David, son of Lewis,
    219
  D.P., 259
  E.A., 94
  Harriet, dau of
    Lewis, 219
  Hugh, 274, 276
  Hugh, son of Lewis,
    219
  Isabella, dau of J.F.
    Wolff, 274
  James, 105
  John, 136
  John, son of C.
    Saxon, 234
  Joshua, 110, 181,
    195
  Joshua, son of
    Lewis, 219
  L., 70
  Lewis, 8, 9, 21, 23,
    24, 27, 53, 61,

    62, 65, 66, 80,
    98, 99, 105, 131,
    178, 217, 218,
    252, 255
  Lydall, son of Lewis,
    219
  Mary, 94
  Mary, dau of Lewis,
    219
  Mary W., wife of
    Benjamin H.,
    136
  Oswald, 136
  S., 131, 220
  Salley, wife of
    Lewis, 53
  Samuel, 64, 131,
    217, 220, 249,
    269
  Samuel, son of
    Lewis, 219
  Sarah McNeese, 219
  Sarah, wife of Lewis,
    219
  Susan, dau of Lewis,
    219
  Suzy, dau of M.
    Swindle, 241
  Tabitha, dau of
    Lewis, 219
  Wm., 269
Saxon & Co., 218
Saxon, C.C.
  Lewis, 44, 67, 207,
    211
Saxon, CC
  Lewis, 95, 236
Saxon, Clerk
  Lewis, 43
Saxon, Dr.
  Hugh, 234
Saxon, Esq.
  Charles, 210, 217
  Lewis, 151
Saxon, J.P.
  Charles, 122, 160,
    189, 210, 213,
    220, 221, 231,

249, 264, 265, 267, 273
James, 39, 160
Joshua, 214
Lewis, 125
Saxon, J.Q.
B.H., 57, 213, 251
James, 250
Scarborough/Scarbrough
Edward, 71, 93, 141
Schaufferburger
Johannes, 220
Scott
Archibald, 210, 211
James, 113
Saml., 30
Samuel, 69, 217, 220, 221, 231
Scurlock
Ann, 107
Frances, 108
John, 107
Scurry
Thomas, 237
Sell, Q.M.
Charles, 163
Sharp
Bettey, wife of Isaac, 213
Isaac, 212, 213, 248, 249
Shaw
Martin, 68, 121, 210

Shelley
Richard, 179, 221
Sherl
John, 260
Sherley
Richard, 179
Sherral/Sherrel/ Sherrell/ Sherrill
Philip, 49, 75, 123, 139, 148, 170, 171, 173, 221, 222
Shirley/Shirly [See Shurley]

Aaron, son of John, 223
Jane, 224
Jane, wife of Robert, 223
John, 2, 3, 18, 46, 176, 222, 223, 224, 260, 275
Mary, 224
Mary, mother of Robert, 223, 224
Mary, wife of Richard, 223
Rebecca, wife of John, 223
Richard, 3, 179, 223, 224, 225
Robert, 3, 223, 224, 275
Robert, son of John, 224
Robert, son of Richard, 223
Thomas, 80
Shirley, Sr.
Jno., 18
Richard, 223
Shoats
Kitt, 59
Shockley
Salatheil, 102, 170
Salethiel, 91
Shote
Elizabeth, 225, 226
Kite, 58
Kitt, 130, 135, 225
Shote/Shoud/Stroud, 225
Shotes
Kitt, 97, 98, 135, 136
Shotwell
Elender, 76
Shroud
Elizabeth, 226
Shubrick/Shurbrick
Thomas, 88, 226, 227, 228, 229
Shurley [See Shirley], 46
Elijah, 224

John, 36, 115, 224, 256
Richard, 43, 224
Robert, 45
Thos., 195
Shurley, Sr.
John, 275
Simmons/Simons
Ann, 231
Charles, 114, 224
John 252
John, 8, 99, 125
William, 30, 100, 229
Wm., 98, 99, 236
Simpson, 231
A.R., 197
James, 14, 199, 229
Jas., 4
John, 158
John B., 92, 228
John F., 216
John W., 197
Mary, wife of John F., 216
R., 259
R.F., 128, 171
Richard F., 171, 259
R.J., 128
Samuel, 40
William, 12, 126
Zachariah, 77, 233
Simpson, Esq.
James, 205, 229
Simpson, J.P.
J. Wislar, 196
Simpson, Jr.
Jno. W., 84, 85
Sims, 45, 231
Drewry, 274
Drury, 41, 42, 231, 273
Easter, 175
Elizabeth, 120, 232
Elizabeth, widow of Zachariah, 232
Elizabeth, wife of J. Sims, 253
Ester, 142

319

Francis, 103
Hiram, 137
James, 175, 232, 233
Joel, 35, 77, 233
John, 35, 185, 220,
   221, 231, 232,
   253
John, son of
   Elizabeth, 232
Micajah, 235
Nathan, 83, 192
Olly Ann, 175
Rebeccah, dau of A.
   Starnes, 238
Robert, 10, 104, 141,
   187, 188, 212,
   213, 235, 236
Robt., 188
Ruth, 231
Sarah, 109
Thaddeus, 66
Thomas, 231, 232
Thomas, son of
   Elizabeth, 232
William, 231, 232
Wm., 45, 212
Zachariah, 232, 233
Zacheriah, son of
   Elizabeth, 77
Sims, Sr.
   Robert, 236
Sims, widow, 174
Simson
   Enos, 36
   John B., 40, 93

Singleton
   Richard, 109
Skeen/Skin
   Jonathan, 103
   Lettey, 256
Slaves, 274 [See
   Negroes]
Smith
   Barnett, 89
   Benjamin, 133, 177,
   233

Charles, 98, 152,
   161, 191, 214,
   254
Daniel, 54, 55
David, 144, 154,
   234, 235, 264
Elijah, 73, 233
James, 40, 93, 235,
   236, 253, 264,
   268
Job, 23
John, 72, 98, 111,
   131
Julius, 250
Lucy, wife of
   Charles, 233/234
Lucy, 28, 233
Mary, wife of David,
   235
Morton W., 163
Wm., 267, 269
Smith, J.P.
   Charles, 23, 51, 65,
   86, 98, 131, 154,
   166, 160, 183,
   214, 264
Smith, Jr.
   Charles, son of
   Charles, 233
Smith, Rev.
   Charles, 14
   David, 22
   Robert, 7, 80
Smith, Sr.
   Charles, 233
Smith, widow
   Lucy, 77, 233

Snead/Sneed
   Jemima, 47
   Jemema, dau of John
   Box, 46
Snetgar
   David, 144
Sooter
   Benjamin, 87, 113,
   160
   William, 160

South
   Caty, 236
   Daniel, 269
   James, 45, 78, 113,
   269
   John, 228
   Joseph, 269
   Molly, 47
   William, 7, 73, 96,
   236
   Wm., 73, 177, 178
Speers
   David, 191
   Robert, 7
Speiring
   Patrick, 122
Spelts
   John, 191
Spence
   David, 237
   Robert, 237
   Sarah, wife of David,
   237
Spence (formerly
   Neilson)
   Sarah, 237
Spierin
   Pat., 45
   Patrick, 78
   Thomas, 78
Sproull
   J., 265
Spurgin
   John, 173, 198
Stain
   William, 242
Stantion
   William, 31
Stanyarne
   James, 259
Starin
   William, 124
Staren/s
   Aaron, 173, 223, 237
   Aaron, son of Ann,
   238
   Ann, 238
   Anna, dau of
   Ebenezer, 237

320

Anna, wife of
    Ebenezer, 237,
    238
Arron, son of
    Ebenezer, 237
Ebenezer, 101, 237,
    238
Ebenezer, son of
    Ann, 238
John, son of Ann,
    238
John, son of
    Ebenezer, 237
Mary, dau of
    Ebenezer, 237
Rebekah, dau of
    Ebenezer, 237
Starns
    Aaron, 101, 253
    Anna, 101
    Ebenezer, 37, 69,
        101, 185, 237
    Jno., 238
    John, 101
    Shubel, 257
Stedman
    Saml. E., 98, 131
Steel/e
    Aaron, 173, 206
    Jane, 173
Stern
    Ebenezer, 36, 179,
        184
Stimpson
    Mary, 239
Stinson
    Enos, 37, 238, 239
    James, 160, 192
    Mary, 238, 239
Stitlius
    John, 239
Stone
    John, 174
Stother
    Kemp T., 98, 131
Strain
    James, 233

Polly, mother of
    Negro Hannah,
    197
William, 196
Strange
    B., 235
    Benj., 82
    John H., 193
    Joseph, 57
Stroud
    John, bro of
        Elizabeth, 226
    Latson, bro of
        Elizabeth, 226
Strum
    Elizabeth, wife of
        Henry, 239, 240
    Henry, 239, 240
Stuart
    Francis, 191
Studdard
    David, 123, 215
    Nancy, wife of
        David, 215
Studdard, Jr.
    David, 215
Sturm
    Henry, 140
Suber
    John, 136
    Uriah, 136
Suillvant
    Chas., 32
Sullivan, Jr.
    James, 122, 142
Sullivant
    Charles, 20, 109,
        182, 208, 212
    Frederick, 122
    Hewlett, 109, 208
    James, 122
    Menoah, 180
    Nancy, dau of S.
        Bolling, 42
    Nathaniel, 109, 208
Sulter
    Wm., 107
Suter/Sutter
    Benjamin, 160

Benjn., 157
William, 107, 122,
    240
Swain, widow, 229
Swancy/Swansey, 213
    J.W., 108
    Samuel, 240
Swering
    Anna, 85
    John, 85
Swindel/Swindle, 165
    Daniel, son of
        Michael, 241
    Delila, dau of
        Michael, 241
    George, 240
    George, bro of
        Michael, 241
    George, son of
        Michael, 241
    John, son of
        Michael, 241
    Michael, 36, 132,
        240, 241
    Mitchell, 132
    Richard, 240

T
Taggart
    James, 66
Taggart, Ord.
    Moses, 8, 177
Tait/Tate
    Isaac, 226
    Robert, 136
    Samuel, 137
    William, 137, 225
Task?
    John, 101, 192
Tavel
    Frederick, 158
Taylor
    Arthur, 24, 61, 63,
        178
    John, 127
    Margaret, 63
    Mary, dau of John,
        127

Mary, wife of C.
Hubbs/Hobbs,
127
Robt., 127
Samuel, 206
William, 7
Teague
George, 187
Teed
James, 248
Tegclaar
Jan Gabriel, 58
Tenant/Tennant/Tennent
Charles, 132, 178,
Chas., 132
Patsey, 132
Patsy, 132
Wm., 132
Tennant, Mr., 132
Terk [See Turk]
Wm., 78
Terry
John, 174
Sarah, 44
Terry, Esq.
Champness, 44
Thomas
Abel, 17, 40, 227,
228, 256
Able, 241, 242, 246
Ann, 242
Cassandra, 242
Daniel, 242
Edward, 17, 227,
228
Evan, 26, 227
G., 180
Isaac, 17, 186, 191,
228
Isaac, son of
Timothy, 242
John, 17, 20, 38,
227, 228
Lavina, 200
Nehemiah, 227, 228
R., 200
Sarah, dau of
Timothy, 241
Timothy, 241, 242

Timothy, bro of
Able, 242
William, 72, 242
Thomas, J.P.
J., 242
Js., 243
Thomas Jr.
Jno., 169
Thomas, Jr.
Timothy, 242
Thomason, 136
Elenor, wife of
Gideon, 215
George, 96, 131, 243
Gideon, 95, 214, 215
James, 214
John, 74, 76, 183,
184, 223, 268
Mourning, wife of
Nathan, 182
Mourning, wife of
Wm., 183
Nathan, 182
Sarah, wife of Wm.,
217
William, 74, 182,
183, 217
Thomason, 2nd, Jr.
William, 183, 184
Thomason, Jr.
William, 182, 217
Thomason, Sr.
William, 182, 183,
184
Wm., 182
Thompson
Flanders, 31
Franklin, 138
Henry, 276
Jno., 185
Robert, 31
Thomson, D.S.
Jas., 107
Tinsley
Elizabeth, wife of
James, 265
James, 265, 266, 268
Toad [See Todd]
Margaret, 243, 244

Robert, 244
Todd [See Toad]
Benjamin, son of
James, 245
Betsey, dau of
James, 245
Daniel, 92
James, 127, 128,
171, 200, 244,
245
John, 157, 161, 255
John, son of James,
245
Margaret, 243, 244
Nancy, dau of James,
245
Polly, 245
R.A., 215
Robert, 85, 128, 156,
157, 160, 171,
244, 255
Robert, son of
James, 245
Samuel, 48, 242
Samuel R., 92
William, 245
William, son of
James, 245
Todd, Dr.
Samuel, 215
Todd, Sr.
Robert, 244
Tomlinson
William, 75
Towles
Oliver, 159
Townsend, 61
Troup, Esq.
John, 271
Troup, Esq., D.S.
General
John, 147
Troup, J.P.
John, 109
Tuckland, 125
Tuft
Simon, 253
Turk/e /Turks[See Terk],
125, 150

John, 1, 3, 52, 241,
242, 245, 246
John, son of John,
245
Neomy, dau of John,
245
Rachel, 168, 247
Theodocius, 245,
246, 247
Theodore, 245
Theodosia, 4, 119,
257
Thomas, son of John,
245
William, 3, 78, 123,
124, 148, 149,
150, 154, 245,
247
William, bro of John,
245
Turkland, 150
Turner
Asa, 89, 275
Benj., 13, 79
Fanny, 120
William, 5, 29
Turnstall, C.P.C.
Will., 120
Turpin
William, 208, 274,
275
Wm., 160
Tweed/Tweedy, 213
Eleanor, 9, 126, 248
Elenor, 247
Ellenor, 248
James, 53, 172, 248,
249
Robert, 58, 59
Tweed/Tweedy, Sr.
James, 248

U
Underwood
Isaac, 34, 71, 158

V
Valk
Jack, 215
Jacob, 249, 250

Vance
David, 252
Vanhorn, 26
Benjamin, 17, 26,
27, 250, 251, 252
Jane, dau of
Benjamin, 250
Joanna, wife of
Benjamin, 251
Joanne, 252
Joanne, wife of
Benjamin, 26, 27
Rebecca, 252
Rebecca, dau of
Benjamin, 250
Rebecca, sister of R.
Vanhorn, 251
Robert, 17, 250, 251
Vanhorn, Mrs.
Joanne, 251
Vaughan/Vaughn
Benj., 197
George, 91, 204, 205
Jonathan, 41, 94
William, 3, 252
Wm., 91
Vines
James, 264
Volk
Jacob, 249

W
Wade, D.S.
Jno., 268
John, 268
Wadkins
Ann, 51
John, 179, 261
William, 121, 227
Wm., 113, 166

Wadsworth
Thomas, 11, 17, 160,
184,187, 188,
208, 221, 226,
227, 274, 275
Wadsworth, J.L.C.
Thomas, 45, 64

Wadsworth, J.P.
Thos., 185
Wagner
John, 97
Wait/Waits/Waite/
Waites
Frances, 77
James, 45, 232, 277
John, 35, 73, 77,
120, 232, 233
Joseph, 3, 4, 252,
253
Philip, 73, 252, 241
Sarah, dau of E.
Sims, 232
Sarah, wife of James,
232
Walden
James, 47
Waldrop/Waldrup
Elizabeth, 269
G.B., 195
Green Berry, 195
Jas., 137, 138
Walker/s, 276
Albert, 76
Cilvenis, 239
Elias, 236
Elijah, 82, 233
Horatio, 161
Joel, 192, 253
John, 7, 96
Mansd., 271, 272
Mansfield, 271, 272
Menn., 80
Silvanus, 96, 146,
190, 237, 239,
240
Tandy, 243
William, 253
Walker, Esq.
Silvanus, 237
Walker, J.P.
Philip, 153, 154
Silvanus, 223
Walker, Jr.
Silvanus, 96
Silvs., 146, 275

Walker, Sr.
Silvanus, 105, 205
Wallace
John, 31, 250
Waller
Ben., 144
Benjamin, 144
Wallis
Jesse, 253
John, 253
Jonathan, 253
Wm., 132
Wallises
William, 131
Wardlaw
David, 250
Waring
Archer, 253
Thomas, 41, 54
Thos., 253
Waring, Sr.
Thomas, 54, 55
Warner
Elizabeth, 243
Wetenhall, 114
Wittenhall, 243
Washington, 165
Wm., 118, 241
Waters
Phillip, 59
Watkins, 51
Anna, wife of Wm.,
122
Charles, 88, 228
James, 81, 232
James, son of Wm.,
122
John, 111
William, 87, 113,
121, 122, 196
Watson
Bena., 239
Elijah, 266, 268
Lewis, 269
Richard, 132
Wm., 188
Weakley
Saml., 133

Weatherall
John, 8, 177
Weathers
Thomas, 196
Weatherspoon
John, 99, 254
Saml., 101
Weaver, 14
A., 254
Frederick, 254
Samuel, 132
Webb
Daniel, 255
David, 254, 255
Weir
James, 125
John, 255
Samuel, 73, 81, 206
Thomas, 256
Weir, Jr.
Thomas, 172, 256
Wells
Clement, 189
James, 46, 192, 193,
195, 256
John, 121, 189
Moses, 189
Rebecca, wife of
John, 189
West
Berry, 197
William, 247
Wm., 247
Wharton
Geo., 35
Maudlin, 238
P.G., 34, 71, 221
Pleasant, 34, 71
Saml., 36, 43, 239
Samuel, 101, 232,
237, 238, 239
Stephen, 83, 193
Whigs, 14
Whitaker, 59
White
Joseph, 105
Wier
James, 8

Wild
Thos., 212
Wild, Esq.
Richard, 205
Willard
Elizabeth, dau of
John, 258
j, 258
John, 36, 54, 78,
247, 257
Macajah, son of
John, 258
Martha, 258
Martha, dau of H.
Hendricks, 257
Martha, dau of M.
Hendrix, 120
Melagah, 258
Micajah, 258
Micajah, wife of
John, 258
Patsy, wife of John,
257
Pattey, 258
Patty, wife of John,
258
Polly, dau of John,
258
Sarah, dau of John,
258
William/Williams, 266
Ben., 65, 198
Benjamin, 46, 62,
66, 97, 192, 193,
256, 259, 268
Benjn., 128
Bn., 193
Daniel, 43, 131, 132,
138, 198, 203,
260, 262
Edward, 198, 260
Elisha, 269
Eliz., 269
Elizabeth, 269
Elizabeth, sister of J
Williams, 265
Elizabeth, wife of
John, 265
Gainer, 273

Hester, wife of
James, 261
J., 192
Jacob, 21, 22, 65,
157
James, 14, 45, 86,
101, 113, 145,
148, 164, 165,
179, 184, 192,
217, 220, 221,
260-262, 265,
271, 272
James A., 262, 266
James At., 266
James Atwood, 265,
266, 268
Jas., 185
Jno., 201
John, 71, 75, 145,
183, 184, 221-
223, 261- 269
Jonathan, 62
Jonathan, son of
Benjamin, 259
Joseph, 239, 240,
268, 269
Lucretia, 259
John, 257, 269
Joseph, 240
Martha, wife of
John, 257
Mary, 21
Mary, sister of John,
265
Mary, wife of James
A., 265
Mary, wife of James
Atwood, 266
Nimrod, 140, 203,
260
Oliver, 260
Saml., 86, 129, 239
Samuel, 22, 49, 75,
86, 240, 269
Thomas, 50
Thomas B., 198
Thomas, grand-son
of James, 261
Washington, 265

William, 46, 181,
270, 275
Wm., 18, 167, 269
Wright, 260
Williams, J.P.
Charles, 232
Williams, J.Q.
James, 265, 268
Williams, J.Q.N.D.
James, 266
Williams, Jr.
Benjamin, 62,
Daniel, 140, 266,
268
John, 265, 266, 268
Saml., 167
Williams, Maj., 213
Williams, Sr.
Samuel, 21
Williamson, 59
Archibald, 213
Ben., 63
Benjamin, 58, 59,
258
Elisha, 47
Elisha, grandson of
John Box, 46
John, 47
W., 176
William, 32, 150,
169, 226, 227,
250, 256, 270-
273
Wm., 123, 147, 149,
227, 249, 270-
273
Williamson, D.S.
William, 176
Williamson, Esq., 256,
Benjamin, 259
William, 94, 146.
172
176
Williamson, Mr., 270
Williamson
William, 125
Wm., 124
Willis
William, 132

Wills
James, 45
John, 150
Wills, J.P.
James, 195
Willson
Hugh, 151
John, 41
Stain, 64
Wilson, 145, 258, 259
Allen, 144
Charles, 190, 248
James, 145, 190, 244
John, 41, 42, 273,
274
Litt. B., 220
Pamela, wife of
Robert, 113
Robert, 113
W., 145
Whitfield, 70
William, 160
Wilson, widow, 244
Winn
Gallanus, 64
Richard, 32, 59, 258,
259
Richd., 58
Winn, D.S.
R., 38
Richard, 32, 96, 146,
236
Richd., 38, 50, 53,
146, 147, 236,
253, 271, 273
Winthrop
Joseph, 272
Wiseman
John, 226
Withers
Thomas, 108
Wofford, D.S.
Js., 189, 198
W., 83, 198
William, 190
Wm., 83, 221, 222
Wolff, 95, 131, 233, 273
G., 233
G.F., 94

George, son of John
F., 274
J.F., 170, 179, 214,
270, 272
John F., 161, 169,
182, 183, 184,
208, 214, 215,
270, 271, 272,
274
John Frances, 74, 76,
161, 182, 183
Mary, wife of John
F., 274
Wolff, Col.
John F., 266, 268
Wolff, Esq.
John Frances, 214
Wolff, Gen.
John F., 273
Wolff, Genl.
J.F., 137
Wood, 10
Ethld., 118
Lazarus, 107
Peter, 120
Robert, 267
Robert Jno., 263
Sarah, wife of
Stephen, 112
Ste. C., 102, 113
Stephen, 102, 112
Stephen C., 112
Thomas, 209
W.C., 56
Woodies
John, 31
Woodin
Jno., 116
Woods
Benjn., 262
Jno., 169
John, 270
Peter, 192
Robert, 69, 174
Robt., 115
Stephen, 34
Woods, J.P.
Saml., 153
Woodward

Thomas, 58, 59, 105,
134, 143, 146,
274
Woody, 118
Isabella, wife of
John, 274
Jno., 84, 85
John, 28, 31, 82, 86,
87, 117, 118,
211, 269, 274
John, son in law of
H. Dial, 88
Sarah, 113
Stephen, 223, 238
Thomas, 36
Woody, Sr.
John, 128
Wooford
James, 59
Wooford, D.S.
Wm., 54
Wooley
John, 118
Word
James, 82
Robert, 231
Word, L.S.
Robert, 231
Wright, 120
Daniel, 224
Edy, 18, 275
Eliza., 120
Elizabeth, 120
Elizabeth, dau of M.
Hendrix, 120
Elizabeth, mother of
George, 275
Elizabeth, widow of
Jacob, 275
George, 10, 18, 34,
42, 43, 96, 112,
222, 223, 238,
260, 274, 275
George, son of
Elizabeth, 275
George, son of
Jacob, 275
Jacob, 36, 156, 275
James, 232, 240

Joseph, 105, 163
Rachel, 17
Robert K., 57
Sarah, 17, 36, 193
Sarah, dau of Jacob
Bowman, 43
Thos., 84, 91, 168,
214, 275
William, 109
Wright, D.S.
Joseph, 137
Wright, J.P.
Daniel, 41, 61, 118,
211, 238, 271
Wright, J.Q.
Daniel, 87, 173, 187
Thomas, 13, 71, 84,
142, 199
Wright, Jr.
George, 203, 262
William, 208
Wright, Q.M.
Danl., 31

Y
Yager
Gray, 269
John, 269
Yarborough, 114
Yeargin
Benjamin, 244
York
Emanuel, 29
Young, 43
Archabald, 95, 191
Archd., 31, 273
Gallaten, son of
James, 276
Gallatin, 76
H.C., 234
Henry C., 97
James, 76, 191, 208,
253, 276, 277
Keturah, 76
Mary Ann, wife of
James, 276
Phebe, 76
Rhoda E.C., 76

Rhoda, wife of
James, 76
Robert, 35
Susannah C., 76
W.A., 276, 277
William Agustin, son
of James, 276
Wm. A., 76, 277

§§§§

PLACE INDEX

A
Abbeville, 276
Alabama, xv
Jackson Co., 47
Sinclair Co., 68
America, 57
Ancient Boundary, 11,
12, 94, 118, 141

B
Baptist, 96
Big Survey, 264
Blockhouse
Kellett's Station, 11
Boundary line, 118
Bounty Land, 20, 49,
129, 167, 168,
185, 199, 235, xv
Branches
Beaver Dam, 59
Beaverdam Branch,
275
Bradshaws Branch,
170, 171, 174, x
Broad and Saludy
Rivers, 31
Bullet Branch, x
Bullets Branch, 50
Bullett Branch, 9,
218, 247, 248
Burrises Branch, 81,
157
Burrisses Creek, x
Calhouns Branch,
69, x
Dry Branch, 59

Durban Branch, 71
Enoree, 59
Guttery's Branch,
266, x
Hallams Branch, 267
Hallams Creek, 263
Hallums Branch, 262
Hellams Branch,
189, 222, 262,
265, 267, x
Helmes Branch, 262
Hendricks Branch,
107
Hilly Branch, 161, x
Indian Hut Branch,
194, x
Jones Branch, 211, x
Kellett Branch, x
Lick Branch, 172
Little Branch, 259
Long Branch, 94,
145, 176, 177
Long Lick, 37
Long Lick Branch,
237, 253
Long Lick Creek, 36
Mill, 20
Moll Kelly's Branch,
270, 271, 272, x
Muddy, 85
O'Daniels Branch,
95, 207, x
Peaching Branch, 87
Peaching Creek, 87
Peachlands/Peachlin
Branch, x, 1, 123
Polks Branch, 107, x
Red Lick Branch,
161
Reyburns Branch,
243
Reynolds Branch,
207
Ritchey's, 101
Ritchey's Branch, x
Rock House Branch,
218, x
Rockey Branch, 78,
x

Sandy Branch, 168,
169
School House
Branch, x
Schoolhouse Branch,
266
Sherrill's Branch, 67,
x
Shirrels Branch, 60,
63
Starnes Branch, x
Steep Hollow
Branch, 249
Still House Branch,
267, x
Todd's Branch, x
Walnut Branch, 139,
140
Widow Reeds/Reids
Branch, x, 204,
205
Williams Branch, x

C
Caintucky [sic]
Mercer Co., 36
Canetuckey
Mercer Co., 208
Cemetery
Babb-Kellett, 11
Rosemont Cemetery,
80
Saxon, Cleveland
Cemetery, 219
Charles Town, 250
Charleston, 58, 60, 80,
144, 149, 211,
216, 229, 272,
xiv
Charlestown, 1, 147, 176
Cherokee Indian
Nations, 15
Cherokee Lands, 11
Churches
Beaverdam Church,
16
Duncan Creek
Presbyterian
Church, 76

327

Poplar Springs, 7, 96
Poplar Spring
  Meeting House,
  73
Rocky Springs
  Presbyterian, 7
Confiscated Estates, 144,
  145
Confiscated Property,
  178
Coppunks Place, 105
Counties
  Abbeville, xiv
  Anderson, 31
  Berkley, 20, 32, 33,
    36, xiv
  Berkley Co., 42, 50,
    55, 70, 71, 83,
    97, 109, 111,
    117, 119, 121,
    125, 135, 137,
    139, 140, 147,
    149, 150, 152,
    153, 157, 158,
    159, 162, 167,
    168, 172, 179,
    189, 193, 194,
    198, 199, 201-
    203, 212, 216,
    223-235, 238,
    241, 252, 254,
    255, 257, 260,
    262, 265, 267,
    269, 274
  Craven, 22, 24, 25,
    32, 35, 37, 58
  Craven Co., 3, 49,
    52, 53, 54, 59,
    67, 69, 78, 85,
    94, 96, 100, 102,
    104, 107, 108,
    110, 119, 120,
    122, 126, 129,
    130, 131, 132,
    143, 146, 148,
    163, 166, 170,
    171, 174, 175,
    176, 181, 185,
    190, 191, 193,

199, 201, 207,
  211, 220, 222,
  226, 230, 237,
  239, 243, 249,
  253, 254, 256,
  257, 260, 261,
  268, 269, 270
Granville Co., 247
Greenville, 15, xiv
Greenville Co., 141
Laurens, 9, 10, 15,
  16, 21, xiv
Laurens Co., 52,
  212, 240, 272
Newberry, 16, 26
Creeks
  Allison's Creek, x
  Allisons Creek, 29,
    30, 159
  Beaver Dam Creek,
    40, 60
  Beaverdam Creek,
    29
  Berkley Co., 116,
    162
  Black Creek, 35
  Brown's Creek, x
  Browns Creek, 59,
    129
  Buckhead Creek,
    115
  Bufflew Creek, 59
  Burreses Creek, 81
  Burress Creek, 81
  Burresses Creek, 244
  Burris Creek, 45, 68,
    81, 122, 180,
    191, 231, 232
  Burrises Creek, 78,
    80, 122, 160, 262
  Burris's Creek, 160
  Burriss Creek, 160
  Burrisses Creek,
    157, 162, x
  Burrisses Creek,
    formerly
    Williams, 68
  Burrows Creek, 262
  Bush Creek, xv

Cain Creek, 80, 102,
  189
Calhouns Creek, 247
Cane Creek, 102,
  275
Craven Co., 161, 213
Dartons Creek, 231
Dirty Creek, 8, 9, 15,
  20, 57, 82, 84,
  85, 86, 87, 88,
  91, 97, 128, 129,
  154, 155, 160,
  161, 171, 180,
  195, 197, 213,
  214, 235, 259,
  263, 267, 269, x,
  xv
Duncans Creek, 30
Durbans Creek, 71
Durbins Creek, 256
Durty Creek, 214
Dutchman's Branch,
  x
Dutchmans Creek,
  59
Elisha Creek, 59
Fergusons Creek, 59
Flat Creek, 268
Flat Rock Creek, 268
Hellams Creek, 222
Hellems Creek, 222
Helms Creek, 221,
  269
Indian Creek, 144,
  201, x
Laurel Creek, 95
Lick Creek, 99, 169,
  249, 256
Long Cane Creek, 5,
  247
Long Lick Creek, 34,
  35, 45, 68, 102,
  112, 147, 184,
  237, 239, 247
Long Oak Creek, 9
McHerg's Creek,
  102, 103
McHurgs Creek,
  170, 263, x

Middle Creek, 136
Mountain Creek, 41,
  95, 131, 170,
  182, x
North Fork, x
Peaching Creek, 137
Peaching Old field or
  Creek, 218
Peachlings Creek,
  192
Poplar Springs
  Baptist, 16
Rabarnes Creek, 71
Rabbins Creek, 13
Rabburn's Creek, 70
Rabens Creek, 9, 84,
  85, 116, 129,
  221, 277
Raberns Creek, 84,
  85
Rabins Creek, 52
Rabon Creek, 20,
  113
Rabons Creek, 45,
  69, 174, 233,
  262, 276, 277
Raborns Creek, 32,
  93, 103, 116,
  121, 136, 141,
  145, 156, 167,
  182, 188, 199,
  218, 242, 248,
  267, 272
Raboruns Creek, 205
Rabouns Creek, 252,
  254
Rabourn Creek, 23,
  26, 33, 88
Rabourns Creek, 5,
  9, 12, 22, 24, 26,
  27, 28, 38, 40,
  44, 46, 52, 57,
  66, 70, 72, 74-
  78, 83, 86, 88,
  94, 101, 103,
  109, 114, 118,
  121, 124, 125,
  128, 131, 139,
  142, 145, 150,

151, 161, 163,
  168, 170-172,
  190, 191, 195,
  202, 204, 205,
  209, 211, 215,
  217, 218, 222,
  223, 225, 228,
  242, 244, 247,
  248, 249, 256,
  262, 266, 268,
  271, 273, 274
Rabourns Creek,
  called Burris, 81
Rabun Creek, 15,
  226, x, xiv
Rabuns Creek, 158
Raburn Creek, 118,
  255, 270, xiv, xv
Raburnes Creek, 171
Raburns Creek, 1, 8,
  10, 14, 17, 18,
  20, 21, 25, 30-
  32, 41, 51, 62,
  63, 67-71, 80,
  81, 84, 87, 89,
  95, 97, 98, 106,
  113, 114, 117,
  120-123, 125,
  126, 128, 130,
  135, 136, 138,
  142-144, 146,
  147, 149, 150,
  154, 155, 157,
  160, 161, 166,
  167, 170-172,
  175, 183, 184,
  185, 186-189,
  191, 192, 197-
  199, 202, 204,
  214, 219, 223-
  225 236, 243-
  245, 247, 249-
  252, 256, 264-
  267, 271, 272
Raibens Creek, 259
Raibons Creek, 138
Raiborns Creek, 22,
  31, 51, 68, 74,
  75, 86, 117, 147,

153, 154, 162,
  166, 183, 186,
  214, 222, 231,
  243, 264, 268,
  271, 273
Raibourn Creek, 97
Raibourns Creek, 54,
  164, 208, 218,
  249
Raiburns Creek, 22,
  24, 25, 52, 55,
  92, 103, 122,
  164, 165, 190,
  201, 254, 264,
  269, 276
Raifords Creek, 108,
  x
Raybans Creek, 28,
  77, 253, 260
Raybons Creek, 126,
  212
Rayborn Creek, 1, 2,
  4
Raybornes Creek,
  55, 83
Rayborns Creek, 14,
  86, 98, 153, 204,
  211, 229, 230
Raybournes Creek,
  50, 52
Raybourns Creek,
  33, 34, 71, 157,
  259
Rayburn Creek, 3,
  252
Rayburnes Creek, 2,
  32, 70, 121, 223,
  239, 260
Rayburn's Creek, xv
Rayburns Creek, 1-4,
  6, 10, 13, 31, 35,
  44, 49, 53, 54,
  56, 83, 86, 95,
  97, 98, 99, 103,
  105, 107, 111,
  114, 116, 117,
  121, 123, 139,
  143, 147, 149,
  158, 161-163,

165, 166, 168,
172, 176, 179,
181, 182, 184,
186, 189, 191,
192, 198, 199,
201-203, 205,
207, 212, 216,
217, 220, 222,
223, 225, 230,
231, 234-236,
240, 243, 244,
247, 249, 252,
256, 260, 261,
267, 270, 277,
xiv
Reabins Creek, 70
Reaborn Creek, 94,
231, 242
Reaborns Creek,
112, 159
Reabourns Creek,
124, 126, 193,
215
Reaburans Creek, 61
Reaburn Creek, 94,
134, 145
Reaburns Creek, 2,
9, 16, 26, 32, 33,
41, 47, 50, 54,
60, 61-66, 70,
72, 83, 86, 87,
94-96, 98-100,
102-107, 109,
116, 122, 128,
130, 133, 134,
148, 151-153,
161, 168, 169-
174, 176, 177,
182-187, 189,
190, 193, 202,
205, 208, 209,
211-214, 217,
220, 221, 224,
225, 230, 236,
239, 240, 241,
243, 245, 251,
252, 254, 255,
258, 259-267,
269-272, x

Reaburns Creek,
called Burrises
branch, 157
Rebans Creek, 245
Rebens Creek, 259
Reborns Creek, 107,
220
Rebourns Creek,
212, 215
Rebuns Creek, 169
Reburns Creek, 48,
75, 135, 139,
143, 148, 175,
179, 203, 204,
244, 254, 256,
260
Red Creek, 215
Reedy and Raiburns
Creek, 121
Reedy Creek, 38, 56,
102, 257
Reedy Creek,
formerly Reedy
River, 159
Reedy Fork Creek,
250
Reedy Lick, 160
Reighburns Creek,
181
Reybornes Creek,
166, 235
Reybourns Creek,
53, 152, 163
Reyburnes Creek,
163
Reyburn's, 41
Reyburns Creek, 25,
31, 71, 94, 125,
126, 130, 135,
139, 148, 151,
170, 174, 176,
179, 207, 211,
220, 243, 253,
254, 261, 269,
270
Rocky Creek, 158
Rubens Creek, 243
South Fork, x
Stevens Creek, 5

Turkey Creek, 8, 80,
194
Walnut Creek, 73,
80, 240
Warrior Creek, 96, x
Williams Creek, 67,
68, 160, 244, x
Williams Creek,
formerly
Raburns, 68
Williamses Creek,
116, 244

D
Dam, 187
Delaware, 16
District
Abbeville, 8
Abbeville Dist., 177
Laurens, 7
Laurens Dist., 232,
235, 242
Newberry Dist., 265
Ninety Six, 17, 41,
101
Ninety Six Dist., 12,
13, 14, 20, 28,
30, 33, 40, 103,
129, 132, 138,
164, 165, 179,
182, 184, 192,
199, 202, 212,
230, 236, 240,
241, 244, 247,
250, 256, 257,
275
Oxford Dist., 164
Dwelling house, 10, 187,
251

E
England, 57, 144

F
Ferry, xv
Field
Peaching Old field or
Creek, 218
Florida
East Florida, 144

Forfeited Estates, 54, 55,
144
Fork
Brown's Fork, x
Forks
Broad and Saluda
River, 59, 137,
144, 177
Broad and Saludy
Rivers, 104, 106,
185, 189, 190,
198, 241, 258,
259
Brown's Fork, 254
Browns Fork, 99
Chesnut Fork, 160
Lockest Fork, 146
Locust, 220
Lokest, 220
North Fork, xv
Raborns Creek, 123
Reedy Fork, 28, 40,
199, 206, 213,
214, 215, 234,
259
Saluda and Broad
River, 33, 99
South Fork, 1, xv
Forts, 5, 14,
Brooks Fort, 6
Hall's Fort, 6
Kellett's Station, 11
Lindley's, 15
Lindleys Fort, xv
Old burnt Fort, xv
France, 123
Frericksbeurg, 11

G
Georgia, 57, 162, 175,
xv
Albert Co., 154
Columbia Co., 184
Decalb Co., 23
Franklin Co., 137,
195, 204
Gwinnette Co., 195
Hall County, 23
Jackson Co., 203

Wrightsboro, 16, 17
Georgia back country, 14
Goundy's House, 5
Graveyard, 9
Great Britain, 55, 57,
123, 205
Great Saludy, 270

H
Hill
Dittany Hill, 220
Holland
Amsterdam, 58
Houses
Norris's house, 125
Goundy's house, 5
House Tract, 9, 84, 85

I
Indian boundary line, 77
Indian Land, 13, 14, 202,
229, xv
Indian Line, 79, 140,
230, 254
Ireland, 7, 76, 123
Antrim, 92
County Carlow, 57
Kings County, 17

J
Jacksonburough, 71,
224
Jamaica, 144

K
Kentucky, 190
Livingston Co., 228
Mercer Co., 36, 208

L
Laurens Court, 91
Laurens Court House, 73

M
Madden track, 68
Maryland, 16, 250, xiv
Meeting house, 8, 96
Bush River Monthly
Meeting, 16, 43

New Garden
Monthly
Meeting, 17
Poplar Spring
Meeting House,
73, 236
Quaker Meeting
house, 8
Quaker meeting
house, 125
Tabernacle Meeting
house, 8
Wrightsboro
Monthly
Meeting, 17
Mills, 10, 84, 85, 187, xv
George Wright's old
mill, 9
Griss Mill, 235
McDaniel's Mill, 20
Old Mill House, 10,
51. 80
Thomasons Mill, 182
Wrights Old Mill,
34, 112
Mount
Mount Warrior, 236,
253
Raburn's Creek
Mount, 96

N
Neighborhood
Raburn Creek, 14
Ninety Six, xiv
North Carolina, 7, 16,
130, 170, 250,
xiv
Anson Co., 76
Asheville, 252
Buncombe Co., 251,
252
Mecklenburg Co.,
220
Mecklinbough Co.,
83
Moore Co., 257
New Garden, 250

New Garden
   Monthly
   Meeting, 17
Orange Co., 226
Tyron, 11

O
Ohio
   Miami Co., 16, xv
   Warren Co., 252
Old Indian Line, 11, 12,
   14, 142, 254
Old Line, 130, 174
Old Survey, 86, 190

P
Parishes
   St. Andrew Parish,
      60
   St. George's Parish,
      144
   St. John's Parish, 202
   St. Mark's Parish,
      257
   St. Pauls Parish, 176,
      211, 257, 259
Peaching Old Field, 22,
   23
Peachlins Old Field, 22
Pearls place, 14
Pennsylvania, 7, 16, 56,
   105, 134, 154,
   250, xiv
   Cumberland Co., 56,
      105, 132, 133,
      134
   Pensborough, 134
   Philadelphia, 57
   West Pennsborough,
      56, 105, 132,
      133, 134

Q
Quaker community, xv

R
Reighburns Creek
      Settlement, 151
Rivers

Broad and Saluday
   Rivers, 30
Broad and Saludy,
   58, 59
Broad and Saludy
   River, 105
Broad and Saludy
   Rivers, 32, 116,
   159, 226, 244
Bush River, 5, 6,
   149, 154
Enoree, 53, 115
Enoree River, 198,
   226, 250
Kings River, 53
Little River, 10, 14,
   53, 59, 69, 76,
   85, 114, 137,
   138, 161, 187,
   213, 215, 216,
   234, 236, 237,
   250
Little River of
   Saluda, 59
Little Saluda River,
   58
Reedi/ie River, 41,
   96
Reedy and Saluda
   River, 80, 224
Reedy River, 1- 3, 9,
   11-13, 21- 24,
   28, 30, 31, 34-
   38, 40, 42-48,
   51, 53, 55, 57-
   59, 62, 71-73,
   76, 77, 79, 82,
   88, 93, 94, 96,
   100, 102, 103,
   107-112, 115,
   118-121, 124,
   126, 128, 129,
   131, 132, 137,
   140, 142, 144,
   146, 147, 156,
   165, 174, 175,
   177, 178, 181,
   184, 185, 187,
   188, 190, 192,

   195, 197, 199,
   202, 203, 205,
   206, 209, 214,
   216, 218, 221,
   223, 225- 229,
   231, 233, 236,
   238-, 242, 246-
   249, 254, 255,
   257, 268, 271-
   276, x, xiv
Saluda and Reedy
   Rivers, 80
Saluda River, 26, 34,
   54, 70, 71, 74,
   99, 111, 122,
   134, 135, 141,
   147, 149, 152,
   153, 162, 181,
   182, 217, 229,
   241, 244, 251,
   271, 273, x, xiv,
   xv
Saluday River, 265
Saludie River, 245
Saludy and Reedy
   Rivers, 115
Saludy River, 10, 31,
   32, 33, 47, 52,
   55, 56, 72, 75,
   78, 98, 99, 104,
   106, 110, 115,
   116, 125, 126,
   130, 135, 143,
   146, 152, 158,
   176, 181, 186,
   189-191, 193,
   194, 203, 212,
   213, 222, 230,
   241, 250, 254,
   260, 267, 269,
   274
Santee, 83, 104, 106
Santee River, 1, 25,
   56, 109, 130,
   143, 164, 241
Savannah, 11
Tyger River, 55, 59
Wateree, 99
Wateree River, 199

Roads
  To Andersons land,
    213
  Cumbia's Road, 244
  George Wright
    Road, 112
  Greenville Road, 91
  Laurens to
    Greenville Court
    House., 91
  Main County, 138
  Old Road, 22, 112,
    213
  Raburns Creek to
    Charleston, 138
  Rebourns Creek to
    Charleston, 138
  Road from fish dam
    ford, 73
  Road to Brocks
    Store, 227
  Road to the Court
    House, 259
  Road to Wolff's
    store, 170
  Swanseys Road, 213
  Waggon Road, 24,
    62, 141, 227,
    228, 241, 270
S
Sawmill, 143
Scotch-Irish, 7
Scotland, 7
Settlements
  Reaburns Creek
    Settlement, 98,
    259
  Reighburns Creek
    Settlement, 151,
    201
Shoals, 243
  Fish Trap Shole, 102
  Tumbling Shoals,
    24, 178
South Carolina, 7, 250
  Abbeville, 276
  Abbeville Co., 133,
    174, 247

Abbeville Dist., 72,
  76, 135, 136,
  165, 175, 193,
  228, 232, 240,
  250
Anderson Co., 31
Berkley Co., 16, 33,
  56, 74, 75, 112,
  114, 132, 167
Cambridge, 144
Cambridge, town of,
  110
Camden, 11, 16, 17
Camden Dist., 106
Camden Parish, 119
Charles Town, 109
Charleston, 21, 72,
  99, 139, 154,
  169, 185, 202,
  227, 248, 259,
  271, 275
Charleston Dist.,
  158, 163
Charlestown, 11, 97,
  271
Chester Co., 114
Colleton Co., 111,
  176
Craven Co., 35, 38,
  44, 56, 75, 115,
  149, 154, 190,
  223, 246, 262
Edgefield, 17, 128
Enoree, 194
Fairfield Co., 130,
  131, 224
Fairfield Dist., 139
Greenville, 165
Greenville Co., 104,
  109, 112, 222,
  225
Greenville Dist., 22,
  136, 137, 139,
  174, 181, 188,
  199, 244
Kershaw Dist., 192
Larrence (sic) Dist.,
  270

Laurance (sic) Dist.,
  42
Laurence (sic) Dist.,
  68, 113, 128
Laurens, 12
Laurens Co., 26, 28,
  34-38, 44, 46,
  48, 53, 56, 57,
  60, 61-66, 69,
  70, 73, 76, 77,
  83, 86, 87, 94,
  98-102, 104,
  105, 107, 108,
  110, 111, 113,
  114, 117, 118,
  120, 122, 134,
  135, 140, 144,
  147, 153-156,
  158, 160-162,
  164, 166, 168,
  170, 171, 174,
  177, 181-183,
  186, 190, 195,
  200, 204, 205,
  208, 209, 211,
  214, 215, 217,
  218, 220-229,
  231, 234-238,
  240, 243, 244,
  246- 248, 251,
  252, 255-257,
  259, 261, 263,
  264, 266-268,
  270-275
Laurens Dist., 23,
  30, 31, 34, 40,
  47, 57, 66, 67,
  71, 78, 81-85,
  88, 89, 91, 93,
  94, 96, 103, 108,
  113-125, 128,
  130-132, 136-
  138, 142, 143,
  145, 149-151,
  157-159, 161,
  163, 165-169,
  174, 175, 177,
  178, 180, 187,
  188, 190-193,

195- 200, 203, 206, 212, 213, 215, 216, 218, 219, 221, 224-226, 228, 231-236, 239-242, 244, 245, 247-251, 253, 257-259, 262, 265-267, 269, 271-273, 276, 277
Lawrence Dist (sic), 87, 113, 262, 265
Newberry, 17, 165
Newberry Co., 26, 136, 138, 209, 226, 227
Newberry Dist., 107, 135, 136, 186, 188, 266, 268
Ninety Six Dist., 30, 33, 38, 41, 43, 49, 50, 55, 64, 68, 79, 99, 100, 106, 110, 119, 138-140, 147, 152, 153, 158, 160, 172, 181, 185, 189, 194, 195, 204, 206, 209, 217, 218, 221, 224, 229, 230, 235-237, 239, 248, 249, 253-255, 261, 262, 267
Orangeburgh, xv
Orangeburgh Dist., 135
Pendleton, 109
Pendleton Co., 195
Pendleton Dist., 179
Pitsylvania [sic] Co., 119
Spartanburg Dist., 172
St. John's Parish, 202
St. Mark's Parish, 257

St. Pauls Parish, 211, 259
Stono, 259
Union Co., 17
Wantook, 202
Washington Dist., 208
Springs
Motes Spring, 171
Rocky Spring, 7
St. Pauls Parish, 259
Stores
Brocks Store, 227
Wolffs Store, 170
Survey
Big Survey, 74, 227
Old Survey, 126

T
Taverns
Hickory Tavern, 225, 226
New Market, 225
Newmarket, 226
Tennessee, xv
Davidson Co., 48, 260
Franklin Co., 47
Ripley Co., 196
Territory
Indian Territory, xiv
Township
Saxegotha, 5

U
United Netherlands, 58
Up Country, 57

V
Village
Laurens Village, 113
Virginia, 7, 16, 43, 64, 65, 70, 125, 183, xiv
Augusta Co., xiv
Campbell Co., 114
Halifax Co., 203
Orange Co., 152, 153
Pittsylvania Co., 120

Spotsylvania Co., 83

W
West Indies, 144

§§§

Meets & Bounds
in Deeds on Pages:
7, 10, 28, 41, 96, 117, 138, 205, 273